Societal Benefits of Freely Accessible Technologies and Knowledge Resources

Oswaldo Terán
Universidad de los Andes, Venezuela

Jose Aguilar
Universidad de los Andes, Venezuela

A volume in the Advances in Knowledge
Acquisition, Transfer, and Management (AKATM)
Book Series

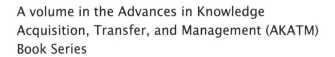

Managing Director:	Lindsay Johnston
Managing Editor:	Austin DeMarco
Director of Intellectual Property & Contracts:	Jan Travers
Acquisitions Editor:	Kayla Wolfe
Production Editor:	Christina Henning
Development Editor:	Brandon Carbaugh
Typesetter:	Cody Page
Cover Design:	Jason Mull

Published in the United States of America by
Information Science Reference (an imprint of IGI Global)
701 E. Chocolate Avenue
Hershey PA, USA 17033
Tel: 717-533-8845
Fax: 717-533-8661
E-mail: cust@igi-global.com
Web site: http://www.igi-global.com

                    Library of Congress Cataloging-in-Publication Data

CIP Data
Societal benefits of freely accessible technologies and knowledge resources / Oswaldo Teran and Jose Aguilar, editors.
    pages cm
 Includes bibliographical references and index.
 ISBN 978-1-4666-8336-5 (hardcover) -- ISBN 978-1-4666-8337-2 (ebook) 1. Technology--Social aspects. 2. Open access publishing. 3. Open source software. 4. Freedom of information. I. Teran, Oswaldo, 1966- II. Aguilar, Jose, 1964-
T14.5.S63836 2015
303.48'3--dc23
                    2015006752

This book is published in the IGI Global book series Advances in Knowledge Acquisition, Transfer, and Management (AKATM) (ISSN: 2326-7607; eISSN: 2326-7615)

British Cataloguing in Publication Data
A Cataloguing in Publication record for this book is available from the British Library.

For electronic access to this publication, please contact: eresources@igi-global.com.

Advances in Knowledge Acquisition, Transfer, and Management (AKATM) Book Series

Murray E. Jennex
San Diego State University, USA

ISSN: 2326-7607
EISSN: 2326-7615

MISSION

Organizations and businesses continue to utilize knowledge management practices in order to streamline processes and procedures. The emergence of web technologies has provided new methods of information usage and knowledge sharing.

The **Advances in Knowledge Acquisition, Transfer, and Management (AKATM) Book Series** brings together research on emerging technologies and their effect on information systems as well as the knowledge society. AKATM will provide researchers, students, practitioners, and industry leaders with research highlights surrounding the knowledge management discipline, including technology support issues and knowledge representation.

COVERAGE

- Cognitive Theories
- Cultural Impacts
- Information and Communication Systems
- Knowledge acquisition and transfer processes
- Knowledge management strategy
- Knowledge sharing
- Organizational learning
- Organizational Memory
- Small and Medium Enterprises
- Virtual Communities

IGI Global is currently accepting manuscripts for publication within this series. To submit a proposal for a volume in this series, please contact our Acquisition Editors at Acquisitions@igi-global.com or visit: http://www.igi-global.com/publish/.

)

Titles in this Series

For a list of additional titles in this series, please visit: www.igi-global.com

Contemporary Issues Surrounding Ethical Research Methods and Practice
Chi B. Anyansi-Archibong (North Carolina A&T State University, USA)
Information Science Reference • copyright 2015 • 331pp • H/C (ISBN: 9781466685628) • US $205.00 (our price)

Organizational Knowledge Dynamics Managing Knowledge Creation, Acquisition, Sharing, and Transformation
Constantin Bratianu (Bucharest University of Economic Studies, Romania)
Information Science Reference • copyright 2015 • 349pp • H/C (ISBN: 9781466683181) • US $210.00 (our price)

Strategic Data-Based Wisdom in the Big Data Era
John Girard (Middle Georgia State College, USA) Deanna Klein (Minot State University, USA) and Kristi Berg (Minot State University, USA)
Information Science Reference • copyright 2015 • 312pp • H/C (ISBN: 9781466681224) • US $205.00 (our price)

Handbook of Research on Maximizing Cognitive Learning through Knowledge Visualization
Anna Ursyn (University of Northern Colorado, USA)
Information Science Reference • copyright 2015 • 572pp • H/C (ISBN: 9781466681422) • US $325.00 (our price)

Information Seeking Behavior and Technology Adoption Theories and Trends
Mohammed Nasser Al-Suqri (Sultan Qaboos University, Oman) and Ali Saif Al-Aufi (Sultan Qaboos University, Oman)
Information Science Reference • copyright 2015 • 321pp • H/C (ISBN: 9781466681569) • US $200.00 (our price)

Handbook of Research on Scholarly Publishing and Research Methods
Victor C.X. Wang (Florida Atlantic University, USA)
Information Science Reference • copyright 2015 • 589pp • H/C (ISBN: 9781466674097) • US $335.00 (our price)

Collaborative Knowledge in Scientific Research Networks
Paolo Diviacco (Istituto Nazionale di Oceanografia e di Geofisica Sperimentale (OGS), Italy) Peter Fox (Rensselaer Polytechnic Institute, USA) Cyril Pshenichny (Geognosis Project, ITMO University, Russia) and Adam Leadbetter (British Oceanographic Data Centre, NERC, UK)
Information Science Reference • copyright 2015 • 461pp • H/C (ISBN: 9781466665675) • US $200.00 (our price)

Enhancing Qualitative and Mixed Methods Research with Technology
Shalin Hai-Jew (Kansas State University, USA)
Information Science Reference • copyright 2015 • 643pp • H/C (ISBN: 9781466664937) • US $225.00 (our price)

www.igi-global.com

701 E. Chocolate Ave., Hershey, PA 17033
Order online at www.igi-global.com or call 717-533-8845 x100
To place a standing order for titles released in this series, contact: cust@igi-global.com
Mon-Fri 8:00 am - 5:00 pm (est) or fax 24 hours a day 717-533-8661

Editorial Advisory Board

Table of Contents

Detailed Table of Contents

Chapter 1

    Jacinto Davila, Universidad de Los Andes, Venezuela

Information technology development is a must for societies in the whole world and, particularly, in the so-called third world. However, which particular research goal and which mode of research are suitable for that development are questions that need careful consideration and reasoning. In this chapter, we try to explore those reasons by visiting the logic in Free, Libre, Open Source Software, FLOSS, as a general concept. It is a political logic, because it clearly interferes and is interfered by dominant economical policies with respect to issues such as knowledge diffusion, copyrights and intellectual property. In the chapter, we explore available evidence over which principles are actually held and how that is done. Our highest goal, however, is to show that information technologies are best understood in the wider context of socio-political games and any suggestion of the opposite is itself a move in some of those games.

Chapter 2

    *Jose Aguilar, Universidad de Los Andes, Venezuela; & Prometeo Researcher, Universidad
        Técnica Particular de Loja, Ecuador*
    Oswaldo Terán, Universidad de Los Andes, Venezuela

This chapter describes an autochthonous system of Knowledge, Science, and Technology (KST): its actors, policies, strategies, and instruments. It is proposed to create it via a continuous reflection-action process. Such a system is aimed at promoting an autonomous nation, and will strongly rest on culturally free KST, beyond its actual conception (as universally valid, and neutral) in the Western Society. We argue that since the culture, problems and needs of the western nations are different from those of the non-western nations, such as Latinamerica, Africa or the Muslim World, the use of western KST in non-western societies without an appropriate reflection about national and local pertinence, generates dependence on KST that has very limited local societal benefits, and prevents developing an autonomous and pertinent KST system – non-western societies can only superficially capture the creations of the western society.

To overcome this, we suggest that non-western nations must generate an autochthonous KST system.

Chapter 3

Sulan Wong, Universidad Católica de Temuco, Chile
Julio Rojas-Mora, Universidad Austral de Chile, Chile
Eitan Altman, INRIA, France

The neutral nature of Internet has allowed its consolidation as a crucial tool in the dissemination of knowledge and access to culture. Due the creation of new business models of Internet access, a debate about the need of keeping a neutral Internet has emerged, leading to a sudden regulatory process that seems to emerge from a process of public consensus. However, participation in this debate requires knowledge in telecommunications, economics, and law, leaving participation to expert actors. In public consultations on Net Neutrality and in the resulting legal documents, three fundamental problems related to net neutrality are studied. Firstly, what constitutes a neutral, open and free Internet? Secondly, what is the effect of traffic management and what are the consequences of providing differentiated services? Finally, can transparency be an efficient tool to curb potential violations of net neutrality? This article presents the historical background that led to this debate and how its main points have been treated primarily in USA and Europe.

Chapter 4

Amir Manzoor, Bahria University, Pakistan

In recent years, several case studies have appeared on how emerging technologies had an impact in bringing grass root political changes. It has been widely argued that emerging technologies are influencing democracy all over the world. This chapter explores how emerging technologies support various pillars of democracy (freedom of expression and freedom of press, rule of law, human rights, and individual liberty) to strengthen and foster the democratic processes. While there exist substantial evidence that technology provides strong support to democracy, significant issues still exist and need to be addressed for emerging technology to contribute to democracy. The chapter discusses these issues and offer recommendations for better use of emerging technologies for democracy.

Chapter 5

Soledad Torrecuadrada García-Lozano, Universidad Autónoma de Madrid, Spain
Vladimir Aguilar Castro, Universidad de Los Andes, Venezuela
Carlos Grimaldo Lorente, Universidad de Los Andes, Venezuela

In this chapter, the authors attempt to demonstrate that respect for cultural identity of all human groups should be seen as a fundamental right. Ignoring Collective rights of indigenous peoples, those related to their cultural traditions, generally causes the lack of respect. Thus, knowledge of the cultural manifestations and their origin and meaning (as part of the history of the territories they inhabit) can conquer this respect on a par with its defense. This obviously with comprehensive training aimed to sensitize the general population in the positive assessment it deserves it different. The actions of nation-states governments with strong indigenous population has been characterized, until recently, by a remarkable disregard for indigenous cultures, having as a result the result of which such attitude, today from the non - indigenous perspective indigenous cultural manifestations are reduced to colorful folklore shows, when not seen as backward and primitive traditions. This chapter delves deeply into the legal framework for the protection of collective and cultural rights of indigenous peoples. The authors also attempt to show the weaknesses of the law and how states should act to strengthen them. Proposed article does emphasis on indigenous traditional knowledge and not in a wider debate on the topic of knowledge in general.

Chapter 6

Sulan Wong, Universidad Católica de Temuco, Chile

It is argued that patents encourage scientific development, benefiting society by creating useful products and services that improve the quality of life. However, by granting exclusive rights of exploitation, patents create situations in which they interfere with the exercise of the freedom of scientific research. This work examines five scenarios where this problem can be seen and the utilitarian function of patents is questioned. Firstly, the effects of research funding in the definition of the lines and research objectives are observed. Secondly, the anticommons is studied, as it is a situation where excessive fragmentation of ownership in scientific knowledge may prevent its use. Thirdly, broad patents and their implications are examined. Fourthly, the deterrent power of patent litigation, which creates an unexpected business model, is analyzed. Fifthly, secrecy is looked upon, as it is encouraged by the logic in which the patent system works.

Chapter 7

Jose Aguilar, Universidad de Los Andes, Venezuela
Oswaldo Terán, Universidad de Los Andes, Venezuela

Mass media (e.g., TV) and social media (e.g., Facebook) have a large utilization nowadays; they are becoming an integral part of our life. This chapter describes the psychological effects of media bias and manipulation, along its impact on public opinion by using "agenda setting" and "prototypes/framing". It shows how media can artificially create feelings and emotions. It will also explore the relationships between free knowledge and media. Free knowledge has a strong potential to prevent media manipulation, and for people emancipation from media control. The paper suggests using media in a more humanistic way, as a space to create knowledge, where social interaction influences knowledge. We talk of communities where people regularly share and create knowledge. The media do not replace existing processes of building knowledge; rather they provide an additional dynamic environment, which must meet certain criteria for what the social knowledge will be emancipator, and not manipulative.

Chapter 8

Vladimir Aguilar Castro, Universidad de Los Andes, Venezuela

Political and legal developments addressed to protect traditional knowledge are the result of huge efforts made by different actors at international and at national level. Nevertheless, traditional knowledge is broadly understood as freely accessible. Intellectual property norms are highly developed and strongly protect some knowledge products that are excluded of public domain, such as new varieties of plants. In light of this situation, political and legal tensions emerge in different countries, especially when it has an impact on areas highly profitable for some industries. This is the case of multinational agricultural companies that act globally by using technologies protected by intellectual property rights, threating traditional expressions applied for the use and conservation of seeds by local communities in different countries. In Venezuela, such tensions are present in the 2002 Law about Seeds, Animal Material and Supplies for Biological Reproduction, which is analyzed in this chapter.

Chapter 9

Giulio Focardi, Osun Solutions, Italy
Lorenza Salati, Bigmagma, Italy

A Multifactory is a new concept of productive environment. This chapter presents what Multifactories are, their constitutive elements and how these interact. In this chapter will be also presented the governance system, that is largely self-generated, and the way knowledge is shared and how this brings to innovative practices in exchanging skills and professional services. The chapter will also present the way the Multifactory Model was developed, from the direct observation of different real cases within Europe to the on-field test of the model. The chapter also suggests how Multifactories can be a possible way to face the needs for job creation and an environment where to experiment innovative ways to share knowledge.

This chapter motivates and discusses the process of making a simulation model available for others to freely inspect and use. Firstly, it outlines the three reasons why this is necessary: democratic right, scientific scrutiny, and public value extraction. Then it describes the basic steps for doing this, including: making code comprehensible, documentation and licensing. It then describes some further things one might do when releasing a complex model to help ensure it is understood and re-used appropriately. It briefly looks as some tools and approaches to help in all this, and ends with a discussion about the change in underlying "modelling culture" that is needed.

This chapter develops a discursive context called "the sawmill metaphor" that interprets the technology as a system of timber production that runs through a river. Trees are cut upstream and transported by the river towards a sawmill in the midstream. The sawmill then transforms trees into logs that are sent down river towards other factories that produce finished products downstream. Using this metaphor a link between technology and production is identified as well as the vital importance that the interlinking networks has on production. This context allows us to propose a diagnosis of the state of technology on Venezuela in 2014, a country which regardless of plans of technological acquisition sets forth since 2003 with sizable investments, far from increase technological sovereignty has lost it. Finally, taking as a basis the Venezuelan case, we present a set of general guidelines to consider in a plan of technological acquisition.

Preface

In general, in human societies knowledge and technology are free. The first is the accumulated social understanding, and the second is its useful application, both in accordance to, and perceived as good from, the perspective of the culture of each society. They exist since the prehistory along all human societies, and also at present in all human social groups (e.g., in any Amazonian tribe). The form they take in any social group depends on the culture and social needs.

However, in the last centuries, *proprietary knowledge and technology* are the forms of knowledge and technology dominating in the western world. Proprietary knowledge and technology are those knowledge and technology protected by copyrights and patents. As an example, in the software ambit, proprietary technology means that software can neither be modified, nor copied, nor distributed.

In part as a reaction against proprietary knowledge and technology, *free and open source knowledge and technology* have appeared. For instance, free software is that software that can not only be used, but also copied, modified and distributed by its users. Free and open knowledge and technology have allowed the emergence of new *forms of creation* of knowledge and technology. These new forms of knowledge and technology are understood and conceptualized differently from their proprietary counterparts. They also have a *different perspective and philosophy about social needs,* and pretend *democratize* their social creation, use and impact.

In particular, freely accessible technologies and knowledge resources have generated important societal benefits and have become highly valuable and promising. They have a strong potential in a diversity of areas, including Endogenous Development, Social Autonomy, Social Self-Organization, Emergent Systems of Health and Education, etc. For instance, Information Communication Technologies (ICT) technologies have already been widely used for government/state/institutions/communities organization, for social production. Their use has contributed to facilitate and increase people participation in public decisions, promote democracy, and strength national sovereignty.

These achievements have been possible thanks to Free and Open Source Technology development projects, involving diverse communities and social processes. Very well known cases are the communities developing Linux, LibreOffice, Wikipedia. The maturity of these communities has allowed the emergence of Associations, Institutions and Foundations, such as, the Free Software Foundation and the Open Source Initiative. Also, communications via conferences, online networks and platforms, have deepened the synergy among and inside diverse groups, in order to share and spread the products of these communities, *e.g.*, the SOURCEFORGE software platform management and repository (see http://sourceforge.net/).

These products freely accessed of these communities, have had relevant impact in public and private organizations, institutions and communities. This impact has been especially valuable in ICT applications, increasing the capabilities for online and electronic business and trade, planning, governance, health services, education, organizational coordination and communication, community planning, etc. It has become important in Europe, U.S., Japan, Australia, but is particularly promising for developing countries. This promise resides in both the potential to create local communities cultivating their own know-how in accordance to the local social needs, and in the applications of their products. In both cases important societal benefits are generated, based on processes locally sustainable, as they produce local adapted capacities and autonomy.

These processes and communities are subjects of active research in order to be better understood and contribute to their progress, especially to further their effect in favor of increasing societal benefit, and improving organizational performance.

This book contributes in understanding better and collect experiences related with the Freely Open Technologies and Knowledge Resources phenomena. It will address relevant issues such as the conceptualization of the phenomena, difficulties and challenges (both in developed and in developing countries), as well as relevant applications. The book explores different domains that traditionally are not considered in the analysis about free knowledge and technology, even without explicitly naming this. It appears as a "natural" or cultural practice where the notion is implicit, such as in the case of indigenous knowledge, native seeds, web neutrality, use of the social networks to increase collective knowledge, and the multifactory model. Thus, such domains include industrial productive models, research issues in free knowledge and technology, ancestral communities rights and traditions, the democratic systems, the Internet and its use, among others. In this sense, it aims at being an essential reference source, building on the literature and experiences going on in Freely Accessible Technologies and Knowledge Resources in general, opening possibilities for further research in this dynamic field.

Consequently, this text not only is useful to the communities and researchers working in the covered issues, but also provides a framework for policy makers, technology developers and managers, to analyze and study the phenomenon around Freely Accessible Technologies and Knowledge Resources. In particular, free and Open Source Knowledge and Technology communities, policy makers, academicians, researchers, advanced-level students, technology developers, and government officials will find this text useful for their work, activity, and research about Freely Accessible Technologies and Knowledge, assisting them in strengthening and advancing their own efforts in this field.

THE CHALENGES

In order to foster the Societal Benefits of Free and Open Knowledge and Technology, as well as the Free and Open Knowledge and Technology community itself, the academic community and the practitioners of Free and Open Knowledge and Technology are called to grasp and conceptualize about the process of development, and the social and organizational forms associated to the production of Free Knowledge and Technology, as well as about its applications and social consequences. The academic community should also examine prospectively the future development and potential application of free knowledge and technology. In particular, the potential of these to promote autochthonous development, democracy, as well as collective education, require careful attention.

Among the diverse topics related with free and open knowledge and technologies that require better understanding we have:

- Freely Accessible Technologies and Societal Benefit
- Freely Accessible Knowledge Resources and Social Impact
- Freely Accessible Technologies and Knowledge and Social Self-Organization
- Freely Accessible Technologies and Knowledge and Cultural/Social Autonomy
- Free and Open Technologies and Public Policy
- Freely Accessible Technology and Knowledge and Education
- Freely Accessible Technologies and Endogenous Development
- Organizational applications and implications of Freely Accesible Technologies and Knowledge
- Free Technologies and Production Chains
- Future of Freely Accessible Technologies and Knowledge (globally or regionally, e.g., in China, in Europe, or in LatinAmerica)
- Legal issues in Freely Accessible Knowledge Resources and Technologies
- Experiences in adopting and promoting Freely Accessible Knowledge
- Free Practices, Knowledge and Technologies in Ancestral Communities and Societies.

Free knowledge and technology is called to take a protagonist role in favor of the autonomy and liberating education of man, in accordance to the culture of each Nation. The dominant character of Science and Technology over western man has already been noticed by Habermas (1968) and Heidegger (1977). Habermas notices how human interaction has been subjugated by the instrumental work category, represented mainly by instrumental science and technology. Similarly, Heidegger considers that western man has become an instrument of technology, as technology in itself has become autonomous: its goal is to create more and more technology, independently of its pertinence for humanity, where man is not appreciated widely as a creature searching for its spiritual and physical well being, but rather as an instrumental entity maximizing the production of material goods.

Some of these themes have already received particular attention in Latin America. For instance, Fuenmayor (2006) observes the important constraints of a deteriorated culture to the development of pertinent science and technology, and suggests some general guidelines and policies to promote a good form of science and technology in a developing country. Fuenmayor suggestions are closely related with Free and Open Science and Technology. Similarly, Varsavsky (2006, 2013) highlights the strongly dependent (neo-colonialist and developmentist) character of Science and Technology in Latin America, what can be overcome via a process of Free and Open Science and Technology.

Related with these requirements, Núñez (1999) describes forms (social processes) of developing pertinent free local science and Technology, and Ochoa (2008, 2006) examines how free knowledge can be connected to endogenous development and public policies. These authors are both concerned with the liberation of man from the dominance of instrumental knowledge, science and technology. Furthermore, Aguilar (2011), and Aguilar and Terán (2011) have conceptualized in relation to how knowledge in general, and in particular science and technology, can promote democracy, social autonomy and free man. Additionally, emergent social processes as forms of developing free knowledge have already been studied, for instance, in Perozo, Aguilar, Terán and Molina (2013) (in particular Wikipedia and the community developing the kernel of Linux are reviewed cases). Finally, Himanen (2001) elaborates an interesting description of the attitudes behind the Hacker´s social action when involved in processes of elaborating free technologies, e.g., Linux. Himanen indicates that hackers have high levels of altruism, solidarity, and collaboration, while enjoying their doing, which is not perceived by them as a mere mean for surviving, but rather as a way to enjoy life and contribute to social well being.

However, still there are plenty of concerns that need careful attention. For instance, in relation to the sense and role of Free and Open Knowledge in general for an autonomous culture. Particularly relevant is Fuenmayor's call for a new social attitude, beyond only instrumental collaboration, which be directed towards caring of well being, including the culture as the fundamental being, via virtuous practices, as described by MacIntyre (1985). Similarly, Varsavsky mentions the need for a creative and pertinent science and technology, supported by a National Plan. Following these and other researchers, other elements that need attention are the study for new organizational forms, the analysis of the consequences and potential for human freedom, among others.

ACHIEVEMENTS AND ORGANIZATION OF THE BOOK

The chapters of this book contribute in understanding better and conceptualizing about the previously needs in relation to the societal benefits of Free and Open Source Knowledge, Science and Technology. The contribution of each chapter can be summarized as follows:

Chapter 1 explores the suitable research goal and the research mode of developing information technology, from the view point of Free, *Libre*, Open Source Software (FLOSS), as a general concept. It also shows that the system of development and use of information technology is well understood if it is seen as a socio-political game, where any suggestion to consider it as something else is in itself a move in that game –the actor might not be aware of the socio-political significance, and implications, of that move. This chapter helps in understanding better the socio-political implications of information technology, knowledge and technology in general, and their role in favor of dominant socio-political actors. Then it makes clear the potential of free and open information technology, as well as free and open knowledge and technology in general, for a fairer society.

Chapter 2 describes limitations and poor benefits of western Knowledge, Science and Technology (KST) for non-western societies, because of its low pertinence for the social problems and situation of non-western societies. Then, it claims for the development of an autochthonous KST system, based a reflection about its local pertinence, and on virtuous practices. It highlights its implication for fostering democracy and cultural autonomy, at the time that is directed in accordance to the local culture. In addition, the chapter reviews the implication of its proposal for Latin America. Alike the previous chapter, this chapter highlights the potential of free knowledge and technology to favor democracy, man freedom, and cultural autonomy.

Chapter 3 address the net neutrality debate appeared in USA and Europe. In particular its historical character is described. It calls attention to the constraints for public participation, as appropriate knowledge in telecommunications, economics, and law are required, leaving the debate in the hands of an elite of "experts". It identifies three particular problems addressed in public consultation on net neutrality and in the resulting legal documents, including the conception of what is a neutral, open and free internet. This chapter also addresses a political issue, and is linked to freedom of internet users and their participation on determining policies regarding the accessibility of the web.

Chapter 4 describes some political changes that emerging freely accessible technologies promote. In particular, it explores how emerging technologies support democracy. However, it recognizes that significant issues still exist and need to be addressed for emerging technology to contribute to democracy, giving recommendations for better use of emerging technologies for fostering democracy. This chapter is strongly linked, alike previous chapters, to the political relevance of freely accessible knowledge and technology, in particular to their potential to support democracy.

Chapter 5 summarizes the political and legal framework regarding cultural and collective rights of indigenous peoples in Venezuela, which recognizes and defends indigenous traditions. It argues that lack of knowledge of cultural traditions, their origin and meaning, generally causes lack of respect for indigenous people. The chapter claims that this knowledge, along appropriate training to sensitize the general population, helps in increasing respect for indigenous peoples. It also points out the common disregard for indigenous traditions in diverse countries with an important indigenous population, in conjunction with lack of respect for these peoples. Alike previous chapters, this chapter deals with a political issue, but differently from previous chapters its focus of attention are the cultural rights of non-western communities, which must be kept free and open in accordance to the perspective of those cultures.

Chapter 6 suggests that by granting exclusive rights of exploitation patents can create situations where they interfere with freedom of research. It considers five scenarios for this problem, in which the utilitarian function of patents is questioned: a) the effects of research funding in the definition of research polices and goals; b) the anticommons – excessive fragmentation of ownership in scientific knowledge may restrict its use; c) broad patents and their repercussions; d) the restrictive power of patent litigation; e) secrecy, as it is encouraged by the logic in which the patent system works. Somewhat similarly to previous chapters this chapter addresses a political issue: how patents constraint freedom of research. However, it gives a more technical treatment to the issue.

Chapter 7 describes the psychological effects of media (both mass media (e.g., TV) and social media (e.g., Facebook)) manipulation, along its impact on public opinion by using agenda-setting and framing. It shows how media can contribute to triggering certain feelings and emotions. It then explores the relationships between free knowledge and knowledge offered by media, arguing that free knowledge has a strong potential to prevent media manipulation, and for people emancipation from media control. It then recommends giving media a more humanistic role, as a space to create knowledge, where social interaction influences knowledge, in line to some suggestions offered in chapter 2. In this case, communities would freely share and create knowledge, and the role of the media is limited to provide an additional dynamic environment to help communities interact in order to create pertinent and emancipating knowledge. Thus, this chapter claims for knowledge and information free from media and groups of power manipulation, which is favored by free and open process of knowledge creation.

Chapter 8 analyzes a case of political and legal tensions emerging in different countries as a consequence of intellectual property norms. Intellectual property norms are highly developed and strongly protect some knowledge products that are excluded of public domain (e.g., new varieties of plants), especially when it has an important impact on highly profitable areas. The chapter examines the 2002 Venezuelan Law about Seeds, Animal Material and Supplies for Biological Reproduction. This case is related with the action of multinational agricultural companies acting globally by using technologies protected by intellectual property rights, threatening traditional practices associated to the use and conservation of seeds by local communities. This chapter also has a political character, addressing an international issue, via a local Venezuelan case. While the interest of transnational companies is in increasing the scope of intellectual property norms, communities' interest is in free and open access to seeds, animal material and supplies, as a mean of liberation from transnational exploitation.

Chapter 9 presents a new concept of a productive environment: the Multifactory model. This is defined as an "Invisible Factory", bottom-up based on a social structure, considered as an archipelago of companies independent and autonomous, which can integrally cooperate among them like divisions of a single company. As a bottom-up generated structure, its governance system is largely self-generated, with a constant circulation of ideas, having innovative practices in sharing knowledge and in exchanging skills and professional services. This model was originated from direct observation of real cases within Europe. Its bottom-up quality is based on free and open social practices. In fact, one of its main targets is to serve as an environment to experiment innovative ways to share knowledge.

Chapter 10 is dedicated to motivate and discuss the process of making a simulation model available for other researchers, stakeholders and users, to freely inspect and use. It considers three motives for this, giving the proposal an important social and political justification, namely: democratic right, scientific scrutiny and public value extraction. The chapter suggests achieving that by making code comprehensible, documentation and licensing. In addition, it gives some further guidelines to follow when releasing a complex model to facilitate its comprehension and re-use; and identifies some tools and approaches to help in all this. It also calls our attention to the need of an appropriated modelling attitude or "culture", in order to make possible the suggested practices in favour of free and open modelling. The chapter shows then that open and free modelling and simulation will contribute to public well being, as suggested also by Terán and Ablan (2013), and many modelling applications have shown.

Chapter 11 gives and interesting discursive context, "the sawmill metaphor", in which technology is interpreted as a system of timber production that flows through a river. The metaphor consists of a process in which, first, trees are cut upstream and transported by the river towards a sawmill (in the midstream), and, second, the sawmill transforms trees into logs, which are sent downward the river towards other factories that produce finished products downstream. This metaphor suggests a link between technology and production, and highlights the importance that the interlinking networks have on production. The metaphor is then used to diagnose the state of technology on Venezuela, concluding that Venezuelan technological sovereignty has decreased despite of recent efforts in the opposite direction. Before finishing, the chapter presents a set of general guidelines to consider in a plan of technological acquisition in order to promote technological sovereignty, emphasising on the potentials of free knowledge and technologies for achieving this goal.

As seen, the present book has covered a diversity of the above mentioned challenging topics and problems associated with free and open knowledge and technology. They range from issues related to socio-political and cultural pertinence of free and open source knowledge and technology to more specific and concrete issues. Among the last, we have tools and metaphors for supporting learning, education and the use of modeling and simulation for policy making. In the middle of this range, the book reviews relevant legal marks associated to free access, not only to knowledge and technology, but also to social practices and traditions (e.g., of indigenous peoples). In doing so, the book goes even beyond the traditionally covered issues of the practice and use of free knowledge in the world, to include elements of non-western cultures (indigenous peoples). All covered themes are associated to concrete experiences and applications, in a variety of fields, situations, for dealing with diverse kind of deeply social (western and non-western) concerns.

Several of the themes relevant for free and open source knowledge and technology identified by, or relevant in accordance to the research of, authors such as Fuenmayor, Varsavsky, Núñez, Ochoa, and Aguilar and Terán have received treatment in the present book. In general, in the chapters, the socio-political and cultural relevance of free and open source knowledge and technologies for fostering national autonomy, democracy, sovereignty, endogenous development, and people public participation, are treated. The chapters offer non-traditional perspectives and go beyond the view point dominating at present in the free and open knowledge and technology communities.

Because of all this, the present book is highly valuable for diverse audiences and communities: practitioners, policy makers, managers, academics, stakeholders and users in general of knowledge and technology.

REFERENCES

Aguilar, J. (2011). Conocimiento libre y educación emancipadora. *Revista EDUCARE, 15*(1), 84–106.

Aguilar, J., & Terán, O. (2011). Ciencia y tecnología liberada y liberadora, para una potencia mediana. In Venezuela: Potencia Emergente (pp. 357-394). Caracas, Venezuela: Monte Ávila Editores, Centro de Estudios Políticos Económicos y Sociales (CEPES).

Fuenmayor, R. (2006). *El estado venezolano y la posibilidad de la ciencia.* Mérida, Venezuela: Fundacite. Gráficas Quintero. Retrieved from http://www.cenditel.gob.ve/node/422

Habermas, J. (1968). *Technik und wissenschaft als "ideologie".* Frankfurt am Main: Suhrkamp.

Heidegger, M. (1977). The question concerning technology. In *The question concerning technology and other essays* (pp. 3–35). New York: Harper Torchbooks.

Himanen, P. (2001). The hacker ethic and the spirit of the information age. New York: Random House; Retrieved from http://portal.feaa.uaic.ro/isg/Shared%20Documents/The.Hacker.Ethic.pdf

MacIntyre, A. (1985). *After virtue: a study in moral theory.* London: Duckworth.

Núñez, J. J. (1999). *La ciencia y la tecnología como procesos sociales: Lo que la educación científica no debería olvidar.* La Habana, Cuba: Editorial Félix Varela.

Ochoa, A. (2006). *Aprendiendo en torno al desarrollo endógeno.* Mérida: CDCHT-ULA.

Ochoa, A. (2008). El sentido de las políticas públicas vinculadas al conocimiento para la transformación social. *Reflexiones desde Cenditel, 4,* 5-31.

Perozo, N., Aguilar, J., Terán, O., & Molina, H. (2013). A verification method for MASOES. *IEEE Transactions on Systems, Man, and Cybernetics. Part B, Cybernetics, 43*(1), 64–76. Retrieved from http://ieeexplore.ieee.org/xpl/articleDetails.jsp?arnumber=6211437

Terán, O., & Ablan, M. (2013). Modelado y simulación de situaciones sociales complejas en Latinoamérica: Contribuyendo al cuidado del bien público. In La emergencia de los enfoques de la complejidad en América Latina: Desafíos, contribuciones y compromisos para abordar los problemas complejos del siglo XXI (pp. 118–135). Buenos Aires: Comunidad de Pensamiento Sistémico; Retrieved from http://www.academia.edu/3366646/Tomo_1._La_emergencia_de_los_enfoques_de_la_complejidad_en_America_Latina._Desafios_contribuciones_y_compromisos_para_abordar_los_problemas_complejos_del_siglo_XXI

Varsavsky, O. (2006). *Hacia una política científica nacional*. Caracas, Venezuela: Monte Avila Editores. (Original work published 1972)

Varsavsky, O. (2013). *Estilos tecnológicos: Propuestas para la selección de tecnologías bajo racionalidad socialista*. Buenos Aires, Argentina: Bibioteca Nacional. Colección PLACTED-Ministerio de Ciencia, Tecnología, e Innovación Productiva, Presidencia de la Nación.

Chapter 1
The Political Logic of Free, Libre, Open Source Software

Jacinto Davila
Universidad de Los Andes, Venezuela

ABSTRACT

Information technology development is a must for societies in the whole world and, particularly, in the so-called third world. However, which particular research goal and which mode of research are suitable for that development are questions that need careful consideration and reasoning. In this chapter, we try to explore those reasons by visiting the logic in Free, Libre, Open Source Software, FLOSS, as a general concept. It is a political logic, because it clearly interferes and is interfered by dominant economical policies with respect to issues such as knowledge diffusion, copyrights and intellectual property. In the chapter, we explore available evidence over which principles are actually held and how that is done. Our highest goal, however, is to show that information technologies are best understood in the wider context of socio-political games and any suggestion of the opposite is itself a move in some of those games.

INTRODUCTION

Barwise, J. and Hammer, E. (1995), in one of a collections of essays, edited by Prof. D. Gabbay, to answer the question: What is a Logical System?, explain that a logical system is a mathematical model of some pre-theoretic notion of consequence coupled with a inferential practice of some sort. We rescued this account to establish that some intuitive notion of logic exists before an actual system is modeled, even though that intuition could be enriched or modified during the modelling process. Axioms, and the principles they formalized are, therefore, important in a logic, but more important are intuitions on their content and on how to reason with them.

In this chapter, we explore the logical intuitions behind the concept of Free, Libre, Open Source Software, FLOSS, For this technological concept, which is defined in due course, we present a set of principles that try to describe the underlying intuitions about what is a free technological device and how users of those devices are affected by the ways in which they have access to those technologies. As the title of the chapter suggests, our hypothesis is that those principles are of a political nature, even

DOI: 10.4018/978-1-4666-8336-5.ch001

though the exchange of technology is normally regarded a mere economic practice and, therefore, neutral in political terms. A key element to support this argument is the insight that software is, unlike other devices, a form of knowledge.

The Driving Forces behind a Road Map for *Libre* Knowledge Management Technology Research and Development

Information technology -IT- development is a must for societies in the whole world and, in particular, in the so-called third world. Then, it is only logical that scientists and technicians from those regions of the world, organize themselves to do the research they require for their development. However, which particular research goal and which mode of research are suitable for those organizations are questions that need careful and independent consideration. By "independent" we mean that for being relevant to their human contexts, those questions should be addressed to their national or permanent human activities taking into account local problems, local priorities and local resources. Scientist do require a mode of research that may guarantee local relevance and open scrutiny to empower communities, which, in turn, may evaluate the real impact of the so-called scientific and technological contributions. This requires a mode of inquiring that should not be biased to a particular, alien or contradictory frame of mind subjected to interests that may not coincide with local needs and demands.

Heidegger, in "the question concerning technology", (Heidegger, 1964) warns us of the difficulties to reveal the essence of technology: it is (technology) a revealing, a particular way of bringing forth. This unusual way of reflection seems appropriate because we are called to explore meanings that are so involved and embedded in complexities, hidden behind the many different language games (Wittgenstein, 2001) in which they are used. To understand those meanings, we have to experience them as directly as possible. Looking for an essence, we go after something in every instance and, yet, different from every one. A technique is a means to an end and a human activity. But it also has an element that transcends them both. Technology is also revealing, but with a certain form and a certain purpose. Heidegger explains: "Whoever builds a house or a ship or forges a sacrificial chalice reveals what is to be brought forth [..]". The technician [who is] designing an "object" unfolds upon it, his/her own under-standing. Then, he adds: "And yet, the revealing that holds sway throughout modern technology does not unfold into a bringing-forth in the sense of poiesis. The revealing that rules in modern technology is a challenging (*Herausfordern*), which puts to nature the unreasonable demand that it supplies energy which can be extracted and stored as such."(Heidegger, 1964).

The peculiar revealing in information technologies and knowledge management is also a challenge. However, it is not the whole mother nature "who" is being challenged. People are. This time is not about transforming raw materials into market products. This time is about what is tradeable in a concept, a method, a sort of mental experience or an idea. We are being challenged to transform these "things" into objects of use and profit.

Knowledge management is a generalized demand upon the academy, where knowledge has been traditionally sought, preserved and spread. Nowadays, however, the demand is for learning objects that can be easily traded in the global market: "To enable a strong and growing economy for Learning Objects that supports and sustains all forms of distribution; non-profit, not-for-profit and for profit" (IEEE, 2002).

How are Academics Supposed to Answer that Challenge?

They must do as requested. Being at universities implies being universal. There is the obligation of endorsing key societal objectives. They must oppose the evolution of education towards making it a mere marketable item, as a prominent knowledge management organization in Europe used to say.

However, support for this objective is not easily obtained. Facing market domination tendencies is just a part of the university tasks. But universities do profit from markets having such features. Some people believe that marketing is inherent to traditional schooling: "Certification constitutes a form of market manipulation [...] Free and competing drill instruction is a subversive blasphemy to the orthodox educator." (Illich, 1971). It is reasonable to expect that all over the world, academics (with sympathetic support from the rest of Society) will reject any explicit attempt to replace the educators as knowledge mediators.

Is there any room for intervention, change or improvement of some sort on this state of affairs?

Free, *Libre*, Open Source Software, FLOSS, is a technological realm in which learning is a fundamental right, well above trade rights. We have reasons to believe that it is a suitable space to challenge Heidegger's frame which seems to be embedded in any form of western technology, particularly in information technology, where the non-tangibility of products makes that challenge more difficult to enforce.

In this chapter, we seek to explain those reasons by visiting the logic in FLOSS as a general concept. It is a political logic, in the sense that it clearly interferes and is interfered by dominant economical policies with respect to issues such as knowledge diffusion, copyrights and intellectual property. Along the chapter, we explore the evidence of these principles and how those interferences happen. Our main goal, however, is to show that information technologies are best understood in the wider context of socio-political games of strategy (Leyton-Brown and Shoham, 2008)s and any suggestion of the opposite is itself a move in some of those games.

First, in the following section (**The copyleft is rightish, too**), we revisit the principle of copyleft originally adopted by the FLOSS movement and how it is used to support and promote the sharing behaviour in IT communities. Then (in **The reasons for FLOSS**), we elaborate on the many reasons to adopt, promote and develop FLOSS. Thirdly (in **About rentism and intellectual property in Venezuela**), we investigate the connections between the sharing-above-selling approach and the highest political decisions, by studying the case of a national economy based on rentism. **Free Quality** introduces the immense challenge being faced by defenders of FLOSS: to show that a successful technical profession on software development is possible without exerting abuse on users and clients. In **Horizontal and Vertical Modules**, we try to clarify the boundaries between FLOSS and the private use of software, an explanation that could help to prevent arguments of all-or-nothing being attributed to FLOSS. The section **Software Wars** is an exercise of reality-check which gives emphasis on the fact that technologies have become a battlefield, and even those that are in search of peaceful developments are forced to take side, as the stakes include their own freedom to think and learn. We summarize the logical principles of FLOSS in the last section before the **Conclusion** which, in turn, restores the main points into the general context.

THE COPYLEFT IS RIGHTISH (TOO)

An Unfortunate Simplification of a Big Step for Humanity

It is not surprising the enthusiasm for free software among socialists. Neither is the interest of the free software community in some socialist ideas, such as cooperation. It is a profound and undeniable affinity, a peculiar one as it unifies the political realm with the technological world, being this normally and naively assumed as neutral.

The truth is that **copyleft**, an important but not compulsory principle found in some variants of FLOSS, is a careful compromise that combines demands from the socialist left wing and the neoliberal right wing. This makes it a great political achievement for the 20th century and an excellent starting point for the new political endeavors of the 21st century.

Copyleft is also a careful compromise between individuals and society. Every FLOSS license entails respect for the individual by helping to preserve, zealously and effectively, the authorship of each work. But even before that respect for the individual sets in, there is respect for the rules in a global society, where everyone can trust the law (and, therefore, licenses) and define the terms by which she or he wants to share a piece of work. This is precisely the spirit of the most popular free software license, one that has become a sort of "constitution" for the whole movement: The General Public License, GPL, originally written by Richard Stallman (FSF, 2007).

The implications of copyleft and FLOSS, in general, are subtle and difficult to grasp at first look. In fact, they can be catastrophically interpreted (as the Spanish parliament attested:A proposal for a law enforcing FLOSS was massively rejected after some confusing arguments about free software not being gratis, not being open source and being no more than a commercial strategy). One element of that confusion is the very term "copyleft". It makes for a fantastic slogan. And it is normally portrayed as an antonym of copyright.. And, of course, it is a sacred term for socialists, ever since their precursors (known as capitalists at that time) sat to the left wing in the mother of parliaments. It is even the case that socialist-leaning premiers are pejoratively called "leftish" by the media. Stallman confirmed that he did intend those effects by using the word left (Stallman, personal communication, November, 1, 2009)..

The truth, however, is that copyleft (Moglen, Sullivan & Sullivan, 2013) is an principle that seeks to counterbalance the concession of *libre*, free and open access to an author's work with a requirement for a similar treatment for whatever improvement is made with the intention of distribution. If an author is asked to share his or her work, an accepted response in the FLOSS community is: "Ok. I'll share it with you, but you should share yours alike". Thus, the more general form of the principle is now known as "share and share alike" and it can be shown in many forms. This is the relevant text that states it in the GPL:

c) You must license the entire work, as a whole, under this License to anyone who comes into possession of a copy. This License will therefore apply, along with any applicable section 7 additional terms, to the whole of the work, and all its parts, regardless of how they are packaged. This License gives no permission to license the work in any other way, but it does not invalidate such permission if you have separately received it.

According to some critics (see, for instance, Golden(2005) and others cited by the Wikipedia), this share-alike feature causes copyleft licenses to behave like a virus, by "infecting" any work derived from the one so licensed (derivative work is any improvement or enhancement of the original work) under the same conditions for *libre*, free and open distribution. One could say that the proper name for this virus would be the virus of solidarity. However, the ascription of the virus condition has been sternly rejected.

Strictly speaking, copyleft licenses are among the more individualistic free software licenses (one could say *selfish* if it were not so easy to insult somebody with this epithet, especially in the socialist community). The key aspect relies on two elements, namely, that an author does not simply concede all permissions to copy and exploit her/his work, and whoever improves on this work (creating a derivative work) and intends to distribute the new solution, must do so as in the original license (an extension of the concept to the case of services is an important but more recent development). Notice that all this conditioning is independent of any other agreement with respect to the work (particularly, of payment).

Thus, in the simplified political spectrum, copyleft could be seen as a left-wing oriented policy but perfectly acceptable, even in zealously individualistic copyright laws (such as the laws in the United States and also in Venezuela, except for the fact this Latin American country does not allow software patents).

However, when compared to most extreme policies of the left (like universal health), copyleft is a move to the right allowing the author to take personal advantage of one aspect of traditional copyright: setting conditions of use. This also explains why copyright and copyleft licenses coexist: an author releases his/her work in agreement with copyright but allowing the use with freedom. But s/he also sets the particular condition of sharing alike on those users. So, this author can label her/his work with both the © of copyright and the symbol facing left for copyleft (See Box 1).

It is worth noticing that changes in copyright laws would most probably have an effect on this situation. For instance, chances advanced by the pirate parties in Europe to have copyright terminated after a period of time, could potentially damage the intended effect of the copyleft, by eliminating its requirements as copyrights expires. See, for instance, Richard Stallman's explanations in this respect.

Interestingly, the principle mutates its form when one goes from a particular community to another. Among free software programmers, the copyleft license marks the boundary for the constraints that can be imposed on the users of a program. That is, the farthest an author can go to limit the use of her/his work is to request from users to behave in the same way (if they want to distribute the original work or derivatives thereof). This agreement is included in all accepted free, *libre*, open-source software (FLOSS) licenses and there is a general criteria for all of them, even among those who defend free access to the source code only for practical reasons. This is the "open-source" sub-community where the basic understanding is that allowing other requirements could be tantamount to creating conditions for cheating by, for instance, reversing the license with subtler proprietary terms. In all this, the free, *libre* and open source movement displays a solid unity around the reasons a programmer would have to share her/his code and their equivalence to an actual gift economy.

However, in other communities of free, *libre* creators, for example, artists using creative commons licenses, the copyleft principle is relaxed to the point of allowing sharing for free, provided that the

Box 1.

receiving user does not get rich. If someone starts making a lot of money out of somebody else' s contribution, apparently some transfer of wealth is expected from the money maker to the original authors. This is the reason for CC-BY-NC type licenses, which state freedom of use, provided the user engages only in non-commercial (NC) activities with the work. The discussion is far from settled, though. A recent court decision in Germany has assumed that non-commercial terms are equivalent to "personal use only", an interpretation which is obviously not intended by many users of the CC-BY-NC license.

This variant of the copyleft principle is normally not disputed, neither by liberals nor by socialists (that is, socialists who agree that authors can or must make profits by any means). However, that variant, as said, is unacceptable for programmers, who can only go as far as requesting share-alike. We argue it is a variant of copyleft because if the user shares her/his improvements in the same terms as the original author, this would be empowered to carry out the same money earning activities the second author may be enjoying. This is true, however, only if those activities involve distributing software (for instance, for a fee or under a contract) as a user is always empowered by the GPL to use the software to do anything (even money earning activities) without reporting to the original author. The license only restricts (re) distribution.

There have been different attempts to explore this conceptual boundary between commercial and non-commercial exploitation of a free, *libre*, open-source software. The Java Research License, JRL (Sun Microsystems, Inc), was one of those attempts, and the introductory argument seemed to have been, at the time, that the now dismantled company (bought by Oracle in 2010), Sun Microsystems had invested a lot of efforts and resources to produce the highly successful Java Language Platform and, although they were willing to open the sources and let them be used for free without other restrictions, they would preserve the right to share any eventual financial benefit for third parties. The answer from the FLOSS developer community was an unanimouy NO: Every user of a program should be empowered to do with the software whatever s/he would want, even a lot of money without paying royalties to the original developers (this is a common requirement in FLOSS[1] and even in Open Hardware licenses).

The underlying reasoning, still valid, seems to go like this: if royalties or other kind of charges are allowed as conditions for software licensing, even in hypothetical scenarios, the temptation to bypass the user's right to free, *libre* use for some subtle "business exchange" would be irresistible.

Certainly, Sun Microsystems, Inc. was no stranger to FLOSS. By the time, it had already released an important system, known as OpenOffice, and used another interesting license: The LGPL, a variant of the GPL which involves a more flexible form of copyleft that does not "infect" a derivative work with the obligation to share unless the original work is actually modified. This makes it particularly suitable for libraries of software and draws a compromise between the original, "strong" copyleft principle and the more permissive free, *libre*, open-source licenses (such as the MIT License). OpenOffice became an extraordinary contribution to the FLOSS community as it was an effective alternative to the reigning proprietary software for office automation, Microsoft Office. Moreover, Sun ended up releasing the whole Java suite with the GPL (version 2), which was modified with a peculiar exception for some of its components. It is called the Classpath Exception for the GPL and it provides a way to link "GPL-ed" components and other components with different licenses without demanding the GPL terms for the latter, similarly to the LGPL.

All these "games" on the edge of acceptability of FLOSS principles helped Sun Microsystems to earn the reputation of having a double standard. This got worse after being sold to Oracle, a traditional skeptic of FLOSS. Double standards have also be attributed to other companies such as IBM and Red Hat (Read & Dew, 2012).

There are, of course, companies that do not care about those standards, but are openly against FLOSS and still keep exploring possibilities. Microsoft has just released the code of the very famous MSDOS, now regarded a piece of museum but still valuable enough, in their mindset, to limit its distribution to non-commercial terms. The Microsoft Research License agreement states (Microsoft, 2014) the following:

"You may use, copy, compile, and create Derivative Works of the software, and run the software and Derivative Works on simulators or hardware solely for non-commercial research, experimentation, and educational purposes. Examples of non-commercial uses are teaching, academic research, public demonstrations, and personal experimentation. "Derivative Works" means modifications to the software, in source code or object code form, made by you pursuant to this agreement".

These terms are not FLOSS and are rejected by FLOSS morals.

Morality is an aspect in which socialism seems to have a clear lead. The socialist morality is rationally perfect. How can one openly and overtly contradict the claim that we all should be generous and care for others?. There is, of course, the issue of whether an ethics can be defined on such a noble purpose. A lot has been written in this respect (see for instance, Trosky, L. (1938) and Ball, S. (1896). Nevertheless, "the devil is in the detail". Respecting this subject, one immediately wonders whether it would suffice to have just one standard of conduct that does not directly contradict that perfect morality.

It can be argued that Sun Microsystems (now Oracle), IBM and other companies do not engage in double standards with those tinkering behaviors around FLOSS. They all have one supreme goal: maximization of economic benefits without (too much) regard for side effects and collateral damage. This is the well known desideratum of the capitalist world and one expression of the challenge mentioned in the introduction. Thus, all those companies go for FLOSS insofar as it is profitable.

This sets the stage for a clear questioning of any intended technologically assisted transition to socialism in the 21st century. Are they actually (re)visiting the issue of the profit as a goal for software (that is knowledge) developing operations? Or are they going to let them carry on business as usual as the side effects keep being cautious and generous? Would this be enough?

THE REASONS FOR FLOSS

Overcoming inertia by means of reason has always been difficult. But, it is even more difficult to argue against a special interest that hides itself from open discussion behind a simulated inertia on those who would be affected should their real goals be exposed.

FLOSS, faces those two kinds of difficulties in a country like Venezuela. First, there are people who do not want to alter the fragile equilibrium they have reached in their work or in their institution with a technological solution, despite (that solution) being proprietary and thus, forced to submit possibilities for development to an external interest. Secondly, there are people who actually harvest some benefits from those solutions and are against any chance of discussing alternatives.

We believe that the former are many, well-meaning officers in many cases. The latter are a few, but well located in key decision-making positions or, at least, positions of influence.

The result, at a first stage, was a country that confused making FLOSS with data migration by starting every system from scratch. Moreover, in many instances, the main criterion for system negotiation was that the programs should "run" on Linux (i.e. Gnu/Linux), disregarding actual access to the code and other terms of licensing. It was a very dramatic reduction of the concept which almost derailed FLOSS government policies, starting with the Decree 3390, issued by President Hugo Chávez.

Fortunately, this trend started to reverse with the approval by the National Assembly (the highest legislative body of the country) of the "info-goverment law" (Asamblea Nacional, 2013) which states a clear commitment to *Libre* technologies, FLOSS in particular, and directs their use to improve public services and to guarantee swift access to official information. Article 35 of this law states that "licenses for software used by the state must allow access to the source code and knowledge transfer associated with their understanding, freedom to modify, freedom of use in any area, application or purpose, and freedom to publish and distribute the source code and changes. Only those licenses guaranteeing derivative works be licensed under the same terms as the original works could possibly be adopted". Therefore, this law enshrines all the FLOSS principles and entails a strong form of copyleft for the public software of the Bolivarian Republic of Venezuela.

Good enough?

In retrospective, one would expect to be able to discuss the underlying reasons to set the whole public sector of a country (letting individuals to choose their personal solutions by themselves) for using and promoting FLOSS. There are academic, social, economical, and political reasons to do so. Far from pretending to be exhaustive, we list and comment on some of them:

1. FLOSS is better because is *libre,* and it works. Users are free to use, study, copy and improve every piece of software without major constraints. But this is not a theoretical statement. There are hundreds of thousands software solutions freely available exactly in FLOSS terms, and many of those are well established developments with continuous support. There are, in fact, stable and specific technological solutions to traditional problems such as the aforementioned office automation, which competes successfully with proprietary solutions.
2. FLOSS does not require payments for use licenses. In fact, FLOSS abhors the concept of charging or otherwise limiting the freedoms to use the software and regards it as unethical. In practice, this makes possible to provide all the software required by an entire institutional infrastructure, such as an University or another education institution, without having to spend huge amounts of money on recurring licensing payments.
3. FLOSS is flexible and adaptable to the needs and resources available at any institution. There have been many institutional experiences in software distribution, that are only possible in practice thanks to the freedoms embedded in FLOSS. Moreover, the costs of software updates, even for a whole institution with many users, are minimal. Upgrades are free too, and institutions can arrange for local repositories and distributions mechanisms that optimally use the channels, so as to save on connections charges to the Internet.
4. The incidence of computer virus on free platforms is negligible. It is true that there is no automatic immunity just by being FLOSS. But it is also true that FLOSS responds very effectively to security threads. This means, of course, that user data is more secure. A network with less incidence of virus is also a network with more capacity for services such as mail transfer, usually heavily degraded by the custodial requirement to search and remove viruses which are being exchanged by users across different platforms.
5. FLOSS clearly establishes the freedom for improvement and innovation. It adds value to local developments which, in turn, add value to the existing pool of solutions and open opportunities for technological sovereignty. This is also the reason why FLOSS is perfect for teaching and promoting the technological development of a nation, a transcendental effect which has been systematically studied and reported (Europe, 2006).

6. Any organization, disregarding how far it is from the centers of powers, can establish and maintain a fully fledged users supporting platform, which may also be escalated to assist the needs of other institutions as well.

7. FLOSS sustains a close relationship with open technological standards. There is no better way to open a software standard than implementing it as FLOSS. Then, anyone could learn the rules in detail, test the solution and immediately deploy it. Open standards are essential for the preservation of institutional memories (the collection of documents and data of an organization), as they provide the base to guarantee safe storage and eventual data and knowledge retrieval without having to depend on external agents.

8. There is a clear trend towards the adoption of FLOSS as a public policy strategy in many countries. We already mentioned that it is law in Venezuela (Asamblea Nacional, 2013). At some point, in 2008, Kerala State in India claimed to have the world largest deployment of FLOSS. This, however, has been clearly surpassed by the Canaima Project in Venezuela, with more than 2.5 million computers running FLOSS (UNESCO, 2012) and used by children at primary school. Furthermore, the great impact on Internet usage in the whole country has been acknowledged by UNESCO. Also in 2008, Ecuador received a presidential decree (N. 1014, 2008) establishing the use of FLOSS in public offices. Nowadays, this country is in the process of developing a new law for what they call *libre* and open knowledge but it is not yet clear how it will connect with FLOSS. Uruguay's legislative body has also approved a very precise law in favour of FLOSS, but it only states that it must be preferred before proprietary software. Brazil was the leading country in adopting FLOSS in Latin America, in 2002. The state of Paraná has issued at least two laws stating the preference for the use of FLOSS over property alternatives, but not mandating it. In fact, the country has witnessed since 1999, at least nine attempts to pass a law in favour of FLOSS, but none of which has succeeded. There are reports showing a brazilian trend toward FLOSS and Free Culture in general, during the terms of President Lula Da Silva. Currently, it is now reversing.

The sheer side of that economy, however, seems to favour a very interesting experiment on sustainable FLOSS identified as Public Software (Alves & Pessôa, 2010). The same concept appears in Bolivia to indicate a combination of a FLOSS license for the source code and a creative commons style license for other components (arguably, documentation and manuals) which would allow non-commercial restrictions on distribution. Bolivia has a law stating higher priority for FLOSS (but not making it compulsory) since 2011 (Asamblea Plurinacional, 2012). Spain, despite failures in passing laws, sustains a permanent effort to promote FLOSS at CENATIC. Argentina has no national law. A project was prepared in 2010; however, there is a regional law at Argentina's Santa Fe province (Legislatura de Santa Fe, 2004). In the rest of the world, notably Russia, has a plan to migrate the software in public offices to FLOSS starting in 2015 (Russian Federation, 2010) apparently as a practical response to financial pressures from proprietary software providers in the West. China, despite reporting an increase in the use and development of FLOSS (Guohua & Bonk, 2007) and an apparently close affinity with its legal and political frameworks (Xia, 2010), has not reported a specific law yet. The United Nations has declared the importance of FLOSS for a sustainable global development (Sowe, Parayil, & Sunami, 2012). Perhaps the strongest statement in favour of FLOSS in Europe is a study requested by the European Commission (Contract ENTR/04/112) which shows its clearly positive economical impact (Europe, 2006).

9.   FLOSS encourages cooperation and solidarity. FLOSS developing communities are well known for their amazing collective productivity. Even other expressions of openness and willingness to share knowledge, such as the Wikipedia, are closely associated with FLOSS.

10. FLOSS coincides to some extent with the principles of Open Access (Suber, 2012), a global initiative which aims to allow wider access to scientific knowledge, particularly by freeing it from commercial restrictions. Scientists are increasingly aware that the results of their work are kept away from potential users, specially other scientists, and for reasons that are not scientific (Guedón, 2001).

Why are these reasons not enough?

In the public realm, there is no excuse. Mixed (public-private) initiatives must be kept open to discussions, to make private initiatives feel they are in their best interest to adopt FLOSS. But even then, reasons are decisive.

However, when faced with a personal, a non-expert perspective or a for-profit commercial software development operation, these (and other) reasons fail to persuade.

Why?

It seems that the notion of a successful and compassionate economy, all at once, is counterintuitive to business people. As if they simply could not believe such a thing: there must be a catch.

Apparently, an economy in which agents constraint themselves for non-economic reasons not to extract maximum benefits out of their clients buying their products -that is not "wanting more rather than less of a good" (Weingast, 2013)- would be a dysfunctional economy as understood by some prevalent schools of economics.

With FLOSS, the developer or the owner (who may not be the same developer but whoever has paid for the development) waives his/her legal right to restrict distribution and elaboration (improvements) of the software sources, to allow those freedoms to its users. FLOSS developers **refrain from refraining**, we could say, as a clear display of respect for the users.

However, "refraining from refraining" does not imply refraining from charging (per development). Nothing in FLOSS prevents a developer from selling her/his work at the price that s/he considers appropriate. Nothing.

The catch, as surely someone would want to call it, is that the developer cannot charge for each copy of the software. The program sold goes with its source code. Once this source code is freed to copy, it makes little sense to pay for it, unless, of course, one pays not just for the software but also for some kind of guarantee. Actually, this kind of agreements with guarantees of functionality, maintenance and upgrades, is a common form of relationship between developers and users of software.

Is this profitable?

We have done some experiments to evaluate the conditions under which these agreements are profitable. However, it is even more persuasive to verify that this kind of agreements is just what the vast majority of software developers do worldwide. The proprietary software market, where they do not refrain from refraining, is, according to some studies (Europe, 2006), at most 20% of the whole software market. The rest is either FLOSS or private software (to be used within an organization, for instance) bought and sold precisely under those guaranteeing conditions.

Should we keep discussing?

Of course. But, it is also reasonable to admit that not everybody is open to consider collective reasons or even abstract concepts such as freedom. It may be necessary to look into personal, even intimate grounds for a discussion, hoping that they actually exist.

ABOUT RENTISM AND INTELLECTUAL PROPERTY IN VENEZUELA

Consider the following definition: "An ideal type is formed by the one-sided accentuation of one or more points of view and by the synthesis of a great many diffuse, discrete, more or less present and occasionally absent concrete individual phenomena, which are arranged according to those onesidedly emphasized viewpoints into a unified analytical construct...".

In what follows, we adopt it as part of a strategy advanced by the German sociologist Max Weber to address organizational complexities: an ideal type model, a clear and emphatic description of an organizational possibility, which may sacrifice accuracy for the sake of a global vision.

Let us use it to explore a context in which the notion of property of knowledge is particularly striking: dependent vs sovereign access to a country's natural resources. The country under study is the oil-rich Bolivarian Republic of Venezuela. A national social reality is bound to be highly complex. It is hard to think and even more to talk about it, especially if one aims to go to the roots of the problem.

Rentismo (rentism) (Neira, 2008) is, not only an established economic practice in Venezuela, but also an intellectual cause: the school of rentism. It basically argues that in Venezuela economic value is illusionary as most goods have been paid, to some extent, by ill-gotten revenues from oil. Petroleum, they explain, is a commodity whose production cost normally varies from 4 to 7 US$ per barrel, irrespective of the technology used to extract it. However, that barrel is nowadays sold for more than 100 US$, making the profit margin of at least two magnitude orders for the, in this case public, national oil industry.

The intellectual cause has even been stripped off all these specific and has been used to study the origins of a form of capitalist economy: the rentist capitalism (Baptista, 2010). The core of rentism seems to be the acquisition, by the State, owner of a **non-produced, production means**, of a income which is paid by international markets in exchange for its property. In short, according to this interpretation, the State acquires a rent out of (practically) no work (nothing). There is, therefore, no real justification for such an income.

That school argues that this becomes an insult with injury from Venezuelans to citizens of the rest of the world, who are forced to pay those prices. An offense that has been repeated for nearly 100 years since the discovery of oil reserves in the country. "We are a parasite country" (Domingo, 2008).

This argument is offered as a justification for punishment of a sort. There is a clear effect of this line of thoughts on the psyche of Venezuelans: an intuitive skepticism about the economic value of things. Venezuelans, following this argument, do not and cannot believe in the value of their economy. Therefore, that economy is doomed to disaster.

Thus, according to this school, Venezuelans do not produce sufficient economic value. Venezuelans cannot justify the living standards of their society, which oil income supports. Moreover, Venezuelans know this well, but instead of taking "real" solutions, they engaged themselves, like spoiled kids, in a fight for the treasure of the forty thieves.

The arguments goes on: Venezuelans do not know how to produce "things" that could be sold for a price sufficiently high to justify their status. For example, they do not know how to address the demand for lavatory facilities, since they import them. They do not even know how to produce pens, as they do not have any national industry with the capacities to make the small ball at the tip of a pen. Any product requiring non-trivial technological facility (like toys, electronics, optical parts, miniatures, biochemical compounds, integrated circuits and, of course, complex software) is beyond the capacities of the country. But even worse, public and private entrepreneurs mislead national public opinion (including themselves) when believing that technological transfer is taking place when they are just buying "ensembles". Those transfers of technology are normally more cosmetic than real.

What Venezuelans are really good at is pretending. It is a crucial skill developed by natural selection, one could say, in an environment characterized by a fratricidal war for oil revenues. We mean fratricidal because it aims to eliminate local competitors: let them die in ill-conditioned hospitals, let them be killed in the streets by "common" crime, let them be squashed on the roads by undetected drunken drivers. All these attacks on people help ("less dog, less hair, less fleas").

Their intellectual effort is focused on finding strategies to skim the government: the "natural" rent manager, using whatever excuse good enough to demand a fair slice. Everyone wants to work for the State, as public officers, with its implied stability (in exchange for having to pretend to serve others, which can become a nuisance), or as private contractors, so long as those contracts are regular and guaranteed.

Each group has its own strategies to bite the rent. Public officers have established a complex system of assessment scoring for personnel, which states two basic requirements: a public servant must always 1) appear to be doing something and 2) appear to achieve some objectives. These conditions seem to be enough to make some public employees climb the scale and earn more and more in their way up (it is normal in a bureaucracy to earn more if one is up in the scale) and simply by aging.

Private contractors have a different strategy. They know they can compensate lack of stability by maintaining a network of relations that increases the probability of being hired over and over again. They sometimes even do the same task, and with such a profit margin that they could easily afford "gifts" for their fellows in the network.

Is this a competition in a free market? Is this a good way to select the best solver for every problem? Only in appearance, of course. There is always an (unfair) advantage when a fellow from the network is part of the evaluation body for a contract. This part of the argument is also useful for those who pretending to defend socialism, argue against unfairness in free competitions.

All of the above elements are but components in an admittedly tabloid-like sketch of a Weberian ideal model of Venezuela's reality according to the school of rentism.

Models are alwayst, approximations to reality. In this case, it is fair to say that not all Venezuelans behave as described. Not even a majority, one could add. However, the model does explain the behaviour of many in "key" positions and allows for some predictions of their behaviour in response to any real or apparent action that may threaten their advantages. Responses will more likely be successful so long as oil keeps flowing through Venezuela's pipelines. Confronting (or correcting) that behaviour would require an enormous effort.

Let us try to use the model by 1) complementing it with some arguable beliefs from agents involved, and 2) make a prediction that will come true if the model turns to be valid in some foreseeable future. The reader is to be advised, however, that a level of higher complexity is introduced in the following statement: the model absorbs its modeller.

Let us complement the model with an account of those who actually reveal a genuine fear and hate for Socialism and regard Chávez' Bolivarian revolution as unnatural. They are by no means a majority of Venezuelans. Between 1998 and 2012 there were 17 national elections in Venezuela. Hugo Chávez and his followers won 16 of them. They lost only one, the referendum that was intended to permit some changes to the letter of the Constitution. This election took place in December 2nd, 2007 after a campaign in which many Venezuelans were persuaded by contrary forces who insisted in showing people that President Chávez was for a perpetual mandate so that the transformation of the country into a communist society where "mine would not be mine" (as some opposition ads announced) or where nobody would own anything as the government (or its feared bureaucracy) would own it all, would be but a sort of nightmare came true. However, Chávez did win another referendum and later, a six-year mandate after that episode (in October 2012) by a clear majority.

Thus, let us concentrate in that proven minority who believes that Chávez was a disaster because he reversed the "right process" of wealth transferring the oil revenues to foreign interests. According to this view, it was wrong to allow Venezuelans to take advantages of this natural resource only because they were born above the well. This should matter less than the fact that resources should belong to inventors of the technology for extracting and exploiting them.

We believe this is the most aggressive interpretation of the raw concept of intellectual property. According to this, children from the first world are entitled to exploit natural resources at will because they (that is, some of them) allegedly discovered or invented how to do it. Followers of this interpretation should necessarily include Venezuelans who actually want (or "accept") the price of a barrel of oil in less than 10 US$, as it was before Chávez, and never above 100 US$, as has been in recent years. Of course, Chavéz' actions were not the only reasons for the price to rise. But he definitely see to it and act accordingly with considerable success. More important for the profile we are writing, a typical opposition representative always tended to blame Chávez of everything "bad" that happened in the country. "Culp'e Chávez" (it's Chávez' fault) is the expression.

And this is how the antisocialist movement connects with the rentist model we have been sketching. This form of Intellectual Property, IP, becomes the guarantee to sustain innovation, because inherently limited, human intelligence (Simon, 1982) may only respond to the desire for profit or individual benefits. This belief in a hard intellectual property right that is seen as a condition for innovation seems to be at the heart of plans for "modernizing" many third world economies.

The reasoning sequence seems to be like this: Hard IP guaranteed →technical staff prosperity guaranteed→initiative and innovation at maximum levels→profit and non-oil revenue for Venezuela→ (economic) prosperity for Venezuela -for a rebuttal of this viewpoint, see Peter Drahos' essay, (2007)-. This would have also implied that, without hard IP, the country would never reach economic prosperity, the only that matters, of course.

How would agents holding these beliefs actually behave?

They would not oppose any contrary policy openly and directly, as their final motivation would be exposed. But they would sabotage it with the simulating strategies that we have just described. And some of them would find personal comfort in the belief that they are fighting for their most basic property rights (intellectual or otherwise), while others would just imitate them.

In this context, any initiative to revisit the concept of intellectual property (as the one represented by the FLOSS movement) will be under siege and attacked by that appearance or simulating strategy.

Venezuela may have escaped to this interpretation of IP with the approval of that explicit mandate for FLOSS for the public sector in the info-goverment law, recently approved by Venezuelan National Assembly. As far as we know, however, this is the only compulsory mandate to use FLOSS. Thus, it may be time to start asking about that hard interpretation of IP in other countries and for other resources, natural or not.

Free Quality: The Stubbornness ON FLOSS and Open Formats

Why this stubborn insistence on changing the software of our computers? What is the point of switching my files in the computer from the well-known .doc format to those new .odt type of files? Why should I not leave my presentations as .ppt?

Let us try a pedagogical strategy of explaining complex ideas by means of metaphors. It is useful as long as the reader may bear in mind that a metaphor is always a loan from a different context and may not be a perfect referent, but a suitable one.

Consider the following scenario: Imagine you agree with one of your neighbours to do something with the space between your houses. Let us imagine that you both order a table in the shared space, so that it may be used whenever it becomes necessary. But, later on, you discover that your neighbour, who kindly commissioned the design and construction work (perhaps with some undetermined help from you), has reserved all access and use of the table for himself. If anybody (you included) need the table, they would have to ask for his explicit permission. If you want to modify or improve the table or its surroundings, you need a permit too. He has even asked you to pay for the permission. And if you want to share the table with other neighbours, you cannot unless you have an explicit authorization from this person, which would set specific times and some kind of payment for him. To make matter worse, whenever your astute neighbour decides to change or fix the table, you are forced to share the bill.

But, of course, you would not stand this situation forever and, at some point, you would decide to fight back. You consult some lawyers. But they explain to you that your neighbour is right in his conduct because, after all, he designed and built the table (or had it built) and what matters is that design, a creative contribution (also known as his intellectual property, IP). This is precisely the intellectual property over the table that grants all the privileges to your neighbour.

Thus, you end up without the table and without the land on which it is located, originally yours too. Very soon you find that the only way for you to use (let alone change) the table is to reach a commercial agreement with your neighbour who would probably want to receive some regular income (a rent) out of the table and whatever else you do with it. IP lawyers will tell you that all this situation may be part of the price to have a table, more likely without acknowledging that this is a very peculiar form of property.

What would you feel if you find out that your neighbour has reached the same deal with many other neighbours over the same table?

Out of the metaphor, one could say that the hardware of your computer is the common ground between the houses (which is even "more" your property than the metaphorical land) and the table corresponds to the software. Your neighbour is the provider of the software. He "made the table", although you may have helped him by paying for the effort to code, for documentation, training and also whenever you cooperated with him by reporting errors.

In an alternative interpretation of the metaphor, the table may stand for all those files, like documents and presentations, that you create and store in formats over which your neighbor has operational and intellectual control. In particular, we are talking about Word, Excel or Power Point files stored in their native formats (.doc, .xls or .ppt) or in the new office collection of self-declared "open XML" that they now want to establish as standards (docx, .xlsx and .pptx). It may even happen that you have to pay for the right to access and use the information you have stored on those formats (which is exactly what you do when you pay for the corresponding update of the license to use the software). To say that the format is less important with respect to the software is like saying that the building matters but not the columns supporting it.

Those are, metaphorically speaking, a set of reasons that makes us stubborn people in search of leaving close formats and proprietary software and adopting open formats and FLOSS.

And if we are stubborn in this search, it is because we acknowledge that we may have not been sufficiently clear, and because this is a subject with subtleties that are difficult to grasp for non-technical people. We think we could divide our world of computer users into the stubborn FLOSS technicians, ST, the "light minded" technicians, LT, and the rest. Those LT are so called because they do not want to argue for their preference on software licensing, although they perfectly understand the details. Actually, they count on those licenses to make a huge profit, charging for every copy of each program and disabling users to understand how those programs work, among other added disabilities.

Meanwhile, users are busy getting along with whatever understanding they may have of the software. Hence, they would not go deeper than necessary. Certainly, users avoid any complication with everything sounding intellectual property, or the like.

This distribution of the universe of users is typical in any countryy, as most people are normally happy being only consumers of technology. But in a country like Venezuela, far from the centers of standardization, conversations around those decisions are normally a joke. How many people in the third world have had anything to say about the form and characteristics of nozzles, plugs, sockets, nuts or razors with the shapes and dimensions that they use? Those decisions are normally made in Europe or in USA.

Thus, in such a context, the FLOSS community has no choice but to remain stubbornly insisting on the reasons for our choices and, therefore, trying to increase the number of FLOSS followers.

Fortunately (and this is something that the LT know very well), neither ST nor any of our users have to sacrifice any possibility for using these technologies: Anything that can be done through software, can be done through FLOSS and open formats. Notice that we use Free, *Libre*, Open source vs Proprietary for software and only Open vs Closed for formats.

However, we are particularly interested in arguing in favour of government officers who fight for adoption of FLOSS and open formats. Officers decide not only for themselves, but on behalf of whole communities. If one of them chooses a particular piece of software and a storage format to manage the information flowing to/from users in the public, s/he is making a decision that affects the public (by forcing some particular decisions on them too).

FLOSS and open formats have a crucial virtue by which they become automatically the best choice: they are the less restrictive. Users of FLOSS and open formats have more rights than users of a corresponding proprietary software with closed formats. Of course, some users might claim that they are entitled to submit some of their rights in exchange for some personal benefit. But public officers are not entitled to waive the rights on behalf of other users without consulting them. And this is exactly what they do when they go for proprietary software or closed formats.

Why then, is people choosing close formats? Because they arrived first and were favoured by the network effects (predicted by Metcalfe's law) and by the lock-in caused by the uses of proprietary software: Once you acquire it and use it for a while, you become dependent upon its provider as improvements can only come from the same source. It is a hard monopoly. Thus, breaking out free from that dependency requires a hard push: stubbornness.

Our stubbornness is not for free, though. It has costs. Shown as a defense against a system that refuses learning, it may be considered arrogant, or aggressive and, therefore, unacceptable. We may end losing adepts. We have to play with the rules of the "enemy" as this anecdote shows: an international expert on methodologies bridging the digital divide, once explained that those communities traditionally excluded from technology would tend to prefer proprietary but well advertised solutions. They naturally aspire to overcome their disadvantages and those products, well marketed, show themselves as the best. "If you offer anything else, they will reject it as it is perceived as of lower quality".

Thus, promoters of FLOSS and open formats have the difficult task of dismounting that advertising manipulation and insisting (reasonably, of course) on showing the results they already have and could have and how they could guarantee our users superior experiences in all cases.

Consider, for instance, the problem with computer viruses: the fear induced by the mere possibility of losing important and urgent information due to a computer virus. With FLOSS as the operating system of your computer, the probability of such event is practically (and comparatively) null. It is not that it is impossible to make viruses for FLOSS. It is possible. Nor it is that FLOSS market attracts so few people that it is unattractive for malignant hackers -the opposite of ethical hackers. The truth is that FLOSS is a public space massively "armored" against malice, because all the systems are open to scrutiny and evolution (correcting) of its functionality by an interested community. For instance, viruses for Linux exist and will continue appearing. But their creators face an unequal fight against a great team of maintainers. Just like any community with a majority favouring a common good and protecting their common spaces. So, this phenomenon of practical immunity to viruses is poorly understood. Promoters must insist on the experience (real and possible) for the end-user. And FLOSS has many other examples of high quality software with superior user experiences -See, for instance, the size and reach of the Debian Community, reported in (Europe, 2006)-.

In our opinion, the biggest challenge is to instill the phrase "free quality" of meaningful support in terms of user experience. The challenge is not technical. As we have argued in a previous section, FLOSS goes against a belief that sounds counterintuitive: a service can be *libre* and of superior quality. And it is perceived as counterintuitive even if *libre* does not correspond with free (null price). A successful technical profession on software development is possible without abuse of users and clients.

As for the dispute between STs and LTs, the latter are right on one crucial point: users will choose. "the market", as some of them call it. STs may well remain with that stubbornness and allege that they do it for the common well-being, as fanatics of any religion would say. It may be a better idea to lead the example. To show that STs can do anything with FLOSS as the other do with other solutions. The stubbornness should be put in terms of a desire to show the possibilities made into realities. Sts should refuse to build on exclusive technology specially in contexts where they could, with some additional effort, provide users with the same or a better experience on FLOSS. A strategy that is, it must be admitted, very hard to implement without societal and political support.

Horizontal and Vertical Modules for Development of FLOSS and Private Software

A software is free when the user is guaranteed with certain rights of use, access, (re)distribution and improvement of the contribution received from a developer or development team (FSF GNU, 2014). Nothing in that statement is contrary to the possibility that a developer decides to become a user of her/his software and dedicate it for private use only. The ethics and morals of FLOSS are opposed to proprietary developments. They do not oppose to the private use of software (FSF, 2014).

An institution developing software by modules can, for example, name **horizontal modules** to those ones that the institution is willing to share with the world because those developments could be useful to different people in different contexts. They could name **vertical modules**, those whose privacy would be preserved for their own reasons. Examples of these organizations abound, including several alleged-FLOSS enthusiasts, such as Google.

It is worth noticing that this classification does not have to be unalterable. The same organization could release their vertical developments as soon as they consider appropriate. Vertical development may, if they serve other users or disciplines, end up becoming horizontal developments.

Horizontal developments are extremely important for the development of free technology, as they always empower a wider community with platforms to solve complex problems without having to start every newly required solution from scratch. FLOSS Operating systems, such as GNU/Linux and its various distributions, are the best example of such horizontal developments.

Several studies provide ample evidence of the dynamic growth of FLOSS, thanks to multi-sectorial contributions, including those from "in house", individuals and companies, developments, with the primary intention of solving an internal problem but with the vision of cooperating on a common platform with other organizations and thus sharing the costs of its development as well as its benefits (Europe, 2006).

The horizontal modular approach is particularly useful for developments addressed to a wide community or a complex enterprise in order to identify features actually required for various software uses by different users. Specific user profiles usually require more development effort, but it can be highly rewarding to have a user-friendly, adaptable and maintainable solution. Maintainability, then, would be induced by the need to explain engineering decisions and crucial details of the platform to developers that are not affiliated to the same organization. This kind of horizontal modularity is also essential to identify interfaces and formats for data and information exchange between different applications and users, thus constituting the starting point of any effort to create **open standards**.

The vertical perspective also offers advantages for targeting well-defined needs with a limited provision of resources, time and workforce. This kind of vertical modularity represents the focus of a development team on a particular target, given a set of constraints and specifications. But this may also include legal, contractual and even strategical considerations that may preclude, even temporally, developers from releasing the software to a wider audience. A vertical development can, despite this restricted focus, respect certain interfaces and protocols to interact and share data, computing power and other resources with a horizontal platform and, through this, with other vertical developments.

The definition of a taxonomy of vertical and horizontal modules developed by an organization or a group has another important practical advantage. It is then possible to define a **scheme of licensing** and distribution of software that may be transparent and fair to all parties. For example, vertical applications would be protected under the terms required by each organization, including confidentiality clauses for developers and other legal provisions. Horizontal applications, in turn, would have all the universe of FLOSS licenses to choose from (FSF Licenses, 2014). Moreover, valuable documentation of the programs and licenses, essential to guarantee confident use by the same or new users -non-experts in many cases-, could also benefit from the range of free, *libre*, open documentation licenses (CC, 2014) with adaptations to local legislations.

The desirability of special restrictions such as copyleft to ensure that subsequent (added value) developments remain free and accessible for the whole community, for instance, may well be considered as part of a strategic plan for a long term defense of free, *libre*, open and sovereign technology, as we have been arguing in this chapter.

In short, the use of horizontal and vertical perspectives in development processes of institutional software may provide a highly effective methodological strategy.

A Statement of Lefts: Logical Principles of FLOSS

Having explored the conceptual space of FLOSS, it should now be clear that it is a political space with connections with economy and society as every one may reasonably expect. In fact, FLOSS represents a rejection of a simplistic tendency to treat software and any other form of knowledge as a commodity in an economy: a merchandise to be exchanged in a value-setting market of deliverables.

There is a very precise definition of **free software** (Stallman, 2010), which struggles against the overload of English word "free" (the reason why we use FLOSS: Free, Libre, Open Source Software). There, the foundational concepts are summarized as the four freedoms of free software:

"A program is free software if the program's users have the four essential freedoms:

- The freedom to run the program, for any purpose (**freedom 0**).
- The freedom to study how the program works, and change it so it does your computing as you wish (**freedom 1**). Access to the source code is a precondition for this.
- The freedom to redistribute copies so you can help your neighbor (**freedom 2**).
- The freedom to distribute copies of your modified versions to others (**freedom 3**). By doing this you can give the whole community a chance to benefit from your changes. Access to the source code is a precondition for this."

Can these be restated in a form that exhibits their political features? We think that they can and to that end we suggest the following principles:

- **Principle of Use**: A user is entitled to know and exploit all the functionalities of every piece of software that he or she uses (freedom 0 and freedom 2) whatever the reason he or she has to use it.
  - *Rationale*: Every piece of software is a collection of ideas. Once in contact with it, a user must be allowed to know it all, build on it, use it at will and share it. This includes a right to economical exploitation as long as this exploitation does not interfere with the principles of knowing and elaboration for others.
- **Principle of Knowing**: A user has the right to know the source codes of the pieces of software he or she uses, to modify them and to adapt them in whatever way he or she regards as convenient. Only when it comes to **share the software or exploit it as a service**, for whatever reason, the user will be obliged by the sharing terms established by the original author-developer, which may include forms of *copyleft* but **may not** include any form of royalty, forced, or recurrent payments (freedoms 1 and 2).
  - *Rationale*: No boundary must be allowed on what any person can possibly learn. Doing otherwise would be a violation of their individual freedom of thought, education and general welfare (Articles 18, 19, 26 and 29 of the Universal Declaration of Human Rights).
- **Principle of Elaboration**: Every user must be allowed to follow and elaborate every idea built in her or his software (freedom 1).
  - *Rationale*: Doing otherwise would imply setting a boundary for what people learn disregarding of what they can actually learn and this would be a violation of their individual freedom of thought, expression, education and general welfare (Articles 18, 19, 26 and 29 of the Universal Declaration of Human Rights)

- **Principle of Tolerance for Copyright Law:** The release of software as FLOSS does not imply a rejection of the author's rights to decide upon some distribution forms or any levels of revenue for her/his work. FLOSS' terms and current copyright laws are compatible for a license of use **as long as the terms of that license do not contradict the principles of use, knowing and elaboration above** mentioned. The programmer or author of a piece of software is still entitled to decide when, how and if he/she will distribute his/her software or use it as a service for others and in exchange for whatever appropriate retribution (freedoms 2 and 3).

  ◦ *Rationale*: FLOSS entails that the author refrains from refraining users from the possibilities opened by the previous principles. FLOSS does not restrict any moral rights whatsoever. It may even be argued that the added visibility of FLOSS will ensure proper recognition and prestige. Other exclusive rights are indeed restricted but with the explicit intention of allowing users a fair chance to use the software freed from recurrent or forced payments of licenses of use or any form of royalty (-ies)[s] to the original authors. Therefore, programmers or software authors are allowed to make money from their work as long as their particular business model does not contradict the aforementioned principles.

As suggested by the text above, there is an order of precedence between the principles. The principles or use, knowing and elaboration can be followed in any other between them, except that, normally in practical terms, knowing precludes elaboration. However, the principle of tolerance of copyright laws has to be subservient to the previous three ones. This is due to the fact that current forms of copyright do not acknowledge any rights for the users of knowledge. Only the economic rights of producers, generators or mere distributors are normally made explicit in copyright laws, sometimes even contradicting the original intentions of those legislations. A change in copyright laws could restore those intentions and may even force some restatement of FLOSS principles (see Stallman, 2013).

Since the reasons to sustain the first three principles and their order of precedes are neither technical nor economical, even less individualistic, we state that they are social and political in nature, having to do with the common challenge of producing, using and sharing knowledge among all humans.

Restating the rights of users and programmers in this way, apart from showing the political substance behind, may also serve other purposes. It makes explicit the stand of the FLOSS community on a subject we have not discussed in this chapter: **Patents,** with their exclusive rights to exploitation. In our restatement is clear that royalties or similar charges, as produced by patents, would not be allowed. This is a subject in which the FLOSS community has not been very clear (however, see section 11 of the GPLv3), probably because there is a tendency to practical solutions. FLOSS licensing, however, is normally very clear with respect to royalties.

Patents and royalties have become, nevertheless, a battlefield between economic powers. Another expression of the actual stakes and the underlying strategic games that model the fight to control and secure them.

Software Wars: The Distance between Public Objectives and the Actual Use of Information Technology

Multiple conflicts do not necessarily entail a war. A war is a state of affairs in which the parties assume and try the others to disappear or to be conquered.

One could say that there is a war between ideological inspired interests -or parties- in the realm of information technologies, except for the fact that at least one of them does not recognize a clear ideology. However, it can be safely stated that it is an economic war, even though the implicit reasoning is notoriously political. But war so redefined would be seen as a constant confrontation between technology agents that aim to defeat the others for good.

The war being depicted in this chapter is the one between those who think that information technology should not be used to enslave its users (an easily assumed public goal of technology) against those who believe it may be necessary in order to sustain technological innovation. According to them, developers should be allowed to request anything as exchange: even the fundamental right of people to learn and know.

Those are the tenets of the war for a free, *libre*, open access to technology. It is a low-intensity war in which many victims become the staunchest defenders of their victimizers, sometimes unwittingly. A form of blindness that allows and even supports converting knowledge into transactional objects that can be marketed piecemeal to provide a regular and highly profitable form of rent for their owners. It is interesting to note that blindness can even be induced as a networking effect in which a community persuades its members, without further thinking, that the best solution is the one that the majority in that community have chosen. Going along with tradition or costumes is, of course, a way to avoid extra thinking which sometimes is useful. Sometimes is not.

A peaceful strategy (it could not be otherwise, as the movement as such has not military and not even media power whatsoever) is what drives the actions of the FLOSS movement. A logic inspired and clearly connected to the belief that making knowledge into trading artifacts inevitably leads to injustice. But, it is also a logic that connects to non-personal and personal reasons to share knowledge as a straightforward path to gain more knowledge.

A priori, this logic seems difficult to grasp. It clearly contradicts the usual but unspoken, marketing *knowhow* which states that one has the right to sell whatever someone else wants to buy. FLOSS logic is intended to engage users in the defense of rights they are not even aware they have or deserve. These kinds of wars are, of course, the most difficult to overcome: wars for awareness. We will win as long as we collectively gain a better understanding. The irony remains, however, in that we are fighting precisely for the freedom to understand.

CONCLUSION

Free, Libre, Open Source Software is software that can be used, known and elaborated upon by any person, who then becomes its free user, above and before any constraint that could be set by means of copyright laws or developers' economic expectations. FLOSS is an expression of a technological solution to restore the rights of users of technologies at the level of the rights to individual freedom of thought, expression, education and general welfare (Articles 18, 19, 26 and 29 of the Universal Declaration of Human Rights). The former have been diminished by a dynamic of trade common to technological artifacts that denies that the nature of software is knowledge and as such must be considered. Therefore, FLOSS is a political cause, even if many participants in its development and deployment are unaware of it.

However, despite its creative legal contributions (besides all the technological advances), FLOSS does not reject the legal *status quo*. It fits in current copyright frameworks and, by doing this, it acknowledges the rights of individuals to establish the value of their contributions in the face of an exchange with others, even though limits for the forms of that exchange are established. Its insistence on "refraining from refraining", despite all the practical and moral support that it receives, remains a choice of each individual.

ACKNOWLEDGMENT

The author wishes to acknowledge and thank Dr. Melva Márquez and two blinded reviewers for their careful and very useful proofreading, critics and comments.

REFERENCES

Alves, A. M., & Pessôa, M. (2010). *Brazilian Public Software: beyond Sharing*. Business Complexity and the Global Leader Conference. Retrieved March 1, 2014, from http://businesscomplexity.com/bizcom2010/papers/p584f01r311ed40c.pdf

Asamblea Legislativa Plurinacional de Bolivia. (2012). *Ley General de Telecomunicaciones, Tecnologías de Información y Comunicación*. Retrieved March 1, 2014, from http://www.softwarelibre.org.bo/wiki/doku.php?id=ley_de_telecomunicaciones_2011

Asamblea Nacional de la RBV. (2013). *Ley de Infogobierno. Gaceta Oficial de la República Bolivariana de Venezuela*. Año CXIII Número 40274. Retrieved March 1, 2014, from http://www.cnti.gob.ve/images/stories/documentos_pdf/leydeinfogob.pdf

Ball, S. (1896). The Moral Aspects of Socialism. *Fabian Track No 72*. London: The Fabian Society. Retrieved August 1, 2014, from http://lib-161.lse.ac.uk/archives/fabian_tracts/072.pdf

Baptista, A. (2010). *Teoría económica del capitalismo rentístico*. Caracas: Banco Central de Venezuela (BCV)p. 306. Retrieved August 1, 2014, from http://www.bcv.org.ve/Upload/Publicaciones/ABaptistateoria.pdf

Barwise, J., & Hammer, E. (1995). *Diagrams and Concept of Logical Systems. What is a Logical System?* (D. Gabbay, Ed.). Oxford, UK: Oxford University Press.

CC. (2014). *Creative Commons License*. Retrieved from http://creativecommons.org/licenses/

Correa, R. (2008). *Decreto 1014 del Rafael Correa Delgado*. Quito, Ecuador: Presidente Constitucional de la República de Ecuador.

Domingo, C. (2008). La Economía de Venezuela. *Entorno-Empresarial.Com*. Retrieved March 1, 2014, from http://www.entorno-empresarial.com/articulo/1769/la-economia-de-venezuela

Drahos, P. (2007). Makind Deals with Al Capone: Paying Protection Money for Intelectual Property in the Global Knowledge Economy. In P. K. Yu (Ed.), Intellectual Property and Information Wealth: Issues and Practices in the Digital Age, Volumen 4. Academic Press.

Europe. (2006). *The impact of Free / Libre / Open Source Software on innovation and Competitiveness of the European Union*. Retrieved March 1, 2007, from http://ec.europa.eu/enterprise/sectors/ict/files/2006-11-20-flossimpact_en.pdf

FSF. (2007). *GNU General Public License Version 3, 29*. Free Software Foundation, Inc. Retrieved from http://fsf.org/

FSF. (2014a). *Categories of free and non-free software*. Retrieved from http://www.gnu.org/philosophy/categories.es.html

FSF. (2014b). *Free Software Licenses*. Retrieved from http://www.gnu.org/licenses/licenses.es.html

FSF. (2014c). *The Free Software Definition, GNU*. Retrieved from http://www.gnu.org/philosophy/free-sw.es.html

Golden, B. (2005). *Succeeding with Open Source*. Addison-Wesley.

Government of the Russian Federation. (2010). *Plan for the transition of federal executive authorities and federal budgetary institutions on the use of free software in 2011 - 2015*. Retrieved March 25, 2014 from http://filearchive.cnews.ru/doc/2010/06/17/2299p.doc

Guedón, J. C. (2001). *In Oldenburg's Long Shadow. Librarians, Research Scientists, Publishers, and the Control of Scientific Publishing*. Association of Research Libraries. Retrieved March 1, 2014, from http://www.arl.org/storage/documents/publications/in-oldenburgs-long-shadow.pdf

IEEE. (2002). *WG12: Learning Object Metadata*. IEEE Standard for Learning Object Metadata. Retrieved July 1, 2009, from http://ltsc.ieee.org/wg12/

Illich, I. (1971). *Deschooling Society*. New York: Harper Colophon Books.

Instituto de Estadística de la UNESCO. (2012). *Uso de TIC en Educación en América Latina y El Caribe. Análisis regional de la integración de las TIC en la educación y de la aptitud digital (e-readiness)*. Retrieved March 25, 2014 from: http://www.uis.unesco.org/Communication/Documents/ict-regional-survey-lac-2012-sp.pdf

Legislatura de la Provincia de Santa Fe. Argentina. (2004). *Ley 12360 del 18 de Noviembre de 2004*. Retrieved March 25, 2014, from http://www.proposicion.org.ar/proyecto/leyes/11134-BRA/texto_aprobado.html

Leyton-Brown, K., & Shoham, Y. (2008). *Essentials of Game Theory*. Morgan and Claypool, Publishers.

Microsoft. (2014). *Microsoft Research Licence Agreement | Microsoft DOS V1.1 and V2.0*. Retrieved March 25, 2014, from http://www.computerhistory.org/_static/atchm/microsoft-ms-dos-early-source-code/agreement/

Microsystems, S. Inc. (n.d.). *Java Research License. Version 1.6*. Retrieved March 1, 2014, from https://www.java.net/jrl.csp

Moglen, E., Sullivan, J. D., & Sullivan, I. (2013). An introduction to the most used FOSS license: the GNU GPL license. In *Legal aspects of free and open source software*. European Commission. Retrieved March 1, 2014, from http://www.europarl.europa.eu/document/activities/cont/201307/20130702ATT6 8998/20130702ATT68998EN.pdf

Neira, E. (2008). *Venezuela: 4th & 5th Republics. The Economic Thing*. Universidad de Los Andes. Retrieved March 1, 2014, from http://www.saber.ula.ve/bitstream/123456789/14622/1/econo.pdf

Pan, G., & Bonk, C. J. (2007). The Emergence of Open-Source Software in China. *International Review of Research in Open and Distance Learning, 8*(1). Retrieved March 1, 2014 from http://www.irrodl.org/index.php/irrodl/article/view/331/0

Read, S., & Dew, N. (2012). *Money from Nothing - The Redhat Story*. British Airways Business Life. Retrieved March 1, 2014, from http://www.effectuation.org/article/money-nothing-redhat-story on March 2014.

Simon, H. A. (1982). *Models of Bounded Rationality: Empirically grounded economic reason*. MIT Press.

Sowe, S. K., Parayil, G., & Sunami, A. (2012). *Free and Open Source Software Technology for Sustainable Development*. United Nations University Press.

Stallman, R. (2013). Misinterpreting Copyright—A Series of Errors. In *Free Software Free Society: Selected Essays of Richard M. Stallman*. Retrieved March 25, 2014, from http://shop.fsf.org/product/free-software-free-society-2/

Suber, P. (2012) *Open Access*. MIT Press. Retrieved March 1, 2014, from https://mitpress.mit.edu/books/open-access

Trosky, L. (1938). Their Morals and Ours. *The New International, 4*(6), 163-173. Retrieved August 1, 2014 from https://www.marxists.org/archive/trotsky/1938/morals/morals.htm

Weingast, B. (2013). e-Study Guide for the Oxford Handbook of Political Economy. Academic Press.

Wittgenstein, L. (1953/2001). *Philosophical Investigations*. Blackwell Publishing.

Xia, Y. (2010). Introduction to software protection under Chinese law. In *The International Free and Open Source Software Law Book*. Open Source Press GmbH. Retrieved March 1, 2014, from http://ifosslawbook.org/china/

KEY TERMS AND DEFINITIONS

Copyleft: It a particular provision in the free software and other types of licenses that request that any improvement on a free work must also be free.

FLOSS: Free, Libre, Open-source Software is software that can be used in freedom, as defined in some free software license.

Free Software License: It is a contract whereby a developer or author presents its work to a user and allow him or her to use, copy, share and improve that work with freedom, as explained in the chapter.

Freedoms in Free Software: A set of well defined rights that an author or developer concedes upon the user of his/her work.

Logical Principles in FLOSS: A set of legal and ethical principles underlying the reasons and reasoning of the actors involved in the free software ecosystem.

Open Formats: Openly defined, data structures used by computer programs to store the particular data their users request or provide. Their openness entails, for users and developers, the possibility of being able to produce or obtain alternative pieces of software to do the job, without being forced to a particular software solution. ec

Rentism: A peculiar economic system in which benefits are obtained with little effort, due to the nature of the good involved which can be easily produced or obtain and are sold a very high prices. Oil is known to have such rentist effects. Software too.

ENDNOTES

[1] "Each contributor grants you a non-exclusive, worldwide, royalty-free patent license under the contributor's essential patent claims, to make, use, sell, offer for sale, import and otherwise run, modify and propagate the contents of its contributor version" (Section 11, GPL, https://www.gnu. org/copyleft/gpl.html).

Chapter 2
Towards a Nationally Pertinent System of Knowledge, Science, and Technology

Jose Aguilar
Universidad de Los Andes, Venezuela; & Prometeo Researcher, Universidad Técnica Particular de Loja, Ecuador

Oswaldo Terán
Universidad de Los Andes, Venezuela

ABSTRACT

This chapter describes an autochthonous system of Knowledge, Science, and Technology (KST): its actors, policies, strategies, and instruments. It is proposed to create it via a continuous reflection-action process. Such a system is aimed at promoting an autonomous nation, and will strongly rest on culturally free KST, beyond its actual conception (as universally valid, and neutral) in the Western Society. We argue that since the culture, problems and needs of the western nations are different from those of the non-western nations, such as Latinamerica, Africa or the Muslim World, the use of western KST in non-western societies without an appropriate reflection about national and local pertinence, generates dependence on KST that has very limited local societal benefits, and prevents developing an autonomous and pertinent KST system – non-western societies can only superficially capture the creations of the western society. To overcome this, we suggest that non-western nations must generate an autochthonous KST system.

INTRODUCTION

The dominant actual meaning and societal role of Knowledge, Science and Technology in general (KST), and of both Free Knowledge, Science and Technology (Free KST, or FKST, which is promoted by, e.g., the Copyleft licenses), and proprietary Knowledge, Science and Technology (or PKST, e.g., that promoted by Copyrights), are creations of the dominant Western Society[1], and are understood as universally valid, and thus neutral. This allows defining the worldwide dominant western models of KST, which are the western KST, western FKST and western PKST).

DOI: 10.4018/978-1-4666-8336-5.ch002

Given that western KST has been created for a (western) society, whose culture and other particular characteristics are different from non-western or peripheral regions and nations, such as Latinamerica, Africa, Asia or the Muslim World, their use in non-western or peripheral societies, without an appropriate reflection about national and local pertinence of such KST, generates dependence (at different levels: economic, political, social, cultural, etc.) on western KST, which has local limited societal benefits. We do not neglect that these non-western or peripheral regions partially share elements of the western world, but they are culturally different and are not leaders in relation to the creation of KST in the world, but rather followers of the western KST and way of life. In this sense they are peripheral, since they are marginal to a dominant western, which imposes them a certain way of life, and a form of KST.

Thus, the western KST promotes a foreign and not pertinent global social model in detriment of the local/autochthonous social model and culture, preventing and precluding the development of an autonomous KST system. A reason for this is that non-western societies can only superficially capture the creations of the western society, viewing from their perspective only the instrumental and passive features, which are easily imitable, while missing its fundamental aspects. Among the aspects missed when coping the western KST are its creative and endogenous character, since western KST appears as a consequence of the western needs and culture, which differ from those in other regions of the world – each region has its own particular local environment, needs and culture –. The most immediate and easiest aspect of KST to be copied is its instrumental use, reduced sometimes to its vacuous employment. This is a use *without any local meaning*, but considered good by the non-autonomous actors (actors who imitate western KST), because actual western KST is fashionable, so it is imitated in order to get *actualized,* and because of the illusion that coping the west KST keeps the non western or peripheral nation "modern", "advanced". Despite of all this, we are not rejecting the fact that some peripheral cultures and societies share in some degree common aspects with western culture and society, and thus western KST has some degree of pertinence with western culture and society. However, such pertinence must be determined and used as a criterion when copying western KST.

This peripheral KST also has some expressions of FKST and PKST (no good copies of the corresponding western FKST and PKST), as well as certain degree of autochthonous KST. Peripheral KST of diverse regions or nations in the world have some relevant common characteristics despite of the differences among such regions or nations. We will centre our attention in such common characteristics, but will describe some particularities specific for the Latinamerican region.

From the point of view of this paper, a common culture defines a Nation. In this sense, the Latinamerican region defines a Nation conformed by several countries (they share a common culture), most of them appearing after the split, into several countries, of the American Spanish Empire in the 19 century. The other country included in this Nation is Brazil, a country coming from the American Portuguese Empire, which also shares the Latinamerican culture. In this chapter we will be using with the same meaning, and indistinctly, the terms national and regional to refer to that which is particular to a Nation (the term regional highlight the fact that the Nation is placed in a certain place, and undergoes some particular situation, in the world).

For this paper, western Knowledge is that theoretical corpus or practical understanding of some subject of interest in the western society. On the other hand, western Science is related to systematic/formal organization of knowledge, in accordance to western social needs and dominant forces (e.g., corporations). Finally, western Technology refers mainly to tools and knowledge useful for solving problems in accordance to western needs, which since several decades are defined mainly by western dominant forces (e.g., industry, corporations, governments, and other actors), and aspire to continuously increase productivity and economical growth, despite of the social and environmental negative effects of this unconstrained increase of economical growth.

Similarly, KST could be developed in a peripheral region in accordance to the social needs of this region. If such development is *autonomous and creative*, i.e., corresponds to the societal needs of the region, we call it *autochthonous*. Usually, KST in a peripheral region is a copy of western KST; in this case, we call it peripheral KST. That autochthonous KST is characterized here as Nationally pertinent, and then *necessarily free* in terms of the culture of the nation. This kind of knowledge in turn promotes an autonomous society with an auto-generative culture.

In order to clarify our argument, we will usually refer to two cases of peripheral societies and KST:

(1) an autonomous society with an autochthonous and creative KST system. This models of society and KST closely linked to the idea of endogenous development suggested in (Ochoa, 2006); to the idea of a creative model of KST described in (Varsavsky, 2006, 2013); and to the idea of a KST as a practice, or as a social process, as described in (Núñez, 1999). Such ideas, can guide application in a particular field of action, such as Social Simulation (Terán & Ablan, 2013). In broad terms, following these authors, we suggest here creatively cultivate KST as a social practice, from the social forms of doing, considering the local know-know. Such a model of KST corresponds to an autonomous, just, democratic, solidary and nationalist society

(2) On the other hand, we have a dependent society and its dependent KST, which we can call "developmentist" case of KST (modelo desarrollista de KST, following Varsavsky 2006, 2013). A developmentist model of KST corresponds to a society culturally dependent on the western culture (its people wish to have the form of live of western people), which attempts to develop by itself all products that the dominant western society elaborates, imitating and copying western KST in its search for economic independence. This form of searching for independence is a trap, given the fact that this nation and its society will never become economically independent: given its cultural dependence. People in this nation necessarily will be always wanting/wishing/desiring what is promoted as good in the western nations, including its KST. The characteristics of this society are a search for economic efficiency, low level of cultural autonomy, and low levels of solidarity and nationalism.

Considering the actual highly interactive and interdependent world, and the historical western domination/exploitation of peripheral nations, it will be impossible to have a totally autochthonous KST system. Thus, in a peripheral nation, an autochthonous KST system has to co-exist with the KST imitated from the west. Given this, the hope is in increasing the level of national pertinence of the KST, measured in terms of the proportion of investment and creation of autochthonous KST in relation to the total KST being in use in the Nation. Because of this, *in this chapter we will usually consider two cases: the western KST and that of a region highly dependent on western KST, such as Latinamerica. Along these two actual cases, for contrasting purposes and clarity in the presentation of our argument, we will manage the two possible models of peripheral KST, named above: the autochthonous and creative one, and the developmentist (imitative) one.*

This chapter will be focuses in *proposing a form of a nationally pertinent (autochthonous) KST system.* In a further work the authors will consider a methodology for developing such a KST system.

The chapter is organized as follows. In the second section, the main characteristics of the western, the imitative peripheral, and the national autochthonous KST systems will be defined. Section three will consider the dominant role of western KST. Afterwards section four offers a wide and concise description of an autochthonous (Nationally Pertinent) KST system. Finally, section five will summarize some characteristics of the actual Latinamerican KST, and will give some guidelines necessary to promote an autochthonous Latinamerican KST system.

TOWARDS A CONCEPTION OF A NATIONAL PERTINENT KST AND FKST

The Western KST

The notions and differences between PKST and FKST appeared in the western society, as part of its actual situation. In this society, both, PKST and FKST, have a clear sense and role, and involve an intricate network of diverse activities.

Amazingly, PKST is developed not only in private organizations, as expected, but also in many public organizations, which get only *partial* "support" from private entities. This fact benefits the private sector in detriment of the public sector, since privative KST gives little recognitions to, while gets strong benefits from, public KST and traditions.

The main feature of privative KST is that it is closed, in the sense that its access is constrained, since the developing entity imposes copyright and other kind of restrictions on its use. Restrictions include constraints on its modification, sharing, studying, redistribution and reverse engineering. Aside this, many international and national legal instruments have been created or modified to protect copyrights of organizations developing privative KST. When such constraints are canceled either partially or totally then open source and free KST, respectively, appear. Open KST means that still some constrains remain. Because of this, in this chapter, open KST will be included as part of privative KST.

We will present a summary of some of the deepest views about technology in the western culture, which is extendible to western KST, following Heidegger (1977), Habermas (1968), and Feenberg (2002). In accordance to these thinkers, the agenda of knowledge and science has become dominated by technology (by the technocratic interest in increasing productivity).

Heidegger (1977) considers that in the western culture technology has become different from technique, as this was known in traditional cultures. Technique in traditional cultures does not depend on high exploitation of energy and nature. The western European culture was traditional until the third quarter of the XIX century. Heidegger considers that western technology dominates man in the sense that man becomes an instrument of technology rather than, as expected, technology being a tool for man. He explains how man serves technology as man makes technology without a clear function for an autonomous humanity, but rather just to make technology, becoming so part of the net of instruments serving technology. In this sense, technology, and western KST in general, has become autonomous from man, and dominates a subjugated man.

Similar ideas are presented by Habermas (1968). Habermas conceives technology as an organic progression of the means people have available, extending their natural capabilities, in order to solve problems. But there is a difference between traditional societies and capitalist modern society in relation to the developed technology, as in the last one the emphasis is on efficiency and individual success.

To explain the differences between a traditional society and the capitalist society in relation to technology, Habermas defines the categories: *Work* and *Interaction*. Work is understood as rational action and choice, or a combination of both, oriented to accomplish tasks with given ends. Thus, Work is based on the *use of the reason to achieve given ends*, and has two components: the *instrumental* one (action: to perform the Work) governed by technical rules based on empirical knowledge, and the *strategic* one (to choose among ways of action, i.e., evaluation of alternatives) supported on analytical knowledge.

Interaction is defined as actions that allow people to engage on socio-political issues. It rests on adherence to social norms of behavior understood and regarded by the involved agents. Violation of norms by an agent has negative consequences for the agent. Interaction is based on human relations, on individual and in-group participation in community activities, in order to increase social benefits. Such activities are mainly publics, but can require the participation of private enterprises (element of Work) as a medium for the achievement of specific ends. National Interaction must be based on the culture while enabling sane cultural change, in the sense that makes possible that the culture keeps its autonomous character. The concrete form of global Interaction (national level of Interaction) emerges from regional and local Interaction.

Under this view, the institutional mark (e.g., the family) of a society rests on Interaction while other subsystems of the society, such as the economical system and the state, which are subsystems of *rational action* respect to given ends, are based on Work. The economical system and the state are *instrumental forms* of organizing and administrating certain aspects of the western society (or an expression of this in a peripheral society), representing a kind of KST (usually called social technology), and, in this sense, are part of Work. In addition, the *learning of rules* of the rational action respect to given ends gives the discipline related with *abilities* useful to solve problems, while the *internalization of norms* of behavior offers the discipline that gives the *structures of the personality*, and the *motivation to conform to the norms*. *This last element represents the force that sustains institutions, and can promote or not emancipation.*

In a traditional society, like the western society before the third quarter of the XIX century (with few exceptions such as France and England), Interaction is the dominant category. In traditional societies, Work is an important force to sustain the society, but it is grounded on traditional values, and subjugated to Interaction. In a traditional society, necessarily the capacities of autonomy of the institutional mark cannot be over passed by the subsystems of rational action.

Different from the case of traditional societies, in capitalist societies (dominant in the west nations) Work is the dominant force, and Interaction is subjugated to it. Habermas observes that Capitalism is the first form of production in world history *institutionalizing* a self-sustaining economic growth, what leads to a fast rate of economic growth, and to a prosperous society in material issues. Nevertheless, at the same time, as growth is unconstrained, many social and cultural attributes are disregarded and even can fall apart.

All this creates individuals without conscience and political willing, i.e., "apolitical" individuals, where the culture is transformed in a view of the world as a thing, while nature and man are disposed in favor of the increase of productivity and technological rationality. This situation is not perceived by the individuals, becoming an unconscious trap for them. In this state of things, science and technology became an ideology, which defines and gives form to such trap. Western KST, then, takes a protagonic role in defining the policies of a society dominated by the interest in increasing productivity, and energetic exploitation of the nature. Consequently, western KST became autonomous, dominating the institutional order and Interaction.

From a point of view close to these of Heidegger and Habermas, Feenberg (2002) offers valuable arguments that help in clarifying the situation about western KST described by the two first authors. He affirms that, in the western capitalist societies, the cultural horizon is characterized and constrained by some beliefs/assumptions and social values respect to the technical objects. These beliefs/assumptions define a technological dimension, which is the base of the actual modern social hegemony. That cultural horizon supports the social hegemony imposed by the technocracy, and give form to many aspects of actual modern life. While establishing the cultural horizon, the technological rationality introduces in the design and structure of the machines and organizational forms social values present in the dominant rationality.

Some actors and specific KST tools have a protagonist role in this situation, getting benefits from and/or promoting the domain of the technocracy, in particular among them we have transnational companies, traditional Economics and Systems Engineering. Some relevant social actors being under the domain of the technocracy are governments, universities, and even international institutions, including organizations regulating commerce or controlling development policies of diverse countries. The domain of Work over Interaction sets the agenda of these institutions, what has important social and cultural consequences.

Finally, among the properties of the western KST we have:

- It is autonomous from other social forces.
- It dominates institutional national and international settings (i.e., norms of behavior, with the help and support of communication media).
- It defines the "cultural horizon", which at the same time supports the social hegemony of KST.
- It proposes and gets advantage of the idea of apolitical individuals and the neutrality of KST.
- Western KST is essentially different from technique in traditional societies (where Interaction (the institutional setting) is the dominant force and KST do not dominate man).
- Western KST represents the interest in increasing productivity.
- Western KST serves to the goal of getting high production of energy, exploiting nature without any limit.
- Transnational enterprises and systems engineering, apart from communication media, are key actors and forces supporting western KST domain.

The Peripheral KST

The fundamental aspect of peripheral KST is its *developmentist and imitative property* (superficially copying western KST). This is part of the strong imitative character of many peripheral societies and nations. This imitative character of peripheral societies appears because actors of the peripheral society see as good and desirable the form of life of the western society, i.e., actors of the peripheral society get a perspective of life, and define their aspiration levels about many issues, in accordance to what they perceive in the western society.

Consequently, peripheral KST's ideal is western KST. Similarly, the ideal for peripheral PKST and FKST are western PKST and western FKST, respectively. However, imitation never can be original, and a peripheral society can only copy the superficial aspects of western KST, failing to notice and take its creative attributes. As said above, peripheral KST has not a good correspondence with, and pertinence for, local needs. It is neither the product of local Interaction, nor of local based or relevant choice. Rather, it is mainly the product of imitative action and decontextualized choice. In this sense, only the form of using knowledge is copied, but the philosophical insight and base/generative KST, existing in the western society, are not, and cannot be, copied by the peripheral society. In fact, from the perspective of the western nations and KST dominant actors, peripheral nations have a marginal role, serving as providers of raw materials and consumers of final goods.

On the other hand, as part of imitation of the domain of technocracy in the western, technocrats in peripheral nations are supposed to have the truth. They imaginarily manage the valid "best" rationality and KST, having the power to design and direct social policies. Their opinion is supposed to be strongly valuable in order to develop the country or nation and so become part of the developed world, for what western KST is a fundamental component. Peripheral KST, including its research and teaching in peripheral universities, is usually reduced to issues of interest in order to serve to applications and research in the west. Knowledge of peripheral technocrats in productive organizations, and to a good extent in the universities is reduced to the ability to apply technology in accordance to some manuals elaborated in the west (Varsavsky, 2006).

Consequently, peripheral technocrats are disconnected from the culture of their society. They are "apolitically sheeps" dominated from external interest, and then become unaware extensions/representantives of foreign dominant technocracy, trans-national enterprises and governments. National KST then becomes dominated by a foreign KST, culturally strange, and which is, at best, instrumentally understood and copied. Even more, culture of peripheral societies becomes dominated by the resulting imitated (superficial and usually mediocre) technocracy, which is supposed to have the truth about political issues.

Given this state of issues, the culture of the nation can become strongly affected, loosing its autogenerative capabilities, if the proportion of autochthonous KST is small in relation to the total KST used in the nation. The country becomes a satellite at the service of the west. In particular, the KST system is dominated by a strongly imitative KST system, which is called interestedly "apolitical", managed by technocrats that serve the interest of transnational companies and foreign nations. Finally, the characteristics of a developmentist society, as mentioned in the introduction above and suggested in Varsavsky (2006), are met: a poorly autonomous, highly dependent, as well as lowly solidary and nationalist society.

First Ideas about a National Pertinent KST

A peripheral nation has both: a) its peripheral KST (PKST and FKST), and b) its autochthonous/pertinent KST. The second is defined as the traditional and culturally congruent KST, in the sense that it serves to solve culturally pertinent problems, corresponding to an autonomous, just, solidary, democratic, and nationalist society.

Given the cultural dependence of peripheral nations, and their developmentist model of KST, in these countries usually western KST is recognized as highly valuable, while autochthonous KST is seen as retrograde and undesirable by the national dominant technocratic actors. This is due to the dominance of the copied western KST over the national interaction category defined by Habermas. A consequence of that is the low pertinence of actual copied KST to solve problems associated to the social reality of peripheral nations.

This chapter suggests reverting such a situation by: a) recognizing the superiority of the national culture, i.e., of Interaction over Work (rationality to achieve given ends); and, b) promoting a Nationally Pertinent KST. In this case the autochthonous KST will prevail over western KST. This KST should necessarily be *culturally free, creative and cultivated from the national social practices.*

THE DOMINANT ROLE OF WESTERN KNOWLEDGE, SCIENCE AND TECHNOLOGY

The Role of Knowledge in Society

In this section, we will discuss about the role of actual dominant western knowledge and the potential of free knowledge to generate societal benefits, especially to peripheral nations. There is an important relationship between the society, and how it uses and builds knowledge (we use here a wide connotation of the knowledge concept encompassing science and technology). Knowledge is one of the dynamic elements in a society, consequently it is valuable to reflect upon it. A society characterizes key elements of its life from the knowledge it manages: their ways of organizing, social rules, educational models, among others. Each of the alternatives, dynamics, etc., in each of these areas is conditioned by the knowledge that constitute them, and the possibilities they allow. This permits us to say that knowledge is political.

Furthermore, a fundamental aspect of any society is its cultural matrix. The cultural matrix is given by, among other things, knowledge, myth, and religion, of the community, what gives meaning to the life in the society (Aguilar & Terán, 2011; Fuenmayor, 2006). For people, for the human being, the more transcendent, fundamental public good, is its cultural matrix, since it is the one that allows him to regenerate, recreating his culture.

In this sense, all what is given to a society in terms of knowledge, should be harmonious with, and must be designed to feed its cultural matrix. But in capitalist societies, knowledge, expressed through technology and science that gives rise to it, is turning everything around it in a tool (Aguilar, 2011a, 2011b). This form of knowledge development has been associated with a deterioration of the cultural matrix (Aguilar & Terán, 2011; Fuenmayor, 2006, 2001).

This shows us that knowledge is not neutral in society, but rather plays a fundamental role in it. Several authors have analyzed this not neutral role of the knowledge from different perspectives; for example, (Núñez, 1999) has proposed look at it from two angles, first, from the point of view that the knowledge is the result of a social activity, and, second, from the point of view of the value of this knowledge in the cultural matrix of a society. Science and technology, as a form of knowledge, is perhaps where more naturally that role in society is expressed (Aguilar, 2011a). For example, authors such as Habermas (1999) argue that technology is a legitimating ideology of a way of acting, in most cases, following other ends alien to society, to the detriment of their culture.

Knowledge not only transforms its relationship with man, but also changes the relationship of man to man himself (Aguilar, 2011b). In particular, capitalist view of knowledge is becoming a society in a tank of "devices ready to use". It is an instrumental view of knowledge, which sees it as cold, outside society, without an historical-social origin.

That is, the most widespread conception of knowledge today is the instrumental one, which serves as a means to achieve predetermined ends. However, knowledge shows other aspects (Aguilar & Terán, 2011; Aguilar, 2011b):

- Define key elements in the life of a society. The forms of governance, the community planning, the political system, the urban modes, to name a few, are mediated by technologies.
- It is not something cold, without a social-historical origin. Knowledge comes from a given cultural matrix.
- It is determined and determines the Science and Technology (there is a feedback among them).

We say there are more democratic ways of approaching knowledge, which opens to a society the possibility of a new form of power that is expressed in their active participation in cognitive activities, in the control of cognitive processes, and not simply watching knowledge as a mediator of social activities.

This requires rethinking the ways of organizing societies, where modes of citizen participation in public life prevail, accompanied by cognitive enrichment processes that feed social dynamics (as suggested in Núñez, 1999). This again leads us to the issue of neutrality of knowledge. We see that knowledge is not indifferent to the set of possible purposes it can serve. Thus, knowledge ends up favoring some and precludes other purposes, so it is not neutral (Varsavsky, 2006).

A major factor in the relationship between society and knowledge is the possible opening of cognitive processes to democratic forms of social control. That is, a "democratic intervention" of the society in the knowledge creation. It allows the apparition of social values of society in social cognitive processes, such as environmental claims, ancestral making, among others, and incorporating them the cognitive processes allowing development of knowledge in harmony with local interests (these ideas are close to those of socially constructed knowledge Núñez, 1999).

This is where the real power of free knowledge appears, in a new kind of society that understands the importance of knowledge in it. We're talking about a public sphere in the political life of the society, in which appears something that until now has been closed to it, the conception of social cognitive processes, including technology assessment, and the design of the scientific-technological agendas, etc. This is not a struggle for wealth, but a dispute for questioning, disassemble and remake, social practices that structure our daily lives, characterizing, challenging and developing the knowledge that is embedded in them (Aguilar, 2010a). That means demystify the universality of the scientific-technological decisions, from a non-dogmatic view of them. To do this, we need to start from the consequences of knowledge (scientific and technological), and questioning the social framework that it generates, something that is allowed only by the potentials free knowledge offers.

But this democratic form of social cognitive processes requires extending the range of interests represented in them, sensitive enough to understand and modify, where necessary, the injurious social dynamics to its cultural matrix. The so-formed social groups are able to generate a reflective environment on their doing, their rationale, and the way they organize, enriched with its own criteria of its social environment. Thus, the decisions, evaluations, and performances of the society are given on a new rational dynamic where the senses are built collectively. From there will emerge a new kind of public life, as part of the democratization of society, typified by ongoing public debate on the knowledge that affects every aspect of social life.

We are talking about an active public participatory democracy, in which the ability to act warranting the decisions that have to take place must be rescued, from such participation. It is not a problem of majorities, as classically tells us the electoral logic that ends up ignoring minorities, but a space for discussion through cognitive analysis and virtuoso collective judgment. This would allow a "multicultural cognition", in which each social context would have its own social interpretation (Aguilar, 2011b).

This process of democratization of knowledge implies that the scientific and technological development is seen as a political process, rather than instrumentally. That scientific- technological development would be a space of social struggle where ideas are discussed, and society is built, being that as it would confer the political nature of this process (Aguilar & Terán, 2011). It is one of the ways to break the cultural dependency in one of the areas where it is most remarkable and least perceived. This would define a scientific-technological culture for a society in which its agendas are discussed from the problems of everyday life, their ways of solution, etc.

We're not talking about isolating the society from the global advances, we are proposing a knowledge that suits the social meanings, that also incorporate the social values of the environment where it will be used. In this way, knowledge becomes meaningful in the culture of each local community, socially conceived and discussed, and not imposed by powers and particular interests.

This idea finds many obstacles, including technocracy, which states that the scientific-technological knowledge is beyond any questioning (forgetting Galileo Galilei). Thus, the actors that are in positions of organizational leadership, public or private, capitalists or communists, are subordinate to that way of thinking. In this sense, the economic importance of knowledge is negligible compared to its human implications, defining lifestyles, forms of social doing, among other things.

Economical Aspects of Knowledge

Knowledge can be stored in digital form, and then be forwarded for productive purposes. From this point of view, knowledge is seen as a means of production, unlike the mass production of the past, it has a defining characteristic: it is reproducible, in unlimited amounts, regardless of whether the research that originates it was expensive. The knowledge, once obtained, can be used indefinitely without losing any of its effectiveness. It does not spend or deteriorate, it may even get richer.

This stage of capitalism has exploited this codified knowledge, given origin to a new type of economy, called by some as Knowledge economy, or Knowledge-Based Economy. This conception of economics assumes that the knowledge is used as a key element to generate value and wealth through its transformation (Aguilar, 2011b). This is what is hidden behind the term "knowledge society", some authors have preferred to call it cognitive capitalism (Aguilar, 2011b), seen as the emergence of a new regime of accumulation in which the object of accumulation is knowledge. Cognitive capitalism has been taking over and privatizing universal knowledge, the common cultural heritage, for its sole benefit. This has been leading to a cultural impoverishment, to spaces of great social dependence, precluding self-generation of culture, because knowledge is been kidnapped (Aguilar, 2011b).

This idea of "knowledge society" has been analyzed by (Núñez, 1999) including several terms to describe it. The term "technoscience" to define the close relationship between science and technology without a clear frontier between them; the term "scientific industry" to describe the new mercantile processes around the science; and the term "scientific migrations" to describe the concentration of the scientific and technologic activity in several poles (North-America, Europe and Japan).

Apart from the idea of Núñez, the term "knowledge society" currently appears as one of the champions of progress, but in fact it seems too superficial and distorted, because knowledge that supports these production processes is being hijacked by artificial forms of access restrictions. The knowledge society has some distinct features compared to previous models of societies. It, without the intention of limiting the subject, has as most significant features: the globalization of knowledge, the prevalence of informational capitalism, the important role of technological infrastructure, the replacement of traditional mechanical production systems, the interactivity, the immediacy of outputs and outcomes, the work flexibility, the commitment to scientific progress, and its strong dependence on information and communication technologies.

Something that merits deep reflection on the concept of knowledge society is the idea of efficiency and progress. It is part of an ongoing struggle to reach the top positions (social, productive, and personal) over any ethical and social value. This clashes with more human schemes and social groups, where cooperation, solidarity and social welfare are the values prevail. This notion of knowledge society has allowed a conception of globalization with the following features:

- The dominant role of the financial world.
- The role of transnational corporations, with ever greater influence in governments and societies.
- The changing notion of time and space due to the use of ICT.
- The deterioration of the nation-state concept.
- The growing involvement of international organizations (UN, IMF, etc.).

The current globalization model of doing science and technology strengthens this new form of capitalism. A model that is based on violence today applies to restrictive policies regarding access to knowledge and creations derived from it, as a way to hijack that knowledge. We talked about a whole space of production and stimulation of business activity in which appear the intellectual property, new forms of monopoly, patents and rights of author, etc., having effects on health, food, etc.

In that sense, cognitive capitalism has elements that characterize it that need to be unveiled (Aguilar, 2011b). First of all, knowledge is merely at the service of capitalist production. Second, it is based on an artificial shortage of knowledge, where some are consumers of knowledge that others create and sell. Third, the economy is based on immediacy, where a consumer-based dynamics is imposed.

This step has been strengthened by the breakthrough of the Internet, which has allowed the dynamic commercial about knowledge to gain a global connotation. Specifically, the Internet has also added communicative element to this dynamic. Communication is crucial, since the new virtual economy is based on language in its different forms: oral, written, digital, becoming a mediator between scientific and technological developments and the social processes, while integrating different global dynamics of construction of knowledge. Nevertheless, as pointed out before, this stage has also been strengthened by the premise that ideas should be private. This privatization process is based on the notion that "ideas should be private property to protect authors, scientists and artists, who generate knowledge, engines of the new society" (Aguilar, 2011b). What they do not say is that by accepting this premise, the freedom of every man to learn what he wants, following the path he wants, limited only by its abilities, vocations, an a culture in a good state, is denied.

The Knowledge Economy profitability of knowledge is a necessity that is possible only when it has been coded (in the form of models, rules, etc.), being available to someone working with the codified knowledge, for its individual or collective benefice. Thus, this stage of capitalism is a new way of using codified knowledge, seeing it now as digital information for production processes (GI, Good Informational), making it an input. But these GI have several characteristics (Aguilar, 2011b):

- They are the result of a collective process of knowledge creation, which includes periods of collection and processing of information, tests and trials, correction and modification.
- They cannot be exhausted; its utilization does not undermine their effectiveness. On the contrary, the utilization can enrich it
- They have the ability to exploit the Internet to their development and dissemination.
- They exhibit the properties of continuity and replicability,
- They have a development trend according to the Moore's Law

In recent decades, investments to develop this type of economy have been significant, even greater than those aimed at producing tangible goods (machinery, raw materials, etc.).

The Knowledge Economy has two new means of production vital to its dynamics, the computer and the Internet, generating knowledge workers, which have reconfigured the social relations of production, distribution and exchange in the world (Aguilar, 2011b). A new division of labor has emerged, which has transgressed the boundaries of nations, assigning roles to diverse regions of the world according to their cognitive, religious, social, and political conditions. The Knowledge Economy defines a new model of industrial development, which is followed by the software and telecommunications industries.

This new way of accumulation, in addition to knowledge requires other types of raw materials: technology, research, information, culture, communication and language. The two last are necessary to enable cooperative work. So, immaterial labor involves the management of information and communication linked to the processes of knowledge production, which introduces a cooperative dimension, which has the form of social interaction through communication, affective networks, among others.

But capitalism uses common cultural heritage for their own exclusive benefit (the human genome, that of plants and animals, among other skills), limiting accessibility, its social utilization, etc. This contributes to a cultural impoverishment that generates social dependence spaces never before imagined. Because of this, the culture is losing its self-generation capacity (Aguilar, 2011b).

However, new forms of resistance to that situation have been emerging. A clear example is the free software community. But many of the actions from the fields of resistance that have been created worldwide (free software movement, the free culture movement) do not question the notion of ownership, nor its idea that "creations" belong by default to the private. They, in some cases, reinforce that notion to build on their arguments. They do not study the social meanings of the restrictions on the access to knowledge (global dependence spaces, dividing citizens between first and second class people) being generated under these schemes. In this sense, these resistors are not a problem for the cognitive capitalism.

Recognize the strengthening of the property from the resistance processes is critical, because it allows us to understand the possible characteristics of the forms of struggle and resistance to fight the cognitive capitalism, and design a more humanistic economical model. This is important from the premise that intellectual private property is a theft of social knowledge, "kidnapping" and veiling its common good character.

Education and Free Knowledge

First of all, it is essential to reveal the political role of the educational processes of domination in terms of social class, race, gender, scientific and technological alienation, among other things, and how the hidden educational model that prevails in them builds a hegemonic culture. At present, in the western culture, all educational models respond to dominant political and economic model (Aguilar, 2011a).

The prevailing educational model imposes in man the law of fear (fear of doing things, afraid to build their truths, etc.), which precludes their emancipation. This educational model aims to fragment, kidnap knowledge, in order to facilitate the process of control, domination, alienation, awareness and, thus, ensure the hegemony of the ruling classes. Thus, education is a form of domination. It is a way of establishing and promoting economic, political, cognitive and cultural hegemonies. Here lies the shallow knowledge neutrality.

Is there a way to subvert it? Yes, through social processes where truth is grown. The culture of truth must lead to a permanent attitude of critical reflection that allows us to keep adding new levels of truth-seeking in each event analyzed. This bustling about the search for truth must be made from our realities, with their edges and importance according to each setting, at each social context. The study of each social problem should arise by local frames of reference, seeking factors and making it appropriate to the particular case, without neglecting the universal experience, but without accepting it a priori. Thus, the value of each scientific-technological activity is particular to each context. In this way, not all research endeavors, and its forms, are equally important; therefore, a scientific activity in a society cannot be chosen randomly.

The philosophy behind free knowledge is the only one that:

- Defends the rights of citizens in relation to technology.
- Facilitates the incorporation of ICT in everyday life as a factor of progress towards a more just and egalitarian society
- Promotes effectiveness, efficiency and transparency in public administration.
- Allows sustainable development and dissemination of knowledge.
- Promotes regional production, endorsing technological sovereignty.

The philosophical principles present in free software communities appear naturally in this conception of knowledge, as pointed out in (Aguilar, 2011a):

- Knowledge must be accessed and used freely, allowing the encounter and using various sources of knowledge (ancient, scientific, etc.).
- Knowledge must be free to adapt to local work patterns.
- Knowledge should be freely shared through a process of collective construction.
- The knowledge gained can be improved freely, and these new versions of knowledge must be able to be shared freely with others, so that the whole world can benefit.

But the idea that knowledge liberates and emancipates the individual, and allows him to break the chains of disposal, requires another look. It must be a knowledge useful to learn and understand the world in which we live, to understand how we become who we are, take a holistic view of our lives, explain the historical causes of current events, establishing a narrative that gives meaning to our lives individually and collectively. And from this, that knowledge should enable action on our realities to transform and rebuild our mother language as an essential element for our cultural transformation. In this sense, the "four freedoms" of free software not realize the freedom of knowledge and technology in a transcendent sense (Aguilar, 2011a).

We are talking about a concept of free knowledge that goes beyond the notion of "accessibility" and "use", which arises as an emergent quality of social dynamics itself, that seeks to integrate and is assimilated as part of social processes, and that is "free" if it provides positive socio-cultural processes of emancipation and integration, and it is based on inputs and modes of knowledge generation understood as common good.

To delve further this idea of emancipatory knowledge, (Aguilar, 2011a) has identified four elements. The first is that knowledge has an ideological component. For example, we have knowledge for the death and for the life, and each of these approaches to knowledge have completely different social dynamics. The next element is the idea of a free relation with the knowledge, which has to do with that we are not abducted for the knowledge, framed for it, because it is questionable, open to criticism, not a ready to use product. The third element is to recognize the role of knowledge in the culture. Finally, the last point is that we must learn to resist the prevailing scientific-technological model.

From the above we can characterize emancipating knowledge as relevant knowledge, built from below in emerging participatory forms (Aguilar, 2011a). To achieve emancipatory knowledge we must break with the current educational model, kidnapped by academic elites, by bureaucratic forms of management, and by educational technocrats. This new educational model requires endogenous dynamics of social construction of knowledge (Aguilar, 2011a). This demands a culture of free movement of knowledge and expertise. It also requires new forms of knowledge construction (e.g., social networks are an example of collective learning spaces. They allow the emergence of native knowledge derived from the needs of the networks). We are talking about a new form of social activity where all participate in building the knowledge required for the implementation and construction of life projects in common.

The philosophy behind the free knowledge contributes to democratize access to knowledge, the social appropriation of knowledge, to facilitate innovation, to promote scientific and technological sovereignty, among other things. The creation of free knowledge is seen as a development strategy, which ensures sharing it and collectivizing the processes of knowledge generation and innovation. This is so because free knowledge:

- Promotes social inclusion.
- Endorses the effectiveness, efficiency and transparency with which the public administration must act.
- Enables accessibility and dissemination of knowledge, framed on the right of citizens to be informed and be partakers of the development process.
- Encourages local production, promoting technological independence.

Thus, the free knowledge is in the path of the Scientific-Technological Independence, because it presents several fundamental principles closely linked to the notion of endogenous development of a nation (Aguilar, 2011a), such as:

- Allows a sustainable development and diffusion of knowledge, framed on the right of citizens to the information
- Defends the rights of citizens in relation to science and technology, particularly on issues such as access to knowledge, rights of fair use media, etc.
- Facilitates the incorporation of knowledge in everyday life as a factor of progress towards a more just and equal society.

The free knowledge raises an interesting way of managing public goods and services, what is a catalyst for future social and organizational changes that are being accelerated by the Internet. This approach of a free society from the knowledge starts from the fact that social activities are cognitive processes. All this requires a reflection that allows us to address issues such as democratic rationality of cognitive processes in the society; demystification of knowledge; and finally, the need for social learning to ensure public participation of citizens in society, etc.

A NATIONALLY PERTINENT (AUTOCHTHONOUS AND CREATIVE) KST SYSTEM

As said in section 1, given the preference for foreign KST, because of the imitation of the west nations, the actual KST in peripheral nations has low pertinence (low cultural sense). That is so because the western way/view of development has been chosen as the reference model. *If we recognize that diverse models of development are possible, in accordance to the culture of each nation, as suggested by (Fuenmayor, 2000), then KST creation can be directed at solving problems in accordance to the nation interest and culture, which would be fundamentally autochthonous and pertinent. In this case, the Interaction would be dominant, as suggested by Habermas, and Work would be subjugated by Interaction.*

An autochthonous KST system must continuously question both, its conceptions and its form to search for KST, i.e., it must be fundamentally critic even about itself. In this sense, Fuenmayor (2006, 2001) recommends to plant and cultivate KST in terms of good and virtuous practices, in accordance to MacIntyre (1985) ideas. I will also be in line with Núñez (1999)'s ideas of building a system of KST from social practices, Varsavsky (2006, 2013) suggestion of a creative and socialist KST system, and Ochoa (2008) ideas of Endogenous development.

Necessarily, a peripheral nation must base its KST on socio-cultural needs, taking a form of constant *reflection-action*, which will rest on mutually supported (recursive feedback) *bottom-up emergent processes and top-down guiding processes*. The emergent bottom-up processes must start from the *internal dynamics* of the local actors and communities, and then go up towards the national level through more local and community levels. On the other hand, the top-down process *guides* and leads the bottom-up processes, increasing synergy, "dialogue" and coordination among several of these processes coming from diverse communities and regions.

The described *creative* and emergent processes, in accordance to cultural and societal pertinence, will construct: a) *a pertinent conceptual framework*, i.e., the meaning of relevant ideas and concepts such as what are "free" and "not free" KST; b) *community, local, national, and international policies, strategies and instruments;* and, c) *the organizational form and structure* of the KST system. Overtime, these processes must lead the nation outside the peripheral dependence on the west, as the nation would have its proper/autochthonous KST and will pursue its own development form, following National/ Regional criteria.

The bottom-up and top-down processes will be described in further research. They are aimed at re-placing the actual non autochthonous, developmentist, KST system, of the peripheral strongly dependent societies. For this, not only new different components and processes of the KST system should appear but also, and fundamentally, a different and appropriated attitude of the actors involved in the system should appear. These issues demand, on one hand, *a structural change* of the actual KST system into a new KST system with a new structure; and, on the other hand, KST actors with a new attitude, based on a better understanding and identification with the new system in construction, recognizing the priorities of the national culture and its institutional autochthonous mark, i.e., it must give an appropriated importance to *Interaction*. This *requires an educative project (an educative mother project[2]), aimed at strengthening an appropriate attitude and perspective in the nation.*

For this last goal, particular attention should be given to those actual imitative (of the west European Science), apolitical and rationalist (prevailing the rationally with given ends) attitudes of the actual tech-nocrats. To overcome such attitudes, it is necessary to promote a change on the culture of the Nation in favor of Interaction. In particular, the process of *creation of the Nationally Pertinent KST System must be guided by virtuous of the national culture*, who must have deep knowledge of the problems of the nation, and have a critical attitude towards the actual KST.

In fact, to increase sovereignty a nation needs an autochthonous KST, in order to sustain itself as an autonomous nation, which defines by itself its form of development. In this sense a KST has a political character, which tributes and contributes to the construction of a sovereign society, while being constructed/created by this society. The virtuous guide of the construction of the KST system should be accompanied by appropriate direction and control of the process, which can be carried on by an *autonomous public organization*. This public organization must be headed by virtuous people, who are compromised with the increase of the societal benefits of a pertinent KST system. They are virtuous in terms of their knowledge of knowing the society, its culture, international context and natural environment (see Fuenmayor, 2006). This organization must promote the auto-generative character of the culture of the society. In this sense, the process of development of a National Pertinent KST system should define its own concepts and practices, creatively, while dealing appropriately with those concepts and practices coming from the western society.

Summarizing, the Nationally Pertinent KST can briefly be defined as: a *Network of actors with the capacities and appropriated attitudes to cover the KST requirements of the nation, in order to solve its autochthonous problems, which includes also the final users, and is permanently adapting itself to the National requirements and interests* (this idea is in line with the proposals of a Virtuous Scientific System (Fuenmayor, 2006); a National Creative Stile of Science and Technology (Varsavsky, 2006, 2013), and the idea of Science and Technology as a Social Process, suggested by Núñez (1999)). This system must be in permanent construction and coupling via flexible change in relation to the National requirements, in a process of *research-action*, and includes the following components:

- A set of KST policies, strategies and instruments
- A group of virtuous actors orienting those processes.
- KST actors with an attitude coherent with the national requirements.
- A public organization of direction and control, which should be under the orientation of the named virtuous group.

These elements will be described in the next section. Finally, we cannot forget that this KST system is subjugated to Interaction , and is built in a process of research-action.

KST Policies, Strategies and Instruments

Organizationally, three elements must be present in all components and sub-components of the system: a) the policy element, which includes a discussion and dialogue about the ends of the KST system and the system being created, related to the analysis of Interaction in the society, and in the particular context of application (i.e., sector or region); b) the management element (about internal and external issues), associated to the strategic aspect of Work, to generate a correct synergy among the different components of the KST system; and, c) the operative element linked to the instrumental aspect of Work.

As said above, the organization of the KST system should be flexible, but also lowly hierarchical, where roles are assigned to actors in accordance to their engagement and virtuosity. Related models of this kind of organization are those used in the systems of free software development and in the systems of knowledge accumulation, such as in the creation of the kernel of Linux, and in the Wikipedia (for more about this, see, for instance, Himanen, 2001; and Perozo, Aguilar, Terán & Molina, 2013). Strategies, policies and instruments are determined at different levels:

Interaction Category: National/Regional and Local Requirements, Criteria, Policies, and Mother Projects

The set of polices subjugates the other elements (strategies and instruments), and is autonomous from external domain. It must be fed from the most important dynamics occurring at the national Interaction.

The set of policies must implicitly recognize that the country's national life is based on a system of *myths/narratives* guiding the culture of the nation. This narrative accounts for the historical-cultural national context, which must make explicit from where the actual national reality comes from. That system evolves over time following an auto-generative dynamic, a sort of mythopoesis. What we mean with the idea of narrative as mythopoesis is similar to the description given by Guss (2014), when explaining the sense of the socio-cultural narrative of the Yekuana tribes of the Amazonian Forests in Guss (1990) and in De Civrieux (1992).

The description of the narrative must be constantly actualized by the national virtuous actors. It must include a description of how the peripheral aspects of the country, including western KST, are seen. Also, it must refer to the level of influence life in the west Europe (including the western KST) has over the socio-culture of the nation, and to the level of dependence (or correspondingly, of its reverse: autonomy) the nation has from such influence. The narrative must account for the present and past of the world in general (as seen from the culture of the nation), and for the nature of changes in present world (including involved actors and forces).

Social processes supported in such a narrative and creating KST must be emergent, involving actors and entities having national autochthonous capacities. They should be able to deal with external stimulus and rethink itself permanently, adapting properly to its context while keeping its autonomy from external forces. The KST will be autochthonous and nationally autonomous as far as it does not imitates foreign forms of doing KST, and rather constructs/cultivates/creates its own form of developing KST.

The socio-cultural narrative should indicate (interpreted by the virtuous group) the fundamental problems of the nation, which will define important needs in terms of food production, health, institutional organization, education, defense, among other basic requirements. The description should be both, general and by communities and sectors. *This set of basic problems allows the virtuous national group to identify the pertinent KST requirements.*

The definition of needs and requirements must regard the high importance that adherence to social norms of behavior has for a good state of the Interaction. In this sense, the organizational culture of the nation including traditional norms of behavior, must be taken into account and promoted by the developed KST system.

From these requirements, a first version of criteria for choosing KST, a set of KST policies and a set of associated KST key or mother projects, will be defined[3]. These criteria, policies and associated mother projects must be defined in order of importance, and necessarily linked, via an explanation, to the historic-cultural narrative. At this point of our discussion, four projects with the following goals can serve as examples of mother projects:

1. To cultivate national education, in order to support national autochthonous development, and increase the public good (this project was named above);
2. to continuously auto-generate the cultural narrative;
3. to conceptualize (including the definition of the structure and processes), and develop strategies and tools for the KST system;
4. and, to continuously update the research-action methodology and tools that guide the development of the autochthonous KST system.

Given that the set of KST requirements, policies and mother projects, should be also aimed at *dealing with the western dominant way of life, and its dominant KST,* in order to increase national socio-cultural autonomy, a mother project can also be created to help in dealing with this specific but fundamental issue.

In order to have a holistic idea about the set of KST policies and KST mother projects, a network of the concrete KST projects should be elaborated. Also, an explanation of the requirements, criteria, set of policies and mother projects, in terms that can be understood by the habitants of the country, must be elaborated. All of these are part of the *national KST plan* (this kind of plan are better explained in Varsavsky, 2006).

The national KST requirements, policies and mother projects, should take into account the communities at the local and regional levels. It must involve all diversity of KST actors, including communities, and especially KST virtuous actors at the corresponding level. It includes actors producing, conceptualizing, or using KST at all the spatial levels. In all levels, the analysis and report should be divided into a general and a by sectors part. Once the consult is made at the local and regional actors, the products of these consults should be unified in a coherent form by selected regional and local actors.

Strategic Element of Work

Once the national and local KST policies (national/regional, and local) have been defined in accordance to the national requirements, the KST strategies are created. I.e., once the fundamental outcome (requirements, criteria, policies, and mother projects) have been generated in accordance to the national Interaction, the following step is to determine the first component of Work. Before this step also the actors, including the virtuous ones, have been identified.

The first component of Work consists in the KST strategies to implement such policies, and move towards the KST national plan to achieve them via KST mother projects, and linked subprojects (both strategic and instrumental ones). During the determination of the "Strategic Element", the set of mother projects is actualized, and projects, aimed at developing and complementing the mother projects, are elaborated. A mother project is carried out via several projects in a certain parallel or sequential order. This order gives a global form of the national KST plan based on all the projects. In order to facilitate the comprehension of the strategies and plan, these must be explained in a document along the KST policies. Such explanation must be based on the socio-cultural narrative (perhaps a summary), the social needs, and the associated KST requirements.

At this level, western form of life, and any kind of influence coming from the western KST system, must be analyzed from a critical point of view, in order to create and implement strategies for increasing national socio-cultural autonomy and an autochthonous KST system. All this will help, for instance, in designing national strategies oriented to control the influence from the west KST and way of life. As part of this control, the national pertinence of western KST must be determined, before western KST is copied and implemented in the nation.

In particular, the social games around KST involving the KST actors and forces must be described, in order to increase its comprehension and help the actors of the KST system in creating and refining strategies to favor a national autochthonous KST system. These games include those actors and forces representing the external influence coming from the western nations, as well as those autochthonous and non-autochthonous KST actors and forces existing in the nation. Strategies, interests, motivations, controlled resources and relations, etc., of these actors must be very well described. The description of the KST strategies and social games has to be made at all levels: national, and local. Tools such as situational planning methodologies and simulation models can help in the comprehension of these games, including the study and analysis of alternative scenarios (ideas from Social Simulation might help, see for instance Terán & Ablan, 2013). The description of the games also considers an explanation of the attitudes of the involved actors, and their relation/gap when compared to the ideal attitude of an actor coherent with a national autonomous culture and an autochthonous KST system.

Instrumental Element of Work

The definition of KST instrumental actions must take into account and improve the autochthonous know-how of the diverse communities, at all levels (local and national). Also, good practices (pertinent) found in particular communities should be recognized, motivated, and promoted/dispersed in other communities.

Virtuous Actors and Strategies of Change

The KST system must be oriented by virtuous actors in the sense of knowing well and caring about the culture of the Nation, while having an attitude coherent with the national pertinent needs, at the same time that are compromised/identified with the spreading of the autochthonous KST. The virtuous actors must be deeply involved in the process of KST creation from the "higher" levels of KST (conceptualizing and elaboration of KST policies), to the lower levels (KST usage by diverse communities), passing through any intermediate steps of KST creation. Among the virtuous actors, especial attention must receive the main actor orienting and coordinating the process of KST creation: *the public organization of direction and control*. Among the fundamental actors and their roles we have the followings:

Communities of Users of the Nation

The communities of the nation represent the main KST users. They face in their everyday life the autochthonous problems and needs, and consequently are the most important actors to define the requirements for the KST system. On one hand, they have to be taken into account by the virtuous actors to define the KST policies, strategies and instruments. On the other hand, they validate the description of such policies, strategies and instruments, collectively constructing the KST system. Consequently, these communities will be fundamental to define the KST local requirements, criteria, policies, strategies and instruments.

Actors in communities share life experiences and goals. They have spaces of collective learning, where KST is seen as a public good, whose property corresponds to the whole nation, or to the whole humanity. The KST system needs to be cultivated, in order to increase national wellbeing. This KST collectively constructed implicitly carries on a proposal of social action, what makes such knowledge pertinent and helps in promoting that proposed endogenous form of social action. This is a strategy of mutual promotion of autochthonous knowledge and social action (for more about these ideas, see Ochoa, 2008).

The KST processes of decision making at all levels must be based on dialogue and consultation, including all social actors. The communities and the virtuous actors must also have control about the process of KST creation, what requires decision spaces, free information flux to allow the virtuous actors and communities to audit that process. The auditing process itself should imply some KST specific requirements (more details about these ideas are proposed for the LA case in Section 5 of this chapter). Some of these requirements are in terms of learning processes and organizational forms, as well as strategic and instrumental tools (they might define a mother project). The answer to these requirements represents a feedback going from the KST system to itself.

The character of these processes of decision making and its products reveals the necessary free nature of the autochthonous KST system.

The State

The state must guarantee the good quality of the process of creation and maintenance of the KST system, favoring its autochthonous character. For that, *virtuous* public administration workers are necessary – they must know very well the culture of the nation and the pertinent requirements for the KST system. Once the KST system become highly autochthonous, the role of the state is reduced to place particular demands/requirements to the KST system, in accordance to its problems and needs, in order to assume its social duties. Aside this, the state must promote a strong educative system, which must be capable of creating the cognitive basic abilities, the necessary language (the language is defined basically as equivalent to the culture of the nation), to start the process of generation of the KST required by the nation.

The Public Organization of Direction and Control of the KST System

This organization must be conformed by those actors having the highest virtuosity (knowledge and practices) in relation to the KST system. It is responsible for the direction of the process of creation and constant adaptation of the KST system to the national requirements, as well as for its excellent virtuous qualities (nationally pertinent practices and products). It must be highly tied to the communities, and characterized by having excellent autochthonous practices.

The Universities and Other ICT Creators

Universities are institutions where universal knowledge is supposed to be cultivated. Universal from the point of view of this chapter means that diverse national development forms, each with its particular narrative or conceptualization, and KST perspectives are taken into account. It does not imply that, initially, a dominant perspective exists, apart from those possible from the point of view of the national narrative. Among the included perspectives are: firstly, the autochthonous perspective of the nation, and, secondly, the western perspective. The cultivated knowledge should spread among the actors of the nationally pertinent KST system. This study must be holistic and explain the cultural origin of each considered perspective, including the associated forms of Interaction and Work.

The university must also help in designing national criteria, policies, strategies and instruments for the national autochthonous KST system. Additionally, the university must contribute to educate actors creating nationally pertinent KST. Moreover, the university must have highly virtuous groups engaged in research-action projects that create pertinent KST to support the KST system in all possible forms.

The Productive Sector: Economic System, Enterprises and Cooperatives

Enterprises and cooperatives must generate products in accordance to the problems and needs of the nation, and thus will have some requirements for the KST system. Simultaneously, the KST practices of these actors must be culturally pertinent and should contribute to improve the national KST practices. This sector must be strengthened in order to export as much as possible the nationally pertinent products, as well as other products helpful to other nations in accordance to their culture.

The KST system should help in designing new organizational forms, aiming at fostering an economy subjugated to the national Interactions, and to a KST generated in the community spaces. The KST must help in creating mechanisms that allow building a social, organizational and economic agenda, from the dynamics of the daily local social activity, as well as mechanisms for auditing the developing of such agenda.

National Integration: A Necessary Police

Historically, dominant nations have being interested in, and have promoted, disintegration/fragmentation of dominated peripheral nations. This, with the help of particular egoist interests of some actors inside the nation, has created disintegration and fragmentation of peripheral nations, and even their split into several countries (e.g., Latin America, or the Arabian countries as they are nowadays). Because of this, national integration polices, as well as strategies and instruments to promote it, must simultaneously endorse the whole national KST system. Without it, nothing nationally significant will be possible, and even less a nationally pertinent KST system.

The integrating action should take the form of resistance against western KST domain, via defining an autochthonous form of KST, and authentic national, and local KST systems. It must promote national autonomy, and a deeply autonomous *mythopoetic* culture.

CURRENT LATIN-AMERICAN SITUATION WITH RESPECT TO FKST AND KST

Characterization of the Actual Situation

We must start by recognizing the role of the Latin American society as consumer and imitator of western knowledge and technology, mainly as a purchaser, but also as a replicator of them. The most popular model in the academic communities of Latin America is scientificism. The absence of moral and political commitment to social models in Latin America, which supposedly should serve the academy, and the strong attraction of the "scientific industry" described by (Núñez, 1999), encourage the scientificist model. This is in accordance with our previous characterization of Latin America, in section 1, as a *developmentist region.*

Apart from its basic imitative character, the current situation in Latin America is, in part, an extension of what happened to the Western world, described by Habermas (1999), Feenberg (2002), among others. According to them, in our time, technocracy has an ideological role, and the social media play a role in control of the masses. In general, technocracy follows interests of transnational and imperialist states.

The lack of a deep analysis about these issues, and in particular about the topic: "knowledge society", is particularly serious in our Latin American countries, which currently is taking a big debate about our future as society. Analyzing the Knowledge Society will give very important inputs to this debate. The apparent progress of the Information Society is part of an inequality, not only in use, but the difficulty of constructing a form of relationship of these advances, apparently neutral, with our cultures and realities. Indeed, these developments have generated profound processes of cultural alienation in Latin America (Aguilar, 2009, 2011a, 2011b).

It has instilled in us a deep admiration for the knowledge society, based on the feeling that we walk towards a fairer world sustained by human knowledge and the capitalist model of production of knowledge, supposedly to be the unique way to ensure the welfare of mankind. But this new form of capitalism has had a major impact in our countries in at least the following dimensions: at technological level, based on the physical infrastructure; at level of knowledge, linked to the skills and knowledge that the citizens must have to appropriate these technologies; and at level of citizen participation, linked to the opportunities of citizens not only to use knowledge in accordance to their needs, but also to intervene in decisions about its developments (Aguilar, 2009, 2011a).

In general, there are not clear policies in LA that resist and subvert this situation, looking for new forms of social activity where the knowledge is considered as a public good heritage. Public policies aimed at developing cognitive skills in order to improve our quality of life, our community life, are needed. The need arises to identify the key elements about the economic, social and humanitarian model, which considers knowledge as a dynamic centerpiece.

Among the current weakest aspects of public policies are the complete disconnection between national economic and social policies, and policies on science and technology. On the other hand, there is not any scientific and technological leadership that talks the need for knowledge to achieve a real emancipation process. Leadership must be understood at two levels: at the institutional level to assert its voice, and at community level to be relevant in its environment, as wise voice, but humble, accompanying the processes of community decision. At present, it has not been able to overcome the exclusionary view of the current model of doing science and technology, a model that approximates the developmental vision described by Varsavsky (2006), not perceived by much of the society, without an important role in the economy, society, politics and culture of Latin America.

They are very shy, or null, integration projects on Sciences and-Technology (ST), and such projects are not seen in the agendas for discussion and cooperation that have been built. The incipient level of agreements of ALBA[4], MERCOSUR[5], etc. in education are not sufficient to build a Latin American System in Science, Technology and Innovation (LSSTI), where we integrate all to share our problems, and from there, build our Latin American (LA) agendas in ST.

While it is true that the ALBA begins to show the rest of the countries in LA that another model of integration is possible, it is necessary to enrich the strategic partnership from people, from the Culture, Science and Technology diversity of our people. It is an American integration, but now from the edge of the ST liberated and liberating, not technocratic. We cannot talk about a Bank of the South[6], PetroCaribe[7] or a single currency, if we do not build spaces for social reflection and to establish new scientific and technological challenges that accompany those polices.

Moreover there have existed attempts to determine the role of a LSSTI in our development model. In this regard, there is not much progress in the construction of a new integrated scientific-technological community for LA, that is in tune with the needs and demands of our society. We continue doing research mainly recognized by developed countries, and in practice, with little connection to the Latin American social, economic and political environment.

The dominant "ideology" of the Latin American scientific and technological community has not suffered a significant change. The current conception has not changed in its atomistic analysis of the phenomena, seen all around us as ready to be used. The new institutionalism in some countries is unable to consolidate methodologies to define scientific-economic agendas, spaces to create high-tech, etc. In addition, institutions tend to become bureaucratic, to be very slow, and do not encourage the appropriation of knowledge, with concrete proposals at the national and local levels. In fewer words, remains the task of reorganizing the LSSTI, based on the recovery of knowledge as a public good, as to make it an emancipatory tool.

There are some interesting LA experiences, but isolated, disjointed between countries, and in some cases without adequate stability for its continuation in time, as the Science Mission in Venezuela, or the Ecuadorian Prometheus program.

Returning to the theme of the scientific-technological appropriation, it has not reversed the idea of latent appropriation. There are not public policies in Latin America to promote a new concept of " appropriation" that goes beyond the mere connotation "transfer", to include other aspects of knowledge: the invention, the copy and the development. Public policies that promote the appropriation must be based on three times: a) learning to use knowledge; b) learning to make knowledge; c) learning to unveil the historical context of knowledge.

Additionally, there are not consolidated technological scientific Latin American networks, and when some are mounted, they are guided by actors from outside the region (as the case of AmSud, proposed by France).

The lack of public policies has created inconsistencies between the Scientific-Technological doing and Latin American economic and social dynamics. It has enabled a scientific-technological Latin American model, whose components have their eyes on other societies, always under the premise of the universality and neutrality of knowledge. That scientific-technological model has allowed, first, an instrumental conception of knowledge as the only legitimate form of knowledge in the present, and second, maintaining a pseudo-LSSTI that continues excluding regional and local actors, with a perspective consumerist of knowledge.

Furthermore, the universally accepted model of neutrality and apolitical knowledge assigns roles to scientists from every part of the world, in some cases as generators of knowledge, in other cases as replicators or as consumers of knowledge, always under the premise that may use knowledge who can afford it, what is impacting the pseudo-LSSTI. In this model, the researcher produces scientific publications, and patents, but has a low relevant participation in community projects. It follows the same 'career researcher' defined by the world model to make science and technology, where publications are essential to promote knowledge. Also, we keep using the same parameters established by UNESCO, which states that "underdeveloped" countries need a scientific per thousand inhabitants or more. From this kind of reasoning, would need to import researchers to complete the quota in order to solve our problems? Of course not (Aguilar & Terán, 2011).

In the Latin American case, and the case of free knowledge, there are already some experiences:

- The Latin American Free Software Foundation.
- ST South American integration projects of cooperation between Venezuela and Bolivia: Infocentro, the agreement to transfer technology and knowledge for technology training under free software.
- Bolivarian Alternative for the Americas of the Free Software Community (ALBASOL).
- Efforts in Latin America to legislate on net neutrality, particularly in Chile and Ecuador.
- Specific efforts, of countries like Brazil and Venezuela, to promote the development of free software institutionally (creating research and development centers, etc.), as well as legal and institutional regulatory incentives to promote the development of free software.
- The creation of strong communities of free software in Argentina and Brazil.

In general, many people in Latin America study the issue of free software and promote good practices derived from it, but without transcending in the search for a society marked by the principles of free knowledge as defined in this chapter (Aguilar, 2011a).

Some Elements for an Integration Process for Latin America from Free Knowledge

The most important issue in a society is the culture, and the public good, in general. Therefore free knowledge must serve to develop the culture, the liberation of man and nature, and an autochthonous knowledge system. To do this, we require a native ST Project with liberating premises.

In this sense, we need to politicize the ST: accepting its non-neutrality, and democratizing its work. We need to understand that the actual ST is not neutral, it does not create any kind of knowledge, but only knowledge stimulated and of interest for the dominant actors of the political system (Aguilar, 2011a). It must be understood that the present global scientific and technological model provides a distribution of intellectual and financial effort as the needs of the dominant system, whose basis is the "consumption" and "technological fashion" model (Aguilar, 2009, 2011a). The essential point is to recognize that ST does not give a universal and neutral product. The results are full of cultural contents, are generated in many ways, and are the result of human actions involving human decisions. Each Scientific-Technological model is produced by men who think in a certain way, live in a certain form, and have some kind of values.

In particular, LA society and culture must recognize this, and ask themselves about which ST they require and should build, with the best talent and scientific-technological practices; i.e., in an local/own and native form, and thus in accordance to their culture. It is a suitable time now to build a new vision for a ST for Latin America.

In all this lies the idea of politicization of ST. We're talking from the ST based on a logic of knowledge that unfolds all social tissue, forming a system of rules that legitimizes and articulates knowledge, providing validation and design guidelines, etc. That ST received feedback and is enriched from the social relationships. This requires breaking with how to manage the current ST in LA, which responds to the prevailing logic of power in capitalism.

Only one ST with these features enables an autonomous process of development for LA. Thus the LSSTI appears with a political sense that contributes to building a sovereign society. We're talking about a Latin American society with a proposal of sovereign scientific and technological development from a democratic rationality (Aguilar, 2009; Feenberg, 2002), i.e., about a Latin American scientific and technological model to withstand the forces, pressures that the scientific-technological globalizing forms have imposed on Latin American agendas. In this regard, it is essential to characterize these forms of resistance from the processes of integration:

- Construction of social knowledge networks that learn to influence the powers that control science and technology;
- Questioning of the scientific-technological reality
- Advance in a model in opposition to the dominant form that has treated to impose the globalization. In this respect, we should strengthen the processes of scientific and technological maturation, denying the scientific-technological fads, and deepen in the theme of scientific-technological appropriation.

That will allow us to respond, under current processes integration of our peoples, to questions like: What is the space to the ancestral knowledge of our people in the LSSTI? How must we share our knowledge in agricultural systems?, And so many more questions. From the integration process?, we must generate forms of resistance to the prevailing scientific-technological model (for more about these ideas, see the role of the "Communities of users of the Nation", in section 4.2.1 above).

These forms of resistance must be based on the liberation of knowledge for collective learning processes, on social networking oriented to achieving forms of Latin American social activity based on reciprocity, honesty, trust and solidarity, among others characteristics. It must be characterized for at least the following four edges (Aguilar & Terán, 2011; Aguilar, 2011a):

- The roots of that task in ST must be in the Latin American context, in terms of its culture, its vocations, its knowledge and potential;
- The control must be in Latin America, specially based on the Latin-American social activity;
- It must take into account Latin American spaces of decision, debate and discussion to ensure the relevance of that task in ST on the Latin-American culture, among other things;
- LA must have an enrichment, tangible or intangible. Within the intangibles, one of the more important is knowledge

This breaks with the classical approaches of social processes, as part of the principle of man making himself (a free man). Then, there appear some knowledge sharing that is collectively constructed, which is not seen as a commodity, but is considered to be at the service of the creation of opportunities for sustainable living, seen as a public good. So, it is free, enriched and enriching the cultural matrix in which we operate, contributing to its self-generation.

An interesting question from the perspective of resistance is: How would free knowledge help in creating conditions for the integration of LA? (in Section 4.3, integration was mentioned as a key element for developing a national autochthonous KST system). It must resist the new power relations that have been established within cognitive capitalism, proposing different logics. For example (Aguilar & Terán, 2011; Aguilar, 2011a), it must:

- Raise community and collective dimension of knowledge.
- Shed the instrumental rationality of knowledge
- Ensure the free movement of knowledge.

Thus, the integration should be an area of struggle for the liberation of knowledge. But its task is not only to make knowledge freely available, but more importantly to liberate the society of a way of life imposed from cognitive capitalism, which imprisons man in an increasingly unjust society. From this view, free knowledge contributes to the creation of a humanistic and social integration based on values of affection, solidarity, collaboration, recognition and delivery.

These are goals that must be achieved through a Latin American plan, goals and guidelines established for the long, the medium and the short term. The ideology of the plan must be clear: based on the cultivation of a Cultural Matrix in a good condition. These guidelines should guide the definition of requirements, selection criteria and projects, definition of concepts such as efficiency, as well as Latin American integration processes, but now from the edge of a ST liberated and liberating.

A native, Latin American, ST should be a tool that facilitates and promotes processes of national/regional integration. We are talking about building a LSSTI to make ST a key element in this new culture of Latin American integration, which allows us to include problems that affect us, starting with the liberation of the cultural matrix.

This requires a LSSTI to generate free knowledge, tied to the care of an autonomous culture (Aguilar & Terán, 2011). Knowledge given in this context must have a high degree of authenticity, i.e., it must have sense in the Latin American culture. Also, this knowledge must be able to account and explain the events of the world. For that, the LSSTI must be composed by emerging social processes, giving it the autonomic capabilities to respond to external stimuli and permanently rethink itself. This will allow the LSSTI auto-adjusting itself endogenous and harmoniously.

This idea gives the knowledge a public good character, a LSSTI with dynamics capable of searching for answers to our needs, and, in that search, building research and appropriate technological agendas. We discussed ways of creating the knowledge embedded in community spaces, with shared common life goals. Also, we have redefined the role of the researcher and technologist, as a social actor, and not just the role of producing and applying knowledge. In that sense, the researcher is not only a seeker of truth, but also he is involved in generating processes that enhance quality of life, the socialization of knowledge attained, etc.

On the other hand, the economic activities in LA should be one of the main aspects to consider in the LSSTI. This should generate mechanisms of accumulation and generation of knowledge to ensure its sustainability. This would lead us to a sustainable endogenous economic model, based on the use of our knowledge.

Overall, it is a new scientific-technological culture, an emancipatory model of doing ST, an instrument for Latin America to change and build a new society with values of collaboration, solidarity, transparency, affection. It will permit to create:

- Relevant knowledge, built from social agendas designed from below, in emerging forms of participation, and social dynamics of endogenous knowledge construction.
- Collective learning processes, to enable the design of a fair world aimed at improving the quality of life, peace, and particularly to meet the needs of society (spiritual, material, etc.).
- Permanently reflection on the educational model of bureaucratic forms of management.
- Knowledge that allows us to cultivate the culture, i.e., free knowledge permitting the society to self-regenerate.
- Promote recognition of the skills of the subjects, establishing horizontal relations.
- Accumulation of native knowledge according to the Latin America cultural matrix.

Finally, given the deterioration of the current cultural matrix, an important part of the initial ST projects in Latin American must conceptualize the current status of its cultural matrix, as well as its possible future cultural matrixes. Using the last one, Latin America could define collectively a ST agenda, one caring of public good, and contributing to create these cultural matrixes. Finally, the scientific and technological development must be seen as a political rather than as an instrumental process.

REFERENCES

Aguilar, J. (2009). Hacia una tecnología democrática para Mérida: Bases para un nuevo paradigma universitario en la creación de una Facultad en Tecnologías Informáticas. *Revista de la Academia de Mérida*, *14*(22), 17–80.

Aguilar, J. (2011a). Conocimiento libre y educación emancipadora. *Revista EDUCARE.*, *15*(1), 84–106.

Aguilar, J. (2011b). Para construir un nuevo tipo de economía social y humanista, se requiere reflexionar sobre el capitalismo cognitivo. *Revista Sistémica Libre*, *1*(1), 3–18.

Aguilar, J., & Terán, O. (2011). Ciencia y tecnología liberada y liberadora, para una potencia mediana. In E. T. Haiman & F. Fernández (Eds.), Venezuela: Potencia emergente (pp. 357-394). Caracas, Venezuela: Monte Ávila Editores, Centro de Estudios Políticos Económicos y Sociales (CEPES).

De Civrieux, M. (1992). *Watunna*. Caracas, Venezuela: Monte Avila Editores.

Feenberg, A. (2002). Democratic rationalization: Technology, power and democracy. In R. Scharff & V. Dusek (Eds.), *Technology and the human condition: A philosophy of technology reader* (pp. 652–665). London: Blackwell.

Fuenmayor, R. (2000). *Sentido y sinsentido del desarrollo*. Mérida, Venezuela: Consejo de Publicaciones y Consejo de Estudios de Postgrado de la Universidad de Los Andes. Retrieved from http://www.saber. ula.ve/db/ssaber/Edocs/centros_investigacion/csi/publicaciones/monografias/sentido_y_sinsentido.pdf

Fuenmayor, R. (2001). Educación y la reconstitución de un lenguaje madre. *LOGOI*, *4*, 39–58.

Fuenmayor, R. (2006). *El estado venezolano y la posibilidad de la ciencia*. Universidad de Los Andes, Mérida, Venezuela: Fundacite & Gráficas Quintero. Retrieved from http://www.cenditel.gob.ve/node/422

Guss, D. (1990). *To weave and sing*. Berkeley, CA: University of California Press.

Guss, D. (2014). Descripción of the book: *To weave and sing: Art, symbol, and narrative in the South American rainforest*. Retrieved from http://www.ucpress.edu/book.php?isbn=9780520071858

Habermas, J. (1968). *Technik und wissenschaft als "ideologie"*. Frankfurt am Main: Suhrkamp.

Habermas, J. (1999). *Ciencia y tecnología como ideología* (2nd ed.). Editorial Tecnos.

Heidegger, M. (1977). The question concerning technology. In *The question concerning technology and other essays* (pp. 3–35). New York, NY: Harper Torchbooks.

Himanen, P. (2001). The hacker ethic and the spirit of the information age. New York, NY: Random House. Retrieved from http://portal.feaa.uaic.ro/isg/Shared%20Documents/The.Hacker.Ethic.pdf

MacIntyre, A. (1985). *After virtue: a study in moral theory*. London: Duckworth.

Núñez, J. J. (1999). *La ciencia y la tecnología como procesos sociales. Lo que la educación científica no debería olvidar*. La Habana, Cuba: Editorial Félix Varela.

Ochoa, A. (2006). *Aprendiendo en torno al Desarrollo Endógeno*. Mérida, Venezuela: CDCHT-ULA.

Ochoa, A. (2008). El sentido de las políticas públicas vinculadas al conocimiento para la transformación social. *Reflexiones desde Cenditel, 4*, 5-31.

Perozo, N., Aguilar, J., Terán, O., & Molina, H. (2013). A verification method for MASOES. *IEEE Transactions on Systems, Man, and Cybernetics. Part B, Cybernetics, 43*(1), 64–76. Retrieved from http://ieeexplore.ieee.org/xpl/articleDetails.jsp?arnumber=6211437

Terán, O., & Ablan, M. (2013). Modelado y simulación de situaciones sociales complejas en Latinoamérica: Contribuyendo al cuidado del Bien Público (Modelling and Simulation of Complex Social Situations in Latinamerica: contributing to caring about public being). In Z. L. Rodríguez (Ed.), La emergencia de los enfoques de la complejidad en América Latina: Desafíos, contribuciones y compromisos para abordar los problemas complejos del siglo XXI (pp. 118–135). Buenos Aires: Comunidad de Pensamiento Sistémico. Retrieved from http://www.academia.edu/3366646/Tomo_1._La_emergencia_de_los_enfoques_de_la_complejidad_en_America_Latina._Desafios_contribuciones_y_compromisos_para_abordar_los_problemas_complejos_del_siglo_XXI

Varsavsky, O. (2006). *Hacia una política científica nacional*. Caracas, Venezuela: Monte Ávila Editores. (Original work published 1972)

Varsavsky, O. (2013). *Estilos tecnológicos. Propuestas para la selección de tecnologías bajo racionalidad socialista*. Buenos Aires, Argentina: Biblioteca Nacional. Colección PLACTED-Ministerio de Ciencia, Tecnología, e Innovación Productiva, Presidencia de la Nación.

KEY TERMS AND DEFINITIONS

Autochthonous and Creative KST: KST developed in a region (e.g., in a peripheral one) in accordance to the social needs and culture of this region.

Cognitive Capitalism: For some authors we are in a third phase of capitalism, where the accumulation is centered on immaterial assets, which follows the previous phases of mercantile and industrial capitalism. Those immaterial assets are protected through Intellectual Property Rights (patents, etc.), in order to create a surplus value resulting from monopolistic rents. It is typical in sectors such as the cultural industry, high-technology industry, the media, business and financial services, etc, and combines digital technologies with high levels of cognitive labors, 'digital labors', etc.

Free Knowledge, Science and Technology (Free KST): Is that kind of Knowledge, Science and Technology (promoted by, e.g., the Copyleft licenses); and opposed to proprietary Knowledge, Science and Technology (promoted by Copyrights). As an example, free software promotes the freedom to run, copy, distribute, study, change and improve the software.

Knowledge Society: In an ideal definition, it is a society which generates and makes available, to all members of the society, the knowledge to improve the human condition. However, the concept of knowledge societies encompasses broader social, ethical and political dimensions. These dimensions rule out the idea of any ready-made definition. Particularly, it is based on the idea that Knowledge has become a key resource. The creation of value is about creating new knowledge and capturing its value. The most important property is the intellectual property. In this way, it actually shows similarities with cognitive capitalism.

Knowledge-Based Economy or Knowledge Economy: The new Economy of the more recent stage of capitalism, in which codified knowledge is exploited. It is based in the fact that knowledge can be stored in digital form, and then be forwarded for productive purposes. Knowledge has become reproducible in unlimited amounts.

Western KST: The KST created by the Western Society, which actually is represented by the dominant European and North American Societies, originated from the Greek Society and Culture.

ENDNOTES

1   The actual dominant European and North American Society, originated from the Greek Society and Culture, at present including both Capitalist and Socialist countries in this area of the world.

2   A *mother project* is a key enterprise to promote key components of an autochthonous and creative KST system. Usually, it is a big project oriented at achieving important services or products for the benefit of the nation.

3   Some of these elements (e.g., criteria and policies) are considered in Varsavsky (2013) as part of the necessary work in the process of constructing a technological style. Such elements are previous to the elaboration of a National Plan for Science and Technology, which in turn is previous to the more operative plan aimed at concretely carrying out the technological style.

4   It is a collaborative and complementary project in political, social and economic between certain countries in Latin America and the Caribbean, which stresses the fight against poverty and social exclusion. The ALBA is based on the creation of mechanisms that exploit the cooperative advantages between different partner nations to offset imbalances between those countries

5   MERCOSUR (the Southern Common Market) is subregional economic bloc composed of Argentina, Brazil, Paraguay, Uruguay and Venezuela.

6   The South Bank is a Latin American monetary fund, whose purpose is to function as a development bank to finance infrastructure and support to public and private companies in the three countries, under the premise of equality, equity and social justice. The bank is proposed as an alternative to the IMF, the World Bank and the Inter-American Development Bank

7   Petrocaribe is an alliance in oil between some Caribbean countries and Venezuela, whose aim is that Caribbean countries buy Venezuelan oil under preferential payment.

Chapter 3
Sleight of Hand or Global Problem:
The Two Sides of the Net Neutrality Debate

Sulan Wong
Universidad Católica de Temuco, Chile

Julio Rojas-Mora
Universidad Austral de Chile, Chile

Eitan Altman
INRIA, France

ABSTRACT

The neutral nature of Internet has allowed its consolidation as a crucial tool in the dissemination of knowledge and access to culture. Due to the creation of new business models of Internet access, a debate about the need of keeping a neutral Internet has emerged, leading to a sudden regulatory process that seems to emerge from a process of public consensus. However, participation in this debate requires knowledge in telecommunications, economics, and law, leaving participation to expert actors. In public consultations on Net Neutrality and in the resulting legal documents, three fundamental problems related to net neutrality are studied. Firstly, what constitutes a neutral, open and free Internet? Secondly, what is the effect of traffic management and what are the consequences of providing differentiated services? Finally, can transparency be an efficient tool to curb potential violations of net neutrality? This article presents the historical background that led to this debate and how its main points have been treated primarily in USA and Europe.

INTRODUCTION

In recent years we have witnessed a public debate on the future of the Internet, between those who defend the principle of net neutrality, which restricts traffic management and promotes free and open access to contents, sites and platforms on the web, and those who support selective traffic management to avoid network congestion, improve security and foster the creation of new business models. Exceptional leg-

DOI: 10.4018/978-1-4666-8336-5.ch003

islative initiatives have been taken, which may pave the way to shape a different future for the Internet. Public consultations about net neutrality were launched in both USA and Europe.

The way in which this debate has been conducted on both sides of the Atlantic has been different. In the United States the government has promoted discussion through the Federal Communications Commission (FCC), recognizing that there is a real problem of discriminative Internet traffic management. In an unprecedented decision that rebuffed the legal authority of the FCC on neutrality issues, a Court in the USA has twice halted its attempts to set up rules on the open nature of Internet. European authorities, however, have consistently denied the existence of a problem of neutrality that could jeopardize their networks. The discussion highlighted that there were large differences in the interpretation of the principle of net neutrality among different stakeholders, ending up focusing more on the importance of maintaining a free and open Internet than a neutral one, in order to avoid addressing the need to formulate clear rules that ensure the net neutrality principle. Only last year, the European Parliament began to discuss about the importance of including the principle of net neutrality in European regulation, while at the same time the freedom to create "specialized services" was also proposed.

We have also seen the first country, Chile, adopting legislation that establishes network neutrality, followed by the Netherlands and Slovenia. Before Snowden's leaks, Brazil had been working since 2011 on a bill in which the principles, guarantees, rights and obligations regarding the use of Internet were established. It was not until this year that this project was pushed through, using the leaks as catalyst for legislative urgency and its prompt approval. Given that Snowden's revelations showed, on one hand, the power of the United States over the Internet and, on the other hand, the weakness of the other governments to protect the private data of their citizens, including that of their leaders, whose vocal protests have been heard from Olympus, Brazil decided to enshrine in its law something more than its commitment to net neutrality, giving the world the first legal recognition of the borderless nature of the Internet. The effect of one country's decision, especially those who happen to host most of the services regularly accessed by users, on any subject that attempts against the net neutrality principle, will undoubtedly affect the entire Internet.

Why do we consider the topic important? Why do we open up the topic into the open knowledge debate? The net neutrality principle touches the heart of the Internet. The Internet has had a huge impact on economy and communication, but also on the exercise of socio-cultural and fundamental rights. In 2009 France passed a law against unauthorized downloading of copyrighted material. It established that measures against piracy, included disconnection from the Internet, could be issued by an administrative authority. The Constitutional Council went back to the Declaration of the Rights of Man and of the Citizen (from the time of the French revolution, two hundred years before Internet's birth) to conclude that the freedom of speech could not be entrusted to a new non-judicial authority in order to protect holders of copyrights and neighboring rights. In its judgment, it recognized that the right to free communication of ideas and opinions implies the freedom to access the Internet (French Constitutional Council, 2009-580 DC §12); in other words, Internet is an instrument for exercising the freedom of speech. In article 19 of Universal Declaration of Human Rights it states: *Everyone has the right to freedom of opinion and expression; this right includes freedom to hold opinions without interference and to seek, receive and impart information and ideas through any media and regardless of frontiers.* Internet has created a legitimate expectation of the right to reliably and securely access information, knowledge and culture. However, the debate continues to focus on issues of technical and economic order, thus moving the discussion on the importance of maintaining an open and neutral Internet to access information, knowledge and culture, as it is undeniable that the practices of sharing and exchanging knowledge have been altered by the Internet.

The specific objective of this chapter is to analyze the arguments, that from the technical, legal and political perspectives, has arisen on both sides of the Atlantic, and which reveals the vast differences in local appreciation of the problem on a resource that is shared globally. The chapter will begin with a review of the different definitions of net neutrality, in which environments they have been used and towards which definition the discourse has tilted. Then we present a brief historical review of the attempts to legislate on net neutrality, emphasizing the American and European attempts. Then, we will discuss the core conceptual elements that are part of the legal and political rhetoric in the debate of the net neutrality as a guiding principle for the operation of the Internet and an indispensable condition for the exercise of civil liberties and fundamental rights in the digital environment. The chapter will end with the conclusions that we reach and a discussion about the possible scenarios that arise with regard to the free communication and access to information that Internet has allowed.

INTERNET'S GOVERNANCE

For the many stakeholders that carry out their economic and research activity with the Internet as their objective, the first view of its governance is the control exerted by the consensus of peers that belong to a small set of private institutions defining only those matters essential for Internet's operation and evolution. According to (Solum, 2009), this is a definition of Internet's governance in the "narrow" sense, since it refers to *[Internet's] current operation, and the processes by which it develops and changes over time*.

Nonetheless, the term "governance" may have a different meaning for different contexts and languages. During the 2003 World Summit on the Information Society (WSIS), many delegations understood it in the sense of those activities implemented by national governments or supranational institutions, as opposed to those delegations that supported the previously defined "narrow" sense. As a matter of fact, it is quite difficult to separate the technological control of Internet with that instituted by governments regulations on any activity carried over its infrastructure. This second sense of Internet's governance, called by Solum the "broad" sense of Internet's governance, is the one that touches fundamental freedoms and rights like those of freedom speech and privacy, and that is carried out, e.g., in the name of the efficiency of the world economic system, the protection of copyrights, and the combat of terrorism.

There is even a third type of governance action on the Internet, that in which national and supranational government institutions request the direct participation of the civil society and stakeholders through the process of public consultation. The objective is to develop regulatory frameworks that are more closely related to the needs and opinions of the participants. According to the European Commission, the "consultation (process) is intended to provide opportunities for input from representatives of regional and local authorities, civil society organizations, undertakings and associations of undertakings, the individual citizens concerned, academics and technical experts, and interested parties in third countries" (COM (2002) 704 final, p. 4). In fact, the European Union, through the Treaty of Lisbon (2007, O.J. (C306) 01), orders the Commission to "carry out broad consultations with parties concerned in order to ensure that the Union's actions are coherent and transparent" (Art. 8,(3) (B)). The United States' agencies -like the FCC-, are ordered by law to "give interested persons an opportunity to participate in the rule making through submission of written data, views, or arguments with or without opportunity for oral presentation (5 USC, §553 (c))".

In the 2005 WSIS, Internet governance was defined in a broader sense:

Internet governance is the development and application by Governments, the private sector and civil society, in their respective roles, of shared principles, norms, rules, decision-making procedures, and programmes that shape the evolution and use of the Internet. (WSIS, 2005, §34)

This definition, nevertheless, seems to leave the architectural decisions out, even if they are inextricably linked to the law and policy decisions that governments, private stakeholders and civil society will take.

ON THE DEFINITION OF "NET NEUTRALITY"

For Hahn and Wallsten (2006) net neutrality "usually means that broadband service providers charge consumers only once for Internet access, do not favor one content provider over another, and do not charge content providers for sending information over broadband lines to end users". Nonetheless, this definition is far from being a standard and has evolved together with the Internet from being a purely technical issue to be a content related one.

One of the main tenets theoretically enshrined by the narrow sense of the Internet governance, a guide to the design of its architecture (Carpenter, 1996), is the "end-to-end principle" (Saltzer, Reed & Clark, 1984). This principle calls for any intelligence to be implemented below the transport layer only if it cannot be implemented effectively in higher layers; intelligence is pushed, thus, to the edges of the network. As the processing needed to forward data packets between network elements is minimal, the network becomes relatively simple and only a "best effort" service is provided. This kind of service does not provide any guarantees on delivery rates, as all packets going through the network will have the same priority and, in case of congestion, the same probability of being dropped. The "net neutrality" principle is firstly based on this behavior, as there is no discrimination between data flows and no quality of service (QoS) level can be guaranteed. We will call this view the "technical sense" of the net neutrality principle.

However, the technical sense of the net neutrality was quickly undermined by the design of real-time services, which require having priority over other types of traffic in order to guarantee QoS. The Integrated Services model (IntServ) was designed to allow for QoS on particular services as well as to control the proportion of a link's bandwidth assigned to each service type (RFC 1633). IntServ was designed to be a rich but complex protocol to guarantee QoS, leaving a "clear need for relatively simple and coarse methods of providing differentiated classes of service for Internet traffic, to support various types of applications, and specific business requirements" (Carpenter & Nichols, 2002); these methods were called the Differential Services enhancements (DiffServ) and were defined in the RFCs 2474 and 2475 (Nichols, Blake, Baker & Black, 1998; Blake, Black, Carlson, Davies, Wang & Weiss, 1998). Even if perpetuated by the idea that ISPs yield too much power to be trusted with the task of performing a "fair discrimination", Hahn and Litan (2007) believe that "net neutrality", in the technical sense, is a myth. In the light of the deployment of more intelligent networks, capable of automatically prioritizing data for applications that critically need it, this myth becomes even clearer. One example of the non-existent neutrality in the technical sense in future networks, as former Commissioner Baker acknowledges while quoting the 3GPP (3rd Generation Partnership Project), is the development of 4G wireless networks which "have prioritization built into the standard to provide optimized service across classes of offerings" (25 FCC Rcd 17905, 2010, p. 18091).

These networks allow the development of many services whose suppliers would be willing to pay more for the ability to provide them in optimal conditions, subsidizing, the services that get satisfied with the "best effort" guarantee. Nevertheless, the idea of a two-tier Internet carries with it the possibility of leaving the lowest level under such conditions that new entrepreneurs will not be able to compete with those in the highest level. Therefore, as Wu (2010) explains, success bestows not the best service, but the service that gets into the highest level, under the best possible deal with its Internet Service Provider (ISP).

A second view of net neutrality, the one that can be called the "content sense", relates to the fact that ISPs cannot favor some Content Provider (CP) over its competitors, due to some signed agreement that might even be exclusive. In this sense, Internet users connected through any ISP are free to choose the contents they require from the CP they like the most among the whole set of CPs available in the Internet, and not from a subset handpicked by the operator. We can see that to define this subset, ISPs will setup their networks with the same tools given to them to discriminate traffic according to priority and QoS concerns.

Building on the third kind of Internet governance, national and supranational governments are trying to control the problem that emerged with the debate on the "network neutrality". The US government, through the FCC (24 FCC Rcd 13064, 2009), has been the first government to tap on the knowledge of the "general public" to resolve this debate quickly followed by the French government (Sécretariat d'Etat à la Prospective et au Dévelopment de l'économie numérique, 2010) and the European Commission (2010a). Nonetheless, the eyes of the world are, as former FCC Commissioner's Robert M. McDowell recognized, all on the steps taken by his agency:

I was reminded how closely the international community watches the FCC's movements. After I spoke with regulators from other nations, it became obvious to me that some countries are waiting for the U.S. to assert more government authority over the Internet to help justify an increased state role over Internet management internationally. It is not an exaggeration to say the world is watching what we do. Although we are proceeding with the best of intentions, as we examine the important issues raised in today's Notice, we should keep in mind that our final actions inadvertently could be setting a precedent for some foreign governments with less pure motives to use in justifying stricter Internet regulation. That would be a mistake. Freedom is best served if we promote abundance, collaboration and competition over regulation and rationing. No government has ever succeeded in mandating innovation and investment. (24 FCC Rcd 13064, 2009, p. 13160)

For Neelie Kroes (SPEECH/10/153, 2010), the European Commissioner for the Digital Agenda, any solution to the net neutrality debate has to take into consideration the respect for the freedom of expression, the transparency of the practices used by operators, the promotion of infrastructure investment as a way to fight "monopolistic gatekeepers", the protection of the fair competition principle for all stakeholders in the value chain, and the promotion of innovative business models in the Internet.

BRIEF BACKGROUND ON THE PUBLIC CONSULTATIONS

It is in the USA that the open and neutral Internet started, and it was there that debate and regulation on neutrality began. At least since 2002, we find references regarding the debate on net neutrality, when a group of the largest American technology and e-commerce companies joined in asking the FCC to "ensure that transmission network operators do not encumber relationships between their customers and destinations on the network" (McCullagh, 2002). However, already in 2000, Lemley and Lessig warned of the attack at the end-to-end principle by the large broadband providers wishing to offer bundled services: *...ISPs would have the power to discriminate in the choice of Internet services they allow, and customers who want broadband access would have to accept that choice.*

Wu (2003) coined "net neutrality", a principle in which ISPs do not favor one application over another, leaving the choice to users, who will use meritocratic arguments to justify their decision on which he will use. Success in the Internet world, thus, becomes a Darwinian subject, as only the fittest survives.

Asked in 2005 about the new Internet services success, then SBC's, and later AT&T's, CEO Edward Whitacre exposed the position of the broadband industry:

How do you think [CPs] are going to get to customers? Through a broadband pipe. Cable companies have them. We have them. Now what they would like to do is use my pipes free, but I ain't going to let them do that because we have spent this capital and we have to have a return on it. So there's going to have to be some mechanism for these people who use these pipes to pay for the portion they're using. Why should they be allowed to use my pipes? The Internet can't be free in that sense, because we and the cable companies have made an investment and for a Google or Yahoo! or Vonage or anybody to expect to use these pipes [for] free is nuts! (O'Connell, 2005).

In these words there was an underlying threat to charge Internet subscribers not only for the traffic they generate, but also CPs for the economic benefit they get from it. Comments like this generated replicas from those who later became the standard bearers of the pro-neutrality movement, such as Michael Geist (2005), who have expressed concerns over the interest of ISPs to create a two-tier Internet.

Nevertheless, in a *Policy Statement* of 2005, the FCC adopted a set of four principles which constituted the germ of the protection of net neutrality in the USA, a model that has been adopted worldwide with changes in form, but not in substance. The four principles entitled consumers to access any lawful content, to run any application or use any service, to connect any lawful device, and to competition among providers of both services and contents, in order to encourage broadband deployment and preserve and promote the open and interconnected nature of the public Internet (20 FCC Rcd 14986 2005, para. 4).

The net neutrality debate permeated into politics, especially in the U.S. during Barack Obama's terms as senator (2005–2008), as two bills that he cosponsored supporting net neutrality, were not finally approved (S. 2917, 109th Cong. 2005-2006; S. 215, 110th Cong. 2007-2008). Simultaneously, the European Commission launched a consultation on online content for *promoting fast and efficient implementation of new business models for the creation and circulation of European content and knowledge online* (European Commission, 2006). Question 20 of this consultation refers, in what appears to be officially the first time for the European Union, to the principle of net neutrality and the position respondents had on it.

While campaigning in 2007, President Obama promised to get federal protection for the net neutrality principle, entrusting the task to the new chairman of the FCC, Julius Genachowski. Obama's stance on the problem, and the priority given to it in his presidency, achieved a media presence that is usually very difficult to reach for such a complex issue that weaves together three different areas of knowledge. Meanwhile, the impact on and coverage by media of the debate in Europe was far from that in the USA, a fact recognized in 2008 in Copenhagen by then Commissioner for Information Society and Media, Viviane Reding. In this speech (SPEECH/08/473, 2008), Reding clearly stated that although the Commission recognized the importance of the principle of neutrality to ensure that the CPs could offer innovative services and that consumers could access the services of their choice, it was also true that the European regulation allowed traffic management as a tool for providers to experiment with different offerings to their customers. However, the Commissioner concluded that traffic management would be controlled by both, the European Commission as well as national governments, to avoid offerings with unacceptably low levels of quality.

The biggest legal case in the net neutrality debate started in 2007, when a group of users of the U.S. broadband provider Comcast, found that downloads made using P2P networks were filtered and throttled. NGOs Free Press and Public Knowledge, among others, introduced a complaint with the FCC for Comcast's violation of the principles set forth in the *Policy Statement*. Comcast expressed that it needed to implement these traffic management policies to limit the congestion that P2P traffic generated. Supporting neutrality, the FCC ruled that ISPs could not arbitrarily discriminate between types of traffic, prompting Comcast to demand a judicial review of this decision. The Court of Appeals for the District of Columbia Circuit finally ruled that the FCC had no legal authority to sanction discriminatory practices of Internet traffic, vacating its order (*Comcast,* 600 F.3d at 642).

In consequence, the FCC presented the general public with a Notice of Proposed Rulemaking (*NPRM*) for "Preserving the Open Internet Broadband Industry Practices" in 2009, intended to codify into obligations for broadband Internet access service providers, the four principles that the FCC previously adopted. Two new principles were also included, those of "non discrimination" of any lawful content, application and service, and "transparency" of "network management and other practices as is reasonably required [...] to enjoy the protections specified in this rulemaking" (24 FCC Rcd 13064, para. 16).

Although the public consultation had not yet yielded results, in May 2010, Chairman Genachowski (2010) issued a statement in which he declared the Commission was going to look for a "third way" to solve the net neutrality debate in the USA. This solution would *recognize the transmission component of broadband access service and only this component as a telecommunications service*, while refraining from *application of the many sections of the Communications Act that are unnecessary and inappropriate for broadband access service*. Immediately, a group of 72 congressmen answered Genachoski's statement with a letter in which they expressed *serious concerns about the proposed new regulatory framework*. For them, the proposal caused both a controversy that distracts from what they see should be the main communications priority, *getting every American online*, and uncertainty that *will jeopardize jobs and deter needed investment for years to come* (Green *et. al*, 2010). They urged Genachowski not to take any step towards reclassification of the broadband service "without additional direction from Congress". In answer, Senator John Kerry asked the FCC to act on its own as there is a "Congressional stalemate" on the issue that will make the *legislative solution increasingly unlikely in the near term*, leaving Genachoswki's "third way" as the *only real option to maintain the proper role of government oversight in communications* (Nagesh, 2010). Nevertheless, this "third way" has never been actively sought by the FCC.

In December 2010, the FCC issued the *Report and Order* as the conclusive and regulatory document obtained from the *NPRM*. In it, the FCC continued to hold that it has authority –mandated on Section 706 of the Communications Act (USC,47 § 1302)– to adopt rules on the open Internet (25 FCC Rcd 17905, 2010, part. IV), although not unanimously as two of its members dissented (25 FCC Rcd 17905, 2010, pp. 18052-18054,18092-18097). It was clear that the debate in the USA was far from a simple issue to settle, because not only was there a wide gap between the positions of the American executive and Congress on the one hand, as well as between the former and the courts, on the other hand, but also inside the federal regulator itself.

In a parallel process in Europe, during the discussion of the Telecom Package[1], the net neutrality debate emerged thanks to news about web sites being blocked and Internet services being throttled, a clear indication that ISPs were trying to discriminate Internet traffic based on source, destination or content (European Commission, 2010a). The European Commission adopted in this context a "Declaration on Net Neutrality" (O.J. (L337), 69), in which the importance of preserving the open and neutral character of Internet is recognized as a policy objective as well as a regulatory principle. This institution commits itself to monitor the impact on "net freedoms" - *the ability of end-users to access and distribute information or run applications and services of their choice*-[2], by market and technological developments. As its flagship on the subject, the Commission issued a public consultation focused on the ISPs' behavior regarding "network management" or "traffic management" policies, as differential treatment of Internet traffic can undermine the social and economic benefits that the Internet's openness has provided. Paradoxically, due to the lobbying that both Telefónica and Vodafone made before the European Commission for the ability to charge content providers accordingly to both the QoS provided as well as the amount of traffic generated, as a way to fund the investment in infrastructure needed for new services –which in practical terms accounts to a "Google Tax" (Gabriel, 2010)–, Commissioner Kroes acknowledged that discussions on this strategy with stakeholders had taken place, and that a couple of models were considered (Basteiro, 2010).

Nevertheless, the European Union, both through the statement issued by the Commission under the Telecom Package, as well as through Commissioners Reding and Kroes, made it clear that the intention of the European Union is to protect the neutrality of the network. Except for these public demonstrations, the public consultation remains the only institutional support for a virtually nonexistent debate in Europe. From the final report on the European consultation (2010b), it can be seen that violations of net neutrality reported in different countries are not seen as generalized problems, but only as eventualities remedied by the stakeholders themselves, without the need for any formal procedures. The Body of European Regulators for Electronic Communications (BEREC) concludes in this document, that until the European regulatory framework for telecommunications, which gives prime importance to competition[3], is transposed into the legal systems of member states, it is premature to speak on the necessity of a directive that targets the issue of the net neutrality (European Commission, 2010b, p. 3). With this conclusion, it seems that European officials acknowledge that there is no net neutrality problem in the EU and that isolated events can be handled by national authorities or, in any case, by the European Court of Justice.

While the European and American regulators were still consulting on the need to protect net neutrality, in 2010, Chile became the first country to give it legal status[4], followed in 2012 by the Netherlands, which also incorporated the principle of net neutrality in the body of its Telecommunications Act (Art. 7.4a) Article 7.4a. and Slovenia, which created a new Electronic Communications Act in which it was included (Art. 203).

In September 2011, FCC's *Report and Order* was published in the *Federal Register* (76 Fed. Reg. 59191, 2011), prompting Verizon to challenge the authority of the FCC to set regulations on ISPs. The D.C. Circuit ruled in 2014 that although the FCC had correctly interpreted Section 706, its regulations could not be contrary to the provisions of the Communications Act. Having classified the ISPs under Title I and not under Title II of that legislation, the FCC had divested itself of all authority to regulate this type of service, being its reclassification required before any regulation (Verizon 740, F.3d at 623). After this defeat, in May 2014, the FCC issued a new *NPRM* in the matter of "Protecting and Promoting the Open Internet" (29 FCC Rcd. 5561, 2014), seeking comments on the exact wording the new rules should have, in light of the Verizon ruling.

In 2011, the European Parliament asked the Commission *to ensure that internet service providers do not block, discriminate against, impair or degrade the ability of any person to use a service to access, use, send, post, receive or offer any content, application or service of their choice, irrespective of source or target* (Resolution on the open internet and net neutrality in Europe, 2011). This request was followed by the European Council's (2011) support of the net neutrality principle as a policy objective. In consequence, the BEREC conducted its own consultation processes, first on the Guidelines on Net Neutrality and Transparency (BEREC, 2011) and then on the Guidelines for Quality of Service in the scope of Net Neutrality (BEREC, 2012).

The European Parliament, suggests that appropriate regulation of the principle of net neutrality promotes the defense of the digital freedoms worldwide (Resolution on a Digital Freedom Strategy in EU Foreign Policy, 2012). This statement was followed by a new European Commission consultation on *transparency, traffic management and switching in an Open Internet* (European Commission, 2012). Then, in 2013, the European Commission presented its new package of proposals "Regulation for a Telecom Single Market" (COM (2013) 627 final) Proposal for a Regulation of the European Parliament and of the Council laying down measures concerning the European single market for electronic communications and to achieve a Connected Continent, and amending Directives 2002/20/EC, 2002/21/EC and 2002/22/EC and Regulations (EC) No 1211/2009 and (EU) No 531/2012. COM(2013) 627 final , in which although the need to regulate the principle of net neutrality is recognized, the liberty to implement differentiated services is also stated.

The most recent and most radical piece of legislation regarding net neutrality, among other rights of Internet users, came from Brazil, where the "Marco Civil da Internet" (known in English as "Internet Bill of Rights") was passed in 2014. The "Marco Civil" was the first legal text for Internet that was completely created through multi-stakeholder collaborative action, mimicking the process used to create content in Wikipedia.

CORE ISSUES

In the debate on net neutrality, we find that the core issues in the different legal and political texts that we have studied are the definition of what constitutes a free, open and neutral Internet, the importance and limits of traffic management as a tool to guarantee broadband service and the creation of new business models, and policy transparency in network management as a guiding principle of the decisions of users and subscribers.

Free, Open and Neutral INTERNET

The policies adopted by the FCC to guarantee *that broadband networks are widely deployed, open, affordable, and accessible to all consumers* have followed, since 2005, the four principles that for it defines an open Internet. These principles, that have guided the ISPs in their relationship with their customers and that have balanced the different interests among stakeholders -consumers, broadband service providers, application and content providers and technology companies- were formulated in the *NPRM* as obligatory for the ISPs. It was the opinion of the FCC that the general shape in which these principles were formulated was kept, only that now there is a clear view on who is the subject of statutory obligation, and of whom it is required to fulfill a certain behavior.

The rules, as presented in the *Report and Order* version[5] published in the *Federal Register* (76 Fed. Reg. 59191, 2011) are:

1. Fixed and mobile broadband providers must disclose the network management practices, performance characteristics, and terms and conditions of their broadband services.
2. Fixed broadband providers may not block lawful content, applications, services, or non-harmful devices; mobile broadband providers may not block lawful Web sites, or block applications that compete with their voice or video telephony services.
3. Fixed broadband providers may not unreasonably discriminate in transmitting lawful network traffic.

Neutrality, thus, was defined in terms of transparency, no blocking and no unreasonable discrimination. Even if this *Report and Order* deals with the "open Internet", throughout the document we can find references to the "free and open" nature of Internet. Nevertheless, only its openness is defined in terms of free markets and free speech (76 Fed. Reg. 59193, 2011), a rather tautological definition in which openness and freedom are like two snakes biting their tails.

In *Verizon* 740 F.3d at 623 the D.C. Circuit decided that due to the classification of ISPs under Title I of the Communications Act, i.e., like "information services[6]", the FCC did not have the authority to establish "common carrier[7]" rules on them, striking both the no blocking and the no unreasonable discrimination rules, but upholding the transparency rule. Taking into account the *Verizon* ruling, Ruane (2010) identified three possible scenarios for the FCC. Firstly, the no blocking rule could be reissued without the no unreasonable discrimination rule, as the Court stated that establishing lower limits to the arrangements between ISPs and CPs leaves plenty of room for other deals, clearly departing from common carriage regulation. Secondly, any redraft of the no unreasonable discrimination rule must leave room for individual arrangements between ISPs and CPs. Thirdly, a reclassification of broadband Internet access services as "common carriers" under Title II of the Communications Act will give the FCC the authority to implement the original rules.

With the *NPRM* of 2014, the FCC asks for comments, among other things, on the three rules. Firstly, the FCC would like to understand both how the transparency rule is helping end users, and what information is needed to provide and in which way should it be provided to end users in order to understand if ISPs are living up to their contracts. Secondly, the FCC asks for comments on whether the minimum level of access required should be included in the wording of the no blocking rule, and whether an express prohibition on priority agreements should be included in this rule, given that it would be difficult to word in such a way that it requires authority under Title II. Thirdly, the FCC wants to understand whether prohibiting only commercially unreasonable practices –with a clear identification of the specific practices that do not satisfy the commercially reasonable legal standard or a case-by-case evaluation for commercial reasonableness– would make the no unreasonable discrimination to comply with the requirement established by the court. In this *NPRM*, the FCC makes an interesting definition of what should constitute the minimum level of access, the "typical" level of the "best effort" Internet. Thus, any ISP could negotiate delivery agreements that provide a better than typical level of access, but are prohibited from delivering a worse than typical service.

The European consultation of 2010, adds, as an annex, the Declaration on Net Neutrality (2009, O.J. (L337) 69) of the European Commission, which upholds the importance of keeping Internet open and neutral. Given that European authorities seem to hold net neutrality in high esteem, the consultation asks if, actually, there are problems with net neutrality and the openness of Internet in Europe. For them, and in the consultation document, the Internet is "open" when it allows "end users in general to access and distribute information or run applications of their choice". In this way, the document separates "neutrality", which implies non-discrimination, from "openness", to which the "net freedoms" of citizens are related; the "openness" affects end users, while the "neutrality" affects operators, although discrimination between operators eventually ends up affecting the ability of end users to access the Internet and what it represents[8]. However in the text we can see that neutrality and openness are concepts that are sometimes used interchangeably[9].

This can be seen, e.g., in a Communication of the Commission (COM (2011) 0222), where it is stated that although there is no set definition of net neutrality in the European regulatory framework, the Framework Directive (2002 O.J. (L 108) 33, Art. 8 (§4) (g)) states that NRA's should promote *the ability of end-users to access and distribute information or run applications and services of their choice*. In essence, we can see that the European Commission implicitly defines net neutrality through this article, following the "content" sense, but also interchanging neutrality and openness as defined in the Declaration.

In the new "Regulation for a Telecom Single Market" (COM (2013) 627 final, Amendments 234 and 241 for Art. 2, 12a) there is a proposal to define the net neutrality principle as *the principle according to which all internet traffic is treated equally, without discrimination, restriction or interference, independently of its sender, recipient, type, content, device, service or application*. This proposal, which was not included in the Commission's original proposal, is defined in the "technical" sense of the net neutrality. Nevertheless, in Amendments 236 and 243 for Art. 23, among other rights *end-users shall have the right to access and distribute information and content [...], via their internet access service*, a net neutrality definition in the "content" sense which is basically that of the Commission[10].

The Brazilian "Marco Civil" of 2014 considers that access to the Internet is essential to the exercise of citizenship, thus it should promote everyone's right to access the Internet; promote access to information, knowledge and participation in cultural life and public affairs; promote innovation and foster the widespread availability of new technologies, as well as their use and access; and promote adherence to open technology standards that enable communication, accessibility and interoperability between applications and databases. Hence, Internet's open nature is highlighted from several perspectives based not only on technical reasons, but also on fundamental rights and how their exercise is intertwined with Internet. Furthermore, this is the first bill in which the global nature of Internet is recognized, i.e., that the actions of countries, like the USA, or supranational institutions, like the EU, with enough power over Internet services, will affect all other countries in the world.

Traffic Management

Reasonable Network Management

In the *NPRM*, the FCC emphasizes that the obligations required of ISPs are subject to "reasonable network management", although they *would not supersede* emergency situations or needs from public authorities, consistent with applicable law. It is unclear from the text, what is for the FCC "reasonable network management", even though there is a rather tautological definition:

Reasonable network management consists of: (a) reasonable practices employed by a provider of broadband Internet access service to (i) reduce or mitigate the effects of congestion on its network or to address quality-of-service concerns; (ii) address traffic that is unwanted by users or harmful; (iii) prevent the transfer of unlawful content; or (iv) prevent the unlawful transfer of content; and (v) other reasonable network management practices *(24 FCC Rcd 13064, 2009, para 16)*.

Nonetheless, the FCC rejects in the *Report and Order* document approved as *NPRM*'s conclusion, that the terms "reasonable" and "unreasonable" are vague and, in fact, that "reasonableness" is a *well-established standard for regulated conduct* (25 FCC Rcd 17905, 2010, para 77).

In defining what constitutes a reasonable management policy, the FCC recognizes deviation from a guideline previously used that considered "reasonable" those practices which *should further a critically important interest and be narrowly or carefully tailored to serve that interest* (24 FCC Rcd 13064, 2009, para 137). This guideline appears as unnecessarily restrictive in the eyes of the Commission, given the flexibility needed to establish what becomes "reasonable" in light of the non-discrimination obligation. Providers have to use a network management practice that is tailored for a specific task, but not necessarily the narrowest practice *theoretically available to them* (25 FCC Rcd 17905, 2010, para 85).

This decision seems to go in the opposite direction to Canada's Telecom Regulatory Policy (2009), the product of a public consultation. When answering a complaint on traffic management, an ISP must describe the practices employed, as well as its need, purpose and effect, identifying whether the practice results in discrimination or preference. If so, the ISP must demonstrate that the practice was designed to address and solve the effect in question, *and nothing else*. Collateral damage to others and resulting discrimination or preference must be as little as possible. Finally, the provider must justify why infrastructure investment is not a reasonable alternative to the implementation of such practices. When these practices lead to blocking traffic, they cannot be implemented without the approval of the CRTC[11] which will ensure that they will be granted only when they further the objectives set out in the Canadian Telecommunications Act (2009).

After reviewing the responses to the consultation, the definition of what constitutes "reasonable network management" was redrafted in an even broader way: *a network management practice is reasonable if it is appropriate and tailored to achieving a legitimate network management purpose, taking into account the particular network architecture and technology of the broadband Internet access service* (25 FCC Rcd 17905, 2010 Appendix A, para. 8.11). Due to the complexity of the Internet, the FCC concluded that it will study the "reasonableness" of network management policies *on a case-by-case basis, as complaints about broadband providers' actual practices arise* (25 FCC Rcd 17905, 2010, para. 83).

In the case of wireless networks (24 FCC Rcd 13064, 2009, para. 172), the FCC understands that the definition of what constitutes reasonable management practices is even more complex. The Commission recognizes that certain "rules of the road" are critical to maximize the performance of the limited spectrum each operator has. It seems that service providers in wireless environments will have an even greater leeway, with respect to the definition of "reasonable". The "rules of the road" would not only be established in a completely arbitrary way for each particular provider, but they may also change in real time, given certain patterns of use that each ISP assesses differently. As it is seen in the new definition of "reasonable network management" and on the case-by-case evaluation policy, it is expected that mobile networks will be treated differently than fixed networks (25 FCC 17905, 2010, paras. 103,105). As a matter of fact, wireless providers have only to comply with a more basic definition of the no blocking rule:

A person engaged in the provision of mobile broadband Internet access service, insofar as such person is so engaged, shall not block consumers from accessing lawful websites, subject to reasonable network management; nor shall such person block applications that compete with the provider's voice or video telephony services, subject to reasonable network management (25 FCC Rcd 17905, 2010 para 99).

On the European Commission consultation of 2012, the traffic management issue also appeared. It follows from the consultative instrument that the term "traffic management" is associated with a number of practices including *prioritization, slowing down, blocking or throttling of certain data packets.* It is understood that such traffic management practices are applied for operational reasons (prevent or control network congestion) or for the implementation of contractual restrictions. Applying them for security and integrity of networks is also accepted, as well as to restrict the transmission of unsolicited communications by end users, or to fulfill a statutory provision or court order.

In the proposed "Regulation for a Telecom Single Market" (2014) currently under discussion in the European Parliament, with Amendment 148, the "reasonable" accompanying the term "traffic management" that was in the original proposal and was promoted in consultations conducted in 2010 and 2012, was later eliminated. Traffic management can be applied, but the measures taken to that end must be transparent, non-discriminatory proportionate and shall not be maintained longer than necessary. Traffic management measures will apply to implement a court order; preserve the integrity and security of network, services provided via this network, and the end-users' terminals and; prevent or mitigate the effects of temporary and exceptional network congestion provided that equivalent types of traffic are treated equally. Both, the Slovenian and Dutch acts follow this same set of instances in which traffic management can be implemented. The Brazilian bill partially follows this blueprint, accepting discriminatory traffic management policies only for the adequate provision of services and applications and for emergency services prioritization.

On the other hand, the Chilean legislation of net neutrality is even simpler, as it states that traffic management can be used by ISPs as long as competition is not affected. The Regulations of the Act on neutrality network identify more clearly the "competition" referred to in the Act, establishing that any prioritization or discrimination action affecting CPs, applications and/or users with respect to others of a similar nature, shall be understood as arbitrary.

Differentiated Services

The provision of differentiated services, in which operators sell access to their "fast lane" to "power buyers", could create the so-called two-tier Internet. In it, innovative services would be restricted to access the market by their ability to compete with large corporations for access to the fast lane. This goes against what has been the traditional way to enter the Internet market, and that has allowed players like Google or Facebook, to fill niches that large corporations could not. As the FCC recognizes, the ISPs may have incentives not to continue investing in the "best effort" Internet, forcing its users and content providers to use their "fast lane" services (24 FCC Rcd 13064, 2009, para. 71).

From all public consultation documents, it is possible to conclude that the argument in favor of setting a two-tier Internet is threefold. As there is always the need for more bandwidth to cope with more demanding applications, providers can invest in infrastructure, oversizing their network by an amount that is enough to provide at least the required throughput. Obviously, the ISPs would like to recoup their investment as fast as possible, but given that the wired broadband Internet access market in the OECD[12] has much less capacity for growth that the mobile one[13] the payback period may not be sufficiently attractive. Hence, one solution is to have a two-tier, cross-subsidized Internet, in which the upper tier would be charged freely, whereas the lower one keeps hosting the neutral Internet. Expensive, non-neutral fast lane will then be the new cow that ISPs would like to milk, while the "best-effort" Internet, the lower tier, will be in peril of being underdeveloped in the long run, and, as the FCC states, providers would have an incentive "to limit the quality of service provided to non-prioritized traffic". Established CPs would love this proposal, as they could broker exclusive deals with ISPs for "fast lane" access, leaving the upper level as a "walled garden", one close to AOL's and which, ironically, was eventually crushed by the appeal of the open and neutral Internet. In this sense, the FCC has already recognized that pay-for-priority deals will not satisfy the "no unreasonable discrimination" standard, as they could "cause great harm to innovation and investment in and on the Internet", particularly affecting non-commercial end users (25 FCC Rcd 17905, 2010, para. 76).

Another solution to recoup investment on their infrastructure is making governments subsidize it through the creation of a usage-based tax that targets CPs, i.e., a "Google tax". This means that every CP will not only have to pay its ISP for the traffic it generates, but for any country that establishes this tax, it will have to pay its customers' ISPs for the traffic they forward. Small start-ups will be seriously discouraged to develop new services if a considerable part of their funding will be used to pay twice for traffic that has not even reached the critical mass needed to generate profit. Either that, or small CPs would filter access from countries where this tax is in place, until market analysis shows that even paying it, its operation might be profitable. Again, CPs with a strong market position would be willing to accept this tax, as it might mean that there will be less challengers that can offer a fight, turning the Internet into the above-mentioned "walled garden".

Finally, if these two solutions to help recoup investment in infrastructure are not accepted, there is a third way to guarantee the required QoS without the need of privately funded expansion plans, the most ancient trick in the ISP's bag: traffic management. By waving the congestion flag, ISPs would be allowed to apply discriminatory traffic management policies to some kind of heavy load traffic, like P2P, video and audio streaming, or VoIP. This behavior, in itself, is a flagrant violation of the net neutrality principle, especially if this kind of policy is applied in an indiscriminate fashion, but it can become even worst if, for a fee, some CPs are allowed to offer their services under a more permissive set of traffic management rules.

A light in this grim scenario might be the proposal formulated in Europe, by which universal service obligations (Directive 2002/22/EC) should be applied to the Internet broadband access. This way, there is a guarantee of a minimum QoS that providers have to honor, while they are compensated if they are subjected to an "unfair burden", by either the provision of public funds[14] or the distribution of the costs between providers (Directive 2002/22/EC, Art. 13 (1)). ANRs are entitled to set the minimum guaranteed rate, but if most of them are going to follow the trail started by Finland (Ministry of Transport and Communications of Finland, 2009) and Spain (Ministerio de Economía y Hacienda del Reino de España,

2011), which guaranteed a rate of 1 Mbps, it seems difficult to see how the new multimedia services that are available through Internet could be provided. Imposing the obligations of the universal service to the broadband Internet access, might only serve to strength the argument that we have presented in this section. At the very least, it might also encourage the development of mobile wireless networks, which have proved to be much more cost effective in covering large areas, but where control over its operation is done with an iron fist, making net neutrality in the content sense a legend of times past.

However, the FCC has stated that it would monitor ISPs to ensure that the rules that govern an open and neutral Internet apply to specialized services that mask preferential Internet access services, to look for any sign the preferential services development hinders the natural growth in the provision of infrastructure and capacity to the Internet access services, and to evaluate the impact of specialized services on last-mile capacity dedicated to Internet access services (Fed. Reg. 76, 2011, p. 59214). On this same line, European authorities seek that differentiated services "shall only be offered if the network capacity is sufficient to provide them in addition to internet access services and they are not to the detriment of the availability or quality of internet access services"[15].

Transparency

As we have seen before, among the new rules that on its *NPRM* the FCC proposed for the ISPs, we can find that of "transparency". The Commission explained that, in response to repeated unilateral decisions taken by ISPs who change service conditions without properly informing their users, it was necessary to require transparency in the traffic management policies that providers need to employ (24 FCC Rcd 13064, 2009, par. 123). For the FCC, completely clear information is not only essential for users while taking the decision to contract an Internet access service, but also for the regulator in the control of abusive or unreasonable practices that operators could apply. Furthermore, in its conclusions, the FCC acknowledges that *[d]ifferential treatment of traffic is more likely to be reasonable the more transparent to the end user the treatment is* (25 FCC Rcd 17905, 2010, par. 70). Transparency is a requirement for both, wired and wireless broadband providers.

The version of the transparency rule upheld by the D.C. Circuit in *Verizon* ask for transparency on network management practices, performance characteristics, and terms and conditions of their broadband services. Nevertheless, in the new *NPRM* (29 FCC Rcd. 5561, 2014), the FCC explains it has received hundreds of complaints about, e.g., the ineffective way the ISPs communicate how access speed is calculated and allocated, how consumption data is calculated for purposes of contractual data caps, why connections are considerable slower than advertised, and why there are disparities between advertised prices and amounts subsequently billed.

For Europe, transparency is nonnegotiable as Internet traffic management is an issue of considerable complexity for the average consumer, making it imperative that *it must be crystal clear what the practices of operators controlling the network mean for all users, including consumers* (SPEECH/10/153, 2010). Article 1(1) of the European Directive 2002/22/CE establishes as its objective "to ensure the availability throughout the Community of good quality publicly available services through effective competition and choice and to deal with circumstances in which the needs of end-users are not satisfactorily met by the market". In order to fulfill this objective, operators should provide information, not only on conditions that limit access or use of services and applications but also about the changes in these conditions (Art. 21 (3) (c) Directive 2002/22/CE). Furthermore, providers should clarify the procedures for measuring and managing traffic so as to avoid congestion, and how those procedures can affect the quality of service (Art. 21 (3) (d) Directive 2002/22/CE). Transparency is a requirement for contracted services in Europe, to protect customers from abuses carried out by ISPs; this is why operators should include in their contracts, in a clear and easily understandable way Art. 20 (1) (b) Directive 2002/22/CE:

- Information on any condition that limits access to, and/or use of, services and applications, provided that such conditions are permitted under national law in accordance with Community law.
- The minimum service quality levels offered, as defined by the National Regulatory Authorities (NRAs)[16].
- Information on any procedures put in place by the provider to measure and shape traffic so as to avoid congestion, and information on how those procedures could impact on service quality.
- Any restrictions imposed by the provider on the use of terminal equipment supplied.

Not only should this information appear perfectly clear in contracts, but NRAs have to encourage providers to publish guides -or if not possible, publish them themselves- with all necessary information for end-users *to make an independent evaluation of the cost of alternative usage patterns* (Art. 21 (2) Directive 2009/22/CE).

While the European norm requires that changes in contract terms are made public, it does not specify when operators should do it, leaving the door open to changes without prior notice or that these are notified *a posteriori*. It is troubling to see that the European consultation does not ask directly about this subject, leaving respondents the burden of its discovery through a thorough review of the existing legislation. It seems that the Commission would not be interested in defining the minimum period in which the operators should inform users about changes in terms of use, entrusting this task to the member states and their regulatory agencies. On the other hand, the FCC consulted in 2010 on this subject, although it left no doubt regarding the *a posteriori* notification (as the European Commission), asking respondents to consider whether ISPs should be obliged to notify changes in traffic management policies within a "period of time" *after* they have been made. In contrast, the Brazilian "Marco Civil" states that ISPs have to notify their users in advance, in a transparent, clear and descriptive enough way, about the practices of traffic management and congestion mitigation adopted, including those related to network security

The issue of transparency was one of the points brought up consulted again in Europe in 2012 (European Commission, 2012). On that occasion, questions where raised about the technical aspects the end user should know to make a properly informed decision (such as latency or network responsiveness, and which services would thereby be affected). It can be seen that transparency is related mostly to technical aspects of the Internet service, implying information of clear value only to the versed subscribers and to the regulator.

For the FCC, transparency is the best incentive to correct policies adopted by ISPs that could affect the neutral and open nature of Internet (29 FCC Rcd. 5561). In this sense, the European Commission consulted in 2010 whether transparency in traffic management practices by operators may reduce network neutrality concerns (European Commission, 2010a, Question 14). Nevertheless, it is our opinion that transparency, in practice, does not prevent operators from abusing network neutrality, since, as explained, whether traffic management policies are reasonable or not is an entirely subjective and arbitrary matter that rests with the regulator. Not only this, but as Candeub and McCartney (2010, p. 234) stated, transparency will only allow people to *gain a better understanding of the extent of their ISP's market power and their own consumer impotence*. Even assuming the best-case scenario, the information provided will consist of algorithms reinterpreted by lawyers, to be reflected in contracts without incurring unforeseen liabilities, so that it can only be fully exploited by network experts that can fluently read legal jargon, being as obscure to the layman as a block of graphite. Thus, we believe that end-user concerns on net neutrality violations by ISPs are neither eradicated nor reduced by transparency requirements.

DISCUSSION AND CONCLUSION

Since its initial conception, the Internet has been designed with the idea of being a neutral network, leaving decisions on the origin and destination of the information that flows through it to the actors who populate its edges. Nevertheless, due to the rapid development of real-time applications that use the network as a platform for communication, it has been necessary to incorporate traffic management protocols that discretely set priorities in the Internet access service. However, these protocols were not designed with the idea of allowing ISPs to flagrantly violate the principle of net neutrality through service agreements that prioritize a CP over its competitors. Because both ISPs and CPs with a dominant market position could be provided an incentive to establish such agreements, civil society stakeholders related to the operation of the Internet have devoted great efforts to seek that the principle of net neutrality, at least in the "content" sense, be enshrined in national laws or supranational rules.

The Internet is a complex environment where the narrow and the broad forms of governance combine to define the rules of its operation. Governance based on public consultation is gradually consolidating, due to its perception by civil society stakeholders as a tool that allows their voices to be heard by political actors, especially in an issue that directly affects the exercise of two fundamental rights, such as those of freedom of expression and access to knowledge and culture.

The rhetoric of the governance presents the public consultation process as a rational discussion, firstly, between stakeholders and, secondly, between stakeholders and the authorities. With this debate it is expected that differences of position evolve from being factors that give rise to stalemates, to becoming elements of debate enrichment. In spite of this, Estevez Araujo (2008) explains that due to the inherent characteristics of the governance process, neither popular participation nor social transformation can be regarded as its main objectives, but only negotiation and problem resolution for stakeholders. Furthermore, the voice of those who respond is not binding on those drafting legislation, so that their answers are only seen as mere advice. Yet, the opportunity to participate in a debate on the rules for regulating the Internet may give the citizens the expectation that they are in political control of its future.

In a clear alignment with this pessimistic view of the public consultation process in general, we have found that the language used in the documents of public consultation on net neutrality, as well as the knowledge needed to answer them, narrows the scope for participation to only those stakeholders fully dedicated to the subject in debate: scientific researchers, industry stakeholders and lobbies, and non-governmental organizations (NGOs). Undeniably, the powerful industrial lobbies, those that Lessig (2011) believes are responsible for the loss of democracy, are the ones who have both the resources and the incentives to invest in advisory teams with the skill required to address the complexity of public consultations conducted on net neutrality. Therefore, the debate has led to attempts to prefer the development of new business models based on non-neutral networks over the protection of our civil liberties and fundamental rights. Perhaps a particular case of participatory governance in this issue has been that of Brazil, in which a collaborative process was used in the drafting of its *Marco Civil da Internet*, allowing that views of actors with different interests were truly heard and reflected in the final text.

The *Marco Civil* is also a "revolutionary" legal instrument as it recognizes the aforementioned fundamental rights of freedom of expression and access to knowledge and culture, also adding as its key principles and objectives to preserve and safeguard the net neutrality principle, to ensure the participatory purpose of Internet, to promote innovation and new technologies and usage models, and the development and adherence to open standards that allow communication, accessibility and interoperability between applications and databases. But one of the most important contributions of the *Marco Civil* is the recognition of one particular aspect of Internet, one that seems evident but is nevertheless in constant struggle with the second view of Internet's governance, that of its global scale.

Given the sudden flood of legislation by major world powers over Internet issues, as well as the indiscriminately invasive character engendered by the control of illegal activities and the protection of national security of these powers, it is clear that any action imposed by them in violation of the principle of net neutrality will have an impact on a global scale, regardless of borders or jurisdictions. It is, therefore, of crucial importance that the principles that define Internet are agreed on a global scale, no matter what the important of a country has been has been a country in its development and operation. Without these agreements, nations with a more significant presence in terms of content will be in an advantageous position against those who use the Internet primarily for content consumption and not its production.

Despite the global nature of both the Internet and the decisions taken on its principles by the governments of the world, it is amazing how the debate on net neutrality differs on both sides of the Atlantic Ocean. In the United States the executive seeks to achieve judicial acceptance of its jurisdiction to issue pro-neutrality rules, while facing a Congress radicalized in its stance against net neutrality. Even if President Obama tried to promote net neutrality through bills during his term as senator and publicly pledged to protect it during his campaign, his political capital has diminished with the arduous battle he fought for the health system reform and the subsequent shutdown his government suffered[17]. Meanwhile in Europe, the Community authorities act with astonishing calm in total contrast to the American turmoil, while awaiting the transposition of the EU telecommunications regulatory framework in the Member States, before deciding whether there is need for action to protect net neutrality.

There are two main themes in the discussion about net neutrality: traffic management and transparency. Traffic management is a sensitive issue in the debate over net neutrality, due to both the original design guidelines that Internet development followed and the Darwinian process that has ruled its market. We understand that due to congestion, some traffic management is inevitable and that certain levels of prioritization have been already defined in the standards that shape the operation of the Internet. What we cannot accept is that discrimination is made for commercial reasons, given the incentive that new business models based on the "walled garden" model made popular by AOL. We must remember that these models became obsolete with the advent of the Internet, so going back to them makes no sense. Regulators need to understand that Internet's economic development is incompatible with these models, which only benefit ISPs and CPs with a dominant market position. Moreover, these models are in stark opposition to the rights of free speech and access to knowledge and culture that the Internet has facilitated and promoted.

Transparency is seen as the silver bullet against all possible incentives for ISPs to violate net neutrality. It is seen as linked to the ability of end users to make a free choice of the products and services to contract or consume. However, information asymmetry is not overcame by the transparent management of ISPs, as without the knowledge to understand what is being transparently disclosed, the user is still unable to exercise real power. In addition, we must remember that the market for Internet access service is an oligopoly with little real competition, as both service offerings and prices are usually very similar between competitors. As traffic management practices are also similar, switching from one operator to another will give end-users no guarantee of improvement in their service or neutrality in traffic management.

We found a partial contradiction in American and European documents concerning the definition of the nature of the Internet; for the former it is a free and open network, whereas for the latter it is an open and neutral network. We believe that besides the "free" and "open" attributes given to Internet, it is important to also add "neutral" to this list, asserting not only the support that the principle of net neutrality has acquired worldwide, but also the implications that for ISPs it has. A neutral Internet, as explained at the beginning of this section, prevents that decisions on origin and destination of the information flowing through it are taken by ISPs. We believe that all CPs can participate in a free Internet without any other requirement than the payment of the costs associated with their connection. We believe in an open Internet too, because its operation is defined by globally agreed technical standards. But we also believe that the saturation of the business model of ISPs and the fictitious axiom of the ever growing economy cannot justify the Internet stops being something that has always been, a neutral space in which access to content is defined solely by the relationship between users with their clients and CPs with their servers. To ensure that the Internet remains the platform that has been the foremost driver to free access to knowledge, it is necessary that it stands as it has always been, neutral. Only a free, open and neutral Internet will be the commons that, as Frischmann (2012, p. 332) says, will allow spillovers effects that increase its social value beyond that of the relationships between users and CPs.

ACKNOWLEDGMENT

Sulan Wong is with the Grupo de Investigaciones Jurídicas (GIJ) of the Universidad Católica de Temuco, Chile.

REFERENCES

Appropiate Framework for Broadband Access to the Internet over Wireline Facilities; Fine Rule 70 Fed. Reg. 60222, 60234 (Oct. 17, 2005) (FCC 05-151) 2005

Appropriate Framework for Broadband Access to the Internet over Wireline Facilities, CC Docket Nos. 02-33, 01-337, 95-20, 98-10, GN Docket No. 00-185, CS Docket No. 02-52, Policy Statement, 20 FCC Rcd 14986 (2005).

Autorité de Régulation des Communications Eléctroniques et des Postes. (2010). *Interview de Stéphane Richard, directeur général de France Télécom.* Retrieved from http://www.arcep.fr/index.php?id=10411

Basteiro, D. (2010, May 5). *Bruselas reconoce que estudia la 'tasa Google'.* Publico.es.

Belson, D. (2010). *The State of the Internet: 3rd Quarter, 2010 Report* (Tech. Rep. No.3 (3)). Cambridge: Akamai.

BEREC (2011). *Guidelines on net neutrality and transparency: Best practices and recommended approaches. Draft for public consultation BOR (11) 44.*

BEREC (2012). *Guidelines for quality of service in the scope of net neutrality: Draft for public consultation BOR (12) 32.*

Blake, S., Black, D., Carlson, M., Davies, E., Wang, Z., & Weiss, W. (1998). *An architecture for differentiated services (RFC 2475).* IETF. Retrieved from http://www.ietf.org/rfc/rfc2475.txt

Braden, R., Clark, D., & Shenker, S. (1994). *Integrated services in the Internet architecture: An overview (RFC 1633).* IETF. Retrieved from http://www.apps.ietf.org/rfc/rfc1633.html

Canadian Radio-television and Telecommunications Commission. (2009). *Telecom Regulatory Policy CRTC 2009-657.* Author.

Candeub, A., & McCartney, D. J. (2010). Network transparency: Seeing the neutral network. *Northwestern University Journal of Technology and Intellectual Property, 8*(2), 227–246.

Carpenter, B. (1996, June). *Architectural principles of the Internet (RFC 1958).* IETF. Retrieved from http://www.ietf.org/rfc/rfc1958.txt

Carpenter, B., & Nichols, K. (2002, March). *Differentiated services (Diffserv) (concluded wg).* IETF. Retrieved from http://datatracker.ietf.org/wg/diffserv/charter/

Comcast v FCC 600 F.3d 642 (D.C. Cir. 2010).

Communication from the Commission to the European Parliament, the Council, the Economic and Social Committee and the Committee of the Regions on the open Internet and net neutrality in Europe. COM (2011) 0222 final.

Council of the European Union. (2011). Council conclusions on the open Internet and net neutrality in Europe. *3134th Transport, Telecommunications and Energy Council meeting.*

de l'Économie, M. de l'industrie et de l'emploi de la République Française. (2010). *Consultation publique sur la neutralité du Net.* telecom.gouv.fr

Directive 2002/21/EC of the European Parliament and of the Council on a common regulatory framework for electronic communications networks and services, 2002 O.J. (L 108) 33. Amended by Directive 2009/140/EC of the European Parliament and of the Council of 25 November 2009, O.J. (L137) 37.

Directive 2002/22/EC of the European Parliament and of the Council of 7 March 2002 on universal service and users' rights relating to electronic communications networks and services (Universal Service Directive), 2002 O.J. (L108) 51. Amended by Directive 2009/136/EC of the European Parliament and of the Council of 25 November 2009, O.J. (L337) 11.

Dorgan, B., Snowe, O., Kerry, J., Boxer, B., Harki, T., Leahy, P., & Clinton, H. et al. (2007). *Internet Freedom Preservation Act.* S. 215, *110th Cong.* (2007-2008)

Estévez Araújo, J. A (2008). Que no te den gobernanza por democracia. *Mientras tanto, 108–109,* 33–49.

European Commission (2002). *Towards a reinforced culture of consultation and dialogue - General principles and minimum standards for consultation of interested parties by the Commission.* COM (2002) 704 final.

European Commission (2006). *Public consultation on content online in the single market.*

European Commission (2009). *Telecom reform 2009: Commission declaration on net neutrality.* Official Journal of the European Communities (L337) 69.

European Commission (2010a). *Questionnaire for the public consultation on the open Internet and net neutrality in Europe.*

European Commission (2010b). *Report on the public consultation on the open Internet and net neutrality in Europe.*

European Commission. (2012). *Public consultation on specifics aspects of transparency, traffic management and switching in an open Internet.*

European Commission Press Release. SPEECH/08/473 (Sept. 09, 2008).

European Commission Press Release. (April. 13, 2010). SPEECH/10/153.

European Commission Press Release. (Sept. 10, 2010) SPEECH/10/434.

European Parliament (2011). Resolution of 17 November 2011 on the open Internet and net neutrality in Europe (P7_TA(2011)0511)

European Parliament. (2012). Resolution of 11 December 2012 on a digital freedom strategy in EU foreign policy. Retrieved at http://www.europarl.europa.eu/sides/getDoc.do?pubRef=-//EP//TEXT+TA+P7-TA-2012-0470+0+DOC+XML+V0//EN

European Parliament (2014). Legislative resolution of 3 April 2014 on the proposal for a regulation of the European Parliament and of the Council laying down measures concerning the European single market for electronic communications and to achieve a connected continent, and amending directives 2002/20/EC, 2002/21/EC, 2002/22/EC, and regulations (EC) N° 1211/2009 and (EU) N° 531/2012 (com(2013)0627- c7-0267/2013 - 2013/0309(cod)) (ordinary legislative procedure: first reading).

Federal Trade Commission. (2006). *FTC to host workshop on broadband connectivity competition policy.* Retrieved from http://www.ftc.gov/opa/2006/12/broadbandworkshop2.shtm

French Constitutional Council. (2009). *Décision Nro. 2009-580 DC du 10 juin (Loi favorisant la diffusion et la protection de la création sur internet).*

Frischmann, B. M. (2012). *Infraestructure: The social value of shared resources.* New York: Oxford University Press. doi:10.1093/acprof:oso/9780199895656.001.0001

Gabriel, C. (2010, April 26,). *Vodafone to petition EU for 'Google tax'.* Rethink Wireless. Geist, M. (200, December 22). *Towards a two-tier Internet.* BBC News. Retrieved from http://news.bbc.co.uk/2/hi/technology/4552138.stm

Genachowski, J. (2010, May 6). *The third way: A narrowly tailored broadband framework.* Federal Communications Commission. Retrieved from http://www.broadband.gov/the-third-way-narrowly-tailored-broadband-framework-chairman-julius-genachowski.html

Green, G., Taylor, G., Murphy, S., Arcuri, M., Kosmas, S., & Wilson, C. … Brown, C. (2010, May 24,). *Letter to Julius Genachowski.* Congress of the United States. Retrieved from http://www.policybytes.org/Blog/PolicyBytes.nsf/dx/TitleII_FCC_24May2010.pdf/$file/TitleII_FC__24May2010.pdf

Grossman, D. (2002, April). *New Terminology and Clarifications for Diffserv (RFC 3260).* IETF. Retrieved from http://www.ietf.org/rfc/rfc2002.txt

Hahn, R. W., & Litan, R. W. (2007). The myth of network neutrality and what we should Do about it. *International Journal of Communication, 1,* 596–606.

Hahn, R. W., & Wallsten, S. (2006). The economics of net neutrality. *The Economists' Voice, 3*(6), 1–7. doi:10.2202/1553-3832.1194

Lemley, M. A., & Lessig, L. (2000). The end of end-to-end: Preserving the architecture of the Internet in the broadband era. *UCLA Law Review. University of California, Los Angeles. School of Law, 48,* 925–972.

McCullagh, D. (2002). *Tech companies ask for unfiltered Net.* CNET News. Retrieved from http://news.cnet.com/2100-1023-966307.html

Ministerio de Economía y Hacienda del Reino de España. (2011). *Proyecto de Ley de Economía Sostenible.*

Ministry of Transport and Communications of Finland (2009). *Decree on the minimum rate of a functional Internet access as a universal service (732/2009).*

Mohammed, A. (2006, February 7). *Verizon executive calls for end to Google's "free lunch".* The Washington Post. Retrieved from http://www.washingtonpost.com/wpdyn/content/article/2006/02/06/AR2006020601624.html

Nagesh, G. (2010, August 5). *Kerry: Net-neutrality legislation unlikely, FCC must act.* The Hill. Retrieved from http://thehill.com/blogs/hillicon-valley/technology/112935-kerry-net-neutrality-legislation-unlikely-fcc-must-act

Nemertes Research. (2007, November 19). *User demand for the Internet could outpace network capacity by 2010.* Retrieved from http://www.nemertes.com/press_releases/user_demand_internet_could_outpace_network_capacity_2010

Nichols, K., Blake, S., Baker, F., & Black, D. (1998, December). *Definition of the Differentiated Services Field (DS Field) in the IPv4 and IPv6 Headers (RFC 2474).* IETF. Retrieved from http://www.ietf.org/rfc/rfc2474.txt

O'Connell, P. (2005, November 7). Online Extra: At SBC, it's all about "scale and scope". *BusinessWeek.* Retrieved from http://www.businessweek.com/print/magazine/content/05_45/b3958092.htm?chan=gl

Obama, B. (2014). Statement on net neutrality. *The White House.* Retrieved from http://www.whitehouse.gov/net-neutrality

OECD. (2010a). *Fixed and wireless broadband subscriptions per 100 inhabitants.* Retrieved from http://www.oecd.org/dataoecd/21/35/39574709.xls

OECD. (2010b). *Households with broadband access.* Retrieved from http:// www.oecd.org/dataoecd/20/59/39574039.xls

Preserving the Open Internet, GN Docket No. 09-191, WC Docket No. 07-52, *Report and Order*, 25 FCC Rcd 17905 (2010).

Preserving the Open Internet. (2011, September 23). *Final Rule.* 76 (185). *Federal Register, 59191, 59235.*

Preserving the Open Internet; Broadband Industry Practices, GN Docket No. 09-191, WC Docket No. 07-52, *Notice of Proposed Rulemaking*, 24 FCC Rcd 13064 (2009).

Proposal for a Regulation of the European Parliament and of the Council laying down measures concerning the European single market for electronic communications and to achieve a Connected Continent, and amending Directives 2002/20/EC, 2002/21/EC and 2002/22/EC and Regulations (EC) No 1211/2009 and (EU) No 531/2012. COM (2013) 627 final.

Protecting and Promoting the Open Internet, GN Docket No. 14-28, *Notice of Proposed Rulemaking* 29 FCC Rcd. 5561 (2014).

Ruane, K. A. (2010). *The FCC's authority to regulate net neutrality after Comcast v. FCC* (Tech. Rep.). Congressional Research Service.

Saltzer, J., Reed, D., & Clark, D. (1984). End-to-end arguments in system design. *ACM Transactions on Computer Systems, 2*(4), 277–288. doi:10.1145/357401.357402

Sandvine. (2008). *Traffic management in a world with network neutrality* (Tech. Rep.).

Sécretariat d'Etat à la Prospective et au Développement de l'économie numérique (2010). *Consultation publique sur la neutralité du net.*

Snowe, O., Dorgan, B., Inouye, D., & Wyden, R., Leahy, Boxer, B., …, Dayton, M. (2006). *Internet Freedom Preservation Act.* S. 2917, 109th Cong. (2005-2006).

Solum, L. B. (2009). Models of Internet governance. In L. A. Bygrave & J. Bing (Eds.), *Internet governance: Infrastructure and institutions* (pp. 48–91). New York: Oxford University Press. doi:10.1093/acprof:oso/9780199561131.003.0003

Treaty of Lisbon. 2007 O.J. (C306) 01. United States Code.

Verizon v. FCC, 740 F.3d 623, D.C. Cir. 2014.

World Summit on the Information Society. (2005, November). *Tunis agenda for the information society.* ITU. Retrieved from http://www.itu.int/wsis/docs2/tunis/off/6rev1.pdf

Wu, T. (2003). Network neutrality, broadband discrimination. *Journal of Telecommunications and High Tecnology Law, 2*, 141–178.

Wu, T. (2010, August 9). Controlling commerce and speech. *The Wall Street Journal*. Retrieved from http://www.nytimes.com/roomfordebate/2010/8/9/who-gets-priority-on-the-web/controlling-commerce-and-speech

KEY TERMS AND DEFINITIONS

Differentiated Services: It is a business model whereby Internet service providers sell preferential access to power users.

Internet: It is a free, open and neutral computer network that interconnects the world.

Internet's Governance: It is the development and application by Governments, the private sector and civil society, in their respective roles, of shared principles, norms, rules, decision-making procedures, and programs that shape the evolution and use of the Internet.

Network Neutrality: It is the principle by which the delivery of content on the Internet is not subject to any discrimination by origin, destination, or protocol used.

Public Consultation: It is a process carried out by national and supranational institutions to gather needs and opinions of stakeholders, in order to develop tailor-made regulatory frameworks.

Traffic Management: It is the set of policies through which ISPs solve congestion problems on Internet connections.

Transparency: It is the openness and accountability, to external control, of the procedures and policies that an institution or firm defines or carries out.

ENDNOTES

[1]   The set of directives governing telecommunications in the European Union. The new legislative measures stated in the Directives 2009/136/CE and 2009/140/CE must be incorporated into the legal framework of each Member State of the European Union by May 25, 2011.

[2]   This new provision that has been included in article 8 (4) (g) of the amended telecommunications Framework Directive, seems to be a synthesis drawn from the first two regulatory principles of the FCC for an open Internet in 20 FCC Rcd 14986 (2005).

[3]   The European consultation uses as legal background, the recently amended regulatory framework for electronic communications that relies upon competition from market forces to ensure the provision of high quality, reasonable priced communications services to the "end user" (European Commission, 2010a, p.3). In this sense, the preamble of Directive 2009/140/EC of the European Parliament and of the Council of 25 November 2009 includes the desire of European authorities that the telecommunications market be solely regulated by competition law, limiting the application of specific regulations to those cases "where there is no effective and sustainable competition."

[4]   Act Nr. 20.453 which enshrines the principle of net neutrality for consumers and Internet users.

[5] The original rules presented in the *NPRM* were:

   ○ Subject to reasonable network management, a provider of broadband Internet access service may not prevent any of its users from sending or receiving the lawful content of the user's choice over the Internet.

   ○ Subject to reasonable network management, a provider of broadband Internet access service may not prevent any of its users from running the lawful applications or using the lawful services of the user's choice.

   ○ Subject to reasonable network management, a provider of broadband Internet access service may not prevent any of its users from connecting to and using on its network the user's choice of lawful devices that do not harm the network.

   ○ Subject to reasonable network management, a provider of broadband Internet access service may not deprive any of its users of the user's entitlement to competition among network providers, application providers, service providers, and content providers.

   ○ Subject to reasonable network management, a provider of broadband Internet access service must treat lawful content, applications, and services in a nondiscriminatory manner.

   ○ Subject to reasonable network management, a provider of broadband Internet access service must disclose such information concerning network management and other practices as is reasonably required for users and content, application, and service providers to enjoy the protections specified in this part.

The FCC believed these obligations provided the best tool to protect consumers from abusive practices and to promote both competition for Internet access and content (24 FCC Rcd 13064, 2009, para 52), and "investment and innovation with respect to the Internet, as with other communications technologies" (24 FCC Rcd 13064, 2009, para 51). The objective was to ensure that users could select any offering available to them, and not only those handpicked by their ISPs (24 FCC Rcd 13064, 2009, para 94). Based on these six obligations, the FCC, through its *NPRM*, sought comments on the best means to ensure an open Internet, in such a way that they "protect the legitimate needs of consumers, broadband service providers, entrepreneurs, investors, and businesses of all sizes that make use of the Internet" (24 FCC Rcd 13064, 2009, para 10) .

In the *Report and Order* (25 FCC Rcd 17905 2010. Appendix A, these obligations are redrafted and condensed in only three rules:

1. A person engaged in the provision of broadband Internet access service shall publicly disclose accurate information regarding the network management practices, performance, and commercial terms of its broadband Internet access services sufficient for consumers to make informed choices regarding use of such services and for content, application, service, and device providers to develop, market, and maintain Internet offerings.

2. A person engaged in the provision of fixed broadband Internet access service, insofar as such person is so engaged, shall not block lawful content, applications, services, or non-harmful devices, subject to reasonable network management.

3. A person engaged in the provision of fixed broadband Internet access service, insofar as such person is so engaged, shall not unreasonably discriminate in transmitting lawful network traffic over a consumer's broadband Internet access service. Reasonable network management shall not constitute unreasonable discrimination.

Nevertheless, the FCC wanted a simpler and more flexible wording, thus changing them into the ones presented in the *Federal Register* (76 Fed. Reg. 59191, 2011).

[6] The Act (47 U.S.C. § 153(20)) defines "information service" as the offering of a capability for generating, acquiring, storing, transforming, processing, retrieving, utilizing, or making available information via telecommunications, and includes electronic publishing, but does not include any use of any such capability for the management, control, or operation of a telecommunications system or the management of a telecommunications service.

[7] In National Association of Regulatory Utility Commissioners v. FCC, 525 F.2d 630 (D.C.Cir.), cert. denied, 425 U.S. 992, 96 S.Ct. 2203, 48 L.Ed.2d 816 (1976) (NARUC I), we observed that the essential element of common carriage is the carrier's undertaking " 'to carry for all people indifferently.' " In the communications context, this means providing a service whereby customers may " 'transmit intelligence of their own design and choosing.' " Computer and Communications Industry Association v. Federal Communications Commission, 693 F.2D 198, 209, 224 U.S.APP.D.C. 83 (D.C. Cir. 1982)

[8] Stéphane Richard, COO of France Telecom, has expressed that his organization supports the concept of an open Internet, where many actors have a responsibility to ensure this character, over the concept of a neutral Internet, in which ISPs are solely responsible for preventing discrimination of data streams (Autorité de Régulation des Communications Eléctroniques et des Postes, 2010).

[9] ... a number of cases have emerged involving the differentiated treatment by network operators of services or traffic which have led some interested parties to question whether the principle of the openness or neutrality of the Internet may be at risk (European Commission, 2010a, p. 5).

[10] Although, ironically, this article's original wording said that end-users were "free" to enter into data cap agreements with their providers.

[11] Canadian Radio-Television and Telecommunications Commission.

[12] Organisation for Economic Co-operation and Development.

[13] Data from the OECD shows that Korea has more that 90% of its households connected with broadband links, while all Nordic countries have more that 70%, USA has 63.5% and the average for EU is 56% (OECD, 2010). There are 27.1 subscriptions to broadband fixed service per 100 inhabitants in the USA and the most developed European countries have more than 30. Actually, the data shows that there is some kind of limit close to 40 subscriptions per 100 inhabitants, probably because there is usually no more than one Internet connection per household. On the other hand, we can see in Korea how the mobile broadband market has been exploited to almost total saturation, as it has 95 mobile broadband subscriptions per 100 inhabitants. While there are some other countries with a high penetration of mobile broadband internet access (Sweden, Japan and Norway all have more than 70 subscriptions per 100 inhabitants), most countries in the OECD have less than 50 subscriptions per 100 inhabitants, leaving a huge space for growth that operators will surely develop (OECD, 2010a).

[14] Commissioner Kroes has made clear that an investment of around 14 bn euros "over a five-year period is needed to secure 2 Megabits per second coverage at an affordable price for all households in the EU", a figure she believes would be "unfair" for providers to bear (SPEECH/10/434). However, without any universal service obligation for broadband operators, broadband average rates are already beyond this level; as Belson reports, in European countries as well as in the USA, more than 60% of their connections are above 2 Mbps, with a the average Internet connections of at least 2.8 Mbps. No country has more that 2.6% of its connections below 256 Kbps, showing, at least partially, how limited the market for such an invasive decision as the declaration of broadband Internet access as a universal service is (Belson, 2010).

[15]   See Amendments 236 and 243 in Proposal for a Regulation of the European Parliament and of the Council laying down measures concerning the European single market for electronic communications and to achieve a Connected Continent, and amending Directives 2002/20/EC, 2002/21/EC and 2002/22/EC and Regulations (EC) No 1211/2009 and (EU) No 531/2012. COM(2013) 627 final.

[16]   As we can find in Art. 22 (3) of Directive 2009/22/CE (Amended). NRAs should be allowed to set the minimum quality of service requirements to avoid degradation of service and traffic throttling. They also have to specify performance parameters that providers have to measure, as well as the way this information should be published, in order to ensure that end-users are able to make comparisons of service.

[17]   Nevertheless, at the moment of this chapter's submission, President Obama (2014) urged the FCC to reclassify broadband Internet service providers under Title II of the Communications Act.

Chapter 4
Impact and Potential of Emerging Technologies for Fostering Democracy

Amir Manzoor
Bahria University, Pakistan

ABSTRACT

In recent years, several case studies have appeared on how emerging technologies had an impact in bringing grass root political changes. It has been widely argued that emerging technologies are influencing democracy all over the world. This chapter explores how emerging technologies support various pillars of democracy (freedom of expression and freedom of press, rule of law, human rights, and individual liberty) to strengthen and foster the democratic processes. While there exist substantial evidence that technology provides strong support to democracy, significant issues still exist and need to be addressed for emerging technology to contribute to democracy. The chapter discusses these issues and offer recommendations for better use of emerging technologies for democracy.

INTRODUCTION

Information and communication technologies (ICTs) are profoundly affecting social, economic and political institutions worldwide, particularly in new and emerging democracies. For reformers and activists, these tools are indispensable to overcome resource disparities and entrenched monopolies of power and voice. The emerging technologies, including web 2.0 technologies, provides their users capability of instant communication with others and content publication that is accessible across borders. Individuals can use the technology to spread their own messages and make their previously silenced voices heard (Chadwick, 2008).

There exist various examples where technology has been used to foster democracy. These examples range from use of technology for promoting citizen advocacy to increasing government transparency and accountability. Public and private organizations, citizens, and politicians are using emerging technologies, including web technologies to enhance communication, improve access to important information, and

DOI: 10.4018/978-1-4666-8336-5.ch004

increase their efficiency. The natural outcome of such enhancements would be strengthened democratic processes and governance that is more effective.

The objective of this chapter is to explore the emerging technologies and their possible impact and potential for fostering democracy. The purpose of the discussion above was to provide a background of the chapter. Next, the chapter shall discuss the use of emerging technologies to foster democracy. Following this discussion, chapter shall explore the link between Leadership, Culture, and Technology. Following this discussion, the next sections will explore the impact and future potential of technologies on individual pillars of democracy. At the end, the chapter will provide implications and recommendations in order for emerging technologies to better support democracy and offer future research directions.

EMERGING TECHNOLOGIES AND DEMOCRACY

Emerging technologies refers to new technologies. These technologies are either currently developing or expected to be developed in the next five to ten years. Emerging technologies has the potential to bring significant changes in the current business and social environment. Some example of emerging technologies include information technology, on-demand printing, robotics, wireless data communication, and biotechnology (Business Dictionary, 2013).

The citizens in democratic societies already regulate emerging technologies through their votes and finance it through their taxes (Strandbakken, 2013). Science and technologies studies have been focused on emerging technologies and their interference with existing conditions of society and technology (Hess, 1997; Latour 2005). While the science and technology should be free, we see that use of technology for democracy is political and awkward and elected democratic governments actually fund the scientific research. This shows that the present republic of science and technology is, at least to a certain degree, is politically controlled or contaminated. Making technology policy an fundamental part of the political debate is one way to democratize this republic of science and technology. The focus on politicizing science and technology clearly make emerging technologies more interesting than the already established and standardized ones (Akrich, 1992).

The positive visions and potential applications for emerging technologies are apparently without limits (Ratner & Ratner, 2003). Emerging technologies are expected to have a substantial influence on the everyday life of individual consumers and households (Ozin & Arsenault, 2006, p. 8). The public concerns about new technologies have strong political potential. One example is the debate about genetically modified crops (Burke, 2004).

There exist two ways emerging technologies can be used to reach people across borders. First by using pre-existing instruments (for example, YouTube and Flickr) and second by using online communities. In first method, we need to maximize the potential of these instruments to respond to the needs of target groups. In the second method, the online communities can be built using social networking tools. Multimedia tools can be very helpful to highlight the activities of various social groups, especially those that cannot be reached using other types of media. Many organizations have created groups on social media. One example is Burma Watch. This Facebook groups was developed to support the monks' protest in Burma. Another group called WLP Lebanon/CRTD.A was created to advocate for equality in citizenship laws of Lebanon. Oxfam, a worldwide development organization that mobilized the power of people against poverty, created Flickr photo pools to petition Starbucks to pay fair prices to Ethiopian coffee farmers. Another group called Nature Conservancy was created on Flickr to create awareness about conservation. Online social networks are an excellent platform for virtual assemblies and campaigns. Online social networks provide immense possibilities for democracy activists. These social networks can help meet new communities, create new and strengthen existing relationships, recruit volunteers to support your cause, and raise funds.

There also exist high-tech approaches to target particular audiences. The first approach is specialized technical applications to promote cooperation among various target groups. There are several examples of use of this approach such as UK school youth, wimps.org.uk, and the Polish portal www.civicportal.org. WIMPS is a website created and managed by young people that seeks to link young people with public servants (politicians and others). Civic Portal is a website of international cooperation and support of civil society in Eastern Europe and Central Asia. Both web portals use advanced Internet technologies, such as multimedia announcement boards and language translation tools. The second approach utilizes technologically advanced portal applications. These applications use a combination of informatics, sociology, psychology, and political science. One such example is Persuasive Technology Lab at Stanford University. This lab carry out various projects of website and mobile apps development. These websites and apps are designed to change what people think and do. For example, the method of "Mobile Persuasion" that uses the TV, radio, and a combination of traditional media and the Internet.

To support cooperation and understanding between countries, there also exist advanced solutions. These solutions are based on identifying and linking local partners from different countries. For example, partners from health sectors in various countries use SMS messaging, a persuasion technology, to increase individual and global health and safety. Many countries opt not to use Internet but other means to transfer less expensive information.

The expansion in people's ability to communicate has always been a revolutionary act. Communication technologies can accelerate the entire process of civic action as we witnessed in the Arab Spring. This acceleration occurs because technology dramatically increases the number of people involved in gathering, distributing and consuming information. Use of technology also provides a positive feedback loop so that people could observe in real-time the effects of their actions. This reinforces commitment and recruits more members into the cause. Even before the advent of Web 2.0 technologies, political movements for a democratic regime were active and running around the globe (Bleicher, 2006). What Internet and technology actually did is to allow them to get organized and strengthen. The dictators with a conventional mind set didn't understand what was happening and unable to control the Internet. The recent Arab Spring revolution provides a very clear message to dictators around the globe. A failure to properly censor and prohibit use of emerging technologies for communication using Internet means the end of dictator's rule (Anderson, 2011). As we can see, Syria has learnt this lesson and we see every possible effort from Syria to stop communication over Internet by its citizens (Al Zoubi & Read, 2013).

ICTs present many possibilities for democracy activists. At the same time, authoritarian governments recognize their potential and are therefore increasingly restricting access and activities in cyberspace. Several restrictions (such as blocking, filtering, and censoring) can be imposed on communication using Internet. There exist tools that can be used to bypass such restrictions e.g. the use of anonymizing services to access restricted information. Users can also remove traces of usage at public Internet centers, by proxy servers that anonymize Web traffic (such as Anonymouse.org); relay networks for hiding Web site access history (such as Tor), and encrypt emails to protect sensitive communications using email encryption tools such as HushMail. Users can use Skype's VoIP and conferencing capabilities to communicate and collaborate. Peer-to-peer technologies provide greater privacy and security than other Internet chat programs.

The new interactive communications technologies can revitalize democracy. We live in a world where we see increasingly negative television commercials and growing cynicism towards governments. Technologies can help by encouraging broader discussions on various issues and dominate positive messages over negative messages. These technologies can uncouple wealth from voter impressions, distribute candidates' messages in multiple languages and formats, and provide two-way communication between the candidate and voters and candidates to candidates.

The present form of digital social media has transformed the ways in which many people communicate and share information. There exist two viewpoints regarding use of social media. According to popular activists, major political changes, such as Arab Spring of 2010, are a direct result of the use of social media (Huffington Post, 2011). The second group of activists think social media as government's means of surveillance and maintaining ever-increasing control over citizens (House, 2011). At the outset, it is necessary to emphasize that technology is not an autonomous power that can inherently be used for 'good' or 'bad'.

Democracy, by definition, is "the rule of the people" from the Greek words "demos" (people) and "kratos" (rule) . The will of the people is manifested most visibly through the electoral process. No democracy can survive without the protection of basic freedom of expression, belief, and press. Another aspect that is considered a litmus test for any democracy is respect for the rule of law. Human rights are another major pillar for any democracy to sustain itself. The last and the most important pillar of democracy is individual liberty or the individual right to choose (Al-Fattal, 2013).

LEADERSHIP, CULTURE, AND TECHNOLOGY

People representatives in a democratic society are their leaders. Technology-assisted revolutions are leader-less revolutions. We also witness that there are far less casualties in technology-assisted revolutions as compared with other revolutions. But another significant fact about these technology-assisted revolutions is that they are quite easy to start but very hard to bring them to their end. Another debate is how we can start and finish a leader-led revolution which is based on technology. Taking the example of Arab Spring revolution we see that in all these countries there were few strong groups who were well-organized and resourceful. When the technology-based revolution was successful in ousting the dictator in the country, one or more powerful groups took control of the government as the result of the election. These groups were not necessarily the representatives of the population. In the aftermath of these elections, differences were visible between the ruling groups and other groups (Roy, 2012).

It can be argued that the culture plays a vital role in a transformation from dictatorship to democratic rule which results from a technology-based revolution. If culture of the country is supportive, the differences among groups become healthy. Democratic process continues in the form of elections and public participation and eventually we can hope that true leaders will emerge. Looking at the example of Egypt, we can see that the culture of the country probably wasn't supportive for this transformation into true democracy. Arab world is composed of tribal and religious structures. There is a long history of significant tribal differences, long lasting wars, and significant racial differences. In Egypt, no emphasis was placed on education and as a matter of fact, higher education meant more difficulties in getting job due to over-qualification. During the dictator's rule of Husseni Mubarak, country ran out of financial reserves. The military industrial complex situation and lack of innovation by Egyptian industry made the situation more difficult (Aouragh & Alexander, 2011).

Can similar type of technology-assisted revolution happen in a much larger country such as China? China is a much bigger country that Egypt or any other country. In China, we have a single repressive party system. While the Arab dictators didn't have the acumen and ability to control the communications on the Internet, China does. The organizational and hierarchical structures in China are over 5,000 years old. We don't see any evidence of Chinese population significant dissatisfaction with Chinese government. In fact, the Chinese culture is supportive of the present system of government in China. In China, unlike most autocracies – including Mubarak's Egypt and Ben Ali's Tunisia—the state is highly decentralized. Local governments have substantial autonomy over decision making related to development policies and social management. As such, while China witnessed very high levels of protest activities during 2011-2012, these political battles were between the protesters and the local authorities and Chinese regime was not directly challenged (Kennedy, 2012; Hess, 2013).

FREEDOM OF EXPRESSION, BELIEF, PRESS AND TECHNOLOGY

In many of the developed world countries, particularly USA, we see homogenous culture and similar values. Political differences exist but people are used to live with them. However, the same situation cannot be taken as granted everywhere. The best possible assistance technology can provide to foster democracy is the education of masses. Education can change the world. Mobile/smart phones are probably the best device for education. Though social media has provided new way to express ideas, evolution of free expression is not just limited to social media. Anyone can easily setup a blog and easily communicate with a large number of potential audience (CNN, 2012).

In early days, people had to publish their ideas in order to communicate the same to a large audience. This required moderation of ones ideas through a system that had strict rules and guidelines. However, this method of communicating the ideas inherently reduced any encountering radical ideas. With the new technologies communication, this is no longer the case. A vast amount of original and unique work can go through avoiding a lengthy and rigorous editing process. This way, technology has opened space for an unimaginable degree of freedom of expression. However, such increased freedom of expression has resulted in an improper fusion of public and private expression. One can write something and share it using Internet. That's a form of self-expression. However, it is quite possible that this writing would never be read by anyone. The technology has made freedom of expression a predominant public phenomenon.

Emerging technologies can have an important impact on privacy and data protection of individuals. Take example of sensors. Individuals concerned may not aware that their personal information is being accessed by using sensors. They are also not as to who controls the sensors, which of their information is sensed and for what purposes, whether this information is permanently stored or not, and who uses this information. While information derived from sensors is very useful, the information is obtained from sensors put in the public places should be readily available to anybody. However, ambiguities exists as to how such information can be shared (Gutwirth, 1993). Sensors that are programmed to detect abnormal behavior and react accordingly are considered a threat to the freedom of speech and particularly the freedom of expression. Another issue is that how these sensors can possibly threaten the fundamental principle of non-discrimination. This is because these sensors can make automated decisions on the basis of genetic features, language, or other features. The privacy issues related to use of RFID have been extensively discussed in academic literature. However, massive deployment of consumer products with small RFID tags can have significant impact on fundamental rights and freedoms. The important issues are similar to the ones that are associated with the use of sensors. One additional issue is that if companies provide product guarantees only if RFID tags must remain attached to the products. In that case, consumers can circumventing their right to remove the tag once the product is bought. The fundamental right of protection of personal data can be compromised using Brain-computer interfacing (BCI) that allows processing of neural signals. These neural signals may represent human thoughts. In a report, Guardian (2007) reported that a team of world-leading neuroscientists had developed a powerful technique that allows them to look deep inside a person's brain and read their intentions before they act. The critical question is under what conditions the use of these neuro-signals can invoke intellectual-property rights. For example can we patent a feeling of happiness created in the mind of human being using neuro-signals? Another issue is the lawfulness of processing of neural signals without consent of the data subject.

The answers to these questions are critical to protect the fundamental human rights of personal life, data protection, freedom of thought, conscience and religion, physical and mental integrity, and human dignity. All these rights are not only at stake through brain 'reading' but also, brain 'writing'. In brain writing, neuro-signals can be used to input information into the brain to trigger certain behavior, thoughts or feelings. Can we allow police to rewrite brain of a criminal to use against criminals? Given this type of brain rewriting may be prone to change the identity of the person, it is important to know if society would allow this to happen at all.

Currently, criminal law only penalizes activities. The law appears to ignore the acts that may not be criminal in nature but pave the way for a criminal activity. Let's suppose the technology enables us to determine the human intentions. Would we penalize an intention to commit a crime or not? Can current criminal law be extended to include criminal thoughts such as "Jihadi thoughts"? In addition, if the law can be extended to punish criminal thoughts are we ready to face its implications for human dignity and freedom of thought?

Body signals can be processed through body-computer interfacing. It is also assumes that these signals may predict human emotions and behavior. In a report, Guardian (2002) reported that British government considered a scheme to implant surgically electronic tags in convicted pedophiles. This scheme was considered due to massive incidents of child abuse. The important question raised here is that in what situation and under which circumstances processing of body signals (personal data) without consent of the data subject can be lawful, if at all. Another question is about the assumption of innocence and the right of defense in a fair trial knowing the fact that technology a priori before the crime was committed. To what extent can having an ICT chip implanted be an obligation de facto or de jure? What would happen if implanting a chip in the body becomes a necessary condition for participation in the information society? What would happen if the same condition is imposed to enjoy emergency healthcare services? Wouldn't the implantation of a chip, in the name of having access to information, be an infringement of the right to human dignity? People may find it horrible to have some silicon in their body. Brain implants can impact physical and mental integrity. Someone cannot be considered free when he must wear an un-removable chip. Brain implants may impede the freedom of thought as unlawful thoughts may be detected (Radoykov et al. 2007).

In short, implanting an ICT chip into human body has serious implications for human various human rights such as right to dignity and the right to physical and mental integrity. These implants can store and process information inside, outside, towards and coming from the human body. Today, law enforcement agencies have access to electronic communication between people and between people and objects (such as websites). However, should the law enforcement agencies be allowed to access that same data if it is stored inside humans? Will the implants be considered as violation of the right of property or right to physical integrity? Should we consider the interaction between technology (the implant inside human body) and outside computers public or private? This aspect is crucial for privacy. The European Group on Ethics in Science and New Technologies (EGE), in its "Ethical Aspects of ICT Implants in the Human Body", discussed the similar questions.

With respect to peer-to-peer networks, a crucial question is the validity of the right to assemble and associate for the virtual assemblies and associations. How we can ensure the freedom of thought, expression and information when the assemblies and associations of people occur in cyberspace where each activity is monitored and the data about activities is stored. Can we have secure virtual places, such as churches or personal rooms, where one can enjoy freedom of thought, expression, and information within the walls of these virtual places?

Use of social worlds and avatars also poses questions. How social worlds can ensure right to physical and mental integrity for users interacting with avatars? What about the intellectual property rights over virtual objects created by avatars? Can the right to freedom of assembly and association be extended to social worlds and, if yes, in what shape? Should expropriation of an object (such as a sword) by avatar be considered a violation of right to property? In Belgium, police was investigating Second Life after getting reports of virtual rape of a female avatar by a user of Second Life. What impact would such news produce on people's behavior and sense of identity? (Virtually Blind, 2007).

The ability to readily acquire factual information is pivotal to the decision making process. Emerging technologies has provided great opportunities for openness as well as misinformation. Despite mass media's large number of audience, professional news outlets continue to represent sources of credible information. In some countries, news outlets are free to report the shortcomings of their governments but the situation is not the same everywhere. In many countries, media is used to manipulate the populous in favor of the government and drive an ethnic conflict. In such cases, media freedom could validate facts and manipulate propaganda and provide a resolution to long-standing insurrection.

Emerging technologies has played a significant role in media freedom. The crackdown in Myanmar (Burma) was only captured because Internet access and digital cameras widely available and individuals were able to provide shocking images of a brutal crackdown. As a result of technological revolution, we see, more and more digitization in the media. Newspapers are no exception. As a result of digitization they continue to face decreasing subscriptions and less cash flows from classifieds. Due to the financial crunch, newspapers are producing less investigative reports (Forbes, 2013b). This is a great loss to democracy.

RULE OF LAW AND TECHNOLOGY

By enhancing the public's access to information and facilitating public participation in government decision-making, the technology has geometrically expanded the scope and reach of the rule of law. The concept of access to information is essential in a democratic society, and core to the rule of law. In order to establish the rule of law in a democratic system, citizens must have access, at the very minimum, to laws of a government. Beyond this, citizens should also have access to the legislative and administrative processes, and transparency should be promoted through providing information of all government activity (Peixoto, 2013).

The Cloud Computing

Law enforcement and government agencies of all sizes can use cloud computing for many potential advantages such as cost savings, rapid deployment of critical resources, off-site storage and disaster recovery, on-demand resource availability, and enhance effectiveness of the marshaling activities. The cloud could enable crowd sourcing of investigatory data, thereby vastly lowering costs of dispute resolution.

Using cloud, government can bring data to secure and authorized endpoints. This helps increase government productivity and interaction with citizens. Government employees can easily and seamlessly manage and access all the information they need to do their job. A move towards paperless environment, enabled by cloud computing, can save government agencies an average of $2,000 to $10,000 annually.

In order meet their dynamic operational needs and keep their systems and data secure, law enforcement agencies using cloud computing must ensure their planning and implementation of cloud computing adheres to some basic principles. These principles include security policy compliance, data ownership, Impermissibility of data mining, Auditing, Portability and interoperability, and Integrity (International Association of Chiefs of Police, 2013). First, the cloud services must comply with the official security policy requirements of the law enforcement agency. Second, law enforcement agencies must retain ownership of their data in the cloud. Third, the cloud services provider must not perform any data mining for any purpose not explicitly authorized by the law enforcement agency. Fourth, law enforcement agencies should be able to conduct audits of the cloud service provider's performance, use, access, and compliance with the terms of any agreement. Fifth, law enforcement agencies should have the facility to port their data stored in the cloud to other systems. This data must also be interoperable with other operating systems to an extent that does not compromise the security and integrity of the data. Sixth, the physical or logical integrity of information must be maintained.

The broader adoption of cloud computing within the law enforcement community offers an opportunity for many agencies to reduce IT costs amid declining budgets. In USA, cloud-computing adoption remains low among law enforcement agencies. One possible reason could be that cloud adoption in law enforcement faces the hurdle of meeting FBI Criminal Justice Information Services security policy standards.

Online and Mobile Applications

Government agencies can use mobile applications (also called mobile apps) to connect with citizens, provide citizens with more information, and to increase engagement and collaboration with the citizens. An estimated 80 percent of population of North America is online. Therefore, effectively leverage this most powerful communications media is vital. With productive citizen participation through mobile apps, governments can improve policy outcomes, and as more voices are heard, a broader perspective is shared and trust is built in the community. Modern online tools and applications make managing citizen input easier. Government organizations can expand their engagement to a wider base of citizens and have a significant impact on the public meeting process - a cornerstone of democracy. The notes of these meetings can be recorded and made accessible to public in timely and accurate manner. This accessibility of information to citizens could help government improve its public police when citizens share their views on government actions and meeting outcomes. The benefits of mobile apps clearly make them a good investment for any government organization.

Mobile apps are available for a variety of application areas such as for language translation, blood-alcohol testing and many other areas relevant to government. New applications continue to come at a staggering pace. The potential benefits of these applications for government use (more importantly for law enforcement) are increased by the emergence of smartphones and tablets.

A location-based service (LBS) is an information service delivered to a mobile device, such as a smartphone or tablet computer. The service is delivered through the wireless data network by utilizing the ability of the mobile device to provide its current geographic position. For law enforcement, LBS has serious implications. Many police departments around the globe have set up automated processes for geocoding crime and incident data in order to feed Internet and intranet mapping applications. These data are typically stored in a cloud (Police Chief Magazine, 2011).

In 2012, Salt Lake City police department in USA implemented "CityConnect" mobile application. CityConnect was the first fully-integrated mobile application that allowed agencies to inform, connect, and engage with their local community through their own agency-branded mobile application. The app features included agency generated alerts, crime alerts page, crime reports map, alerts, and report a problem (Public Engines, 2012). In 2013, The Worcester police department in USA, unveiled a free police app to any resident of the city hoping to access police-related news, crime maps, social media alerts, a police scanner and the ability to submit an anonymous tip to the department.

Apple provides hundreds of apps for citizens to use for better law abiding. CopLogger ($.99) is an app that provides a pocket-sized version of mobile computing terminals (MCT) found in police vehicles. Users can use it to track an entire day's activity and archive or e-mail it. Police Codes ($.99) is an app that will list medical/fire codes, police 10 codes, police 11 codes and scanner color codes. Miranda Warning ($.99) is an app that informs citizens of their rights.

Responsive Web Design

According to Business Insider (Heggestuen, 2013), one in every five people in the world owned a smartphone and one in every 17 owned a tablet. It is very likely that the audience you are trying to reach is not accessing your website through a standard computer. Responsive web design enables the design of a website to adjust from one device to another so that the user experience is seamless and homogenous. Being aware of the need for this and investing some of your dollars into making sure you have a responsive web design is important to convey a professional and educated appearance to the public.

In 2013, Boston, USA police department launched a new website. This new website allowed information, including crime reports and community alerts, to be posted faster and read more easily. The new website (bpdnews.com) featured a responsive design, which refitted content on the website to match the screen size of each user, making it easier to navigate for both desktop and mobile users. Along with a fresh look and color scheme, the website was also simpler for department personnel to update and had better security and reliability.

High-Performance Data Analytics

The amount of data that is attainable through data analytics and big data mining is beyond comprehension for many government organizations - and those that have begun using it at the federal level have only started to scratch the surface. High-performance data analytics can help government agencies make proactive response and decisions, perform time-saving analysis, and accomplish goals through trend information.

Today's law enforcement decision-makers are held accountable for knowing what data needs to be gathered, the appropriate analysis of the data and the interpretation of the results of that analysis. They must also be able to translate those results into both tactical prediction and strategic forecasting.

To protect the public, access to the right information when and where it is needed is crucial for law enforcement officials. Such information can help officers not only solve cases, but also prevent crimes. Over the time, the gathering, assessing, and sharing of this information has become a complex endeavor. Very large amounts of data are available to law enforcement agencies today from various sources such as geographic profiling techniques, video CCTV footage etc. Great data analysis tools are needed to analyze this data and identify reliable intelligence.

With flat or declining budgets and limited human resources, many police departments are struggling to manage this wealth of information. Police departments are using predictive analytics and similar tools for quicker, smarter, and more accurate analysis of this data to help them make informed daily operational decisions and enable more effective day-to-day policing. By combining new digital technologies with analytics capabilities, police forces can, for the first time, generate important intelligence insights without the help of large teams of intelligence analysts.

Predictive analytics techniques build on information shared between different government agencies such as police departments and courts. These techniques can help identify locations where crimes are most likely to occur, help officers identify offenders and even prevent future criminal activity, conduct investigations more efficiently, deploy the right people where they are needed, examine security threats and behavior patterns, and deliver intelligence to officers when and where they need it.

Los Angeles Police Department (LAPD) ran a successful trial of PredPol analytics software and reported that property crime rates fell 12% within six months. The Memphis Police department reported that use of predictive analytics resulted in 30% decrease in serious crimes between 2006 and 2010, The Metropolitan Police of UK, used an automated analytics system and were able to reducing criminal activities in seven neighborhood crime areas. Metropolitan police also reported that use of predictive analytics made it easier for them to prioritize and deploy limited resources. City authorities in Singapore ran an innovative pilot program to integrate advanced analytic capabilities into existing CCTV systems. When an incident was identified, an alert was issued to the government agency or authority required. The objective of this program was to improve response times to public safety incidents.

For law enforcement agencies, provision of right information, at the right, and in the right format remains a significant challenge. To gain maximum strategic value from new technologies, law enforcement agencies need to consider the impact of these technologies the way the way law enforcement resources are organized and deployed. New technologies, such as data analytics, can be most beneficial to government organizations provided these organizations structure themselves to exploit technological benefits, trained its workforce in how to use the technology, and provide appropriate tools for workforce to access the technology. Organizations that seek to preserve traditional organizational structures and practices will struggle to maximize returns on investments in analytics or any other technology.

Data analytics is a technique that can be managed relatively easily, provided centralized and interoperable systems are in place. However, data analytics technique requires constant adjustments and analytics parameters and results must be continuously reviewed and refreshed.

Social Media

Social media advertising allows government to interact and connect with citizens on specific issues affecting them. For instance, if you are running a campaign to figure out what citizens want to do with a city park, you can link the ads directly to a landing page seeking feedback from citizens.

From Facebook to twitter, MySpace and LinkedIn, social media is changing the way business is done across the professional spectrum. This is particularly evident in the areas of criminology and criminal justice, where law enforcement officers and researchers alike are finding new and unique ways to put social networking to use, both to solve crimes and hire candidates.

Social networking is providing officers new avenues and tools to help them solve crimes. With such a large member bases of social networking sites, investigators are able to gain new tips and insights into crimes committed in their communities. Cops can use social media sites to gather valuable intelligence on suspected criminals. Sometimes, police are able to get tips from suspects' "friends" after the suspect inevitably brags about his deviant behavior on the social networking site. Other times, detectives can gather evidence from pictures or video posted on sites like MySpace and YouTube. Even more valuable is the ability to track and gain insight into a suspect's mentality, simply by monitoring their posts.

Besides solving crimes, police can also use it to help find missing, endangered or distressed people. What people post on their sites can often provide helpful insight into their state of mind and their intentions. Social media can also give law enforcement officers important clues as to where runaways or people who are in distress may be headed. By looking at friends lists, 'likes', posts and comments, police can establish a reasonable idea of their plans.

Community outreach is an important step to solve crimes. To achieve this goal, police departments across the globe are creating an online presence of their own. Social media outlets take community-oriented policing to a new level by providing quick, cheap and easy ways to get important information out to followers and concerned citizens.

Law enforcement agencies can also use social media to show human side of police department and show that law enforcement officers are also members of the community they serve. Law enforcement agencies can use social media to highlight their officer's accomplishments, make announcements regarding enforcement campaigns, provide messages about safety, ask followers for tips on crimes, and to provide important warnings or alerts regarding missing children or suspected criminals who may be on the loose.

Selection of right people for their workforce is essential for law enforcement agencies in order solve crimes and maintain trust in the community. Social media sites, such as Facebook, allows background investigation checks. Investigators can gain new and valuable insight into the character of their law enforcement candidates.

Law enforcement agencies and officers use social media to gain access to information and colleagues from across the country and around the world. This practice has encouraged new discussions on officer tactics and techniques. It has also helped to increase the spread of new ideas throughout law enforcement agencies.

HUMAN RIGHTS AND TECHNOLOGY

A democracy is not the tyranny of the majority. To the contrary, a modern democracy is measured by how much the majority in power is restrained by its respect for minority rights. different minority rights that should be protected and society can call itself a democracy when these rights, such as gender rights, are not protected.

Social media helps monitor emerging human rights emergencies and uncover incorrect information. Human rights activists may not reach all places and may be denied access to a potential crime scene altogether. At the same time, recent surge in citizen journalism and social media platforms has led to a flood of potential evidence of human rights violations. Investigator now have access to powerful tools, such as Google Earth, to have hundreds of potential crime scenes at their fingertips.

There exist several examples of emerging technology use for promoting human rights. Amnesty International USA used Twitter and Storify to get the attention of the US State Department to respond to the human rights violations in Bahrain (Newtactics.org, 2011). To honor people and cities that had a profound effect on the course of the Syrian revolution, anonymous artists created special stamps and published them on Facebook. Stamps of the Syrian Revolution are mock postage "stamps" that feature photos of events ripped from the headlines, or of influential people in the uprising. Sometimes the stamps feature key figures suggested by the fans of the page themselves. With over 400 stamps and counting, the page represents a major visual archive and timeline that documents the revolution as it unfolds, and pays tribute to its supporters (informationactivism.org, n.d.). The Facebook campaign "Kurd Men for Equality" was launched to send a message to authorities in Iran: Being a woman is not a tool to humiliate or punish anyone. The campaign was launched in response to a court case in which a man, convicted of domestic abuse, was ordered to wear women's clothing as punishment. This punishment was meant to be a form of public humiliation. But instead, because of this campaign, this punishment has been transformed into an opportunity for men to show their support and solidarity with the women in their communities (CNN, 2013). Thousands of people downloading and sharing a GMO-free consumer guide helped pressure Hungarian companies to come clean on their supply chains. While the genetically modified food is banned in Hungary, many imported ingredients used in Hungarian food and beverages could contain genetically modified organisms without consumers knowing. Greenpeace Hungary, an NGO, pressured Hungarian companies to make a public statement that their products were free from genetically modified organisms. Greenpeace Hungary developed the answers from companies into a free consumer food guide that was shared offline and available online and for download. Products with a green label were safe. Red products were questionable, and implied the company didn't respond to Greenpeace's multiple queries (Team, 2013).

Following years of conflict between the Orma and Pokomo groups in Tana Delta, Kenya, a string of massacres and displacements were galvanized by malicious rumor spreading. These included beliefs held by the Orma community that Pokoma health workers intended to poison their children, alongside Pokomo allegations that the Orma had been given weaponry to destroy Pokomo communities. While there was no evidence to support these claims, intentional disinformation had the advantage of benefit for those with a political agenda. Sentinel Project launched a fact-checking mobile phone initiative for genocide prevention. This application enabled individuals to report incidents or allegations and to receive verification of its accuracy. Importantly, the project acted as a template for other conflict settings, whereby political pursuits of power and propagandist slander could be confronted before violent escalation.

In Kenya, mobile network Safaricom introduced a service called M-Pesa which allowed users to store money on their mobiles. Kenyans used this resource to pay utilities bill and send money to friends. Individuals simply stated the amount they wish to pay by text and the recipient converted it into cash at their local M-Pesa office. The device proved to be invaluable to some of the poorest individuals who were unable to access bank accounts. It is a clear example of technology support to empower individuals with tools to rise above their economic and social disadvantage.

Web 2.0 applications that facilitate participatory online information sharing and collaboration have transformed the human rights community. Often, bloggers are the first to present evidence of human rights violations publicly. These bloggers either witness and document the violations themselves or post someone else's information. Aggregation bloggers like Global Voices Online (http://globalvoicesonline. org) amplify this information so that it is more accessible. International NGOs and libraries also publish and translate selected blogs.

Human rights activists have used emerging technologies for long time to cut the time in transmission of their response to human rights violations (Halpin and Fisher, 1998). With time, this trend has been continued and now it includes use of GPS, crowd sourcing, blogs, tweets etc. Mobile technologies are also playing important role in human rights protection. During Arab Spring of 2011, YouTube was used as a human rights advocacy resource in in Egypt, Libya, Syria, and Tunisia to publicize Arab regimes' human rights abuses both locally and globally.

The use of these technologies resulted in unprecedented era of virtual politics and activism took shape within Arab societies. The Internet and other new communication technologies have been central forces for this change. Preliminary evidence suggested that YouTube was effective in highlighting police abuse cases and prosecuting perpetrators (Lannon and Halpin, 2012). Real-time reports on what was happening on the streets went out on these social networks. Heartbreaking images of suffering, such as the video of the death of Neda Agha-Soltan, an Irani protester who shot dead on her way to the 2009 Iranian presidential election protests, or photographs of Mohamed Bouazizi, a street vendor who burned himself to death to protest harassment by the Tunisian authorities—were seen by millions of people around the world. In the aftermath of Arab Spring, Arab citizens harnessed the YouTube's to capabilities to expose political corruption and police brutality. YouTube and the new breed of social media have grown more effective as favorite political instruments. This is because these tools provide high levels of anonymity, have global reach, and requires no professional prerequisites. As Rosneau (2003, p. 149) argues that with globalization of communication technologies "the misdeeds of human rights violators no longer pass from human kind's conscience." Take example of YouTube videos law enforcement agencies abuse, corruption, and other human rights violations in Arab countries which was a major factor in publicizing misdeeds by the Arab governments. The more shocking the video evidence was, the louder was the public and global outcry against the government abuses. The permanency of the record at these sites also made the fight more salient and constant since the internationalization of human rights abuses builds on a well-proven record of transnational solidarity movements(Keck and Sikkink, 1998).

Social media and emerging mobile ICT have been used to develop human rights organizations and campaigns e.g. the Ushahidi organization developed in Kenya. This organization produced a Web site to map the violence that was occurring in Kenya in 2008. The Web site mapped incidents of violence using reports submitted via mobile phones and the Web, accumulating approximately 45,000 users who provided evidence of the violence. Free open source software help human rights activists achieve a high level of data gathering and analysis and hold perpetrators of human rights abuses accountable. However, in response to human activists, states do involve in repressive action of surveillance and monitoring of citizens and human rights activists.

Biometric technologies can be used to identify a person based on some aspect of their biology. The ever-growing number of video surveillance systems in cities around the globe has caused privacy and human rights storms. Following 9/11 terrorists attacks in USA, the increased use of facial recognition, as a means of detecting possible threats, is also under heavy criticism. Another concern is that, to put such a database together, security agencies seldom seek permission to keep people's records in their data repositories. In 2012, New York Police announced a new police surveillance infrastructure called the Domain Awareness System, which links existing police databases with live video feeds from a variety of different sources. Governments are spending billions of dollars to develop various biometric technologies capable of identifying anyone anywhere in the world (Wolf, 2012).

While a justification can be made for use of these technologies against crime, there is very little doubt that such data can also be easily used to violate individual's rights and freedoms. In USA, there is a growing issue of federal and local law enforcement agencies requesting mobile providers to hand over their data for various requests. According to Thornburgh (2005), digital mobile device networks … "knows where you are, and—the more you text, tweet, shop, take pictures and navigate your surroundings using a smart phone—it knows an awful lot about what you are doing". In USA, federal, state, and local law enforcement officials made 1.3 million requests for cell-phone tracking data in 2011. This shows the growing problems and issues related to the private and personal data held by mobile carriers.

Though there is consensus over the importance of gathering proper information that could be used by the various entities the collection of such information is not always systematic and rapid enough. Yet, the development of technology is extremely fast. Therefore a first measure should be aimed at enhancing the flow of information between the relevant entities and institutions. A second step would be to carry out the analysis of the possible impact of technological developments on human rights. In absence of any regulatory action undertaken at institutional level, private companies will take self-regulatory action and it will probably not be oriented towards the protection of human rights.

Phishing activities and social networks provide potential access to a 3-dimensional datasets of users i.e. friends, links, and habits. Location-based technologies, such as Google Maps and satellites, can be used to determine not only the location of places but also the location of a person, thanks to the smart phone technology. US law enforcement agencies use GPS technology to track criminal suspects and parolees without their awareness. It is normally done by attaching a device, such as Trackstick, with the car. Trackstick is GPS data logger integrated with GoogleEarth. Global System for Mobile Communications (GSM) can be used to track GSM signals transmitted from mobile devices to track individuals carrying the mobile device.

INDIVIDUAL LIBERTY AND TECHNOLOGY

Technology for individual liberty is a two-edged sword. Take social media technologies for example. In many cases, social media platforms can be a profoundly pro-liberty force, as when a Facebook page helped build support for last year's revolution in Egypt. However, China figured out how to use the social media revolution to their own advantage (Forbes, 2012). In China, access to Facebook and Twitter appears to be limited and people use homegrown alternatives (such as Weibo and Renren). It is argued that these homegrown alternative sites actively assist Chinese government's surveillance and censorship efforts. It is further argued that these sites automated filtering and manual human review to steer online discussion away from topics disfavored by the Chinese government. Apparently, this approach might give the Chinese government fine-grained control over online discussions,

Open Knowledge

Technology in fast going out of the hands of governments and empowering normal people with the knowledge previously limited in the hands of few. Mass political mobilization through the internet and disclosures of US government web surveillance of citizens of all countries are clear examples of this trend. From such trends, we can expect further advancements in the democratization of technology. Traditionally, technologies were located within strong political and economic centers of the world and patents and protectionism were used for the justification of these monopolistic technological advantages of certain countries. Access to this previously restricted by the common people helps them confront the more powerful actors.

Governments have responded back by devising systems that prevent users from getting "inside information" and sharing it with other users. Take example of many police departments in USA are relying on technology that allows police to turn off or block data transmission whenever they like, including blocking mobile phones from taking photos and videos. Apple patented such a technology in 2012. Once the police officer designated an area "sensitive", Apple allowed the officers to switch off all data transmission capabilities. Privacy advocates are critical of this technology on fears that the technology may be used to keep whistleblowers such as Edward Snowden from sharing any information. However, as law enforcement's technology increases, so does that of the public. As reported by a local San Francisco news outlet, many criminals are using "scanner" apps on their smartphones in an effort to elude the police. The apps, which range in price from free to 99 cents to $1.99 allow a person to listen in on police communications.

Democracy is entering a new era: one permeated by technology and open knowledge. The values of transparency and accountability in government are fundamental to the democratic ideal, but it is only with recent technological revolutions that their potential has really begun to be tapped. It's fair to say citizens' expectations for transparency and accountability, and for their own opportunity to participate, are rising. Government will be providing more services with less money to go around, so the only way is to apply technology in a transformative way." (Spengler, 2014). With new technological advancements coming out almost everyday, and citizens constantly "plugged in," many government organizations are simply trying to keep up while figuring out the best solutions to use. Following are some of the ways governments are using technology to enforce rule of law.

For the first time, citizens can access the government information including the texts of the laws that govern them with just a click of a button. This has profound implications for the relationship between governments and their citizens. For the very first time, we see a society where many have to the knowledge they need to understand and effect change. To build a deep democracy, this equality of knowledge is vital. The open knowledge enable citizens to answer the questions that matter to them like where my tax money is going. They can have a voice that their leaders can hear and build a world in which they want to live. They can expose and prevent the corruption, both financial and electoral, which can fundamentally undermine democratic institutions.

The role of Wikipedia and other freely licensed/commons-based projects (such as open access scientific publishing) in the context of global development is important. These technologies provide a context in which we can say that improving democracy can further development. Open access publishing can lower the costs of entry into the global information economy, and more basically, can allow people to live a richer life--informed and educated about their own culture and the world in which they live. Innovation and education are core components of development. The governments of western world are also facing serious challenges with respect to the increased citizens' access to government records that were held confidential for a long time. More recently, we saw how WikiLeaks improved the access to information by providing access to public records in ways that are adequate to the technological culture of the present i.e. by putting them online and made them searchable, machine-readable, downloadable, and available to anyone, for any purpose, without registration or other access controls. WikiLeaks also provided access to records of public interest that had been shielded from the public, even in the face of explicit FOI requests. Despite the controversy about and hostility against WikiLeaks stirred up by angry officials and envious media, as well as considerable tensions and contradictions inside the project itself, the public response to the releases was overwhelmingly positive. Its editor in chief, Julian Assange, became a global celebrity and a hero to many. WikiLeaks relied on a widespread sentiment that public institutions were not transparent enough and that unconventional means of providing transparency were necessary. This sentiment was latent before WikiLeaks came into being, but the project brought it to the fore and at the same time radicalized demand for new forms of transparency. While WikiLeaks itself is currently somewhat in limbo (it has not accepted new submissions since late 2010), the dynamics it accelerated are now propelling other initiatives forward. On the one hand, existing initiatives that seek to renew the official mechanisms for generating transparency have received a boost and new ones are springing up. For example, government open-data initiatives have been created all over the world over the last year or two. The idea here is that instead of granting access to individual (paper) records, governments should provide access to entire databases in open and machine-readable formats over the Internet, so that third parties can take and interpret this data in any way they see fit.

Privacy

Increased use of web-based storage services has given rise to privacy concerns. Data stored in the cloud isn't legally protected in the same way that it would be if it were located on a storage device user own. The current US law treats data stored on a server for more than 180 days as abandoned. The current law's definition of such data is vague enough to cover not just email messages but (potentially) other kinds of data stored on servers. A vast amount of data resides on servers owned by cloud-based services. A large number of people keep content in the cloud for years. That means a lot of long-stored files that people haven't abandoned could be a legal target for the government. According to Google's Transparency Report, the number of law-enforcement agencies requests to access cloud-based data increased 70 percent during 2010-2013. Twitter's transparency reporting site offers similar statistics.

Our cell phone and the location data we post to social networking sites are revealing sources about us. Imagine the world with new location-beaming devices coming online, from smarter cars to smarter watches to Google Glass. Users are increasingly worried about their privacy while using mobile phones. According to a 2011 report by Gartner, 41 percent of consumers were concerned about advertising they receive through mobile location-based services. In another survey, 80 percent of consumers aged 20-40 in the United States and the United Kingdom believed that total privacy in the digital world was a thing of the past, and 49 percent said they would not object to having their buying behavior tracked if it would result in relevant offers from brands and suppliers (Accenture, 2014). Similar to the requirements for accessing cloud-based data, the legal requirements for obtaining location data from your mobile service provider are not very stringent.

Posting and tagging photos online may feel like innocent fun. What we might not know that it helps build a facial recognition database. Facebook is considered the world's largest facial recognition database. In 2012, Facebook users were uploading about 300 million photos to Facebook site. Facebook uses tags on photos to build to build a more-detailed database of faceprints. One major concern is that Facebook sells its user data to third parties and photo data may be included. Although Facebook claims that it takes care to protect the data but the sanctity of the data after the sale is uncertain. US government also review or request Facebook data for purposes such as citizenship applications, criminal cases, and security checks. Besides Facebook, Google and Apple have facial-recognition technology built into some of their applications most notably online photo sites. It is possible that photo of an individual be taken and then this photo can be used to track that individual by matching it with some other photos of individual that might have been posted on the web.

Open Government, E-Government, and E-Democracy

Open government is the governing doctrine which holds that citizens have the right to access the documents and proceedings of the government to allow for effective public oversight. In its broadest construction it opposes reason of state and other considerations, which have tended to legitimize extensive state secrecy.. Open government mechanisms including those for public participation and engagement, such as the use of IdeaScale, Google Moderator, Semantic MediaWiki, GitHub, and other software by actual ruling governments – these mechanisms are well developed especially in the UK and the USA. Transparency and democracy are mutually reinforcing. It is hard for a democracy to survive without informed consent. Given that, many well-established democracies still struggling to have more transparency. However, the idea that open governments can flourish in non-democracies is still questionable. To realize the full potential of technology and transparency, it is important to have fundamental political rights and civil liberties.

Across the globe, governments are recognizing the importance of open government. It was emphasized by Hillary Clinton during Open Government Partnership Opening Session in April 2012 when she said, "In the 21st century, the United States is convinced that one of the most significant divisions among nations will not be north/south, east/west, religious, or any other category so much as whether they are open or closed societies. We believe that countries with open governments, open economies, and open societies will increasingly flourish. They will become more prosperous, healthier, more secure, and more peaceful." (Department Of State. The Office of Website Management, 2011). The Open Government Partnership is a new multilateral initiative that aims to secure concrete commitments from governments to promote transparency, empower citizens, fight corruption, and harness new technologies to strengthen governance. In the spirit of multi-stakeholder collaboration, OGP is overseen by a Steering Committee of governments and civil society organizations.

The focus of E-government is on use of technology for routine activities undertaken by public organizations. The focus of e-democracy is on political realm. Historically, e-government and e-democracy have largely been separated but now open government bringing them together by reconciling their divergent paths. Transparency, participation, and collaboration may take some more time and resources. However, they are vital for achieving the historic focus of e-government i.e. improving policy performance. This would be possible because transparency, participation, and collaboration together can create shared understandings of current performance and generating pressure to improve, increasing the pool of applicable ideas, tapping into new sources of expertise, and building civic capacity. All these may ultimately turn out to be the key to concrete improvements in policy outcomes and the quality of government services.

Civic Insurgency

Civic insurgency, generated by means of the social networks, has made the individuals less vulnerable to the oppressive or coercive power of the State. It is a positive aspect of the development of the existing technology, which is already servicing all of us, making a citizen better informed and conscious of his stellar role. For example, several groups of Mexican Internet users and activists took to social networks to protest against a bill put forward by Mexican president that proposed disproportionate powers to the government to control TV content and Internet access (Montes, 2014). This civic, digital insurgency brought together many groups politically opposed to Mexican president. Yosoy132, a social media movement of young Mexicans that criticized Mr. Peña Nieto during the presidential campaign in 2012, formed part of the protests. As a result, the Senate Communications Committee of Mexico proposed a modified bill that striped out the obligation for telecom firms to provide the geographical location of users if requested by intelligence services, as originally proposed. Also, authorities won't be able to temporarily block signals at events or places that authorities consider put national security at risk. Some analysts regarded this civic digital insurgency as a sign of the pluralism of Mexico's young democracy, which opened to political competition in the late 1990s after close to seven decades of authoritarian rule by the Institutional Revolutionary Party, or PRI.

TECHNOLOGY AND DEMOCRACY: IMPLICATIONS/RECOMMENDATIONS

The experience provides evidence that governments wax and wane in their concern for civil liberties and human rights. Emerging technologies are undoubtedly provide a medium to promote civil liberty, free expression, and better government. However, to make that happen there is a need of regulations to maintain the dynamic, emergent and decentralized properties of these technologies so that any government or corporation has a limited ability to act in a crisis to limit or stop the use of these technologies by people.

According to Uandnwin (2012b), Cummings (2010), Westaen (1998), Harari (2013), and Carmouche (2013) following broad sets of significant issues will need to be addressed for technology to contribute to democracy:

Digital Access for All

For technology to contribute to democracy, broadband for all is essential. Public spaces such as libraries and schools should provide access as a way of communication. Appropriate content is necessary, and the digital systems should be affordable and sustainable.

Sociology of Technology and Democracy

There exist many different kinds of democracy. Technologies should be used to support those systems that serve the interests of all people. Technology itself cannot necessarily lead to the introduction or enhancement of democratic processes. Technologies should not be controlled by a small number of organizations, governments and individuals.

The Dark Side of Technology

It is not just companies and governments that can use technology for negative purposes. Individuals and small groups intent on using it for illicit purposes are equally problematic. It is important for governments to actively to engage in responding to 'negative' uses of technology. We have witnessed the dark side of new technologies with the proliferation of new spyware technology, as used by repressive regimes such as the United Arab Emirates and Bahrain. In such cases, individuals have been monitored, dispersed and controlled with greater 'efficiency'. The sad consequence of this is an intensified fear of retribution for those seeking justice, a mockery of accountability measures, and an asymmetrical power dynamic between the citizen and state. To ensure democracy, the ownership of the technology, and those who control it, needs to be much more democratic.

Privacy and Security

It is evident that there are very different views as to what is and should be private both within and between different cultures. Four important principles for governments in this connection are: don't censor, don't spy on your own people, educate people on safe social media usage, and require companies to be transparent about privacy and security. The dangers around the rapid spread of technologies through development initiatives are also evident such as the hazards of technological developments where the rule of law is absent and where access to information is collected and used against individuals.

Technology as the Change Agent

Technology makes it easy to engage people, e.g. in politics, but it doesn't provide answers to the hard questions about how to make a better society. One clear example is Obama's presidential election campaign in which millions of young people enthusiastically campaigned online to spread Obama's message of hope and change. Few years down the road, the lack of substance in that message caused people discontent. Technology itself cannot save democracy. That task in the end will be determined by the spirit and skills of the people themselves. But technology can provide the electorate with the ability to make improved decisions.

Technology is Neither Good Nor Bad, it's the Planning

Intrinsically, technology is neither good nor bad. It is how we use it, which may lead to far-reaching benefits or to negative results. Technology applications are often planned and deliberate, but sometimes unintended and accidental. The survival of democracy is in conflict with consequences of modern technology. This is unintended but expected with many threats.

Short Term Solutions for Long-Terms Issues

Over the years, the longer years of education, work, and retirement has increased an average person's ability to analyze long-term issues. Consequently, people take more time to move from discussion to decision, and then execution. On the other hand, politicians have a short time horizon generally the time until next election takes place. Modern technologies produces longer time scales for problems but provides instant popularity ratings for politicians. Consequently, politicians are forced to adopt short-term solutions for issues influencing us for decades. The lesson to learn here is that while we live longer but technology has made us think shorter.

Technology Literacy and Quantitative Thinking for Decision Makers

Today's world introduces us to numerous issues that cannot be tackled by people lacking a minimal ability to comprehend scientific arguments, accompanied by simple quantitative considerations. These issues may include energy issues, water problems, intellectual property, global warming etc. The vast majority of senior decision makers in most democracies do not possess these fundamental abilities. Lacking such abilities, these decision makers are prone to make gross errors of judgment and historic mistakes, which will impact many generations. One implication here is that, in future, we need decision makers who are proficient in use of technology and able to avoid such mistakes.

Short Attention Span of Public

Twitter, texting and other similar types of one-liners have become very famous and have made traditional TV news item look like eternity. However, such micro pieces of communication cannot summarize the real public issues. This type of communication has encouraged politicians to exercise extremism and superficially express themselves in in the standard 140 characters of Twitter. The voters are exposed only to ultra-brief slogans. A serious implication is that the younger generation is developing a brief attention span and affinity to one-liners seriously threatens their ability to gain a deep understanding of the public issues in hand.

The Rush for Transparency

Increased public desire for transparency, fueled by immediate web dissemination of all disclosed information, it is almost impossible for someone to express his honest opinion, such as a thorough well-balanced evaluation of an organization. In the era confidentiality of information is not just compromised rather the public disclosure is idolized. One implication of this trend is that the talented and experienced people in any field would shy away from expressing their honest opinion knowing the fact that "transparency" can destroy their careers.

Public Desire for All Freedoms

All freedoms guaranteed by a proper democracy, when carried to unacceptable extremes, may lead to grave distortions. The recent increase in disclosure of national security may be necessary to promote open knowledge but at the same time, such disclosure may put many lives in danger. Technology has not only created opportunities for such disclosures but also offered ways for fast and wide dissemination of these disclosures across borders. In a nutshell, by fulfilling public desires of open knowledge technology has turned the sacred human rights and civil freedoms into a double edged sword.

Globalization

Political boundaries cover a political unit and every political unit has a certain set of rules. Two countries may differ significantly with respect to the state of democracy. Both regimes can survive, using their own rules and with no cross talk between the two countries. Globalization helps in the spread of progressive ideas into dark political corners. The denial of the holocaust can be a criminal offense if Germany but what we should knowing that satellite communication can directly reach every house in Germany. Modern technology may allow fast and efficient money laundering, performed among numerous international banks. This is a new challenge. World may try to make international decisions and treaties by majority votes of countries, most of which have never seen any democratic rule. However, this practice would enforce global anti-democratic standards. The situation gets more complicated when we see that fast mobility and modern communication, offered by today's technology, has amplified numerous phenomena such as illegal immigration, cross boundary racism, international tax evasion, drug trafficking, and child labor..

Inequalities in Voice

Inequalities in voice thwart the potential for inclusivity through new technologies. As with some cases of mobile phone usage in the developing world, social media participation tells a familiar tale of educational, urban and gender advantage. Consider the demographics of India's second largest social media platform, Facebook. Accordingly 76% males use this platform, compared with a meagre 24% of females, while the common user is said to be a graduate degree holder. More alarmingly, Internet penetration among India's rural population is just one-twelfth that of the urban population - a big concern when a majority of Indians live in the countryside.

Apparently, the only way we can deal with these issues is by having the structure of modern liberal democracy to evolve and adapt to the new technologies. However, this has not yet begun to happen. We need to come up with ways to preserve the basic features of democracy, while fine-tuning its detailed rules and patterns. This way we can minimize the negative effects and let the modern technology to do more good than harm. Emerging technologies have the capacity to both emancipate and weaken individuals and their choices. It is crucial then, that we do not confuse the proliferation of technology as the main issue at stake. Human rights abuses have occurred with or without these tools. Importantly, technologies cannot substitute political will, nor can they remedy the inherent injustices within a society; most often they will only serve to reproduce inequalities in voice across the spectrum of gender, religious and economic divides.

Transparent Technologies

New digital technologies, especially the Internet, are providing novel types of business enterprises, organizational practices and social connections. These technologies are affecting market structures, the ways democracy functions, and the types of cultural spaces and public conversations. Among many complex forces driving the fast-paced changes in the digital world today, transparent technologies are the ones that has exerted a clear, almost decisive influence. A transparent technology is a technology whose development is supported by an architecture of open access, open standards and open communication so that anyone can gain access to the inner blueprints of the technology. It also means that anyone can learn and use the technical standards upon which the technology is based.

Transparent technology can refer to any technical system that would allow fair and competitive access to the technological platform. This radical idea of keeping open to everyone all aspects of design and technical detail of technology is what has made the Internet such an explosive force for innovation, information exchange, entrepreneurialism and economic development.

Some software developed for use on the Internet, such as social software, have particularly democratizing properties. This social software facilitates open publishing, online assemblies, collaboration, and interaction. This software give voice to the people, provide meeting opportunities, and facilitate new forms of political organizing and activism that were not possible without the technology. Democratizing software often has overlapping properties: for example, many versions of social software are also open source.

In order to flourish, technology needs an architecture of open access, open standards and open communications. Transparent technologies are not meant to put proprietary technologies out of business but to promote a more open, competitive platform for value-added competition. Transparent technologies can accelerate the development and expansion of innovations.

Transparent technology can be regarded as a strategy for advancing education, science and democracy. However, we must understand that certain technology foster certain types of social relationships and values. Technology is a kind of architecture for our personal lives, economy and society. As such technology can not only orient us but also push us in certain directions.

FUTURE RESEARCH DIRECTIONS

According to Moore's law, in every two years, the performance of every device either doubles or its cost becomes half. The pace of current technological change is very high. We see a continued explosion in both connectivity and access technologies. In USA, Google launched Gigabit Fiber project (Google, 2014). In the future, it is predicted that iPhones and Tablets would be available in hundreds of sizes. There would be lot of specialty devices. It is anticipated that personal computer industry would exist but new players and startups would emerge that combine hardware/software to develop various consumer devices. Research is required to investigate how this emerging trend of new devices would facilitate democracy.

Ever increasing speed of information has brought another challenge for democracy. Technology is generating information at a much higher speed than the processing ability of the national leaders. Increased information has opened up new ways of human contact. It is estimated that by 2016, the wireless networks will be saturated because of the rate at which iPhones, Tablets, and Smart Phones are being sold. The United States government recently issued a report outlining a plan for efficient frequency allocation for better bandwidth management (Forbes, 2013a). There is a growing concern whether technology has developed to a scale where it provides its users (politicians) the ability to absorb such enormous amount of information. Research is required to investigate the possible strategies for political leaders to effectively analyze this ever increasing amount of data.

Technologies are also dependent on their creators. Technologies are made for particular reasons, such as ideological, and most most technologies have unintended consequences. For example, mobile phone developers probably never thought of using mobile phones for mobile banking such as the case of MPESA in Kenya. One clear implication of this is that the same technologies can be used by different governments and different individuals and groups in different ways. Since poor and the marginalized do not create technologies, in order benefit them from use of technology some powerful external entity is needed that could ensure technology use in the interest of poor, be that political, social or economic (Unwin, 2014). Research is also needed to understand how specific technologies can influence freedom of expression and democracy in each country: i.e. the impact of context on the impact of technology on democracy. Specific emphasis could be placed on the possible external entities and their and the extent to which they can ensure use of technology in the interest of the needy people.

Research is also required to investigate whether the existing laws can be extended to cover use of emerging technologies is issues such as processing of neural signals and whether the law can be extended to include 'criminal thoughts' such as Jihadi thoughts.

The emergence of Wikipedia and WikiLeaks has generated an increased interest in what we call open knowledge. While we looking at supply of open knowledge, one interesting area that needs further investigation is the relationship between supply and use of open knowledge. This investigation would support more comprehensive analysis of ideologies driving use of open knowledge, and how actors and technologies are interacting, whilst also drawing attention to the actors missing from, or peripheral to, networks around open knowledge.

CONCLUSION

The emerging technologies, including web 2.0 technologies, allow their patrons to instantly connect with other users as well as publish content that can be accessed by individuals around the globe. Individuals can use the technology to spread their own messages and make their previously silenced voices heard (Chadwick, 2008). There exist many examples of technology use for fostering democracy such as use of technology to promote citizen advocacy and to increase government transparency and accountability. The technologies are expected to alter substantially the business and social environment.

The political and awkward debate of technology use for democracy has made emerging technologies more interesting than the already established and standardized ones. The positive visions and potential applications for emerging technology are apparently without limits (Ratner & Ratner, 2003). Emerging technologies are expected to have a substantial influence on the everyday life of individual consumers and households.

Both authoritarian and so call democratic governments recognize the potential of emerging technologies and are increasingly restricting access and activities in cyberspace. We have witnessed examples from many parts of the world including China, Arab world, and Western world where governments tried to curb citizens' access to government information in the name of national security. The new interactive ICTs offer tremendous opportunities for revitalizing democracy. Now days, we see escalating campaign contributions, negative television commercials, and increasing skepticism toward candidates and government officials. Technology can help encourage broader issue discussions and promote positive messages over negative ones.

No democracy can survive without the protection of basic freedom of expression, belief, and press. Technology has allowed space for a previously unthinkable amount of freedom of expression. In order to have the freedom of expression we don't necessarily need to have the ability to share that expression. Technology has transformed freedom of expression from a largely private phenomenon into a predominantly public one.

Emerging technologies can have an important impact on privacy and data protection of individuals. However, the fundamental right of protection of personal data can be compromised by using emerging technologies such as Brain-computer interfacing (BCI) that allows processing of neural signals.

Emerging technologies has provided great opportunities for openness as well as misinformation. In many countries, media is used to manipulate the populous in favor of the government and drive an ethnic conflict. Media freedom could validate facts and manipulate propaganda and provide a resolution to long-standing insurrection. Emerging technologies has played a significant role in media freedom.

By enhancing the public's access to information and facilitating public participation in government decision-making, the technology has geometrically expanded the scope and reach of the rule of law. The concept of access to information is essential in a democratic society, and core to the rule of law.

Governments are using technology in many ways to enforce rule of law. Using cloud, governments are bringing data to secure and authorized endpoints. This increases government's productivity and interaction with citizens. Governments are also using mobile applications to connect to citizens. However, governments need carefully consider the way these technologies are organized and deployed in order to gain their maximum strategic value.

There exist several examples of emerging technology use for promoting human rights. Human rights activists have used emerging technologies for long time to cut the time in transmission of their response to human rights violations (Halpin and Fisher, 1998). During Arab Spring of 2011, YouTube was used as a human rights advocacy resource in in Egypt, Libya, Syria, and Tunisia to publicize Arab regimes' human rights abuses both locally and globally.

Technology in fast going out of the hands of governments and empowering normal people with the knowledge previously limited in the hands of few. Emerging technologies are undoubtedly provide a medium to promote civil liberty, free expression, and better government.

In order for technology to continue support democracy, there is a need of regulations to maintain the dynamic, emergent and decentralized properties of these technologies so that any government or corporation has a limited ability to act in a crisis to limit or stop the use of these technologies by people. Technologies should be used to support those systems that serve the interests of all people. Technologies should not be controlled by a small number of organizations, governments and individuals. It is not just companies and governments that can use technology for negative purposes. It is important for governments to actively to engage in responding to 'negative' uses of technology.

We have witnessed the dark side of new technologies with the proliferation of new spyware technology, as used by repressive regimes such as the United Arab Emirates and Bahrain. The dangers around the rapid spread of technologies through development initiatives are also evident such as the hazards of technological developments where the rule of law is absent and where access to information is collected and used against individuals.

Emerging technologies have the capacity to both emancipate and weaken individuals and their choices. Technologies cannot substitute political will, nor can they remedy the inherent injustices within a society; most often they will only serve to reproduce inequalities in voice across the spectrum of gender, religious and economic divides.

Increased information has opened up new ways of human contact. There is a growing concern whether technology has developed to a scale where it provides its users (politicians) the ability to absorb such enormous amount of information. Research is required to investigate the possible strategies for political leaders to effectively analyze this ever increasing amount of data. Research is also required to investigate whether the existing laws can be extended to cover use of emerging technologies is issues such as processing of neural signals and whether the law can be extended to include 'criminal thoughts' such as Jihadi thoughts.

Most technologies have unintended consequences. Adaptive human beings frequently find new and different uses of technology. For example, the outcomes of social media use in northern Africa and the Middle East in recent years were quite different from the outcomes of use of social media in Tunisia, Egypt, Libya, Syria and Iran.

Though, the poor and the marginalized are not generally those who develop new technologies. If they are to benefit from new technologies, there needs to be some powerful external entity that explicitly seeks to ensure that such technologies can be used in their interest, be that political, social or economic (Unwin, 2014).

REFERENCES

Accenture. (2014). *Eighty Percent of Consumers Believe Total Data Privacy No Longer Exists, Accenture Survey Finds*. Retrieved July 26, 2014, from http://www.accenture.com/SiteCollectionDocuments/PDF/Accenture-Survey-Eighty-Percent-Consumers-Believe-Total-Data-Privacy-No-Longer-Exists.pdf

Akrich, M. (1992). The De-scription of technical objects. In W. E. Bijker & J. Law (Eds.), *Shaping Technology/Building Society: Studies in Socio-technical Change*. Cambridge, MA: MIT Press.

Al-Fattal, R. (2013, May 7). *Why the Arab Uprising Will Not Lead to Democracy Any Time Soon - The Métropolitain*. Retrieved February 27, 2015, from http://themetropolitain.ca/articles/view/1285

Al Zoubi, O., & Read, R. (2013). Unrest uprising, or revolution? *The Philosophers' Magazine, 2013*(60), 28–29.

Anderson, L. (2011). Demystifying the Arab Spring: Parsing the Differences between Tunisia, Egypt, and Libya. *Foreign Affairs, 90*, 2.

Aouragh, M., & Alexander, A. (2011). The Arab Spring| The Egyptian Experience: Sense and Nonsense of the Internet Revolution. *International Journal of Communication, 5*(0), 15.

Bleicher, P. (2006). Web 2.0 revolution: Power to the people. *Applied Clinical Trials, 15*(8), 34.

Burke, D. (2004). GM food and crops: What went wrong in the UK? *EMBO Reports, 5*(5), 432–436. doi:10.1038/sj.embor.7400160 PMID:15184970

Business Dictionary. (n.d.). *What are emerging technologies? definition and meaning. BusinessDictionary.com*. Retrieved August 1, 2014, from http://www.businessdictionary.com/definition/emerging-technologies.html

Carmouche, A. (2013, November 29). *New technologies cannot substitute political will.* Retrieved February 27, 2015, from https://www.opendemocracy.net/opensecurity/ayesha-carmouche/new-technologies-cannot-substitute-political-will

Chadwick, A. (2008). Web 2.0: New Challenges for the Study of E-Democracy in an Era of Informational Exuberance. *I/S: A Journal of Law and Policy for the Information Society, 5*, 9.

CNN. (2012). *"Father of the internet": Why we must fight for its freedom.* Retrieved July 26, 2014, from http://edition.cnn.com/2012/11/29/business/opinion-cerf-google-internet-freedom/index.html

CNN. (2013). *Kurdish men in drag promote feminism in the region.* Retrieved July 26, 2014, from http://www.cnn.com/2013/09/11/world/meast/kurd-drag-campaign/index.html

Cummings, D. (2010, November 10). *A new technological democracy? | Dolan Cummings | Independent Battle of Ideas Blogs.* Retrieved July 26, 2014, from http://blogs.independent.co.uk/2010/11/10/a-new-technological-democracy/

Department Of State, The Office of Website Management, B. of P. A. (2011, July 6). *The Open Government Partnership.* Retrieved February 27, 2015, from http://www.state.gov/j/ogp/

Forbes. (2012). *Social Media Platforms and Liberty: A Two-Edged Sword. Forbes.* Retrieved July 26, 2014, from http://www.forbes.com/sites/timothylee/2012/09/11/social-media-platforms-and-liberty-a-two-edged-sword/

Forbes. (2013a). *Obama Seeks To Free Up Wireless Spectrum (Updated).* Retrieved July 26, 2014, from http://www.forbes.com/sites/larrymagid/2013/06/14/obama-seeks-to-free-up-wireless-spectrum/

Forbes. (2013b). *The Impact Of Mobile On Publishers -- More Consumption, Less Revenue - Forbes.* Retrieved July 26, 2014, from http://www.forbes.com/sites/benjaminboxer/2013/11/14/the-impact-of-mobile-on-publishers-more-consumption-less-revenue/

Google. (2014). *Google Fiber.* Retrieved July 26, 2014, from https://fiber.google.com/about2/

Harari, H. (2013, June). *Technology May Endanger Democracy.* Retrieved February 27, 2015, from http://edge.org/response-detail/23835

Heggestuen, J. (2013, December 15). *One In Every 5 People In The World Own A Smartphone, One In Every 17 Own A Tablet* [CHART]. Retrieved February 27, 2015, from http://www.businessinsider.com/smartphone-and-tablet-penetration-2013-10

Hess, D. J. (1997). *Science studies: An advanced introduction.* New York: NYU press.

Hess, S. (2013, February 22). *Why Wasn't There a Chinese Spring?* Retrieved February 27, 2015, from http://thediplomat.com/2013/02/why-wasnt-there-a-chinese-spring/

House, F. (2011). *Freedom on the net 2011: A global assessment of internet and digital media.* New York: Freedom House.

Huffington Post. (2011, February 11). *Egypt's Facebook Revolution: Wael Ghonim Thanks The Social Network.* Retrieved July 26, 2014, from http://www.huffingtonpost.com/2011/02/11/egypt-facebook-revolution-wael-ghonim_n_822078.html informationactivism.org. (n.d.). *Postage Stamps Document the Revolution*. Retrieved July 26, 2014, from https://informationactivism.org/en/postage-stamps-document-revolution

International Association of Chiefs of Police. (2013). *Guiding Principles on Cloud Computing in Law Enforcement*. Retrieved 26 February, 2015 from http://www.theiacp.org/Portals/0/documents/pdfs/CloudComputingPrinciples.pdf

Kennedy, J. J. (2012). What Is the Color of a Non-Revolution: Why the Jasmine Revolution and Arab Spring Did Not Spread to China. *Whitehead Journal of Diplomacy and International Relations, 13*, 63.

Latour, B. (2005). *Reassembling the Social: An Introduction to Actor-Network-Theory*. New York: Oxford University Press.

mobilisationlab.org. (2013). *Facebook users convince Hungarian companies to wash GMOs from food supply*. Retrieved July 26, 2014, from http://www.mobilisationlab.org/facebook-users-convince-hungarian-companies-to-wash-gmos-from-food-supply/

Montes, J. (2014, April 23). Social Media Protests in Mexico Shape Telecom Bill. *Wall Street Journal*. Retrieved July 26, 2014, from http://www.wsj.com/articles/SB10001424052702304788404579519633220313644

Newtactics.org. (2011). *Mobilizing supporters on social media to get the attention of strategic targets | New Tactics in Human Rights*. Retrieved July 26, 2014, from https://www.newtactics.org/tactic/mobilizing-supporters-social-media-get-attention-strategic-targets

Police Chief Magazine. (2011). *How Location-Based Services Can Improve Policing*. Retrieved August 5, 2014, from http://www.policechiefmagazine.org/magazine/index.cfm?fuseaction=display_arch&article_id=2402&issue_id=62011

Public Engines. (2012, September 18). *New Mobile App CityConnect™ Lets Local Law Enforcement Connect Directly to Communities*. Retrieved February 27, 2015, from http://www.publicengines.com/company/press/cityconnect-lets-local-law-enforcement-connect-to-communities.php

Roy, O. (2012). The Transformation of the Arab World. *Journal of Democracy, 23*(3), 5–18. doi:10.1353/jod.2012.0056

Spengler, T. (2014, April 30). *5 Technology Solutions Worth Government Spending*. Retrieved February 27, 2015, from http://politix.topix.com/story/11820-5-technology-solutions-worth-government-spending

Team, M. (2013, April 29). *Facebook users convince Hungarian companies to wash GMOs from food supply*. Retrieved February 27, 2015, from http://www.mobilisationlab.org/facebook-users-convince-hungarian-companies-to-wash-gmos-from-food-supply/

Unwin, T. (2014). *Social media and democracy: Critical reflections*. Paper presented at the Commonwealth Parliamentary Conference (Colombo). Retrieved from http://www.cpahq.org/cpahq/cpadocs/Unwin%20CPA%20Social%20media%20and%20democracy.pdf

Virtually Blind. (2007, April 24). *Reader Roundtable: "Virtual Rape" Claim Brings Belgian Police to Second Life | Virtually Blind | Virtual Law | Benjamin Duranske*. Retrieved July 26, 2014, from http://virtuallyblind.com/2007/04/24/open-roundtable-allegations-of-virtual-rape-bring-belgian-police-to-second-life/

ADDITIONAL READING

Edwards, S. A. (2006). The Nanotech Pioneers-Where Are They Taking Us? *Environmental Science and Pollution Research International, 13*(2), 144. doi:10.1065/espr2006.02.004

Einsiedel, E. F. (2009). *Emerging Technologies: From Hindsight to Foresight*. Vancouver: UBC Press.

Hildebrandt, M. (2013). *The Rule of Law in Cyberspace*. Retrieved 26 February, 2015 from http://works.bepress.com/mireille_hildebrandt/48

Information Week. (2014). *Big Data Analytics Helps Protect Communities. InformationWeek.* Retrieved August 5, 2014, from http://www.informationweek.com/government/big-data-analytics/big-data-analytics-helps-protect-communities/d/d-id/1113720

Rassmussen College. (2013). *33 Police Apps for Law Enforcement Officers & Future Crime Fighters*. Retrieved August 5, 2014, from http://www.rasmussen.edu/degrees/justice-studies/blog/police-apps-law-enforcement-officers-criminal-justice-students/

Ratner, M. A., & Ratner, D. (2003). *Nanotechnology: A Gentle Introduction to the Next Big Idea*. New York: Prentice Hall Professional.

The Guardian. (2002, November 17). Surgical tags plan for sex offenders. *The Guardian*. Retrieved 26 February, 2015 from http://www.theguardian.com/society/2002/nov/17/childrensservices.crime

The Guardian. (2007, February 9). The brain scan that can read people's intentions. *The Guardian*. Retrieved 26 February, 2015 from http://www.theguardian.com/science/2007/feb/09/neuroscience.ethicsofscience

Unwin, T. (2012) Google and Facebook: privacy and security, 5 February 2012 http://unwin.wordpress.com/2012/02/05/google-and-facebookprivacy-and-security/

World, P. C. (2013, April 8). *The 5 biggest online privacy threats of 2013. PCWorld*. Retrieved August 2, 2014, from http://www.pcworld.com/article/2031908/the-5-biggest-online-privacy-threats-of-2013.html

KEY TERMS AND DEFINITIONS

Cloud Computing: Cloud computing is is typically defined as a type of computing that relies on sharing computing resources rather than having local servers or personal devices to handle applications. (http://www.webopedia.com/TERM/C/cloud_computing.html)

Democracy: The term democracy comes from the Greek language and means "rule by the (simple) people" (http://www.democracy-building.info/definition-democracy.html)

E-Democracy: E-democracy incorporates information and communications technology to promote democracy. It is a form of government in which all citizens are presumed to be eligible to participate equally in the proposal, development, and creation of laws. (http://en.wikipedia.org/wiki/E-democracy)

E-Government: E-Government refers to the use by government agencies of information technologies that have the ability to transform relations with citizens, businesses, and other arms of government. (http://web.worldbank.org/WBSITE/EXTERNAL/TOPICS/EXTINFORMATIONANDCOMMUNI-CATIONANDTECHNOLOGIES/EXTEGOVERNMENT/0,,contentMDK:20507153~menuPK:702592~pagePK:148956~piPK:216618~theSitePK:702586,00.html)

Emerging Technology: Emerging technology refers to new technologies that are currently developing or will be developed over the next five to ten years, and which will substantially alter the business and social environment. (http://www.businessdictionary.com/definition/emerging-technologies.html)

Globalization: Globalization is a process of interaction and integration among the people, companies, and governments of different nations, a process driven by international trade and investment and aided by information technology. (http://www.globalization101.org/what-is-globalization/)

Governance: Governance (as opposed to "good" governance) can be defined as the rule of the rulers, typically within a given set of rules. (http://web.worldbank.org/WBSITE/EXTERNAL/COUNTRIES/MENAEXT/EXTMNAREGTOPGOVERNANCE/0,,contentMDK:20513159~pagePK:34004173~piPK:34003707~theSitePK:497024,00.html)

Open Government: In general, terms, an open government is one with high levels of transparency and mechanisms for public scrutiny and oversight in place, with an emphasis on government accountability.(http://opensource.com/resources/open-government)

Privacy: In Constitutional Law, privacy is defined as the right of people to make personal decisions regarding intimate matters; under the Common Law, privacy is defined as the right of people to lead their lives in a manner that is reasonably secluded from public scrutiny. (http://legal-dictionary.thefree-dictionary.com/privacy)

Social Media: Social media is an Internet-based software and interfaces that allow individuals to interact with one another, exchanging details about their lives such as biographical data, professional information, personal photos and up-to-the-minute thoughts. (http://www.investopedia.com/terms/s/social-media.asp)

Chapter 5
Cultural and Collective Rights of Indigenous Peoples in Venezuela:
Political and Legal Framework

Soledad Torrecuadrada García-Lozano
Universidad Autónoma de Madrid, Spain

Vladimir Aguilar Castro
Universidad de Los Andes, Venezuela

Carlos Grimaldo Lorente
Universidad de Los Andes, Venezuela

ABSTRACT

In this chapter, the authors attempt to demonstrate that respect for cultural identity of all human groups should be seen as a fundamental right. Ignoring Collective rights of indigenous peoples, those related to their cultural traditions, generally causes the lack of respect. Thus, knowledge of the cultural manifestations and their origin and meaning (as part of the history of the territories they inhabit) can conquer this respect on a par with its defense. This obviously with comprehensive training aimed to sensitize the general population in the positive assessment it deserves it different. The actions of nation-states governments with strong indigenous population has been characterized, until recently, by a remarkable disregard for indigenous cultures, having as a result the result of which such attitude, today from the non - indigenous perspective indigenous cultural manifestations are reduced to colorful folklore shows, when not seen as backward and primitive traditions. This chapter delves deeply into the legal framework for the protection of collective and cultural rights of indigenous peoples. The authors also attempt to show the weaknesses of the law and how states should act to strengthen them. Proposed article does emphasis on indigenous traditional knowledge and not in a wider debate on the topic of knowledge in general.

DOI: 10.4018/978-1-4666-8336-5.ch005

INTRODUCTION

Respect for indigenous peoples cultural identity is far from being a trivial matter, as long as its absence generates cultural disappearance of human groups. Special relator, Cobo described its importance in its final report named *Study on treaties celebrated between indigenous peoples and States* emphasizing extinction of some indigenous peoples as social entities with different identities (Ibid. 1987).[1]

At present time it is not possible to calculate or approximate the number of human groups that were missing from the first contact with "civilization"[2]. According to the Population Atlas of the Amazon, only in the Peruvian Amazon, over the last half of the twentieth century, eleven ethnic groups have disappeared [3].

Moreover, respect for the cultural identity of human groups necessarily means the criminalization of all practices that can be targeted, explicit or not, forced assimilation (UN, 1999)[4], since any measure pursuing this effect necessarily violates the right to cultural identity. Clearly the assimilationist processes are based on the denial of diversity, making them incompatible with the content of the statement right. The main effect of these practices is assimilating easily imaginable: they produce the breaking of the transmission of traditional culture - usually orally- between generations, which prevent the cultural identification of indigenous youth with the human group that originally belong to. For this reason, they are forced to overcome problems of integration in non - indigenous social sectors that are equally alien to them. As a result of all this has a greatly increased rate of alcoholism and suicide, and other serious social problems (United Nations, 1998)[5].

In order to avoid this behavior, it has been coined recently the category of *ethnocide* or *cultural genocide*, indicating, as deserving behaviors of this denomination those that have as purpose or consequence *"of depriving them of their integrity as distinct peoples, or of their cultural values or ethnic identity"* or assimilate them, also incorporating in these categories the propaganda that can be directed at these groups (United Nations, 2007)[6].

BACKGROUND

From the reading of the Venezuelan Constitution, and more specifically article 119, recognition of indigenous cultures is clear, which corresponds to a prior conceptual stage to that occupied by the respect for cultural identity of indigenous peoples or different forms of manifestation that integrates it, since respect presupposes recognition but not to on the contrary. Despite that, the entry into force of 1999 Constitution marks only the starting point in which the system of protection and guarantee of indigenous peoples' rights concerns and, although it has not yet managed to reach its goal, solid progress has being made as far as Venezuelan society has demand it. If such respect is not certainly proclaimed in the constitutional rule, it can be clearly be found in the right that develops it, and it starts from the right of free indigenous cultural practice and development of the characteristics that define their traditions, along with the state's obligation to foster and protect them[7].

Besides, indigenous cultures can be characterized as roots of *venezolanidad*[8], statement which is supposed to provide them with a positive value, while the Venezuelan indigenous cultures are native/initial and are recognized as the foundation upon which has been built awareness of the Venezuelan homeland[9] Indigenous cultural identity[10] and, therefore, its integrity, is legally guaranteed by recognition of the right to its maintenance and strengthening and development, occurring within their own cultural models[11].

Consequently, the State is legally liable to promote and support processes aimed at recovering its own *"historical memory as a people"*, goal which is not difficult at all, due to several factors, one of them is that the indigenous historical tradition is usually oral and therefore, they can only be transmitted by members of indigenous communities, and not all of them. Let us think, for example, of the inability to recover historical memory of the missing communities, product of urban migration; other not negligible factor for this purpose can be found in the multiple processes of evangelization-integration-assimilation, prevailing until recently, which may have occurred as a result of the loss of the necessary elements to carry out the recovery.

Consequently, the Venezuelan domestic law on this point must be assessed very positively, due to the spirit it reflects. Let us not forget that a few years before the adoption of the 1999 Constitution, specifically in 1992, the Human Rights Committee in its conclusions on the Venezuela report indicated that *"Under Article 27 of the Covenant should take some measures to ensure to indigenous peoples to have their own culture and use their own language"* (United Nations, 1992)[12]. Despite all the progress made, we cannot ignore the inexistence of a practical realization of its formulation, due to the lacking of mechanisms to control the effective exercise of these rights, the lack in identifying the sanctions that may involve the violation nor the established means to ensure effectiveness, beyond the general measures established.

RIGHT TO COLLECTIVE INDIGENOUS HERITAGE

The *collective Indian heritage* denomination is a complex concept that comprehends all elements of various natures (material, intangible, historical, artistic or natural, for example) (Daes, 1993)[13] that determine its cultural identity[14]. These human groups consider "heritage" as part of their culture, and it can be shared -provisional y revocable- with other peoples. Indigenous' perspective does not distinguish between cultural and intellectual heritage. Despite that, the structure of this section deals with those categories, inasmuch as we pretend to analyze the protection that western rules –they do contemplate such differentiation- give to the indigenous collective heritage.

Cultural Heritage

Indigenous peoples have been stripped over time of much of its historical and cultural heritage: they have been victims of the desecration of cemeteries and sacred and culturally relevant sites. At present, there are even museums exhibiting in their rooms indigenous ancestors, ignoring, in most cases, claims for repayment of their descendants. In response, indigenous groups claim recognition of the exclusive right to protect places considered sacred, and the return of ancestral remains of their people to provide burial according to their beliefs[15]. At this point we must observe that most state constitutions, among which is Venezuela's, proclaim the reserve of state control of culture heritage[16].

What happens with the Venezuelan law? Protection of the Venezuelan indigenous cultural heritage is partially recognized in the Constitution. The Constitution (art. 121) incorporates some elements that make up what are known as cultural heritage and sacred places of worship, but not others that deserve this protection, such as archaeological remains, for example. Venezuelan cardinal rule refers to the cultural heritage in several articles by proclaiming that Indigenous languages are part of the cultural heritage, not only of the Venezuelan nation, but also of humanity (art. 9) and establishes that the State is responsible to protect, preserve, enhance, preserve and restore the Venezuelan cultural heritage, whether tangible or intangible[17], as well as historical memory of the nation (art. 99). It also indicates that, among others, is the legislative responsibility of the National Government on intellectual, artistic and industrial property; cultural and archaeological heritage (art. 156.32).

In accordance with the provisions of the Venezuelan Constitution, is understood that the Venezuelan indigenous' cultural heritage is part of the nation and as such, it benefits from the protection provided for the latter.

Intellectual and Industrial Property

We will now turn our attention to another aspect of the indigenous collective heritage: the protection that deserves songs, symbols, herbal formulas, specific types of plants or their use (De la Cruz, 2007) [18]. Certainly at this point, in relation to intellectual property rights in general, they have proven to be inadequate and ineffective to protect indigenous rights, due to the constant abuse that have and continues to happen with provisions that should therefore be formulated for special protection purpose. We cannot forget that there are many Western plant's patents or medical remedies used since immemorial times by indigenous groups, without any economic compensation provided to them for the original formula (El Pais, 1999)[19].

Venezuelan Constitution (Article 124) forbids patenting of genetic resources in indigenous habitats lands and ancestral knowledge associated with them. This means that any patent derived from indigenous "*technological and scientific knowledge of animal and plant life, designs, traditional methods, and in general, all ancestral and traditional knowledge associated with genetic resources and biodiversity*"[20], is reached by the constitutional proscription. On the other hand, is not enough to prohibit non-Indian registration of such patents, because in any case, the perception by others of potential benefits derived from indigenous traditional knowledge is avoided, then it must be ensured the benefit of the heirs of those who obtained from being benefited by it. For this purpose, a register of collective rights of indigenous peoples and communities related to biodiversity has been established, in charge of the National Office of Biological Diversity[21].

Is well known that indigenous medicinal formulations are not only useful, but also it has been observed that certain plant species grown only in indigenous territories may have a commercial interest[22], cultivation techniques based on traditional ecological knowledge[23] or others that are equally novel for the non-Indian world, from which indigenous peoples could obtain significant income[24], despite being not patentable[25].

Venezuelan law does depend on the prior consent of these groups in order to access to their lands and habitats to collect biotic materials and genetic resources as well as to study them. At this point, indigenous peoples have direct recognition on the right to withhold consent to authorize collection of both biotic and genetic materials such as to have access to traditional knowledge of the group, only in the case they have not been properly informed "about use and benefit of all"[26].

Above-mentioned previous consultation and informed process are generally established by law, without adding customized requisites to those generally required. Thus, in the first place, mandatory presentation of the research project must be submitted to the indigenous peoples concerned, containing in detail all aspects of research with relevance to the indigenous group considered (working relationships to be build, aspects that will be under investigation, proceeds to be received by the community participation ...); in second place, whether under traditional standards the project under consideration is approved, an agreement in written form in which the conditions for the implementation of the proposed project are contained is performed. The determination of indigenous participation in the economic benefits will be decided by applying the process of prior consultation, as defined and set for in the same Organic Law of indigenous peoples and communities. Finally, it should be carried out a joint study between the interested company or entity and the indigenous peoples and communities of the impact that the research intended can potentially produce on these human groups[27].

Once the consent is obtained and once the requirements are evaluated in the presence of the indigenous people, corresponds to the executor entity of Indigenous Policy to grant permission. If the procedure established for this purpose is not complied and despite all permissions have been granted or their beneficiaries exceed the scope of it, the affected ones have the opportunity to try a constitutional remedy[28].

It is also possible that a project`s implementation aspects vary for many reasons once authorized. In these cases, the indigenous peoples concerned, this is, those who have authorized, may urge the invalidity of those permits by applying procedures generally provided to try this type of legal actions. This, despite the fact that the Executing Entity is responsible for granting licenses and concessions, and not indigenous peoples exclusively entitled to this claim[29], but also is a limited protection at this point, since we recognize that the practical effects of the potential claimers and others are not exactly the same.

Since intellectual property has divergent premises in Indigenous and non-indigenous law, it is no wonder that most national statutes in this area are inadequate for the protection of the rights claimed by indigenous peoples. From the indigenous perspective, the rights holder is always a collective subject, the community, the only one with decision-making about it, and not an individual, no matter the belonging within the group. If this statement is true, we find constitutional texts that seek to establish appropriate mechanisms for protecting intellectual property of indigenous peoples living in their territories. Among them is that of Venezuela (art. 124), which recognizes the collective nature of the intellectual property of indigenous peoples[30].

Venezuelan legislation that implements constitutional statement[31] starting from this formulation explicitly recognizes the right to collective intellectual property[32] of indigenous peoples. This with two nuances of extraordinary importance because, on the one hand, proclaims a state guarantee in regard to the exercise of these rights *"in accordance with their customs and traditions"*, hence its non-lapsable action is clear and holds responsible to the State not only on the regulative mechanisms needed to achieve the goals, but also on the control of its use[33] as well as for the state in guaranteeing the indigenous exercise of the right to establish and protect cultural heritage in its entirety.

Specifically regarding to genetic resources it is conditioned on the pursuit of collective benefits both the activities related to these assets, such as knowledge of indigenous peoples and their associated communities. In any case, to the extent that these resources are part of their intellectual property, they may be developed, utilized and protected by these human groups, only according to indigenous uses and customs, always aiming at the collective good of the specific community[34].

One issue to solve is the definition of what is meant by collective benefit. According to the Biological Diversity Act, there are two types[35]: 1) individual, identified with indigenous group in question; and 2) general, in this case, statewide. The first is identified as the *"right to collectively enjoy the benefits derived therefrom and to be compensated for conserving their natural environments"*. The second, meanwhile, follows the establishment of the State's obligation to promote the use of this knowledge *"oriented to the collective benefit of the country"*.

We tend to understand that when it comes to collective benefit it refers, first, to indigenous peoples, although the relationship is closer than it may seem, because the benefit of the indigenous community always and necessarily results in the State's in which they live in; and the realization of the first will result in achieving the second. While this equation is correct, reverse situation is not always so, as not all the general interest results is in the one of culturally distinct human groups, as discussed *supra*, in most cases, are sacrificed to the general interest.

Concerning the protection of industrial property, the existing sectorial law is in force since September 2nd, 1955[36], reason why it does not provide protection for indigenous industrial designs or those that can be based on indigenous knowledge, hence the content of this Act must be interpreted in light of Decision 486 of the Commission of the Andean Community that contains the common system of industrial property[37], in which Member States are required to ensure defense of industrial property by protecting "*traditional knowledge of their indigenous communities*". Discoveries which are based on indigenous knowledge could be patented, having been acquired "*in accordance with international, community and national legal provisions*", without referring to indigenous law, therefore, they shall be patented from an indigenous perspective even if the acquisition has been acquired illegally.

Finally, it is noted that through the processes of self-demarcation is possible to protect traditional knowledge expressed in each of the mental maps created by indigenous peoples and communities they express cultural works. This is the case of:

Collective marks of Pemon people were the result of the products obtained in the second phase of the project 'Indigenous Law and public policy' developed in the process of self-demarcation of Pemon people's habitat. The creation of a total of eighty-four (84) mind maps, true works of visual art that contain in graphic language, the history and cultural heritage of the Pemon, and a family of brands designed and developed as tools linking the Indigenous with their habitat strengthen on one hand, the real possibility of administration of the auto demarcated territory, and the other, justifying the need for recovery and protection of land and traditional cultural expressions, essential elements in the development of specific forms of Aboriginal life, which allows us to show how through the development of the renowned law is possible through the exercise of rights reach its materialization (Aguilar & Uzcategui, 2010) "[38].

With this, the possibility of practical applications to protect the right to collective intellectual property, recognized in the Venezuelan Constitution to indigenous peoples and communities nationwide, through which the conditions for the exercise of the rights are created, it is demonstrated.

COLLECTIVE'S RIGHTS AS A POINT OF ARRIVAL OF THE PRINCIPLE OF SELF-DETERMINATION[39]

We have seen how the right to self-determination has a high regard in various agreements and international declarations. It has also become clear that its inclusion in various legal instruments and the need to respect and implementation by other non-state actors has marked the evolution of international law in general. However, it is also important to determine how upon recognition of the right of indigenous peoples to self-determination a set of collective rights are derived from the ratio of these peoples and their habitats.

The foundation of this relationship and the rights arising there is the land, this is, the ancestral lands claimed by indigenous peoples that are located in the center of the demands and claims of international and national negotiations. However, the collective rights of indigenous peoples go beyond the environmental issue as they have relationship to the original law and human rights in general, based on recognition of cultural plurality (Aguilar, 2001).

We start from the premise that the rights of indigenous peoples in general within its international scope, are inseparable from a collective dimension that is inherent[40], as the way they are designed and become effective on the principle of collective identity with land, for example, a relationship that determines its *modus vivendi* and influence the human condition.

Commitments of Agriculture Organization (FAO) and The First Manifestations of Collectives' Rights

Within FAO two international engagements have been produced in which the basis for the consecration of collective rights sit through the recognition of so-called "farmers' rights". These, though are not expressly rights of a collective character make a good precedent for future codification process. Indeed, the First International Undertaking on Plant Genetic Resources of 1983 (FAO)[41] sets as goal to ensure that plant genetic resources of economic and social interest are exploited, preserved, evaluated and made available for selection and scientific research.

This agreement is based on the universally accepted principle under which genetic resources are the common heritage of mankind[42], and therefore are accessible without restriction. This consideration involving free access to genetic resources and materials required the transfer of technology from the North to the South. The latter would exchange genetic resources within their territory for technology selection (Noiville, 1997, p. 178)[43].

Thus, free access would mean double trouble: from a legal point of view, the common heritage involved the free movement of genetic resources while IP enshrine their monopolization. From the political point of view, the Northern States refuse to consider their improved varieties as the common heritage of humanity and the Southern States would oppose unlimited and free access to their genetic resources. This framework of FAO disputes forced a re-interpretation of the Compromise of 1983 the other in 1989[44].

This new agreement was an attempt to reconcile the logic of free access to genetic resources and earn a profit from holder countries. Innovation trying to catch up with conservation. The intellectual property rights were pressing for tacitly or expressly recognition follow from the interpretation of the new text, through a mechanism using a breeder's certificate that would support two schemes: the recognition of a property right for breeder's new varieties (linking it to the existing Convention on the subject[45]) and compensation to the countries of genetic resources origin. This payment also imply a recognition of the so-called "farmers' rights".

Rio Declaration on Environment and Development of 1992 and Collective's Rights

This important document was signed in the framework of the World Summit on Environment and Development in 1992 in Rio de Janeiro, and highlights the role of indigenous peoples and their contribution to sustainable development.

In this sense, Principle 22 states: *"Indigenous people and their communities, and other local communities, have a vital role in environmental management and development because of their knowledge and traditional practices. States should recognize and duly support their identity, culture and interests and enable their effective participation in the achievement of sustainable development"*.

Collective`s Rights in the Convention on Biological Diversity

This Convention was signed in 1992 in the framework of the Earth Summit, recognizes in Article 8 (j) the importance of indigenous and local communities in the conservation and sustainable use of biodiversity. In turn, recognizes its share of the benefits arising from the utilization of traditional knowledge associated summoning States to protect and encourage customary use of biological resources in accordance with the conservation compatible with cultural practices.

Collective's Rights in the Declaration on the Rights of Indigenous Peoples[46]

Article 7 highlights more clearly the basis of collective rights. The same states that "Indigenous peoples have the collective and individual right not to be subjected to ethnic or cultural genocide, with special prevention and repair of: a) Any action which has the aim or effect of depriving them of their integrity as distinct peoples of their cultural values or ethnic identities of their respective; b) Any action which has the aim or effect of depriving all of their lands, territories and resources; c) Any form of population transfer with the purpose or effect of violating or undermining any of their rights; d) any mode of assimilation or integration by other cultures or ways of life imposed by legislative, administrative or other measures; e) Any form of propaganda directed against them."[47].

Article 8, which complements the aforementioned, states that indigenous peoples have the individual and collective right to maintain and develop their distinct identities and characteristics right, including the right to identify themselves as indigenous and to be recognized as such.

Collective's Rights in Other International Legal Instruments (ILO Convention No. 169)

This convention recognizes the right of indigenous peoples to control their economy; determine their development priorities in the social and cultural fields; a collective relationship with their lands and territories, demanding governments, inter alia, the value of respecting the cultural and spiritual values of indigenous peoples.

As stated by Posey (2004, p.44)[48], recognition of collective rights under this convention includes intergenerational transmission, use and protection of traditional knowledge, therefore, the issue of collective intellectual property gains importance.

Collective's Rights in Other Regional Legal Instruments (Decision 391 of the Andean Community of Nations)

Decision 391 signed by member countries of the Andean Community of Nations (CAN) was passed in 1996 as part of the negotiation of a Common Regime on Access to Genetic Resources. The Decision recognizes and values the rights and the authority of the native, African-American and local communities to decide about their Know-How, innovations and traditional practices associated with genetic resources and their by-products.

To conclude this first part, we have seen the evolution of the Indigenous question dates from long ago. Two of his most controversial aspects (the rights of peoples to self-determination as the basis of the right to self-determination of indigenous peoples and collective rights as arrival point above) contained in the agenda of negotiations between the States and indigenous peoples, have been a constant of international relations and are tacitly or expressly inserted in various agreements, declarations and instruments of regional and international nature. Although not all are mandatory and consecration - strict sense - is not sufficient to create or deny rights, recognition marks a path to its realization. However, these rights will remain the subject of controversy since the provision of the rule per se has only declaratory. Then it will take political complement and completion of the legal will.

Some Considerations on Indigenous Issues as Problems of International Relations and Public International Law and Its Impact on the Domestic Level

The relevance of the topic is based on the way the problem is to be inserted in the domestic context, looking at the processes at the international level are given around the Indian question and how it plays nationally. Indeed, studies and negotiations that are taking place within the framework of international politics circumscribe the right to self-determination of indigenous peoples to two main streams[49]:

1. The maximalist or external component, which provides that the right to self-determination of indigenous peoples must be understood in its fullest expression, i.e., including the possibility of secession of those peoples whose constant and repeated violation of their rights as minorities or people are constantly violated or stalking;
2. Minimalist or internal dimension, which states that self-determination must be understood and conceived in the framework of self-determination of peoples, the possibility that they, once recognized as such, acquire maximum autonomy (fundamentally political) to manage their affairs.
3. Generally this debate has been extrapolated to the internal order with errors, gaps and inconsistencies that have been settled externally. This paper will attempt to respond also to notions of autonomy and the of peoples' right to decide for themselves as the content of the right to self-determination[50]. But to get an elaboration of the latter is necessary to specify the nature of the category "people", not only in international debates, but essentially the way it has been built internally. It is known the difficulty around achieving a consensual definition of this category. Following Torrecuadra (2001) we can ask ourselves the next questions: What is a "people" with its own characteristics? Is it several "peoples" that have common characteristics and that these traits separate them from the rest of the population? Are the minority groups with specific characteristics that make them indigenous? Do they belong to a certain category legally? Trying a system of protection for indigenous peoples is determined largely by consideration as subjects of national and international law. Hence the importance of the distinction[51] with other minority groups such as from a "strictly technical perspective we believe that the indigenous groups, differentiating features are closer to the category of people that the minority, although the use of that political connotations have not always desired by the States (Ibid.)".

For conceptualizing the notion of "people" we should take into account the different definitions and considerations that exist on the subject. Among the most important we shall quote that of Miguel Alfonso Martinez, of the Working Expert Group on Indigenous Peoples in the study on treaties between indigenous peoples and States (1999)[52].

Another is that used by the ILO Convention 169 concerning Indigenous and Tribal Peoples in Independent Countries, and finally, the Directive which stipulates the Operational Manual 4.20 of the World Bank 1991. All this to recognize "that there is no consensus on the use of the term indigenous peoples" in the Working Group (Commission on Human Rights Draft United Nations Declaration on the Rights of Indigenous Peoples), in part, because of the implications that this term may have in international law, including with respect to self-determination and individual and collective rights" (UN, 2000)[53]. However the absence of definition, international practice has shown that this has not been an obstacle in the recognition of common rights, unnamed or undefined. It is the case of minorities, in which the absence of a consensual definition has been no impediment for the protection of their rights and the adoption of international agreements that recognize them (Capotorti, 1991, p. 119).

In the case of Venezuela, these criteria were included in the negotiation process that has been led around indigenous issues at the time of the formulation of the new constitution in 1999. How has this principle designed? How is inserted? What is the state of the current debate?

Negotiation which indigenous peoples of Venezuela on the development and implementation is present in the Demarcation and Protection of habitat and lands of indigenous peoples law (21 December 2000) on one hand, and political participation on the other, in which in this and other processes are concerned, is a good expression of how the international subject is inserted internally. Also the national indigenous position on the internal-external criterion of self-determination appears in several documents of interest for the analysis of indigenous issues. For political attitudes and positions taken by indigenous representatives in the constitutional process of 1999 and then as deputy to the National Assembly, once elected in 2000, one can discern that lean toward the second side (internal).

Once stated that, it is necessary to make a clarification on the content of the indigenous question. The latter is understood as the set of controversial issues affecting directly or indirectly the indigenous peoples, determining the place indigenous issues have occupied in international and national policy agenda. The analysis of indigenous peoples and new social actors lets us understand that they "are the political expression of "*cleavages*" of a society and designate groups excluded from the political system throwing challenges to the political authorities for their demands to be taken into account in the scope of the national policy agenda" (Kriesi, H. 1998, p. 423). Either authorities' responses formulated at a given moment or claims of social actors can be expressed in various ways (Ibid.). The emergence of social actors and their forms of protest depend largely on the political system itself, in particular as regards the configuration of power and institutional framework (Tarrow, 1994, p. 251). In turn, the study of the type of state can see the possible forms of protest and political opportunities that may influence the processes of political decision (Ibid).

In this context we want to clarify that the right to self-determination of indigenous peoples (as the source of all other rights) and collective rights derive from the exercise of this principle. We could add that the evolution of the claims of indigenous peoples in the international context has been matched by demands of minorities. The lack of an explicit and consensual definition of both concepts (people and minority) is a characteristic element of the development of both subjects. Indigenous peoples have expressed that the situation they live and suffer requires special attention from the state and the United Nations (Stavenhagen, 2001, p.119). Thus indicates:

Indigenous peoples themselves (...) have been able to present their views (holding) that their situation is different from the generality of minorities and to be accorded special attention. To begin with, in certain Latin American countries, indigenous people are not a minority, but rather form a numerical majority. Secondly, indigenous are the descendants of the original inhabitants of a country colonized by immigrants or conquered by force. Thirdly, they have been victims of certain processes of economic and political development that have been placed in a position of subordination and dependence in relation to the dominant society within their own territories. Indigenous peoples argue that they are the original nations, the first, and that their human rights have been systematically violated by the dominant states, whose legitimacy is not recognized in certain cases (Ibid.)

Based on the true fact that the colonial powers held treaties with indigenous peoples that were subsequently broken unilaterally, indigenous claim their "peoples" status rather than minorities. It is the argument of the previous occupation as a source of other collective rights attached to the relationship of indigenous peoples to land (Ibid, p.120).

As stated before and as we have said, with the creation of the Working Group on Indigenous Populations in 1982[54], under the Sub commission on Prevention of Discrimination and Protection of Minorities, indigenous issues have acquired its own development (See Supra). Then, within the same, Sub-Working Group on Minorities is also created in the year 1995, at which time official and institutional issues diverged in form and content, at least in their treatment in the field of this UN body.

Since then, progress that had been made about the Indian question was well advanced within the Subcommittee. The Draft Declaration on the Rights of Indigenous Peoples had already been approved and the General Assembly of the United Nations and had also been declared the International Decade of Indigenous Peoples. Notwithstanding the fact that this development was printing out content and specificity to the indigenous issue, there were some aspects that were still pending on the international agenda: first, the scope and content of the principle of self-determination and on the other, the dimension of collective rights enshrined in various international legal instruments relating to indigenous peoples.

But fundamentally, what would be concerned is how these issues would be incorporated in the domestic legislation and how they could affect and be affected by the evolution of the problem internationally. This is the latest venture that is still valid today.

The Latin America Case

One of the main challenges of the American agenda in our times is to include the indigenous question into the discussion of states, mainly after the political and legal changes in the international arena with the adoption of the UN Declaration on the Rights of Indigenous Peoples (United Nations, 2007).

The Declaration of the United Nations constitutes the outcome of new demands of the international system after World War II. In this postwar context, international law and their international relations have suffer changes derivate from the new world dynamics, being one of its features polymorphism as subjects of law and international actors respectively, since the state would not be the only international actor along with we can find the peoples, minorities and the international organizations among others that generate life within the international system.

Regarding peoples in general, and indigenous peoples in particular, after the approval of the UN Charter and the International Covenants on Human Rights, Indigenous Peoples began a new phase which translates in the claiming of their rights. This is based on the legal principle of "self-determination of peoples", which recognizes the right of all peoples to freely determine their political, economic and social future, which hitherto has been subjugated by the States. This principle begins to materialize in the context of decolonization.

However, the indigenous reality continues to be characterized by continued and progressive violations of human rights to these populations. For this reason the United Nations, inserted since 1980 the indigenous issue as an international problem starting the development of the draft Declaration on the Rights of Indigenous Peoples. This inclusion of indigenous issues in the international system is the result of a study by the Special Rapporteur Cobo, appointed by the (former) Subcommittee for the Prevention of Discrimination and Protection of Minorities of the former Commission on Human Rights, who would be responsible to do a study "*in situ*" on the situation of indigenous peoples and communities worldwide.

One of the conclusions that were reached in what later became known as "The Cobo Report" stated that "*indigenous peoples were at the bottom of the socio-economic scale. They did not have the same opportunity for employment and the same access as other groups to public services and/or protection in the fields of health, living conditions, culture, religion and the administration of justice. They could not participate meaningfully in political life* "(Preamble to Resolution 1999/20 of the General Assembly of the United Nations).

This study was important for two aspects: first, as it introduces indigenous issues on the international agenda, and second, for the creation of the United Nations Working Group on Indigenous Affairs, which works since 1980 in the draft Declaration on the Rights of Indigenous Peoples, finally approved in 2007.

As part of the international indigenous legal framework is also the Convention 169 of the International Labour Organization (ILO)[55], which has been ratified by the majority of American States, which "*recognizes the aspirations of these of these peoples to exercise control over their own institutions, ways of life and economic development and to maintain and develop their identities, languages and religions, within the framework of the States in which they live* "(Preamble of ILO Convention 169).

On a regional level, the Organization of American States (OAS) has been working on the Draft American Declaration on the Rights of Indigenous Peoples, which would address more than 670 indigenous peoples with a huge biodiversity, fighting for their rights, which have mostly been violated since the arrival of the colonizers

While some States have developed indigenous laws in their domestic sphere and ratified international indigenous law[56], it is necessary, at the American States level, of a legal framework to strengthen the rights of the indigenous peoples of the region and also of regional policies giving effect to those, having clear that even when the statements come with no legal force at the time of creation, these can become binding upon states where there is consensus and practice thereof, to the extent that respond to human rights standards (*ius cogens*).

Due to the situation where most of the indigenous peoples of the region find themselves, which are still at the lowest ranking of all social stratification and their rights continue to be violated, and in "best" cases are threatened by the State or by any third party who is present in its territory, being victims of social exclusion, it is necessary to be included in the American agenda that the Indian question in that relationship to be constructed between indigenous rights and democracy in America.

SOLUTIONS AND RECOMMENDATIONS

America is a multiethnic and multicultural continent with more than 670 indigenous peoples. Of the 6,000 cultures existing in the world (approximate figure) between 4000 and 5000 are indigenous cultures. In a study conducted by FAO (1990), indigenous people were distributed in Latin America as follows:

- More than 40%: Bolivia, Guatemala, Peru and Ecuador.
- 20% to 5%: Belize, Honduras, Mexico, Chile, El Salvador, Guyana, Panama, Suriname, Nicaragua.

- From 4% to 1%: French Guiana, Paraguay, Colombia, Venezuela, Jamaica, Puerto Rico, Trinidad and Tobago, Dominica, Costa Rica.
- From 0.1% to 0.9%: Brazil, Uruguay, Canada and the United States.

This allows us to determine that approximately 10% of the population of Latin America and the Caribbean belong to indigenous peoples. Also, the global distribution of these indigenous peoples under review shows that there is a strong correlation between regions of high biological diversity and regions of intense cultural diversity.

FUTURE RESEARCH DIRECTIONS

- Indigenous peoples and communities in the Americas are immersed into a social exclusion issue, inherited by the nation-state that can then derive in social conflicts as in the case of Bolivia.
- The difficulty of governance, access to political spaces, decision-making, remains outside of the democratic political system of claim all the demands of indigenous peoples and communities.
- The various constitutions in the American States, which have included the rights of indigenous peoples (noting in its preamble that are multiethnic and multicultural societies), represents a breakthrough in the creation of indigenous movements and parties base to work on their demands through the elections and their representatives or through other mechanisms, marches, protests, etc. However, opening the political system to these villages has resulted in the partisanship of indigenous issues in the areas of power, homogenizing the needs, thoughts and decision making between indigenous and non-indigenous. This recognition (not only political, but also economic, social and cultural rights) has not extended to the exercise thereof, for example, it has failed to create areas of interest where there was a real indigenous representation.
- For democracy to be meaningful, indigenous peoples must have not only the recognition of rights but also a political space that grant them equal (for those non-indigenous) to claim their collective demands emanating from their own worldview and life plans and building programs, alongside; formulate public policies to meet those needs.

In conclusion, there must be an effective representation within the state (equal to formulate preferences) for indigenous representatives to act as interlocutor between indigenous demands and satisfaction thereof by the State.

Five Reasons to Include Indigenous Issues within a Latin American Agenda

1. **The Principle of Self-Determination of Peoples:** which from the inner side states that indigenous peoples once recognized as such, acquire maximum autonomy to manage their affairs? Based on this principle indigenous peoples have incorporated political autonomy to the political system according to their traditions and collective demands.
2. The problem of democracy between States and indigenous peoples has as its starting point the *recognition and realization of indigenous land rights*, as it is in the territory where other rights such as education, health, work including the right to political life become effective.

3. The United Nations said the languages spoken by indigenous peoples are disappearing rapidly. The disappearance of these languages would result in the loss of ecological knowledge accumulated by indigenous people and transmitted from generation to generation. Biodiversity cannot be conserved without cultural diversity and the long-term safety of food and medicines depend on the maintenance of this complex relationship.

4. From a more general perspective, the process of dispossession inflicted to the land can be mitigated through exercise and realization of indigenous land rights. In the words of Alamo (2014) "the state modernization projects have failed to be combined with respect for ancestral lands and the environment, two pillars of the indigenous world and its survival as a people. Inequalities and social imbalances resulting from the exclusion and marginalization of indigenous peoples are directly related to the deterioration of its natural resources as well as the reduction and loss of their ancestral lands" (Alamo, n.d.)[57].

5. Indigenous peoples and communities have organized themselves as social movements seeking social claim, and their expression in the actual moment has taken different types of transactions within the political system. The political moment that indigenous peoples have passed has allowed us to characterize three political transactions:

    a. **Violent Transaction:** occurs when the conflicting parties fail to reach any agreement on a particular issue or claim. Example of this is the initial phase of the conflict in Venezuela around Decree 1850 between 1996 and 1998, the case of the Zapatista uprising in Mexico in 1994, the case of the indigenous uprising in Ecuador in 2000, or the case of the indigenous uprising in Bolivia in 2003.

    b. **The Negotiated Transaction:** the result of the negotiation of all claims in the short or medium term mechanism offered as solution to a conflict party. Example of this is the second phase of the conflict over the Decree 1850 in Venezuela, the case of the Zapatistas in Mexico in 2002 and the case of Ecuador in 2003.

    c. **Institutionalized Transaction:** the cooptation of the original claims of a particular conflict in the public sphere of the state and institutional. Institutionalized transaction may take the form of public policy.

In a democratic system with equal opportunities, indigenous peoples and communities exercise their political transaction according to their traditional structures and class actions, as part of the autonomy granted to it by the international principle of self-determination of peoples.

CONCLUSION

*   There are more than 670 indigenous peoples in Latin America. An estimated 10% in Indian population distributed in the American states. The above shows that a significant population is required to claim their rights and needs a political and legal support of States to carry it out.

*   The right to self-determination of peoples should be recognized, setting aside the fear of territorial disintegration, to the extent that this makes clear the exercise of autonomy that have these peoples to their territories and may request that only those people whose secession violation human rights is repeatedly and systematically.

- The recognition and exercise of the rights of indigenous peoples in a democratic system has as its starting point the specific, identity and cultural status of indigenous peoples. Indigenous peoples and communities through exercise and realization of land rights allow conservation of natural resources for the development of civilization.

- A democratic system that includes indigenous peoples should be aware of the difference of these subjects having visions of law in the creation of political spaces, in the management of social demands and the mechanisms of decision making.

- Finally, a democratic system with a commitment to promote homogeneous cultures poses a great threat to human survival in general.

REFERENCES

Aguilar Castro, V. (2001). *Preliminary thesis report entitled between resistance and dissent. The indigenous questions and challenges current international relations. Tensions and conflicts in Venezuela.* Geneva: HEID.

Aguilar Castro, V. (2001). *Informe preliminar "Proyecto reconocimiento efectivo de los derechos Ye'kwana y Sanemá sobre los hábitats ocupados en el Caura, Venezuela y elaboración de un programa de manejo sostenible de sus recursos".* Venezuela: Kuyujani, CIAG-UNEG, FPP, ULA.

Capotorti, F. (1991). *Etude des droits des personnes appartenant aux minorités ethniques, religieuses et linguistiques.* New York: ONU.

Daes, E. I. (2000). *Prevention of discrimination and protection of indigenous peoples and minorities, working paper on discrimination against indigenous peoples submitted by Mrs Erica-Irene Daes, chairperson-rapporteur of the Working Group on Indigenous Populations, in accordance with Subcommission resolution 1999/20.* Economic and Social Council, United Nations.

Kriesi, H. (1998). *Le système politique suisse* (2nd ed.). Paris: Económica.

Cobo, J. (1987). *Estudio del problema de la discriminación contra las poblaciones indígenas.* New York: Organización de las Naciones Unidas.

Noiville, C. (1997). *Ressources génétiques et droit. Essai sur les régimes juridiques des ressources génétiques marines.* Paris: Editions Pedone.

Posey, D. (2004). International Agreements and intellectual property right protection for indigenous peoples. In *COICA, biodiversity, collective rights and sui generis intellectual property regime.* Ecuador: COICA.

Stavenhagen, R. (2001). *The ethnic question.* Colegio de México.

Tarrow, S. (1994). *Power in movement: Social movements, collective action and politics.* New York: Cambridge University Press.

Torrecuadrada, S. (2001). *Los pueblos indígenas en el orden internacional.* Madrid: Editorial Dykinson.

De la Cruz, R. (2007). The rights of indigenous intellectual property and traditional knowledge of indigenous peoples. In L. Giraudo (Ed.), *Citizenship and indigenous rights in Latin America: Population, states and international order*. Madrid: Academic Press.

Uzcátegui, A., & Aguilar, V. (2010). Collective indigenous rights and intellectual property in Venezuela. The case of the Pemon people. *Year, 27*(27), 161–201.

ADDITIONAL READING

Aguilar Castro, V. & Bustillos, L. (2006). Transversalización de la política (pública) para pueblos indígenas. Hacia una definición del poder popular para los pueblos indígenas de la República Bolivariana de Venezuela. Mérida, Mérida: Consejo de publicaciones. ULA.

Aguilar Castro, V. (2000). La posibilidad de seguir soñando. S. Rodríguez. (Ed.) Diversidad biológica y derechos indígenas: Un debate inacabado. Madrid, España: Literastur.

Carrillo, J. (1969). *Soberanía del estado y derecho internacional*. Madrid, Madrid: Editorial Tecnos.

Clavero, B. (1994). *Derecho indígena y cultura constitucional en América*. Madrid, Madrid: Siglo XXI en España Editores.

Díaz, H., & Sánchez, C. (1999). Autodemarcación y autonomía: Logros e incertidumbre. Burguete A., & Mayor. (Ed.) Experiencias de autonomía indígena. México: IWGIA.

González, P., Carpizo, J., & Fajnzylber, F. (1983). *No intervención autodeterminación y democracia en América latina*. D.F, Mexico: Siglo Veintiuno Editores.

IWGIA (2001). El mundo indígena 2000-2001. Dinamarca: Grupo internacional de trabajo sobre asuntos indígenas.

IWGIA (2002). El mundo indígena 2001-2002. Dinamarca: Grupo internacional de trabajo sobre asuntos indígenas.

Mariño, F., & Fernández, C., & Díaz, C. (2001). La protección internacional de las minorías y organizaciones internacionales. Madrid, Madrid: Ministerio de trabajos y asuntos sociales.

Medina, J., & Aguilar, V. (2008). *Conservación de la biodiversidad en los territorios indígenas Pemón de Venezuela*. Mérida, Mérida: The Nature Conservancy-ULA.

Medina, J., Croes, G., & Piña, I. (2007). *Evaluación de políticas públicas del pueblo Pemon*. Caracas, DC: The Nature Conservancy.

Tardieu, V. (1999). *The Indians discovered the antidote*. El Pais. Retrieved June 4, 2014, from www.elpais.com

Aguilar Castro, V., & Bustillos Ramírez, L. (2007). Oportunidad política en Venezuela. La cuestión indígena entre continuidades y rupturas institucionales (1999-2005). In Revista Venezolana de Ciencia Política, 30, 227-247.

Aguilar Castro, V. (2008). Pueblos Indígenas y Biodiversidad. Paper presented at *I Encuentro por el derecho a la demarcación*, Mérida, Mérida, (Publishing pending).

United Nations. (1992). Concluding observations of the Human Rights Committee: Venezuela. (CCPR/79/Add.13), New York, N.Y.

United Nations. (2014) *Draft report of the expert mechanism on the rights of indigenous peoples on its seventh session*. Geneva, Switzerland.

E/CN.4/Sub.2/1993/28, 1993.

United Nations. (1994). *Technical review of the United Nations draft declaration on the rights of indigenous peoples.* (E / CN.4 / SUB.2 /1994/ 2 /Add.1)

United Nations (1998) E / CN.4 / SUB.2 / AC.4/ 1998/9 June 24, 1998.

United Nations. (1996). *Working paper by the Chairperson-Rapporteur, Erica-Irene A. Daes, on the concept of indigoenous peoples.* (E / CN.4 / SUB.2 / AC.4/ 1996/)

United Nations (2004) Human Rights Commission. Resolution 1995/ September 13 to 24, 2004.

United Nations (1999) Resolution 1999. Promotion and protection of Human Rights Subcommission.

United Nations (1983) Resolution 8/83 of the 22 Session of the FAO conference.

United Nations. (1989) Resolution 4/89 25 Session of the FAO Conference

United Nations. (1948). *Universal Declaration of Human Rights.* New York, N.Y.

United Nations. (1960). Resolution 1514 General Assembly (A / 4684). New York, N.Y.

United Nations. (1966). *Resolution 2200 General Assembly.* New York, N.Y.: XXI.

United Nations. (2001). *United Nations Guidelines for indigenous peoples.* Geneva, Switzerland.

United Nations. (1985). *World Intellectual Property Organization (WIPO). The elements of industrial property.* (Doc. WIPO/IP/AR/85/7).

OAS / Ser.G / CP / CAPJP-1576 /99, October 8th, 1999.

Aramburu, E. (2000). *Aproximación a una definición de "pueblo" en derecho internacional.* Retrieved March 15, 2015, from: http://www.oocities.org/enriquearamburu/DIA/mia17.html

Álamo, O. (n.d). *Pueblos indígenas, Democracia y gobernabilidad en la región andina.* Retrieved March 15, 2015, from: www.focal.ca/pdf/alamo.pdf

Alegrett, R. *(n.d.). Evolución y tendencias de las reformas agrarias en América Latina.* Retrieved December 10, 2014, from http://www.fao.org/docrep/006/j0415t/j0415t0b.htm

CELADE. (n.d). *50 años de demografía en América Latina y el Caribe.* Retrieved March 15, 2015, from: www.inegi.gob.mx/inegi/contenidos/espanol/eventos/VIgen07/doctos/6%20de%20sep/panel%20 3%20B/F

Martínez, M. & IDB *Report on indigenous peoples developed in 1999*. Retrieved December 9, 2014, from http://www.iadb.org/exr/IDB/stories/1999/esp/c1099s3.html

James, A. (1996). *Derecho de autodeterminación de los pueblos*. Retrieved October 12, 2014, from: www.geocites.com/tayacan_2000/autodeter.htm-11K

Provea (2000). *Derecho de los pueblos indios*. Retrieved June 15, 2014, from: www.derechos.org.ve/ publicaciones/ infatuar/2000_01/derecho_pueb_indios.htm-68k

Remiro Brotons, A. (2004). *Derecho internacional. Monografía: Civilizados, bárbaros y salvajes en el nuevo orden internacional*. Retrieved July 5, 2014, from: www.civilizados-barbaros-y-salvajes-en-el-nuevo-orden-internacional_remiro-brotons.html

United Nations. (1998). *Report of the UN Working Group on Indigenous Populations*. Retrieved January 3, 2014, from http://www.puebloindio.org/ONU_Docs/WGIP98_Report2b.htm

Wals, C. (2002*). Interculturalidad, reformas constitucionales y pluralismo jurídico*. Retrieved from: www.icci.nativeweb.org/boletín/36/walsh.html-34k

KEY TERMS AND DEFINITIONS

Collective Rights: Are those rights that belong to an indigenous community that cannot be objects of private property because they have been handed down from generation to generation. These rights are the result of social practices arising from the relationship between indigenous peoples with their environment in general and biodiversity in particular. The basis of this social relationship is their territories. According Fergus Mackay, the right holder may be the group (not individual members) unless an individual has been designated as a representative or received express permission of the latter; or an individual member of the group, who acts either on its own behalf or on behalf of other group members or the group as a whole (collective right dual position).

Cultural Rights: The right to practice and revitalize their cultural traditions and customs.

Determination of Indigenous Peoples: Self-determination in its many forms is, consequently, the fundamental precondition for indigenous peoples to enjoy their fundamental rights and determine their future, while preserve, develop and transmit their ethnic specificity future generations (Cobo Report).

Indigenous Lands and Territories: Places in which indigenous peoples inhabit and develop their ancient ways of life, their cosmogony, their culture, folklore and expressions and their economy.

Indigenous Peoples: Notes that it is the people or people originating from the country in which they live, or who is born or originated in the same place where you are (Dictionary of the Spanish Language).

National Agenda: Is the implicit or explicit inclusion of indigenous and controversial issue in defining national policies (public or not) and in various decisions of legislative, executive and judicial issues.

Traditional Knowledge: According to WIPO, implies knowledge, know-how, skills and practices that are developed, sustained and passed on from generation to generation within a community, often forming part of its cultural or spiritual identity. They also have a vital role in environmental management and development because of their knowledge and traditional practices. States should recognize and duly support their identity, culture and interests and enable their effective participation in the achievement of sustainable development, as stated in the Rio Declaration on Environment and Development.

ENDNOTES

[1]   This work is part of a more extensive currently under review on cultural rights of indigenous peoples in Venezuela. Its authors are Torrecuadrada Soledad García-Lozano, of the Autonomous University of Madrid, Spain, and Vladimir Aguilar Castro of the University of Los Andes, Mérida, Venezuela.

[2]   Vid. Final Report of the *Study on treaties between indigenous peoples and States*, paragraphs 206, 207 and 208. According to the same source there are today villages that can be considered endangered, including the original inhabitants of the Carolina Island found up to the coast of California and the Yanomami in Roraima, Brazil.

[3]   The Population Atlas of the Amazon (available in http://amazonas.rds.org.co/Atlas/cap1/fracap1. htm) reports that in the last half of the twentieth century have disappeared at least "eleven ethnic groups Peruvian Amazonia from seven linguistic families ... - either physically or culturally - and eighteen groups and subgroups in five linguistic families are in danger of extinction". If we consider that amount (11 groups every 50 years) as an index to estimate the number of missing indigenous groups and multiply by the centuries since the first contacts with Europeans, is that the number of indigenous people who perished in the geographical area indicated surpass hundred. We are aware of the inaccuracy of the result, since as a consequence of the first contacts with the colonists the number could be substantially higher, we due to transmission of diseases for which the natives had no antibodies.

[4]   Among the most reprehensible practices emphasizes the separation of children from their human origin groups in order to achieve assimilation to the dominant social sector, relatively recent practice developed among other places in Australia or the United States. In this regard paragraph 238 of the Final Report on *Study on treaties between indigenous peoples and States*, conducted by Miguel Alfonso Martinez or IDB report on indigenous peoples developed in 1999 http://www.iadb.org/ exr/IDB/stories/1999/esp/c1099s3.html

[5]   See the Report of the UN Working Group on Indigenous Populations, 1998, in: http://www.puebloindio.org/ONU_Docs/WGIP98_Report2b.htm

[6]   See in this sense, Article 8 of the UN Declaration incorporating both individual and collective right not to be subjected to indicating some behaviors that are considered constitutive of these types.

[7]   In Venezuela, the strongest initial criticisms to the environmental depredation during the first government of Commander Hugo Chávez Frías were deep during 2004 when the "Oil Opening" begun in Delta Amacuro and the "Power Line" (Tendido Eléctrico) in the Gran Sabana, Bolivar State, but recently (2nd Government of Chávez and continuation of Maduro`s), we have danger of coal exploitation in the Guasare mines region in the border of Zulia State and Colombia. One important Non-Governmental Organization (NGO) which has made serious criticisms to the Government is "Homo et Natura" who attacked the extraction of coal besides of support the indian movement of Perijá to keep their traditional lands. In Guayana we also find other NGO`s who support Pemon Indians in their fight against the National Bolivarian Guard who has the "Plan Caura", a extractive program of minerals in indian territories which increases the raid against original indian peoples of Guiana.

[8]   We refer specifically to the Organic Law on Indigenous Peoples and Communities, which devotes Chapter Two of Title IV (*From education and culture*), to the indigenous culture. Recognition as

venezolanidad roots found in Article 87. The Constitution assumes the above statement, referring to them as "*The folk cultures of venezolanidad*" to say that must be the subject of specific attention.

9   A slightest recognition is contained in Article 126 of the Constitution which proclaims that indigenous cultures as "*ancestral roots.*" Certainly the constitutional purpose is to proclaim that despite the cultural characteristics, the Nation is unique and also the Venezuelan people, to be part of it indigenous peoples.

10   The Constitution, in Article 121 expressly recognizes the right to cultural identity of indigenous groups and their members (affirming the right to maintain and develop cultural identity '*worldview, values, spirituality and sacred places and worship* ... '), which is an expression of the right to culture. The scope of this specific recognition (just as we've seen in the past and especially in the preceding paragraph) of the Organic Law of Indigenous Peoples and Communities, whose article 86 reiterates the constitutional provision substantively indicated.

11   See especially Article 88 of the Organic Law on Indigenous Peoples and Communities.

12   See concluding observations of the Human Rights Committee: Venezuela, 28/12/1992. CCPR/79/Add.13, paragraph. 10.

13   Paragraph 24 of the *Study on the protection of cultural and intellectual property*, prepared by Erica-Irene Daes, Special Rapporteur of the Sub-Commission on Prevention of Discrimination and Protection of Minorities and Chairperson of the Working Group on Indigenous Populations, was issued on July 28, 1993 in E/CN.4/Sub.2/1993/28 UN Doc

14   According to article 41 of the Biological Diversity Act Venezuelan, economic rights are "collective property and control of resources rights associated with forms of life, physically and intellectually that belong to the unique identity of a traditional community, indigenous people or community, of which their own existential and cultural events are released.

15   Article 15.3 of the American Declaration as drafted reduces the scope of indigenous participation in decision under Art. 10.3 of the initial version of this Statement. Then it stated of "*collaboration*" with indigenous peoples, which is more involved than mere "*consultation*" built now. Also, before the state's obligation to adopt "effective" measures are provided, while the current wording refers to '*appropriate measures*'. Finally, in those cases in which state institutions have appropriated "*sacred graves and relics*" belonging to indigenous peoples, the obligation to return them to the rightful heirs stated, content now gone.

16   See the constitutions of Bolivia (191.I), Colombia (arts. 8 and 72), Costa Rica (art. 89), Ecuador (art. 62), Guatemala (art. 60), Nicaragua (art. 128), Panama (art. 80), Paraguay (art. 81), Peru (art. 21), Uruguay (art. 34) and Venezuela (art. 99).

17   Assertion qualified by the Organic Law of Indigenous Peoples and Communities, whose art. 93 establishes the obligation of the State jointly with indigenous peoples and communities to protect and preserve "the archaeological sites located in their habitat and land, promoting knowledge and cultural heritage of every people and nation".

18   See Among recent studies conducted by De la Cruz, R. (2007). The rights of indigenous intellectual property and traditional knowledge of indigenous peoples. In L. Giraudo, *Citizenship and indigenous rights in Latin America: population, states and international order,* (p. 237). Madrid.

19   On 6 September 1999, the daily El PAIS published an article entitled "The Indians discovered the antidote, " in which the author (V. Tardieu) realizes that a French chemist who worked in the Bolivian Institute for Altitude Biology, patented a plant whose bark powder use by Chimanos Indians of Bolivia as a poultice to treat leishmaniasis, one of the worst parasitic diseases known, affecting

about three hundred fifty million people worldwide, according to that information, and transmits a mosquito. For this reason, the said chemical is accused of confiscating property which belongs to the Bolivian Indians. However, despite the importance of the patented product, no pharmaceutical company wanted to market it, since the vast majority of people who develop the disease are poor, earning of wages (in the case of Bolivia) of about 8,000 pesetas per month. Hard money to pay the 40,000 pesetas which may cost product.

[20] Articles 101 and 103 of the organic law of indigenous peoples and communities of Venezuela.

[21] Pursuant to the provisions of Article 86 of the Biodiversity Act. According to Article. 88, National Bureau of Biodiversity has a period of three years from the entry into force of the Law (produced in May 2000) to develop programs for the recognition of the rights of indigenous peoples at this point and proceed its execution. Within the National Office it has been produced a first draft of the decree creating the National Commission on Genetic Resources, in which indigenous peoples participate, along with representatives of the scientific community and public bodies (according to the information contained in the Annual Report 2002 of the Ministry of Environment and Natural Resources, p. 100-106). It has also had a very active participation " *in the National Committee on Traditional Knowledge and Intellectual Property, along with the National Assembly, Ministry of Science and Technology, Ministry of Education Culture and Sports, Self Service for Intellectual Property of the Ministry of Production and Commerce, Ombudsman, National Indigenous Council of Venezuelan and the Organization of Indigenous Peoples of the Amazon. The Commission's main purpose is to develop, together with indigenous peoples and local communities, the mechanisms for participation in decision-making concerning the Previous Informed Consent; the fair and equitable sharing of benefits; and the protection of traditional knowledge associated with biological diversity*".

[22] As the so-called "Peach Palm", a fruit tree cultivated by indigenous peoples of the Amazon, in relation to which, it is stated in paragraph 103 of the study "*funded by USAID, agronomists have collected different genetic varieties of peach palm in order to develop a variety with commercial potential*". Although it is unknown when indigenous peoples began to cultivate this species, they will not receive any economic benefit that can be derived directly from that marketing. Rights to plant varieties that are unknown in any other part of the world due to natural changes in the original or artificially species may be protected by attending the 1961 International Plant Protection Convention. This conventional text requires that the plant remains "*according to its description after repeatedly reproduced and spread*". However, this text poses two problems: one, conceptual, since the Convention regulates the rights of individuals, and not of human groups; other economic, who seeks the protection must first meet the costs arising from the culture of the sample and subsequent tests that clearly show that the variety in question is stable and homogeneous.

[23] For example, in the 70s, the Mikmaqs fishermen of Nova Scotia, Canada, solved the problems caused by the cultivation of oysters in muddy places. Having regard to the result, the "*non-indigenous traders quickly copied his method, however, with better access to financial market. Consequently, fishermen got limited economic benefits with their discovery*" (Paragraph 104 Study of the Special Rapporteur). In these cases, indigenous peoples could have used –by knowing the possibility- the Geneva Treaty on the International Registration of scientific discovery (1978). However, the problem of such use is what a scientific discovery is, in accordance to Article 1: "*the recognition of phenomena, properties or laws of the material universe that had not been recognized or could not verify to date*" definition in which there is not always room for traditional indigenous knowledge.

If these practices lie outside its protection, it could be possible to try to patent this knowledge as "technology". The World Intellectual Property Organization (WIPO) document entitled "Elements of Industrial property" - published as Doc. WIPO/IP/AR/85/7-, understands technology as all knowledge to be useful, systematic and organized, capable of solving a specific problem and that can be transmitted to others. However, the patenting or not these traditional knowledge and technology will depend on what national legislation considers traditional knowledge sufficiently novel and inventive to be patentable.

24   The Convention on Biological Diversity (art. 8) establishes the obligation (flexible to the extent that it is an obligation of conduct and not of result) of States Parties ("as far as possible and as appropriate") to respect, preserve and maintain indigenous knowledge, taking appropriate measures in their legislations-with the participation of the peoples concerned-, although without any reference to the patentability thereof. The Venezuelan Biodiversity Act establishes the recognition of indigenous relevance on material scope regulated by it (as proclaimed in the art. 13).

25   According to WIPO Document entitled "Protection of inventions in the fields of biotechnology," published in Doc WIPO/IP/ND/87/2, the European Patent Convention prohibits the registration of species and biological processes, although legal systems in some countries allow patenting of modified or altered organisms, i.e., those who, as a result of human intervention, have different characteristics to those directly provided by nature.

26   Agreeing basis is in Decision 391 of the Cartagena Agreement Commission containing the Common Regime on Access to Genetic Resources. The article 7 states that Member States "*recognize and value the rights and authority of the native... to decide.... about their know-how, innovations and traditional practices associated with genetic resources and their products*".

27   In this regard to Articles 14, 17, 57 and 55 respectively of the Organic Law on Indigenous Peoples and Communities.

28   Specifically, see. Article 59 of the organic law on indigenous peoples and communities. Among the objectives of the National Bureau of Biological Diversity in 2003 the "*Study on the mechanisms for obtaining Previous and Informed Consent, and the Fair and equitable sharing of benefits arising from the use of biodiversity for peoples was indigenous and local communities* ", as referred to in the Annual Report 2002 of the Ministry of Environment and Natural Resources, p. 100-106. Also Article 11 regarding prior procedure and informed consultation with indigenous peoples and Article 146.16 both of the same Organic Law of Indigenous Peoples and Communities.

29   Data included in the text is found in Articles 19 and 17 respectively of the Organic Law on Indigenous Peoples and Communities. Meanwhile, the Kuna people of Panama has chosen to require all those who intend to conduct research in their territory "to pay an entrance fee, hire Kuna staff as guides and assistants, form Kuna scientists, submit copies of research reports to Kuna authorities, such as photographs and plant specimens". See this information in paragraph 108 of the study of the Special Rapporteur.

30   Against this is the Constitution of Bolivia (Article 171.I), incorporates the recognition of economic rights of indigenous peoples, without reference to the type of protection provided in relation to intellectual property of these groups or even, there are generally proclaiming a unique system for protecting intellectual property. What mean the recognition of the individual nature of these rights and the temporal limitation of its protection, as is the case of the Constitutions of Brazil (art. 5), Chile (art. 19), Colombia (art. 61), Costa Rica (art. 121), Guatemala (art. 42), Nicaragua (art. 125), Panama (art. 49), Paraguay (art. 119) and Peru (art. 2.8).

[31] Specifically, we refer to Chapter V, of the collective knowledge and intellectual property of indigenous peoples under Title IV, from education and culture, of the Organic Law on Indigenous Peoples and Communities.

[32] The Biodiversity Act (Article 85) states to be considered other than the right of private property *"when they correspond to a cumulative process of use and conservation of biological diversity."* Restricted to the material field covered in the Act but may be extrapolated to the general area.

[33] See Article 103 of the Organic Law on Indigenous Peoples and Communities. Also article 84 of the Law on biodiversity, that reflects the State's commitment to *"promote and protect the rights of indigenous peoples and local communities over their traditional knowledge related to biodiversity and the rights they enjoy collectively the benefits derived from them and be compensated for conserving their natural environments.*

[34] See Article 124 of the Constitution. Not to mention at this point that the objectives of the National Strategy for Biological Diversity (art. 17) is to establish the necessary mechanisms for the fair distribution of the benefits to be derived from biodiversity, especially *«in knowledge traditional, local and indigenous communities and their participation in the benefits».*

[35] This is in accordance with Articles 84 respectively and 45 of the said Act.

[36] Official Gazette No. 25,227 dated December 10, 1956. However, is to remember that Venezuela is not part of the Andean Community of Nations (ACN).

[37] Venezuela withdrew from CAN when President Hugo Chavez announced it at an April 19, 2006 meeting, and subsequently, in July 2006, Venezuela was admitted as full member of Mercosur. In this sense, a legal void could exist on the specific legal topic of intellectual property resulting from the non-applicability in Venezuela of Andean Community Decisions.

[38] Uzcátegui, A. & Aguilar, V. (2010). Indigenous collective rights and intellectual property in Venezuela. The case of the Pemon people . Yearbook of Law Legal Research Center at the University of the Andes, Mérida, Venezuela, 27, pp.161-201.

[39] For a more extended view of the problem and its constituents see our Preliminary thesis report entitled Aguilar, V. (2001). Between resistance and dissent. The indigenous question and challenges in current international relations. Tensions and conflicts in Venezuela, Geneva: IHEID. Collective rights can also be derived in relation to biodiversity.

[40] We were inspired by the notion used by Norbert Rouland for minorities. In our case, we propose to extend indigenous peoples since, as problematic, the right of indigenous peoples has as its starting point the principle of the right of peoples to self-determination.

[41] Resolution 8/83 of the 22 session of the FAO Conference, November, 1983.

[42] The notion of common heritage of mankind has a double meaning: from the point of view of development, the use of resources by all States is the "guarantee" that will not be over exploited by a single state. This is the standard set out in the Convention on the Law of the Sea 1982. From the ecological point of view, the non-appropriation of resources is the "guarantee" that will not be over used by the State in which they are located. This is the standard set out in the Antarctic Treaty of 1959. Thus, both notions underline the principle of use and resource exploitation over conservation.

[43] The consideration of the common heritage of humanity and repositories posed a problem in the field of intellectual property for the innovations resulting from research, which do not belong to humanity to be patent. In this sense, rooted in their biological support, the genetic resource would be declared the common heritage of mankind; worked, the genetic resource to be integrated protected by a variety breeder's certificate; isolated from their biological and capable of industrial

application support would become a patentable invention. The common heritage of mankind might work for genetic resources considered only from the physical point of the term. Noiville, C. (1997). *Ressources génétiques et droit. Essai sur les régimes juridiques des ressources génétiques marines*, Paris: Editions Pedone, pp.178.

[44] See also Resolution 4/89 25 Session of the FAO Conference, November 1989.

[45] The Convention is on the International Union for the Protection of New Varieties of Plants (UPOV), 1961.

[46] Aguilar, (2001). Ibid.p15.

[47] Although there is no explicit definition of what are collective rights in the declaration, the interpretation of several articles (6, 7, 8, 9, 32) that is not individualized set of rights whose violation affects a community or indigenous people. Ibid.

[48] Posey, D. (2004). International agreements and intellectual property right protection for indigenous peoples. In COICA, *Biodiversity, collective rights and sui generis intellectual property regime*, Ibid.44.

[49] Many authors give different rankings on the principle of self-determination. As for this general study and its application in the field of colonized peoples, in addition to the above at the end in the literature, we can mention among others: Crawford, J. (1988). *The Rights of peoples.* Oxford, England: Clarendon Press, p. 236; Obieta, J. (1993). *El derecho humano de la autodeterminación de los pueblos*, Madrid, Spain: Tecnos, p.251; Remiro-Brotons, A. (1982). *Derecho internacional. Principios fundamentales.* Madrid, Spain: Tecnos, p.341; Davies, E. W. (1995). *The legal status of british dependent territories. The West Indies and North Atlantic Region*, New York, N.Y.: Cambridge University Press, p. 376; Pomerance, M. (1982). *Self-determination in Law and Practice. The New doctrine in United Nations.* The Hague, Switzerland: Martinus Nijhoff, p. 154. As for the principle of self-determination in the context of states, we can mention among others, Brolmann, C., Lefeber & R., Zieck, M. (ed.) (1993). *Peoples and minorities in international law.* Amsterdam, Netherland: Martinus Nijhoff, p. 364; Chandra, S. (ed.) (1985). *Minorities in national and international laws.* New Delhi, India: Deep and Deep Publication, p. 376; Gurr, T. (1993). *Minorities at risk: A Global view of ethnopolitical conflicts.* Washington, DC: United States Institute of Peace Press, p. 427; Gurr, T. (1980). *Handbook of political conflict: Theory and research.* New York, N.Y.: Free Press, p. 566; Gnanapala, W. (2000). *Minorities claims: From autonomy to secession: International law and state practice.* Aldershot, England: Ashgate, p. 339; Hannum, H. (1990). *Autonomy, sovereignty and self-determination: The accomodation of conflicting rights.* Philadelphia, P.A.: University of Pennsylvania Press, p. 503; Thornberry, P. (1992). *International Law and the rights of minorities.* Oxford, England: Clarendon Press, p. 451; Oraa, J. (2000). *Textos básicos de derecho internacional público.* Bilbao: Universidad de Deusto, p. 374; Azcarate, P. (1998). *Minorías nacionales y derechos humanos.* Madrid, Spain: Congreso de los Diputados-Universidad Carlos III, p. 329; Hannum, H. (ed.) (1993). *Documents on autonomy and minority rights.* Dordrecht, Netherland: Martinus Nijhoff, p. 779. Finally, properly referring to self-determination of indigenous peoples, see: Kingsburry, B. & Roberts, A. (1994). *Presiding over a divided world: Changing UN roles 1945-1993.* London, England: International Peace Academy, p. 95; Hurrel, A. & Kingsburry, B. (ed.) (1992). *International politics of the environment: Actors, interest and institutions.* New York, N.Y., Oxford: University Press, p. 492; Tomuschat, C. (ed.) (1992). *Modern law of self-determination.* Dordrecht, Netherland: Martinus Nijhoff, p. 347; Brownlie, I. (1992). *Treaties and indigenous peoples.* Oxford, England: Clarendon Press, p. 105; Brownlie, I. (1999). *Los derechos*

humanos en un mundo dividido. Bilbao: Universidad de Deusto, p. 304; Fenet, A.; Koubi, Geneviève & Schulte-Tenckhoff, Isabelle (2000). *Le droit et les minorités. Analyses et textes.* (2ème Edition). Bruselles, Belgium: Bruylant, p. 661; Lerner, N. (1991). *Minorías y grupos en el derecho internacional: derecho y determinación.* México: Comisión Nacional de Derechos Humanos, p. 227; Mavian, L. (2000). *At the edge of the state: Indigenous peoples and self-determination.* New York, N.Y.: Transnational Publishers, p. 231; Duncan, I; Patton, P. & Sanders, W. (2000). *Political theory and the rights of indigenous peoples.* Cambridge-New York, N.Y.: Cambridge University Press, p. 323; Urban, G. & Sherzer, J. (1991). *Nations-States and indians in Latin America.* Austin, T.X.: University of Texas Press, p. 335. The Human Rights Commission also established a criterion in this issue by performing two interpretations as to self: one internal self-determination (autonomy), and the other the right of people to freely choose their international status (free external determination) .See ECOSOC, Doc. E/2256, Suplemento No.4, XIV Sessions. For purposes of this paper we have drawn on the classification made by Torrecuadrada, S. (2001). *Los pueblos indígenas en el orden internacional.* Madrid: Editorial Dykinson, p. 192.

[50] For authors such as Stavenhagen self-determination and free-determination are used interchangeably. C.f. Stavenhagen, R. (2001). The ethnic question. México: Colegio de México, p.111. However, in the discussion of the right to self-determination as the main feature of free-determination, experts insist that in the latter range is also contained.

[51] Among the most important distinguishing features are: the relationship with the land by indigenous peoples; self-identification; claim the principle of self-determination in their condition as 'peoples', relying on Article 1 common to the two international human rights covenants and not only in Article 27 of the International Covenant on Civil and Political Rights; treaties between indigenous peoples and their predecessors with the colonial powers of the time; historical continuity with the original inhabitants of the region.

[52] Doc. UN E/CN.4/Sub.2/1999/18.

[53] Doc. UN E/CN.4/2000/84.

[54] Later in the year 1993 will be renamed the Working Group on Indigenous Peoples.

[55] Before the ILO Convention 169 was elaborated, Convention 107 had been developed within the same institution. With the evolution of international law, changes occurring on indigenous and tribal peoples are given worldwide, which begin to be addressed from a new law that fits the new context, becoming a rethinking of the principles of the Convention adopting the convention 107 and 169.

[56] Convention No. 169 has been ratified in Venezuela in2001 and the UN Declaration on the Rights of Indigenous Peoples in 2007. It has also been developed a whole national indigenous legal framework which is enshrined in the Constitution of the Bolivarian Republic of Venezuela, the Organic Law of Indigenous Peoples and Communities and in the Special Law of Demarcation and Guarantee of Habitat and Lands of Indigenous Peoples and Communities among others.

[57] Álamo, O. (n.d). *Pueblos Indígenas, Democracia y Gobernabilidad en la Región Andina.* Retrieved from: www.focal.ca/pdf/alamo.pdf

Chapter 6
Patents and Scientific Research:
Five Paradoxical Scenarios

Sulan Wong
Universidad Católica de Temuco, Chile

ABSTRACT

It is argued that patents encourage scientific development, benefiting society by creating useful products and services that improve the quality of life. However, by granting exclusive rights of exploitation, patents create situations in which they interfere with the exercise of the freedom of scientific research. This work examines five scenarios where this problem can be seen and the utilitarian function of patents is questioned. Firstly, the effects of research funding in the definition of the lines and research objectives are observed. Secondly, the anticommons is studied, as it is a situation where excessive fragmentation of ownership in scientific knowledge may prevent its use. Thirdly, broad patents and their implications are examined. Fourthly, the deterrent power of patent litigation, which creates an unexpected business model, is analyzed. Fifthly, secrecy is looked upon, as it is encouraged by the logic in which the patent system works.

INTRODUCTION

Intellectual property rights, in general, and patents, in particular, give their holders exclusive rights over creations and discoveries. This legal right, or *ius prohibendi*, conferred with a patent, implies that no one can legally use an invention without prior permission from its holder. These exclusive rights are granted as an incentive for the return of investment made in research, in exchange for the disclosure of the invention so that others can use it.

However, if patents would promote innovation in the terms in which it is said, one must ask why there are groups who claim that the open and free access to knowledge is essential to the advancement of science. For them, patents have not been the main incentive for scientific and technological innovation. By contrast, patents create situations in science that challenge their utilitarian purpose, since the *ius prohibendi* granted to the patent holder enables the flow of ideas to be blocked, hindering the exercise of the freedom of scientific research.

DOI: 10.4018/978-1-4666-8336-5.ch006

Indeed, in the scientific community there are initiatives to migrate to platforms that ensure the free exchange of scientific results, offering incentives different to those of the patent. A paradigmatic example is the free software movement, where creators collaborate on improving and expanding the available knowledge base by ensuring the so-called "four freedoms": use, study and modification, redistribution, and improvement and publication.

The romantic notion of science, in which the scientist is lost in thought searching for a "eureka" moment, provides an individualistic view of the intellectual creation that denies any possibility of defining knowledge as a collective and cumulative process. As such, science requires full and open communication of their findings. This requirement does not arise from selfish whims, but both from the requirements of the scientific method, and an inherent need for the production of scientific knowledge: knowledge requires knowledge to be created.

In practice, patentes generate a series of situations that reveal a conflict between intellectual property rights, freedom of scientific research and free exchange of knowledge in science. The situations encountered in which patents interfere with the free exercise of scientific research are presented in this chapter as follows. Firstly, the effects of public research funding in the definition of the lines and research objectives are observed. Secondly, the *anticommons* is studied, as it is a situation where excessive fragmentation of ownership in scientific knowledge may prevent its use. Thirdly, broad patents and their implications are examined. Fourthly, the deterrent power of patent litigation is analyzed, as it may discourage research, while creating an unexpected business model. Fifthly, secrecy is looked upon, as it is encouraged by the logic in which the patent system works. Finally, the last section is composed of some discussion and the conclusions reached in this work.

FUNDING

Independently of the domain, scientific research "economics" includes a series of expenditures to completely fulfill the objectives of a research project. Any project will require the acquisition of books, journals, equipment and supplies, the payment of wages, travel expenses and institutional overheads. For any researcher willing to carry on his line of research, the logical question would be "where do I find the required economic resources?" Thus, the long pilgrimage of researchers and research institutions begins.

Not all universities or research centers have the same infrastructure and budget to execute research projects proposed by their researchers, so lines of research are carefully selected. Nevertheless, belonging to one of the selected lines of research does not ensure financial support of a researcher's project. In some domains of science, competition for funding can be so frustrating that researchers feel their peers systematically shun them out. Even if funded, the amount assigned to a research project delimits a hard boundary to its scope. Furthermore, competition is also increased by research teams that belong to the industrial sector, more focused in "products" that could be profitable and, therefore, more attractive to investment[1].

Funding must come from an actor with a clear interest in the line of research followed by a researcher. The State tries to partially cover the lines of research that are more adapted to its strategic planning, leaving the rest behind. Private sector, through nonprofit foundations, philanthropic grants, crowdfunding[2] or NGO-backed initiatives, finances some other research lines. However, those with more profitability potential are usually funded by the industry, which offers support in exchange for a participation in the potential economic benefits derived from the commercialization of the intellectual products[3]; access to intellectual property rights on the results of scientific research are deemed as an strong incentive to corporate funding of science (Azagra-Caro, Carayol, & Llerena, 2006) .

The relations between industry, university and government institutions have been reinforced and encouraged by governments through R&D plans that are aimed to partially unload the funding burden into the private sector[4]. Nevertheless, it is possible that hidden indirect costs might be indirectly transferred from funding firms to universities, as the former would not have to incur in recurrent costs generated by the installation and maintenance of their own research laboratories (Godin & Gingras, 2000, p. 277; Barge Gil, Modrego Rico, & Santamaría Sánchez, 2006, p. 58).

Moreover, due to private funding, university research groups would have to align their research topics with those of private funding groups. What apparently is not taken into account in the public-private relations of scientific research, is that interest from different actors are no necessarily the same: the industry obviously wants to ensure a return of its investment, while universities -at least the public ones- want to generate knowledge that contributes to social wellbeing. Despite this difference in objectives, we can see how the public sector pursues the private sector, and R&D programs have successfully get this imperfect match work, with the end result that publicly funded research products leave the public sphere to become private[5].

In exchange over control of the direction and subjects of a research project, corporations offer irresistible incentives to their academic partners (Evans, 2001): money for facilities, equipment, experiments, tests and personnel. Universities provide knowledge and technology for industrial and economic development. Thus, the work of a research team ends up with some discovery of certain industrial application. Industry does not risk capital investing in projects whose results, at the very least, do not offer the possibility of obtaining a patent and, primarily, a new product for the market. As Krimsky (2003) explains, universities primarily exist to offer a highly trained workforce to the industrial sector, one that helps in the transformation of knowledge in technology, technology in productivity, and productivity in revenues. In this sense, and before university-industry relationships are deemed "profitable", it would be good to ask ourselves, who funds whom (Olivieri, 2003, p. 37)?

In the scientific and academic world, private investment should not replace public expenditure[6], nor should it be tolerated or legalized that the results of publicly funded research is privatized through technological transfer processes. When this happens, when the conception of science as a social process which is both collective and cumulative, where achievements are products of trust relationships, the rhetoric of the scarcity of "intellectual products" is introduced and the free flow of scientific results is hindered by private interests. Freedom of research is left to a rhetorically loaded expectation, where the research is bounded to the "will" of technoscience.

ANTICOMMONS

In medieval England, the common fields were fields for plowing, on which, once the crop was raised, a common right of open grazing was established for all members of a community. Hardin (1968) developed a metaphor based on this traditional form of resource management to establish the hypothesis of its essay "The tragedy of the *commons*". The "tragedy" makes reference to a situation of overuse of a resource shared in an open access regime[7], i.e., a resource on which nobody could legally exclude someone else from using it. To avoid resource depletion by overexploitation or overuse, Hardin proposed privatization as a solution. Now, what happens when establishing proprietary forms excessively fragments resources? Heller (1998) believes that the evolution of common resources to proprietary forms can cause another problem, which he coined, in contrast to the Hardian tragedy, the "tragedy of the *anticommons*".

Heller explains that if there is a regime in which everybody has the privilege of using the resource as much as they want and in which no one has a right to exclude, as in the *commons*, then there may be a regime in which no one has the privilege to use the resource and everyone has the right of exclusion. Because in an *anticommons* regime there is a right of exclusion, using the resource is conditional upon the consent of all the commoners; this means that at times the ability to effectively use a scarce resource can be denied. The right of exclusion, acquired with the establishment of private property over the resource, has value, because those who want to use the resource must pay for the right to use it. When the amount to pay exceeds the payment capacity of the interested party, which often occurs because owners tend to overvalue their right of exclusion or the value of their property, we find the emergence of an *anticommons*.

The tragic sense of the anticommons is determined by the extreme difficulty of getting out once it has occurred[8]. As we see, if the tragedy of the *commons* arises from overuse of the resource, that of the *anticommons* arises from its underutilization[9].

It was also Heller who, with Eisenberg (1998), extrapolated the tragedy of the *anticommons* to the contemporary debate on intellectual property, wondering whether patents could discourage innovation and, therefore, scientific research. The example used in their article is the privatization of biomedical research, either through the system of intellectual property protection, through private financing of research conducted in public institutions or arrangements that restrict the use of materials and data. Through these forms of private appropriation of knowledge the result of research is claimed, blocking access to knowledge that not so long ago might have been freely available in the public domain.

Privatization can lead to serious problems when too many owners hold rights on previous findings that constitute obstacles to future research. Upstream patent rights[10], initially offered to help attract more private investment and in the public sector encouraged by laws such as the U.S. Bayh-Dole Act[11], give researchers a new incentive beyond recognition and esteem; the researcher becomes co-inventor on a patent, with the benefit of any royalties generated under material transfer agreement[12]. Consequently, an overwhelming number of patent applications, each having a different owner, has reached even higher in the flow of scientific research. Then, there arises a tragedy in the form of an *anticommons*, which is even more critical than the simple underuse of knowledge.

With each patent granted on basic research, another toll appears on the course of the research cycle, adding costs and slowing the pace of downstream research. The result is the delay and cancellation of development projects of useful products.

In their work, Heller and Eisenberg (1998) point out that transaction costs of grouping rights can have a long-term effect. Public institutions have limited resources to address them and usually give up quickly, unlike private companies, which have strong legal teams dedicated to negotiate agreements. This heterogeneity of interests and resources among rightholders difficults the application of standard solutions to reduce transaction costs[13].

Transaction costs appear early in the flow of R&D, when there is high uncertainty in project's profit, so it is unknown if in solving the *anticommons* one ends up with a product too expensive. For this reason, patent owners tend to overvalue their inventions, so that each one believes patent is the gateway to a research area, requiring downstream product developers a higher price than that of the market.

Anticommons in research may occur in the form of concurrent fragments or stacked licenses. The former is found when in the course of a research project, licenses from a myriad of patent holders, each owning a piece of the technology required for the creation process, are required. The later arises when in a project it is required to license technologies which in turn have required *Reach-through Licence Agreements* (RTLA). This type of licenses, allows the patentee to obtain royalties for any development that depends directly or indirectly on his patent. In practice, RTLAs can lead to an *anticommons,* as upstream owners stack their overlapped and inconsistent claims about products that are developed downstream. Patent thickets[14] may lead to negotiate with innumerable and unknown upstream patent holders, which can render downstream research impractical[15].

In both cases, the licensing of patents in upstream research creates high transaction costs, long before anyone can tell whether the investigation will generate sufficient income to carry it out. Transaction costs grow quickly when discoveries in basic research, necessary for the subsequent work, belong to many actors (Rai & Eisenberg, 2003). Given the difficulty of solving the problem of high transaction costs, the emergence of an *anticommons* will be very difficult to overcome[16].

Rationality, in the economic sense, is the engine that drives patent owners to make the decision that gives more financial benefits, even if it means closing every access to a line of research to all stakeholders, placing freedom of research at serious risk.

BROAD PATENTS

A patent gives its owner the right to prohibit, that without his authorization, third parties from using the patented invention. This *ius prohibendi* will be as broad as the patent's claims, as they define the scope of legal protection; thus, a patent can be able to block whole areas of research. The problem of broad patents is that they can stretch into a variety of products or applications, including those in scientific and industrial sectors initially unconnected with the patentees, even if these products or applications were not enabled in their patents (Barton, 1996-1997, p. 459). The broader the claims in a patent, the more likely is for a researcher to incur in an infringement while working on ideas close to them. Hence, it is asserted that broad patents often discourage further innovation[17] by other researchers in the general field of the patent (Commission on Intellectual Property Rights, 2002; Barbosa & Grau-Kuntz, 2009) and create dependency issues (COM(2002) 545 Final). For example, the discussion on broad patents is common in research related to software, genetics and chemistry, because these areas of science are based on basic and primordial structures that, once fenced, could discourage or prevent subsequent research[18].

Moreover, as the success of the legal protection of an invention depends on the claims, the rational behavior is to seek a scope of protection that is as wide as possible, obtaining rights beyond what was originally described in the invention. Barton (1996-1997, p. 456) founds an explanation for this, derived from the inefficiency of the system to limit the scope of what is patentable when the burden of proof lies with patent offices. The applicant obtains a broad patent, because he is not required to demonstrate that the scope of what is claimed was not sufficiently described, as this is an obligation of the patent office, which must review and determine if some claims in the patent application are unfounded.

Instead, patent offices, as revealed by Drahos (2010), have allowed that the "art" of writing broad patents is inserted into patent systems, through the acceptance of standard claiming formats[19], that once accepted by those offices will begin to be used by patent attorneys. The goal is no other than seeking to legally guarantee, by administrative authority, the broadest control over future research. Patent offices, which do not have the means to restrict broad claims through a costly comprehensive review, end up granting patents whose exploitation rights go beyond what is claimed. The problem emerges *a posteriori*, when another inventor is denied the possibility of carrying out an investigation, because the holder of a broad patent argues that the invention of the former is included in his claims. Therefore, is only subsequent research that reveals the breadth of the claims granted by a patent office[20].

A patent discloses only one or a few embodiments of invention in a patent's specification, but will claim often thousands of various embodiments in a claim (Sichelman, 2010, pp. 356-357). For example, a recent study by Kepler, Crossman and Cook-Deegan (2010) on the scope of the claims of patent 4,747,282 on the BRCA1 gene[21], has found that chromosome 1 (which does not contain the BRCA genes) comprises 300,000,000 oligonucleotides covered by these claims, and that 80% of the sequences of cDNA and mRNA contributed to GenBank before the patent was requested, also contained at least one oligonucleotide claimed by the patent. In summary, any isolated DNA molecule comprising the nucleotide sequences 15bp would fall under the claims granted by the USPTO[22].

This case is hardly an exception in biotechnology. When researchers introduce a patent application, it would be virtually impossible to know all the functions of a genetic sequence; however, this issue does not prevent researchers from seeking broad claims that will not coincide with that described in the application. Many researchers have expressed concerns about the patentability of genes whose precise function is unknown at the time of patent application, as this will impede future research to discover the detailed and substantial functional role of this gene (Jackson, 2010, p. 13). In a letter to Mark Nagumo, then commissioner of USPTO, twelve scientists in genetics of National Advisory Council for Human Genome Research expressed concern about the breadth of claims allowed in patents of genes. They argued that these claims discouraged research, stifling scientific discovery, because recognizing broad and poorly substantiated claims creates, as a matter of fact, an unacceptable monopoly in every field in which the new gene could be used (Burke et al., 2000). This concern is confirmed in the econometric study of Huang and Murray (2009), who concluded that gene patents reduce public knowledge in genetics. This is an effect exacerbated by the breadth of patents, the appropriation by the private sector, the complexity of the patent landscape and the commercial relevance of genes[23].

Due to broad patents, the original incentive that is theoretically seeked, that of giving encouragement to research, becomes meaningless or self-contradictory, as they seem to cause the opposite effect when used to prevent the entry of new actors in specific areas of research.

LITIGATION CULTURE

A patent is a legal instrument that gives its holder[24] a set of rights enforceable against third parties. These rights allow the holder of the patent, unless otherwise provided, to prevent any uses of the invention without permission. In the event that a third party uses the invention without the authorization of the patent holder, he can go to court to enforce his rights. Understanding the power conferred by this legal privilege, together with how costly it can be to stand trial and the difficulty of knowing whether a patent is being infringed[25], in practice, litigation has become a clear business strategy for financial gain and to maintain a dominant position in the market. This being so, we wonder in this section if this strategy, which some might see as a simple abuse of the system weaknesses, leads patents to work out, rather than as an incentive, as a barrier to innovation and access to knowledge.

The fact that any inventor who has improved an invention, may be involved in a patent litigation causes that strengthening intellectual property rights does not always provide an incentive for research (Merges & Nelson, 1990, p. 616). Since in some areas of science development is done at a fast pace, it is possible that among the different competitors it is established a real litigation network, in which all sides accuse each other of violating their patent portfolio. A case is shown by Heller (2008), who offers a snapshot of a litigation network arising around genetic microarrays, diagnostic tools in which multiple genetic probes attached to microchips are used to screen the information contained in a genome.

Each area of science and technology develops its own network of litigation, although in recent times the one that has captured the world's attention is that which arose around mobile devices and their operating systems. Nokia, Apple, Samsung, Microsoft and Google, for example, have been directly or indirectly entangled in their own judicial and administrative litigation network, before both local and international courts. Corporations often fall into asymmetric games in patent litigation (Chien, 2009, p. 1610). Apple, with a broad portfolio of patents, probably started its "battle" with HTC because this was a relatively new and small company with little innovation, compared to giants like Samsung and Google; with fewer patents to face judicial actions, it was, therefore, an easier piece to remove from the game. Even if Samsung's important size as an actor in the telecommunications and consumer electronics market is not disputed, before getting in the ring with Google, Apple prefers to face it; the result has been a series of defeats for the Korean transnational, although at a considerable cost to both firms.

Google does not sue Apple for patent infringement perhaps for the same reason that Apple does not sue Google. It is a similar scenario to that experienced in the Cold War, as both contenders are putting together their patent portfolios to avoid an attack from the other, and each one is deterred from attacking the other for fear of the outcome. Google, which has acquired patents from Motorola and IBM, gave patents to HTC and Samsung so that they could face litigation brought by Apple, and in response could countersue. However, Google has been sued by Oracle, who accuses it that its Android operating system infringe certain patents that the latter has on Java, a programming language used to develop Android. On the other hand, and parallel to litigation, HTC agreed to pay Microsoft (2010) some preemptive compensation, consisting on royalties for each Android phone sold by HTC, thus avoiding to open another front of battle.

In this legal maelstrom, Microsoft, RIM, Sony Ericsson and Apple beat Google in the acquisition of a large batch of patents from Nortel, the Canadian telecommunications transnational; Rockstar, the consortium responsible for the administration of these patents, has served as a facade for indirect litigation of Apple-Microsoft against Google-Samsung as well as other smaller manufacturers of Android-based devices. Google, in turn, has responded with a lawsuit against Rockstar. As observed in this last case, patents have also been used to create a business model that was not foreseen, becoming an interesting phenomenon. We refer to the derogatorily called "patent troll"[26], a company or individual in the private sector who does not conduct research to obtain patents, but that acquires patents from other inventors, usually in financial distress, in order to enforce them against third parties when infringement of the claims has already been allegedly committed[27], obtaining economic benefits through licensing, royalties and compensation (McDonough, 2006–2007, p. 189). This behavior, abusive even for advocates of the IP system, makes trolls being characterized as actors in bad faith[28]. Therefore, trolls are actors in the patent system that, by developing an opportunistic behavior, interfere with innovation (Lemley, 2008).

A troll takes advantage of the fact that going to court for patent infringement can generate large costs for the parties involved. Therefore, it seems valid to think that, given the threat of patent infringement, anyone being accused of it eventually abandons his research, the provision of a service or the manufacture of a product, thus avoiding litigation[29], either because he does not have the resources needed to face it, or because though he has them, the risk of losing the case and the amount of compensation sought are very high. Even if he can continue with his research, in order to end litigation he must reach agreements that may not be favorable (Holman, 2008).

One argument used in defense of trolls is that they help independent inventors to defend their intellectual property. Bessen, Ford, and Meurer (2011) explain that lawsuits filed in American courts have cost mainly technology corporations nearly 80 billion dollars a year, from 2007 to 2010. For these authors, such losses of wealth become, in fact, an irreparable social loss, for less than 2% of the defendants' losses are transferred from trolls to independent inventors. Although this figure seems small, some doubt lingers on over whether it would drive innovation. Bessen et al. (2011) refute the argument, explaining that, firstly, such a large loss is a disincentive for large corporations with a large investment in R&D. Moreover, defendants rarely have deliberately copied the technology, but rather it has been infringed accidentally, so they have to estimate the risk of losses from future claims as part of the costs of their product and technology developments. This disincentive would be much larger than any of the possible incentives generated by transfers to independent inventors through the trolls. Secondly, due to the risk of lawsuits filed by trolls, corporations would reduce what they would pay to independent inventors for licenses. Finally, intensive litigation by trolls encourages them to get extremely broad and vague patents that, as we have seen, seem to be legitimized by the courts. Therefore, investment in innovation of products useful to society would be reduced.

SECRECY

The exchange of ideas, research results and knowledge has been consistent practice in science. Conferences, seminars and publications in journals are some of the natural mechanisms of communication in science. A quick and direct access to any scientific communication, regardless of origin or destination, can be guaranteed thanks to the development of Internet. One can say that both sharing and communicating are part of the *ethos* of science (Merton, 1973; Guédon, 2001).

Science as a social institution implies that its findings should not be assigned to a particular researcher, but rather to the scientific community[30]. The fact that science acquires a communal nature implies that its findings should be shared, and thus their full and open communication is required. Furthermore, if the recognition of peers and society in general for contributing to the common pool of knowledge is expected, the findings should be reported to the scientific community as soon as obtained (Ziman, 2000). Therefore, publishing serves as an incentive for the recognition and appreciation of achievements in science. Nevertheless, other incentives in science seem to curb the practice of communalism, encouraging scientists to keep their work secret[31]: patenting and commercial exploitation of research results.

Disclosure

It is argued that patents allow the transfer and incorporation of knowledge into the public domain, once the legal period of protection of the invention has expired. The disclosure of the invention in exchange for the legal monopoly conferred may meet this objective, if the patents were drafted in full, clear, accurate and simple terms, if the inventor would not withhold for himself any relevant information and if any person skilled on the subject could replicate the invention.

Patent documents, however seem to show that this objective is not entirely achieved, as patent drafters use a language that is rather vague (Lemley, 2011, p. 72), omitting details essential to replicate the invention (Feldman, 2009), i.e., they provide an incomprehensible revelation. Using as an example the controversial US Patent 5,960,411, granted to Amazon for its Internet one-click shopping system, Boldrin and Levine (2008, p. 189) show how software patent claims do not include any information that a programmer could use to continue developing systems on the same line of work. The source code for the specific implementation of Amazon is not even included in the patent document as it is not required.

The lack of a legal requirement becomes a clear incentive not to disclose the source code in software patents, but instead claims are established through functional description of the software, since this way all its possible implementations, regardless of the programming language used, are included (Canfield, 2006, p. 15). In addition, patent offices seem to ignore their role as guarantors of the contract the inventor enters into with society, collaborating with the obscurity of the patent by not requiring the disclosure of the invention in a clear language (Drahos, 2010, pp. 29–30). The art of drafting obscure patents, which the Supreme Court of the United States (Brenner v. Manson 383 U.S. 519, § 24) interpreted as the ability to write patent claims that would not disclose the information needed to replicate the invention, in addition ends imposing itself on a global level through the recognition of the invention in the regional and national patent offices, showing that patents could hardly be useful tools for knowledge transfer[32].

Novelty

For an invention to qualify as patentable, among other requirements it must be novel[33]. This requirement, which is common among intellectual property laws throughout the world, means that the invention has not been disclosed previously. This requirement, in practice, encourages researchers seeking to patent the results of their research, not to disclose them. Even where legislation allows publication prior to a patent application, the usual legal advice is not publishing before the patent application is introduced. Thus, to ensure novelty, the natural mechanisms of communication in science are affected, because they are seen as conducive to waiving the patentability requirement[34].

Secrecy is not attacked[35] in research conducted in both public and private academic circles, as not all universities have established clear policies requiring disclosure of research. For example, a study by the American NIH found that 55% of all American universities required disclosure for the research made by their entire faculty, while 45% required it only for the principal investigator (Krimsky, 2003, p. 207). In today's academic world, it is difficult to find an academic center with policies contrary to the logic of patenting-then-publishing.

Conflicts of interest arise in the decision between publishing or patenting the results of scientific research as a strategy to manage intellectual property (European Commission, 2002b). As Kenney (1987, p. 129) explains, the primary "duty" and main concern of the industry to its investors is to achieve benefits. This concern leads to an ethical conflict in relations between industry and academia, especially with regard to freedom of scientific research, as for the purposes of a patent, industry's best strategy will be secrecy[36].

In contrast, it is expected of a scientist who believes in open science and the free exchange of research results, disclosure of the results of the investigation as soon as they have been obtained[37]. When these competing interests coincide in an R&D project, conflict arises as the academic researcher tries to follow the ethical norm of communalism and strictly comply with the industrial required secrecy,

Patents and Scientific Research

which is enforced by confidentiality clauses. If a researcher under these restrictions attempts to publish the results of his research, considering them in the public interest, the paper can be blocked and he can be threatened with the enforcement of confidentiality agreements[38]. It is no longer the researcher who decides how far he goes with his work and what will he do with the results. The funding partners are the ones who, with their contractual restrictions, decide where the freedom of the researcher ends. Hence, the researcher should not expect that a funding partner, with a clear commercial interest in the results of the research, allows their publication without permission. The researcher should never give veto power over his publication rights, because expecting the veto holder not to use it to protect his interests is acting naively (Drummond, 1997).

DISCUSSION AND CONCLUDING REMARKS

In science, intellectual property rights in general and patents in particular impose restrictions which prevent that knowledge could be of open access and diffusion. When in science, researchers are unable to access the knowledge needed to build more knowledge, the exercise of the right of freedom of scientific research is reduced to sheer expectation. Individualistic claims on knowledge, which are sheltered under the cloak of intellectual property rights, tend to ignore its social nature, disregarding the contribution made by others in its construction. It is, as Shiva (2001, p. 21) explained:

The myth that patents contribute to the stimulation of creativity and inventiveness [...] is based on an artificial construction of knowledge and innovation –that of knowledge being isolated in time and space, without being connected to the social fabric and contributions from the past.

Whether patents encourage or impede the progress of scientific development is a debate that is still open. In this chapter we contribute to it by showing that there are five paradoxical scenarios that allow us to support the thesis that patents, rather than encouraging innovation, creation and progress in science, becomes an obstacle in the exercise of the freedom of scientific research.

Firstly, scientific funding policies continue to identify the scientific production mode under the linear model that separates basic from applied research, feeding the latter with the results of the former. This conventional taxonomy reflects the need to quantify results and establish research priorities in purely economic terms, with which funding can be allocated. Programs promoted under the label R&D, derived from this taxonomy, allow private ownership of scientific research developed in academia. Before participating in a research project, the industry seeks to ensure the return on investment in R&D, requiring, e.g. the exclusive rights of commercial exploitation of the invention. This requirement is not left to chance, but is the result of the careful choice made by industry of the research lines whose results are potentially patentable. Knowledge is reduced to a purely mercantile expression and once patented, it would be no longer available[39], becoming a product that allows the industry to control a market.

Secondly, the desire to obtain patents in areas such as biotechnology and information technology can lead to the excessive proprietary fragmentation of scientific knowledge, which may even prevent knowledge's use as a fundamental tool for the development of new inventions. The so-called anticommons is configured as a minefield that facilitates infringement, since it would be impossible for a researcher to know both every patent holder and all patented inventions, before he begins with his research. Furthermore, when scientific research depends on multiple licenses to move forward, the scientist is subject to a licensing game with multiple owners. Therefore, transaction costs in time and money are increased, slowing down progress. In addition, negotiations can be complex since they involve many and sometimes diffuse owners. Research then leaves the lab to be set at the negotiating table, a field where it is clearly at a disadvantage.

Thirdly, with the provision of "broad" patents, which ensure that the scope of protection goes beyond that originally described in claims, entire research lines can be blocked, even in unrelated areas. Patents are usually granted on building blocks for scientific progress, even on those that even the inventors are unaware of all their properties; trying to invent around the patent, reverse engineer it or develop applications not covered by the patent is not possible, as the building blocks of knowledge are fenced for any use in any area of science.

Fourthly, the litigation culture inherent to the patent system has given rise to two unintended effects; on one hand there are dynamic networks of litigation in which the dominant firms of an area of high technological development and competitiveness are involved, due to the patent minefield in which scientific research is carried out. On the other hand, we find the so-called "patent trolls", entities that are not dedicated to scientific research, but that hoard a broad portfolio of patents with which they harass researchers and firms with the threat of litigation. In both cases, the high costs involved in facing litigation for patent infringement, the consequences of judicial action to order the cessation of the research activity and the bargaining power that grants a large portfolio of patents, may lead to the abandonment of research. Otherwise, researchers are forced to negotiate licensing agreements at a disadvantage.

Fifthly, it is said that patents encourage the disclosure of the invention, which would otherwise remain secret. Disclosure would assist in the transfer of knowledge into the public domain, but this could only be achieved when it would be made in a manner understandable to a person skilled on the subject, so that, from it, anyone can really study, learn, create and innovate. A patent drafted in vague, ambiguous and abstract terms cannot be disclosing an invention on the terms expected by society. The trust relationship between the inventor and society, that leads to tolerate the good monopoly in knowledge, is broken. When this point is reached, patents lose all value as incentives to disclosure, because it does not really happen. The requirement of novelty of the invention and patentability requirement, neither contributes to strengthen open access nor dissemination of knowledge. It reinforces, however, secrecy, altering the natural communication channels of the open science. Given the need to ensure the novelty, the researcher must avoid by any means, the dissemination of research results. Before submitting a simple abstract to a conference, the researcher may have to review the confidentiality provisions set out in his contract, unless he wants to get involved in a litigious situation.

With the situations discussed here, it appears that the legal-political-philosophical foundations of modernity that paved the way for the appropriation of knowledge through the patent, emphasizing its role in promoting innovation and the progress of science, can hardly stand today. Free software can announce it: patents have not been, and will not be the engine that drives software developers to progress, create and innovate. The General Purpose License (GPL[40]) has allowed innovating as much or even more than large technology industries. Free software keeps open the debate between those who defend and promote the need for patents as an incentive to scientific innovation and those for which the patent is an obstacle to free and open access to knowledge. In this discussion, there is an underlying problem of restriction of liberty that has been given little attention, being displaced by the emphasis given to the alleged practical benefits of the patent for social welfare. Having the right to freedom of scientific research means to have the tools to make this right attainable, otherwise, it will be reduced to sheer expectation.

ACKNOWLEDGMENT

This paper is part of the project "Análisis, sistematización, fundamentación y evaluación de las nuevas formas de regulación jurídica" (DER2011-28594) of the Universitat de Barcelona, which was supported by the Spanish Ministry of Science and Innovation.

Sulan Wong is with the Grupo de Investigaciones Jurídicas (GIJ) of the Universidad Católica de Temuco, Chile.

REFERENCES

Arrow, K. J. (1962). Economic welfare and the allocation of resources for invention. In he rate and direction of inventive activity: economic and social factors (pp. 609–626). Princeton, NJ: Princeton University Press.

Azagra-Caro, J. M., Carayol, N., & Llerena, P. (2006). Patent production at a European research university: Exploratory evidence at the laboratory level. *The Journal of Technology Transfer, 31*(2), 257–268. doi:10.1007/s10961-005-6110-3

Baldini, N., Grimaldi, R., & Sobrero, M. (2007). To patent or not to patent? A survey of Italian inventors on motivations, incentive and obstacles to university patenting. *Scientometrics, 70*(2), 333–354. doi:10.1007/s11192-007-0206-5

Barge Gil, A., Modrego Rico, A., & Santamaría Sánchez, L. (2006). *El proceso de transferencia tecnológica universidad-empresa*. Barcelona: Fundaciò Empresa i Ciéncia.

Barton, J. H. (1996-1997). Patents and antitrust: A rethinking in light of patent breadth and sequential innovation. *Antitrust Law Journal, 65*, 449–466.

Bessen, J., Ford, J., & Meurer, M. (2012). The private and social costs of patent trolls. *Regulation, 34*(4), 26–35.

Boldrin, M., & Levine, D. K. (2008). *Against intellectual monopoly*. Cambridge, UK: Cambridge University Press.

Borges Barbosa, D., & Grau-Kuntz, K. (2009). *Exclusions from patentable subject matter and exceptions and limitations to the rights*. WIPO SCP/15/3, Annex III. Retrieved from http://www.wipo.int/edocs/mdocs/scp/en/scp_15/scp_15_3-annex3.pdf

Brenner *v.* Manson 383 U.S. 519 (1966)

Bruce, J. W. (1998). Review of tenure terminology. *Tenure Brief, 1*, 1–8.

Buck Cox, S. J. (1985). No tragedy on the commons. *Environmental Ethics, 7*.

Burke, W., Buxbaum, J. N., Chakravarti, A., Horvitz, H. R., Kucherlapati, R., Lawrence, J., … Williamson, A. (2000, March 21). *Letter to the commissioner of patents and trademarks*. Retrieved from http://www.uspto.gov/web/offices/com/sol/comments/utilguide/nih.pdf

Canfield, K. (2006). The disclosure of source code in software patents: Should software patents be open source? *The Columbia Science and Technology Law Review, 7*, 1–25.

Capel, H. (2003). El drama de los bienes comunes. la necesidad de un programa de investigación. *Biblio 3W, Revista Bibliográfica de Geografía y Ciencias Sociales, 8*(458).

Chien, C. V. (2009). Of Trolls, Davids, Goliaths, and Kings: Narratives and evidence in the litigation of high-tech patents. *North Carolina Law Review, 87*, 1571–1615.

Cho, M., Illangasekare, S., Weaver, M. A., Leonard, D. G. B., & Merz, J. F. (2003). Effects of patents and licenses on the provision of clinical genetic testing services. *The Journal of Molecular Diagnostics, 5*(1), 3–8. doi:10.1016/S1525-1578(10)60444-8 PMID:12552073

Clarkson, G., & Dekorte, D. (2006). The problem of patent thickets in convergent technologies. *Annals of the New York Academy of Sciences: Covergent Technologies, 1093*(1), 180–200. doi:10.1196/annals.1382.014 PMID:17312259

Commission on Intellectual Property Rights. (2002). *Report of the commission on intellectual property rights: Integrating intellectual property rights and development policy.* Retrieved from http://www.iprcommission.org/papers/pdfs/final_report/ciprfullfinal.pdf

Drahos, P. (2010). *The global governance of knowledge: Patent offices and their clients.* New York: Cambridge University Press.

Drummond, R. (1997). Thyroid storm. *Journal of the American Medical Association, 277*(15), 1238–1243. doi:10.1001/jama.1997.03540390068038 PMID:9103350

Eggertsson, T. (2003). Open access versus common property. In T. L. Anderson & F. S. McChesney (Eds.), Property rights: Cooperation, conflict and law (pp. 73–89). Princeton, NJ: Princeton University Press.

Eisenberg, R. (1987). Propietary rights and the norms of science in biotechnology research. *The Yale Law Journal, 97*(2), 177–231. doi:10.2307/796481 PMID:11660398

Eisenberg, R. (1996). Public research and private development: Patents and technology transfer in government-sponsored research. *Virginia Journal of Law, 8*(8), 1663–1727. doi:10.2307/1073686

Eisenberg, R. (2003). Science and law: Patent swords and shields. *Science, 229*(5609), 1018–1019. doi:10.1126/science.1081790 PMID:12586927

Ellickson, R. C. (1993). Property in land. *The Yale Law Journal, 102*(6), 1315–1400. doi:10.2307/796972

Elliot, V. (2001). Who calls the tune? *The Unesco Courier, 54*(11), 21–22.

European Commission. (2002a). *Development and implications of patent law in the field of biotechnology and genetic engineering.* COM(2002) 545 Final.

European Commission (2002b). *An assessment of the implications for basic genetic engineering research of failure to publish, or late publication of, papers on subjects which could be patentable as required under Article 16(b) of Directive 98/44/EC on the legal protection of biotechnological inventions* [SEC(2002) 50]. COM / 2002/0002 final*/.*

Evans, G. (2001). Leaving room for dissent. *The Unesco Courier, 54*(11), 17.

Feeny, D., Berkes, F., McCay, B. J., & Acheson, J. M. (1990). The tragedy of the commons: Twenty-two years later. *Human Ecology, 18*(1), 1–19. doi:10.1007/BF00889070 PMID:12316894

Feldman, R. (2009). Plain language patents. *Texas Intellectual Property Law Journal, 17*(2), 289–304.

Fromer, J. C. (2009). Patent disclosure. *Iowa Law Review, 94*, 539–606.

Garabedian, T. E. (2002). Nontraditional publications and their effect on patentable inventions. *Nature Biotechnology, 20*(4), 401–402. doi:10.1038/nbt0402-401 PMID:11923849

Gibbs, W. (1996, November). The price of silence: Does profit-minded secrecy retard scientific progress? *Scientific American, 275*(5), 15–16. doi:10.1038/scientificamerican1196-15

Godin, B., & Gingras, Y. (2000). The place of universities in the system of knowledge production. *Research Policy, 29*(2), 273–278. doi:10.1016/S0048-7333(99)00065-7

Guédon, J. C. (2001). *A l'ombre d'Oldenburg: Bibliothecaires, chercheurs scientifiques, maisons d'edition et le controle des publications scientifiques*. Paper presented at the Association of Research Libraries Meeting, Toronto, Canada. Retrieved from https://halshs.archives-ouvertes.fr/halshs-00395366/document

Hardin, G. (1968, December). The tragedy of commons. *Science, 162*(3859), 1243–1248. doi:10.1126/science.162.3859.1243 PMID:5699198

Heller, M. (1998). The tragedy of the anticommons: Property in the transition from Marx to markets. *Harvard Law Review, 111*(3), 621–688. doi:10.2307/1342203

Heller, M. (2008). *The gridlock economy: How too much ownership wrecks markets, stops innovation and costs lives*. New York: Basic Books.

Heller, M., & Eisenberg, R. (1998). Can patents deter innovation? The anticommons in biomedical research. *Science, 280*(5364), 698–701. doi:10.1126/science.280.5364.698 PMID:9563938

Henkel, J., & Reitzgi, M. (2010). *Patent Trolls, the sustainability of 'locking-in-to-extort' strategies, and implications for innovating firms*. Retrieved from http://ssrn.com/abstract=985602

Hess, C., & Ostrom, E. (2001). Artifacts, facilities, and content: Information as a common-pool resource. *Law and Contemporary Problems, 66*, 111–145.

Hettinger, E. C. (1989). Justifying intellectual property. *Philosophy & Public Affairs, 18*(1), 31–52.

Holman, C. M. (2008). Trends in human gene patent litigation. *Science, 322*(5899), 198–199. doi:10.1126/science.1160687 PMID:18845733

Huang, K. G., & Murray, F. E. (2009). Does patent strategy shape the long-run supply of public knowledge? Evidence from human genetics. *Academy of Management Journal, 52*(6), 1139–1221. doi:10.5465/AMJ.2009.47084665

Jackson, M. W. (2010). The patenting of human genes: a cautionary tale. *Cable, 37*(2), 11–14.

Jacobs, P., & Gosselin, P. G. (2000, March 21). Profiteering & shoddy science: Error found in patent of aids gene. *Los Angeles Times*. Retrieved from http://articles.latimes.com/2000/mar/21/news/mn-11091

Jaffe, A. B., & Lerner, J. (2001). Reinventing public R&D: Patent policy and the commercialization of national laboratory technologies. *The Rand Journal of Economics*, *32*(1), 167–198. doi:10.2307/2696403

Kenney, M. (1987). The ethical dilemmas of university - industry collaborations. *Journal of Business Ethics*, *6*(2), 127–135. doi:10.1007/BF00382026

Kepler, T. B., Crossman, C., & Cook-Deegan, R. (2010). Metastasizing patent claims on BRCA1. *Genomics*, *95*(5), 312–314. doi:10.1016/j.ygeno.2010.03.003 PMID:20226239

Krimsky, S. (2003). *Science in the private interest: Has the lure of profits corrupted biomedical research*. Lanham: Rowman & Littlefield Publishers.

Lemley, M. A. (2008). Are universties patents trolls? *Fordham Intellectual Property*. *Media & Entertainment Law Journal*, *18*, 611–631.

Lemley, M. A. (2011). *The myth of the sole inventor*. Stanford Public Law Working Paper No. 1856610. Retrieved from http://ssrn.com/abstract=1856610

Madey v. Duke 307 F.3d 1351, (Fed. Cir. 2002).

Maurer, S. M. (2006). Inside the anticommons: Academic scientists' struggle to build a commercially self-supporting human mutations database, 1999–2001. *Research Policy*, *35*(6), 839–853. doi:10.1016/j.respol.2006.04.008

McDonough, J. F. (2006–2007). The myth of the patent troll: An alternative view of the function of patent dealers in an idea economy. *Emory Law Journal*, *56*, 189–228.

McManis, C. R., & Noh, S. (2011). *The impact of the Bayh-Dole act on genetic research and development: Evaluating the arguments and empirical evidence*. Washington University in St. Louis Legal Studies Research Paper Series.

Merges, R. P., & Nelson, R. R. (1990). On the complex economics of patent scope. *Columbia Law Review*, *90*(4), 839–916. doi:10.2307/1122920

Merton, R. K. (1973). *The sociology of science: Theoretical and empirical investigations*. The University Chicago Press.

Microsoft Corporation. (2010). *Microsoft Announces Patent Agreement With HTC*. Retrieved from http://news.microsoft.com/2010/04/27/microsoft-announces-patent-agreement-with-htc/

Morgan, M. (2008). Stop looking under the bridge for imaginary creatures: A comment examining who really deserves the title patent troll. *The Federal Circuit Bar Journal*, *17*(2), 165–180.

Mulligan, C., & Lee, T. B. (2012). Scaling the patent system. *NYU Annual Survey of American Law, 68*, 289. Retrieved from http://ssrn.com/abstract=2016968

Munzer, S. R. (2005). The commons and the anticommons in the law and theory of property. In *The Blackwell Guide to the Philosophy of Law and Legal Theory*. Retrieved from http://ssrn.com/abstract=647063

Nelson, R. R. (1959). The simple economics of basic scientific research. *Journal of Political Economy*, *67*(3), 297–306. doi:10.1086/258177

OCDE. (2004). *Patents and innovation: Trends and policy challenges.* Retrieved from http://www.oecd.org/science/sci-tech/24508541.pdf

Olivieri, N. F. (2003). Patients' health or company profits? The commercialisation of academic research. *Science and Engineering Ethics*, *9*(1), 29–41. doi:10.1007/s11948-003-0017-x PMID:12645227

Pascual, R. (2011, July 16). Con las patentes no habría sido posible la Capilla Sixtina. *El País.com.*

Rai, A. K., & Eisenberg, R. (2003). Bayh-Dole: Reform and the progress of biomedicine. *Law and Contemporary Problems*, *66*(1/2), 289–334.

Rifkin, J. (1998). *The biotech century.* New York: Tarcher/Putnam.

Risch, M. (2011). Patent troll myths. *Seton Hall Law Review*, *42*, 457–499.

Shapiro, C. (2000). Navigating the patent thicket: Cross licenses, patent pools, and standard-setting. In A. Jaffe, J. Lerner, & S. Stern (Eds.), *Innovation policy and the economy, 1.* Cambridge, MA: MIT Press.

Shiva, V. (2001). *Protect or plunder: Understanding intellectual property rights.* New York: Zed Books.

Sichelman, T. (2010). Commercializing patents. *Stanford Law Review*, *62*(2), 341–413.

Thomas, S. M., Hopkins, M. M., & Brady, M. (2002). Shares in the human genome; the future of patenting DNA. *Nature Biotechnology*, *20*(12), 1185–1188. doi:10.1038/nbt1202-1185 PMID:12454661

UNESCO. (1999). *Declaration on science and the use of scientific knowledge.* Paper presented at the World Conference on Science. Definitive version. Retrieved from http://www.unesco.org/science/wcs/eng/declaration_e.htm

Vanneste, S., Van Hiel, A., Parisi, F., & Depoorter, B. (2006). From 'tragedy' to 'disaster': Welfare effects of commons and anticommons dilemmas. *International Review of Law and Economics*, *26*(1), 104–122. doi:10.1016/j.irle.2006.05.008

Williams, H. (2010). *Intellectual property rights and innovation: Evidence from the human genome.* National Bureau of Economic Research, Tech. Rep. No. 16213.

Wilson, R. (2012). *GPL V3 - What's New?* OSS Watch. Retrieved from http://oss-watch.ac.uk/resources/gpl3final

WIPO. (2004). *Enlarged Concept of Novelty: Initial Study Concerning Novelty and the Prior Art Effect of Certain Applications under draft Article 8(2) of the Substantive Patent Law Treaty (SPLT).* Retrieved from http://www.wipo.int/export/sites/www/scp/en/novelty/documents/5prov.pdf

WIPO. (2010). *World intellectual property indicators.* Retrieved from http://www.wipo.int/edocs/pubdocs/en/intproperty/941/wipo_pub_941_2010.pdf

WIPO. (2011). *World intellectual property report: The changing face of innovation*. Retrieved from http://www.wipo.int/edocs/pubdocs/en/intproperty/944/wipo_pub_944_2011.pdf

Ziman, J. (2000). *Real Science: What it is, and what it means*. Cambridge, UK: Cambridge University Press.

KEY TERMS AND DEFINITIONS

Anticommons: Proprietary regime in which no one has the privilege to use the resource and everyone has the right of exclusion.

Broad Patents: Patents that can stretch into a variety of products or applications, including those in scientific and industrial sectors initially unconnected with the patentees, even if these products or applications were not enabled in their patents.

Free Knowledge: It is the knowledge that is not subject to restrictions imposed by intellectual property rights.

Freedom of Scientific Research: It is the fundamental right of all scientific researchers to conduct the research of their choosing.

Funding: It is the provision of economic resources for a scientific project.

Patent Troll: Actors in the patent system that, by developing an opportunistic behavior, interfere with innovation.

Patent: Legal title through which the state gives its holder exclusive rights to exploit his creation or invention.

Secrecy: Behavior originated by legal or economic incentives that lead a scientist to curb the practice of communalism, i.e., to fully and openly communicate his work.

ENDNOTES

[1]   In biotechnology, chemical and pharmaceutical multinationals have invested heavily to get research time at major academic laboratories worldwide (Kenney, 1987, p. 130).

[2]   For different reasons and through crowdfunding, individual citizens are backing obligations that belong to States People who suffer from rare deceases, those which affect a very small percentage of a country's population and, therefore, are not profitable to pharmaceuticals, are not being included in R&D governmental programs. One should ask if the right to health does in reality exist, *ergo*, who should provide the means to make this right attainable.

[3]   For example, the agreement between the University of California, Berkeley, and the Swiss pharmaceutical conglomerate Novartis, has been considered a landmark in the univesity-industry relations. For US$ 25 million, the equivalent to one third of the budget of the Department of Plant & Microbial Biology, Novartis, through its Novartis Agricultural Discovery Institute (NADI), had a five-year period in which the complete work of an academic department would be closely monitored by the multinational company. UC Berkeley also gave Novartis and unprecedented privilege: first-rights to licenses for patentable discoveries produced in any of the laboratories of the department. Furthermore, and against UC Berkeley's policy of freedom to publish scientific research, Novartis

could demand a delay of up to 120 days in the publication of any new research in which it would introduce a patent application. See Elliot (2001, pp 21-22) and Krimsky (2003, pp 35-38).

[4] During the 1980's, with the *Stevenson-Wydler Technology Transfer Act* (15 USC 3701) and the *Bay-Dole Act* (35 USC 200–212), the US Congress established the adequate environment to foster cooperation between the public and private sector for the commercialization of research results of publicly funded projects. See McManis and Noh (2011) and Eisenberg (1996). Inspired by this model, OCDE members modified their laws and regulations to encourage universities in pursuing the exploitation of patent derived rights obtained in their publicly funded projects. See OCDE (2004, p. 20).

[5] Many of the main investors on R&D programs are also the main worldwide patent applicants, e.g., Toyota, Nokia, Roche, Novartis, Microsoft y General Motors. See WIPO (2010, p. 20).

[6] See UNESCO (1999, §30). During the 1980's, when public funding decreased in the US, private sector seized the opportunity to increase its contribution and participation on academic research. See Gibbs (1996, p. 15). In the OCDE countries, the national expenditure in R&D decreased from 40.9% to a 34.5% of their GDP between 1986 and 1995, leaving a gap that was filled by the industrial sector. See Godin and Gingras (2000).

[7] Hardin's methaphor has generated in the specialized literature a broad and long debate on the nature and regimen of the resource that generates the tragedy. Much of the discussion has focused on whether the tragedy, modeled with reference to the English *commons*, takes place under an open access regime (open fields) or a *commons*. For more information on this discussion see Buck Cox (1985); Feeny, Berkes, McCay and Acheson (1990); Ellickson (1993); Bruce (1998); Hess and Ostrom (2001); Capel (2003); Eggertsson (2003); Munzer (2005).

[8] Heller explains that even in developed market economies it may become encysted, requiring government action to overcome it. Vanneste, Van Hiel, Parisi and Depoorter (2006, p. 21), with a more pessimistic view, add that if the *commons* regime leads to a "tragedy", the *anticommons* can lead to "disaster". This is because in an *anticommons*, regime owners, while exercising their prerogative - the right of exclusion - have no sense of harm associated to it, even if the other owners may suffer economic loss.

[9] Moreover, that Heller himself asserts that an *anticommons* property can not always be seen as a tragedy. In a world without transaction costs agreements to use efficiently a valuable resource can be achieved *a posteriori*. However, such a world does not exist and the interested party must face *a priori* the costs of obtaining the right to use the resource.

[10] *Upstream* research can be seen as that carried out by scientists working in basic research lines and tools that allow applied scientific research. Similarly, the work done at the end of the research process is presented *downstream*. This research can be seen as that made by technologists and engineers who develop new products.

[11] With this legislative measure the number patents granted to American universities increased from 1.1% of all those generated between 1969 and 1986, to 4.8% between 1987 and 1999. See Eisenberg (2003); Rai and Eisenberg (2003); Krimsky (2003).

[12] For Rifkin (1998), the reward of research is no longer simply the respect and admiration of those who share the scientific activity around a given topic, nor the satisfaction of contributing to knowledge, but patenting inventions that can be very lucrative.

[13] An example of this problem can see it in the initiative of one hundred scholars of the biological sciences to create a global Data Repository of Human Mutations - the Mutations Database Initia-

tive - negotiated in accordance with business partners, and capable of self-financing. Although the group achieved a significant economic offer, information costs were too high for the majority of the members who could not make a sufficiently informed decision. To reduce this effect, the project proponents made information more accessible, but opponents introduced information that could not be easily corroborated. The result was an *anticommons* that could not be unlocked and that prevented the realization of the project. See Maures (2006).

[14] Shapiro (2001) developed the term patent thicket as analogous to Heller's *anticommons*. See also Clarkson and Dekorte (2006).

[15] DuPont, for example, has offered non-commercial licenses to use their "oncomouse" on research projects, but in return demands to be present at the negotiations when derivative products are discussed or obtained through it. See Heller and Eisenberg (1998, p. 699). This kind of "deals" which threatened to become unmanageable, led to some action taken, e.g., by the U.S. National Institute of Health (NIH). In its guidelines to license genomics research tools that it had funded, the NIH suggests broad and non-exclusive licensing. In 2001, the patent offices of the United States, Japan and Europe decided that certain claims in DNA research tools must not reach the drugs that are subsequently created. See Heller (2008, p. 63).

[16] Shapiro (2001) has suggested three solutions to the anticommons: (1) Cross-licensing, especially useful if it does not include the payment of royalties, because final prices are not affected. (2) Patent pools, which allow their members unlimited access to the patented research committed to it. Access is subject only to the payment of established royalties. (3) License packs, which consist of agreements between two or more joint holders to license their technologies and how they distribute royalties.

[17] The economic literature that has treated the subject is abundant, but it is suggested to see Merges and Nelson (1990, p. 916); Heller (2008, pp. 51–52).

[18] Research in these areas is also known as "cummulative" or "complex" (WIPO, 2011).

[19] Patent formats are recognized forms of claims that patent offices accept as valid. Patent attorneys make constant changes to unrecognized formats, often for being vague or broad, seeking acceptance from reviewers. Thus, a claim that was originally regarded as too broad, with a cosmetic change can become accepted, establishing a standard claiming format for broad patents (Drahos, 2010).

[20] For example, the CCR5 receptor, on which Human Genome Sciences obtained a patent, only later, and thanks to the work of other researchers, was known that it was the main point of entry of the HIV / AIDS virus. See Jacobs and Gosselin (2000); Thomas, Hopkins, and Brady (2002).

[21] The BRCA1/2 genes belong to a class of suppressor genes, whose mutations are correlated with susceptibility of women to develop breast and ovarian cancer.

[22] The implications of the patents granted on the BRCA1/2 genes were highlighted in Association for Molecular Pathology, *et al. v.* United States Patent and Trademark Office, *et al.* (09 Civ. 4515).

[23] On this issue, see the studies conducted by Williams (2010) and Cho, Illangasekare, Weaver, Leonard, and Merz (2003).

[24] In this section, we prefer to speak of "holder" rather than "inventor" because not always the inventor retains the exploitation rights of the invention.

[25] Jon Hall, executive director of Linux International, explained that given the number of patents, for example, exist in software, people not only waste time and money trying to find out if a part of their development is under patent, but it also is impossible to memorize them all, and so not infringe any (Pascual, 2011). See also Mulligan and Lee (2012).

[26] In the Anglo-Saxon tradition, a troll is a kind of ogre, of great strength and frightening physical appearance, often prowling under bridges for unsuspecting pedestrians trying to cross it, demanding a toll from them. The term patent troll was coined in 2001 by Peter Detkin, then Assistant General Counsel at Intel, as an alternative to the more derogatory term patent extortionist. The patent troll tag was placed by Detkin on Tech-Search, a firm that in 1998 had acquired the patent 5,574,927 on a microprocessor. Search Tech-Intel warned that it was infringing the patent, offering a license. Intel rejected the proposal and accordingly Search Tech-sued, claiming that the products of the Pentium Pro and Pentium II line infringed the patent. Since then, the term has been used to signal those who acquire patents to enforce them, but with no intention of using them to develop new products. See Morgan (2008, pp. 166-167).

[27] Waiting for an alleged infringement is part of the strategy of the trolls, as alleged infringers are placed in a position of dependency that forces them into disadvantageous agreements. See Henkel and Reitzgi (2010, pp. 5–6).

[28] See Morgan (2008, pp. 179-180). Nevertheless, Lemley suggests that the issue is not to identify if someone is acting in bad faith or not, since for him, everyone at some point behave like trolls (troll is as troll does), but rather to focus on predatory acts and legal rules that make them possible. See Lemley (2008, p. 19). Furthermore, Risch (2011, p. 3) believes that it is wrong to think of trolls in Manichean terms, since qualifying a patent holder as such, in the absence of evidence that supports the opposing camps, depends on who is placing the label.

[29] It is estimated that in the United States the cost of a patent trial can vary from US$ 350,000 to 6,000,000, the defense for a typical case may be around US$ 1.5 million, while it may reach US$ 4 million when damages of about US$ 25 million are claimed. See Morgan (2008, p. 169). Also, it must be remembered that associated indirect costs arising from the pre-trial preparation activities also exist. See Jaffe and Lerner (2001, p. 14).

[30] Hettinger (1989) explained that it is precisely the social value in creation what prevents the identification of the value of the work added with the value of the product. When this identification is made, the vast contributions that others have carried out are not recognized.

[31] A real "epistemic pollution" that, according to Ziman (2000), increases the subordination of science to corporate and political interests.

[32] Different studies show that the performance of the patent system as a disseminator of knowledge has been, at the very least, disappointing. Refer, for example, to Fromer (2009, pp. 560-562). Also see the Report from the Commission to the European Parliament and Council: An assessment of the implications for basic genetic engineering research of failure to publish, or late publication of, papers on subjects which could be patentable as required under Article 16(b) of Directive 98/44/EC on the legal protection of biotechnological inventions (SEC, 2002: 50).

[33] For a reference on the configuration of the novelty requirement in some jurisdictions see WIPO (2004). Internationally see 54 of European Patent Convention of 5 October 1973 as revised by the Act revising Article 63 EPC of 17 December 1991 and the Act revising the EPC of 29 November 2000 and 3 of Directive 98/44/EC of the European Parliament and of the Council of 6 July 1998 on the legal protection of biotechnological inventions.

[34] In addition, novelty could be affected by the publication in non-traditional outlets such as conference proceedings, posters, internship reports, oral presentations, public records of calls for research project grants, or posting in open digital repositories (Garabedian, 2002).

35   Ziman's (2000) "epistemic pollution" concept seems to explain why secrecy is not even noticed in scientific environments, preventing its combat.

36   Two Nobel laureates in economics have addressed this concern on their research. Nelson (1959, p. 306) stated that when knowledge has been produced, its marginal cost is zero, which implies that the economic optimum is reached when it is freely exchanged. However, this would reduce the incentives for private firms to produce knowledge. Arrow (1962, pp. 616-617) concurs, explaining that the restriction on the use of the results of scientific research is, in economic terms, suboptimal but necessary to the interests of the industry, enabling it to create an artificial scarcity.

37   The mentality of open science in universities is described as one of the main problems that hinder the participation of Italian professors in activities aimed at obtaining a patent. See Baldini, Grimaldi, and Sobrero (2007, p. 334). Before the rise of commercial interest in biotechnology, neither the scientists nor the institutions of basic research in biomedical sciences were very keen to defend the results of basic research through patent rights. On the contrary, sometimes they showed aversion to patents on their work. See Eisenberg (1987, p. 181).

38   See the cases of Nancy F. Olivieri (2003) and Betty J. Dong (Drummond, 1997).

39   A case can be made that the research exemption covers non-commercial and academic uses. The research exemption is explicitly enshrined in Chile or Monaco. In other countries, such as Brazil, Denmark and Mexico is established, but not explicitly defined. In Australia, it would be argued under the guise of "private and non-commercial use." However, even the research exemption may be subject to the interpretation of the "benefit" obtained with the use of the patented invention. For example, a broad interpretation of the benefit that Duke University obtained was made in Madey v. Duke (307 F.3d 1351, Fed. Cir. 2002). For the Court, the status of the institution -for-profit or not- would be irrelevant, since a university is in the "business" of gaining prestige to get better students, better researchers and better grants.

40   Specially the GPLv3. For more information, see Wilson (2012)

Chapter 7
Social Media and Free Knowledge:
Case Study – Public Opinion Formation

Jose Aguilar
Universidad de Los Andes, Venezuela

Oswaldo Terán
Universidad de Los Andes, Venezuela

ABSTRACT

Mass media (e.g., TV) and social media (e.g., Facebook) have a large utilization nowadays; they are becoming an integral part of our life. This chapter describes the psychological effects of media bias and manipulation, along its impact on public opinion by using "agenda setting" and "prototypes/framing". It shows how media can artificially create feelings and emotions. It will also explore the relationships between free knowledge and media. Free knowledge has a strong potential to prevent media manipulation, and for people emancipation from media control. The paper suggests using media in a more humanistic way, as a space to create knowledge, where social interaction influences knowledge. We talk of communities where people regularly share and create knowledge. The media do not replace existing processes of building knowledge; rather they provide an additional dynamic environment, which must meet certain criteria for what the social knowledge will be emancipator, and not manipulative.

MASS MEDIA AND SOCIAL MEDIA IN OUR LIVES

Introduction to Mass Media and Social Media

With social media and mass media we refer basically to communication media, i.e., to the storage, organization, processing and delivering of information or data. There are two kinds of media, the old media or legacy media and the new media. The old media are traditional means of communication and expression existing before the internet, while the new media are those media appearing after and based on the internet. Among the old media we have broadcast and cable television, radio, movie studios, music

DOI: 10.4018/978-1-4666-8336-5.ch007

studios, newspapers, magazines, books and other print publications. On the other hand, among the new media we have Facebook, blogs, wikis, Tweeter, Skype, email, and many other internet based media. *In this chapter, we will use the names: mass media for old media, and social media for new media.*

New media or social media shows properties allowed by the internet, such as on-demand access to content at anytime, anywhere, by using any digital device. It allows interactive feedback and "creative" participation. It includes the real-time generation of news and unregulated content. New media has increased its coverage and impact in the last decades, but it still is far from replacing old media yet. For instance, TV is even now having and strong impact around the world. Similarly, other old media are also quite influential in diverse parts of the world.

Given the fact that old media or mass media are widely known since many years ago, and very concrete, while new media is recent, spreading and complex, presenting a wide diversity of forms to get, process, transmit, and deliver information and data, the following of this chapter will be devoted mainly to new media (it is enough to mention the main cases of old media (TV, etc.)).

The widespread use of information technologies and communication technologies (ICTs), especially the web, is a reality. The Web is based on light-weight web services, and provides browser-for the interaction with the end users. The Web technologies include the Internet enabled Web as the native platform. Internet is the more frequent source of information. The problem of using the Internet is the quality and security of the information. Doubts about the quality of online information are given by the lack of control over their scientific and professional rigor.

The last years the web has shifted towards user-driven technologies such as social networks, video-sharing, etc. These social technologies have enabled a revolution in User Generated Content (UGC) and the publishing of consumer opinion. This is dominating the way we use the internet, and the social media (YouTube, Twitter, Facebook, etc.) is redefining how the internet works.

Particularly, social networks emerged in recent years as one of the main uses of Internet. Social networks have been growth by the users' actions. It is currently estimated that 53% of Internet users participate in social networks generally (Smith, 2009; Treem & Leonardi, 2012). The social media incorporate features to allow users to produce and share content, to build communities, to discuss about specific topics, to publish opinions, to build relationships, or in general to connect and interact.

The first known use of the term social media occurred in 1997, by the executive of AOL Ted Leons when he commented that the consumers needed "social media" (Smith, 2009; Treem & Leonardi, 2012). During the decade of 2000, a number of social media technologies made their debuts: Facebook, Twitter, Blogger (a blogging platform), Wikipedia, etc.

There is not a clear definition of social media. Kaplan and Haenlein (Braun, 2012; Smith, 2009; Treem & Leonardi, 2012) refer to social media as "Internet-based applications that build on the ideological and technological foundations of Web 2.0, and that allow the creation and exchange of UGC". We can consider social media like a human communication mediated through social software. A social software facilitates the creation of social networks in a digital environment, in order to allow the interaction, the content-sharing and the collaboration. Social media are designed to promote the content generation by the users and to facilitate the sharing and diffusion of information. The Organization for Economic Cooperation and Development has defined three basic requirements for UGC (OECD, 2007) (Braun, 2012):

- The content must be made available, for instance on a social network service accessible to a selected group of people, or on a public website.

- The content creation must involve creative effort. Copying content and publishing it on another website is not UGC.
- The motivations for the creation of UGC are personals like achieving a certain level of fame, work with peer, etc.

There are different technologies to implement social media (or social web applications) like wikis, microblogs (e.g., twitter), Web-based communication systems, photo-sharing, video casting and sharing (e.g., YouTube), networking systems (e.g., Facebook), social annotation, social bookmarking, social networking, etc. In (Chun & Luna-Reyes, 2012) the next social media characteristics are distinguished:

- Digital space for collaboration: co-create content, collective actions, etc.
- Digital space for meeting and exchanging ideas, products, and information with others.
- Cross-platform data sharing in order to share content by transferring data across sites.
- User-generated social content that others can view.

The usage of social media has grown at staggering rates. The social media impact is being felt across the globe. The social media are adopted as a form of social community. This social revolution has changed the form of life in present days, even if we are not involved in social media. Particularly interesting are the changes in our relationship to content and other aspects of information. Videos focused on users' personal lives outpaced all professional content. The content is built bottom up based on two premises (Chun & Luna-Reyes, 2012):

- The networks of influence are dominated by strangers who share digital spaces (e.g. Facebook).
- Our opinions are influenced by the online users' opinions

Kaplan and Haenlein define five types of social media (Braun, 2012):

- *Social Network Services.* Communities where the social network itself is the core functionality. These services, such as Facebook, offer its users a variety of features which facilitate public and private communication, self-presentation, etc.
- *Content Communities.* These are similar to a social network service, but the intention of the user is different. In this case, the users' main goal is to consume and share content, like YouTube for videos, and what is not the case in social networks.
- *Blogs and Micro-blogs.* Blogs are special websites that allow the creation of articles or "posts". Blogs are platforms for UGC. Micro-blogs are a sub-genre of weblogs limited to a defined number of characters like Twitter.
- *Collaborative Projects.* It is a platform where users create, organize, and edit content. The multitude of users allows a very extensive collection of knowledge. The technology normally used on these platforms is called wiki. The most famous example is Wikipedia.
- *Virtual Social Worlds.* They are platforms that replicate real environments, and in which users can appear as avatars and interact with others.

In (Chun & Luna-Reyes, 2012) the social media depending on the activities, products and behaviors of the users are categorized as follows:

- Building physical products such as software, knowledge bases, etc.
- Building social networks
- Reviewing, tagging, etc. web content, products or users.
- Sharing information.

Some examples of social media are:

- LinkedIn is a social networking site for the business community to establish networks of people with their professional links.
- Twitter is a microblogging service to broadcast short posts and follow other users.
- Facebook allows users to create profiles, keep in touch with friends, send messages, etc.

In (Braun, 2012) some researchers have developed a framework for the characterization of social media. The framework consists of seven "functional blocks": Identity, Conversations, Sharing, Presence, Relationships, Reputation, and Groups. These blocks are neither mutually exclusive, nor do they all have to be present in a social media activity. These blocks describe social media aspects like end-user participation, problem solving based on collaboration, etc. For example, YouTube focuses primarily on Sharing, secondary on Conversations, Groups, and Reputation, but it does not focus much on Identity, Relationships, and Presence. On the other hand, Facebook focuses primary on Relationships, secondary on Identity, Reputation, Presence, and Conversations, and less on Groups and Sharing.

Social Media Technology

The form social media has today is the result of years of development, of policing, cultural and economic factors, and personal preferences. As we said previously, Social Media is human communication mediated through social software. This mediation depends on the specific social media software. A social software is characterized by a "bottom-up" process, in contrast with the classical software based on the "top-down" paradigms. Braun (2012) defines specific features of the social software:

- *Support "human communication"* (which would also apply to e-mail).
- *Support all interaction types between individuals or groups*: synchronously, asynchronously, one-to-one, one-to-many, many-to-one, many-to-many.
- *Support social feedback.*
- *Support social networks.*

According to Braun (2012), the entirety of all communication forms is what makes software social, and can be formed by the combination of many: e-mail and instant messaging (one-to-one), web pages and blogs (one-to-many), and wikis (many-to-many). In this sense, we can add a "Social Layer" to Internet, which has the totality of social software.

Social infrastructure is a more general term that describes services which allow software developers to integrate social functionalities. Social software, social layer, and APIs, are part of the social infrastructure. The problem with the social layer paradigm is the environments in which most social media takes place. In contrast to the early Internet, which was open and free, some functionalities of existent social network are private. For example, Graph API is proprietary of Facebook (this API gives a view of the Facebooks Social Graph: people, friends, events, photos, etc.). Every social network service provides APIs to build applications on top of them. No industry standard has been developed yet. Social network services (like API) are not inter-operable, in comparison to e-mail. A Facebook user cannot send a direct message to a Google+ user and vice-versa. The reasons for this lack of inter-operability are economical. The possibility that proprietary social network services open up their infrastructure seems unlikely, since the value of such services derives directly from the data of their users (a value impossible to define and calculate).

Social Media are Not Neutral

The result of social media communication depends greatly on the design of social media products. Just comparing the two most popular social media services, Facebook and Twitter, we immediately discover great difference in communication. Not only the social network topology is different, but the way the users communicate with each other is very different.

Twitters are limited to a length of 140 characters, due to historical reasons (it is derived from the limited character of SMS). The limitation to 140 characters forces Twitter users to "make it short". It is less intrusive and also forces Twitter users to think about the necessity of their next tweet. To follow a Twitter user who writes about uninteresting topics is ineffective. The Facebook's communication culture is quite different. The bad comments are easier to ignore, filter, or hide. Annoying comments from a specific user can be hidden without the necessity to break up the relationship. While the act of unfollowing a user is very common on Twitter, on Facebook is rather an exception.

An important but hidden issue in social media is that its usage leaves a trace in relation to how it is used, i.e., about the behavior of the user and its links, contacts or partners (e.g., about the information that is handled with who someone communicates, follows, etc.). This information is currently used for "social intelligence". In particular, in the social media data mining techniques are used in order to extract knowledge about the behavior of individuals. In certain countries we can find agencies dedicated to this, among other related tasks. These agencies are interested in analyzing and inferring in relation to how individuals act, and behave, to favor the interest of those who can afford to pay for, or have the power to get access to, that knowledge.

Another very important aspect of the social networks is real-time. That allows people leverage expertise of others through social networks. The power of the real-time online social networks is that they create a continuous expertise, without replace the existing knowledge. It provides a dynamic environment which people can use to make decisions. Additionally, in a social network a person can tag their interests. This allows the creation of a pool of people with similar interests. Some knowledge can be generated from that. Human activities have changed as a result. The social interaction is influencing people, their knowledge, etc. Since the arrival of the social networking sites there is so much information to consume that we rarely spend any time exploring any of it in great depth. Other aspects hidden in the social media are:

- The social media tries to seduce us into wasting time.
- The social media allow over-sharing and loss of privacy, in a way the concept of privacy seems to lose.
- The social media tries to influence our personal opinion.

All these aspects are hidden behind social media, no one is not visible, we act and we are not aware of this reality, we cease to be conscious of our starring, assuming the social media are neutral (Aguilar, 2009, 2012).

Particularly, the last aspect is very important to study, specially the process of opinion formation on social media. This process is more complicated than in real society, due to that the information is fuzzy and evolves more rapidly. There are several reasons for this: users discuss with others anonymously, users do not know the personality and internal opinions of the others, etc. There are recent works of sociologists, computists, psychologists, etc. to understand and predict the behavior of the opinions throughout social networks. Many good features of inter-personal communication are cancelled, and a sort of blind interaction appears. We learn and shape our cognition, perspective, opinions, feelings and behavior in part from such a blind and des-contextualized communication.

In this paper we are going to study the process of opinion formation on social media. Opinion is composed by the aggregate of dominant opinions within a society, where the culture and ideology play a key role. Social communication through social media is increasing. The way public opinion is formed is strongly influenced by these new media. Social media are being used to seek information about topics. But an important question about social media as an information source is how people assess the source credibility of this information. There are new criteria for the credibility judgments, such as the ability to see how quickly a page is updated.

In general, there is a huge amount of research about social media as a communicational mechanism. Some researches study how a subject is trendy in a community. Other studies examine how pieces of information impact the opinion (Agrawal, 2011; Braun, 2012; Green, 2010; Treem & Leonardi, 2012). Other works center theirs studies on social processes related to the diffusion of information and opinions in social media (Canals, 2005; Hogg & Huberman, 2007; Smith, 2009). Other researches have shown how social media can be used to direct public opinion toward topics of interest to social groups (Braun, 2012; Helms, Ignacio, Brinkkemper, & Zonneveld, 2010; Smith, 2009).

About this last aspect, an example is how twitter has been used on the public protests in some countries (such as the recent case of the Venezuelan opposition), using bots that circulate fake pictures and videos about what is happening, from other countries, performing a disinformation campaign. Many Anonymous twitter accounts involve in the dissemination of street protests. To verify their origin we can use the metadata of the image, and determine that the information does not correspond to what is stated, or the examination of the temporary time of occurrence (for example, pictures of invasions using airplanes correspond to a forum exhibition).

Huesmann (2007)'s paper is particularly related to the present chapter. He argues that media, both new and old media, have had and important effect in generating social aggressive behavior and social violent behavior. Video games are found as especially effective in influencing social behavior of children. For supporting his conclusion, he cites diverse surveys and studies. His work is particularly relevant when considering children's education. Three mechanisms of psychological influence of mass media, namely priming[1], arousal[2] and mimicry[3], and three long processes, through which mass media influence in children, to be exact Observational Learning[4], Desensitization[5], and Enactive Learning[6], are pointed out.

In "observation learning" behavior of a person is understood as generated by the interplay between the individual's social situation and the individual's emotional state, the social cognitive schemas about the world, the normative beliefs about what is good in the present situation, and the social scripts (which he has learned). Huesmann argues that social scripts of children, while children grow up, become affected by mass media messages and examples about aggressive and violent behavior. Afterwards, children imitate aggressive and violent behavior observed in media, what in turn affects the social cognitive schemas they are creating about the world around them. Once the children mature, their normative beliefs are constructed in accordance with this kind of schemas and scripts. Finally, they behave in accordance to these normative beliefs. In particular, citing diverse studies, Huesmann concludes that media (e.g., video games, cinema or TV) violent and aggressive acts justified because they are carried out by charismatic "heroes", who are rewarded, have a high potential to increase the viewers' aggressive and violent behavior.

Via observational learning then media increases aggressive and violent behavior by affecting and altering not only the children's opinion (e.g., schemas about the world), but also their behavior (e.g., via social scripts and normative beliefs). Similarly, desensitization (about consequences of aggressive and violent behavior) and enactive learning (of aggressive and violent behavior) increase aggressive and violent behavior in our societies.

Huesmann's work strengthens the thesis of the present chapter, namely: that media influences public opinion formation, in relation to aggressive and violent behavior. The present chapter, differently from Hussmann's, is interested in the influence of media in public opinion in general. Another difference between this chapter and Hussmann´s work is that we are also interested in the non obvious influence of media message, e.g., in the effect of subliminal messages, which seem to be mediated sometimes by psychological mechanisms different from those considered by Huesmann. Finally, in this chapter we focus specially in new media.

Despite of all this, can the social networking sites have a positive influence on humanity? We think that the answer is affirmative, of course, if we made an intelligent (informed, contextualized) use of them, i.e., if we are more aware and cautious about why, how and for what we use them.

Democracy and Social Media

During the 1990s, due to the spread of popular access to new information and communication technologies, in part due to the Internet, optimistic people believed we were on the beginning of a new era of social and political democratization (Chun & Luna-Reyes, 2012). Benjamin Barber speculated that ICT had the potential to strengthen democracy by increasing public access to information (Chun & Luna-Reyes, 2012).

Rheingold predicted that "cyber communities" could challenge the political and economic elite's control (Braun, 2012; Chun & Luna-Reyes, 2012). Grossman predicted the emergence of what he called an "electronic republic" based on Internet-based dialogue and a reflexive process of public opinion formation. Weitzner characterized the Internet as "a vast forum for political discourse and activism" (Chun& Luna-Reyes, 2012).

In terms of electoral politics, the impact of the Internet is similar to that of the television in the mid 20th century. In this case, social media not only allow parties spread their word in entirely new ways", but it also allows an interactive two-way communication.

At the level of the democracy, an important aspect to study is the censorship. It is a topic that is strongly connected to human communication. Sometimes, it is seen as necessary or as dangerous. Sometimes it is illegal, or it is not. Sometimes it is precisely regulated; or it is difficult to define. Sometimes it is accepted, or it is not. It depends on the local social and political circumstances as well as the ideological believes of the society where censorship is applied. The OpenNet Initiative has identified four approaches to Internet filtering (Chun & Luna-Reyes, 2012):

- **Technical Blocking:** Used to block users access to specific websites.
- **Induced Self-Censorship:** The promotion of social norms or intimidation to favor self-censorship.
- **Take-Down:** When a website is forced to be taken down by its administrator.
- **Search Result Removals:** Remove specific sites from the listings of search engines.

In recent years many situations have occurred where social media played an essential role in the organization of social movements (the protests in Arab countries, or in Venezuela). Social media is a sophisticated tool to organize protests, campaigns, and circulate information. The blocking of social media sites is already a common practice. Some countries have adopted filtering as a standard activity. Live-streaming sites and social networks are often the most affected. Additionally, often social media are being monitored by police to identify possible protesters or antigovernment activists.

In this way, a new software industrial is been deployed to monitor and filter, but also to overcome filtering and to anonymize. The development goes even further, because there are intentions of building alternative "Internets".

Other important aspect at the level of democracy is the regulation of the Internet through laws. In recent years this topic has received increasing attention. Many of these laws have not been invented by the politicians who promoted them, but they have derived from entities, in some cases privates and/or foreigns, who influence these politicians.

The most recent and famous examples are SOPA (Stop Online Piracy Act) and ACTA (Anti-Counterfeiting Trade Agreement). These are two laws about the treatment of intellectual property, but really with the goal of a wide regulation of Internet content. These laws were deliberately formulated imprecisely and openly, just like Facebook's terms of service.

Social Media, knowledge Engineering, and the Economy

Social Network Analysis (SNA) is a domain of research coming from Sociology, which studies social relations between people (Jones, 2011). Also, it is a technique for analyzing social networks based on graph theory, using typical measures like distance and centrality. It can carry out a more qualitative analysis based on this visual representation of the social network, to reveal patterns such as connectedness of the network or social cohesiveness within and between sub-groups.

Several authors have used SNA to study knowledge sharing in social media. In (Jones, 2011) SNA is applied to informal networks of knowledge sharing. They study the application of SNA to analyze knowledge sharing at the British Council. (Helms et al., 2010) presents Knowledge Network Analysis techniques that focus on study relations in defined knowledge areas within an organization.

Also, social media is reorientating the economy. Now every online consumer is a commentator, reviewer and publisher. In this way, all organizations must stop talking and start listening to how it is perceived. Listening is just the start; it is about actively taking part and engaging consumers directly.

People listen and then they talk. This engagement with consumers online will be a key way to build long-term advocates of the brand, who not only purchase their products, but also recommend them on and offline. This orientation away from talking through social media, it is more of listen and converse through it, shifting the whole focus of economy, making the research about the information, utilization, etc., of the social media is more important. This is a huge opportunity for research about issues such as the followings (Smith, 2009):

- In an economy driven by consumer opinion, we need to understand the reasons behind trends in opinion.
- It is now possible to build a brand through listening, and asking questions in a social media environment become a way to start listening and build relationships.
- Social platforms (Facebook, LinkedIn, etc.) become research platforms about interests of the people. etc.
- We publish our opinions, we leave a trail of data, we need research about this data to understand why things happen.

PSYCHOLOGICAL INFLUENCE IN THE PUBLIC OPINION FORMATION

In this chapter we will study how the psychology on the mass media and the social media drives opinions, beliefs, meanings and emotions until behavior. Psychology does play a huge role on mass media and social media. For that, we must understand the person's psychology. For instance, it is important to take into account the role having the basic neuroanatomical substratum, which is somewhat at the limbic system, as a set of structures that influences not only in the emotions per se, but also in the cognitive functions (Chronister & Hardy, 1997). The basic neuroanatomical substratum includes: a) the prefrontal cortexes (orbito-frontal cortex-OFC, cingulate cortices), which are association cortices that are linked in the brain-mediated frontal-limbic modulation, what maximizes the likelihood that behavioral aggression occurs in response to provocation in an appropriate context (Lee & Coccaro, 2007); b) the reticular formation (SRA), which plays an active role in generating and maintaining the arousal state and its vegetative functions in the hypothalamus; c) the hippocampus, which appears to be associated to the consolidation of long-term memories from immediate and short-term memories (this refers to types of memories that persist for seconds and minutes); and, finally, d) the amygdala and its sensory information processes, which in turn participate in the creation of emotionally conditioned object memories (Lee & Coccaro, 2007). As a whole, all this allows us to "get used to" something that has happened all of life, which mediates in human decision making, giving sense, feelings and moods. On the other hand, it will shake us out when we hear an unfamiliar opinion. In general, reticular formation cans (frames) us out the things that are not important, and also cans us shake when something unfamiliar happens. That is, people are unconsciously making decisions based on psychological impulses of the brain. Specifically, our psychological make-up based on the reticular formation tells us to our think (psychological influence).

Particularly, via the neuroanatomical substratum the mass media can generate the activation of arousal: biological, automatic and unconscious biological preparation/activation for action, through (either negative or positive) emotions. This activation is slow in its process of going to its basal functional state of activation. Because of this, constant messages in the form of new stimulus can generate in the individual a prolonged state of stress (hypersensitization), and an acquired hopelessness, or an aggressive response focused over particular objects, which have been intentionally focused from such messages. Alternatively, such messages along prolonged states of stress could create in the individual desensitization in the form of apathy.

Similarly, the locale system and the taxon system have important functions of memory related with the influence of the media (with media we mean both, mass media and social media). The locale system is concerned with episodic or contextual aspects of meaning; and the taxon system is associated with a stimulus without relating it with constrains of context (here concepts and feelings are recorded but not the spatio-temporal context of the issue of the case). Clore and Ortony (2000) argue that the *hippocampus* serves the function of the locale system. If the hippocampus does not works well, or if the information does not arrives or is not recorded correctly at it, the person will be des-contextualized about the issue of the case. Decontextualized meaning and emotions generates reinstatements of emotions without the use of cognition. These emotions are not controlled. The media can use decontextualizations to direct public opinion in accordance to certain interests. In this section we will analyze the consequences of decontextualized information as an example of how media could manipulate people's feeling, situations of meaning, and drive public opinion.

We part from the hypothesis that we can create the feelings and emotions artificially using media. Emotion is often defined as "a complex state of feeling that results in physical and psychological changes that influence thought and behavior". That means, with the media we can bias the user to do what we want them to do. For that, media could direct certain messages to exploit some functions of the brain of the users, such as those of the reticular formation and the hippocampus, by getting people step by step from the familiar to the unfamiliar, by capitalizing on the emotional perspective and other feelings of the reader.

Appraising, and Affective Feelings: Emotions, and Moods

As said above, we are interested in explaining how media affects public opinion, which, we can say, is a widespread tendency in the public (a community, or a society) to give meaning in a certain form, i.e., from some perspective. In accordance to Clore and Ortony (2000) both emotions and moods are relevant feelings when people give meaning. Even more, emotions and moods interact and feedback each other. Clore and Ortony (2000) affirm that appraisal is always present in what we can call normal emotions, but that some emotions are recorded without the appropriated/necessary context, and then when reinstated (with little or null intervention of cognition/appraisal) they can generate decontextualized, unconscious, and perhaps amaising, emotions. Alongside, moods affect considerably the disposition of a person when giving meaning, and consequently his opinion and emotions.

All these three kinds of feelings, namely, moods, normal emotions and decontextualized emotions can be capitalized from the media in favor of the spreading of certain opinions, and, similarly, against the spreading of others. In order to explain this, we will first describe (in this section), following Clore and Ortony (2000), how these feelings appear, as well as their possible physiological origins, and relationship with appraisal.

Moods, Emotions and Appraisal

Clore and Ortony (2000) argue that some affective feelings and moods such as those related with anxiety and depression can have only purely biochemical causes, and that they can occur without any cognitive appraisal. This is not the *normal* case for emotions, which are based on cognitive appraisal. To differentiate better between moods, other affective feelings and emotions, Clore and Ortony (2000) define normal emotions as: "affective (i.e., positively or negatively balanced) states that have objects (what philosophers call "intentional" states)" (Clore & Ortony, 2000, pp. 26). On the other hand, other affective feelings, such as the anxiety or depression, do not have any reference object, but rather are vague about a reference. This is related with their *persistence and free-floating character*. Consequently, no evaluation of any object is required for such kind of affective feelings.

A third characteristics that difference emotions from moods (apart from appraisal and the referenced objects), is that moods do not have implications for personal coping (conscious effort and strategies to solve personal and interpersonal problems, and facilitate solving conflicts and surviving), while emotions do have. *Information that generates moods is not feedback from a current situation, while information conveying emotions is feedback from situations.* However, *free-floating (objectless) feelings* can be transformed in emotions. This can occur as follows: after being plagued by an anxious feeling (e.g., about our child safety), we could develop a particular feeling about an object (stones of some bench as a potential risk for our child), and then we attempt to avoid or eliminate this object (break up the bench and carry away the stones and rest of the rubble). Thus, moods though being biologically indistinguishable from emotions (which have reference objects) have different psychological implications.

Clore and Ortony (2000) give a possible explanation for this influence of the mood on a subsequent emotion: *the effect-as-information hypothesis.* In accordance to this hypothesis, affective feelings tend to appear as reactions to whatever is in focus in a certain situation. Consequently, chronic feelings that are incidentally present during judgment and decision making are probably feedback about the object of decision making or the alternative being considered. In this sense, people who have anxious feeling will increase their likelihood of perceiving threatening events. The anxious feelings (in a form of feedback) are taken as the information that a threatening event is imminent.

Summarizing, moods and other affective feelings, differently from (normal) emotions, neither have an object reference nor have implications for coping, but rather are free-floating, and are not based on appraisal. Also, they have different psychological implications, as we will see below. However, they can be transformed in emotions, in specific situations; i.e., the non cognitive feelings can provide information for cognitive appraisal, informing situations of meaning, from where certain emotions and opinion tendencies appear, in accordance to the effect-as-information hypothesis.

The Two Routes to Appraisal in Emotions

We need to differentiate about two kinds of emotions: some emotions that do not surprise us (to which we have referred before as normal emotions, because they have a reference object, and involve appraisal), and emotions that often conflict with our beliefs, are elicited by stimuli outside of awareness and are outside of our control (appear without appraisal). For this, we will differentiate about two forms of giving meaning (appraising) associated to emotions. Despite of their differences, both are related with the activation of deep structures of situational meaning. Also we will refer to some associated physiological research results that help us understanding the role for giving meaning and behavior that those amazing emotions have. This will help in understanding better possible forms how such emotions can be used by media to drive public opinion.

The first route to appraisal is called **Bottom-up or situational analysis,** and consists in *assembling of relevant interpretations of the world, which involves a continuous (on-line) computation of whether situations are desirable or undesirable, and in which way.* Desirability or undesirability is associated to how the event or object linked to the assembling favors (disfavors) or is coherent (incoherent/contrary) with our goals and/or norms/moral. The actor then feels pleased or displeased, and emotional meaning appears.

The second route to appraisal is the called **top-down route or appraisal reinstatement**. In this case meaning, and emotions appear from similarity (association) of a current situation to a past situation. For instance, appraisal of threat and reaction of fear could appear in a current situation via restatement of a past situation, which in some aspects (at least those related with threat and fear) is similar to the present situation. Earlier experiences (situations of meaning) with their significance, including the emotional one, are reinstated. This kind of experience seems to be more related to procedural knowledge, heuristics[7], customs, and fast response as reaction to certain issues of situations requiring it. Clore and Ortony (2000) emphasize the importance of "the idea that a current situation can bring back whole prior episodes rather than some generalization derived from them or abstract rule implicit in them." (Clore & Ortony, 2000, pp. 34). Automated, conditioned, imitated, and reinstated emotions are associated to this kind of cognitive appraisal.

Related Dichotomies

The above described two routes to emotions are also routes to situational meaning and cognition in general. Those routes do not have to be pure and exclude each other, but rather it is supposed that there exists interplay between anew computation and previously learned significance. The distinction between these two forms of appraisals is clearer when considering what Clore and Ortony (2000) call *dual processes* or related dichotomies, which are also present in any process of meaning and of appraisal. Those dichotomies are shown in Table 1. Each route to appraisal corresponds to a kind of categorization, a form of reasoning and a behavioral function. In fact, reinstated (resp. computed) appraisal appears in a prototype-based (resp. theory-based) categorization, which is governed by associative (resp. rule-based) reasoning, and, which promotes behavioral preparedness (resp. flexibility).

Theory-Based vs. Prototype-Based Categorization

In prototype-based categorization (actual) situations are categorized in accordance to their *similarity* to a *prototype* or *best example* (strong significance in previous experiences) of a *category of situa-*

Table 1. Dual processes (taken from Clore & Ortony, 2000, pp. 37)

	Bottom-Up Processes	**Top-Down Processes**
Routes of appraisal	Computed	reinstated
Kind of categorization	theory-based	prototype-based
Forms of reasoning	rule-based	associative
Behavioral function	Flexibility	preparedness

tions, while in theory-based categorization actual situations are categorized by their *underlying aspects (properties),*conditions necessary and sufficient, in accordance to a certain *theory*.

Prototype-based categorization consists in matching a collection of ***perceptibly*** *available features* that usually are found among exemplars of a category (pattern), to those of the prototype, without regards to whether they are central or peripheral. On the other hand, theory-based categorization consists in reasoning about what the case seems to be and conceptual definitions of what the cases are. For instance, someone can be categorized: (1) as a person that has to be avoided because of the way he talks (loud, etc.), in accordance to a prototype-based previous experiences involving people with a *similar* attitude; or, (2) in accordance to what the person is doing (selling something in the street) and other *properties* of someone who does this kind of work (theory-based categorization).

Prototype-based categorization is useful for identification, *classification*, fast reasoning/heuristics and action – it is based on superficial issues; while theory-based categorization is useful for reasoning and *explanation*. They can complement each other. For instance, in a risky situation or in a situation of life requiring high mental concentration (*e.g.*, driving), while things are as expected (normal), prototype-based categorization, and the unconscious choice, would be more appropriated. On the other hand, after or in parallel to an unsatisfactory prototype-based output, the theory-based categorization or situational analysis might generate a *better* answer (e.g., when driving and something mechanical appears to be wrong in the car, and then this does not answer properly/as expected. In these cases, after the application of a heuristic the consequences are surprising, and not expected, and then we will reason about the situation in which we are in order to find a better answer/behavior).

Rule-Based vs. Associative Forms of Reasoning

Reinstated-based elicited meaning and appraisal, and prototype-based categorization are coherent with associative processing or reasoning, where objects or what have been the cases are organized according *to subjective similarity and temporal contiguity in experience*. On the other hand, anew computed elicited meaning, and theory-based categorization are coherent to rule-based reasoning or processing, which consist on *manipulation of symbolic structures*. Both of them can appear either consciously or unconsciously.

Flexibility vs. Preparedness Behavioral Function

The previous emotion and meaning elicitation forms, as well as the linked dichotomies, serve for rapid action and/or for flexible action, which might occur separately, in parallel or sequentially. Clore and Ortony (2000, pp. 41) suggest an example of the last one (the sequential manner): first *perceptual processes* (associative reasoning) identify stimuli with emotional value and actives preparation for action, and then *cognitive processes* (theory-based reasoning) verify the stimulus, situate it in context, and appraise its value. Additionally, in accordance to these authors such elicitation forms are related with evolution of humans, and flexibility appears along an expanded capacity for subjective experience. Being this the case, rule-based reasoning is a newer capacity than associative reasoning.

Finally, the impact of language in people ways to give meaning and emotions is important for opinion formation. To choose the appropriate language is important. Clore and Ortony (2000) suggest that *connotative language*[8] allows communicating emotions and experiences better than *denotative language* (alike it is well communicated in the raw in music and in the prosody of speech), which captures the physical and descriptive attributes of the objects in order to discriminate among them. It is highly probably that media recurs to this kind of language, in order to impact on and bias public opinion.

Truncated/Deconcextualized Cognition and Emotions

Clore and Ortony (2000) consider that emotions are reactions to personal meaning and the significance of a situation, and that they can be either conscious or unconscious. Unconscious emotions are elicited in a precognitive process, before the cerebral cortex is involved, and so awareness, but not before without the occurrence of the process giving meaning or significance. Because some significance is involved, the process is cognitive, though unaware. Thus, some surprising emotions can occur because they are elicited in a precortical process. An example of this is the reaction generated by a snake, which can occur through the direct hippocampus route before we fully realize about the presence of the snake.

Even more, sometimes emotions elicited almost without involvement of a cognitive process, as happens in the case of emotions promoted by subliminal messages, are sometimes used by media to promote certain opinions. Subliminal messages consist in stimulus (primus) involving a person for only a few milliseconds, and which is *masked* by another larger message. *Awareness of the primus is blocked by this second message.* Clore and Ortony (2000) recognize that *the effect of primes disappear when people are aware of them, however usually such awareness is missing.*

We will briefly describe what happens in this case (effects of subliminal messages), and then will mention other kind of cases used in media to favor certain opinions, and even manipulate people. How these forms of generating emotions, and other seen before, can be used for favoring certain opinions and manipulating people will be presented in the next sections.

In subliminal messages, the primus adheres to the subsequent messages/stimulus, so that it is overrated (either positively or negatively). Its effect could affects behavior and even dreams, as well as other aspects of life.

For explaining the different effects between unconscious subliminal primus and conscious primus, Clore and Ortony (2000) suggest that there is nothing precognitive involved in subliminal priming: the visual mask, which allows the image to be seen by only a few milliseconds, on one hand, interferes with the *episodic knowledge* of having seen the *stimulus*, but, on the other hand, does not interferes with the *semantic knowledge* of having seen *the image*. Consequently, the meaning is activated but the memory is not informed about the origin of the meaning, as this has been blocked. Thus, the particularities of meaning, which are highly important, are lost, and only the general aspects of meaning are kept. Diverse contextual elements of experience are lost including time and place.

Clore and Ortony (2000) relate these findings with certain neuroanatomical considerations, and in particular with two types of learning systems, each one having a separate neuroanatomical structure. These structures are: a) *the locale system*, concerned with episodic or contextual aspects of meaning; and b) *the taxon system*, associated with an stimulus without relating it with constrains of context (here concepts, categories, feelings, etc., can be recorded but not the spatio-temporal context).

Clore and Ortony (2000) argue that the *hippocampus* serves the function of the locale system. If the hippocampus does not work well, the person is decontextualized. Also, Clore and Ortony (2000) affirm that under stress the hippocampus can be suppressed, the person can be decontextualized and some phobias can reemerge. Clore and Ortony (2000) argue that the effect of primes in subliminal messages is then recorded in the taxon system, but not in the locale system or in the hippocampus. Ideas coming from primes become powerful not because anything to do with affect, but because their semantic meaning is not constrained. All this could be used by media, for instance, to created situations that can artificially genera stress, or frightens people, which then can be associated with new situations and generate unconscious surprising emotions, which promote certain behavior of interest for the media and for the elites that control it. We consider that media transmits two kinds of information: semantic information, generating semantic knowledge and meaning; and contextual information, associated with episodic and in general contextual knowledge and meaning.

An important conclusion of Clore and Ortony (2000) study is that the effect of subliminal messages is similar to that effect found in other phenomena, with supraliminal messages (differently from subliminal messages, supraliminal messages involve people for much longer periods than a few milliseconds, and are neither *masked* nor blocked by another message). All what is important, they say, is *whether the individual is able to fully parse the information stream into semantic (taxon) and episodic (local) information.* Among the situations, where an effect similar to that of subliminal messages, are those supraliminal messages in which the primed mining is obvious and related to a first issue, but people are distracted by other secondary issue, which attracts the *focus* of attention. In similar cases, the prime can appear as incidental, or some distraction interfere with episodic registration of the priming. Then emotions without appraisal can occur to the extent that they are reinstated obviating the differences between the contexts of the original situations (those creating the prototype, and which have not been properly recorded) and the actual situation. These emotions are promoted by media semantic information, where contextual information is missing, blocked, hidden or veiled.

These feelings associated with *primes, alike those related with moods, can have runaway affective meaning because they are not constrained by any episodic attachment.* In both cases, the *meaning associated to the experience is widely or indiscriminately applied.* This is a fact favoring certain media practices oriented to spread and strengthen certain opinions, as will be seen below.

Media Process of Inducing Opinion via Decontextualized Meanings and Emotions

Situations of meaning without context might be deliberately created, for instance, when an important issue related with priming is shown (either subliminally or supraliminally), and there is a certain interest in avoiding people having some reasoning, and/or searching for explanations, about the priming information. In these cases, as said above, another (distracting) issue is placed to *capture* the person's focus of attention. This is related with the form media operates sometimes in order to promote certain opinions. *Some media can influence people step by step, making the context less and less relevant, until it fades, while simultaneously creating certain prototypes of their interests to be used as a mean to match certain situations, generating decontextualized semantics and affective unconstrained meanings, being possible to manipulate and direct emotions and opinions in the direction of the media and elites' wish.* Prototypes in media can be associated to *Frames* (see section 3). Figure 1 shows how this process could occur based on the descriptions given in the previous subsection.

Prototype-based categorization is associated with framing (and planned in Agenda-setting, to be described in Section 3 below). Situations of real life are categorized in accordance to the interest of some elites and groups specialized in 4th generation war and manipulation[9], highlighting some features of interest for such elites and groups. Framing is the process of selecting certain aspects (attributes) of an issue to bring people's attention and to lead them a particular line of *interpretation*. Frames are simplifications or representations and interpretations of situations of interest, especially of particular political or economical relevance for elites and groups of power. These elites and groups of power can be globally relevant and associated with world media such as CNN (see section 3) or locally relevant and related with regional media.

Figure 1. A general model of the role of social media for creating public opinion. The media can promotes certain decontextualized information, by managing the context appropriately in order to put the focus in a process different from the prime, or to hide this, so that only semantic information is recorded (the episodic or local element of inf. is missing), and later on reinstated. Simultaneously, the media promote certain prototypes. These are used to generate some situations of meaning, and affective feelings (including emotions), without appraisal/reasoning, which can increase people's stress and raise certain moods (anxiety, for instance). These situations of meaning, affective feelings, and perhaps anxiety and moods, favor certain opinions. Such opinions generate social effects which feedback the described process, which afterwards strengthen such opinions.

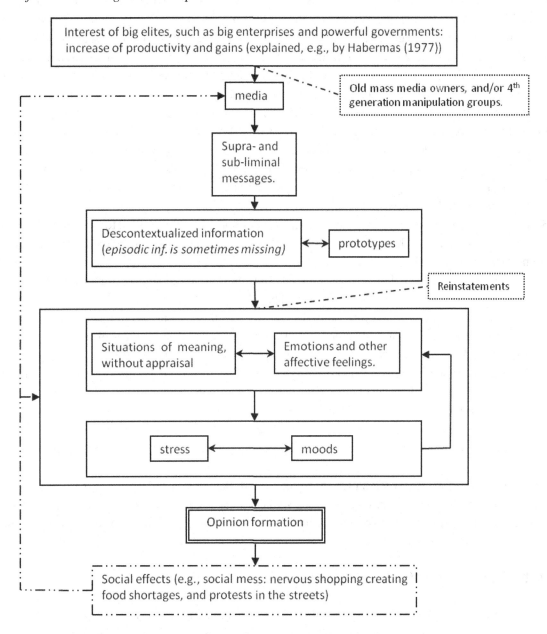

For instance, a government contrary to the interest of international elites can be prototyped/framed as *terrorist*; or, particular actors such as the head of the government, or the head of the army, can be framed as *dictators, illegitimate, oppressive or human rights violators*. Simultaneously, the opposition members (supported by the elites) can be framed as *freedom fighters*. These frames highlights some attributes that might either be little relevant, or perhaps false, but whose unfair public spread is of the interest for international powers, and so are put in the *agenda* of media, and used to manipulated public opinion by using framing strategies. Some people reached by such frames will reinstate them, and judge the framed actor either negatively (the head of the government) or positively (the opposition leader) in accordance to the assigned frame. In this form, prototypes/frames are used by mass 4th generation manipulation.

There is evidence that such model of the media has been applied to influence public opinion in relation to some countries whose governments (or social processes) (e.g., Venezuela, Russia, or Libya) affect the interest of, and are considered not friendly to, powerful elites, governments and companies (e.g., the U.S. government, the Oil companies) (these themes are treated in different web sites, see, for instance: http://www.globalresearch.ca/theme/media-disinformation).

In Venezuela and in several Arabian countries particular forms of protest are used to feedback media action, in favor of certain opinions and creating chaos (some of these cases will receive further description in the next section). For instance, in Venezuela barricades and *guarimbas* (Ross, 2013; Pardo, 2014) are activated by some groups that include hired delinquents, whose actions are contrary to local and national common good, for organizing local protests in some neighborhoods. These groups close streets, bridges, and local food supplies.

Some proves have being given that these groups get support from powerful actors in the local society and from foreign countries. These actions, barricades and guarimbas, along some media arguing in their favor and other media arguing against them, induce stress and moods (e.g., anxiety) in people, fostering particular opinion tendencies. For instance, media controlled by the opposition favor the idea that the authorities are the only actor guilty of the chaos and problematic situations of the country. The generated stress and moods (e.g. anxiety) has important effects on the life of people in the country (e.g., higher levels of chaos and negative feeling affect the population), what feedbacks the process of opinion formation, following the media reports of the chaos, what directly impacts on people' wellbeing (see Figure 1).[10]

In the case of the social networks and other types of social (new) media, prototypes are created and quickly (in real time) spread via short messages, which creates a reactive effect that feedbacks (as social media users reproduce them) the spreading process itself. In this sense, social media users help in promoting frames or media prototypes. The real time character of this spreading process helps in inhibiting the context of the original situation. The so created media prototypes, alike other prototypes, generate decontextualized emotions.

Prototypes spread by social media are often planned in the agenda-setting process (to be described in section 3), but also can appear/emerge from social media users interaction. In any case emerging prototypes are part of the perspective about certain situation, or state of issues, fostered by the media to favor certain elites' interests.

How to Cancel the Effects of the Media?

Clore and Ortony recommend not use the theory-based categorization alone, but also involving the alterative prototype based categorization. This will allow creating explanations about the situations of meaning and emotions, and keep them along the prototypes in order to give sense to what is happening beyond the decontextualized information prototypes alone give. In theory-based categorization, deep properties of the situation have to be searched for and involved in the explanation. Explanations must give sense to the properties of the prototypes.

A practical form to give contextual meaning to situations is talking about our feelings to a specialist, to a member of the family, to a friend or to oneself (Clore & Ortony, 2000). This helps to organize our thought, to explain, and to contextualize problematic decontextualized feelings. It is important to explain the context, and episodic aspects, of the situations of the past (history) constituting the origin of such feelings. To remember such past history and events, and become conscious of their association with those feelings, will help in resituating and constraining them, while importantly decreasing their subjective effects. As a consequence, the false forms of giving meaning, and decontextualized feelings will decrease, increasing fairness and better judgment /opinion about actual situations, liberating people from the effect of past distressing situations, as well as from media manipulation.

The consequences of decontextualized feelings have been largely studied since Sigmund Freud time. Similarly, to talk about our feelings in order to improve our psychological health and give sense to our feelings, becoming aware of them and their context, at the time that we decrease their indiscriminated application, is an old technique in Psychology and in some old practices, such as Yoga. What is new in Clore and Ortony paper is the explanation of how decontextualized feelings appear, and their relation with Neuroanatomical issues. What is new in this chapter is the application of Clore and Ortony (2000) ideas to show how media can promote bias and manipulate opinion formation, as illustrated in Figure 1.

MEDIA (BIAS) AND PUBLIC OPINION FORMATION

Media are considered as having an important influence on public opinion in a diversity of fields, including political science, communication studies, and more recently also computer based models. A high amount of research in this subject draws on psychological research on attitudes.

Agenda setting, framing and *social desirability (creation)* are some well known theories explaining the influence of media on public opinion (Public opinion, n.d.). To understand these and some related issues will allow us to comprehend better the influence of media on public opinion formation. Let us briefly defines these notions and then later, in the next sections, describe the first two and their implications in more detail. Agenda setting suggests that world media agenda is under control of major world media enterprises and some elites, and so has a high potential to effect on the formation of public opinion. This determines which stories will be newsworthy in accordance to the concern of powerful actors such as transnational companies, governments of developed countries, and groups of interest (e.g., religious). Clearly, this implies that there is some intentionality of influencing and manipulating public opinion by media.

Framing consists in portraying a story or a piece of news in a particular way in order to sway the consumer's attitude in a particular form. Thus, this is a way of stereotyping situations, actors, etc, and promoting certain interpretations, i.e., this is a second mode of effecting on public opinion. It is an old form of manipulation present in mass media, being now reproduced in social media.

Such media biases are facilitated by social desirability. Social desirability is based on the wish of people to be recognized and become part of the group they identify with. People then behave and form their opinions in accordance to the behavior and opinions they believe are the behavior and opinions prevalent in that social group. However, many times the behavior and opinion people believe is the dominant one in that group, is not; but rather some behavior and opinion (point of view/perspective) repeated throughout a diversity of news mediums and social networking sites have created a false perception of what is considered as prevalent behavior and opinion in the group people identify with.

As said above, the diversity of media and social networking sites promoting this kind of behavior includes both: a) old media or mass media such as TV, radio, newspapers, journals, books, etc.; and, b) new media, or social media, or internet based media such as tweeter, Facebook, and blogs. In particular, in social media stories and opinions (what includes frames) are placed by some users/actors (individuals or groups) to which other users virtually associate/identify with, usually without an appropriate discernment about the intensions of those actors, the context of the stories, and the veracity of the opinions. This allows a fast spreading of frames, and of effects of manipulation.

Agenda Setting

This theory describes the ability of the media to influence the topics appearing in public agenda. To be in this agenda ensures an item to be frequently and prominently covered, and then the audience will consider it as important. This theory was developed by McCombs and Shaw (see for instance, McCombs and Reynolds, 2002; McCombs and Shaw, 1972; McCombs, 2005; and Rogers, 1993), in their study about the 1968 U.S. presidential election called "Chapel Hill Study". This study showed a strong correlation (r above 0.9) between: a) what 100 neighbors of Chapel Hill in North Caroline thought was the most important election issue, and b) what the local and the national media news reported was the most important issue. Here the named researchers were able to show the degree to which media determine public opinion (McCombs & Shaw, 1972). This work has generated plenty of further research (more than 400 studies), which have confirmed the theory. Nowadays this theory continues being relevant and influential. Similar but independent results were got by Ray Funkhouser (see for instance, Funkhouser, 1973).

The origin of the ideas of this theory can be traced to the work of Lippmann (1922), in a chapter titled "The World Outside the Picture in Our Heads" published in Lippmann edited book: Public Opinion (Lippmann, 1922). Inspired in Lippman's ideas, Cohen (1963) pointed out how successful the media is in suggesting people *what to think about,* depending on the map that is drawn for them by writers, editors, and publishers. More recently researchers such as Craig Roberts Paul have shown why disinformation work in the U.S. (see, for instance, Craig (2013)). Craig highlights the role of agenda-setting.

Some key assumptions or findings of this theory are: a) the media do not reflect reality, they filter and shape, so they are intentionally biased; b) media concentration on few issues and subjects leads the public to consider those issues as more important than others, some of which are even forgotten and are not part of public concern despite of their social importance. It is a clear fact that mass media impacts a longer fraction of people around the world in present time than in the last century, that the agenda is set in the most powerful countries (at the called developed world, and mainly in the U.S.), and that the intensity of messages, or number of messages per unit of time, from the media increases over time.

This is being reproduced in social media, where stories (tales) are made and some frames are placed, via which certain features of people, and events, are highlighted by elites and especially from organizations specialized in 4th generation war and manipulation. Such stories and frames are reproduced by followers of who creates them. Afterwards, other people (e.g., friends, colleagues, supporters, etc., in twitter, or in Facebook) will also imitate, quickly spreading the story and frames. Similarly, institutions specialized in 4th generation war and manipulation can neutralize and deactivate certain stories and frames contrary to the interest of the institutions they favor. Thus, nowadays prototypes can be created or deactivated/ neutralized almost instantaneously (in a very short time, i.e., in real time).

Some authors suggest that agenda setting is operativized via *accessibility*: media covers and issue in the agenda frequently and prominently, so that a high number of instances of the issue become accessible to the audience memories. The aggregated impact of a large number of messages is very important, even if the messages have different content but they deal with the same general issue, and share a similar perspective about the issue (Iyengar & Kinder, 1987, Iyengar, 1990; Dearing & Rogers, 1988). Media also has an important impact in what people think that others think (Dearing & Rogers, 1988; Noelle-Neumann (1977). This has influence in social *norms*, as people tend to behave in the form they think other expect from them.

An alternative media (as we will mention in the next section) will be one in which agenda elaboration has *important* participation and feedback from people/users. This mode is called *Agenda Building*. The agenda building mode recognizes the importance of users and of their participation. Some web tools are useful for this purpose because of their facilities for interaction and feedback, such as the blogs. Other related notion is *agenda melding* (Ragas & Roberts, 2009), which consists in adapting our agenda and the agenda of diverse free media that serve specialized interest groups. In this case, individual join groups and blend their agendas with those of the groups. This allows creating communities of interest whose members share values, attitudes and opinions. These other two types of agenda have the potential to modify the impact of the media in the public, what can be combined with free technologies in order to create a media with a different, more critical, impact. This will be the issue of the next section.

Some researchers describe two levels of agenda-setting: the first level tells us *what* to think about, and the second level tells us about *how* to think about. The first one centers on issue salience, and the second one gives more importance to attributes salience (Balmas & Sheafer, 2010). Attributes can be either properties or tones (positive, negative, neutral), which are more related with emotions. Some authors argue in favor of recognizing the second level of agenda setting as similar to framing. However, researchers such as Scheufele (2000) say that framing and agenda-setting possess distinct theoretical boundaries, operate via distinct cognitive processes (accessibility vs. attribution), and relate to different outcomes (perceptions of issue importance vs. interpretation of news issue).

Framing

The concept of framing was first elaborated by Bateson (1972). He considers frames as spatial and temporal attachments (bonds) of a set of interactive messages. Framing refers to the social construction of social phenomena and understanding, often conducted by media. Media promotes particular definitions, interpretations, evaluations and recommendations (Entman, 1993; Nelson, Clawson, & Oxley, 1997). Framing defines, for instance, how news coverage shapes public opinion. Some authors consider framing as the process of selecting certain aspects (attributes) of an issue to bring people's attention and to lead them a particular line of *interpretation*. The influence of frames is considered in two ways: 1) frames in thought, consisting of the mental simplifications, and interpretations of reality; and, 2) frames in communication, consisting of the communication of frames among actors.

Framing complements agenda-setting. While agenda settings focuses on defining "what to think about", framing tells us "how to think about" that previously defined and planned in the agenda setting, or emerging in social media, and of interest for elites and groups specialized in 4th generation manipulation.

By using frames (as well as by agenda-setting), the media gets advantage of the fact that there is an inevitable influence on individuals and groups perception and perspective of the meaning of words and phrases. In fact, media often goes intentionally beyond any candid attitude, as it is driven by and responds to commercial and elitist interests. Media require monetary support, which usually is got via advertising, or collaboration of some actors. However, such advertising usually is given only if the media satisfy certain policies of interest for the supporter. Such support can be either promoted or prevented/blocked by elites and other groups, such as groups specialized in 4th generation manipulation, in accordance to their interest.

Frames usually emphasize (positive or negative) connotative meanings of an object or situation by focusing on certain attributes, while given less importance or obviating others. There are also diverse framing strategies. For instance, the equivalence frame, which consists in presenting information based on the same facts but the frame in which it is based changes, thus creating a *reference dependent perception*.

A frame consists basically in an element of rhetoric to encourage certain interpretations and discourage others. Many examples have been studies as we will show below. To give a short idea of the cases: in journalist applications, it has been shown that the frame surrounding the issue can change the reader's perception (see, e.g., Framing (social sciences) (n.d.)). Several other cases can be found at this web site, with the appropriate reference to the supporting research papers, and books.

A frame can also be defined as a collection of anecdotes and *stereotypes* on which individuals rely on, and use to respond to events. Under this view, a frame is a *schema of interpretation*. Frames usually describe aspects of objects and situations in accordance to its importance for an individual or group, in order to achieve a certain goal in terms of effecting on (constructing different or changing existing) perceptions in a community.

This effect will then affect the psychology of people, in terms of creating certain prototypes which are easily reinstated, as explained in the previous section. Some of those prototypes or stereotypes recur to manipulation of emotions via decontextualized situations of meanings and emotions. In this sense, sometimes framing seem to follow schemas similar to that one presented in Figure 1 of the previous section, as will be suggested in the examples below.

The social media are an excellent way to develop framing strategies in accordance to the interest of the groups specialized in 4th generation war, and particularly to manipulate public opinion, telling us "how to think about" the issues selected in agenda setting

Diverse media could compete with somewhat different frames. One of the competing frames will prevail. Among the factors that affect the prevalence of a frame are: support from powerful groups such as elites, groups of interest, or political actors; and the cultural context (or previous frames people already manage).

Psychological Effects of Framing

A well-known study about the psychological effects of media frames is that carried out by Iyengar (1991). This study examines the impact of *episodic* and *thematic* news frames on viewer's attributions of responsibility for political issues such as crime, poverty, unemployment and racial inequality in U.S. An episodic news frame is understood as a case study *or event-oriented report* depicting public issues in terms of *concrete instances*. Differently, a thematic news frame is more argumentative/explicative and places public issues in terms of a more general and abstract context, arguing in terms of outcomes or conditions (Entman, 1993; Iyengar, 1991) (this is more theory-based). Iyengar (1991) shows in his research covering six years of TV coverage that the majority of television news of poverty was episodic. His experiments indicate that people who watch episode news about poverty are more than twice probable, than those who watch thematic news, to attribute poverty responsibility to poor people themselves rather than to society and politicians. This has important consequences in politics, favoring the position of politicians who do not address the poverty issue widely as a social problem. This study shows that episodic news frames, which hide the context more than thematic news frames, promote certain kind of perspectives. When hiding part of the context, episodic news might be following a strategy to bias opinion formation close to that process shown in Figure 1.

Social media can produce the same effect, perhaps with less effort and more effectively, because of some characteristics of the episodic frames used in social media; for instance, the restricted allowed length of a twitter message does not allow thematic frames. In this way, social media decontextualize reality fostering impulsive/reactive behavior in the target society.

Other cases will be shown below. This has many consequences, including moral ones. For instance, Entman (1993) suggests that by selecting some features of a perceived reality and making them more salient, frames *promote a particular problem definition, causal interpretation, and even moral evaluation* for the object or situation of the case. Even more, Kuypers (2009) suggests that frames (both episodic and thematic) operate in four key ways, which together imply a wide impact in, and even manipulation of, social life: define problems, diagnose causes, make moral judgments, and suggest remedies. Consequently, frames manipulate first to introduce a problem, and then to suggest a solution.

Recent research that involves empirical studies (Nelson et al., 1997; Scheufele, 2000) indicate that the more effective aspect of framing is *applicability* rather than accessibility. Applicability is associated with the existence in the individual of previous schemes related with the information he receives. Those studies suggest that by making particular considerations more applicable and therefore more relevant to the judgment process framings are effective. On the other hand, accessibility is associated with how recent and how often the information has been given, and thus it is accessible to the individual in his mind. Applicability is favored by the process described in Figure 1, where decontextualized messages will create certain beliefs that are widely applied by the individual, via unconstrained (without appraisal) reinstatement, as in episodic news appraisal described above. Applicability and accessibility are both related to the use of the Availability Heuristic/Proposition: "if you can think of it, it must be important."

Consequently, to favor accessibility in order to manipulate public opinion, frames should be repeated as often as possible, and nude of (without) context as much as feasible (e.g., twitter messages or facebook wall messages). Similarly, in order to favor accessibility that fosters public opinion, frames should be elaborated in a way that matches as much as possible previous schemas of knowledge of the individuals.

Finally, it is worth saying that via diverse mediums (e.g., magnetic resonance imaging) cognitive neuroscientists have showed the effect of frames on the amygdale and other areas of the human brain (see, for instance, Framing (social communication theory) (n.d.).

Examples of the Media Bias and Influence in Public Opinion

Media seems to have effects in a diversity of social issues such as Culture, Health, Nutrition, Education, Politics, Economics, and even in violence, conflicts and wars, among many others. A fact related with this issue is that about 90% of the total news outputs of the world press are *managed* by only four media actors: AP, UPI, Reuters, and Agence-France-Presse, which usually reflect the point of view of the status quo, or dominant and elite western countries (as an example, see Media influence (n.d.)). Mass media has had an important impact both in western culture (some researchers talk about social control), and in non-western cultures, to the point of *westernizing* different regions of the world in a sort of cultural-imperialism (Schiller, 1975).

Similar effects have been created by social media, which are also managed from the western countries, and strongly influenced by elites, as well as by groups specialized in the 4th generation war and manipulation. In social media, frames spread quickly and usually have a high level of decontextualisation, what gives the social networks a high strategic importance to manipulate public opinion, in parallel and complementing mass media. Such strategic power is given by the fact that, at present, a high percentage of young people around the world uses the social networks without any deliberation/questioning.

Some concrete examples of manipulation by the media are:

Use of Frames

1. The use of some words by the U.S. government, such as:
    a. "Crime" and "War on Terror" after the September 11, 2001 attacks against the World Trade Center. The first word is a call for justice applied towards someone who is already supposed to be guilty, and the second for action to bring in justice, by strong and dangerous acting against other countries (war), to what public support in the U.S. is already implicit. In this sense frames are a sort of pre-fabricated public opinion, based on stereotypes of other actors (muslim people are characterized as terrorists, and U.S. and western people are stereotyped as fighters for freedom).
    b. "Foreign aid", which implies that the money given will help foreigner rather than harming them.
    c. "Stabilization policy", which assumes that a certain policy will have an stabilization effect.
2. Framing the "other" as primitive, pre-modern and not human, as western media do, for instance, to characterise the Muslims during the Iraq war, as showed by Butler (2009).
3. Placing in social media manipulated stories with false frames about social events arising in certain countries (in the last years, e.g., Ukraine, Venezuela, Libya, and Syria). Sometimes such events are also generated by social media manipulation. This manipulation is strategically planned (included in agenda) and carried on by elites and 4th generation war groups.

The Availability Heuristic

Use of the heuristic named above: "if you can think of it, it must be important." It suggests that whatever issue about which we think is important. However, sometimes the frequencies that events come to mind are usually not accurate reflections of their actual probability in real life. This might happens in media (both mass media and social media) manipulation as described above when using the ideas of "Applicability" and "Accessibility". Media manipulation promotes wrong extrapolations. For instance: when an example of characteristic of a known person is extrapolated to a whole group, what can create a strongly biased positive or a negative perspective about the group. This can happen in developed countries in relation to Muslims who are usually considered as potential "terrorists" because of a relatively small number of cases, of which, even some are doubtful. The same happens in countries such as Venezuela where the government and the opposition usually promotes certain negative qualification of each other, and a positive qualification of itself in the media by using some specific cases or examples that can be considered as good or bad behavior, but which do not support the generalization (in Venezuela, both, the opposition and the government, have some important controlled media).

The CNN Effect

This is an explanation of the impact of TV and other media in countries foreign policy. Initially, it described the effect of Cable News Network CNN) on some states foreign policies during the Cold War. This effect of the TV has continued after the Cold War. Examples of this effect have occurred during the fall of Communism in Eastern Europe, the Gulf War, the War against Libya, the war in Syria, and the promoted prototyping as the "evil" or "bad guy" of Iran and other countries.

Steven Livington (Livington, 1997) is one of the more relevant researchers in this issue. He identifies three CNN kinds of effects: a) policy agenda setting, b) impediment to the achievement of desired policy goals, and c) accelerant to policy decision making.

CNN and similar media focuses on instantaneous and ongoing media coverage on particular conflicts, international incident, etc, what requires political attention, as governing politicians of many countries attempt to demonstrate that they are aware of, and act in accordance to, "the development of current situations". The effect, according to Belknap (2001), is that real time news coverage has led to almost instantaneous public awareness and governmental responses, as events are still going on. In this sense, the media sets the agenda of the politicians. For this, CNN, alike other mass media, is also using the social media; e.g., to make public their agenda, and to place stories and videos in accordance to this agenda, and in real time. This significantly increases CNN's effectiveness in biasing public opinion.

Disinformation

Disinformation or black propaganda is intentionally false or inaccurate information that is deliberately spread in the media. A disinformation practice consists in mixing truth with false conclusions and lies, or showing partially some truth while presenting it as the whole truth. Recent cases of media disinformation campaigns carried on by powerful western actors (agenda-setting and frames likely were elaborated by powerful governments, media companies and other elites) have contributed to increase the proportion of public opinion in favor of some wars the western have been carrying on against several countries, such as Iraq and Libya. In the case of Iraq it is well known the misinformation about the existence of an arsenal of chemical weapons, which was probed to be false once the invasion was carried out. Another case of misinformation is the hiding of the strongly negative consequences of some weapon used by western countries, and of all the war, for the Iraqi people.

Again, social media also can be used in this domain. As an example, recently during the guarimbas in Venezuela, in the social media false photos (e.g., photos from other countries) and other inaccurate information was used to manipulate certain sectors of the Venezuelan and international public in order to impulse bad opinion about the Venezuelan Police (see, e.g., Combs (2014)). Such excess occurred few times, however *they were far from being general*. This fact is veiled by some false photos showing police men mistreating people, and framing/prototyping them as violent and oppressive *in general*. Additionally, this social media did not say that violence was *initiated* from groups doing the guarimbas, who the police attempted to control in order to protect the Venezuelan population, and that even some police men were killed by them; or, that public spaces were kidnapped by people doing the guarimbas.

SOCIAL KNOWLEDGE: TOWARDS AN EMANCIPATE UTILIZATION OF THE SOCIAL MEDIA

Social Media for Knowledge Generation

In general, Web 2.0 and Web 3.0 tools are essential for the consolidation of a democratic technological rationality. They enable social emergency (Aguilar, 2012). In this sense, the social media become a learning space based on the premise: "knowledge to those who need it". Web must be discovered as tool for the social interaction, collective knowledge creation, i.e., as a catalyst for social emergent processes.

The tools around Web 2.0, or social Web, and Web 3.0, or Web intelligent, as they are known, allow the use and creation of knowledge, based on collaboration and flexibility of learning processes. The tools around Web 2.0 and Web 3.0 enable large participation and, most importantly, new ways of relating.

The human emancipation process requires a new relationship between man and the technologies. This new model should allow the construction of a liberating knowledge in a participatory manner (Aguilar, 2011a). This vision must develop in the users a critical awareness, social awareness, and common sense, in order to promote new ways of seeing social reality. All this should allow the users to transform their reality.

This would facilitate the ongoing search for the truth, from the local, as the cornerstone of the process. A model of a relationship between man and the technologies that favors spaces of collective work, of equality and of solidarity is required. Spaces, in order to develop a sense of community, with critical values about the individualism, the profit and commodity fetishism, should be developed. Also, spaces that allow all of us to take an active role in solving collective problems of the community in which we live, and in which we can all participate in the construction and implementation of community life projects. This requires social practices based on coexistence, cooperation and mutual aid, key factors that have already been present in social networks.

This new technology model requires a kind of horizontal relationship among men (Aguilar, 2009, 2012). According to (Aguilar, 2009), this is possible "through a direct and profound communication in which we can re-learn and re-create". From this relationship is defined a mutual creation in which participants are involved. Thus, human interaction is not merely a certain kind of economic development, but a creation of self in community with the other.

It should be clear that a model of man's relationship with the emancipatory technologies is not neutral, it is a space of struggles, debates and social construction, for learning, not hijacked by technocrats (Aguilar, 2011a). We are talking about a model that generates capacities from below. To do that, open spaces of permanent construction from below are required, allowing democratizing knowledge and breaking the technical mediation of technocrats. It also requires learning processes, and not only merely contemplative knowledge acquisition but also processes of knowledge creation and questioning . We are talking about processes that recover the ideological character of technology, understanding this as an ideological activity. In fact, there are several ways to do it, some of which help in sustaining the existing social system, and impede its replacement or evolution towards a form of technology supporting a more just society, while some of these other forms of technology support a more just society and goes against existing privileges of some actors and societies, as expounded in (Aguilar, 2011b; Varsavsky, 1974). From this ideological view of technology, each type of society requires its own model of man's relationship with the technologies, one different in content; a technology for the particular problems faced and studied in each society, which supports the methods used, their practical criteria of truth, as well as the sociological characteristics of the members of the society.

How serious is the role of the social networks in these emancipated societies?. They are, as forms of collective social construction of knowledge, and socialization of knowledge. We are talking about a new form of work, where all stakeholders participate together in building the knowledge required for the implementation and construction of projects of life, using social networks.

To give coherence and ability to materialize the model relationship between man and the technology requires a new type of rationality. In an emancipator context, this new rationality must be based on the principles of review and action for change. In this regard, it is essential that all people actively participate in the process of knowledge production. The tools around the Web 2.0 and 3.0 allow great participation and, most importantly, new ways of people inter-relating.

This new rationality constructs the social networks in terms of interest and experience of social actors, from the problems of everyday life and what has shaped our past and present. This new rationality requires that we can say our own stories, and not as now, when these histories and our language are eliminated product of technocratic imposition and education. This new rationality is seen as a dialectical process of critical analysis and transformation of the social, political and cultural reality.

Social Knowledge Networks

People must recognize that there are many different social networks and communities and that, like e-mail, it is up to users to decide how to use them (Helms et al., 2010). Sharing of knowledge is an important part of social media to learn and innovate. Sharing of knowledge typically occurs in the informal networks by means of social interaction. One extension of the social media that some communities have applied is called Social Knowledge Networks (SKNs) (Green, 2010; Helms et al., 2010). This is a virtual environment around a social process that combines content, human resources, and expertise on the problem, in order to increase performance, preserve knowledge, and allow innovation. Contents as data, documents, etc. are the resources of a successful Social Knowledge Network, while people and their expertise are the lifeblood. Collaboration is natural and happens because people are socially connected based on their interests. Several aspects can be considered for a successful SKN (Green, 2010; Helms et al., 2010):

- **Define the Problem:** This is probably the most important aspect because gives the goal to reach as a collective agreement of what that problem is. It represents the issue to address by way of implementing a Social Knowledge Network.
- **Pick your People:** It is important to explicitly define a community of people focusing on an objective. They will understand the value of sharing knowledge and ideas, to cooperate to solve real problems, etc.
- **Find Leaders:** One successful social network need a culture of a collaborative leadership. The idea is to combine the top-down studied content with the bottom-up wisdom of the community.

Some aspects to study in KNA if used for emancipation are (Green, 2010; Helms et al., 2010):

- **Master-Apprenticeship:** Learning is possible if there are connections between experts and non-experts, and higher levels of connections are reached if the transfers are of high viscosity.

- **Sub-Community:** A learning network must be one cohesive group so that knowledge can flow freely throughout the network.
- *Knowledge drain & knowledge brokers* concerns risks, and focuses on the impact of the sudden (or planned, when is a retirement) departure of employees. A knowledge broker occurs when employees that leave have a brokering role in the organization. Without this knowledge connectedness can decrease and even disconnect sub communities. A knowledge drain typically occurs when an expert leaves the organization and he has null or low viscosity knowledge transfer relations.

Social media offer new possibilities to structure and perform learning processes. Social media can be used by educators, institutions, and individual students to support particular teaching and learning experiences and to organize individual availability. Challenges for educators and institutions using social media for knowledge generation in teaching could be summarized under the following keywords: transferability, security and privacy issues and content issues (Canals, 2005).

There are four characteristics of social media (Canals, 2005; Chun & Luna-Reyes, 2012; Treem & Leonardi, 2012): visibility, persistence, editability, and association. Traditional web tools enable some of them, but lack some of them. For example, e-mail affords editability because users can carefully craft messages prior to sending, and the medium has high persistence for individual users who can save, store, and search through their own messages. However, e-mail does not afford much visibility (the messages a person receives are limited to those addresses indicated by the message's sender). Social media, by contrast, have rate uniformly high on their four characteristics. These aspects must be analyzed in a free relationship with the Social Media, in order to exploit the next characteristics (Treem & Leonardi, 2012).

- *Social Connection.* Social media allow making associations more explicit.
- *Emergent Connection.* Features such as rankings and recommendations in social media afford forms of associations and suggest ways to improve existing associations or initiate new ones.
- *Access to Relevant Information.* Individuals establish associations with the content in social media.
- *Robust Forms of Communication.* Robust" means how difficult it is to destroy, or abandon content. Keeping existing contents and their tags, makes reuse easier and increases the likelihood to popularize material through ongoing use.
- *Metaknowledge.* The visibility of social media provides metaknowledge about people.
- *Improving Information Quality.* By the editability of the social media, individuals have the opportunity to revise, reshape, and coordinate content.
- *Sustaining Knowledge Over Time.* The persistence of content created and stored in social media allows that knowledge contributes to the technological development and remains available over time.
- *Targeting Content.* Users of social media often tailor messages for specific audiences.
- *Growing Content.* The nearly limitless space afforded by social media, facilitates the growth of communication. But, this unlimited storage generates that the content embedded in social media tools can become unwieldy over time. For that, social media also provide individuals with the means to find content with filters and search tools.
- *Regulating Personal Expressions.* The editability of content into social media allows us to strategically define forms favor sharing of personal information.

Social Media on Intelligent Communication Processes

The social media results have the next characteristics: a high degree of visibility, persistence, editability, and association. Other technologies have features that instance some of these characteristics. A database system may have the same visibility of a blog, a worker may carefully craft an e-mail just as he would a wiki entry. However, social media differ in that they afford all of these four communicative outcomes simultaneously and consistently in an organizational setting.

These four social media characteristics can alter three processes that have, historically, a high importance for the communication: socialization, information sharing, and power relations (Treem & Leonardi, 2012). Particularly, in a free relationship with social media, thinking in an emancipatory utilization, these processes must be redefined as:

Socialization: Communication is the primary way through which individuals manage the uncertainty. The three most commonly discussed topics related to socialization must be:

- *Information seeking.* Users use a variety of communication tactics to gather information, and the usefulness of information for socialization is closely related to the communication technology people use to find it. In this way, it is necessary to consider how social media afford individuals novel ways to search information.
- *People processing tactics.* Both the visibility and persistence of information can result in diverse socialization experiences, and allow greater choice of the material that someone can access or encounter.
- *Relationship formation.* The associations of the social media are a powerful way to establish relationships with others. Social media offer the opportunity to find individuals with similar interests, or discover potential mentors.

Knowledge Sharing: Many researchers are interested in the processes by which people create and transfer knowledge. The characteristics offered by social media may affect four processes, which must be analyzed for a free relationship with them:

- *Capturing tacit knowledge.* One of the paramount challenges is how to capture and learn from the tacit knowledge held by users. The visibility afforded by social media allows presenting personal information publicly.
- *Identifying expertise.* The ability to identify the expertise of people allows assigning individuals to appropriate tasks and, improving group performance. The visibility of the social media allows that, but also can block that.
- *Motivating knowledge contributions.* Given the ways that social media support relations, motivating contributions may merely increase social exchanges and not necessarily increase organizational knowledge.
- *Overcoming organizational boundaries.* Social media are commonly viewed as means to organize knowledge and place it in a form accessible to other organizational members. However, individuals often have trouble understanding communications from other people because they have different vocabularies. One way that social media can address this issue is through the visibility. Another way is through easy associations that encourage people to explore new relationships.

Power: The processes of managerial power, and resistance to it, have occupied a lot of studies about communication. Four processes are often discussed in the relationship between power and communication, which must be analyzed for a free relationship with them:

- *Surveillance.* Social media, by making the practices and contributions of people more visible, may increase surveillance of them. Additionally, social media creates a record of activity that may be used for a variety of surveillance purposes.
- *Filtering of social content on the Internet by country.* Internet Censorship is not a static phenomena, it is evolving, rising and/or falling, depending on politics, societies and jurisdictions all over the world.
- *Resource dependency.* The knowledge contained in social media is a potential source of power for individuals. By making information visible to others, individuals may be able to subtly signal that they possess knowledge. If that knowledge is then perceived as valuable, it can be a source of power that can result in increased influence in decision making
- *Participation in discursive construction.* Social media, by facilitating visible text, can be viewed as an inherently discursive space where individuals are able to put forth arguments and engage in public deliberation.

Democratization of Communication

Not only social media fosters a process of democratization of communication. The Internet itself and the possibility to communicate thought computer mediated channels over distance have started the process. During the pre-Internet era communication was limited to certain forms. For instance, via one-to-many industrial mass media communication, or via one-to-one individual media interaction, such as via the telephone. Because of the cost of distribution, the possibility to communicate to a great amount of people was available to only small elite. But even then the individual media producer was limited in her freedom of expression by external factors such as the market situation and the ideologies of her superior and the company.

Internet has overcome another limitation to communication: the inflexibility of space and time. The invention of e-mail, and later the SMS, created ways of overcoming previous space and time constrains. With email it was suddenly possible to communicate with a great amount of people. Social Media share similar characteristics with e-mail, but they are much more effective. This has redefined a new space where a free relationship can be defined with the Social Media.

But we need to analyze the Citizen Media. They are media that are strongly connected with the topic of social media founded on citizenship in a society. Although citizen media were already existent before the advent of social media, it is only through social media that citizen media have become a significant part of todays media environment. Citizen media content is often (but not exclusively) based on local topics in a specific society. This content does not necessarily find its way into industrial media since it is not of general interest and therefore economically unsustainable. The technological advancements and the decreasing cost of audio visual equipment in combination with the Internet and social media have favored the rise of this new form of journalism, where special interest topics have found a new platform.

A camera phones, smart phones and video cameras with Internet accessibility become ubiquitous, and every citizen becomes a potential producer of citizen media, even if it is only for a short time. An example of this phenomenon is: Citizens who film a certain event, share it via social media, and become producers of citizen media. This social behavior must be analyzed, and a new citizenship must be considered associated with a critical, conscious, and not manipulator use of social media.

REFERENCES

Agrawal, D., Bamieh, B., Budak, C., El Abbadi, A., Flanagin, A., & Patterson, S. (2011). Data-Driven Modeling and Analysis of Online Social Networks. In H. Wang, S. Li, S. Oyama, X. Hu, & T. Qian (Eds.), *Web-Age Information Management: Proceedings of the 2011 International Conference* (LNCS) (Vol. 6897, pp. 3-17). Berlin, Germany: Springer.

Aguilar, J. (2009). Hacia una Tecnología Democrática para Mérida: Bases para un nuevo Paradigma Universitario en la creación de una Facultad en Tecnologías Informáticas. *Revista de la Academia de Mérida, 14*(22), 17–80.

Aguilar, J. (2011a). Conocimiento Libre y Educación Emancipadora. *Revista EDUCARE, 15*(1), 84–106.

Aguilar, J. (2011b). Para construir un nuevo tipo de Economía Social y Humanista, se requiere reflexionar sobre el Capitalismo Cognitivo. *Revista Sistémica Libre, 1*(1), 3–18.

Aguilar, J. (2012). Autonomía Tecnológica vs. Tecnocracia. In J. Medina & M. Salazar (Eds.), *Tecnología y Poder: Una mirada a las Telecomunicaciones* (pp. 37–60). Caracas, Venezuela: Ediciones A Desalambrar.

Balmas, M., & Sheafer, T. (2010). Candidate Image in Election Campaigns: Attribute Agenda Setting, Affective Priming, and Voting Intentions. *International Journal of Public Opinion Research, 22*(2), 204–229. doi:10.1093/ijpor/edq009

Bateson, G. (1972). *Steps to an Ecology of Mind*. New York: Ballantine Books.

Belknap, M. H. (2001). *The CNN Effect: Strategic Enabler or Operational Risk?* U.S. Army War College Strategy Research Project.

Braun, L. (2012). Social Media and Public Opinion. In *Master's Thesis: Interculturalitat i Polítiques Comunicatives en la Societat de la Informaciò*. University of Valencia.

Butler, J. (2009). *Frames of War*. London: Verso.

Canals, A. (2005). Knowledge diffusion and complex networks: a model of high-tech geographical industrial clusters. *The Network Science Society*. Retrieved from: http://www.netscisociety.net/biblio?page=1

Chronister, R., & Hardy, S. (1997). The Limbic System. In D. Haines (Ed.), *Fundamental neuroscience* (pp. 443–454). New York: Churchill Livingstone Inc.

Chun, S., & Luna-Reyes, L. (2012). Social Media in Government. *Government Information Quarterly, 29*(4), 441–445. doi:10.1016/j.giq.2012.07.003

Clore, G., & Ortony, A. (2000). Cognition in Emotion: 1, Sometimes or Never? In R. Lane, L. Nadel, G. Ahern, J. Allen, & A. Kaszniak (Eds.), *Cognitive Neuroscience of Emotion* (pp. 24–61). Oxford University Press.

Cohen, B. (1963). *The press and foreign policy*. New York: Harcourt.

Combs, C. (2014). These Photos Being Shared From Venezuela Are Fake. *Global Research. Global Research News*. Retrieved from: http://www.globalresearch.ca/these-photos-being-shared-from-venezuela-are-fake/5370091

Connotation. (n.d.). *Wikipedia*. Retrieved from: http://en.wikipedia.org/wiki/Connotative

Craig, R. P. (2013). Why Disinformation Works. In America "Truth has no Relevance. Only Agendas are Important". *Global Research*. Retrieved from: http://www.globalresearch.ca/why-disinformation-works-in-america-truth-has-no-relevance-only-agendas-are-important/5336335

Dearing, J., & Rogers, E. (1988). Agenda-setting research: Where has it been, where is it going? *Communication Yearbook*, *11*, 555–594.

Ellner, S. (2014). Terrorism in Venezuela and Its "Regime Change" Accomplices. *Global Research*. Retrieved from: http://www.globalresearch.ca/terrorism-in-venezuela-and-its-regime-change-accomplices/5383291

Entman, R. M. (1993). Framing: Toward clarification of a fractured paradigm. *Journal of Communication*, *43*(4), 51–58. doi:10.1111/j.1460-2466.1993.tb01304.x

Framing (social communication theory). (n.d.). *The Free Dictionary*. Retrieved from: http://encyclopedia.thefreedictionary.com/Framing+(communication+theory)

Framing (social sciences). (n.d.), *Wikipedia*. Retrieved from: http://en.wikipedia.org/wiki/Framing_(social_communication_theory)

Funkhouser, G. (1973). The issues of the sixties: An exploratory study in the dynamics of public opinion. *Public Opinion Quarterly*, *37*(1), 62–75. doi:10.1086/268060

Gaudichaud, F. (2014). Street Violence and the Political Destabilization of Venezuela. US Sponsored "Color Revolution". *Global Research*. Retrieved from: http://www.globalresearch.ca/street-violence-and-the-political-destabilization-of-venezuela-us-sponsored-color-revolution/5376339

Golinger, E. (2014). Agents of Destabilization in Venezuela: The Dirty Hand of the National Endowment for Democracy. *Global Research*. Retrieved from: http://www.globalresearch.ca/agents-of-destabilization-the-dirty-hand-of-the-national-endowment-for-democracy-in-venezuela/5379325

Green, P. (2010). *5 Steps for a Successful Social Knowledge Network Implementation*. Retrieved from: http://www.cmswire.com/cms/enterprise-20/5-steps-for-a-successful-social-knowledge-network-implementation-008423.php

Helms, R., Ignacio, R., Brinkkemper, S., & Zonneveld, A. (2010). Limitations of Network Analysis for Studying Efficiency and Effectiveness of Knowledge Sharing. *Electronic Journal of Knowledge Management*, *8*(1), 53–67.

Herman, E., & Chomsky, N. (2010). *Manufacturing Consent: The Political Economy of the Mass Media*. New York: Pantheon Books.

Hogg, T., & Huberman, B. (2007). *Solving the organizational free riding problem with social networks.* Technical Report. HP Labs, American Association for Artificial Intelligence. Retrieved from: http://www.hpl.hp.com/research/scl/papers/insurance/AAAIinsurance.pdf

Huesmann, R. (2007). The Impact of Electronic Media Violence: Scientific Theory and Research. *The Journal of Adolescent Health, 41*(6Supplement), S6–S13. doi:10.1016/j.jadohealth.2007.09.005 PMID:18047947

Iyengar, S. (1990). The accessibility bias in politics: Television news and public opinion. *International Journal of Public Opinion Research, 2*(1), 1–15. doi:10.1093/ijpor/2.1.1

Iyengar, S. (1991). *Is Anyone Responsible? How Television Frames Political Issues.* Chicago: University of Chicago Press.

Iyengar, S., & Kinder, D. (1987). *News that matters: Television and American opinion.* Chicago, IL: University of Chicago Press.

Jones, P. (2001). Collaborative Knowledge Management, Social Networks, and Organizational Learning. In *Proceedings of the Ninth International Conference on Human-Computer Interaction* (pp. 310-314). Academic Press.

Kathleen, J. (2000). *The interplay of influence.* Belmont, UK: Wadsworth.

Katzman, J. (2002). *4GW: What is 4th generation warfare?.* Retrieved from: http://windsofchange.net/archives/002736.html

Kuypers, J. (2009). Framing Analysis. In K. Jim (Ed.), *Rhetorical Criticism: Perspectives in Action.* Lexington Books.

Lee, R., & Coccaro, E. (2007). Neurobiology of Impulsive Aggression: Focus on serotonin and the orbitofrontal cortex. In D. Flannery, A. Vazsonyi & I. Waldman (Eds.), The Cambridge Handbook of Violent Behavior and Aggression (pp. 170-186). Cambridge, UK: Cambridge University Press.

Lippmann, W. (1922). *Public Opinion.* New York: Harcourt.

Livingston, S. (1997). Clarifying the CNN Effect: An Examination of Media Effects According to Type of Military Intervention. Cambridge, MA: John F. Kennedy School of Government's. Joan Shorenstein Center on the Press, Politics and Public Policy at Harvard University. Retrieved from http://genocide-watch.info/images/1997ClarifyingtheCNNEffect-Livingston.pdf

McCombs, M. (2005). A look at agenda-setting: Past, present and future. *Journalism Studies, 6*(4), 543–557. doi:10.1080/14616700500250438

McCombs, M., & Reynolds, A. (2002). News influence on our pictures of the world. In J. Bryant, & M. Oliver (Eds.), *Media effects: Advances in theory and research* (pp. 1-18). Retrieved from: http://www.asc.upenn.edu/gerbner/Asset.aspx?assetID=1617

McCombs, M., & Shaw, D. (1972). The agenda-setting function of mass media. *Public Opinion Quarterly, 36*(2), 176–187. doi:10.1086/267990

McCombs, M., Shaw, D., & Weaver, D. (Eds.). (1997). *Communication and democracy: exploring the intellectual frontiers in agenda-setting theory*. Mahwah, NJ: Lawrence Erlbaum Associates.

Media Influence. (n.d.). *The Free Dictionary*. Retrieved from: http://encyclopedia.thefreedictionary.com/media+influence

Nazemroava, M. D. (2014). Rise of the Anti-Government Flash Mobs: First Ukraine, Now Venezuela. *Global Research*. Retrieved from: http://www.globalresearch.ca/rise-of-the-anti-government-flash-mobs-first-ukraine-now-venezuela/5369691

Nelson, T. E., Clawson, R. A., & Oxley, Z. M. (1997). Media framing of a civil liberties conflict and its effect on tolerance. *The American Political Science Review*, *91*(3), 567–583. doi:10.2307/2952075

Noelle-Neumann, E. (1977). Turbulances in the climate of opinion: Methodological applications of the spiral of silence theory. *Public Opinion Quarterly*, *4*(2), 143–158. doi:10.1086/268371

Pardo, D. (2014). Los opositores venezolanos que están hartos de las protestas violentas. *BBC Mundo*. Caracas. Retrieved from: http://www.bbc.co.uk/mundo/noticias/2014/04/140409_venezuela_12_guarimba_oposicion_dp.shtml

Public Opinion. (n.d.). *Wikipedia*. Retrieved from: http://en.wikipedia.org/wiki/Public_opinion

Ragas, M., & Roberts, M. (2009). Agenda Setting and Agenda Melding in an Age of Horizontal and Vertical Media: A New Theoretical Lens for Virtual Brand Communities. *Journalism & Mass Communication Quarterly*, *86*(1), 45–64. doi:10.1177/107769900908600104

Rogers, E., Dearing, J. W., & Bregman, D. (1993). The anatomy of agenda-setting research. *Journal of Communication*, *43*(2), 68–84. doi:10.1111/j.1460-2466.1993.tb01263.x

Ross, C. (2013). *The Venezuelan Guarimba (Into Bizarro World)*. Retrieved from: http://www.counterpunch.org/2013/04/17/the-venezuelan-guarimba/

Scheufele, D. (2000). Agenda-setting, priming, and framing revisited: Another look at cognitive effects of political communication. *Mass Communication & Society*, *3*(2), 297–316. doi:10.1207/S15327825MCS0323_07

Schiller, H. I. (1976). *Communication and cultural domination*. New York: International Arts and Sciences Press.

Smith, T. (2009). The social media revolution. *International Journal of Market Research*, *51*(4), 559–561. doi:10.2501/S1470785309200773

The C. I. A.'s Plan to Create a "Destabilizing Student Opposition in Venezuela": Interview with Ex-CIA Collaborator. (2014). *Global Research*: *Global Research News*. Retrieved from: http://www.globalresearch.ca/the-cias-plan-to-create-a-destabilizing-student-opposition-in-venezuela/5376807

Treem, J., & Leonardi, P. (2012). Social Media Use in Organizations: Exploring the Affordances of Visibility, Editability, Persistence, and Association. *Communication Yearbook*, *36*, 143–189.

Varsavsky, O. (1974). *Estilos Tecnológicos*. Buenos Aires, Argentina: Ediciones Periferia S.R.L.

KEY TERMS AND DEFINITIONS

Agenda Building: Agenda elaboration has important participation and feedback from people/users. Some web tools are useful for this purpose, because of their facilities for interaction and feedback, e.g., blogs. It, and agenda melding, can be combined with free technologies in order to create media with critical impact.

Agenda Melding: It consists in adapting our agenda and the agenda of diverse free media that serve specialized interest groups. Individuals join groups and blend their agendas with those of the groups. This allows creating communities of interest whose members share values, attitudes and opinions.

Agenda Setting: Suggests that world media agenda is under control of major world media enterprises and some elites, and so has a high potential to effect on the formation of public opinion. This implies that there is some intentionality of influencing and manipulating public opinion by media.

Framing: Consists in portraying a story or a piece of news in a particular way in order to sway the consumer's attitude in a particular form. This is a way of stereotyping situations, actors, etc, and promoting certain interpretations of interest for certain powerful actors.

New (or Social) Media: Media based on the internet (e.g., Facebook, blogs, and wikis).

Old (or Mass) Media: Traditional means of communication and expression existing before the internet (e.g., Television and newspapers).

Reticular Formation: a set of interconnected nuclei located throughout the brainstream. It is not anatomically well defined, since it includes neurons located in diverse parts of the brain. Its neurons all play a crucial role in maintaining behavioral arousal and consciousness. It also cans (frames) us out the things that are not important, and cans us shake when something unfamiliar happens.

Subliminal Messages: Consist in stimulus (primus) involving a person for only a few milliseconds, which is masked by another larger message. Awareness of the primus is blocked by this second message.

Supraliminal Messages: Involve people for much longer periods than a few milliseconds, and are neither masked nor blocked by another message.

ENDNOTES

[1]   Via this process, a spreading activation in the neural network, created by an external stimulus, excites a brain node representing cognition, emotion and/or behavior. The external stimulus can be the sight of a gun, or a certain aggressive form of driving, promoted in media, and the primed (excitation) could be a certain aggressive behavior. Media priming of aggressive concepts increases aggressive behavior.

[2]   It is associated with being awake or reactive to stimuli. Media messages can arouse people, and excite them towards aggressive and violent behavior. An example of a consequence of this is that a stimulus could be seen as more severe when it is miss-attributed to some emotions that have been recurrently provoked and linked to the stimulus by the media.

[3]   It consists in imitation (mimic) of specific behavior, and can be understood as a particular case of observational learning. Children have a tendency to mimic aggressive and violent behavior shown in the media.

[4]   Children learn in their situation while observing others and media. Thus, media aggressive and violent messages strongly influence children negatively.

⁵ Repetitive exposure to media that activates certain emotions can lead to habituation of certain "natural" emotional reactions. In particular, children repeatedly exposed to negative emotions via aggressive and violent media messages, become habituated to the negative situations shown in the messages, then the intensity of the emotions decrease, and they become desensitized about such negative situations. The children then could actively plan and participate in similar negative situations, without experiencing negative emotions.

⁶ Children learning is conditioned and reinforced in certain directions. In this learning media takes part. Aggressive and violent behavior is enacted by aggressive and violent media. In video games this issue is very relevant, as children are active participants in the game.

⁷ Heuristics are also called "rules of thumb" (Rules of Thumb, n.d.). The first time certain knowledge appears or is applied, we are using the situational analysis, but afterwards, as this knowledge is *reinstated* as a rule, it becomes a heuristic that appears somewhat automatically.

⁸ "A **connotation** is a commonly understood cultural or emotional association that some word or phrase carries, in addition to the word's or phrase's explicit or literal meaning, which is its denotation.

A connotation is frequently described as either positive or negative, with regards to its pleasing or displeasing emotional connection. For example, a stubborn person may be described as being either *strong-willed* or *pig-headed*; although these have the same literal meaning (*stubborn*), *strong-willed* connotes admiration for the level of someone's will (a positive connotation), while *pig-headed* connotes frustration in dealing with someone (a negative connotation)." (Connotation, n.d.)

⁹ 4th generation war and manipulation refers to war based especially on communication media, and on dispersion that removes the battle front entirely (in the form it is traditionally known). Attackers rely on media manipulation, and cultural destruction or degradation, what collapses the enemy's moral and political motivation. A somewhat similar notion is broadly managed, see, for instance, Katzman (2002).

¹⁰ For more about the Venezuelan case, see, for instance: The CIA's Plan to Create a "Destabilizing Student Opposition in Venezuela": Interview with Ex-CIA Collaborator (2014, Retrieved from: http://www.globalresearch.ca/the-cias-plan-to-create-a-destabilizing-student-opposition-in-venezuela/5376807), Combs (2014), Nazemroava (2014), Golinger (2014), Gaudichaud (2014), Steve (2014).

Chapter 8
Political Framework of the Production and Use of Seeds in Venezuela:
Approaches at the International Regime

Vladimir Aguilar Castro
Universidad de Los Andes, Venezuela

ABSTRACT

Political and legal developments addressed to protect traditional knowledge are the result of huge efforts made by different actors at international and at national level. Nevertheless, traditional knowledge is broadly understood as freely accessible. Intellectual property norms are highly developed and strongly protect some knowledge products that are excluded of public domain, such as new varieties of plants. In light of this situation, political and legal tensions emerge in different countries, especially when it has an impact on areas highly profitable for some industries. This is the case of multinational agricultural companies that act globally by using technologies protected by intellectual property rights, threating traditional expressions applied for the use and conservation of seeds by local communities in different countries. In Venezuela, such tensions are present in the 2002 Law about Seeds, Animal Material and Supplies for Biological Reproduction, which is analyzed in this chapter.

INTRODUCTION

Currently, issues linked to production, distribution, and consumption of food, are the most prominent, strategic and vital for human survival. Thus, these issues have to be resolved by some governments, while it is impossible to be resolved by others, and it is used as a weapon of war by developed countries. The fact is that all over the world, these issues are observed and actions surrounding them are taken.

In recent years, in Venezuela there have been severe political disputes and a clash of two economic models has taken place. As a result, large extensions of land and food processing industries have been subject to expropriation. During decades, a single business consortium called Agroisleña monopolized

DOI: 10.4018/978-1-4666-8336-5.ch008

the entire distribution of seeds and agricultural supplies. The process how the Venezuela's government intended to transit from Agroisleña to Agropatria is an example of how public policy about food industry has been understood by the current Venezuelan government.

Asides political and economic aspects, at national level and at international level there are in this context several legal realms involved, which can roughly be put into two groups: one is the protection of biological diversity and security in biotechnology, and the other one is the protection of knowledge forms, i.e.: intellectual property rights, and protection of traditional knowledge pertaining to indigenous and local communities. Focusing on the Venezuelan context, this chapter looks at how the legal regime on seeds recognizes different sources of knowledge, and the preference shown for certain forms of it, especially those protected by intellectual property rights, in particular the so-called "breeder's rights". Intellectual property system excludes, on the one hand, the free access to some knowledge and technologies, and on the other hand, neglects traditional forms of knowledge and technologies as such. Several norms into the Venezuelan national legal order refer to the aforementioned issues. Thus, the 1999 Venezuelan Constitution includes some fundamental rights and general principles, which have been developed by different legal (sub-constitutional) mechanisms. This chapter will deal with the 2002 Law about Seeds, Animal Material and Supplies for Biological Reproduction.

BACKGROUND

Agricultural production, and especially distribution of food, is one of the most pressing concerns for governmental institutions, scholars, as well as general public. Harmful production practices have over-exploited the environment and produced, among other things, soil depletion. Where massive forms of production have taken place, soils that were fertile are infertile now, and water sources that were abundant and suitable for human consumption and agriculture are scarce or polluted.

One of the main indicators of such a rather bleak reality is the shortage and maldistribution of food, which entails, on the one hand, absence of some commodities and, on the other hand, excessive monetary gain at the food production chain. This situation is based on the way the food production industry operates, and the way scientific procedures create genetically modified products or biofuels. This forms a backdrop together with intellectual property system, cartelization of food prices and other components of the aforementioned chain, for the analysis of the political aspects of production and distribution seeds in Venezuela.

POLITICAL ASPECTS OF THE PRODUCTION AND USE OF SEEDS IN VENEZUELA

Currently, agricultural production and, above all, food distribution are perhaps the most pressing concerns of governments, institutions, academicians, as well as most common people. This is due to the effects that some harmful production practices have had on the environment, such as soil depletion from mass production practices, that is, soils that at one time were fertile and are now barren, and water sources that were once abundant and suitable for human consumption and agriculture, but are now scarce or have become polluted.

One of the main indicators that show the rather bleak reality of food shortages or food misdistribution, is, firstly, the absence of some basic commodities or the excessive price increases at all levels of the food chain, that is, the so called "high cost of living".

Understanding how the food production industry operates, the scientific procedures required to create genetically modified foods, biofuels, storage in silos, patent ownership, the *cartelization* of food prices and other elements of this chain, constitute the context of the political aspects related to seed production in Venezuela.

Therefore, understanding that the question of foodstuff is the most prominent, strategic and vital for human survival at present is to recognize that we are witnessing a very difficult and sometimes impossible issue to resolve for many of the world's governments. An issue that has become a problem which is used as a weapon of war by more developed countries and also by those who foresaw the problem in time to take necessary action.

In Venezuela, and because of political disputes and the apparent clash of two economic models, many acres of land, food processing plants, and distributors (including the Agroisleña corporation, a business consortium that had a monopoly on the entire seed distribution and other agricultural products), have been nationalized via expropriation, as in the case of Agrosileña, in recent years. The transition of Agroisleña to Agropatria can serve as an example to better comprehend how the food industry works as well as understanding what a public policy for this sector would entail.

An examination of the history of agro-food policies in some countries compels us to draw lessons that may be useful in our understanding of the Venezuelan state's interest in this key production sector of the national economy. At present, agro-ecological policies not isolated issues for individual countries, nor can they be kept obscure for long, particularly in this age of excessive media outlets and international offices, both of whom encourage and fixate on this information, such as the United Nations Food and Agriculture Organization (FAO). The initiatives carried out in different world contexts places us within a standardized handling of knowledge, of the details regarding the concerns and mechanisms implemented, and of the achievements and consequences gained from each experience.

Therefore, we consider it vital to explain agro-ecology as a fundamental aspect to contextualize the issue of production and utilization of seeds in Venezuela. Indeed, if we were to list the aspects related to the agro-ecological issue, we might first consider the following: environmental pollution, hunger, food shortages, equitable distribution of resources, biogenetic manipulation, "agriculture ports", land ownership (*latifundio*), single products, mechanization of agriculture, seeds licenses, etc.

We believe then that the selected topic is of great importance, and we must acknowledge the doctrines that support each production system and how to understand the related policies, whether they be developmental, technological, massifying, highly technical and perfectionist, of "tonnage increase" production statistics, etc.

In light of the aforementioned, the Seed Projects Law (2014) currently being debated at the Venezuelan National Assembly considers that:

- The overall objective of this Law is to regulate the endorsement, certification, distribution and marketing of seeds in the Bolivarian Republic of Venezuela from an agro-ecological perspective, as a strategic basis for overall rural development in order to strengthen our food sovereignty and thus contribute to the national economic and social development, and in agreement with Article 305 of the Constitution. This proposed bill promotes the development of a system of seed production which is: modern, anti-transgenic, high in quality, sovereign, democratic, participatory, mutually responsible and solidary, and which advocates the protection of biodiversity and helps preserve life on the planet.

- As an element of biodiversity, each seed contains centuries of evolution, a process during which the genetic code that determined its essence, reproduction and wealth was transmitted. Today, large global corporations threaten the disruption of this natural cycle, with the market approach to scientific changes that alter its nature, genetic makeup and the essential characteristics that have allowed it to exist for millions of years.

- The industrial processes of genetic seed modification alter the natural life cycle and jeopardize the best interests of the Venezuelan state. Neoliberalism encourages both a farce and a new green revolution, which thrusts seeds into the center of the global debate. The pretense of helping to eliminate hunger in the world with seeds that have been subjected to a horizontal transgenesis, means to strike an irreparable blow to the Latin American countryside. Large transnational biogenetic corporations are leading aggressive productive and trade endeavors that seek to, once again, plunge our countries into models of agricultural, biogenetic, economic, political, technological and food dependency, which will drive us farther from agro-sustainable rural development that is also respectful of the ecosystem.

At present, and because of the effect of globalization, the agro-ecological issue is understood not as an isolated field within nation-states' constitutions (at least in theory), but as part of the whole of social and environmental identity and diversity, which is summarized in the theory of sustainability.

However, there has not always been talk of sustainability. On the contrary, throughout history, almost all modern production models have been highly detrimental to the environment. Both in the socialist philosophy of the Soviet Union, and its counterpart principle of "progress" in the United States and Europe, the model was based on the destruction of forests by large machinery that allowed the development and occupation of large tracts of land for industries and large edifices. The notion of sustainability is not contained within the treaties and theories that have been developed by the modern world. Historically, the colonization of human settlements has always been associated with the conditions offered by the environment: water, fertile soils, climate, control over possible environmental accidents, timing of crop sewing and harvesting, and adaptation to the environment, which has ultimately driven the birth of cultures and other manifestations such as religion.

The most recent backdrop to this issue is found in the latest reports by the FAO and similar organizations, as well as in the reports by the Human Rights Council of the United Nations. In its segment on the promotion and protection of all human, civil, political, economic, social, and cultural rights, it contemplates steering the main international Forum to persuade its constituting countries to include in their constitutions the right to water and food as inalienable rights for every human being, along with the protection of biodiversity.

The contrast of policies and government strategies have been successful in some countries, whereas not in others, such as the anti-hunger food aid campaign in Africa, which went from being a well intentioned global effort, to a perverse impoverishment mechanism which discourages locally produced harvests and demotivates the locals to the point of expecting everything from international charity. The result of such campaigns is to discourage individual and family work, going from being autonomous productive farmers to peasant laborers, or in the worst case, to being unemployed or displaced.

Agro-Ecology as a Foundation for the Sustainable Production and Use of Seeds: A Pending Case in Venezuela

With a view set on reviewing policies implemented throughout the world which are intended to strengthen food production, or at the least, to alleviate its absence, the problem that arises in Venezuela is facing the negative balance left by the expropriation of properties, farms, food distributors and companies selling seeds and agricultural products. All of which has led to question whether or not the effects of nationalization have allowed these large tracts of farmland and private companies to be more productive and efficient under the administration of the Venezuelan State.

Moreover, globally and therefore, for Venezuela, the issues of global warming, environmental disasters linked to this imbalance, the loss of biological species, soil depletion, rising food prices, the limited maneuverability that governments have with which to respond to their people and other related problems, position agro-ecology as the research area that currently merits the greatest worldwide effort, not just to meet the food quotas required by six billion people, but rather to satisfy the need to change the production patterns used so far.

In his article, Núñez (2007) says that:

Agro-ecology and technical scaffolding, in addition to raising new forms of social organization emerges as the only scientifically valid option to overcome the various challenges, threats and weaknesses in agricultural production. Just as millions of farmers have claimed and affirmed in other international forums, food sovereignty must necessarily be viewed and operated from the agro-ecological prism (p.43).

Familiarizing oneself with these new forms of social organization, which is a necessary condition for understanding the changes and learning to live, alternatively in harmony with the environment, must also be the purpose of any investigation.

According to Leff (2003), agro-ecological knowledge is summarized as follows:

Agro-ecological knowledge is a constellation of knowledge, techniques, and scattered skills and practices that respond to ecological, economic, technical and cultural conditions particular to each geography and population. This knowledge and these practices are not unified around a science; the historical conditions of its production are expressed at different levels of theoretical production and political action that paves the way for the implementation of its methods and the execution of their proposals. Agro-ecological knowledge is forged at the merger of worldviews, theories and practices. Agro-ecology as a reaction to greedy agricultural models is configured through a new field of practical skills for sustainable agriculture for the common good and the ecological balance of the planet, and as a tool for self-sufficiency and food security of rural communities (p.76).

This constellation of agro-ecological knowledge enables accounting for the tangible productive, cognitive and organizational dimensions that will continue to emerge spontaneously in rural societies, without rules or laws to ascertain its appearance, as well as the social relevance that also arises in those spaces. Acknowledging agro-ecology as the current most pressing issue for humanity and for setting public policy in Venezuela is one of the remaining tasks for the future. In addition, determining the characteristics of agro-ecology so as to construct emerging public policies within the country which specify the subsystems it contains, identifying international laws that guarantee food as a fundamental human right, agro-ecology as an emerging right and as a foundation for building a post-rents society, are all crucial in our country's coming days.

THE INTERNATIONAL REGIMES OF THE PRODUCTION AND USE OF SEEDS: ECO-POLITICS AND SOCIAL MOVEMENTS (PARADOXES, PARADIGMS AND ANTIPODES)

Premises and Basis (Figure 1)

1. When referring to eco-politics, we are referring to the turning points that have made the ecological crisis a matter of global human concern.
2. Drawing from the aforementioned, we refer to social movements as key players of those turning points.

Figure 1. Eco politics chronology and social movements

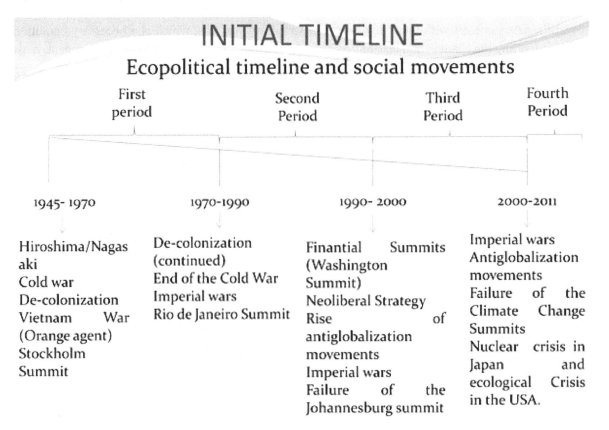

3. As a third aspect, we will attempt to look at the relationship between ecology, war, social movements and popular rebellions to pinpoint the characteristics of the anti-status quo and anti-system ecological clash and of the social insurgencies.

What Does This Timeline Demonstrate?

1. The ecological crisis is inseparable from current production organization structures, which excessively pollute and impact on the environment.
2. Whereas at first glance nuclear diplomacy would appear to be a mechanism for preserving a post WWII international status quo through a balance of world power, nuclear energy today has become a problem for global peace and security since its negative impact on the environment has exceeded the carrying capacity of the planet.
3. Apparently, within the present state of things, no energy exists which can replace fossil fuels in terms of the profit margins they generate.
4. The commitment to "change life becomes a change of life" (Saramago), that is, it becomes necessary to set aside the current patterns of production and consumption as these are untenable with the biosphere and the planet in general.

Social Movements Typology (Touraine, 1991)

Alain Touraine proposes a categorization of social movements, which, though not definitive, gives us a broad idea of the role that they have developed in the *ecological shift generated by politics and in the shift generated by ecology, which we can also refer to as eco-politics.*

1. Social movements in and of themselves have been defined as "both the culturally oriented and socially conflictive action of a collective social actor, thus defined by the historically appropriated dominant or dependent world position, cultural investment models of knowledge and morality, towards which it (the actor) is oriented" (Table 1). This definition presents social movements as agents of structural conflicts within a social system.
2. Social movements are also critical cultural players, which are important at the beginning of new historical periods when political actors are still not representative of the demand and new movements (Table 2).
3. Historical social movements that are at the crossroads between one societal type and another (Table 3).

Political Action According to Wallerstein (1991)

Based on the above, Wallerstein offers the following as elements of the anti- political action movements:

a. A re-politicization of the foundation of the movements and their schemes.
b. A new system of concepts for understanding the processes of social transformation in themselves.
c. The movements as non-geocentric global movements.

Table 1. State-centric world vs. Multi-centric world (actors)

	State-centric world	Multi-centric world
Actors	less than 200	several thousands.
Dilemma	security	autonomy
Resources for the fulfillment of the goals	armed forces	cooperation and consensus.
Guiding priorities	those that protect sovereignity and the rule of law.	cooperation and consensus.
Collaboration models	fromal alliances when possible.	temporary coallitions

Table 2. State-centric world vs. Multi-centric world (agendas)

	State-centric world	Multi-centric world
Agenda	limited	limitless
Norms regulating interaction among actors	diplomatic practices	ad hoc polices (situational)
Distribution of power among actors	hierarchical (amount of power)	relative equality in what concerns the start of the action
Interaction model	asymmetrical.	simmetrical
Leadership	position great powers	emerging actors.

Table 3. State-centric world vs. Multi-centric world (structures)

	State-centric world	Multi-centric world
Regrading Institucionalization	well stablished	emerging
Vulnerability in the light of change	relatively reduced	relatively high
Deciding structures	formal authority (law)	different types of authority
Results (outputs) control	concentrated	scattered

Towards a Strategy of Eco-Politics as the Action of Social Movements

After the fall of the Berlin Wall, George Bush Sr. promised a new world order that was more just, more stable and more peaceful. Twenty years later (Bensaid, 2003):

1) The world is becoming increasingly unfair and out of proportion.
2) The world is becoming more violent as there are more and more permanent civil conflicts.
3) The world is unstable because it is diluted by an increasingly dangerous planetary chaos.
4) After twenty years, the world would appear to give continuity to the thesis of "total war".
5) This idea of "total war", coined in 1935 by Ludendorf, Head of the German armed forces at the time, referred to two aspects:
   a. The playing field in question would extend to the whole territory of the warring nations;

b. The population from that point on would be involved in the war, both in the forefront and in the rear.

6) In the "total war" context, eco-politics as resistance establishes itself on several fronts:
   a. Any crisis must represent the key moment of unity (Marx in the Grundrisse);
   b. Therefore, it is the partisan subjectivity (that which arises when one takes sides) that determines the magnitude of the crisis;
   c. It is from within the crisis that an underlying subjectivity must emerge, for example, the assurance of a "change of direction" (Walter Benjamin) "from below";
   d. The core social relationship within valuable relationships is not an abridgment, but rather the final contradiction of class rivalries;
   e. Such being the case, the crisis is revealed as the moment of truth of the social actor, whom no longer subject to the law, becomes subject to the (eco) policy.

SOMES LEGAL ASPECTS OF THE PRODUCTION AND USE OF SEEDS IN VENEZUELA[1]

During the last seventeen years, modern biotechnology has increasingly been used in agriculture worldwide. According to FEDEAGRO, a Venezuelan civil association of farmers, forty percent of the 170 millions of hectares, where genetically modified seeds are currently sowed worldwide, are in Mercosur countries. The association affirms that the soy and maize seeds imported to Venezuela from Argentina, as well as from Bolivia and Brazil, are genetically modified. In different parts of the world, political as well as legal frameworks come together with this reality. During 2012, a total of 2,497 authorizations, including twenty five genetically modifies crops, have been issued by the competent authorities in fifty nine countries, of which 1,129 are for food use (for direct use or for processing), 813 are for use as fodder (for direct use or for processing) and 555 are for planting or release to the environment (James, 2013, p. 9; Díaz, 2013).

As it has been highlighted through social movements (Ley que privatiza la semilla campesina, 2013), that context underlines an expansion of "new" genetically modified plant varieties versus the traditional ones, that is, those produced by local and indigenous communities in different countries through generations. Each of such kinds of plant varieties implies different kinds of knowledge and technologies related to production and use of seeds. It is important to say that genetically modified seeds are not prohibited according to the 2002 Law about seeds, whose articles 15 and 16 state that their use shall be authorized by the Ministry of Environment, when it proof they are biologically and environmentally harmless. No prohibition of genetically modified seeds is also the FAO´s position (Cevallos, 2014).

At national level as well as at international level, there are several legal realms involved, which can roughly be put into two groups: one is the protection of biological diversity and security in biotechnology, and the other one is the protection of knowledge forms, i.e.: intellectual property rights, and protection of traditional knowledge pertaining to indigenous and local communities. Focusing on the Venezuelan context, the following part of the chapter looks at how the legal regime on seeds recognizes different sources of seed related knowledge, and the preference shown for certain forms of it, especially those protected by intellectual property rights (in particular the so-called "breeder´s rights"). Intellectual property system excludes, on the one hand, the free access to some knowledge and technologies, and on the other hand, neglects traditional forms of knowledge and technologies as such.

Several norms into the Venezuelan national legal order refer to the aforementioned issues. Thus, the 1999 Venezuelan Constitution (CRBV) includes some fundamental rights and different laws have developed mechanisms for their respect. This has clearly been a reflection of international trends.

The legal system in the Seed Projects Law (2014) currently being debated at the Venezuelan National Assembly necessarily touches several of the cornerstones of the Bolivarian Constitution it develops the economic regime of the nation while its successful implementation depends on the full enjoyment of various social, economic and cultural.

In this regard, the Bolivarian Constitution of Venezuela contains an evolution in its standards on economic activity since it does not conceive but to satisfy social needs, respecting ethical, moral and legal imperatives. Which consider the economy is not a closed, self-contained system; that the interest generated competitive behaviors are not necessarily complementary and harmonious. Why, the Venezuelan state retains the ability to make a series of activities and to intervene in several ways, among which limit the ability of individuals to develop economic activities that jeopardize the health of people or interests nationals.

The contents of the chapter will be noted that since the supreme standard features of agriculture listed in Article 305 which called it sustainable and is the strategic basis for overall rural development. Must be considered in this regard, that agriculture has to serve social and development of our peasantry, in rejecting constitutional forms of economic participation such as monopoly, oligopoly and other unfair practices.

CRITICAL APPRAISAL, SOLUTIONS AND RECOMMENDATIONS

The project of law, seeks to implement in relation to seed food sovereignty, understood as the right of the republic to define their own agricultural, fishing, food and land policies so that these are ecologically, socially, economically and culturally appropriate for the people. Consequently, the full recognition of the right to food and national food production, including what is consumed is healthy, nutritious and culturally appropriate.

It is the central idea of this bill protecting seeds as staple food and the right to life, for free use under the terms of social justice, the peasants, and declaring rule the Venezuelan state as a territory free of patent life and genetically modified species get the irreversible pollution of essential genetic diversity of plants and animals.

Since mid-2013 (Venezuela Libre de Transgénicos, 2013), the so-called popular movement is mobilizing to exercise social control and constituent power facing the legislative process of the new law seed. So the contributions and observations initiated by the Economic Development Commission of the National Assembly to ensure four key elements in this new law, which must transcend the economist and technocratic view of the law in force since 2002 were sent legislative process (Seeds Act and biological materials inputs).

These key elements are:

- The non-privatization of the seed through patents and PBR determined by transnational agribusiness.
- The prohibition of entry, release, use, propagation and production of genetically modified seeds (GM) in the country.

- The recognition of native seeds from a new logic that exceed the control and certification criteria imposed by the contaminating conventional farming.
- Ensuring constituent protagonist and popular participation of a diverse and sovereign new agricultural model.

That is why the country urgently demands a set of rules capable of fighting plans Imperialist offensive expressed in the imposition of genetically modified seed and the apparent improvements that are performed on them, which results in high biological cost to the humanity. The use of this type of seed would cause high costs to nature and humanity, in our case would generate irreparable damage and loss of incalculable dimensions for our farmers, peasants, indigenous and African (producers and producers).

To guarantee and give adequate response to the considerations and requirements outlined above, you have a seed Act (Venezuela Libre de Transgénicos, 2013):

a) ensure the availability of sufficient and timely seed in time and space.

b) ensure availability of a suitable seed production performance without negative effects on the environment

c) favors domestic supply of seed and food, and reduce the vulnerability of agriculture and the economy in general.

d) strengthen the autonomy in production, packaging and local supply of seed with endogenous technologies, appropriate and appropriable.

e) implant and strengthen the national seed system to achieve national independence and sovereignty technology and agribusiness.

f) promote and defend the conservation, propagation and multiplication of peasant, indigenous and Afro seed.

g) defends endogenous initiatives and ventures in production and procurement of seeds

h) promote quality assurance seed through a decentralized, flexible and participatory approach to organized popular power and the state.

i) prohibit the release, use, multiplication, enter the country and domestic production of LMOs and GMOs.

j) promote the exchange of knowledge and practice on agroecological shaped seed throughout the national level, including formal education.

k) guarantees the rights of Mother Earth, agro-biodiversity, the health of farmers and consumers of food.

l) develop human rights recognized in the CRBV and international instruments. These rights are environmental human rights that recognize the rights of present and future generations, biodiversity and environmental preservation.

m) consider the seed as a living organism and therefore free of patents and plant breeders' rights or any other form of intellectual property

n) ensure the protection of peasant, indigenous and Afro seed.

o) protection mechanisms of free knowledge associated with the seed is generated.

p) facilitates and fosters a new institutional architecture set seed management in accordance with the needs of the seed system and strengthening (p.8)

In light of the foregoing, the regulation of seeds contained in the new law aligns with the concepts underpinning the democratic and social state of law and justice, advocating the primacy of human rights, conceived as inherent and indivisible, all covered by Venezuelan law.

FUTURE RESEARCH DIRECTIONS

For future research should advance the relationship between law and institutions. We believe that 15 years of new social contract in Venezuela, the main constraint on the development of the rights is constitutionally the absence of exercise. Much of the latter is mainly due to the absence, in turn, of institutions to implement them.

One of the main challenges of this law is to advance the creation of appropriate institutions to guarantee the exercise of rights recognized.

For nobody is a secret relationship between indigenous peoples and conservation work and use of seeds through their traditional knowledge. Indeed, the importance of indigenous traditional knowledge appears in Venezuela for several decades already. In a paper published in the early 50s, for example, spoke Tamayo (1952) on "indigenous medical science" and said:

That is all secular phytological investigation of those men who discovered and used the effects of rotenone, strychnine, cocaine, quinine and a thousand other drugs, analyzed a longer by modern science and more confused yet in that nebulous botanist folklore of the New Continent is the legitimate child of indigenous wisdom world. So farmers Paraguana heal the states of nervous overexcitation with teas flower patches, knowing without knowing what the sedative effects of "pasiflorina" are; why the rustic farmers Tocuyo "úbeda" allowed to grow in impoverished lands for a few years after good harvests of corn, without discovering the action of nitrifying bacteria "men who also" discovered the cropping system in the mountains and sandy desert plains and created social-based agricultural economy and communal ownership of arable land structures (p.75).

While one might note that such studies produced mostly in scientific and academic circles did not influence the legislative activities of the country directly - for then were preserved in official sectors very different positions - must be recognized that contributed as a spur to Once helped lay a platform that could support movements that contributed to express recognition of certain rights of indigenous communities subsequently produced mainly from the 1999 Constitution, particularly the recognition of the protection of "property collective intellectual knowledge, technologies and innovations of indigenous peoples "(art.124 CRBV).

For the above and further research, for the indigenous peoples of Venezuela theme seeds I is linked to the demarcation of their territory. In this regard: what are the principles and international political and legal instruments to implement the demarcation process?

1. The formulation of policies, plans or programs for recognition and demarcation of indigenous lands is of sovereignty and responsibility of each State. However, implementation of the right to participation and the principle to free and informed recognized in numerous international instruments and the domestic legislation of some countries (e.g. Venezuela), is mandatory participation of indigenous peoples. In the case of Venezuela is the state that guarantees and title.

2. The demarcation should be part of a state policy (public policy), agreed with the indigenous peoples themselves to ensure that the process is outside the contingencies and changes of government, or

alteration of the instances that manage the indigenous question in each country. It is a political process, the territorial issue is a subject of political order however should not depend on the contingencies of time and therefore should be reinforced politically and legally.

3. Attempts should be a review of interim titles granted to indigenous peoples in the past, in cases where the award was made on insufficient areas for their survival.

4. Consideration should be given priority to the recognition of ancestral lands traditionally occupied as required by the law of demarcation. This, in a strategy of demarcation, can be part of the guidelines to continue the process depending on the stage of the process of demarcation. It is logical that it will not be the same strategy for a community that is in an urban area than in one that is located in a rural area or in protected areas. The demarcation must be differentiated. They may be as many districts as indigenous peoples and communities exist. Consequently, there is no univocal boundaries much less homogeneous.

5. Break the process of demarcation and titling for indigenous to the traditional legal order stipulated in ordinary legislation and in the agricultural or civil law. The problem we have in Venezuela is that recognition has been done under the aegis of ordinary law, and has not innovated to the right of demarcation should respond to the traditional indigenous law according to their specific realities. This is an issue that needs to take into account the Agricultural Minister and, consequently, is the condition for its facilitation in the process.

6. The full and absolute ownership cannot give rise to doubts and cannot be subjected to acts of revocation of securities or granting of land for other purposes. The Venezuelan State recognizes entitled but in turn also recognizes the interests to third parties, causing them to be their own peoples and indigenous communities who face the third in ordinary courts.

7. Acts of full ownership must incorporate social and environmental obligations all property generally must be (even collective). It will take a collective property title but is implicit in a number of obligations inherent in the title.

8. Titration should be direct, full and final without recourse to mechanisms attempt or provisional award or the performance of previous mechanisms. The title is always given as preceding stages are met. Accordingly, it is proposed that the condition for awarding the title does not necessarily pass through the recognition of others or Areas Under Special Administration Regime (ABRAEs).

9. Achieve balance between recognition of indigenous land rights with other legislation aimed at regulating agricultural, forestry or soil and water issue and generally relating to natural resources and the environment. It is proposed that indigenous and environmental rights under a new legal system is harmonized.

10. The process of recognition and protection of the demarcated territories should above other laws within the framework of necessary reconciliation between complementary legal systems (where possible)

11. Insert the indigenous issue within the domestic legal and political system without establishing rules or policies of special character, but as part of the institutional system of a country. The indigenous peoples come to be a recognized legal status within the national legal system, not as special legislation but as a transversal entitled to all the CRBV.

12. Creating conditions for restitution in the best possible terms of fragmented or damaged indigenous territories, whether by settlement or by the exploitation of natural resources and the biodiversity. Even established the Convention 169 of the ILO and the Declaration of Rights of Indigenous Peoples of the United Nations, which must be paid back the lands of indigenous peoples and communities who have been displaced by force majeure.

13. Promote and respect the traditional management models indigenous territories based on customary rights of indigenous peoples. Incorporate this right within the domestic legal system of each country recognizing the value of their own institutions and legal forms. Article 260 of the CRBV develops models of indigenous legal administration and Article 119 claims the traditional character of the ways to manage indigenous territories.

14. Once the territories have been demarcated should ensure that management of these areas, as well as its internal dynamics, commensurate with the demands and conditions set by the people themselves who live there. It's necessary make a distinction between what is the demarcation and titling habitat, which may be part of a recognition strategy for dialogue with the state. The foundation of each other could be determined by limiting the area. In any case, land management (subsequent phase to the demarcation and titling) should in principle be sustained in Life Plans.

15. Delegate to the indigenous peoples and communities in the territories demarcated certain functions of public authority in the context of territorial management. There is a principle of shared responsibility laid down in Article 326 CRBV in which you can draw a parallel between indigenous territories demarcated areas in the public domain.

16. Incorporate the principle of free and informed consent for indigenous peoples within the plans, projects and policies that may affect their demarcated or to demarcate territories.

17. The creation of efficient mechanisms for the demarcation of indigenous territories and the concentration of this process into a single entity. In the case of Venezuela, inasmuch as the Attorney General's Office is going to issue the title, it must be in the process of demarcation but using flexible mechanisms and not to hinder it. In the demarcation process, therefore, should involve the competent authorities in order to give effect to the rights recognized.

18. It should be taken into account in the process of demarcating the traditional forms of representation and government of the indigenous peoples concerned. Both the process of demarcation and self-demarcation should be a space for the enforcement of rights, because it is not demarcating the land to the State but to the indigenous peoples and communities. This is a new notion of nation-state that is held in the framework of a Multicultural and Postcolonial Constitutionalism.

19. In the land titling and recognition is made of indigenous territories must guarantee the right of access of these peoples to natural resources with the obligations relating to the conservation of natural heritage and biodiversity.

20. Ensure the adequacy of natural resources in recognized or demarcated to ensure the survival of indigenous peoples areas.

21. Incorporate the recognition of the territories or areas demarcated within legal initiatives under domestic law or according to ILO Convention 169 and the Convention on Biological Diversity and national laws of biodiversity, which are necessary to protecting biological resources on them as a fundamental part of national and community heritage.

22. To protect the collective rights of indigenous peoples that emerges from the associated biological and traditional management systems and sustainable use of natural resources diversity knowledge. On experience with the mental maps created with some indigenous peoples, we can say that is a basis for setting the record, and associated knowledge should be part of the accompaniment of the demarcation process and self-demarcation.

23. The territorial recognition and demarcation should be given priority over the unilateral declaration of the respective environmental authorities, natural parks or any other form of protection, within defined spaces and indigenous areas. Not enough for the State to provide the title. Most importantly,

land management from the habits and customs that may have on these lands, as this is what opposes the right of indigenous peoples and communities with the interests of third parties.

It is important to note that these third parties can become agents of recognition of indigenous land rights, coupled with a mechanism of arbitration roundtable to conflict with the interest of third parties. The latter can be carried out by the regional commissions of demarcation. What cannot be accepted is that the interest of third remains embedded in the degree.

24. Find the reconciliation of protected areas with recognized, demarcated and demarcates and harmonization of overlapping spaces through complementary regimes, based on local experiences of self-demarcation indigenous territories. The self-demarcation and delimitation you are looking to give consistency to what the national territory, to show that what is sought is to harmonize what is the country with demarcate indigenous territories.

25. Development of new strategies of cooperation and co-management of lands and protected areas between indigenous peoples and the State, including the declaration of areas of national interest such as cultural and natural heritage. In the Venezuelan State must establish strategies that will reconcile indigenous rights against the State's position. From this point of view should be possible to develop a strategy for joint management and cooperation.

26. Explore the possibility of keeping the united ownership of subsoil resources, indigenous peoples recognize the right of access and benefit to the resources found therein and preferential right for communities to exploit those that are within their recognized or demarcated territories.

How then under specific actions like these principles we turn it into a mechanism of enforcement of law?

1. From a strategy of demarcation or self-demarcation long as there is a (territorial) space to realize rights recognized.

2. It is necessary to specify which are the foundations of a demarcation process has already been recognized as legitimate by the state and includes a time of award, but not before noting that there are a set of variations in land titling. Among them we can mention:

   a. Where the recipient of the degree is recognized as a distinct social sector and the delivery of the land is made in order to ensure their survival.

   b. When the award is given in the terms in which it establishes the positive law of a country, for example, the Civil Code.

   c. 1) The delivery is full of property; 2) that entitle the holder a right of use in perpetuity reserving the state supreme dominion; 3) That a right of usufruct is transferred revocable at any time and circumstance; 4) That the award is merely declaratory.

   d. That the allotted lands are inalienable, subject to liens, prescriptive and subject to law.

   e. In the case of Venezuela, there is a legal framework for three stages of the process are foreseen: demarcation (it is proposed that through self-demarcation validated in cases that do concur); Certification and finally land management through the Life Plans of each indigenous people.

CONCLUSION

The new management of existing resources on planet earth, by either states or international organizations, has been clashing with the interests of local actors whose ancestral or traditional relationship with these resources are threatened by the ever-increasing action government, state or supra-state actors. The global ecological governance imply a level of consensus at the time of access to natural resources that are located in areas that have repeatedly been occupying local, rural and indigenous communities among others.

The new challenges that are imposed on these local actors is to establish a catalog of rights that emerge when instant access to natural resources threatens the exercise of historical or territorial rights.

Three notions should go hand in hand when accounting for the rights emerging relationship and global ecological governance: one, to understand the law as a social construct and not as an end in itself; two governance as intermediary mechanisms and actions to seek consensus; and three, the possibility that the definition, execution and implementation of public policies "from the local" can become a mechanism and the exercise of rights recognized.

Concerning the debate on the seeds in Venezuela, there are several aspects to reveal: first, the parliamentary debate has not been sufficient in relation to an issue that still has many limitations in other areas of development. In this regard, it is noted that the large agribusiness projects in the framework of strategic alliances in our country, do not take into account the essential elements that were underlying in the parliamentary debate. In other words, the fact that Venezuela a country dependent on food imports makes it equally dependent on exogenous dynamics in terms of seeds concerns that the country itself cannot control.

Second, the absence of pacing between law, rights and institutions makes the right which can be recognized by standard does not necessarily can be exercised, for being the Venezuelan State guarantor character institutions must be sufficiently solid to ensure the rights recognized.

This is one of the main unresolved debates in the country for the next time.

The legal system developed in Venezuela, referring to the seeds, necessarily touches several of the cornerstones of the Bolivarian Constitution it develops the economic regime of the nation while its successful implementation depends on the full enjoyment of various social, economic and cultural.

In this regard, the Bolivarian Constitution of Venezuela contains an evolution in its standards on economic activity since it does not conceive but to satisfy social needs, respecting ethical, moral and legal imperatives. Which consider (Venezuela Libre de Transgénicos, 2013):

- The economy is not a closed, self-contained system.
- That the interest generated competitive behaviors are not necessarily complementary and harmonious.

Why, the Venezuelan state retains the ability to make a series of activities and to intervene in several ways, among which limit the ability of individuals to develop economic activities that jeopardize the health of people or interests nationals.

The contents of the chapter will be noted that since the supreme standard features of agriculture listed in Article 305 which called it sustainable and is the strategic basis for overall rural development. Must be considered in this regard, that agriculture has to serve social and development of our peasantry, in the constitutional rejection under Article 113 concerning forms of economic participation such as monopoly, oligopoly and other unfair practices.

Therefore, agricultural activity has to be developed in accordance with the content of these articles and maximum respect and protection of our national sovereignty and social justice. Since the practices that have developed within the framework of the so-called Second Green Revolution lay in between that it is the duty of the Republic to consolidate legislation will not only the technical aspect but consider how the field will contribute to achieving the supreme interests of the nation, hence, that the rule propose a legal regime that protects local seed, peasant, indigenous and Afro as part of Venezuela's biodiversity and to guarantee better living conditions for peasants in Venezuela .

It is there when you notice that with this bill not just a regulation of seed in economic terms is sought, but progress on the idea of consolidating a rigid legal framework to protect biodiversity in constitutional terms of Article 127 (p.4).

Similarly, this bill seeks to implement in relation to seed food sovereignty, understood as the right of the Republic to define their own agricultural, fishing, food and land policies so that these are ecologically, socially, economically and culturally suitable for the Venezuelan people. Consequently, the full recognition of the right to food and national food production, including what is consumed is healthy, nutritious and culturally appropriate (Venezuela Libre de Transgénicos, 2013).

Consequently, it is the central idea of this bill protecting seeds as staple food and the right to life, for free use under the terms of social justice, the peasants, and declaring rule the Venezuelan state as a territory free of patent life and genetically modified species get the irreversible pollution of essential genetic diversity of plants and animals.

Additionally, this law states ban the release, use, multiplication, enter the country and domestic production of LMOs and GMOs as these instead of improving food security, seriously put at risk. Any time you have studies on health impact that associated with diseases such as cancer, birth defects and other pathologies of severe consequences for public health (p.6).

While seeks (Venezuela Libre de Transgénicos, 2013) to incorporate the protection of innovative and traditional knowledge systems linked to the improvement, management, production and circulation of seed to ensure they can be used, studied, shared and improved freely, like its improvements are free to use, study, share and improve (p.3).

Faced with the threat of GM and agribusiness in general (Venezuela Libre de Transgénicos, 2013), it is necessary to recognize, value and revitalize the practices of farmers, indigenous and African descent, part of the historical, cultural, environmental heritage of humanity. In this sense, the conception of this Act contemplates Seed legitimacy of indigenous peoples as the first historical moment, multi-ethnic and multi-cultural roots of our people as well as the cultural, social and environmental assets of communities in each region of the country. The peoples originating from a close relationship with the seed have ensured their conservation, breeding, production and reproduction. That is why the valuation of our traditional peoples, indigenous, peasant and Afro is necessary for the understanding of our agro-biodiversity threatened by climate change and other severe environmental stresses (p.12).

Another aspect of agribusiness linked to the seed is the desire of its privatization through patents and plant breeders' rights, which are nothing but forms of commodification of the seed that lead to monopoly of these, trapping them all agrifood chain. That is why this law raises find ways to protecting knowledge, knowledge, practices and beliefs, ancestral associated with the seed, for the defense of national sovereignty and sovereignty of indigenous peoples, Afro-descendants and peasants, guardians, fathers and mothers historical entire agro-biodiversity as well as the knowledge and skills obtained by local creators and producers. In this sense, an attempt to rescue craft practices and techniques agro-ecological production of harvestable seed for a new model of socialist agricultural production, rescued from farming activity in the culture of *conuco* (p.13).

Agricultural biodiversity is intrinsically linked to peasant agriculture, indigenous and Afro therefore their conservation depends on these agricultures are maintained. On the other hand, there are geographical and climatic conditions which allowed the existence of a wide bio-diversity. These conditions have been exploited by local cultures to develop agro ecosystems and diverse food systems. These comprise dozens of species and varieties in a complex web of technology, culture and spirituality. That is why the zoning of eco-regions or socio-bio-regions where species diversity is integrated into the indigenous-peasant farming is an important aspect that will guide the diagnosis, monitoring, development and revitalization of agro-biodiversity and seed under this Act (p.15).

Moreover, in terms of associated traditional knowledge to seed, it should be noted that the possibility of protecting traditional knowledge is directly related to the recognition of indigenous land rights, since the latter is not only the field of application but basically I exercise of such knowledge.

The realization and realization of any indigenous law passed by the need to develop indigenous public policies that are defined not "top down" (the state toward indigenous peoples and communities), but primarily "bottom up" (of indigenous peoples and communities to the state).

The scope for progress in defining and implementing mechanisms to protect the collective intellectual property of indigenous peoples is the national, which should serve as a starting point for advancing other regional and international levels, where mechanisms are harmonized, joint strategies are established and where customary law to become the impetus for the realization of the protection of traditional knowledge, for the realization of the territorial rights and indigenous implementing public policies.

REFERENCES

Cevallos, R. (2014). FAO no descarta transgénicos en lalucha contra el hambre. La República.pe. Retrieved from http://www.larepublica.pe/08-05-2014/fao-no-descarta-transgenicos-en-la-lucha-contra-el-hambre

Díaz, L. (2013). Detección de secuencias asociadas a organismos vivos modificados en semillas de maíz (Zea mays L.) y Soya (Glycine max L. Merryl). Master Degree Work. Facultad de Agronomía. Universidad Central de Venezuela. Maracay. Retrieved from http://saber.ucv.ve/xmlui/bitstream/123456789/4520/1/T026800007886-0-Trabajo_de_grado_Luis_Diaz-000.pdf

James, C. (2013). Situación mundial de los cultivos biotecnológicos/GM: 2012. Executive summary. International Service for the Acquisition of Agri-Biotech Applications. Retrieved from http://www.isaaa.org/resources/publications/briefs/44/executivesummary/pdf/Brief%2044%20-%20Executive%20Summary%20-%20Spanish.pdf

Leff, E. (2003). *Epistemología ambiental*. Sao Paulo: Cortez Editora.

Ley que privatiza la semilla campesina. (2013, 22 October) [Video file]. Retrieved from http://www.youtube.com/watch?v=uWoZIM0QkdU

Núñez, M. (2007). *La agroecología en la soberanía alimentaria venezolana*. Mérida: Ed. IPIAT.

Tamayo, F. (1952). Introducción alestudio del fitofolklore venezolano. In *Archivos Venezolanos de Folklore. Year 1, N° 1. Universidad Central de Venezuela. Facultad de Filosofía y Letras*. Caracas: Faculty of Pharmacy and Language.

Touraine, A. (1984). *Le retour de l'acteur*. Paris: Fayard.

Wallerstein, I. (1991). *Histoire et dilemmes des mouvements antisystemiques*. Paris: La Decouverte.

ADDITIONAL READING

Aponte, A. (Ed.). (2009). Manual de Semilla Solidaria. Instituto Nacional de Investigaciones Agrícolas. Plan Nacional de Semillas (National Plan of Seeds). Maracay. Retrieved from http://www.sian.inia.gob.ve/repositorio/noperiodicas/pdf/Manual_semilla_solidaria.pdf

Daniel, B. (2003). *Le nouvel internationalisme*. Paris: Textuel.

Daniel, B. (2006). *Clases, plebes, multitudes*. Caracas: El Perro y La Rana.

Intergovernmental committee on intellectual property and genetic resources, traditional knowledge and folklore (2013, 19-21 April). Indigenous Expert Workshop on Intellectual Property and Genetic Resources, Traditional Knowledge and Traditional Cultural Expressions. Workshop Report. Doc. WIPO/GRTKF/IC/28/INF/9, Annex I. Geneva.

Karl, M. (1980). Los grundrisse. España: Viejo Topo.

Ministerio del Poder Popular para el Ambiente. (2012). Estrategia nacional para la conservación de la diversidad biológica 2010-2020 y su plan de acción nacional. Caracas.

Revue Contretemps. (2003). *Changer le monde sans prendre le pouvoir?* Paris: Textuel.

Taibo, C. (2005). Movimientos de resistencia frente a la globalización capitalista. España: Ediciones B. Venezuela: http://venezuelalibredetransgenicos.blogspot.com/

World Trade Organization (2001, 9-14 November). WTO Ministerial Declaration. Doc. WT/MIN(01)/DEC/1. Doha.

KEY TERMS AND DEFINITIONS

Biodiversity: Usually called "biological diversity". It is the diversity of life in all its forms, at all levels and in all combinations. It includes genetic diversity, species diversity and ecosystem diversity (Posey and Dutfield / Claude Auroi).

Controversial Issues: Are those transcendental aspects that play a specific agenda and are the subject of ongoing debate in the international and national levels, can be both a source of tensions and conflicts on both levels, at different times or simultaneously.

Farmers' Rights: Have been enshrined in various resolutions of the FAO. These, though not expressly rights of a collective nature, are a good variant of them as precedent for future coding process.

International Agenda: Are those issues that are part and impact the dynamics of international relations in a given historical moment.

International Regime: Set of principles, norms, conventions and decision-making procedures, explicit or not, governing a particular field of international relations (Stephen Krasner).

Seed Bill In Venezuela: Bill who seeks to erect a new legislation on the use and disposal of seeds in the country. Part of the idea of ensuring food security in the country despite being a nation that depends essentially on the importation of food.

Social Movements: Are those that generate responses "from below" against changes in the international system. Included in these indigenous peoples as new international actors.

ENDNOTES

[1]   From here we have relied in parliamentary debates on the law. Cf. National Assembly. Seed Bill. September 2013.

Chapter 9
A New Approach to Knowledge Sharing:
The Multifactory Model

Giulio Focardi
Osun Solutions, Italy

Lorenza Salati
Bigmagma, Italy

ABSTRACT

A Multifactory is a new concept of productive environment. This chapter presents what Multifactories are, their constitutive elements and how these interact. In this chapter will be also presented the governance system, that is largely self-generated, and the way knowledge is shared and how this brings to innovative practices in exchanging skills and professional services. The chapter will also present the way the Multifactory Model was developed, from the direct observation of different real cases within Europe to the on-field test of the model. The chapter also suggests how Multifactories can be a possible way to face the needs for job creation and an environment where to experiment innovative ways to share knowledge.

INTRODUCTION

"Many people say do it yourself, we say do it together, make things together and share knowledge."
Parade, M. (2013, July 15). Personal interview.

The debate about freely accessible knowledge refers most often to something that happens on, applies to, or is somehow related to the web and the world of Internet and digital technologies.

These are environments where collaboration between individuals prove to work and to produce resources of free knowledge available to almost everybody.

Outside the web groups, companies, and institutions have an increased interest in sharing environments and cooperative networks.

DOI: 10.4018/978-1-4666-8336-5.ch009

Box 1. Crowdworkers' Voice on Expectations

> *"In a way, MOB is a channel for me to get closer to people related to innovation and open collaborative systems, and that's why it makes sense for me being into MOB. I didn't have any expectations, at the beginning. I was working at home, but I realized it was too hard to spend so much time at home, alone, I was completely isolated and I was completely out of the world. I was spending 14 hours a day in my living room. It was unhealthy. At first, I started looking for an office, then I found MOB, and I felt it was different. My expectations were like a coworking space, with many people going around, but then, I think, MOB has exceeded my expectations in many ways. Especially for the workshops, and then I started getting familiar with these Makers, a movement I was completely ignorant about. Like in a way you're working, but while working you keep yourself updated and connected to the world, so that's the part that's exceeding my expectations." Rius, C. (2013, September 10). Personal interview.*

For example, the European Union alongside the Horizon 2020 program brings attention to Sharing Economy and Social Business, as these are seen as relevant points to support the economic and social development of European Countries.

This chapter focuses on Multifactories, which are a type of collaborative environment where free access to common resources and free exchange of knowledge between people are key factors in the establishment and development of economic activities.

Multifactories are environments that prove that the concepts at the base of free knowledge sharing and free access to resources can apply to physical places and spread into "common" society, or people not involved in specific movements, or driven by a particular ethic purpose.

Multifactories also exemplify the social benefit of free knowledge sharing and how to make possible a tangible improvement in social assets through collaborative environments.

Multifactories are emerging working environments that present peculiar elements of innovation: a Multifactory is a shared workspace, different from a classical Coworking space, as it's not intended as a "desk farm," but an environment dedicated both to the development of services and to the production of material goods.

A Multifactory is a Community of Purpose, where the purpose is job creation and the concretization of better working conditions. It takes form as a Community Project, where all the stakeholders take an active part in designing its shape and in the shared definition of norms, rules, and governance system.

Multifactories are multi-competency environments, which allow for a creative reuse of competencies and lead to product innovation and scope economies in small-scale businesses.

A Multifactory generates more value than the sum of companies' individual values and is a completely new form of territorial entity that allows local governments and institutions to interact with a single economic and social agent. Therefore, it is not a "Factory," but something close to the idea of a "village." It gives back to single workers a collective representativeness and the consciousness to belong to a specific new and innovative Social Class (see Box 1).

Multifactories are examples of social innovation, a new way to face the needs for job consolidation and job creation. The challenge to the base of this work is to understand what defines a Multifactory, to underline its constitutive elements, and to highlight the main dynamics that take form in it, in order to develop a model that can be replicable, scalable, reproducible, and customizable.

In this work, eight Multifactories were taken into account:

Made in Ma.Ge. (MAGE) - Multifactory of 15 companies near Milan, in Sesto San Giovanni (IT), in a 2,000 square meters space previously part of the Falk steel factory. It can accommodate up to 50 people. Most of Litefactories are artisans, companies and freelancers.

Pollino - Multifactory system located in Basilicata (IT) and geographically spread over a dozen municipalities, consisting of about 20 production facilities involving about 100 people. It's an example of Multifactory mainly made of companies in the agricultural market.

Table 1. Different kinds of Internal Stakeholders in the analyzed Multifactories

Internal Stakeholder	Multifactories							
	MAGE	Pollino	Building Bloqs	Balneário	Oficina Colectiva	Agora	FreiLand	MOB
Initiator	University	District + one LF	NP association	One of the LF	One of the LF	NP association	NP association	Private
Strategist	NP association	District + one LF	NP association	One of the LF	One of the LF	NP association	LF plenary session	Private
Formal coordinator	NP association	District	NP association	One of the LF	One of the LF	NP association	NP association	Private
Administrator	NP association	/	NP association	NP association	One of the LF	NP association	NP association	Private
Supervisor	University	/	/	/	/	/	Municipality	/
Litefactories	17	20	30	8	8	40	40	30
Institutions	Municipality	District	/	/	/	/	Municipality	/
Owner	Municipality	/	Private	Private	Private	Private	Municipality	Private

Building Bloqs - Multifactory located in London (UK), in a 1,000 square meters space. It can accommodate up to 100 people, most of them are artisans or artists.

Balnéario - Multifactory located in Lisbon (PT), in a 300 square meters space, which is part of LX Factory, a former industrial complex. It can accommodate up to 20 people (artisans, artists and freelancers).

Oficina Colectiva - Multifactory located in Lisbon (PT), in a 200 square meters space (a former industrial bakery) in the city center with windows on the street. Oficina Colectiva includes 8 different LiteFactories (artisans, companies and freelancers) and accommodates 16 people.

FreiLand - Multifactory located in Potsdam (DE), situated in a 15,000 square meters area formerly owned by the local gas and water company. Freiland includes companies, artisans, artists, makers, associations, a FabLab, a café, a club for concerts and events, a guest house, an area for conferences and workshops. Freiland includes 40 different LiteFactories and it can accommodate up to 120 people.

MOB (Makers of Barcelona) - Multifactory located in Barcelona (ES), in a 800 square meters space (a former warehouse). MOB includes a café, a FabLab and accommodates up to 120 people. MOB is highly focused on Makers, digital fabrication and smart manufacturing.

Agora - Multifactory located in Berlin (DE), in a 800 square meters space, includes a café and an event space. In Agora most of Litefactories are freelancers and artists, but there is also a workshop for manual works. Agora can accommodate up to 80 people on four floors.

A Different Way to Produce

A Multifactory is a Complex System that involves several different elements. These elements are heterogeneous, may interact in several different ways, and can be seen as nodes of a socio-economic system within the dynamics taking place.

To start a new Multifactory and to make it grow and develop, it's needed to properly define the main characteristics of each node and the conditions under which the desired dynamics take place.

Box 2. Crowdworkers' Voice on WORKING TOGETHER

> *"Oficina Colectiva is not a Company, it's a place. But when we work together on the same projects, we don't even have to separate the teams, as we're from the same space, the same environment. We don't have to say: "these are the guys from Toyno, these are the guys from Nambana". Quinta, R. (2013, May 5). Personal interview.*
> *"We collaborate with other people here, we use our experience to help them, and they do the same.*
> *We had a side project when we first came here, we were redesigning the brand for a restaurant and we needed someone who designed the interiors of the restaurant, so we cooperated, they designed the restaurant interior and in exchange we're redesigning their brand for the notebook." Quinta, R. (2013, May 5). Personal interview.*
> *"MOB is a strange beast, in a sense that from the very beginning we wanted to apply this mentality of the Makers, as a mentality, not simply as the act of making, so as we know makers are people making manual things, actually using their hands, physically building something, which is great, but want a kind to define it on a different level, meaning that we want to change into an attitude. While changing people attitude, you can change movements, and society." Tham, C. (2013, September 18). Personal interview.*

A Multifactory is a shared working environment aimed at the production of goods and the supply of services, both in B2C and B2B fields, and is structured as a microcosm of many different economic agents.

These agents have separate properties and operate in an independent way, fully autonomous under an operational, fiscal, commercial, and strategic point of view. But at the same time, they are able to cooperate and share resources in such an integrated way that they can be considered divisions of a single large company. A Multifactory may be seen as an "Invisible Factory," that is an archipelago of independent companies that can, if needed, operate as a single entity.

A Multifactory does not provide a unified direction at the strategic level, or at the level of operations. When working on common projects, the participation of each company in the joint project is completely spontaneous and organized on the basis of bilateral or multilateral, formal or informal agreements.

The economic subjects that constitute a Multifactory belong to a wide range of industries; they can be SME, craftsmen, or creative companies. They can operate in the art field, in the third sector, or in services like Architects, Web Developers, Video Makers, Photographers, Specialists in Communication, Consultants and free lances (see Box 2). Most of them are devoted to project, product, or distribution of physical goods. So a Multifactory has to contemplate an adequate fraction of the available space for production and prototyping purposes.

A NEW WAY TO SHARE KNOWLEDGE

Which Kind of Knowledge?

In a Multifactory there are digital enterprises, traditional companies, artisans, smart factories, freelancers, and all shades and hybridizations between these categories.

All these subjects own a wide range of skills and competencies, but lack many others.

There are "old style" artisans, who have huge amounts of experience and know very well how to use specific equipments and machinery, but who don't know anything about marketing or have never used Social Networks.

There are experienced professionals, who have all the skills needed to shape and project an object, but who don't know how to realize a physical prototype by hands.

The "knowledge" all these subjects may exchange can be of several types, and can cover a wide range of activities. Just to exemplify, knowledge of new materials and techniques (like 3D modeling and

Table 2. Main tasks of the managing entity and involved activities

Tasks	Main Activities Involved
Ordinary administration	To pay bills, to pay services (surveillance, cleaning, waste charges).
Non-ordinary administration	To make the calls to fill the space, to sign the contracts with the Litefactories.
General services	To choose and monitor surveillance, cleaning service, etc…
High level coordination	To organize meetings and plenary sessions, to coordinate the working groups on joint projects, monitor the progress of joint projects, to solve conflicts.
Everyday coordination	To coordinate the use of common areas, of the kitchen (supplying, cooking), of shared tools.
Events organization	To decide, organize, and manage common events and exploitation activities.
Supervision	To solve difficult situations of Litefactories, to collectively pool negative situations.
Strategic planning	To define the strategic guidelines, objectives, and actions to achieve them, seek funding, to define new entries, to decide which joint projects to start, to decide marketing and promotion, to decide common actions.
Routine maintenance	To solve small practical problems (leaking pipe, lock to change)
Emergency maintenance	To solve big practical problems (broken heating, broken electric gate).
General rules setting	To set rules about space allocation, opening hours, allowed activities.
Everyday rules setting	To set rules about common area booking, kitchen usage, shared tools booking.

printing, laser cutting, fast prototyping in general), knowledge on traditional techniques (like soldering, woodworking, sewing, and so on), immaterial knowledge (like copywriting, project writing, proofreading, etc), digital knowledge (like web design, SEO, programming) or other technical skills (like video-making, music composing, event organization).

All those people are much more interested on a learning process that allow them to experiment and to try by their own rather that following some set rules (see Box 3). They have chosen a place without any expensive learning program also because they have inside this "maker attitude" that bring them to find, trough Internet and trough a process of trial and errors, solutions to theirs everyday challenges.

Box 3. Crowdworkers' Voice on LEARNING

"I don't think I have to go to workshops or courses of illustration to improve my job but I think I have to do a lot to make experiments, it's like a trial, I say "Ok it works, or it doesn't work", I find that producing and drawing every day and trying different things I can learn more than if I would go to any courses." Lapo. (2013, May 3). Personal interview.
"I watch tutorials. I see how people do things, and then I try to do the same, and I try, I try until it works." Oliveira, F. (2013, May, 3). Personal interview.
"This is an open space and open space means also open knowledge. People should try to transfer their knowledge to other people.
It's not so important to have very expensive tools, as you can't use these tools if you don't understand how to operate them. This is for us very important: we try to make a new way to find new technologies and open these technologies to other people, and we're not alone in doing this". Parade, M. (2013, July 15). Personal interview.
We like to promote peer-to-peer learning, we work with university abroad and they send us their students, they come to study inside our facility instead of going to university, they actually look for a non academic environment and instead of teachers we pair them up with members. It's not exactly coworking, it's not exactly a school; it's a kind of a new environment for learning. Thum, C. (2013, September 18). Personal interview.

Table 3. Different kinds of managing entities in the analyzed Multifactories

		Managing Entity Composition								
		MAGE	Pollino	BuildingBloqs	Balneário	Oficina Colectiva	Agora	FreiLand	MOB	
	Kind of *	Shared	Shared	Constituted (association)	Constituted (association)	Constituted (private)	Constituted (collective)	Constituted (association)	Constituted (private)	
Includes (formally or informally)	Litefactories	X						X	X	
	Initiator		X	X	X	X	X	X	X	
	Strategist	X	X	X	X	X	X	X	X	
	Formal Coordinator	X	X	X	X	X	X	X	X	
	Administrator	X		X	X	X	X	X	X	
	Supervisor									
	Institutions	X	X							
	Owner	X	X							

*

Shared: Managing Entity is the result of an informal (but coordinated) interaction of the Internal Stakeholders, or some of them.
Constituted: Managing Entity is formalized and its role is formally recognized by all the Stakeholders.

The Need to Exchange Knowledge

Within a Multifactory, there are two main reasons for which that put in evidence the need to exchange knowledge.

A – the solopreneurs, entrepreneurs, SMEs, and artisans who are members of a Multifactory in most cases are startups and come from previous jobs as employees, and/or completely different sectors. This means that they have ideas and most of the technical skills needed to start their own business, but they miss many other skills.

So, they face problems they don't know how to solve, and an exchange of knowledge can directly solve them, or help them to retrieve the required information to autonomously find a solution.

B – There used to be a time when it was very important to protect an idea, let it grow internally in the company and then to develop an exclusive product/service that could last for years.

Nowadays, the life cycle of ideas, products, and services is so fast that it's less important to protect them. It's much more important to develop them as fast as possible, in a very reliable and flexible way, to target the market as fast as possible.

A single small or medium company, an artisan or a pro should have many good ideas throughout the years, and they can be very different from others, so they can't rely only on their knowledge, skills and experience, but they need an easy, fast, reliable ways to get competencies.

If they're part of a system where they're used to an everyday free exchange of knowledge between well known subjects, they can find the resources they need, saving financial expenses and avoiding the cost of retrieving resources (for instance, to obtain a loan), and the cost of creating a completely new coordinating structure for each single project.

Box 4. Crowdworkers' Voice on SHARING

> *Often I go to other people here and I ask for help, or for ideas, I'm not alone. Ribbe, S. (2013, July 14) Personal interview.*
>
> *It's not about me, us, we live in a network society, we're all networked, but we don't have a place to meet. This is a perfect place to establish discussions about any topic and we do that a lot, it's a different way to educate yourself. Tizzi, C. (2013, July 12). Personal interview.*
>
> *"We've access to internet and to every single tutorial you can imagine, we've access to very cheap technology, we've access to knowledge, and if you combine them, every individual has the power to manufacture things that are mind blowing. I googled "nuclear reactor" and there are the instructions to build your own, in your kitchen. This would be impossible 50 years ago, you wouldn't be able to do this. This is the direction we're moving towards and this is the way to get out of our crisis, nowadays, with 55% of youths in Barcelona and in Spain who are unemployed. I think, instead of giving them a job, we teach them the tools, we give them the knowledge, we give them the resources that they need to invent their own jobs, I think this is the only way.*
>
> *Tham, C. (2013, September 18). Personal interview.*

Advantages to Exchange Knowledge

A crucial issue in a system where free exchange of knowledge is an important aspect of how relationships are regulated between nodes is that whoever spreads competencies, or suggestions, should have some form of non-monetary return.

In most cases, the "knowledge exchange" also requires some labor, sometimes the use of their equipment and machines, and at least the use of an (many times small) amount of time.

Many people, in their private lives, share knowledge for philanthropic reasons, or because it's something that belongs to their values, or beliefs, or just use it as a way to spend some spare time. In this sense, the return of sharing could also be just the proud of being part of a movement, or the consciousness of being useful for someone else. This obviously should not apply to entrepreneurs, professionals, or artisans; at least not as a strategy of growth.

At first sight, the return should be intended as a mere exchange of professional services, a way to offer and get services without money, or a kind of barter: "I have a need, I looked for a skill, I found it, I offer something in change."

This is something that happens, but there is something hidden much more interesting, that's the capability of the system to increase through knowledge sharing the opportunities of growth of the Companies that are part of the system (see Box 4).

What happens is that availability of competencies enables and leads people to think in a different way. They know that when they face some problems, or professional challenges, they can count on a wide range of capabilities and skills that are available and reliable, and this constant, continuous availability of resources enables entrepreneurs to think in a wider way.

It's a buffet of skills. Entrepreneurs know which resources are available and how to get them. Maybe they don't need them for a long time, but they are aware of the availability and this leads them to take on big projects because they know that they will have access to all what they will need.

So, when they put knowledge into the system, what they're doing is raising the global potential of the system by itself, and if everyone in the system offers something different, the result is that every node in the system can grow faster and steadier.

It's a way to build a system where all the players give their contribution to increase the capabilities of every single node of the system itself.

Box 5. Crowdworkers' Voice on MULTIFACTORY'S ADVANTAGES

"Money in its basic form is about exchange: a token for some work and some work for a token and in this form it's a great thing. But it has been taken a funny road. BB is a great opportunity for people to exchange skills, rather than money." Nichols, A. (2013, February 27). Personal interview.

"People like to share their knowledge, so we do a lot of workshops where members present themselves, and maybe someone says "oh, you're an expert in social media, could you help me with this project?" and they start to collaborate.

There are situations where someone from the outside says: "I have a product, I just came up with this new wine, but I need a team, can you put a team together? So we say, yes, what do you need? I need a photographer, a graphic designer, a marketing person, and we have all of that here, in MOB. So we build a team and sell it as a package." Then there's a third kind of collaboration when someone has just a really brilliant idea and just writes it on a board asking who is interested in it. It's very organic, we don't really have rules and instructions, people just grow as they like, and this was pretty effective until now." Tham, C. (2013, September 18). Personal interview.

"...Then other collaborations, trivially common interests in trade fairs, sharing costs and making a joint logistics. Then there are thousands of examples in everyday life, trivialities perhaps, as exchange information on the suppliers, or on the development of a small solution that is implemented thanks to the intuition of a neighbour and maybe it's something that for you alone it would have required days of study. Or a mutual exchange of instruments and equipment. These are aspects that you don't even notice, because they are part of the daily." Colombo, S. (2012, October 13). Personal interview.

This is an emerging property of the system, which comes from the interaction between elements of the system, and that increases the possibilities of each node of the system to afford new and bigger projects, which means an increased possibility for success on the market.

CONSTITUTIVE ELEMENTS OF A MULTIFACTORY AND DYNAMICS BETWEEN AGENTS

Light and Flexible Economic Subjects: The Litefactories

The average dimension of the companies included in a Multifactory ranges from micro to small, as they are often start-ups.

They are open to new opportunities and able to make changes very fast, according to the situational needs. They are flexible, innovative, sustainable, and "thin" under dimensional, strategic, operative, and structural points of view. Their competitiveness is mainly based on their immaterial assets and on a mix of quality, innovation, customer care, and the construction of a network of partner companies.

They are companies that by structure, style and perspective are in a grey zone between the word of craftsmanship, the free lances, and the SMEs. They are a new class of economical subjects that refer to past productive categories, but at the same time express specific characters. To identify these companies in one word, the choice was to introduce the term "Litefactory." It effectively expresses the "lightness" and flexibility of these economic agents, joint in their propensity to act in the production field.

In a Multifactory the presence of some artistic or creative Litefactories is very common, but a Multifactory is not an ensemble of creative companies; it's a system of companies that act in a creative way.

Nowadays flexibility is a need and is a transversal characteristic of SMEs, craftsmen, and free lances, but in the traditional production model "flexibility" often involves a condition of weakness, as it means just a margin contraction and a higher risk assumption to stay on the market. In a Multifactory this weakness can be mitigated, as "flexibility" takes form as the possibility for each Litefactory to offer a wider range of products/services as they can rely on the competencies and cooperation of other Litefactories that operate as partners, not as suppliers.

Box 6. Crowdworkers' Voice on DIVERSITY

> *"I think I'm really lucky that I can work in a space were everyone is different and has got his own specialty and I can learn from them."*
> *Lapo. (2013, May 3). Personal interview.*
> *"There are people doing different things here at Oficina Colectiva, and we're very different. They have stuff we don't have, 'cause they're more rational, more organized than we're here upstairs. Downstairs they're more logical, and they think much better than us. And this infects us in a good way. I think we both inspire each other in some way. It's really good to see the reactions: if we start putting post-it on the walls, they first react a little bit strangely to that, and after a month you see they're doing the same thing. If they start doing a commercial work, we think "damn, we should do a commercial work also" and we start following them and they start following us. It's a kind of a really healthy competition when they do something we have to positively react and do something good, and it's the same for them. It's a kind of creating that feeling like "let's move, let's move let's move, let's do stuff, let's do things!!" This is the kind of feeling I feel here." Quinta, R. (2013, May 5). Personal interview.*

The continuous exchange of knowledge and professional suggestions coming from people working in different sectors, but within the same environment, helps to find innovative and creative solutions and helps to solve problems in a faster, easier way.

The availability of knowledge, equipments, and tools helps in widening each Company's offer, without additional costs.

This makes possible for a Litefactory to meet its customer's need for flexibility without the costs and problems of searching for and coordinating external unknown suppliers, offering a better quality as well as sharing investments and risks (see Box 5).

A New Productive Social Class

"One day you make a thing, another day you do something else, but I can use the same stuff I learnt at the University to have a different perspective on what I'm doing." Oliveira, F. (2013, May, 3). Personal interview.

People who establish and animate the Litefactories have a high level of personal commitment, show a medium-high to very high education level, and they usually come from very diversified previous work experiences. They face challenges as opportunities for growth and believe it is important to have satisfaction in what they do, regardless of the economic return, which is generally relegated to second place with respect to the return in terms of quality of life.

In general, the entrepreneurial spirit is very strong, as is the idea to achieve something concrete, So is the awareness to be social actors, both as promoters of culture rather than as individuals able to give employment and generate well-being.

In most cases, they are not entrepreneurs or artisans by vocation or family tradition, but in response to the crisis in the labor market. Some of them are reluctant to accept a subordinate position as an employee, but many were expelled from the labor market, or never had the opportunity to enter it. In general, they are people who, after evaluating several other options, chose to try to make their passion a profession.

Some of them have solid theoretical and practical skills, others only partial specific ones, supported by good will, commitment and a strong personal network.

All, however, are reluctant to be framed in precise patterns. Formally are entrepreneurs, artisans, professionals, but when they work together they continuously mix roles, areas of expertise, and methods (see Box 6).

So, the authors decided to refer to these people as "Crowdworkers", as they usually share and mix skills and resources between Litefactories, and their products and services come from a continuous confrontation with others.

Internal Stakeholders

Internal Stakeholders: these Agents are directly involved in the construction, development and management of a Multifactory. They are different in size, structure, scope, but have to interact and cooperate to make a Multifactory work. The presence of all of them is not strictly required and their specific roles and areas of responsibility may change according to the specific needs of each different situation.

- Initiator: who has to initiate the process that leads to the birth of a Multifactory, to write the project, to create consensus, to analyze the socio economical situation, to choose the place where the Multifactory will be established, to make the first selection of Litefactories
- Strategist: who has to define the overall strategic guidelines, objectives, and actions to achieve them, seek funding.
- Formal Coordinator: who has to organize meetings and Plenary Sessions, to coordinate the working groups on joint projects, monitor the progress of joint projects, to solve conflicts
- Administrator: who has to pay bills, to choose, monitor, and pay services (surveillance, cleaning, waste charges).
- Supervisor: who has to solve difficult situations of Litefactories, to collectively pool negative situations, to monitor the development phases of the Multifactory
- Litefactories: companies, associations, free lancers included in a Multifactory
- Institutions: public or private institutional stakeholders, as municipality, foundations, district governor, other public entities
- Owner: who has the right to properties on the area where the Multifactory is established.

The Table 1 shows which are the Internal Stakeholders in the analyzed Multifactories:

Managing Entity

A Multifactory requires a Managing Entity, which by itself is a complex system. The Managing Entity is constituted by several agents and has to deal with several tasks.

Main Tasks are listed in the Table2:

The Managing Entity can be formal, as an association, or can be the result of the informal (but coordinated) interaction of the Internal Stakeholders that decide to share the managing roles under competence and convenience criterions. So, the key point is that the roles have to be allocated on a combination of competencies, time availability, and interests base.

In the analyzed Multifactories, the Managing Entity takes form in many different ways, that are shown in the Table3:

In the Multifactory Model, the suggested option is to establish an association made by at least the most directly involved internal stakeholders (Initiator, Strategist, Formal Coordinator, Administrator and Litefactories). The board of the association should not exclude Litefactories, Strategist, and Coordinator. This association should then distribute the tasks to single persons/entities and keep them under control.

Box 7. Crowdworkers' Voice on COMMUNITY

> *"It's very difficult to go along and find somebody who says: "ok, yes, I really, really want to give my time and help with my efforts in order for you to get wealthy", as soon as we made it a non for profit organization suddenly the flat doors opened and people become investing time and ideas to help us create the vision we had in mind and when we removed money as the primary objective of the company suddenly the development possibilities grew enormously" Parra-Mussel, A. (2013 February 26). Personal interview.*
> *"We talked together in plenary and we said "ok, we can imagine to create an association only to organize this project". The plenary decided it was a good idea, to have a structure that is just organizing the place, to be sure that rooms are ok, that people are paying the rent, to talk to politics and the electricity company." Trautvetter, A. (2013, July 15). Personal interview.*

Once a month there should be a plenary session with all the Litefactories of the Multifactory, to discuss and decide strategic guidelines, to decide about common projects and proposals coming from outside, and to accept new Litefactories into the Multifactory.

This is a desired situation, but it is difficult to gain it from the beginning because Litefactories have to settle down, and the institutions and the owner have to fully understand the advantages of being part of a Multifactory. Therefore, some very important activities such as to define new entries, to decide which joint projects to start, to decide marketing and promotion, and to decide common actions can be performed by the Strategist, or the Initiator, or the Formal Coordinator, but it's important that this situation should last for a short period, and as soon as possible, these activities should be managed in a collective way (see Box 7).

Institutions

Looking at the analyzed Multifactories, small and medium ones can be established following a private initiative without the intervention of Institutions. However, a large Multifactory can't exist without the support and involvement of Institutions: they create the conditions for the birth of a Multifactory by direct interventions (i.e. tenders, grants, premises, and others facilitations such as the utilization of public spaces) or indirect interventions (i.e. acting as a mediator with territory and private investors).

A key point is that Institutions have to be a social glue and implement facilitating actions, but the socio-economic structure of the Multifactory should develop and configure by itself.

A Multifactory can exist only if the institutions are not invasive, but remain in the background.

So, institutions can be part of the managing association, as they are important stakeholders, but they should not be part of the board.

As examples, at the Made in Ma.Ge. municipality and other public institutions promote the events and participate to the initiatives, but don't give directions. Sometimes they make proposals, for instance when there are tenders or grants that can be interesting for the Litefactories, but the implementation is left to the Litefactories.

In Potsdam, the municipality economically supports FreiLand with a relatively small annual amount (around 100.000 €/year), but activities, governance system, strategy are self organized and municipality doesn't interfere with the decision processes.

In London, local authority knows what Building Bloqs is doing, they appreciate their work and also gave a 15.000£ grant, but don't interfere on how the project develops.

Box 8. Crowdworkers' Voice on DEMOCRACY

"We're utilizing our strengths as we do have a flat management structure. We have a chair of each of our meetings but we don't want to institute a hierarchy where we have a managing director and then subordinate. Being as democratic organization as we can is important for us. As we're founders, we have to carry the vision, but not necessarily direct everything" Nichols, A. (2013, February 27). Personal interview.

Owner of the Area

The owner of the area can be public or private. Usually these areas are abandoned, as not suitable anymore for the needs of a single large company, and for this reason the property is willing to grant them for free with a low rent. Usually they are former empty factories just outside the town, but easy to reach. These are ideal places to produce and host a number of different professions and equipment and to use noisy machinery, also because the owner is usually not interested in preserving the internal structure, so that can be adapted by Litefactories according to their needs.

As Rivas (2011) says, linking heritage to the contemporary is another highly demanded value for those facilities seeking some differentiation and offering a unique experience as working environment. Thus giving full meaning to Jacobs' forward-looking opinion: *"old ideas can sometimes use new buildings but new ideas must use old buildings,"* (1961).

Governance

Governance of a Multifactory relates to general management, cohesive policies within Litefactories, relationships among stakeholders, sustainability, strategic planning, defining organization guidelines and processes, and the allocation of areas of responsibility.

The governance system doesn't involve internal affairs of Litefactories, as each one is an autonomous agent that decides by itself, but refers to all that is needed to facilitate the Litefactories in gaining their own goals.

Organization of economic and operative relations between Litefactories is based on bilateral or multilateral agreements and is not top-down managed.

Internal organization of Litefactories is entirely left to individual actors, and each one has a completely different internal organization model. This heterogeneity is important, as it allows a deep confrontation of different points of view. This leads to an adaptive change of each Litefactory, that is not conscious, but is the result of the incorporation of other's best practices, as Litefactories can see what happens around them in a transparent environment (see Box 8). It's not an explicit adoption of external models, but a slow, deep process that starts from the emulation and proceeds through trials and errors.

The overall organization of a Multifactory is also the result of an adaptive process.

A Multifactory is a system of heterogeneous interacting agents, with an emerging Multi-Stakeholder, collaborative, self-adaptive and self-organized system of governance. Shared rules emerge from the resolution of specific cases. This is a slow process, but important for what concerns the construction of the group (see Box 9).

Some basic rules, that are needed to channel processes and provide the basis to allow the Litefactories to begin their activity are set in a top-down way by the Initiator, the Formal Coordinator or the Managing Entity. These are requirements and conditions to be part of the Multifactory, the basic rules for the usage

Box 9. Crowdworkers' Voice on BOTTOM UP APPROACH

> *"I imagine an organic community. A community that creates itself through the people who get involved with that. It's not a community that we decided the goal would be. It will grow of its own: the people will come and get involved with it, with the things created here, with the way they interact with the outside world. This will create a community in itself and I don't think there is any plan exactly on how it will end up. It's an open ended project." Nichols, A. (2013, February 27). Personal interview.*

of common areas, rights and duties of being part of the Community, but the agents are free to define by themselves the micro social rules and the system of governance is largely bottom-up.

Coordinating Structure

A Multifactory requires reference entities to coordinate activities and to act as glue between Stakeholders. Coordination aspects are formal, informal and communicative.

Formal Coordination

The Formal Coordinator has the function of a facilitator and should be a territorial entity. The Formal Coordinator is the grant of the overall operations, but doesn't interfere with any activity of individual actors and its interests don't overlap to the specific interests of Litefactories.

Formal Coordination may refer to specific projects, use of common areas, facilities or equipment, general inquiries, technical questions, or relational aspects between Litefactories and other stakeholders. The coordinating process is not intended to be as an animation activity, that is an activity intended to start specific interactions, but the construction of the right environmental conditions where dynamics can originate from different starting points. For instance, collaborative processes must lead to a business development, but this doesn't mean that they have to begin within the boundaries of business field. They can originate from a cooperation in the micro-social field, as the management of the common facilities, or from a confrontation on the governance system, as the internal rules definitions, or from a cooperation on a cultural project, as an exploitation action towards external stakeholders.

Different Litefactories will act autonomously and in a locally unpredictable way, and so the aim is not to lead people to do certain things, but to set up an environment where a desired final situation can be gained from different starting points.

The Formal Coordinator can be a public institution, or a private organization with an institutional nature. The Formal Coordinator can also be an association constituted by the Lite Factories themselves, that is an association in which Lite Factories are members and constitute the board. An association can be easily set up after the establishment of the Multifactory, this allows for an easy turnover of associates and managing roles. On the other hand, it requires a high level of commitment and trust, as in an association all responsibilities fall on members of the managing board (see Box 10).

Informal Coordination

Many activities are coordinated by persons belonging to a Litefactory. Coordination of a common area usually starts from a single agent, a person who has a need or passion and acts as an attractor, then other elements of the system give help, or at least don't interfere.

Box 10. Crowdworkers' Voice on MANAGING ENTITY

> *"Maybe I'm a catalyst, a sort of instigator, helping to make things happen. Essentially somebody that sets the ball rolling. We don't'*
> *know where it's gonna go, and that's exciting. I'm quite confident in lots of interesting and amazing things will come from. But the way*
> *I see myself in it, if it was a stage play I'd like to be the guy who lays on the back. The shine on the stars...because the people will be the*
> *stars. The people are the stars, absolutely. And if we get to the point in the future when BB pays for itself and pays for its own rent and*
> *pays for its own energy supplies maintenance and everything goes with it, I'll be delighted and that would be enough for me." Nanray, S.*
> *A. (2013, February 27). Personal interview.*

Informal Coordinators are trusted by the peer group on a competency base, after a long process of incremental accreditation, then they become the referees for the formal coordinator, and everybody refers to them within a specific area.

Informal Coordinators don't get a direct specific or economic income from their coordinating activity, so what they gain is the chance to deeper influence the organization system, an increased visibility, and the opportunity to better interact with other Litefactories.

For this reason it's highly probable that Informal Coordinators don't belong to the bigger and more developed Litefactories, but to the smallest and newest ones, that need to grow up.

So, a Multifactory is a system where also the weakest elements (under an economic or development point of view) can directly influence the overall system and become referees of important areas.

Internal Communication

Mailing lists and open groups on social networks realize a circular communication that not only keeps everyone up to date, but allows a direct comparison of how other companies are organized, and everybody can review the internal coordination method of each company. This allows for the definition of the coordination guidelines in a shared way, and allows the community to decide which questions have to be considered of common interest or not (see Box 11).

Norms, Rules, Conventions

For what concerns laws and labor regulations, each agent in a Multifactory operates independently and assumes the burden to comply with the rules and laws related to its business. Each agent is, therefore, responsible for itself.

Internal norms and rules refer to the use of common spaces, meeting rooms, and common facilities such as the kitchen, the way to organize and conduct meetings, organization of events, the use of other's tools and consumables, and other aspects related to everyday life.

So norms and rules, as a whole, constitute a unique corpus of behavioral directions that are the result of agreements between Litefactories, but also of compromises between different moral codes. This enables people not only to accept compromises on specific issues, but also to be part of shared ethics.

There are no (or few) rules derived from a regulation, but the rules are self-generated by the everyday confrontation between different points of view. In general, the micro-social rules are subsumed by the sense of belonging that defines individual behaviors that are beneficial to the community, but every agent has its own idea of what is good or bad for the community and these ideas sometimes don't coincide.

Box 11. Crowdworkers' Voice on COWORKING

> *"We're free to make our own rules, that's very nice." Clac, E. (2013, July 14). Personal interview.*
> *"A coworking place for me is more a service for people for renting an office place, there are also places to make real coworking and to make projects, but in Freiland we have a more bottom up approach, we are a coworking place, but coworking place developed by itself. We didn't start with a future projection to make a coworking place, but after three years in Freiland we're a coworking place." Parade, M. (2013, July 15). Personal interview.*
> *"If you want to have a room here you have to come to the monthly plenary, to explain what you want to do and then the plenary decides if it fits with the FreiLand Project and if it fits you can have a space." Trautvetter, A. (2013, July 15). Personal interview.*
> *"We don't have very strict criteria for the selection of other people but we like to know the person, see what he does, the interest he has and see if it is a person who can be comfortable in this environment. We give priority to those who do creative activities, however if comes a lawyer who is interested in working in such an environment and can also give some contribution, why not." Brazao, R. (2013, May 5). Personal interview.*

In that case, the starting point is the opinion belonging to the majority, but the final rule is always the result of a mediation with the minority, because it's important that nobody feels the rules as an enforcement, because rules and norms self-generated by the community make sense only if all the members feel a moral obligation to respect them.

Control

In this scenario, control system takes an important role.

All the agents control the others according to their morals, identifying for themselves what is right or wrong according to their own standards. This is not enough, because it is then necessary to mediate their beliefs with others both personally and as a comparison with the ethics of the whole group.

In practice, it is a system that is based on a hetero-control with respect to each person/group, but also based on self-control with respect to the Multifactory system by itself (see Box 12).

Effectiveness of control is granted by the fact that other agents have an immediate interest. The consequences of loss of control are immediate, then the control is fast and accurate.

It is a system of mutual control much closer to what happens in small towns rather than what is usually expected in a workplace.

Participation and Knowledge Sharing

There is a strong link between the way Multifactories are organized and the kind of relationships that can be established.

First of all, the physical presence of people in the same environment results in everyday contact between members, and the fact that they are in the same working space helps them explore different ways to cooperate, as there are many opportunities to increase the mutual knowledge, mostly in informal occasions, as it should be during lunchtime.

But, on the other side, the participatory Governance that rules Multifactories builds up a System where everyone is somehow involved in the conduction of the space and has the responsibility to make something for and with others. This helps to turn the informal relationships into structured collaborations between economical subjects.

Box 12. Crowdworkers' Voice on FREEDOM

> *"Control? We're telling you our grown ups, you know in what kind of place you're working. We don't have bosses around here, people decide if they want to work here or not and so if you want to work here to good work and it works, everybody is responsible for himself or herself. And we do a good work, most of the times." Clac, E. (2013, July 14). Personal interview.*
> *"For what concern control, we're four people who control if everything is in the right place. If there are some beginners we make courses and classes for beginners, but then is self-responsibility of the users. When they use the tools, we're hoping that they're using the open workshop in the right way, but we had no negative experiences." Riboni, U. (2013, September 18). Personal interview.*

THE RESEARCH PROJECT

The Multifactory Model is the result of hundreds of interviews and the direct observation of many different cases in several European Countries (Italy, Spain, Portugal, United Kingdom, Germany), making use of a visual anthropology method and assuming an ethnographic point of view.

The research started in 2012 from a single case, the MAGE in Sesto San Giovanni (Milan – IT).

The MAGE is a community project and its experimental character lead to the emergence of a specific way to organize relationships between the companies and associations hosted and to interact with the territorial stakeholders.

The first trip took place in Basilicata, in South Italy, where the unemployment is an endemic problem, and the answers collected there were surprisingly similar to the answers gained from people working in the MAGE. At that point, it wasn't already clear if it would have been possible to build a model that could constitute a theoretical structure, but there was the feeling that these experiences could be a change of paradigm in the way to intend work organization and job creation.

It was time to see if something similar could exist outside Italy, and so the research moved to London, as the UK capital is a European trendsetter for cultural and social movements. In London, in February 2013, it was possible to find a Multifactory in start-up phase, Building Bloqs, and again the direct observation and what people told in the interviews was surprisingly similar to what was observed before.

During the trip to Building Bloqs, the Multifactory Model took its early form and the following travels to Lisbon, Berlin, and Potsdam allowed to refine it and to define the Intervention Model.

The Multifactories found around Europe were not built on an existing model, following given guidelines. They are totally self-made, mainly on a trial and error basis, and developed by people who never met and who didn't know anything about each other. So, it was somehow surprising to discover that the Multifactories faced the same problems and they presented many similarities in structure, organization and governance. Moreover, also the self-perception of people involved in different Multifactories is very similar, as is the overall ethical point of view.

None of the Multifactories included in the research wrote anything about their experience, and they never theorized anything on their intervention scheme. Sometimes they have some theoretical reference models coming from the US, but these models were completely changed as the socio-economical environment is radically different. As a matter of fact, all of the analyzed Multifactories are managing their growth by themselves, as if they have no idea that there are other similar places to compare with (see Box 13).

On one hand, this has been a great advantage for the research development, as Multifactories always were very welcoming, and it was possible to make shootings and interviews without restraints. It was possible to freely move inside the Multifactories and to see the everyday life for several days, and this allowed for a deep understanding of their characteristics. Moreover, as each Multifactory didn't know anything about others, the answers from interviewed people are expressions of truly personal points of view.

On the other hand, it was also clear that the lack of reference models leads the Multifactories to carry forward their own projects on a trial and error basis, so a systemization of these experiences and the development of a coherent model should have been very helpful to support the establishment of new ones, especially because places similar to the eight included in the research are in project or under construction, or open to the public every month, and a unifying intellectual framework could help their development.

Research Actions

The research work is divided into four main parallel Actions. Each Action has a defined goal and is intended to produce tangible outputs.

- Action Output

1) On field research. This research was conducted from autumn 2012 to summer 2013 and was intended to visit several Multifactories within Europe to understand how they work and their characteristics. During this Action several days were spent in each Multifactory, taking part in the everyday life interviewing the people managing them and working there.

2) Development of the Multifactory Model. This Action is intended to systemize the collected data, to understand, underline, and categorize the main common characteristics that describe a Multifactory and the emerging dynamics that take place. The output is the Multifactory Model, which describes the profile and the role of the key elements constituting a Multifactory and the dynamics that take place in it.

3) Development of the Intervention Model. The Multifactory Intervention describes the steps that can lead to the constitution of a Multifactory. This model should describe the desired characteristics of the agents, strategy, methods, and actions to build up a Multifactory starting from scratch.

4) Development of the Computational Model. This Action has the aim to build a Dynamic Simulation Model that can help Social Designers developing a Multifactory to forecast the emerging dynamics within agents at the change of some parameters in order to give them suggestions about the proper strategies to implement to manage the process.

Ethical Issues

Around the World, and also in Europe, many researchers and intellectuals are trying to find creative, sustainable and effective solutions to emerging issues related to new concepts in Economy, as to the present situation of the labor market. Many of these solutions take form as experimental models that have to be put into practice to see if they work and under which conditions, but this process is not risk-free.

Researchers have an enormous responsibility, as in case their assumptions are wrong, or they are not able to properly manage unexpected dynamics, their intellectual failure means also an economical and personal defeat for many people, who not necessarily have all the instruments to correctly evaluate in advance the risk of joining an experimental project based on an innovative, not fully tested intervention model.

Under this point of view, the necessity to make predictions as accurate as possible is a moral need, and thought that all the socio-economic environments are complex systems, characterized by emerging

Box 13: Crowdworkers' Voice on MODELS

"We arrived through a process of many months of brain cuddling and mind maps and discussions." Parra-Mussel, A. (2013 February 26). Personal interview.

"My dream is that we create something here which proves to be so useful, so beneficial, so interesting, and innovative that is only a question of time before we ourselves or somebody else builds the next BB so we can spread the benefit of what we are achieving here as fine as well as possible we will not necessarily be employing people directly as an organization but what we are doing is job creation and this is so necessary here right across the UK, but also right across Europe now." Nichols, A. (2013, February 27). Personal interview.

The interviews were taken from October 2012 to September 2014:

Made in Ma.Ge. (Milano, IT) October-December 2012

Pollino (Basilicata, IT) 22-27 January 2013

Building Bloqs (London, UK) first trip February-March 2013

Balnéario and Oficina Colectiva (Lisboa, PT) May-June 2013

Agora (Berlin, D) and FreiLand (Potsdam, D) July 2013

Building Bloqs (London, UK) second trip September 2013

MOB (Barcelona, ES) September 2013

behaviors that are impossible to forecast with intuition, the use of Simulation Environments to support the development and management of these social experiments seemed to be an innovative and effective way to reduce the risk of failure and to fully accomplish the social role that Researchers have to play.

But this was not enough. Each new idea, each new model related to Social Innovation needs to be tested. This lead to set up an experimental environment, based upon the Multifactory Intervention Model, where several people decided to work and somehow to risk on their own, and to establish their own activities.

This environment is called Bigmagma and is a self-financed, self-regulated Multifactory based in Milan and built following the Multifactory Model, as it was defined by this research.

Bigmagma was an experiment to check if it would have been possible to build a Multifactory from scratch, and if that environment should effectively support the growth of the Litefactories which compose it. People who joined Bigmagma are small entrepreneurs, designers, craftsmen, musicians, a drawer, an oenologist and an artist. Researchers who developed the Multifactory Model are part of it, and contribute to the community of workers exactly as every other member.

After one year, Bigmagma is a fully functional Multifactory, which has grown from four to ten Litefactories and is still growing. All the Litefactories which are part of Bigmagma are going quite well on the market and self sufficient. All the activities are self organized and regulated by few democratic concepts, which were formalized in a collective Manifesto. Bigmagma is also part of a free exchange program within Multifactories, aimed to support the exchange of experiences and knowledge, which allows people from Multifactories to spend working periods in other ones for free.

Future Research Directions

Multifactories are a particular kind of productive environments, but the Multifactory Model promotes a way to organize workplaces that goes beyond the analyzed experiences.

Corporations, Huge institutions, Schools and Universities, NGO are economic and social systems that have to manage complexity, balancing the effort to gain stability, to build upon their own experience, to incorporate new ideas, and to experiment new ways to develop and produce goods and services.

The Multifactory Model seems able to counterbalance these aspects, and it would be interesting to apply it to different environments.

The Multifactory Model could also be seen as a new approach to service training. It could be a model to replace the old ways of postgraduate curriculum activating the work places as academic places. This would allow to better integrate academic needs and requirements coming from the private sector, and it could lead to a situation where people can easily shift from Companies to Universities several times during their lives, improving their skills in several different ways. This would not only allow to mix practical and theoretical skills, but also to reduce segregation of knowledge.

These are suggestions coming from the actual research and they would require further analysis, but they seem to be very promising and not so hard to verify.

BACKGROUND

Obviously, there isn't any specific reference on Multifactories, as it is a completely new concept. The general framework assumed as background refers to Sustainable Development, with particular regard to:

- Creative Industries
- Workplace Innovation
- Sharing Economy

The basic assumption of the work presented in this chapter is the need for a change from a Taylorist work organization; characterized by task specialization, a pyramidal hierarchical structure, and a centralization of responsibilities; to a holistic organization, featuring flat hierarchical structures, job rotation, flexi-time, self-responsible multi-skilled teams, worker empowerment, and the change from vertical to horizontal organization models.

The labor market changes reflect not only an economic crisis but also a social one, and the international *World of Work Report (2013)* gives a wide view about the social impact of the rise of long-term joblessness and problems related to job quality in Europe. It also composes the general framework to be considered, which include the official European Commission legislation and reports as *A European strategy for smart, sustainable and inclusive growth (2010)*, the *Agenda for new skills and job (2010)*, and *Social innovation as part of the Europe 2020 strategy (2010)* as well as the International Institute for Labor Studies Working towards sustainable development: *Opportunities for decent work and social inclusion in a green economy (2012)*.

Creative Industries

According to Howkins (2005), The Creative Economy is a comprehensive kind of new economy, based on creative people, creative industries, and creative cities. That means revitalizing manufacturing, services, retailing, and entertainment industries, leading to a change of where people want to live, work and learn, where they think, invent and produce. Howkins (2005) recognizes all kinds of creativity, not only the arts, as major cultural and economic processes. *"Success in the creative economy will come to the organizations that recognize and reconcile the personal, the spiritual, and the economic."*

Living out the debate on which activities have to be included in the concept of "creative industries," there are interesting concrete platforms to apply this concept in concrete projects such as URBACT, an European exchange and learning program promoting sustainable urban development.

The URBACT Creative Clusters Project analyzes the crossroad between the creative economy and the economy of culture. Multifactories are an example of successful creative-based strategies on local public policies and how those strategies, trying to promote a local creative ecosystem, rapidly take the shape of a social innovation strategy. *"Creative industries is not limited to arts and culture, it extends to fields where creative individual, managers and technologists meet together. Moreover, the creative entrepreneur comprises much more than people working in cultural and creative industries."* (Rivas, 2011, p. 92)

Referring to Nordström & Ridderstrale (2007), the Multifactory model is an example of a creative-based business model and proposes new ways of organizing work in general, rather than focusing on how creative class is exploring new ways of working. Most of the interviewed people can be considered part of the creative class, but not because they do creative jobs, as this is not the most relevant characteristic: the focus is not to be creative or not, but to be productive in a creative way, as a Multifactory is aimed to economic development, rather than to cultural development.

Workplace Innovation

A lot of literature is focusing on workplace innovation as directly linked to the technological changes. More in general, one can say that there is a strong correlation between the introduction of new technologies and work reorganization. The development of information technology has induced managers to rethink the way work has traditionally been organized (Beblavy, Maselli, & Martellucci, 2012) and this is an important framework that has to be kept in consideration.

To the extent of the Multifactory Model, Workplace Innovation is intended in the way Pot (2011) suggests, *"the idea behind is to combine economic and social goals."* As Cressey & Kellher (2003, p. 93-107) pointed out, innovative work practices represent a radical change in the production process. This implies the shift from a static type of organization, where tasks and processes are continually replicated, to a transformative learning organization, where relationships and connections matter, and the action is the core of the processes. *"Transformative action requires a focus on human beings and the organization must be viewed not as a machine but as 'living' entities."*

Sharing Economy

The sharing economy business models are an answer to a rising need to make businesses cooperate and share. The most common examples of sharing economy are the Crowdfounding platforms (such as Kickstarter and Indiegogo), which are instruments often used by Litefactories, or the Multifactory by themselves, but sharing economy is a concept that can refer to a much wider range of experiences, as can be a Multifactory, that is a small community, like a village, and a natural place for sharing resources, competences, and experiences within all the involved agents.

There are recent interesting studies about the collaborative economy, commissioned by the newest giants of P2P marketplaces and synergic platforms on the web (as Airbnb), as well as studies in general about social media (Maineri, 2013).

Talking about sharing experiences related to work, there are many different models and answers, from the territorial networks to the shared working places. The first ones have existed a long time and take form as associations of enterprises, industrial districts, and corporations. Shared working places can take many forms, as Coworking places, Maker Spaces, Creative Hubs, Fab Labs, or Startups Farms, and are new answers to the disintegration of the labor market. They are experiencing dramatic growth and increasing structuring, assuming well-defined specificities that are very clear to those who are part of these cultural movements, but often escape the understanding of those who are not directly involved and engender errors and misunderstandings.

Usually, shared environments for workers are a solution for work-at-home professionals, independent contractors, or people who travel frequently who end up working in relative isolation. Unlike a typical office environment, those places are not employed by the same organization. They are also the social gathering of a group of people who are still working independently, but who share values and who are interested in the synergy that can happen from working with like-minded talented people in the same space. The most studied is the coworking movement that has roughly doubled in size each year since 2006. The latest *Global Coworking Survey* (2012) carried out by Deskmag shows there are now more than 1100 spaces worldwide.

As said before, at first sight the MF could seem similar to a coworking space, but every time the Multifactory Model was presented to people involved in the coworking movement they refused every similarity.

During the National Day of Social Security 2013, a public debate was organized at the Milan Stock Exchange between the developers of the Multifactory Model and the founders of the three main coworking spaces in Milan and they affirmed they could not link the Multifactories to their experience or, at least, they associated more to a new kind of working space for the new craftsmen (GNP, 2013) which is in line with the theoretical frame well underlined by Micelli (2011).

Another confirmation came from the interview to Carsten Foertsch, the founder of *deskmag.com,* the most relevant European on-line magazine about coworking that is based in Betahaus, the most famous coworking space in Berlin, as the Multifactory Model wasn't absolutely comprehensible from his point of view, *"It is not possible for me, that I have to write at the computer all day long, to share the space with a carpenter who produces dust." Foertsch, C. (2013, July 13). Personal Interview.*

CONCLUSION

A Multifactory is an environment where knowledge sharing happens "naturally" and involves a circular engagement.

People who have a strong competence in new technologies may lack competencies in traditional techniques, and vice versa.

They both need each others, but it's hard to meet together as they belong to very different social circles and they speak different technical languages.

A Multifactory allows them to freely meet and share ideas and Skills. This leads to new projects and collaborations.

A Multifactory is an environment that makes the knowledge available in the right place and at the right time, in a simple, easy, effective and self-regulated way.

A Multifactory is an opportunity for retired people or old craft men to share knowledge with young entrepreneurs, as it's a simple way to give them access to the net economy by using native digitals.

Multifactories are also an effective, sustainable and viable way to help people to invent or reinvent their job and proved to work in different cultural contexts.

Multifactories are the proof that different kinds of knowledge can be exchanged between people in a working environment, and that this exchange doesn't require any special value engagement. In a Multifactory, it's all about structure, not values, and this means they are a way to extend the participative concept of Shared Knowledge and Collaborative Economy to people who are not explicitly involved in groups or projects ethically labeled.

An innovative concept demonstrates that it really works when becomes an opportunity for everybody, as is when it works because of its structure, not because involves people who have the exact extent to make it working.

Multifactories are not utopian places, where "special", high motivated people try to set up a parallel world, but "common" working environments where "common" people keep on their own activities, but in a different way.

Multifactories are places where social innovation is not expressed as an attack to the system, but as a leverage to change it, and prove that the concepts explored by this book are far behind the pioneering stage and can coexist with the mainstream system and become part of it.

REFERENCES

Cressey, P., & Kelleher, M. (2003). The conundrum of the learning organization: Instrumental and emancipatory theories of learning. In B. Nyhan, P. Cressey, M. Kelleher, & R. Poell (Eds.), Learning organisations: European perspectives, theories and practices. Luxembourg: CEDEFOP.

Deskmag, C. E. (2012). *The 2nd Global Coworking Survey*. Retrieved July. 1, 2013, from http://www.deskmag.com/en/first-results-of-global-coworking-survey-171

GNP. (2013). *Tem(p)i e luoghi del lavoro flessibile*. Retrieved July, 1, 2013, from http://www.giornatanazionaledellaprevidenza.it/terza-giornata-gnp2013

Howkins, J. (2005, September). Enhancing creativity. In Creative Industries: A symposium on culture based development strategies. New Delhi, India: Malvika Singh Editor.

Maineri, M. (2013). Collaboriamo! Come i social media ci aiutano a lavorare e a vivere bene in tempo di crisi. Milano, Italy: Hoepli.

Micelli, S. (2011). Futuro artigiano. Venezia, Italy: Marsilio Editore.

Nordström, K. A., & Ridderstrale, J. (2007). *Funky business forever: How to enjoy capitalism*. Upper Saddle River, NJ: Pearson Education.

Pot, F., & Associates. (2011 September). *Social innovation of work and employment, challenge social innovation*. Paper presented at Workshop: Social Innovation at Work, Wien.

Rivas, M. (2011). *From creative industries to the creative place: Refreshing the local development agenda in small and medium size towns*. URBACT creative clusters project final report. Óbidos, PT.

ADDITIONAL READING

Aigrain, P. (2014). Sharing: Culture and the economy in the internet age. Amsterdam, NL: Amsterdam university press.

Amidon, D. M., Formica, P., & Mercier-Laurent, E. (2005). *Readings on knowledge economics: Emerging principles, practices and policies.* Tartu, EE: Tartu University Press.

Anderson, C. (2010). How web video powers global innovation. *TEDGlobal.* Retrieved June, 12, 2013 from http://www.ted.com/talks/chris_anderson_how_web_video_powers_global_innovation.html

Anderson, R. (1999). *Mid-course correction: Toward a sustainable enterprise.* Chelsea, MA: Green publishing Company.

Anderson, R. (2009). The business logic of sustainability. *TEDX.* Retrieved July, 1, 2013, from http://www.ted.com/talks/ray_anderson_on_the_business_logic_of_sustainability.html

Antagata, W. (2007). Libro Bianco sulla creatività. Roma, IT: Commissione sulla Creatività e Produzione di Cultura in Italia/Ministero per i Beni e le Attività Culturali.

Ariely, D. (2012). What make us feel good about our work. *TED talk. Rio de la Plata.* Retrieved July, 23, 2013, from http://www.ted.com/talks/dan_ariely_what_makes_us_feel_good_about_our_work.html

Bettoni M. C., The Essence of knowledge management: A constructivist approach. *Institute for Methods and Structures*, Basel, CH, 1-6.

Bollier, D. (2008). *Viral spiral. How the commoners built a digital republic of their own.* New York, NY: The new Press. Retrieved July, 1, 2013, from http://www.viralspiral.cc/sites/default/files/ViralSpiral.pdf

Broderick, D. (2001). *The spike: How our lives are being transformed by rapidly advancing technologies.* New York, NY: Tom Doherty Associated.

Caves, R. E. (2000). *Creative industries: Contracts between art and commerce.* Cambridge, MA: Harvard University Press.

Chapain, C., Comunian, R., & Clifton, R. (2011). Location, location, location: Exploring the complex relationship between creative industries and place. *Creative Industries Journal*, 1(3), 5-10. Retrieved July, 1, 2013, from http://www.ingentaconnect.com/content/intellect/cij/2010/00000003/00000001/art00002

Christopher, A., & Dominique, C. (2007). The strength of weak cooperation: An attempt to understand the meaning of web 2.0. *International Journal of Digital Economics*, 65, 51–65.

Communication from the Commission to the European Parliament. the Council, the European economic and social Committee and the Committee of the regions. (2011). *A renewed EU strategy 2011-14 for corporate social responsibility.* {COM(2011) 681 final}, Brussels, BE: Retrieved July, 1, 2013, from http://eur-lex.europa.eu/LexUriServ/LexUriServ.do?uri=COM:2011:0681:FIN:EN:PDF

Communication from the Commission to the European Parliament. the Council, the European economic and social Committee and the Committee of the regions. Social Business Initiative. (2011). *Creating a favorable climate for social enterprises, key stakeholders in the social economy and innovation.* {SEC(2011) 1278 final}, Brussels, BE: Retrieved July, 1, 2013, from http://eur-lex.europa.eu/LexUriServ/LexUriServ.do?uri=COM:2011:0682:FIN:EN:PDF

Communication from the Commission to the European Parliament. the Council, the European economic and social Committee and the Committee of the regions. (2011). *An agenda for new skills and jobs: A European contribution towards full employment.* {26.11.2010 COM(2010) 682 final/2} Strasbourg, FR: Retrieved July, 1, 2013, from http://eur-lex.europa.eu/LexUriServ/LexUriServ.do?uri=COM:2010 :0682:REV1:EN:PDF

Coy, P. The creative economy. Which companies will thrive in the coming years? Those that value ideas above all else. *Business Week Magazine.* 2000-08-28.

Creative metropoles. Situation Analysis of 11 Cities: Final Report. (2010). Retrieved July, 1, 2013, from Creative Metropoles Interreg IVC Programme web site www.creativemetropoles.eu

Drew, J., Sundsted, T., & Bacigalupo, T. (2009). *I'm outta here: How coworking is making the office obsolete.* Austin, TX: NotanMBA Press.

Drucker, P. (1993). *Post-capitalist society.* Oxford, UK: Butterworth Heinemann.

Eck, J. (2005). Struggling with the creative class. *International Journal of Urban and Regional Research, 29*(4), 740–770. doi:10.1111/j.1468-2427.2005.00620.x

European Commission. (2010). Green paper. Unlocking the potential of cultural and creative industries. Brussels, BE: COM (2010).

European Commission. (2010). Europe 2020. A European strategy for smart, sustainable and inclusive growth. Brussels, BE: COM (2010).

Gansky, L. (2012). *The mesh: Why the future of business is sharing.* New York, NY: Portfolio Trade, Penguin Group.

Genevieve, V. DeGuzman & Andrew, I., (2011). Working in the unoffice: A guide to coworking for indie workers, small businesses, and nonprofits. San Francisco, CA: Night Owls press.

Gordon, R., & Brynjolfsson, E. (2013). The future of work and innovation debate. *Ted2013*, Retrieved July, 15, from http://blog.ted.com/2013/04/23/the-future-of-work-and-innovation-robert-gordon-and-erik-brynjolfsson-debate-at-ted2013/

Howkins, J. (2001). *The creative economy: How people make money from ideas.* New York, NY: Penguin Group.

Jackson, T. (2005). *Motivating sustainable consumption: A review of evidence on consumer behavior and behavioral change, Paper published by the Centre for Environmental Strategy,* University of Surrey Retrieved July, 1, 2013, from www.epa.gov/sustainability/workshop0505/5d_Jackson_Tim.pdf

Jacobs, J. (1961). *The death and life of great American cities.* New York, NY: The Random House.

Kurki, L., & Manoliu, M. (2011). Opinion of the European Economic and Social Committee on Innovative workplaces as a source of productivity and quality jobs (own-initiative opinion) *Official Journal of the European Union* (2011/C 132/05) Retrieved July, 1, 2013, from http://eur-lex.europa.eu/LexUriServ/LexUriServ.do?uri=OJ:C:2011:132:0022:0025:EN:PDF

Miroslav, B., Maselli, I., & Martellucci, E. (2012). *Workplace innovation and technological change*, Brussels, BG: Centre for European Policy Studies Special Reports. Retrieved July 15, 2013, from http://ssrn.com/abstract=2147619

Morace, F. (2011). I paradigmi del futuro. Lo scenario dei trends. Busto Arsizio, IT: Nomos Edizioni.

Rombie, D. (2010). *The entrepreneurial dimension of the cultural and creative industries*. Utrecht, NL: European Commission. Utrecht School of the Arts.

Rushkoff, D. (2011). *Life inc: How corporatism conquered the world, and how we can take it back*. New York, NY: Penguin Random House Trade Paperbacks.

Shirky, C. (2008). *Here comes everybody: The power of organizing without organizations*. New York, NY: Penguin Group.

Tapscott, D., & Williams, A. D. (2007). *Wikinomics: How mass collaboration changes everything*. New York, NY: Portfolio Penguin Group.

Towse, R. (2002). Book review of creative industries. *Journal of Political Economy, 110*(1), 234–237. doi:10.1086/324388

Van Heur, B. (2010). *Creative networks and the city: Towards a cultural political economy of aesthetic production*. Bielefeld, DE: Transcript Verlag.

Verwijnen, J. (1999). The creative city's new field condition. Can urban innovation and creativity overcome bureaucracy and technocracy? In J. Verwijnen & P. Lehtovuori (Eds.), *Creative cities. Cultural industries e urban development and the information society*. Helsinki, FI: UIAH Publications.

KEY TERMS AND DEFINITIONS

Crowdworker: People who run the Litefactories and who usually put their skills together to run joined projects.

Litefactory: Every Company, Craftman, Freelance, Artist, Association which is constitutive part of a Multifactory.

Multifactory: Self regulated shared working environment for both those into intellectual jobs and practical professions.

Sharing Economy: An economical paradigm based upon the opportunity and potentialities of sharing knowledge, ideas, equipments and resources.

Social Business: A business whose aim is to address wealth for investors and shareholders, and to gain social improvements for Society and stakeholders.

Sustainability: While running a Company, a condition that is reached when the economical situation of the company is good, the company has good development opportunities, people who work in and for the company are safe, personally satisfied and paid according to their needs, the company respects the environment, doesn't create pollution and doesn't waste non-renewable resources, customers are given high value for money products and services.

Work Life Balance: The balance between the aspects related to work and to private life. Crowdworkers usually agree to shift the balance towards private life aspects.

Chapter 10
Open Modelling for Simulators

Bruce Edmonds
Centre for Policy Modelling, Manchester Metropolitan University, UK

Gary Polhill
The James Hutton Institute, UK

ABSTRACT

This chapter motivates and discusses the process of making a simulation model available for others to freely inspect and use. Firstly, it outlines the three reasons why this is necessary: democratic right, scientific scrutiny, and public value extraction. Then it describes the basic steps for doing this, including: making code comprehensible, documentation and licensing. It then describes some further things one might do when releasing a complex model to help ensure it is understood and re-used appropriately. It briefly looks as some tools and approaches to help in all this, and ends with a discussion about the change in underlying "modelling culture" that is needed.

INTRODUCTION

While preparing and making ones simulation model public might be at the last thing on the mind of its developer, this is a crucial step in terms of the public benefit to be gained from their effort. This chapter looks at this in the context of simulation modelling, discusses the arguments for it and then outlines some of the necessary steps to make it effective. In particular, it aims to do the following.

- Motivate the reader as to the importance of open modelling practices
- Help the reader understand the various steps that are necessary to making this a reality
- Suggest further steps to help ensure that particularly complex models are understood
- Describe some tools and approaches that will aid in this process
- Discuss some of the underlining changes to the "culture of modelling" needed

DOI: 10.4018/978-1-4666-8336-5.ch010

BACKGROUND

The phrase "Open Data" has become a banner under which a campaign has developed to make the data gathered by various institutions available to the public with relatively light conditions upon its subsequent use (Auer et al. 2007). The campaign has focussed upon publicly funded institutions, such as government authorities and universities but has also included government subcontractors and even private companies.

Open Data allows for the development of several benefits, namely that the data are available for checking against other sources of evidence; that any mistakes or distortions are more likely to be detected; it allows a better understanding of the recommendations that such institutions make through access to the underlying data; it allows a deeper democratic debate; and finally the extraction of further value from that data is possible via subsequent use, allowing for a wealth of secondary services to be built.

The reasons put forward against opening access to data might include worries over privacy; the wish to protect internal processes; the subsequent reluctance to collect data that might be embarrassing in the first place; the cost of preparing data for release; and a wish to commercially exploit or sell the data themselves. However, it is being increasingly realised that data can be a valuable public asset and that the people who have ultimately paid for the data have a greater right to it than the particular institutions who created it.

Here we intend the phrase "Open Modelling" to be similar to that of "Open Data", except that in this case it is indicated that it is the models rather than the data that are to be made widely accessible. Thus Open Modelling is the practice of making ones models available to others. Here we are mostly concerned with simulation models, but a lot of what is discussed below would apply to any kind of complex model.

MAIN FOCUS OF THE CHAPTER

The Purposes of Open Modelling

Similar to Open Data, Open Modelling has the potential to deliver a number of benefits to wider society, with the underlying motivations of democratic right, scientific scrutiny and public value extraction, which are now discussed.

Democratic right. Citizens have a right to understand how the decisions that affect them are made. If models are being used as part of the policy development process, then the formulation of those models will have an impact on those decisions. In this case, if citizens are not to be disadvantaged in the debate over policy, they need access to the same range of evidence and tools as those proposing policy, including the details of any models used.

There are two, closely related, arguments against this: that the wider public will not be able to understand such models (so it is a waste of time to provide access), and that they will misinterpret/use them (in other words, these matters are best left to the institutional experts). However these arguments could be made against the release of any technical or statistical data. In practice what happens is that a variety of specialists from pressure groups or academia, who have the skills, will inspect, analyse and critique the models and present their conclusions to each other and, if they have enough public import, to a wider audience. These practices mediate the understanding and critique of models, just as academics and journalists might do for other technical information. The value to the wider public is still real, even if it is (as with many aspects of life) mediated and provided by an "ecology" of information analysts, brokers and political actors. This is how an open and democratic society should ideally work, and the inclusion of models in the mix would simply extend the openness and the scope of potential debate[1].

Scientific scrutiny. Modelling is a technically tricky process – one in which it is easy to make unintentional mistakes. It is easy to fool yourself with models and come to false conclusions from them, even if the papers and other documents about them have been extensively reviewed (e.g. as documented in Edmonds and Hales 2003). The fact is that models are increasingly complex objects that are impossible to *completely* check by inspection or testing of their code.

Ultimately the most thorough way of checking models is by having an independent, or even hostile, modeller inspect, re-implement and re-analyse the properties of a model, looking for bugs, hidden assumptions, vulnerabilities and contestable interpretations of its properties. Making sufficient documentation of the code available to potential critics is essential for this purpose. However models can be so complex that it is likely that not all details might be so adequately described, so it is important that the code should be accessible to check details when other means fail.

In this way models can be the unambiguous elements in a wider social process of analysis and improvement, resulting in a higher quality and reliability of models, with a greater understanding of their assumptions and conditions of application. This is the key importance of using formal models within the scientific process (Edmonds 2000). Unless models and sufficient documentation are made available this cannot happen.

There are no substantial arguments against this purpose, apart from the potential embarrassment from model developers about mistakes and weaknesses being exposed. This is a matter of maturity; of an acceptance that one will necessarily not be able to evaluate one's own creation completely, any more than poets or authors will be able to evaluate their own work. We contend that modelling is better done as a collective exercise than one characterised by "heroic" individual achievement. The wish to manage one's own reputation by preventing mistakes being discovered is easily trumped by the need for better tested, better understood and more reliable models.

Both the purposes of democratic right and scientific scrutiny can be seen as special cases of Popper's arguments for the falsifiability of statements (Popper 1963) and the desirability for openness within a democratic society (Popper 1967). The more a model is open to its deficiencies being revealed, the better the public, longer-term, outcome. Thus merely making a model available, whilst seeking to control and limit criticism of it (e.g. by making the code obscure or impossible to run), is not attaining the ideal of open modelling. Openness that borders on *seeking* criticism (rather than merely tolerating it) marks out science from other social phenomena.

Public value extraction. Rigorous modelling requires a great deal of effort. There are many stages to good modelling practice (including exploration, design, implementation, verification, validation, documentation, publication) each of which require time and skill, and many of which are tedious to do properly. Thus, if a model achieves something substantial, it can be a thing of considerable value, enabling its owners to forecast and/or understand processes that others cannot (without expending the same level of effort). If this has been developed using private resources, then it is understandable that its developers might wish to have a monopoly over the use and/or licensing of their code to gain profit from this investment[2]. However, if it is ultimately public money that has funded the development of a model (e.g. within a government or academic institution) then, usually, the public has a right to access the value created.

Thus the ability to reuse a model (or parts of it) for new purposes by other people can allow more value to be gained from modelling effort. For example: a simplified version of a well-known model might be used for teaching purposes, the model combined with others to make a composite model, or a particularly useful set of routines in the model extracted for reuse elsewhere.

Reusing models or parts of them is not without difficulty or its own dangers. A model produced for one purpose in one context may be subtly unsuitable for another (Edmonds & Hales 2005). To safely reuse a model for another purpose requires understanding the assumptions and limitations of a model, so the standard of the documentation is important. Similar dangers are inherent in the use of any analytic tool that is widely available, such as statistical techniques, but these are relatively generic so that the effort in understanding when and how they can be used is more likely to be worth it. However, even if a model is of use to only one other purpose, for someone who puts in the effort of understanding it sufficiently, making it open has created value that would otherwise have been lost.

The benefits of scientific scrutiny and public value extraction lie behind all open source software, and so many of the same protocols and techniques used there apply to Open Modelling. However, as we shall see, the particular complexities and uses of models do create some differences and difficulties that need to be addressed.

Basic Steps for Making Models Open

Current practice in opening models is to accompany academic papers using them with making them publicly available on an internet page, archive or repository using an appropriate software licence. Popularly used repositories include GitHub and SourceForge, and there are specialist archives such as openabm. org, which can be used for agent-based models. Some practitioners make use of their own personal or institutional webpages for releasing software. There are advantages and disadvantages with each. Institutional or personal webpages provide the licensor with greater control over the release of software and tracking downloads, but web addresses are less likely to be permanent, and they do not provide an opportunity for others to make contributions or 'fork' the product in a transparent way. Repositories such as openabm.org are useful for developing a community of practice in a particular modelling approach, but may also have issues with persistence if funding to support them is not maintained. Other software repositories offer tools to help with bug-tracking and community contributions, but are vulnerable to institutional changes, such as a previously free service being changed to one that is available for a fee.

Licensing is a very important, but often overlooked, aspect of making software open. The default position, without any specific licence, is that software is not open from the instant it is created. In earlier work (Polhill & Edmonds 2007), we reviewed the requirements for licensing modelling software needed to ensure that proper scientific discourse can be conducted legally. All these rights, necessary for science, are prohibited by default without a licence explicitly permitting them:

- the unrestricted right to run the software, possibly under 'perverse' conditions, to understand how it works;
- inspecting the source code;
- modifying the source code;
- redistributing the software and any modifications thereof;
- obliging the licensee to redistribute the software under an equivalent licence (so-called 'copyleft' protection).

Arguably some of these rights need to be strengthened to obligations for the purposes of scientific discourse, and there may be further obligations that should be placed on the licensee for these purposes. For example:

- If you take someone else's software, make modifications to it and publish the results in a journal article, then you should be obliged to redistribute the modified version.
- If you use someone else's software in a journal article, with or without modifications, then there may be articles in the literature you should be obliged to cite.

Our earlier review did not find any licence that met all these criteria, but the Academic Free and GNU General Public Licences were closest.

Releasing models used in academic literature on the web using an appropriate licence, though it includes a number of important steps, is still insufficient to make models open. Effectively, the only guaranteed documentation for the model is the academic paper accompanying it. If the paper is only available for subscribers of the journal, then that documentation, even if it were adequate, is not universally accessible, particularly to members of the public whose taxes may have funded the work. If the model has been used for several such papers, the associated software may have been revised, so it is not necessarily clear which version of the software is associated with which paper. The kind of detail required to understand a computer program is in any case not typically available in a journal article. Documentation protocols for journal articles such as Grimm et al.'s (2006, 2010) ODD[3] protocol only ensure (if properly followed) that the reader could re-implement the model the authors describe; they do not guarantee that the particular software used will be comprehensible. ODD already includes more detail than journal editors are typically willing to tolerate, so it is clear that making further documentation available is necessary to make a model open.

NetLogo (Wilensky, 1999) is a popularly used rapid prototyping environment for agent-based models that encourages model developers to provide more documentation by including an 'info' tab on its GUI.[4] The info tab provides suggested sections for the developer to complete, including a brief description of what the model is for, how it works and how to use it, as well as suggested experiments with model parameters and extensions to the model that would improve it in some way.

Volker Grimm, Amelie Schmolke and colleagues (2010, 2011) have devised the TRACE protocol to outline the documentation needed for accessible modelling. The protocol outlines an eleven-section document grouped into three areas: model development, model testing and analysis, and model application. Though this may seem unduly burdensome to time-pressed academics, the TRACE protocol was devised from a review of the literature on good modelling practice when using ecological and environmental models for decision support (Schmolke et al. 2010). The protocol also follows their particular conceptualisation of the modelling cycle. Though there are several such conceptualisations (e.g. Jakeman et al. 2006; Dray et al. 2006; Livet et al. 2010), the more general point is that any perceived burden in providing such documentation can be lessened if it is embedded into the model development process.

Interestingly, the TRACE documentation does not include provision of standard computing documentation such as a user guide or programmer's guide. Both are arguably important in improving the accessibility of modelling software. A user guide makes it easier for someone to get the model working – something particularly important for larger scale models that may have several input data or configuration files. A programmer's guide (rarely if ever provided for models) facilitates making changes to model code. Unlike TRACE, documentation such as user and programmer's guides may need to be modified by someone making modifications to the code, and the revised documentation redistributed. Here again the default legal situation prohibits such actions, and the GNU Free Documentation Licence[5] was devised to allow the legal rights needed to make and redistribute modifications in this situation.

It is rare nowadays for anyone to argue that software used to generate scientific results should not be open source, not least because reports from those attempting replication typically state that access to the source code has been important (e.g. Wilensky & Rand 2007). However, researchers can find themselves coming into conflict with their employer's intellectual property protection policies when trying to release source code from software they have developed. Institutional obstacles such as this require a community effort to overcome, and include a culture in which scientific publications using modelling software are not accepted without accompanying source code, and funding bodies (especially those using taxpayers' money) make the public release of modelling software a contractual obligation.

There is more to the release of the source code in opening models than implied by a strict interpretation of the word 'release'. The source code is a document itself, and if made publicly available, should be written such that others can read it. Most programming languages provide syntax for comments in the source code (text in the source code that is ignored by the compiler or interpreter), and such comments are another aspect of documentation. The Java programming language provides tools that if properly used can be used to develop programmer's guides automatically from comments in the code. As modellers, however, there are further potential uses for comments in identifying the provenance of the code: the theories or interview and survey data on which specific sections of it may be based. This can be critical in understanding (and debating) why a model was implemented in a particular way, or a certain algorithm was chosen for some aspect of the model rather than any of the other options available. The social sciences are not (yet[6]) sufficiently settled that one algorithm for representing such things as decision-making or social interaction is clearly superior to all other options in all cases.

More generally, good programming practice is a very important aspect of making a model open. The tongue-in-cheek International Obfuscated C Code Contest[7] is a testament to the fact that it is possible to write computer programs in ways that are difficult to understand. Many of the tricks used by entries to this contest, such as unreadable code layout (typically to make a piece of ASCII art[8]) or using obscure or non-standard language features, can be instructive in learning how to write better, more readable code. The role of laying code out neatly in facilitating its comprehensibility is often underestimated. IDEs[9] such as Eclipse[10] provide tools to specify code layout rules allowing automatic formatting of the source code text, and programming languages such as Python[11] enforce some aspects of good code layout practice syntactically.

More formally, the concept of 'anti-patterns' (Brown et al. 1998), though applied more broadly than programming, can be helpful in outlining practices to *avoid* because they are known through extensive experience in software development to cause problems in debugging, extending and maintaining code. The literature on automatically identifying authors by examining source code (e.g. Krsul & Spafford 1997; Ding & Samadzadeh 2004) suggests that programmers have sufficiently idiomatic styles to make this feasible. Guidance on avoiding pitfalls that make code difficult to understand may therefore be more useful than prescriptive standards forcing people to write programs in a manner that does not support the way they think. Fowler's (2000) edited collection of tips for improving ('refactoring') code, though focused on object-oriented programming languages, makes concrete suggestions for how to avoid anti-patterns.

One of the most important anti-patterns is the 'magic number', which entails the unexplained appearance of a number in source code. In modelling software, this could apply to parameters or input data being hard-coded as literals, e.g. "if(income < 10000) { look_for_another_job(); }". One way of detecting the problem is if you find yourself recompiling your model each time you want to run it with different settings. The danger with this is that you lose the particular configuration of the code that led to a reported result.[12] Most agent-based modelling software tools and libraries help avoid this by providing utilities to specify parameters on the model GUI, or load them in from a file. However, this shifts the problem to remembering which parameter and/or input data files were associated with which output from the model. Although metadata tools can be deployed to assist with this problem, it can also be avoided by recording parameter and input data settings in model output files. NetLogo's "BehaviorSpace" tool, for example, records the parameter settings associated with each measured output.

Hence, best practice with modelling is that the program itself doesn't stand alone, but should be expected to have numbers of supporting files that the program reads to configure its behaviour and that of the model it implements. A mature piece of modelling software that has been used for a number of pieces of work may have several options for implementing submodels in different ways, each of which may have different parameterisation requirements and associated files. Similarly, models making extensive use of empirical data may need several files containing these data, which are used to initialise different objects or agents in the model, and to provide time-series data for exogenous variables (those that influence, but are not influenced by the model's dynamics). Ideally, these files would all be in standard formats that can be read and edited by other software, such as CSV,[13] XML[14] or JSON.[15] Binary formats (as opposed to plain text) are particularly to be avoided, both because they are difficult to read (without specialist supporting software), and because the way different computing architectures store numbers affects their portability unless appropriate precautions are taken when reading and writing the files in a program operating on them.

Providing open access to the model therefore entails providing the supporting files as well as the source code of the software itself. This is a potentially contentious issue, particularly for social simulations, where there may be confidentiality agreements with respondents modelled in the software that preclude providing the supporting files actually used in generating a reported result. Further, and more generally, the model may have used supporting data (e.g. map data) under a licence that prohibits its redistribution. Both these issues can be circumvented by providing examples supporting files that have statistically similar properties to those originally used, and when used with the model, generate similar output.[16] Though it may seem burdensome to do so, it is arguably a useful exercise as part of the sensitivity analysis of the model – something the TRACE protocol gives an entire section of documentation to in the area of 'model testing and analysis' (Schmolke et al. 2010).

For some models, supporting files may include 'scripts'[17] deployed to prepare input data for use by the model, run sensitivity analyses exploring parameter space, and process and analyse output files generated by the model. These scripts (for those able to read the language in which they are written) can themselves act as documentation of use cases of the model, and are particularly useful in recording exactly how a particular result was generated, from source data to the graph or table of results in the journal article. Since they are computer programs, they too will be covered by copyright legislation, and making them available will require their release using an appropriate licence.

To summarise the above, the following steps should be taken to make a model open:

- Ensure the source code is well structured, neatly laid out and commented. Use comments not only to assist with understanding what the code is doing, but also to annotate the code where appropriate with any provenance explaining how the model came to be implemented in a particular way.

- Self-archive journal articles based on the model as soon as the copyright transfer agreement with the journal allows, or publish them in open-access journals.
- Release the software on the web at an address that you reasonably expect to have a degree of permanence, using a suitable software licence. If you do not use a repository or archive, then you should make a reasonable effort to link from your personal page to other webpages that release subsequent versions of your software.
- Apply version management to the software to ensure that access can be provided to the specific software used for a particular publication.
- Accompany the release of the software with any supporting input data or parameter files and scripts used to set up, run or analyse the results of the model.
- Provide supporting documentation on the software, using a suitable licence if that documentation might need to be amended or redistributed by anyone modifying your software.

Further Issues for Complex Models

However, models are becoming increasingly complex. So that even given that all of the above steps are taken, a model may be still difficult to understand and reliably use by anyone else. (Of course the creators of a model might find it difficult to understand and use their own models, but we are not concentrating on that case here.) If such complex models are to be reused, we are faced with the inevitability of have to use models we do not fully understand and cannot fully analyse. That is, the models are to different extents, opaque to us. This 'opaqueness' causes new problems for the sharing of knowledge encapsulated as very complex simulation models. In particular, if a model is developed for one purpose/context but then reapplied in another, how are we to know if we can rely upon its results? There are no final answers to these further difficulties, but some directions of travel are discussed in this section. Each of these goes a little way towards ameliorating the problem without completely solving it.

Post-Implementation Simulation Behaviour

With a complex model, the code and the specification is not enough to give a good understanding of what happens when this is run. Rather we need to give as many "views" of the model as possible, with its explicit, micro-level, description only being one (however theoretically complete). These views could include:

- A characterisation of some typical behaviour, including textual description, graphs, and other values, that give a feel for what sort of simulation one might expect
- Tables of the average values of measurements on the outcomes that encapsulate what has been claimed as the key properties of the simulation. This can be used to check a reimplementation, or show how simulation behaviour has changed when the model is adapted or used on new data
- A sensitivity analysis composed of graphs showing how relevant indicators of outcomes change with the variation of parameters. This may be either shown using an average of these measures with indicators of the spread of these, or the individual trajectories shown for chosen parameter values
- Visualisations of the outcomes that give more of a 'holistic' picture of the behaviour of the simulation under different circumstances.

- Case studies of some of the micro-level behaviour that can result, for example the history of a single agent or group in the simulation.

In this way a more complete idea of the simulation can be formed by the next user of the simulation, and thus be more likely to be understood and thus mistakes concerning its use and interpretation avoided.

Relationship with Other Models

Another way of ensuring the integrity of model use and adaption is by specifying its relationship with other models. This can be done in a variety of ways, relating models of different kinds, granularities and levels of abstraction. We will only discuss a few of the possibilities here, but the general idea is that the more closely related another model is, and the more formally is the relationship specified then the more helpful this is.

Often there might be some formal, or semi-formal, documentation made in the process of the development of the model – something akin to a specification, plan or ontology for the model. The simulation model should be an instantiation of this – some code that is consistent with that, more abstract, model. There may be more than one kind of specification, for example, the spatial structure, algorithms for sub-processes and a systems-view of the simulation showing the main feedback loops. Exhibiting such specifications along with the eventual model is helpful for imparting the intentions behind the development and provides extra consistency checks.

Sometimes a simulation uses another simulation as a sub-model, but where the processes of the sub-model are embedded in a wider set of interactions. In this case, the target model is some kind of composite, using other models as sub-modules as well as some extra code. Here, even if the documentation of these sub-models is clear and the code open, how it interfaces to the whole model can be crucial to the behaviour of the whole. The messages/data passed back and forth between sub-models, and in what form needs to be carefully documented. In particular any assumptions made about the interpretation or use of the sub-model in the composite needs documenting. Ideally the behaviour of the composite model should be compared when the sub-model is replaced by some kind of null model (e.g. one giving random or constant outputs).

Another kind of relation is when there is a post-hoc abstraction of the original model. For example, this might be a future version of the model where some of the less important mechanisms have been eliminated or an approximation of it using mathematical equations. This model of the model, may allow for a more rigorous understanding of the key dynamics and may be an analytic solution. The behaviour of the more abstract model can be checked against the behaviour of the original, maybe revealing some of the conditions under which it is a good approximation. These kinds of model can include: individual-based models, system dynamic models of the aggregate behaviour, analytic models (such as systems of differential equations), or network models. Access to these model abstractions might allow for a deeper understanding of the original and yet another check on any future variations or applications.

A very simple kind of representation of a model is the sets of data it may produce when run with different random seeds and different parameter settings. Archiving sets of the output data for different parameter sweeps along with the model is very helpful for others to analyse (maybe using hypotheses about model behaviour the developer has not guessed) and check against new runs of the model.

Finally there can be different kinds of model that purport to model the same phenomena in different ways. For example one might be an agent-based model and one an analytic one, or they may just focus on different aspects of the same phenomena: one looking at the geographic distribution and one the social interactions. Whilst it may be helpful to list models with the same target, they are not easy to directly relate unless they relate to the same set of data (e.g. validation data). Here it may be that the different models capture different aspects of the data, or for different parameter ranges (such as one for low numbers, and one for high).

Capturing Model Development

Lastly, with very complex artefacts it is often impossible to completely divorce the context and trajectory of its development with its properties, due to the impossibility of completely understanding complex models (Edmonds 2012). In these cases it can be very helpful to also make available some documentation as to this origins and history.

A simple electronic diary, documenting the versions of the simulation that were made, the results obtained, and the reasons for developmental choices can be helpful to subsequent users of the model in order to further understand the model and its assumptions. In particular it can be as useful to know what did *not* work in the past, as to what did. This might not be normally read, but might be referred back to by subsequent users when considering future variations. Such a diary would not only document the development of the, more formal and careful phase where a model and its results are being prepared for public consumption, but also the more informal and private exploratory phase that often precedes this (Norling, Edmonds & Meyer 2013).

Another useful document is one that keeps track of the evidential provenance of different parts or design decisions in the model. That is what kind of evidence (if any) supports which design decisions and how. Thus a certain probabilistic process might be specified according to well-known statistics (say birth and death rates in a population). There may be some broad evidence for the characteristics of a process from the research literature (say evidence from psychological experiments for a mental process). The specification of some processes might be based upon observational or first person narrative data. Some processes or parts of a model may come from previous models or authorities. Other values or processes might be discovered through trial and error to fit validation data in the process of model tuning. Finally and inevitably, some parts of a simulation will be as the result of common sense or plausible guesses by the modeller, in which case it is equally important to flag this fact (so that future modellers can inspect, critique and improve upon these). Over all this kind of documentation gives information as to the reliability of assumptions made in the modelling, and, equally importantly, some indication of their conditions of application. This can help to guide the re-use of models to a new situation.

FUTURE RESEARCH: TOOLS TO AID OPEN MODELLING

A common complaint about agent-based modelling (especially among social scientists with no background in computer programming) is that the huge learning curve associated with engaging with it, no matter how interesting it may seem, poses a considerable obstacle to its wider adoption (Janssen et al. 2008; Alessa et al. 2006). The requirements for open modelling, particularly if enforced by a strong cultural norm, can only add to such a perception. Insofar as they impose constraints on modelling practice, however, such norms can assist in narrowing what needs to be learned. On the other hand, where they require the provision of materials not currently stipulated by journal editors and other gatekeepers of the tokens of academic esteem, they create the impression of extra work to be done that isn't strictly necessary and can hence be ignored. It is natural therefore to consider software facilitation of open modelling practices as a means of encouraging its wider adoption.

Development of further software tools is a double-edged sword. A degree of confidence is needed by the user to allow the investment associated with learning a tool, much of which is associated with whether there is a significant community also using it, and a development community providing training, maintenance, enhancements and bug fixes. The former is a classic problem of innovation adoption. For tools developed with research funding, the latter aspect of software sustainability is missing from funding infrastructure, and cannot be ignored as an institutional obstacle to open modelling.

With this in mind, there are a number of technologies in various stages of development that could facilitate open modelling practices if appropriately integrated with existing modelling tools, and offer potential directions for enhancing functionality they provide.

- Version control software has been a bedrock of professional programming for decades, and there are popular web-based version control tools that can be deployed to assist with version management. Many are particularly useful for collaborative model development. Embedding version control facilities in agent-based modelling toolkits would allow a version to be 'locked off' for later retrieval as the program responsible for creating results, whilst permitting continuing development of the software. Such embedding would enable the version associated with output files to be automatically included in their metadata.

- Virtualisation is the provision of a simulation of a computer system in a host computer running appropriate software. Embedding model development within a virtual machine enables its deployment on any host running virtualisation software, and also facilitates replication for large-scale parameter exploration on suitably-configured cloud infrastructure. This latter point is likely to be increasingly significant in conducting proper sensitivity analyses of agent-based models, yet is also associated with institutional and knowledge barriers to more widespread adoption.

- Provenance capture could replace much of the documentation required for open modelling with a dataset that can be queried and reasoned with. Pignotti et al. (2013) identify three kinds of provenance relevant for social simulation: (i) provenance about the process of model construction; (ii) provenance about running the model; (iii) provenance about how the model itself reached a particular result from its input data. Significant changes to the way agent-based models are built and used would be needed to capture all three kinds of provenance.

- Using ontologies to represent the state and structure of the model at any one time allows more transparent representation of the model, as has been argued by Polhill and Gotts (2009), and ontologies have also been argued to have an important role in the model development process (Dray et al. 2006; Livet et al. 2010; Gotts & Polhill 2009). Ontologies can also be used to describe constraints on simulations that capture the intent of the modeller (Pignotti et al. 2011).

- Recording metadata on models, including their inputs and outputs, and describing what the models do could, with appropriate metadata standards, replace some of the need for documentation as well as facilitating model reuse. There is a significant body of work on this in the integrated modelling literature (e.g. Rizzoli et al. 2008), and several existing proposals for metadata standards for documenting models (e.g. Richiardi et al. 2006; Treibig & Klugl 2009).

- Extra checks on a simulation model – either in terms of limits upon its specification, or error checking on the outcomes – are useful in checking simulation integrity and reliable use. For example, it might be known that the energy of animals is always above zero, or that each bank account has an associated agent who owns it. This kind of knowledge is often in a declarative form, that is they can be expressed as general relationships or statements, which should always hold. Declarative and constraint programming allow for such statements to be encoded as part of the specification of the computer program[18]. Such statements can be seen as an extension of the idea of strong typing, which is known to reduce errors in code and whose use can aid the development of reliable code (Pierce 2002). This style of programming (maybe in combination with imperative styles for specifying processes) could aid in the specification and checking of simulation models – maybe as a kind of wrapper that continually checks the simulation against defined statements that should always be true.

- Literate programming (Knuth 1992) is a form of computer programming in which natural language text and formal programming code are interspersed. The source code and documentation would be a single document that is both a program that can be run and readable by humans. We know of no efforts to embed literate programming principles in agent-based modelling tools and libraries, though this could be a significant contribution to the open modelling agenda.

CONCLUSION

The Need for a Change in Modelling Culture

Despite the above considerations, good practice in making models available and new tools to make these processes more effective are probably less important than the underlying culture and attitudes that lie behind the decision as to whether to make models openly accessible. Constructing a model is a labour-intensive process, but also a creative one. In addition to this one typically spends an extended period of time thinking about, interacting with, analysing and writing about one's models. Thus there is a considerable amount of personal investment in a model one creates, and the quality of that simulation can affect ones status as a modeller. In other words, one feels one owns the models one makes and that they are part of ones "extended phenotype" in the social sphere.

This feeling of individual ownership of models might make one reluctant to release it into the public sphere where it might be misused or judged harshly. Rather one might (in effect) find it more comfortable to retain control over the IP encapsulated in the model, and only make selected details openly available. This might not be a conscious decision, but rather simply reflected in a lack of motivation to release models. In this case, one might always intend to make the model open but put off by even small difficulties and barriers, and then experience a lack of negative consequences as a result (people not finding bugs or weaknesses in the model, and no lack of citation or publication due to a failure to archive).

Of course, in some cases there are some very obvious reasons why models might not be made open, contradicting the three purposes for open modelling discussed at the beginning of this chapter. A government using a model as part of the policy making or evaluation process might wish to insulate themselves against methodological criticism. A company using a model might wish to keep this secret in order to maintain competitive advantage. A modeller might not want others to gain the value from a model that they have put such effort into. It is likely that in such cases the real reason will not be given to justify this choice, but rather other rationales, such as privacy concerns, the effort required, or that they are awaiting for the model to "mature".

However, the weakness of these rationales is readily apparent if one substitutes "knowledge" whenever the term "model" arises. Would it be acceptable for a government to hide knowledge due to the effort involved in releasing it or because general access to this knowledge would make it more criticisable? Would it be acceptable for a researcher to hoard "knowledge" indefinitely in order to perfect it or to avoid critique of this knowledge? The answers are then obviously "no". We accept that (in general) making knowledge openly available is such an overwhelming public good that it overrides any selfish reasons for keeping it secret. Models are an encapsulation of knowledge – a representation of how its processes interact and their eventual outcomes – so there is no fundamental reason why models should be treated differently from other kinds of knowledge.

In contrast to models, we do not view knowledge as something we can own. Rather we see the development of knowledge as a, largely, collective knowledge. We acknowledge and celebrate those that make significant discoveries, but the knowledge itself is a public good. We now need the culture of modelling to shift more towards this collective view, where models are significantly developed by individuals but not owned by them. This shift would facilitate the collective development, critique, improvement and use of these models. This openness is exactly what has occurred in other areas of open source software, and has resulted in high quality and reliable code, produced and corrected collectively[19].

How This Change Might Be Encouraged

Although it may be that underlying changes in the background culture, shown in the expectations of the internet generation, there are some steps that would help encourage and maintain such a cooperative culture.

- *Firstly*, researchers can simply state their expectations of their peers that models will be made open, putting soft social pressure on each other[20].
- *Secondly*, journals could stipulate that any models central to academic papers are made publically available as a condition of publication.
- *Thirdly*, a condition of public funding could include that any models are publically archived.

These are directly analogous to the requirement that core data behind scientific publications are made publically available by the journals themselves or as a condition of receiving public money for the research. However as with open data, the proof is in the practice, since even with journals where data is supposed to be freely available there are often considerable problems and barriers to obtaining it.

- *Fourthly*, on the positive side, we can help ensure that researchers get due credit for making their models open.

Models in public archives being citable and the habit of citing models as well as papers becoming established can facilitate this. This requires that there be an established method for citing models[21]. Taken individually, these may not have much impact upon the prevailing culture but, taken together, may help speed its development.

A Vision of an Open Modelling Future

In many ways a future where openness is the norm and artefacts for the public good are collectively developed already exist in terms of the open source communities that produce much of the software that runs the web; the entries of Wikipedia (Goldspink, Edmonds & Gilbert 2008); and many areas of science itself[22]. It is a future where the benefits to society far outweigh those that might otherwise have been harvested by individual entities. It is a future which allows a far greater external scrutiny of the complex constructions we know as simulation models, resulting in better and more reliable models. It is a future in which the fruits of research are freely available outside the high-tech countries that tend to produce such artefacts. It is a future to be desired.

REFERENCES

Alessa, L. N., Laituri, M., & Barton, M. (2006). An "all hands" call to the social science community: Establishing a community framework for complexity modeling using agent based models and cyberinfrastructure. *Journal of Artificial Societies and Social Simulation, 9*(4), 6. Retrieved from http://jasss.soc.surrey.ac.uk/9/4/6.html

Apt, K. R. (1991). Logic programming. In *Handbook of theoretical computer science* (Vol. B, pp. 493–574). Cambridge, MA: MIT Press.

Auer, S., Bizer, C., Kobilarov, G., Lehmann, J., Cyganiak, R., & Ives, Z. (2007). Dbpedia: A nucleus for a web of open data. In The semantic web (pp. 722-735). Springer Berlin Heidelberg.

Axtell, R., Axelrod, R., Epstein, J. M., & Cohen, M. D. (1996). Aligning simulation models: A case study and results. *Computational & Mathematical Organization Theory, 1*(2), 123–141. doi:10.1007/BF01299065

Brown, W. J., Malveau, R. C., McCormick, H. W., & Mowbray, T. J. (1998). *Anti patterns: refactoring software, architectures, and projects in crisis.* New York, NY: John Wiley & Sons.

Ding, H., & Samadzadeh, M. H. (2004). Extraction of Java program fingerprints for software authorship identification. *Journal of Systems and Software, 72*(1), 49–57. doi:10.1016/S0164-1212(03)00049-9

Dray, A., Perez, P., Jones, N., Le Page, C., D'Aquino, P., White, I., & Auatabu, T. (2006). The AtollGame experience: from knowledge engineering to a computer-assisted role playing game. *Journal of Artificial Societies and Social Simulation, 9*(1), 6. Retrieved from http://jasss.soc.surrey.ac.uk/9/1/6.html

Edmonds, B. (2000). *The purpose and place of formal systems in the development of science, CPM Report 00-75, MMU, UK.* Retrieved from http://cfpm.org/cpmrep75.html

Edmonds, B. (2012). Context in social simulation: Why it can't be wished away. *Computational & Mathematical Organization Theory, 18*(1), 5–21. doi:10.1007/s10588-011-9100-z

Edmonds, B., & Hales, D. (2003). Replication, replication and replication - some hard lessons from model alignment. *Journal of Artificial Societies and Social Simulation, 6*(4), 11. Retrieved from http://jasss.soc.surrey.ac.uk/6/4/11.html

Edmonds, B., & Hales, D. (2005). Computational simulation as theoretical experiment. *The Journal of Mathematical Sociology, 29*(3), 209–232. doi:10.1080/00222500590921283

Fowler, M. (2000). *Refactoring: improving the design of existing code*. Upper Saddle River, NJ: Addison-Wesley.

Frühwirth, T., & Abdennadher, S. (2003). *Essentials of constraint programming*. Springer.

Goldspink, C., Edmonds, B., & Gilbert, N. (2008). *Normative behaviour in Wikipedia*. Paper presented at the 4th International Conference on e-Social Science, Manchester, UK. Retrieved from http://cfpm.org/cpmrep190.html

Gotts, N. M., & Polhill, J. G. (2009). *Narrative scenarios, mediating formalisms, and the agent-based simulation of land use change. In Epistemological Aspects of Computer Simulation in the Social Sciences* (pp. 99–116). Berlin: Springer-Verlag.

Grimm, V., Berger, U., Bastiansen, F., Eliassen, S., Ginot, V., Giske, J., & DeAngelis, D. L. et al. (2006). A standard protocol for describing individual-based and agent-based models. *Ecological Modelling, 198*(1–2), 115–126. doi:10.1016/j.ecolmodel.2006.04.023

Grimm, V., Berger, U., DeAngelis, D. L., Polhill, J. G., Giske, J., & Railsback, S. F. (2010). The ODD protocol: A review and first update. *Ecological Modelling, 221*(23), 2760–2768. doi:10.1016/j.ecolmodel.2010.08.019

Grimm, V., & Schmolke, A. (2011). *How to read and write TRACE documents*. Helmholtz Centre for Environmental Research – UFZ, Department of Ecological Modelling, Permoserstr. 15, 04318 Leipzig, Germany. Retrieved from http://cream-itn.eu/creamwp/wp-content/uploads/Trace-Guidance-11-03-04.pdf

Jakeman, A. J., Letcher, R. A., & Norton, J. P. (2006). Ten iterative steps in development and evaluation of environmental models. *Environmental Modelling & Software, 21*(5), 602–614. doi:10.1016/j.envsoft.2006.01.004

Janssen, M. A., Alessa, L. N., Barton, M., Bergin, S., & Lee, A. (2008). Towards a community framework for agent-based modelling. *Journal of Artificial Societies and Social Simulation, 11*(2), 6. Retrieved from http://jasss.soc.surrey.ac.uk/11/2/6.html

Knuth, D. E. (1992). *Literate Programming*. Center for the Study of Language and Information Publications, Stanford University.

Krsul, I., & Spafford, E. H. (1997). Authorship analysis: Identifying the author of a program. *Computers & Security, 16*(3), 233–257. doi:10.1016/S0167-4048(97)00005-9

Livet, P., Müller, J.-P., Phan, D., & Sanders, L. (2010). Ontology, a mediator for agent-based modeling in social science. *Journal of Artificial Societies and Social Simulation, 13*(1), 3. Retrieved from http://jasss.soc.surrey.ac.uk/13/1/3.html

Norling, E., Edmonds, B., & Meyer, R. (2013). Informal approaches to developing simulation models. In B. Edmonds & R. Meyer (Eds.), *Simulating Social Complexity - A Handbook* (pp. 39–55). Springer. doi:10.1007/978-3-540-93813-2_4

Pierce, B. C. (2002). *Types and programming languages*. Cambridge, MA: MIT Press.

Pignotti, E., Edwards, P., Gotts, N., & Polhill, G. (2010). Enhancing workflow with a semantic description of scientific intent. *Journal of Web Semantics, 9*(2), 222–244. doi:10.1016/j.websem.2011.05.001

Pignotti, E., Polhill, G., & Edwards, P. (2013). Using provenance to analyse agent-based simulations. In *EDBT '13 Proceedings of the Joint EDBT/ICDT 2013 Workshops* (pp. 319-322). New York, NY: ACM. Retrieved from http://www.edbt.org/Proceedings/2013-Genova/papers/workshops/a46-pignotti.pdf

Polhill, J. G., & Edmonds, B. (2007). Open access for social simulation. *Journal of Artificial Societies and Social Simulation, 10*(3), 10. Retrieved from http://jasss.soc.surrey.ac.uk/10/3/10.html

Polhill, J. G., & Gotts, N. M. (2009). Ontologies for transparent integrated human-natural system modelling. *Landscape Ecology, 24*(9), 1255–1267. doi:10.1007/s10980-009-9381-5

Popper, K. (1963). *Conjectures and refutations*. London: Routledge.

Popper, K. (1967). *The open society and its enemies*. London: Hutchinson.

Richiardi, M., Leombruni, R., Saam, N., & Sonnessa, M. (2006). A common protocol for agent-based social simulation. *Journal of Artificial Societies and Social Simulation, 9*(1), 15. Retrieved from http://jasss.soc.surrey.ac.uk/9/1/15.html

Rizzoli, A. E., Donatelli, M., Athanasiadis, I. N., Villa, F., & Huber, D. (2008). Semantic links in integrated modelling frameworks. *Mathematics and Computers in Simulation, 78*(2-3), 412–423. doi:10.1016/j.matcom.2008.01.017

Schmolke, A., Thorbek, P., DeAngelis, D. L., & Grimm, V. (2010). Ecological models supporting environmental decision-making: A strategy for the future. *Trends in Ecology & Evolution, 25*(8), 479–486. doi:10.1016/j.tree.2010.05.001 PMID:20605251

Treibig, C., & Klugl, F. (2009). Elements of a documentation framework for agent-based simulation models. *Cybernetics and Systems, 40*(5), 441–474. doi:10.1080/01969720902922459

Wilenski, U. (1999). *NetLogo*. Center for Connected Learning and Computer-Based Modeling, Northwestern University, Evanston, IL. Retrieved from http://ccl.northwestern.edu/netlogo/

Wilenski, U. (2007). Making models match: Replicating an agent-based model. *Journal of Artificial Societies and Social Simulation, 10*(4), 2. Retrieved from http://jasss.soc.surrey.ac.uk/10/4/2.html

ADDITIONAL READING

Polhill, J. Gary (2010). *ODD updated. Journal of Artificial Societies and Social Simulation, 13*(4), 9 Retrieved from http://jasss.soc.surrey.ac.uk/13/4/9.html

Polhill, J. G., & Edmonds, B. (2007). Open access for social simulation. *Journal of Artificial Societies and Social Simulation, 10*(3), 10. Retrieved from http://jasss.soc.surrey.ac.uk/10/3/10.html

Suber, P. (2012). Open access. Cambridge, MA: MIT Press; Retrieved from http://mitpress.mit.edu/books/open-access

The Open Knowledge Foundation. (2010-2012) *The open data handbook.* Retrieved from http://opendatahandbook.org

KEY TERMS AND DEFINITIONS

Agent-Based Model: (also Agent-Based Simulation) is a simulation where the entities being represented are represented as separate objects in the simulation, and these objects are usefully interpreted as having some kind of cognitive processes.

Anti-Pattern: A pattern of code that should be avoided due to the problems it is known to cause.

Model: A representation of something else (the target) that can be used to make inferences about that target. In the context of this chapter we mean a simulation model.

Open Modelling: The practice of making ones simulation model effectively open to inspection, critique, reuse and adaption by others.

Provenance: The source of some data or bit of code. In the case of code, what motivated or justified each design decision in the program's construction.

Simulation Model: A computer program intended as a model of something.

Software License: The legal conditions imposed on an object of Intellectual Property (such as a simulation) upon a subsequent user of that object.

ENDNOTES

1. Arguably, this is how science itself works.
2. However in this case there must be a doubt concerning the extent to which such a product could be trusted without scientific scrutiny, and a lack of openness should limit its role in democratic debates, following the above arguments.
3. Overview, Design concepts and Details
4. Graphical User Interface
5. http://www.gnu.org/copyleft/fdl.html
6. ... or rather, arguably never will be ...
7. http://www.ioccc.org/
8. ASCII art is an art form in which alphanumeric and other characters in the American Standard Code for Information Interchange character set are used to make a picture. Possibly the most extreme example is its use to make an animation of a well-known science fiction film stereotypically popular among people who write computer programs: http://www.asciimation.co.nz/
9. Integrated Development Environment
10. http://www.eclipse.org/
11. http://www.python.org/

[12]   The anti-pattern of using comments to enable/disable pieces of code can also lead to this problem. If you find yourself wanting to do this, consider using a parameter to select which option you want to use.

[13]   Comma Separated Values – can be imported to and exported from most spreadsheet and database software.

[14]   eXstensible Markup Language – a rather verbose machine-readable format with a tree-like document structure and metadata 'tags' providing some description of what the data in the file are.

[15]   JavaScript Object Notation – a more efficient format for metadata-tagged tree-like documents often used instead of XML.

[16]   Axtell et al. (1996) identify levels of similarity that could apply, from exact numerical replication (an unrealistic goal for all but the simplest models) to qualitative similarity.

[17]   A script is a relatively short computer program written in an interpreted language such as Shell, Perl or (for statistical analysis) R that is typically used to automate a series of operations performed by the user.

[18]   For an introduction to these areas see (Apt 1991) and (Frühwirth & Abdennadher 2003).

[19]   However, open source communities are not anarchies and have evolved a considerable degree of social structure, including norms, reputation, group membership and varying levels of edit and versioning rights.

[20]   Of course, this is the primary purpose of this chapter.

[21]   Such as the one available via sites such as http://openabm.org

[22]   At least the ones with low immediate commercial interest

Chapter 11
The State of Technology in Venezuela in the Context of Production Chains

Leandro Rabindranath León
Universidad de Los Andes, Colombia

ABSTRACT

This chapter develops a discursive context called "the sawmill metaphor" that interprets the technology as a system of timber production that runs through a river. Trees are cut upstream and transported by the river towards a sawmill in the midstream. The sawmill then transforms trees into logs that are sent down river towards other factories that produce finished products downstream. Using this metaphor a link between technology and production is identified as well as the vital importance that the interlinking networks has on production. This context allows us to propose a diagnosis of the state of technology on Venezuela in 2014, a country which regardless of plans of technological acquisition sets forth since 2003 with sizable investments, far from increase technological sovereignty has lost it. Finally, taking as a basis the Venezuelan case, we present a set of general guidelines to consider in a plan of technological acquisition.

INTRODUCTION

Over the past twelve years, one of the main political aims of the Venezuelan government has been to establish independent production systems through the development of technology in Venezuela. To this end, several different strategies have been implemented, such as: the establishment of monetary policies aimed at preventing capital flight from Venezuela, the inauguration of numerous new universities, the implementation of incentives for local production (subsidies, tax incentives, etc.), attempts to improve the transport system, the promotion of foreign capital investment, especially from China, and the generation of open knowledge.

Nevertheless, twelve years on, the situation regarding Venezuelan based technology is now more precarious than when the plans for technological development were initiated. While domestic demand for staple goods has risen considerably, particularly in the food sector, imports of these essential items have also dramatically increased.

DOI: 10.4018/978-1-4666-8336-5.ch011

As we discuss below, a technological system requires interlinking networks; for example, transport systems, telecommunication networks, or those related to the generation and transmission of electricity. While these networks are accessible to almost all Venezuelans, both as regards their availability and their cost, their use has been oriented towards individual consumption in detriment of industrial use. To date, the national transport system is on the edge of collapse due to excessive traffic, lack of maintenance, and especially a failure to expand. Similarly, there is currently a deficit of approximately 20% in the generation and transmission of electricity caused by a very strong domestic demand, which has resulted in repeated rationing and power cuts. The same could be said of the telecommunications sector, which suffers from interruptions in both the telephone and internet services.

Perhaps the most eye-catching aspect of this situation is that the Venezuelan government has shown a very clear desire to develop Venezuelan based technology, as demonstrated by the implementation of policies to promote its acquisition that have been successful elsewhere, particularly in South Korea and India (Adelman & Yeldan, 2000). Despite this, however, Venezuela, far from having progressed towards developing its own technology, has actually increased its dependence on foreign technologies.

The question therefore, whilst wishing to avoid political proselytism, is: Why, in spite of the political will and the implementation of policies that have been successful in other countries, has Venezuela not only failed in its objective to gain technological independence, but has also moved even further backwards? What mistakes have been made? What is it that the Venezuelan leadership responsible for technology has not perceived? Why have they not perceived it?

We suggest that the lack of success that Venezuela has had in developing its own technology is largely due to the fact that the authorities responsible have made many misguided interpretations of what technology actually is. This has led to a "fragmented vision"[1] of the technological situation in this country. Potentially effective formulas and protocols have not been successful because no-one is clear what they are for. This lack of clarity about how to define technology has meant that is has been very difficult to identify clear objectives and reach agreement on the best way to acquire it.

In this chapter we attempt to identify the possible misinterpretations that have led to the failure of Venezuela to acquire a technological base. This is intended to serve as a framework for further discussion.

Before proceeding we would like to clarify that this essay is of a subjective rather than an objective nature based on the modest experiences and personal impressions of the author in his role as a director in centers for the research and development of Venezuelan technology, as well as his participation in discussions about Venezuela's strategies for the acquisition of technology.

This essay is divided into three parts: In the first part **"What is technology?"** we discuss the general framework of the article and use this to give a clear definition of technology in order to avoid confusion surrounding this term and its use. With a clear definition in hand, in the second part **"Technology in Venezuela"** we outline, in very broad terms, the technological situation in Venezuela. Finally, in third and last part **"General recommendations for the acquisition of technology"**, we provide some general guidelines and political priorities for a plan for the acquisition of technology in Venezuela.

WHAT IS TECHNOLOGY?

Possibly the main obstacle to an appropriate and sensible policy for technological development is the diversity of mistaken interpretations as to what technology actually is. For the most part, the misconceptions consist in confusing an essential component of technology with technology itself.

Thus, before we attempt a definition of technology, we must first identify these misunderstandings and clarify from them what technology is and what it is not.

TECHNOLOGY AS KNOWLEDGE

One of the characteristics of technology as an ubiquitous historical phenomenon is that it is built from a vast store of knowledge, especially but not limited to, scientific knowledge. In other words, technology is the result of what we know today as modern science.

Can we then define technology as the sum of the knowledge we need in order to produce a good or a service? To develop this approach we will briefly mention three examples of "technology" as knowledge: automotive "technology", mobile phone "technology" and satellite "technology".

Taking the example of automotive "technology", it is probable that because cars and other vehicles are now so much part of our daily lives, we are unaware of the vast amount of scientific knowledge from many different fields of study that is required for their manufacture: mechanics, metallurgy, electricity, thermodynamics, organic chemistry, to mention just a few. It is relevant at this point to mention that "technology" as knowledge does not consist of one area of knowledge only. In fact, as we have just seen for the automotive industry, it is an amalgamation of many areas of knowledge that historically were unrelated to each other.

The different areas of knowledge involved in the manufacture of the motor vehicle have been developed over thousands of years, firstly with the emergence of the wheel and simple mechanics, passing through the era of Newtonian physics 500 years ago, and lastly about 120 years ago, with the appearance of the steel industry and the exploitation of hydrocarbons.

As regards our second example: mobile phone "technology", we can see that not only several areas of knowledge are involved, but also that some of these areas are more recent than those involved with automotive technology. This is particularly true for those areas associated with electromagnetic theory, whose formal origins, although dating back some 400 years, were not theoretically unified until 1865 by the famous James Clerk Maxwell.

Finally, our last example "satellite technology", which as well as sharing some of the "technologies" with the mobile phone and automotive industries, requires other, more recently developed "technologies", such as rocket science and the well-known theories of relativity and quantum physics developed in the early 20th century.

With these examples in mind, let us return to the question: is technology the sum total of the body of knowledge required in order to produce a good or service? In other words, when someone says they "have the technology", do they mean that they dominate the knowledge inherent to that technology? For example, does saying that we have "automotive technology" mean that we have mastered the mechanical, metallurgical, electrical, etc. knowledge required to produce automobiles?

Knowledge, interpreted as the unbiased judgment and reasoning behind any human endeavor, and necessary for mastering the vast majority of "technologies" is mostly freely available in books and libraries and taught in traditional educational institutions, such as universities and technological institutes. Regarding specifically our three example "technologies", all the knowledge required for their implementation, including that inherent to the most complex of them: satellite technology, are available to anyone who has sufficient training to understand them.

In Venezuela, however, despite the availability of the relevant knowledge and the fact that it is taught in Venezuelan universities, very few products linked to the technologies described are manufactured in this country.

This fact leads us to doubt the belief that mastering a particular technology consists merely in obtaining the relevant knowledge. If this was so, then it could be said that Venezuela has all the technology it needs, because it possesses the educational institutions to teach the knowledge required.

Another necessary condition for mastering a technology is that knowledge should be freely available; this is also true of Venezuela.

Are there then, individuals in Venezuela within the educational system who have mastered the knowledge required to generate new knowledge whilst preserving the old, and who can pass this down through the generations? If knowledge is vital for the development of technology, it is evident that these individuals and institutions are also vital. In Venezuela, however, educational institutions do exist where the knowledge required for "technology" is understood and taught. This requirement then, although essential, is not enough in itself for the development of technology.

Finally, technology has been interpreted as "research", defined here as the work that is undertaken, traditionally but not exclusively by the universities, for the creation of new knowledge. It is here, if we take into account the low amount of research undertaken in Venezuela compared with other countries, that we might make the mistake of thinking that in research lies the key to obtaining technology. We can see, however, if we look at our three examples that this is a mistaken conclusion: the relevant knowledge has already been acquired, is fully available and there are institutions in Venezuela that teach it.

In short, while the transfer of knowledge, research, and the existence of institutions associated with its generation and teaching, are necessary for the development of technology, they do not define it completely.

Technology is not (only) based on knowledge.

TECHNOLOGY AS INFRASTRUCTURE

The next source of confusion may best be unraveled by posing the question: does infrastructure (buildings, machines, devices, etc.) define "technology? Considering the complexity of what is produced in our examples: automobiles, mobile phones and satellites, we can see that manufacturing infrastructure is a strong component of technology.

In order to make an automobile we need assembly lines, which in turn require factories that produce steel, glass, plastic, engines, gear boxes, suspension systems and many other parts. The manufacture of these components in their turn depends on the manufacture of other components and so on until you reach the extraction of the raw materials.

There is another side to infrastructure associated with "technology" that tends to go unnoticed and which consists of other necessary "technologies". For example, in order to be able to drive cars we need a road network along which they can travel. The road network is also based on infrastructure and thus "technology". In addition, automotive technology is essential to other technologies, for example, the transport of parts and raw materials between factories is often done using some kind of road-bound vehicle; several agricultural "technologies" require the use of vehicles, for example tractors and combine harvesters.

To all the above considerations we must add the fact that for many, the automobile is part of our individual daily lives.

As regards telecommunications, we can also appreciate its relevance to other technologies, for example, television, and public and private computer systems. The telephone industry also requires infrastructure for its operation: switchboards, repeater stations, antennae, help centers, etc. In turn, the telephone depends on other technologies: computer systems, electronics, semiconductors, etc.

The dependence of satellites on other technologies and their infrastructure is more obvious: computing, optics, telecommunications, aerospace, rocket science, relativity, etc. Similarly, telecommunications and other technologies rely on satellite technology. Satellite technology is the latest and most sophisticated of our examples, but it is also the one that requires the most infrastructure with respect to the scale of the final product.

Let us now return to the initial question and ask ourselves whether Venezuela has the infrastructure described above.

As regards "having" in the sense of ownership, Venezuela "has" automotive technology. We (Venezuelans) have an extensive road network and several systems that depend on automobiles that we use to an excessive degree. We also manufacture some of our own components and assemble some cars from start to finish. The components that we don't make are imported. So since we, albeit only partially, manufacture automobiles within the national territory, we can say that we possess an automotive infrastructure, both as regards the infrastructure to support other technologies and the infrastructure for vehicle manufacture itself.

The same can be said for the mobile phone industry. We are one of the countries with the highest number of users per capita in Latin America, suggesting that we also possess cross-support technology in this area. We also have factories that make telephones, especially mobile phones.

Looking now at satellite technology in Venezuela, we find that we do have some shortcomings as regards ownership. We have two satellites in operation, but do not yet produce them, although we are in the process of learning how to. In addition, we depend on others to launch the satellites into space. In consequence, under this definition of ownership, although we cannot say we have satellite technology yet, we can say we are on the way to having it.

There is a crucial observation in this definition of the ownership of technology associated with infrastructure: we also have the economic capacity to acquire the infrastructure.

This being so, we could say that we (as Venezuelans) do have technological infrastructure, and even when we do not, we have the capacity to acquire it. Now, does this really mean that Venezuela has the technologies needed to produce automobiles, mobile phones and satellites? This is easier to answer if we consider what would happen if the foreign companies who manufacture the infrastructure denied it to us. Would we be able to build and maintain our own infrastructure? Probably not.

It is thus evident that infrastructure is not enough *per se* to completely define technology, although, as for knowledge, it is certainly a necessary condition for it.

A variation on the theme of technology as infrastructure is the knowledge of how to use it. Since there it is obvious that infrastructure has no value if it is not used, it is clear that knowing how to use it is fundamental to the development of technology, but this still does not complete the full picture. Going back to our three examples: we have factories operated by Venezuelan staff and can thus say that we do know how to use this infrastructure.

We thus have infrastructure and know how to operate it, but when we observe our reliance on foreign goods, we must conclude that even this is not enough to assert that we "have technology".

Infrastructure and knowing how to use it are essential for technology, but neither its presence nor its operation defines it.

THE SAWMILL (PRODUCTION CHAIN) METAPHOR

In order to continue to sift through the discussion of the nature of technology proposed here, we will introduce the so-called sawmill metaphor, as illustrated in Figure 1. This shows a "simple" technological system for the production of goods based on logging.

In this system, production is divided into three zones. The first zone, on the far left hand side of Figure 1, represents the forest from which the timber is cut. Note that several fields of knowledge are necessary to maintain this forest; for example, the knowledge of how to plant the trees, care for them and then log them at the appropriate time.

The entire area is crossed by a river that serves as a means of transport. The forest lies in the upper reaches of the river or "upstream".

The felled trees are thrown into the river and transported by it to the sawmills located "midstream". The mills partially process the logs, for example by removing the bark and leaves, leaving them as what are known as intermediate goods.

Finally, these intermediate goods are sent down river to the factories that produce the finished products (located to the right of the figure: "downstream").

Figure 1. The sawmill metaphor

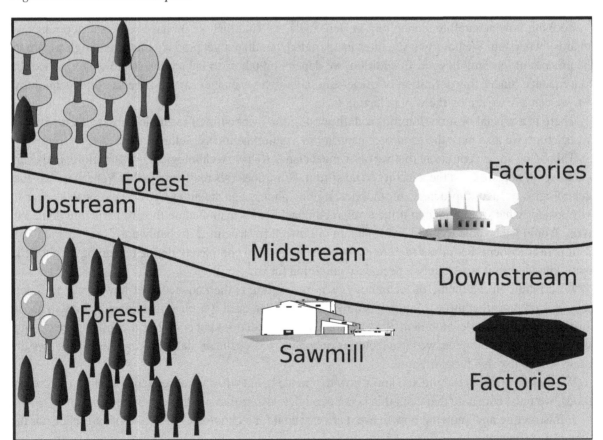

This metaphor allows us to introduce several ideas of interest surrounding a technological system; which we will explore in the following sections.

The All-Embracing Nature of the Network (The River)

The transport of goods within this simple technological system is essential for its proper functioning. Under the terms of the metaphor, the transport medium is provided, at least in part, by the river. The goods produced within the different zones crossed by the river must be transported at the appropriate rate along it.

Any change to the river upstream or midstream could thus affect the rate of production and compromise the system.

In order that the technological world based on this metaphor can operate properly and efficiently over long distances and between agents that are unknown to each other, we need the river. Without it, the agents with their own different interests, knowledge and production infrastructures would find it much more difficult, perhaps impossible, to communicate with each other. The river connects different interests around activities that are especially noticeable downstream, as this is where the final products appear and consequently, the customers.

At this point, it is important to emphasize that without the river as a means of communication it is impossible to maintain the system. The river then, represents a kind of **"linkage network"** between the different production entities without which goods could not travel between zones.

Linkage networks are readily apparent in technological systems: networks for the supply of electricity, rail and road (transport) networks, telephone networks or the INTERNET for business and e-Government.

The Interdependency between the Links and Zones

Although changes in the transport network could affect the entire system, modifications to some of the links could also have an impact. The magnitude of these modifications depends on the zone where the affected part of the system is situated. If for example, a factory downstream interrupts its operations, then the consumers of the goods produced by the factory will be affected. But if the change occurs at a sawmill midstream, then this will proportionally affect all the factories downstream. Any changes that occur upstream will have an impact on the entire system.

It is essential to grasp at this point is that the further upstream the production entity is situated, the greater the impact any change to it would have on the entire production system.

The Feedback

Obviously, the metaphor allows for thinking on a return of finished goods from downstream to the upstream. Nevertheless, this does not seem convenient for the purpose of our discourse for at least two reasons. The first one is that it limits the didactic value of the metaphor since it makes more complex and confusing its understanding, specially regarding the role of the river as a mean of transportation. The second is that, for reasons that will be presented later in the background section, the return of goods occurs with a lower flow rate than the one in the river flow direction.

Care and Sustainability

The interdependent relationship between the components means that if this production system is to last over generations, both production and consumption patterns must be carried out at rates at which the resources upstream are not destroyed or depleted. This leads us to a concept of care and maintenance that needs to be upheld by all the parties involved so as to ensure the sustainability of the system over time.

There are several considerations surrounding the idea of care, which we will use to establish priorities and responsibilities.

Firstly, we have to care for the forest that produces the wood. It should be obvious that felling the entire forest would lead to a radical and destructive transformation of the whole production system. A similar case could be made for the river which is vital both as a means of transport and for the health of the forest, and as such is as important to the system as the forest itself.

Although less essential than those parts of the system located upstream, the components midstream should also be properly cared for and maintained. This maintenance, however, is exercised more at an infrastructural level with the aim of ensuring or improving the quality of the intermediate goods.

While it is clear that the factories located downstream should also be adequately maintained, the components at this level are more resilient, as they are more diverse and easier to replace.

Finally, the need to protect the network itself (the river) must be apparent. Partial damages or faults within a particular zone may be tolerated to a degree, because they only affect the surrounding zones. But a complete failure could cause the system to collapse.

With regard to the network then, it is important to consider two often disregarded points:

1. As the interconnecting factor in the production chain, the proper maintenance of the links within the network is essential. This should be orientated towards strengthening resilience and the capacity for connection according to particular requirements (transport in the simplest sense).
2. The linkage capacity of the network limits the production capacity. Therefore, any desire to increase the rate of production requires an evaluation of the efficiency at which the network is currently operating, and a means of increasing this if necessary.

The components of this metaphorical system are then, in order of priority: the network (or transport system), followed by the elements upstream, then midstream, and finally downstream. Any strategy for technological acquisition must take this sequence into account. Thus, a factory downstream, as well as ensuring a secure market, must also consider the suppliers upstream. If the factory relies on foreign inputs then these should be secured and/or a plan for the local replacement of these inputs put in place for the future.

Knowledge on the Sawmill Metaphor

Under the conditions of our metaphor, the role of teaching and research may be interpreted in several ways.

Potential staff should be trained to work in the different zones within the system. This requires a training process and thus institutions devoted to that purpose. Under this perspective, staff would need to be instructed in the following areas: operation, maintenance, repair and manufacturing, both of the goods that circulate within the system and of the corresponding infrastructure.

Research, generating new knowledge, is also required. This should be aimed at firstly, improving the quality of the goods produced, and secondly to ensure the proper maintenance of all the processes within the system. These processes can be seen both as separate components and as a whole: two quite different visions that must not be dissociated from each other. This type of research is very important, as it provides us with the appropriate tools to identify threats to the system, detect problems and find solutions.

Infrastructure

It should also be clear that infrastructure and the capacity to use and maintain it, is essential at all levels. It follows that care of the system must also include care of the infrastructure, because without it the system cannot be maintained.

The Concept of Institution

For our metaphorical system to be stable and sustainable there must be institutions in all the production zones, engaged in the tasks inherent to that zone. We refer here to institutions from a social perspective; that is, organizations and governing bodies within the communities of workers that guarantee and regulate individual behavior for the good of the system.

We can appreciate this from looking at the different zones within the metaphor. Each institution could be seen as a separate entity. However, the entire system can also be considered a single institution.

It must be noted that without an institution, whether it be explicit in the form of a legal organization or implicit as a set of uniform behaviors, the stability of the system is at risk.

Awareness of the System

Let us imagine one of the workers in our sawmill system. How much information will he or she have about the whole system? We call this kind of knowledge "system awareness".

Suppose, for example, we imagine a lumberjack. Now, if our lumberjack has "an awareness" of the whole system, we would expect him to do his job in a way that does not put the rest of the system at risk. However, if he focuses all his attention on his immediate surroundings, he will become unaware of events that occur down river. In consequence, when faced with an unplanned situation, it will be more difficult for him to make decisions that take these events into account. For example, let us suppose that the sawmill breaks down. In order to relieve congestion midstream whilst the problem is being solved, the best course of action the lumberjack could take would be to stop working, or at least slow the rate of logging. Now, for our hypothetical lumberjack to listen to and understand the person who reports the fault, he must be aware of the system as a whole. Without this awareness, the lumberjack will be less willing to cooperate.

The workers located midstream will be more likely to better understand the system as they act as both consumers and producers.

The level of awareness tends to be most limited at the downstream end of the system. To understand why this should be, we need to explain that workers in this zone could have one of two perspectives. Firstly the worker that is aware of one of the factories. As a consumer of intermediate goods from the sawmill and a producer of an end product, this individual could have a perspective comparable to that of a worker midstream, although this will depend on how aware he is of the existence of other end products.

The second perspective is that of an individual that is a mere consumer of the finished goods. Note that out of all those that make up the system, this is the individual least capable of understanding it. In fact, he or she might be completely uninformed of what goes on upstream. Worse still, this individual is not tied to any of the production units that make up the sawmill system, and may not even be aware of the existence of nearby downstream units.

Perhaps the element we are least aware of is the network itself; which in the case of our metaphor would be an awareness of the existence and importance of the river.

There are two additional observations that are important to mention here. The first is that the longer and wider our metaphorical system, the harder it is to gain a global awareness of it. The second, no less important, is that a customer who acquires products mainly produced downstream is far less likely to attain a global understanding of the system.

The Concept of Property

In this section, regarding the sawmill system we have described, we discuss what conditions must be met before we can say that it is ours. Insofar of course that we can say that it is ours: a better form of expression is to say that we exercise sovereignty over it. To understand sovereignty we must understand two concepts: autochthony and autonomy.

By autochthony we mean that which originates in our culture.

By autonomy we mean that decisions of government are made within the culture in which the system is located

Note that these two aspects are interrelated and to some extent could be considered two sides of the same coin. It is difficult to govern what one does not possess and difficult to possess what one does not govern.

There are several sides to consider when answering the question of whether or not we exercise sovereignty.

Evidently within the system, territory is essential to the idea of property. From this perspective the more we possess, geographically speaking, of the different sectors and zones within the system, the more autochthonous the system is. If for example, the sawmill is located in another region, this would probably incur higher transport costs and greater dependence on foreign elements, which is of course when the greatest loss of autochthony and autonomy would occur.

Autochthony also implies that the development and use of infrastructure should also have their origin in our culture. At all levels.

At this stage of the argument, it should be clearly understood that any concept of the ownership of a technological system must include the ownership of the network which links the producers across all zones. Without full possession of this linkage network, it is difficult to discuss aspects of autonomy and autochthony.

The exercising of autonomy requires an understanding of the system, or "system awareness" mentioned in section **"Awareness of the system"**. In turn, this awareness requires the presence of a network of institutions which preserve the relevant areas of knowledge. These institutions must also be capable of undertaking research so that threats to the system can be identified and defense strategies and contingency plans implemented.

WHAT IS TECHNOLOGY?

At this stage, now that we have clarified the main areas of confusion and discussed the metaphor of the sawmill, we are ready to formally define what we mean by technology within the scope of this article.

Technology is the organizational supra-institution that governs individuals within production entities necessary to our way of life (depending on our specific culture).

According to this definition and following on from the sawmill metaphor, we can understand technology as a network of relationships between production entities that manufacture goods and services. This is shown in figure 2 as a graph where the nodes represent the producers (ellipses), and the arrows the relationships between producers through which circulate goods and services.

There is a parallel between the network in figure 2 and the sawmill metaphor. Ellipses (nodes) with arrows only pointing away from them (outputs), situated at the far left of figure 2 represent activities that take place in the upper reaches of the river; i.e., the extraction of raw materials. Terminal nodes, located at the far right and with arrows only pointing towards them (inputs), represent th producers down river. The remaining nodes represent those situated midstream, with their intermediate status a function of their proximity to nodes situated either "upstream" or "downstream" of them.

The arrows represent the links between the production entities. Note that in the same way as for real technological systems, special attention must be paid to the river, that is, the means by which the producers are linked.

Apart from the complexity and vastness of technology as a supra-institution, technology seen in this way helps us to identify priority areas according to their importance in our lives: food, transport, maintenance of our standard of living (health, clothing, basic services, etc.), government, education, etc. For simplicity, we can consider separate production networks for each category (although in many cases this is not strictly correct).

Considering our way of life and the world geopolitical situation, technology as a supra-institution has a global character. In a sense, and however authentic a culture likes to pretend it is, all are subject to the technological arsenal produced by this supra-institution.

If then, technology acts as a global supra-institution, it is very difficult to imagine that one culture or nation could have absolute sovereignty over it. In fact, it could be said that it is technology that exercises sovereignty over cultures. Despite this, however, it is both desirable and feasible for a culture to gain

Figure 2. Technology as a network of production entities

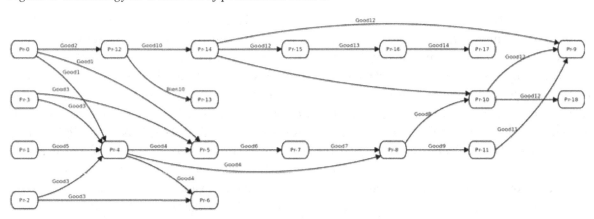

technological sovereignty over staple goods, especially food, as well as services associated with the basic needs of life such as health, education, electricity, water, telecommunications, waste management, etc., including the establishment and maintenance of linkage networks between producers.

Gaining sovereignty over technology is thus equivalent to gaining sovereignty over our way of life. Seen in this way, it is pertinent to observe briefly, as a full discussion falls beyond the scope of this essay, that we should reflect deeply on the benefits of living under the rule of technology.

THE TYPES OF FORCES IN PLAY

Following on from the idea that the technological system of a country or culture can be interpreted as a supra-institution, we can start to ask ourselves questions about how stable "technology as an institution" actually is. Fuenmayor (2000) suggested that institutions may be subject to different types of forces: perpetuating forces that work to preserve the institution and transforming forces that may act in either a positive or destructive way.

Within technology-as-an-institution, or more accurately, within its sub-institutions, there are habits, behavior patterns, rules of government, social orders and critically, power games that are played out at all levels, among both individuals and groups. These elements can be either perpetuating or transforming.

Since technology is a global supra-institution these social games have geopolitical scope and, according to how critically linked they are with production entities, can become geopolitical power issues. Once again, the driving forces can be either perpetuating or transforming.

Following on from the above, we can also divide the forces that operate on technology into domestic and foreign ones. Domestic forces are those that emerge from and operate within a nation. Within our scenario of technology-as-an-institution these forces can arise in two ways: actions that take place within the sub-institutions and cultural attitudes.

Foreign forces are those that come from regions outside the nation and tend to be represented as actions. They may be either geopolitical or environmental_[2].

There is one kind of force whose importance will become more apparent in the following section: the ownership of the linkage network, its type and capacity.

LINKAGE NETWORKS AS SUPERSTRUCTURES

Different types of technological systems are organized in linkage networks, especially transport, communication and information systems. To understand why, it is useful to look back at the history of some of the systems and institutions relevant to what today we associate with modern technology.

Historically, England is considered the first country to become industrialized and has since become the most emblematic country of the industrial revolution. It is no coincidence that by the time this revolution took place in the18th century, England already possessed an established national transport network and the world's largest maritime network. In this regard, neither does it seem to be a coincidence that during its most frenzied industrialized period, the 19th century, this country already possessed an extensive railway network created and maintained using autochthonous technology. We should also highlight the fact that during this period England also possessed, albeit only available to an elite class, teaching, publication and academic research networks. This is especially relevant when we consider that much of the inventions that enabled the industrial revolution to take place were built on engineering research.

The industrialization of the erstwhile Soviet Union was preceded by the construction and consolidation of their transport, communication and electricity networks. Parallel to this, the country also concentrated on developing an academic network for the acquisition and generation of knowledge.

The USA at the time of the Bretton Woods Agreement was the country with the highest rates of production in the world. The strategy employed by the Government through this treaty consisted in establishing a worldwide commercial network to ensure the supply of raw materials for their manufacturing industries and sales markets. In parallel, in the years following the agreement, the USA successfully encouraged, and still does, a flow of intellectual immigration to support it academic needs.

Most of the cultures that today are considered to be "developed" especially the most recent ones, such as South Korea, have begun by establishing local linkage networks followed by their insertion in global networks and the construction of academic networks.

Today, despite the economic growth of many cultures and the displacement of the USA as the most industrialized nation on the planet, very few doubt the "technological and commercial superiority" of the latter. Currently, networks linked to information technologies are intrinsic to all areas of life: education, culture, research, manufacturing, etc. It is noteworthy then that USA based institutions are at the forefront of information technology. In this regard, when we look at the history of computer science we can see that the USA is the country that has invested most in the research and development of information technologies. Without trying to qualify this, our way of life has certainly undergone structural changes brought about by the emergence of a new computer science based network that appeared between the late 1980s and early 1990s.

We can thus observe that the generation of a new network brings with it new forces that often motorize structural change and create new important variables within geopolitical power games.

The network (the river) linking the production entities (or nodes), constitutes a superstructure on which they depend. It follows that any modification to the network will result in a structural change to the production system and thus the technological system. In order to more easily understand this relationship of cause and effect, we have only to refer to the metaphor of the sawmill and look at the effect a change in the nature of the river would have on the rest of the system. For example, if the direction of the channel is altered the location of the sawmill would have to be changed. Similarly, changes in flow could involve changes in the speed of transport of the logs. As an extreme case, we could consider a radical transformation of the river, for example, if it dried up completely. In this case, the system would be completely transformed and perhaps even cease to exist.

In some way, changes in technology lead to changes in the capacity of the network and the degree of ownership, but more especially in the emergence of a new class of network.

THE ROAD TO TECHNOLOGICAL SOVEREIGNTY

Within the context of technology as a supra-institution, we propose a new idea of sovereignty. Thus, under the terms of a production network, sovereignty would be a function of:

- **Autochthony:** the territorial ownership and control of the development and use of production nodes, from the highest point upstream to the lowest point downstream, in the areas essential to our way of life. The greater number of links owned in a production chain, the greater the independence obtained, and therefore the greater the sovereignty over that production chain.

- **Autonomy:** the capacity to manage and control the various forces (perpetuating and transforming; domestic and foreign) that act on the production chains.
- **Structure:** the ownership of the linkage network (the river) between the (autochthonous) production nodes. Here, ownership is defined as the degree of management and control that is held over the network and its capacity. Given the global nature of technology, this aspect contemplates the degree of interconnection with other worldwide infrastructural networks. Consider for example, the power a nation has on its merchant navy.

Under these conditions, a strategy for the acquisition of technology or the preservation of sovereignty should take into account the following guidelines:

1. If the linkage network is the superstructure upon which the technological system rests, a nation must guarantee, as far as possible, the acquisition of the linkage networks related to the supply of staple goods and services. Similarly, if a weak or non-existent good or service is considered a national priority as much as possible of the linkage network needed in order to produce that item should be acquired.
2. There should be an awareness of the importance of acquiring and owning the production nodes from the furthest point upstream to the lowest point downstream. Nevertheless, the nodes further upstream are more important than those midstream which in turn are more important than those downstream. The reason for this prioritization is explained by independence. The nodes furthest upstream are the least dependent nodes, not only from the other production entities within the system, but also from foreign forces.
3. The technological systems to be developed should be prioritized according to the local culture and needs of the nation. These may not necessarily be universal, but rather could be very specific to a particular culture.

A culture that is not capable of producing its own essential products (food and basic services) is more likely to find itself at the mercy of destructive domestic and foreign forces.

Alongside these guidelines, particular attention must be paid to two aspects of the care of technological heritage.

The Role of Government in Technology

With technology as a supra-institution that for good or ill dominates our way of life, governs our production and therefore our economic activities, we should be clear that the government of a culture is related to the government of technology.

From our representation of technology as a production network, we can see that it is in the interests of the Government to acquire production nodes at all levels as well as the linkage networks between them.

Thus, we can separate two modes of government. The first of these refers to the development of cultural attitudes. In this aspect, and adhering to the established norms of the Republic, the principal methods lie in the elaboration and advocacy of laws aimed at the care and maintenance of technology.

The second mode is to draw up guidelines and implement economic policies. Since economic issues lie outside the scope of this essay, we will mention only the main aspects that should be examined before preparing economic policies oriented towards the acquisition of technology.

Government actions are more immediately perceived by the majority of the population, usually customers, on the nodes downstream. Due to their dependence on the nodes upstream, however, the operating margins are lower at this point along the river. Note that if customer satisfaction is to be met downstream, production midstream and therefore upstream must be maintained or increased. As, generally speaking, the majority of the consumers within a culture are found downstream, there could be a propensity to bias policy towards activities in this zone, in detriment of production upstream. This will lead to immediate, but sadly short lived, customer satisfaction.

Other dangers of only taking the lower reaches of the river into account, especially if the linkage network is neglected, are the exacerbation of consumerism and political clientelism, coupled with a failure to maintain a perspective of the global nature of technological systems.

There are many things that a government must ensure when it undertakes a plan for the acquisition of technology. One of the most important of these is to guarantee that production moves directly through the various autochthonous production entities, until it finally reaches the end consumers. A government that for the sake of the welfare of the country favors business by offering incentives and privileges must make sure that production flows endogenously: that is, through own-culture linkage networks towards nationally based nodes or end consumers.

At times, due to lack of a structure (network) or for a strategic reason, this is neither possible nor desirable. For example, the production of goods for export, which even though they will not be consumed locally should be encouraged as long as the channels of return on investment are directed towards nodes within the national production system.

The Role of Teaching and Research

In section **"Technology as knowledge"**, we noted that while knowledge is not equivalent to technology, it is essential to it. Although knowledge is often confused with technology, at other times it is neglected, and institutions devoted to the cultivation of knowledge and research are considered unimportant and unnecessary. Nevertheless, the presence of these institutions is even more essential than infrastructure, as they enable the creation and maintenance of production, ergo technology. Special attention must, therefore, be paid to the cultivation and care of our technological assets through research and education without discriminating between areas of knowledge.

Here we can consider three categories of research. Firstly, that which aims to improve a technological process (for example by making it more efficient), or create a new one. Secondly, and vitally, research involved with the care and maintenance of the system. This consists in identifying the potential forces (domestic and foreign, perpetuating and transforming) that have an influence on the productive nodes, as well as determining how to manage them. Finally, a third and also important category is prospective and consists in identifying the structural forces that could affect the system especially the linkage network.

Since knowledge is essential for the institutionalization and preservation of technology, areas and methods of research should not be restricted. Of course, this does not mean that certain productive nodes, or more importantly, the care or creation of linkage networks linked to the generation or dissemination of knowledge itself, cannot be encouraged. An example of this is the Wikipedia network, whose uses and benefits seem obvious in spite of the criticism sometimes leveled at it.

Historically, the institutions in charge of the cultivation and care of cultural issues and thus, in this case, of technology are the Universities or Academies. Nevertheless, we should mention that currently these institutions seem to focus more on research that aims to improve local aspects, particularly the efficiency and economic gain related to one of the goods/services or nodes, rather than being concerned with the care of the production system as a whole, even though this last should have a much higher priority.

The Relationship between Technology, Economics and Politics

With all this in mind, we can now discuss with less risk of misunderstanding, the three-way relationship between technology, economics and politics.

Firstly, technology and the economy are closely related, especially when attempting to develop the former. As a result, the issue of the acquisition of technology is also an economic one.

Secondly, since we are dealing with an economic problem within a supra-institution (technology) that dominates our whole way of life technology is, whether we like it or not, also a political issue.

Finally, and this is perhaps the most controversial point to accept, politics is subject to technology. Thus, production capacity and the means to co-act with other production systems are dependent on the degree to which technology is acquired.

BACKGROUND

Background Over the Sawmill Metaphor

The terms upstream and downstream are part of common industry jargon. Upstream refers to suppliers or parts of the industrial system that sell or produce inputs while downstream refers to the clients or parts of the system that receive the manufactured goods. Surely, these expressions have been used in other contexts with a meaning very close to the metaphor. For example, they have been used in the field of hydrology.

That being said and without any pretensions of awarding us the originality of this standpoint, in the literature search undertaken we have not found any formal proposal similar in the idea of using the metaphor of the sawmill applied to the idea of technology.

Background on Mathematical Models of Production Chains

Production systems at the micro and macro levels have been modeled on ways that seem inspired directly or indirectly in the terms of our metaphor. In this sub-section we will mention very briefly the various models that we know. It should be noticed the emphasis on production systems in contrast to what commonly is known as technology. In this regard, an interpretation of technology strongly associated with production as set forth in this paper is unknown to us.

Network Flows

The most precise way of modeling a production chain is using a multi-commodity network flow (Ahuja, Magnati & Orlin, 1993). The nodes of the network represent the production entities, generally factories, while the arcs represent the potential flow relationships. Figure two shows in practical terms a network flow based on the system "Mapa Productivo of Venezuela" (Mapa productivo de Venezuela, 2014) which is a set of systems currently under development that relies on this type of model.

Models based on network flows allow for optimal decision making regarding production according to the accuracy of the data used to build the network. Nevertheless due to its scale, computational complexity and the difficulties associated with obtaining all the data required they are not suited to study dynamical behavior. Its main use is in gaining knowledge of the situation and as an aid in decision making.

Cellular Automata

A second alternative, probably the most suited to simulate and evaluate scenarios consist of modeling the production chain as a cellular automata (Wolfram, 2002). Broadly speaking the cells represent the production entities and the rules governing its behavior the potential exchange relationships.

This type of models is much more convenient to study scenarios for understanding and planning.

Simulation Models

Simulation models, both continuous and discrete events, can be used to model supply chains. In the continuous domain, system dynamics (Forrester, 1971; Sterman, 2000), has gained some popularity for modeling supply chains. Although less popular, oriented discrete event models have also been used to study supply chains (Law & Kelton, 2000; Robinson, 2004).

Input-Output Matrices

The input-output model developed during three centuries by Francois Quesnay, Léon Walras and Wassily Leontief (Input–output model, 2014) presents a network of producers as a matrix that encodes the relationships between supply and demand of the producers. In this way it produces a system of linear equations that allows to study the demand in a situation of equilibrium.

A great advantage of this model is that is computationally very manageable. Its disadvantage lies in the lack of precision. This model is popular in macro-planning.

About Feedback in The Different Model Types

Regardless of the model used to study the production chain it is important to be careful regarding feedback, that is to say, the river flow from downstream to upstream. Placing temporarily on the side the fact that it increases substantially model complexity since the feedback occurs against the current it has a greater cost. Also, physical considerations (thermodynamics second law) ensure that *"perpetuum mobile"* (perpetual movement) is impossible and modeling the feedback entails the risk of losing the importance that is given to the care of the system in the sawmill metaphor.

TECHNOLOGY IN VENEZUELA

In spite of the current situation, when we look at Venezuela's economic policies we find that these same policies have been used successfully in other countries to generate production and technology. To try to understand this apparent contradiction, we will briefly mention them here.

Summary of Current Development-Oriented Policies in Venezuela

Perhaps the greatest danger to developing economies is the volatility of foreign investment and capital flight. To mitigate this risk, the Venezuelan Government has imposed restrictions on the convertibility of its currency through currency exchange control. This type of control has been applied as a temporary measure in many countries, including some economies of the so-called developed countries. Currency control should normally only be used as a temporary measure as long-term exchange control tends to discourage foreign investment, which is possibly what has occurred in Venezuela.

Nevertheless, despite exchange control, Venezuela has received considerable foreign investment. Whilst much of this has been in the oil sector, other areas involving technology have also benefitted such as, for example, telecommunications, infrastructure, agriculture and some new factories in different sectors within the production network.

In the education sector significant investments have been made at all levels: from primary and secondary schools to universities, to the point at which Venezuela has become one of the countries with the highest number of university students.

Free and open access to information has also been strongly encouraged. The use of free software in the public administration sector is nominally mandatory.

The Government has also shown wide ranging interventionist policies. This is important to note because, in an attempt to be fair and in order to find appropriate business substitutes, the Government has intervened rapidly and effectively in inefficient production nodes. This has occurred with companies in various sectors that have been deemed unproductive or speculative, to the extent that several companies in the agriculture, food and civil construction sectors have been expropriated. Unfortunately, judging by the subsequent shortages in the sectors associated with these companies, it seems that the Government has failed to find effective surrogate managements.

Finally, the Government has openly promoted national sovereignty and independence. This at least suggests, although does not in itself prove, the political will to obtain them.

Policies of this type have been applied successfully in South Korea, during the Menji era in Japan, Communist China, the former Soviet Union, India and Brazil.

In addition to the aforementioned policies, Venezuela in the last decade has received substantial capital input from oil revenues. We can thus affirm, without risk of contradiction, that Venezuela has not lacked capital to invest in the acquisition of technology.

Nevertheless, it is clear that Venezuela today is suffering from serious economic and production problems and consequently political and therefore technological ones.

A critique of possible incompetence, errors of government and the domestic and foreign forces that have acted against Venezuela in the economic field is outside the scope of this essay. Our interest in briefly describing Venezuela's economic policies is to demonstrate that the Government has provided many of the tools necessary for the acquisition of technology (Adelman & Yeldan, 2000). So what is it then that the Venezuelan techno-political leadership has failed to understand, and why is it that, even with the available resources and implementation of policies that have been successful elsewhere, inroads into the acquisition of technological sovereignty have not been made?

In the next section we propose and discuss a very brief and general diagnosis of the technological situation in Venezuela based on the definition of technology given in section "**What is technology?**". The intention is to provide a contextual backdrop, open to questioning, that it is hoped will lead to further discussion. It should not be considered as the final word on the subject, but is presented rather as a testable hypothesis which attempts to shed some light on the matter.

Overview of Venezuela Technology

The general state of technology in Venezuela can be summed up in one expression: **"technological fragmentation"**. This is illustrated in Figure 3 which shows the technological situation in Venezuela, based on the information given in figure 2, and represented as a network. By fragmentation we mean an inability to understand the system as a complete national unit, as well as the cultural inability of the country to project itself within the scenario of a global technological system.

The Zones within the Production Network

To summarize, for nearly all of the critical goods and services, i.e. those that are essential to the Venezuelan way of life, the production network in Venezuela contains very few nodes with respect to the global technological network inherent to each product.

We will mention here the areas of production that seem to us to be of greatest interest.

There are a few "upstream" nodes that correspond to the extraction of raw minerals, for example, iron and aluminum. Except in the civil construction sector, the market for these raw materials is external.

As regards food production, there are certainly enough high quality agricultural resources in the "upstream" zone of the system to be fully sovereign. These valuable resources are, however, woefully under used as there are neither sufficient production nodes upstream nor an established production network downstream that can adequately take advantage of them to ensure self-sufficiency.

In the health sector the production network is virtually non-existent, which has resulted in a complete dependence on imports of pharmacological and medical supplies. This is so acute that, in a similar way to the situation in Iraq after the first Gulf war, the mortality rate in Venezuela would increase considerably if those imports were suddenly interrupted.

We cannot fail to mention a very particular and critical node: oil extraction. This is a node located in the furthest upper reaches of the river that constitutes the primary energy input of technology itself; that is, of the global production network. But even within this industry, the production network is fragmented with an absolute dependence on foreign inputs and technologies.

Midstream, there are some industries that, although geographically located within the national territory, cannot be considered wholly national as they are still dependent on foreign inputs. It would seem that most of these production nodes are geared towards providing some supplies for basic services. Here we would like to make an interesting observation. Despite all the criticism whether valid or not, Venezuela, as for the majority of Latin American countries and in contrast to other cultures (especially some of the African ones) possesses relatively stable institutions that do provide basic services. This is an important point because it denotes a cultural capacity to build institutions and maintain them.

With respect to production nodes "downstream", where arguably the majority of Venezuelan industries are located, these are overwhelmingly dependent on imported materials.

Most technologically sophisticated end products, for example those from the world of electronics, are manufactured outside Venezuela. The current Government has encouraged the local assembly of some of these goods, but without a visible plan for acquiring the rest of the production chain. Examples

Figure 3. Technological fragmentation in Venezuelan

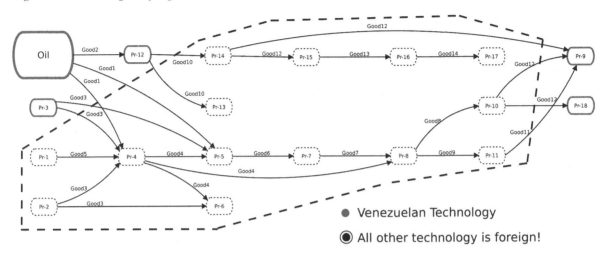

of this include cell phones, computers, digital TV set top boxes and locally assembled cars. However, if it were not for the presence of a local market that consumes them, these plants would serve only as maquila industries.

It is worth remembering that, as we observed in section **"The road to technological sovereignty"**, most of the goods produced "downstream" are oriented towards individual, non-public consumption. If production is only stimulated at this level, the chances of a rise in consumerism, clientelism and imports greatly increase. In addition, our cultural ability to critically appraise the use of national technology becomes limited. Both customers and consumers tend to only perceive, and partially at that, the production nodes located downstream. Nevertheless, it must be granted that as regards political moral, achievements downstream can result in a kind of "short-term fix".

The Linkage Network

If stimulating production downstream leads to risks regarding consumerism this is further exacerbated by neglect of the linkage networks which, as they become less efficient, severely increases technological fragmentation. To understand this, it is useful to examine the principal and most obvious linkage networks.

Materials were first transported using land based networks: either by rail or by means of heavy goods vehicles along a road network.

Although modest projects have been undertaken, Venezuela still does not have an extensive rail network. What it does have is a good road network. In addition, fuel (petrol) costs are very low, about US $0.14 per liter. Venezuela should thus in principle have low transport costs.

One of the policies of the current Government has been to promote the purchase of motor vehicles for individual use. From 1991 to 1998, before the Government came into power, a total of 886,286 vehicles were sold, at a mean rate of 110,786 vehicles per year. In contrast from 1999 to 2008, 2,487,874 vehicles were sold, more than doubling the mean annual rate to 248,787 vehicles per year (Ramírez, 2012)

One of the effects of this rise in car sales has been a noticeable increase in the amount of road traffic, both within the city and on the national highways. This has led to a decline in the provision of both urban public transport services and the deterioration of the national road network for the transport of goods. As a result, roads collapse, transport costs have increased and the quality of city life is negatively affected by the increase in urban traffic and pollution levels.

This is then an indication of the effects caused by an increase in activities downstream, in this case those corresponding to the transport system, with no consideration of either production upstream or the performance of the linkage networks.

Another important linkage network comprises the generation, transmission and distribution of electricity. As an energy consuming technology, one would expect that an increase in production implies an increase in electrical power requirements. In addition, the cost of a kilowatt/hour of electricity is approximately 3.1 cents, one of the cheapest in the world.

Owing to the strong incentives for the purchase of end products for individual use, particularly electronic home appliances, air conditioners, etc. the demand for electricity has risen considerably. Note that this demand is not driven by an increase in production but rather by an increase in individual consumption. This has led to a decline in the national minimum reserve and made the country vulnerable to electrical faults resulting from normal wear and tear and climatic variations such as drought, excessive rainfall etc. As a result, both the rationing of electricity and unplanned power cuts have increased dramatically, which has led to interruptions in the functioning of public and private institutions.

Once again, we can see the effects that the up-scaling of production nodes downstream coupled with the neglect of production nodes upstream and the linkage network, can have on the system.

There are other examples of the negative effects of the policy of promoting production nodes, such as those related to the telephone system and INTERNET, downstream, but for reasons of space these are not discussed here.

Knowledge and Venezuelan Technology

As far as knowledge is concerned, there are a series of explicit decrees and laws that have been passed by the current Government. Specifically, Decree N^0 3390 regarding the use of free software in the public administration sector and more recently the *Ley de Infogobierno* (Freedom of Information Act). These policies are important because they stipulate that knowledge is free and open, i.e. that its ownership is not restricted by private economic powers. They also promote and facilitate national projects regarding the freedom of information and other aspects relating to Venezuelan national identity. Recently, albeit in an imitation of strategies implemented by other countries, the Venezuelan Government has approved the granting of "Creative Commons" licenses. These policies should be considered as positive as they act to oppose domestic and especially foreign "forces" supporting the privatization of knowledge. But beyond these considerations, the emphasis on this political guidelines, that are important, suggests that perhaps Venezuelan technological leadership have mistaken the problem of the unleashing of technology as supra-institution, which have to be referred to the generation of production capacity, with the interpretation of technology as knowledge.

Regarding the Universities, these do not seem to have undergone any significant changes towards the construction of a technological identity. With regard to education, universities have tended to interpret themselves as suppliers of qualified personnel, which, although important and consistent with their role as regards the provision of high-level training, does not form part of their mission as guardians and cultivators of cultural identity. The Government has thus promoted the creation of new universities, in an effort to massify the higher education system, with a low (or null) emphasis on the generation of knowledge. In spite of this, we must underline the fact that this has meant that a substantial portion of the Venezuelan youth population is in education.

As far as research goes; the situation is pathetic. Since more or less the 1980's, University research in Venezuela has become mostly investigation "for export"; i.e., the knowledge generated is relevant to problems and demands outside the country. In the absence of projects and national agendas that identify with Venezuela itself, the policies and actions of the current Government have failed to change this situation. Under the headings of "programme" or "project", grants have been made to support research and innovation. However, the lack of concrete and tangible objectives, as well as timelines and specific production obligations, has meant that these projects have often been reduced to mere share-outs of financial resources, whose allocation in many cases has been mediated by lobbying. Much of this problem can be explained by the absence of a Venezuelan technological identity.

High-level research centers have seen their production reduced, probably due to two factors. On the one hand, the Government has restricted their fields of research by interpreting them as mere problem-solvers without contemplating their potential to investigate mechanisms that would aid Venezuela´s insertion in the production system. On the other, some research institutions, particularly some of the autonomous universities, have become proselyting agents serving the interests of particular political parties.

The universities as centers for the cultivation and preservation of Venezuelan cultural identity have indeed fallen very low.

The Global Context

It is clear from the previous section that technology-as-an-institution does not exist in Venezuela. This is understandable given its history and geopolitical circumstances as a supplier of oil to the global industry. However, and especially in light of government speeches promoting technological sovereignty, we would expect a strategic plan for the acquisition of technology and some indication of progress towards the incorporation of Venezuela in the global production system.

Virtually the only instances of international connections are those of oil exports. In this regard, one of the few instances of techno-political clarity was shown by President Chávez in his efforts to establish an oil supply network, through a three-tier strategic plan. In the first tier, preferential sales were set up with Latin American and Caribbean countries. The second tier consisted of Venezuela's insertion in MERCOSUR, with an aim to be the main supplier of oil to the MERCOSUR countries. Finally, the third tier consisted of the diversification of the market to large volume buyers in Asia where future sales were agreed in exchange for loans and technological knowledge. Especially successful agreements have been made with China, which has established several factories in Venezuela, the vast majority concerned with production nodes upstream. These strategies have resulted in an increase of geopolitical power, which is important for the defense of Venezuela against foreign forces.

If we look at the technology network from a global perspective, Venezuela's production nodes lie at the two extremes. Firstly, there are the nodes far upstream pertaining to the extraction of oil and minerals essential for global technology, and from which large amounts of oil and minerals are exported. At the other extreme, far downstream, we find the nodes which receive the majority of the manufactured goods, some of which have been produced with Venezuelan raw materials. The midstream part of the network is however empty, devoid of industrial activity.

In the upstream areas of the river, this imbalance suggests the presence of foreign forces and interests in pursuit of the control of oil resources. In contrast, at the downstream end we can observe the strong dependency Venezuela has on the global production system.

Thus, leaving aside the importance of oil as a resource, although not the considerable economic power it exerts on the world market, Venezuelan society for the most part is seen as being even further down the river than "downstream": as mere consumers of imported end-products.

CONCLUSION ABOUT THE VENEZUELA TECHNOLOGICAL FAILURE

In this article we have looked at a variety of ways technology has been defined, most of these incorrect. We have also discussed the small number of institutions that deal with technology in Venezuela, many of these diminished or in crisis and disassociated from the production system, as well as a notable lack of productivity which would permit the Venezuelan nation a minimum of autonomy. We cannot thus but conclude that production as a supra-institution in Venezuela is practically non-existent and has worsened in recent years. All this in spite of the executive and political will for this country to attain greater technological sovereignty. Enough capital investment has been made available and economic and executive policies implemented that have been successful in other countries, to expect more positive results.

What is it then that has not worked?

In previous papers (Fuenmayor, 1999; León, 2004; Fuenmayor, Aguilar, Anzola, Delgado, Mendialdúa & Terán, 2007), it has been argued, as in this text, that Venezuela has been, and remains, a victim of a deep and blatant cultural theft. The first aspect of this theft is material and consists of the massive capital flight - from oil revenues - that this country has suffered for approximately forty years. Despite exchange control and other economic policies, the current Government has not only been unable to stop this flight, but has aggravated it by supporting financial solutions without national production. The second aspect is far more serious: Venezuelan society has become less and less aware of this theft. One of the best indications of this is the consumer frenzy that has resulted from the policies of importation and an emphasis on developing production nodes downstream, without considering the impact this may have on the linkage networks or how to incorporate and build production chains upstream. The autochthony of the Venezuelan culture has diminished as it has become more dependent on foreign technology, which in turn has caused the country to lose its autonomy. The possibility of Venezuela constructing a technological superstructure is now further away than ever.

Thus, in terms of technology, Venezuela does not possess any kind of superstructure that provides an identity as regards production. Venezuela also suffers from a lack of awareness of the existence of technology, not only because it does not have it or has ever had it, but also because it lacks the capacity to recognize it in the global cultural context and see itself within this context.

There are several forces at work that have prevented the vision and cultivation of technology in Venezuela. To describe and discuss each one of these is outside the scope of this chaper. Fundamentally however, we could say that both in a domestic and a foreign context, the main force that acts against technology in Venezuela is, perhaps paradoxically, the revenue gained (or rather stolen) from the oil industry which continues today.

On the domestic side, income from oil has awarded the country unprecedented economic power compared to the total value of the rest of its weak production capacity. This has made it easy to financially sustain a way of life based on imports rather than national production. This practice has in turn led to a vicious circle of preferring imported goods over those produced nationally, thus eliminating or severely limiting the cultural forces favoring local production and further fragmenting the country's capacity to visualize its production system as a whole.

Looking outside of Venezuela, oil, essential for global technology, attracts coercive foreign powers that compete with local producers. The companies initially interested in oil extraction in Venezuela were all foreign. This is understandable as at that time oil extraction technology as we know it today was unknown in Venezuela. For this reason, there was no national interest to study or carry out oil extraction. It must also be mentioned that during those early days, foreign powers explicitly impeded the establishment of local oil companies.

Gradually, Venezuela began to gain some income and gain some autonomy in decision-making as regards extraction. However, up until now, in spite of nominally owning one of the world´s largest oil companies, it still cannot be said that Venezuela has sovereignly over its oil production. This can be demonstrated by the mixed contracts that are being made with foreign companies for the exploitation of the Orinoco Oil Belt, which contains the largest proven reserves on the planet. If Venezuela had a stronger cultural identity, domestic companies, instead of foreign ones, would have appeared to exploit the reserves. That the conditions of contract, the royalties obtained and their distribution are much improved compared to the past is positive step in the right direction, but it would be infinitely preferable if Venezuelan oil was extracted by Venezuelans.

The fact that after more than a century of oil exploitation, Venezuela is not yet able by itself to extract its own oil, demonstrates that it does not have technological sovereignty in this field. If we add this to the historical "century old" shrinkage of the other areas of national production we can understand, in part, the theft we have already mentioned.

GENERAL RECOMMENDATIONS FOR THE ACQUISITION OF TECHNOLOGY

It is not the purpose of this essay to propose a plan for the acquisition or recovery of technology. However, we do offer some considerations and guidelines that could be used to counteract the main causes that impede the acquisition of technology within a culture. Most of these guidelines are based on not repeating the mistakes made by Venezuela, and always with the understanding that the elimination of the causes of a problem does not necessarily solve it.

The Problem of the Attitude towards Technology

Ways must be found to make public and private executive leadership, as well as Venezuelan society in general, aware that technology is a high priority as well as a political issue, and that its acquisition is closely related to the generation of a cultural capacity for production. In addition to fostering this awareness, mechanisms should be found to question it - another reason why technology is a very political issue. In fact, some thinkers have argued that technology itself may be culturally dangerous (Heidegger, 1982).

In cultural terms, the development of technological awareness is not a mere linguistic problem in the sense of being able to articulate our eventual understanding of things. Interpreting awareness in this way can, in fact, be a burden that has resulted in linguistic abuse and the false idea that awareness and its attendant attitudes may be acquired simply through schooling or propaganda. This in turn, in the absence or misrepresentation of the facts, has led to a misunderstanding of what awareness means. In a culture, awareness should translate into concrete actions carried out by institutions to produce specific goods or services. In the case of technology these actions should give rise to sustainable production entities that form part of linkage networks and which can operate either upstream or downstream. To summarize, technological cultural awareness is demonstrated by deeds, not words.

Venezuelan culture, with decades of very low productivity and consumption habits fueled by oil revenues, suffers from a lack of technological awareness.

This leads us to a difficult question: how can we generate awareness about something that is culturally unknown? The German and Japanese cultures are often branded as miraculous or heroic by the fact that, even after having been defeated and devastated during WWII, they managed in a very short time to place themselves among the principal productive powers in the world. Nevertheless, much of this well-deserved praise ignores the fact that before the war these cultures already possessed technological awareness.

Eastern cultures that have acquired their own technology, for example, India, China and South Korea, have as a common trait, a national cultural identity which, although assaulted by the processes of colonization, was not destroyed.

We believe that cultural roots are very important because they, wholly or partly, make possible the awareness of public assets and cultural heritage [3].

We suggest that Venezuelan society, like that of other Latin American nations, has lost the idea of what a public asset is. This loss, closely linked with the alienation referred to in section "**Conclusion about the Venezuela technological failure**" has been caused by several cultural attacks throughout its history. Firstly, the entire American continent, including Venezuela, was subject to extensive looting by European invaders. Many ethnic groups were exterminated, and those that survived became enslaved during the colonization process which lasted centuries. Then came the American War of Independence. Some of these newly independent cultures, in particular the United States, managed to develop a technological base because the colonists brought with them their European identity. Latin American cultures, labeled as a "second Europe" (Briceño Guerrero, 1977), were however, considered by the rest of the world as mere providers of raw materials. In Venezuela, a process of transformation began at the beginning of the last century, in which income from oil rose to the extent that it displaced, practically to annihilation, traditional agricultural production inherited from colonial times.

Any plan for the acquisition of technology must be made with the conviction that without local production there can be no technology. But initially this conviction must exist in the absence of technological awareness. How then to develop technology and at the same time acquire an awareness of it? We think that an answer could be through the rescue or cultivation of the idea of public technological assets or technological heritage.

THE IMPORTANCE OF PUBLIC ASSETS

A concise way to exemplify the idea of a public asset, although incomplete with respect to the richness of its meaning, is by reference to the traditional "public services": urban and intercity transport, electricity, urban rubbish disposal, telecommunications, postal systems, etc. In this regard, it is appropriate to note that the majority of technological cultures can be characterized by the high performance of their public services.

By public we do not necessarily mean that the services are free, but that they are efficient and available to the entire population.

Have you ever wondered what would happen in a technological culture if any of these services were suddenly severely cut or lost completely? Although it is impossible to give a detailed answer, we can state that yes it is feasible to expect that the culture would react in some way to repair or renew the service concerned.

Now, and taking as an example urban public transport systems, we can ask ourselves: what would have happened if twelve years ago the Venezuelan Government - instead of establishing production nodes downstream, oriented towards individual consumption and supported mostly by imports, which as we have seen has resulted in the deterioration of urban public spaces and an increase in traffic - had devoted its resources to establishing high quality and efficient urban public transport services? Again it is not possible to answer this question in detail, but if we assume that the Venezuelan Government had showed sufficient leadership to convince the population to wait a few more years in order to fully enjoy a decent public transport service, then it would seem plausible to expect Venezuelans to have attained a cultural technological awareness around public transport issues.

We have found, therefore a subtle argument to suggest that any plans for the acquisition of technology must be aimed towards building cultural spaces to engage with that which is public. One of the ways to tackle this is through the development of public services, which, uncoincidentally, are based on technology.

THE CULTIVATION OF TECHNOLOGY AND PRACTICAL LEADERSHIP

Given that technology can be seen as a supra-institution made up of sub-institutions, it seems obvious that in order to acquire it, institutions must be developed in different areas: education, production and the service industries.

New institutions do not, however, appear "on command" or merely by the construction of an infrastructure for them. On the contrary, they develop slowly, patiently and without initially having an exact image of what the final results will be. Before this unavoidable uncertainty, and in general for the issues raised in this section, it is very important to have an idea of what cultivation or "nurture" means, in the sense that results can be appreciated and awareness raised only when, to continue with the metaphor, the fruits are harvested, not when the seeds are planted.

Bearing this in mind, we believe it very important that projects for technological acquisition are headed by people with excellent leadership skills. Both charisma and leadership are extremely important management skills, especially during the initial stages of a project. Since it takes time for crops to grow and ripen, it is essential they be given time. At a time of uncertainty, it is normal that those in charge be seen as "authoritarian", especially when difficult decisions have to be made. But beyond this temporary "authoritarianism" it is vital that the leader shows practical authority, in other words, that he or she has a wide experience and knowledge of the field the institution is involved with. The non-observance of this is perhaps one of the major flaws in Venezuela's strategic plan.

Often, there is a deep set belief that authoritarianism is a necessary or desirable condition for the development of technology. This is possibly due to the authoritarian behavior of the leaders of some countries that have been successful in acquiring technology. For example, the monopolies of power observed at the beginning of the technological era in England and the USA, or the systems of authoritarian government found in the Soviet Union, Chile, China, etc. Nevertheless, a closer look at the technological history of these cultures reveals notable failures during the times when technology projects were headed by individuals without practical authority. Conversely, technological triumphs were generally led by people with a deep practical knowledge of the programmes they were in charge of.

Practical authority is thus absolutely necessary for proper leadership, in addition to the other skills inherent to successful management.

Areas of Priority

Technology includes a myriad of areas and products, but among these there are some that are vital for any culture. In this regard we wish to consider three areas:

1. Food sovereignty: a culture must pursue complete food sovereignty, based of course on national agricultural capacities.
2. Basic services, understood to be those services that enable a reasonable standard of living.
3. Health and education. These must be treated separately from the basic services to avoid the risk of doubling-up or confusion between their production chains.

Provided that at least part of the return on investment is used to subsidize projects in the priority areas, the development of technologies in other fields should be supported.

The Importance of the Network

In section **"Care and sustainability"** we established the essential role played by linkage networks in technological systems. Planners and stakeholders must accept that, whatever the area or product, technological sovereignty can only be attained by controlling the linkage network associated with it. We will illustrate the importance of this with the following examples:

National heavy industry cannot be developed without an adequate power supply. However, it is possible to have heavy industry, as indeed occurs in many countries, provided there is a market for it, by importing the raw materials needed.

It is not feasible to maintain businesses or e-government institutions that depend on the INTERNET without a reliable and efficient telecommunications network.

Neither can a large scale self-reliant food system be achieved without the associated networks for obtaining the inputs necessary (fertilizers, agricultural machinery, etc.), the distribution of the harvested crops and the transport of other necessary products.

The characteristics of the networks required depend on the relative importance of the products and the resources available. This should be studied in a detailed and responsible manner before developing any product or service.

Under the terms of the sawmill metaphor, the network acts as a river; that is, as a means of communication between all the production nodes in the system. As such, its care and maintenance requires the involvement of other systems and areas of production. We cannot emphasize enough the essential character of linkage networks: they act as fertilizer that feeds the technological crops associated with them, triggering the generation and growth of further technological projects in the production chains tied to the network infrastructures and the areas linked by this network along the river. As examples of this effect we could mention the role the railway has played in different cultures, the development of the electricity network in the Soviet Union and the French telecommunications system.

One way adopted by many economies to take advantage of the trigger-like nature of network building is to establish industrial parks on the outskirts of the areas of production that have access to the network.

Finally, while it is strategic that these projects are public in the sense we have already discussed, note that this should neither dissuade nor exclude private investment or monopolies. The first priority is to establish the network; making it fully public or freeing it from monopolies are problems that can be dealt with at a later date, depending on the circumstances.

Priorities between Areas of Production

Given the global complexity of technology it is difficult, and probably impractical, to attempt to acquire all of it, even within a single supply chain. Nevertheless, priorities should be established within each area of production.

In the light of this, it is highly desirable, once the goods to be produced are determined according to the priorities and projects established around their linkage networks, that the order in which the production nodes are developed is from upstream to downstream. If, however, due to circumstances, the order of production has to be changed, then a feasible and detailed schedule of import substitution must be implemented. In the event that it is impossible to establish one of the upstream nodes, for example due to the lack of a raw material in the national territory, a plan must be drawn up to ensure the availability of several alternative suppliers.

The tendency of Venezuela to initiate the acquisition of technology downstream instead of upstream, that as was noted in section **"Overview of Venezuela Technology"** has unleashed a frenzy of consumerism, provides us with a good example of what can happen when this order is reversed. That is why, amongst other reasons, it is imperative that the Government stop intervening in downstream production nodes that produce non-priority goods, especially as it monitors and supervises private companies.

Ideally, any intervention the Government makes should be oriented towards the strict supervision of the development of technology around priority areas: further intervention is unnecessary. Nevertheless, we must recognize that sometimes, as was the case in the development of some Asian economies, Government intervention can quickly correct problems, always assuming that effective surrogate management is found. Here, and bearing in mind that the order of priority should always be: the network, followed by upstream, midstream and downstream production nodes, any intervention should be to ensure the effectiveness of surrogate management. This, in turn, requires practical authority.

TEACHING AND RESEARCH

If sovereignty over technology is really desired, in the sense of ownership discussed in section **"The road to technological sovereignty"** regarding autochthony, autonomy and infrastructure, an excellent education system, that as well as primary, secondary and tertiary schooling also includes fourth level education, is vital. The main reason for this, although it is a means rather that an end, is if autochthony and autonomy is to be achieved, the products and/or services developed must be competitive in relation to foreign technological forces. This would not only result in a greater resistance to these forces, but also could eventually lead to the export of the technology.

Thus, any nation interested in the acquisition of technology must understand that in order to be competitive high level research must be undertaken. The establishment of advanced teaching and research institutes is thus essential.

Although there are certainly cases where these institutes need to specialize in a particular field, we believe it counterproductive for the government to impose areas of research, as they, and the inspiration behind them cannot be subject to government decree, especially when the country has not attained technological sovereignty. The institutes must then, be granted a degree of autonomy from the Government, even though they are financed by it. The main incentives that the Government could offer would be the opportunity to apply the results of projects involved to the development of technology in the real world. It is worth mentioning once again the importance of establishing technological parks within the boundaries of the linkage networks, as they could attract entrepreneurs trained in these institutes.

It is not absolutely necessary that the research institutes themselves be close to the centers of production. On the contrary, the distance between them and the production centers could help them to maintain their autonomy. In addition it is preferable that the institutes be located close to other centers of knowledge, such as universities.

It is important that the Government carry out rigorous monitoring and evaluations of all state educational institutions and check the results against their strategic plans for technological advancement. These evaluations should not be confused with incentives or awards.

To the extent that circumstances permit, and with the aim of capturing more stakeholders interested in the generation of knowledge, the results of the investigations undertaken must be freely available for their consultation and application. Of course, against the possibility of being subject to the GATT/WTO treaties, patenting research results should be seriously considered.

REFERENCES

Adelman, I., & Yeldan, E. (2000). Is this the end of economic development? In *Structural Change and Economic Dynamic* (pp. 95-109). Elselvier.

Briceño Guerrero, J. (1977). *La identificación Americana con la Europa Segunda*. Universidad de Los Andes.

Forrester, J. (1971). Counterintuitive behavior of social systems. *Technology Review, 73*(3), 52–68.

Fuenmayor, R. (1999). Venezuela: su enfermedad y crisis actual. *Estudios de Derecho P*, 335-358.

Fuenmayor, R. (2000). *Sentido y sinsentido del desarrollo*. Universidad de Los Andes - Consejo de publicaciones - Consejo de Estudios de Postgrado.

Fuenmayor, R., Aguilar, J., Anzola, M., Delgado, M., León, L., Mendialdúa, J., & Terán, O. (2007). *El estado venezolano y la posibilidad de la ciencia. En Debate abierto sobre misión ciencia*. Ediciones del Ministerio del Poder Popular para Ciencia y Tecnología.

Heidegger, M. (1982). The Question Concerning Technology. In M. Heidegger (Ed.), The Question Concerning Technology, and Other Essays (p. 224). Perennial.

Input–Output Model. (2014). Retrieved from http://en.wikipedia.org/wiki/Input-output_model

Law, A. M., & Kelton, W. D. (2000). *Simulation Modelling and Analysis*. McGraw Hill Higher Education.

León, L. (2004). Software libre y su rol en el desarrollo tecnológico del País. In *Software libre - Uso y desarrollo en la administración pública venezolana. Serie Conocimiento para el desarrollo sustentable*. Caracas, Venezuela: Ministerio de Ciencia y Tecnología.

Mapa Productivo de Venezuela. (2014). Retrieved from http://http://miv.cenditel.gob.ve/

Ramírez, L. (2012). *El parque automotor en la República Bolivariana de Venezuela, estratos medios de la población y elecciones 2012. período 1990-2011*. Retrieved from http://despertaruniversitario. org/2011/12/24/el-parque-automotor-en-la-republica-bolivariana-de-venezuela-estratos-medios-de-la-poblacion-y-elecciones-2012-periodo-1990-2011-y-parte-ii/

Robinson, S. (2004). *Simulation – The practice of model development and use*. Wiley.

Sterman, J. D. (2000). *Business Dynamics: Systems Thinking and Modeling for a Complex World*. New York: McGraw.

Wolfram, S. (2002). *A new kind of science*. Wolfram Media.

KEY TERMS AND DEFINITIONS

Downstream: Area where finished goods are produced.

Infrastructure: Physical structure needed for producing a given good.

Knowledge: Theoretical and technical understanding that is needed for producing a given good. In this context it is not about facts or information.

Linkage Network: Network interrelating productive entities, either as transportation, communication or institution. The direction of flow through the network is upstrem then midstream and finally downstream. Although feedback is possible, for simplicity it is not considered.

Midstream: Area where intermediate goods are produced. These serve as inputs to manufacturate terminal goods,.

Sawmill (Production Chain) Metaphor: Metaphor that interprets technology as a system of timber production that runs through a river. Trees are cut upstream and transported by the river towards a sawmill in the midstream. The sawmill then transforms trees into logs that are sent down river towards other factories that produce finished products downstream.

Upstream: Area associated with the exploitation of raw materials.

END NOTES

[1]   Quote from the Venezuelan philosopher José Manuel Briceño Guerrero.

[2]   From a local perspective, the environment could be considered as a "domestic force". It qualifies as "foreign", however, when we consider the environment in a global sense.

[3]   A far more detailed discussion of the concept of a public asset and of the process of alienation Venezuela has suffered is given in (Fuenmayor, et al., 2007)

Related References

To continue our tradition of advancing information science and technology research, we have compiled a list of recommended IGI Global readings. These references will provide additional information and guidance to further enrich your knowledge and assist you with your own research and future publications.

Aayeshah, W., & Bebawi, S. (2014). The Use of Facebook as a Pedagogical Platform for Developing Investigative Journalism Skills. In G. Mallia (Ed.), *The Social Classroom: Integrating Social Network Use in Education* (pp. 83–99). Hershey, PA: Information Science Reference; doi:10.4018/978-1-4666-4904-0.ch005

Adi, A., & Scotte, C. G. (2013). Barriers to Emerging Technology and Social Media Integration in Higher Education: Three Case Studies. In M. Pătruţ & B. Pătruţ (Eds.), *Social Media in Higher Education: Teaching in Web 2.0* (pp. 334–354). Hershey, PA: Information Science Reference; doi:10.4018/978-1-4666-2970-7.ch017

Agazzi, E. (2012). How Can the Problems of An Ethical Judgment on Science and Technology Be Correctly Approached? In R. Luppicini (Ed.), *Ethical Impact of Technological Advancements and Applications in Society* (pp. 30–38). Hershey, PA: Information Science Reference; doi:10.4018/978-1-4666-1773-5.ch003

Agina, A. M., Tennyson, R. D., & Kommers, P. (2013). Understanding Children's Private Speech and Self-Regulation Learning in Web 2.0: Updates of Vygotsky through Piaget and Future Recommendations. In P. Ordóñez de Pablos, H. Nigro, R. Tennyson, S. Gonzalez Cisaro, & W. Karwowski (Eds.), *Advancing Information Management through Semantic Web Concepts and Ontologies* (pp. 1–53). Hershey, PA: Information Science Reference; doi:10.4018/978-1-4666-2494-8.ch001

Ahrens, A., Bassus, O., & Zaščerinska, J. (2014). Enterprise 2.0 in Engineering Curriculum. In M. Cruz-Cunha, F. Moreira, & J. Varajão (Eds.), *Handbook of Research on Enterprise 2.0: Technological, Social, and Organizational Dimensions* (pp. 599–617). Hershey, PA: Business Science Reference; doi:10.4018/978-1-4666-4373-4.ch031

Akputu, O. K., Seng, K. P., & Lee, Y. L. (2014). Affect Recognition for Web 2.0 Intelligent E-Tutoring Systems: Exploration of Students' Emotional Feedback. In J. Pelet (Ed.), *E-Learning 2.0 Technologies and Web Applications in Higher Education* (pp. 188–215). Hershey, PA: Information Science Reference; doi:10.4018/978-1-4666-4876-0.ch010

Al-Hajri, S., & Tatnall, A. (2013). A Socio-Technical Study of the Adoption of Internet Technology in Banking, Re-Interpreted as an Innovation Using Innovation Translation. In A. Tatnall (Ed.), *Social and Professional Applications of Actor-Network Theory for Technology Development* (pp. 207–220). Hershey, PA: Information Science Reference; doi:10.4018/978-1-4666-2166-4.ch016

Al Hujran, O., Aloudat, A., & Altarawneh, I. (2013). Factors Influencing Citizen Adoption of E-Government in Developing Countries: The Case of Jordan. [IJTHI]. *International Journal of Technology and Human Interaction, 9*(2), 1–19. doi:10.4018/jthi.2013040101

Alavi, R., Islam, S., Jahankhani, H., & Al-Nemrat, A. (2013). Analyzing Human Factors for an Effective Information Security Management System. [IJSSE]. *International Journal of Secure Software Engineering, 4*(1), 50–74. doi:10.4018/jsse.2013010104

Altun, N. E., & Yildiz, S. (2013). Effects of Different Types of Tasks on Junior ELT Students' Use of Communication Strategies in Computer-Mediated Communication. [IJCALLT]. *International Journal of Computer-Assisted Language Learning and Teaching, 3*(2), 17–40. doi:10.4018/ijcallt.2013040102

Amaldi, P., & Smoker, A. (2013). An Organizational Study into the Concept of "Automation Policy" in a Safety Critical Socio-Technical System. [IJSKD]. *International Journal of Sociotechnology and Knowledge Development, 5*(2), 1–17. doi:10.4018/jskd.2013040101

An, I. S. (2013). Integrating Technology-Enhanced Student Self-Regulated Tasks into University Chinese Language Course. [IJCALLT]. *International Journal of Computer-Assisted Language Learning and Teaching, 3*(1), 1–15. doi:10.4018/ijcallt.2013010101

Andacht, F. (2013). The Tangible Lure of the Technoself in the Age of Reality Television. In R. Luppicini (Ed.), *Handbook of Research on Technoself: Identity in a Technological Society* (pp. 360–381). Hershey, PA: Information Science Reference; doi:10.4018/978-1-4666-2211-1.ch020

Anderson, A., & Petersen, A. (2012). Shaping the Ethics of an Emergent Field: Scientists' and Policymakers' Representations of Nanotechnologies. In R. Luppicini (Ed.), *Ethical Impact of Technological Advancements and Applications in Society* (pp. 219–231). Hershey, PA: Information Science Reference; doi:10.4018/978-1-4666-1773-5.ch017

Anderson, J. L. (2014). Games and the Development of Students' Civic Engagement and Ecological Stewardship. In J. Bishop (Ed.), *Gamification for Human Factors Integration: Social, Education, and Psychological Issues* (pp. 199–215). Hershey, PA: Information Science Reference; doi:10.4018/978-1-4666-5071-8.ch012

Ann, O. C., Lu, M. V., & Theng, L. B. (2014). A Face Based Real Time Communication for Physically and Speech Disabled People. In Assistive Technologies: Concepts, Methodologies, Tools, and Applications (pp. 1434-1460). Hershey, PA: Information Science Reference. doi:10.4018/978-1-4666-4422-9.ch075

Aricak, O. T., Tanrikulu, T., Siyahhan, S., & Kinay, H. (2013). Cyberbullying: The Bad and the Ugly Side of Information Age. In M. Pătruț & B. Pătruț (Eds.), *Social Media in Higher Education: Teaching in Web 2.0* (pp. 318–333). Hershey, PA: Information Science Reference; doi:10.4018/978-1-4666-2970-7.ch016

Ariely, G. (2011). Boundaries of Socio-Technical Systems and IT for Knowledge Development in Military Environments. [IJSKD]. *International Journal of Sociotechnology and Knowledge Development, 3*(3), 1–14. doi:10.4018/jskd.2011070101

Ariely, G. (2013). Boundaries of Socio-Technical Systems and IT for Knowledge Development in Military Environments. In J. Abdelnour-Nocera (Ed.), *Knowledge and Technological Development Effects on Organizational and Social Structures* (pp. 224–238). Hershey, PA: Information Science Reference; doi:10.4018/978-1-4666-2151-0.ch014

Arjunan, S., Kumar, D. K., Weghorn, H., & Naik, G. (2014). Facial Muscle Activity Patterns for Recognition of Utterances in Native and Foreign Language: Testing for its Reliability and Flexibility. In Assistive Technologies: Concepts, Methodologies, Tools, and Applications (pp. 1462-1480). Hershey, PA: Information Science Reference. doi:10.4018/978-1-4666-4422-9.ch076

Arling, P. A., Miech, E. J., & Arling, G. W. (2013). Comparing Electronic and Face-to-Face Communication in the Success of a Long-Term Care Quality Improvement Collaborative. [IJRQEH]. *International Journal of Reliable and Quality E-Healthcare*, 2(1), 1–10. doi:10.4018/ijrqeh.2013010101

Asghari-Oskoei, M., & Hu, H. (2014). Using Myoelectric Signals to Manipulate Assisting Robots and Rehabilitation Devices. In Assistive Technologies: Concepts, Methodologies, Tools, and Applications (pp. 970-990). Hershey, PA: Information Science Reference. doi:10.4018/978-1-4666-4422-9.ch049

Aspradaki, A. A. (2013). Deliberative Democracy and Nanotechnologies in Health. [IJT]. *International Journal of Technoethics*, 4(2), 1–14. doi:10.4018/jte.2013070101

Asselin, S. B. (2014). Assistive Technology in Higher Education. In Assistive Technologies: Concepts, Methodologies, Tools, and Applications (pp. 1196-1208). Hershey, PA: Information Science Reference. doi:10.4018/978-1-4666-4422-9.ch062

Auld, G., & Henderson, M. (2014). The Ethical Dilemmas of Social Networking Sites in Classroom Contexts. In G. Mallia (Ed.), *The Social Classroom: Integrating Social Network Use in Education* (pp. 192–207). Hershey, PA: Information Science Reference; doi:10.4018/978-1-4666-4904-0.ch010

Awwal, M. A. (2012). Influence of Age and Genders on the Relationship between Computer Self-Efficacy and Information Privacy Concerns. [IJTHI]. *International Journal of Technology and Human Interaction*, 8(1), 14–37. doi:10.4018/jthi.2012010102

Ballesté, F., & Torras, C. (2013). Effects of Human-Machine Integration on the Construction of Identity. In R. Luppicini (Ed.), *Handbook of Research on Technoself: Identity in a Technological Society* (pp. 574–591). Hershey, PA: Information Science Reference; doi:10.4018/978-1-4666-2211-1.ch030

Baporikar, N. (2014). Effective E-Learning Strategies for a Borderless World. In J. Pelet (Ed.), *E-Learning 2.0 Technologies and Web Applications in Higher Education* (pp. 22–44). Hershey, PA: Information Science Reference; doi:10.4018/978-1-4666-4876-0.ch002

Bardone, E. (2011). Unintended Affordances as Violent Mediators: Maladaptive Effects of Technologically Enriched Human Niches. [IJT]. *International Journal of Technoethics*, 2(4), 37–52. doi:10.4018/jte.2011100103

Basham, R. (2014). Surveilling the Elderly: Emerging Demographic Needs and Social Implications of RFID Chip Technology Use. In M. Michael & K. Michael (Eds.), *Uberveillance and the Social Implications of Microchip Implants: Emerging Technologies* (pp. 169–185). Hershey, PA: Information Science Reference; doi:10.4018/978-1-4666-4582-0.ch007

Bates, M. (2013). The Ur-Real Sonorous Envelope: Bridge between the Corporeal and the Online Technoself. In R. Luppicini (Ed.), *Handbook of Research on Technoself: Identity in a Technological Society* (pp. 272–292). Hershey, PA: Information Science Reference; doi:10.4018/978-1-4666-2211-1.ch015

Bauer, K. A. (2012). Transhumanism and Its Critics: Five Arguments against a Posthuman Future. In R. Luppicini (Ed.), *Ethical Impact of Technological Advancements and Applications in Society* (pp. 232–242). Hershey, PA: Information Science Reference; doi:10.4018/978-1-4666-1773-5.ch018

Bax, S. (2011). Normalisation Revisited: The Effective Use of Technology in Language Education. [IJCALLT]. *International Journal of Computer-Assisted Language Learning and Teaching*, *1*(2), 1–15. doi:10.4018/ijcallt.2011040101

Baya'a, N., & Daher, W. (2014). Facebook as an Educational Environment for Mathematics Learning. In G. Mallia (Ed.), *The Social Classroom: Integrating Social Network Use in Education* (pp. 171–190). Hershey, PA: Information Science Reference; doi:10.4018/978-1-4666-4904-0.ch009

Bayerl, P. S., & Janneck, M. (2013). Professional Online Profiles: The Impact of Personalization and Visual Gender Cues on Online Impression Formation. [IJSKD]. *International Journal of Sociotechnology and Knowledge Development*, *5*(3), 1–16. doi:10.4018/ijskd.2013070101

Bell, D., & Shirzad, S. R. (2013). Social Media Business Intelligence: A Pharmaceutical Domain Analysis Study. [IJSKD]. *International Journal of Sociotechnology and Knowledge Development*, *5*(3), 51–73. doi:10.4018/ijskd.2013070104

Bergmann, N. W. (2014). Ubiquitous Computing for Independent Living. In Assistive Technologies: Concepts, Methodologies, Tools, and Applications (pp. 679-692). Hershey, PA: Information Science Reference. doi:10.4018/978-1-4666-4422-9.ch033

Bertolotti, T. (2011). Facebook Has It: The Irresistible Violence of Social Cognition in the Age of Social Networking. [IJT]. *International Journal of Technoethics*, *2*(4), 71–83. doi:10.4018/jte.2011100105

Berzsenyi, C. (2014). Writing to Meet Your Match: Rhetoric and Self-Presentation for Four Online Daters. In H. Lim & F. Sudweeks (Eds.), *Innovative Methods and Technologies for Electronic Discourse Analysis* (pp. 210–234). Hershey, PA: Information Science Reference; doi:10.4018/978-1-4666-4426-7.ch010

Best, L. A., Buhay, D. N., McGuire, K., Gurholt, S., & Foley, S. (2014). The Use of Web 2.0 Technologies in Formal and Informal Learning Settings. In G. Mallia (Ed.), *The Social Classroom: Integrating Social Network Use in Education* (pp. 1–22). Hershey, PA: Information Science Reference; doi:10.4018/978-1-4666-4904-0.ch001

Bhattacharya, S. (2014). Model-Based Approaches for Scanning Keyboard Design: Present State and Future Directions. In Assistive Technologies: Concepts, Methodologies, Tools, and Applications (pp. 1497-1515). Hershey, PA: Information Science Reference. doi:10.4018/978-1-4666-4422-9.ch078

Bibby, S. (2011). Do Students Wish to 'Go Mobile'?: An Investigation into Student Use of PCs and Cell Phones. [IJCALLT]. *International Journal of Computer-Assisted Language Learning and Teaching*, *1*(2), 43–54. doi:10.4018/ijcallt.2011040104

Bishop, J. (2014). The Psychology of Trolling and Lurking: The Role of Defriending and Gamification for Increasing Participation in Online Communities Using Seductive Narratives. In J. Bishop (Ed.), *Gamification for Human Factors Integration: Social, Education, and Psychological Issues* (pp. 162–179). Hershey, PA: Information Science Reference; doi:10.4018/978-1-4666-5071-8.ch010

Bishop, J., & Goode, M. M. (2014). Towards a Subjectively Devised Parametric User Model for Analysing and Influencing Behaviour Online Using Neuroeconomics. In J. Bishop (Ed.), *Gamification for Human Factors Integration: Social, Education, and Psychological Issues* (pp. 80–95). Hershey, PA: Information Science Reference; doi:10.4018/978-1-4666-5071-8.ch005

Biswas, P. (2014). A Brief Survey on User Modelling in Human Computer Interaction. In Assistive Technologies: Concepts, Methodologies, Tools, and Applications (pp. 102-119). Hershey, PA: Information Science Reference. doi:10.4018/978-1-4666-4422-9.ch006

Black, D. (2013). The Digital Soul. In R. Luppicini (Ed.), *Handbook of Research on Technoself: Identity in a Technological Society* (pp. 157–174). Hershey, PA: Information Science Reference; doi:10.4018/978-1-4666-2211-1.ch009

Blake, S., Winsor, D. L., Burkett, C., & Allen, L. (2014). iPods, Internet and Apps, Oh My: Age Appropriate Technology in Early Childhood Educational Environments. In K-12 Education: Concepts, Methodologies, Tools, and Applications (pp. 1650-1668). Hershey, PA: Information Science Reference. doi:10.4018/978-1-4666-4502-8.ch095

Boghian, I. (2013). Using Facebook in Teaching. In M. Pătruţ & B. Pătruţ (Eds.), *Social Media in Higher Education: Teaching in Web 2.0* (pp. 86–103). Hershey, PA: Information Science Reference; doi:10.4018/978-1-4666-2970-7.ch005

Boling, E. C., & Beatty, J. (2014). Overcoming the Tensions and Challenges of Technology Integration: How Can We Best Support our Teachers? In K-12 Education: Concepts, Methodologies, Tools, and Applications (pp. 1504-1524). Hershey, PA: Information Science Reference. doi:10.4018/978-1-4666-4502-8.ch087

Bonanno, P. (2014). Designing Learning in Social Online Learning Environments: A Process-Oriented Approach. In G. Mallia (Ed.), *The Social Classroom: Integrating Social Network Use in Education* (pp. 40–61). Hershey, PA: Information Science Reference; doi:10.4018/978-1-4666-4904-0.ch003

Bongers, B., & Smith, S. (2014). Interactivating Rehabilitation through Active Multimodal Feedback and Guidance. In Assistive Technologies: Concepts, Methodologies, Tools, and Applications (pp. 1650-1674). Hershey, PA: Information Science Reference. doi:10.4018/978-1-4666-4422-9.ch087

Bottino, R. M., Ott, M., & Tavella, M. (2014). Serious Gaming at School: Reflections on Students' Performance, Engagement and Motivation. [IJGBL]. *International Journal of Game-Based Learning, 4*(1), 21–36. doi:10.4018/IJGBL.2014010102

Brad, S. (2014). Design for Quality of ICT-Aided Engineering Course Units. [IJQAETE]. *International Journal of Quality Assurance in Engineering and Technology Education, 3*(1), 52–80. doi:10.4018/ijqaete.2014010103

Braman, J., Thomas, U., Vincenti, G., Dudley, A., & Rodgers, K. (2014). Preparing Your Digital Legacy: Assessing Awareness of Digital Natives. In G. Mallia (Ed.), *The Social Classroom: Integrating Social Network Use in Education* (pp. 208–223). Hershey, PA: Information Science Reference; doi:10.4018/978-1-4666-4904-0.ch011

Bratitsis, T., & Demetriadis, S. (2013). Research Approaches in Computer-Supported Collaborative Learning. [IJeC]. *International Journal of e-Collaboration*, *9*(1), 1–8. doi:10.4018/jec.2013010101

Brick, B. (2012). The Role of Social Networking Sites for Language Learning in UK Higher Education: The Views of Learners and Practitioners. [IJCALLT]. *International Journal of Computer-Assisted Language Learning and Teaching*, *2*(3), 35–53. doi:10.4018/ijcallt.2012070103

Burke, M. E., & Speed, C. (2014). Knowledge Recovery: Applications of Technology and Memory. In M. Michael & K. Michael (Eds.), *Uberveillance and the Social Implications of Microchip Implants: Emerging Technologies* (pp. 133–142). Hershey, PA: Information Science Reference; doi:10.4018/978-1-4666-4582-0.ch005

Burton, A. M., Liu, H., Battersby, S., Brown, D., Sherkat, N., Standen, P., & Walker, M. (2014). The Use of Motion Tracking Technologies in Serious Games to Enhance Rehabilitation in Stroke Patients. In J. Bishop (Ed.), *Gamification for Human Factors Integration: Social, Education, and Psychological Issues* (pp. 148–161). Hershey, PA: Information Science Reference; doi:10.4018/978-1-4666-5071-8.ch009

Burusic, J., & Karabegovic, M. (2014). The Role of Students' Personality Traits in the Effective Use of Social Networking Sites in the Educational Context. In G. Mallia (Ed.), *The Social Classroom: Integrating Social Network Use in Education* (pp. 224–243). Hershey, PA: Information Science Reference; doi:10.4018/978-1-4666-4904-0.ch012

Busch, C. D., Lorenzo, A. M., Sánchez, I. M., González, B. G., García, T. P., Riveiro, L. N., & Loureiro, J. P. (2014). In-TIC for Mobile Devices: Support System for Communication with Mobile Devices for the Disabled. In Assistive Technologies: Concepts, Methodologies, Tools, and Applications (pp. 345-356). Hershey, PA: Information Science Reference. doi:10.4018/978-1-4666-4422-9.ch017

Bute, S. J. (2013). Integrating Social Media and Traditional Media within the Academic Environment. In M. Pătruţ & B. Pătruţ (Eds.), *Social Media in Higher Education: Teaching in Web 2.0* (pp. 75–85). Hershey, PA: Information Science Reference; doi:10.4018/978-1-4666-2970-7.ch004

Butler-Pascoe, M. E. (2011). The History of CALL: The Intertwining Paths of Technology and Second/Foreign Language Teaching. [IJCALLT]. *International Journal of Computer-Assisted Language Learning and Teaching*, *1*(1), 16–32. doi:10.4018/ijcallt.2011010102

Cabrera, L. (2012). Human Implants: A Suggested Framework to Set Priorities. In R. Luppicini (Ed.), *Ethical Impact of Technological Advancements and Applications in Society* (pp. 243–253). Hershey, PA: Information Science Reference; doi:10.4018/978-1-4666-1773-5.ch019

Cacho-Elizondo, S., Shahidi, N., & Tossan, V. (2013). Intention to Adopt a Text Message-based Mobile Coaching Service to Help Stop Smoking: Which Explanatory Variables? [IJTHI]. *International Journal of Technology and Human Interaction*, *9*(4), 1–19. doi:10.4018/ijthi.2013100101

Caldelli, R., Becarelli, R., Filippini, F., Picchioni, F., & Giorgetti, R. (2014). Electronic Voting by Means of Digital Terrestrial Television: The Infrastructure, Security Issues and a Real Test-Bed. In Assistive Technologies: Concepts, Methodologies, Tools, and Applications (pp. 905-915). Hershey, PA: Information Science Reference. doi:10.4018/978-1-4666-4422-9.ch045

Camacho, M. (2013). Making the Most of Informal and Situated Learning Opportunities through Mobile Learning. In M. Pătruţ & B. Pătruţ (Eds.), *Social Media in Higher Education: Teaching in Web 2.0* (pp. 355–370). Hershey, PA: Information Science Reference; doi:10.4018/978-1-4666-2970-7.ch018

Camilleri, V., Busuttil, L., & Montebello, M. (2014). MOOCs: Exploiting Networks for the Education of the Masses or Just a Trend? In G. Mallia (Ed.), *The Social Classroom: Integrating Social Network Use in Education* (pp. 348–366). Hershey, PA: Information Science Reference; doi:10.4018/978-1-4666-4904-0.ch018

Campos, P., Noronha, H., & Lopes, A. (2013). Work Analysis Methods in Practice: The Context of Collaborative Review of CAD Models. [IJSKD]. *International Journal of Sociotechnology and Knowledge Development*, 5(2), 34–44. doi:10.4018/jskd.2013040103

Cao, G. (2013). A Paradox Between Technological Autonomy and Ethical Heteronomy of Philosophy of Technology: Social Control System. [IJT]. *International Journal of Technoethics*, 4(1), 52–66. doi:10.4018/jte.2013010105

Carofiglio, V., & Abbattista, F. (2013). BCI-Based User-Centered Design for Emotionally-Driven User Experience. In M. Garcia-Ruiz (Ed.), *Cases on Usability Engineering: Design and Development of Digital Products* (pp. 299–320). Hershey, PA: Information Science Reference; doi:10.4018/978-1-4666-4046-7.ch013

Carpenter, J. (2013). Just Doesn't Look Right: Exploring the Impact of Humanoid Robot Integration into Explosive Ordnance Disposal Teams. In R. Luppicini (Ed.), *Handbook of Research on Technoself: Identity in a Technological Society* (pp. 609–636). Hershey, PA: Information Science Reference; doi:10.4018/978-1-4666-2211-1.ch032

Carroll, J. L. (2014). Wheelchairs as Assistive Technology: What a Special Educator Should Know. In Assistive Technologies: Concepts, Methodologies, Tools, and Applications (pp. 623-633). Hershey, PA: Information Science Reference. doi:10.4018/978-1-4666-4422-9.ch030

Casey, L. B., & Williamson, R. L. (2014). A Parent's Guide to Support Technologies for Preschool Students with Disabilities. In Assistive Technologies: Concepts, Methodologies, Tools, and Applications (pp. 1340-1356). Hershey, PA: Information Science Reference. doi:10.4018/978-1-4666-4422-9.ch071

Caviglione, L., Coccoli, M., & Merlo, A. (2013). On Social Network Engineering for Secure Web Data and Services. In L. Caviglione, M. Coccoli, & A. Merlo (Eds.), *Social Network Engineering for Secure Web Data and Services* (pp. 1–4). Hershey, PA: Information Science Reference; doi:10.4018/978-1-4666-3926-3.ch001

Chadwick, D. D., Fullwood, C., & Wesson, C. J. (2014). Intellectual Disability, Identity, and the Internet. In Assistive Technologies: Concepts, Methodologies, Tools, and Applications (pp. 198-223). Hershey, PA: Information Science Reference. doi:10.4018/978-1-4666-4422-9.ch011

Chao, L., Wen, Y., Chen, P., Lin, C., Lin, S., Guo, C., & Wang, W. (2012). The Development and Learning Effectiveness of a Teaching Module for the Algal Fuel Cell: A Renewable and Sustainable Battery. [IJTHI]. *International Journal of Technology and Human Interaction*, 8(4), 1–15. doi:10.4018/jthi.2012100101

Charnkit, P., & Tatnall, A. (2013). Knowledge Conversion Processes in Thai Public Organisations Seen as an Innovation: The Re-Analysis of a TAM Study Using Innovation Translation. In A. Tatnall (Ed.), *Social and Professional Applications of Actor-Network Theory for Technology Development* (pp. 88–102). Hershey, PA: Information Science Reference; doi:10.4018/978-1-4666-2166-4.ch008

Chen, E. T. (2014). Challenge and Complexity of Virtual Team Management. In E. Nikoi & K. Boateng (Eds.), *Collaborative Communication Processes and Decision Making in Organizations* (pp. 109–120). Hershey, PA: Business Science Reference; doi:10.4018/978-1-4666-4478-6.ch006

Chen, R., Xie, T., Lin, T., & Chen, Y. (2013). Adaptive Windows Layout Based on Evolutionary Multi-Objective Optimization. [IJTHI]. *International Journal of Technology and Human Interaction*, *9*(3), 63–72. doi:10.4018/jthi.2013070105

Chen, W., Juang, Y., Chang, S., & Wang, P. (2012). Informal Education of Energy Conservation: Theory, Promotion, and Policy Implication. [IJTHI]. *International Journal of Technology and Human Interaction*, *8*(4), 16–44. doi:10.4018/jthi.2012100102

Chino, T., Torii, K., Uchihira, N., & Hirabayashi, Y. (2013). Speech Interaction Analysis on Collaborative Work at an Elderly Care Facility. [IJSKD]. *International Journal of Sociotechnology and Knowledge Development*, *5*(2), 18–33. doi:10.4018/jskd.2013040102

Chiu, M. (2013). Gaps Between Valuing and Purchasing Green-Technology Products: Product and Gender Differences. [IJTHI]. *International Journal of Technology and Human Interaction*, *8*(3), 54–68. doi:10.4018/jthi.2012070106

Chivukula, V., & Shur, M. (2014). Web-Based Experimentation for Students with Learning Disabilities. In Assistive Technologies: Concepts, Methodologies, Tools, and Applications (pp. 1156-1172). Hershey, PA: Information Science Reference. doi:10.4018/978-1-4666-4422-9.ch060

Coakes, E., Bryant, A., Land, F., & Phippen, A. (2011). The Dark Side of Technology: Some Sociotechnical Reflections. [IJSKD]. *International Journal of Sociotechnology and Knowledge Development*, *3*(4), 40–51. doi:10.4018/ijskd.2011100104

Cole, I. J. (2013). Usability of Online Virtual Learning Environments: Key Issues for Instructors and Learners. In C. Gonzalez (Ed.), *Student Usability in Educational Software and Games: Improving Experiences* (pp. 41–58). Hershey, PA: Information Science Reference; doi:10.4018/978-1-4666-1987-6.ch002

Colombo, B., Antonietti, A., Sala, R., & Caravita, S. C. (2013). Blog Content and Structure, Cognitive Style and Metacognition. [IJTHI]. *International Journal of Technology and Human Interaction*, *9*(3), 1–17. doi:10.4018/jthi.2013070101

Constantinides, M. (2011). Integrating Technology on Initial Training Courses: A Survey Amongst CELTA Tutors. [IJCALLT]. *International Journal of Computer-Assisted Language Learning and Teaching*, *1*(2), 55–71. doi:10.4018/ijcallt.2011040105

Cook, R. G., & Crawford, C. M. (2013). Addressing Online Student Learning Environments and Socialization Through Developmental Research. In M. Khosrow-Pour (Ed.), *Cases on Assessment and Evaluation in Education* (pp. 504–536). Hershey, PA: Information Science Reference; doi:10.4018/978-1-4666-2621-8.ch021

Corritore, C. L., Wiedenbeck, S., Kracher, B., & Marble, R. P. (2012). Online Trust and Health Information Websites. [IJTHI]. *International Journal of Technology and Human Interaction, 8*(4), 92–115. doi:10.4018/jthi.2012100106

Covarrubias, M., Bordegoni, M., Cugini, U., & Gatti, E. (2014). Supporting Unskilled People in Manual Tasks through Haptic-Based Guidance. In Assistive Technologies: Concepts, Methodologies, Tools, and Applications (pp. 947-969). Hershey, PA: Information Science Reference. doi:10.4018/978-1-4666-4422-9.ch048

Coverdale, T. S., & Wilbon, A. D. (2013). The Impact of In-Group Membership on e-Loyalty of Women Online Shoppers: An Application of the Social Identity Approach to Website Design. [IJEA]. *International Journal of E-Adoption, 5*(1), 17–36. doi:10.4018/jea.2013010102

Crabb, P. B., & Stern, S. E. (2012). Technology Traps: Who Is Responsible? In R. Luppicini (Ed.), *Ethical Impact of Technological Advancements and Applications in Society* (pp. 39–46). Hershey, PA: Information Science Reference; doi:10.4018/978-1-4666-1773-5.ch004

Crespo, R. G., Martíne, O. S., Lovelle, J. M., García-Bustelo, B. C., Díaz, V. G., & Ordoñez de Pablos, P. (2014). Improving Cognitive Load on Students with Disabilities through Software Aids. In Assistive Technologies: Concepts, Methodologies, Tools, and Applications (pp. 1255-1268). Hershey, PA: Information Science Reference. doi:10.4018/978-1-4666-4422-9.ch066

Croasdaile, S., Jones, S., Ligon, K., Oggel, L., & Pruett, M. (2014). Supports for and Barriers to Implementing Assistive Technology in Schools. In Assistive Technologies: Concepts, Methodologies, Tools, and Applications (pp. 1118-1130). Hershey, PA: Information Science Reference. doi:10.4018/978-1-4666-4422-9.ch058

Cucchiarini, C., & Strik, H. (2014). Second Language Learners' Spoken Discourse: Practice and Corrective Feedback through Automatic Speech Recognition. In H. Lim & F. Sudweeks (Eds.), *Innovative Methods and Technologies for Electronic Discourse Analysis* (pp. 169–189). Hershey, PA: Information Science Reference; doi:10.4018/978-1-4666-4426-7.ch008

Dafoulas, G. A., & Saleeb, N. (2014). 3D Assistive Technologies and Advantageous Themes for Collaboration and Blended Learning of Users with Disabilities. In Assistive Technologies: Concepts, Methodologies, Tools, and Applications (pp. 421-453). Hershey, PA: Information Science Reference. doi:10.4018/978-1-4666-4422-9.ch021

Dai, Z., & Paasch, K. (2013). A Web-Based Interactive Questionnaire for PV Application. [IJSKD]. *International Journal of Sociotechnology and Knowledge Development, 5*(2), 82–93. doi:10.4018/jskd.2013040106

Daradoumis, T., & Lafuente, M. M. (2014). Studying the Suitability of Discourse Analysis Methods for Emotion Detection and Interpretation in Computer-Mediated Educational Discourse. In H. Lim & F. Sudweeks (Eds.), *Innovative Methods and Technologies for Electronic Discourse Analysis* (pp. 119–143). Hershey, PA: Information Science Reference; doi:10.4018/978-1-4666-4426-7.ch006

Davis, B., & Mason, P. (2014). Positioning Goes to Work: Computer-Aided Identification of Stance Shifts and Semantic Themes in Electronic Discourse Analysis. In H. Lim & F. Sudweeks (Eds.), *Innovative Methods and Technologies for Electronic Discourse Analysis* (pp. 394–413). Hershey, PA: Information Science Reference; doi:10.4018/978-1-4666-4426-7.ch018

Dogoriti, E., & Pange, J. (2014). Considerations for Online English Language Learning: The Use of Facebook in Formal and Informal Settings in Higher Education. In G. Mallia (Ed.), *The Social Classroom: Integrating Social Network Use in Education* (pp. 147–170). Hershey, PA: Information Science Reference; doi:10.4018/978-1-4666-4904-0.ch008

Donegan, M. (2014). Features of Gaze Control Systems. In Assistive Technologies: Concepts, Methodologies, Tools, and Applications (pp. 1055-1061). Hershey, PA: Information Science Reference. doi:10.4018/978-1-4666-4422-9.ch054

Douglas, G., Morton, H., & Jack, M. (2012). Remote Channel Customer Contact Strategies for Complaint Update Messages. [IJTHI]. *International Journal of Technology and Human Interaction*, *8*(2), 43–55. doi:10.4018/jthi.2012040103

Drake, J. R., & Byrd, T. A. (2013). Searching for Alternatives: Does Your Disposition Matter? [IJTHI]. *International Journal of Technology and Human Interaction*, *9*(1), 18–36. doi:10.4018/jthi.2013010102

Driouchi, A. (2013). ICTs and Socioeconomic Performance with Focus on ICTs and Health. In ICTs for Health, Education, and Socioeconomic Policies: Regional Cases (pp. 104-125). Hershey, PA: Information Science Reference. doi:10.4018/978-1-4666-3643-9.ch005

Driouchi, A. (2013). Social Deficits, Social Cohesion, and Prospects from ICTs. In ICTs for Health, Education, and Socioeconomic Policies: Regional Cases (pp. 230-251). Hershey, PA: Information Science Reference. doi:10.4018/978-1-4666-3643-9.ch011

Driouchi, A. (2013). Socioeconomic Reforms, Human Development, and the Millennium Development Goals with ICTs for Coordination. In ICTs for Health, Education, and Socioeconomic Policies: Regional Cases (pp. 211-229). Hershey, PA: Information Science Reference. doi:10.4018/978-1-4666-3643-9.ch010

Drula, G. (2013). Media and Communication Research Facing Social Media. In M. Pătruţ & B. Pătruţ (Eds.), *Social Media in Higher Education: Teaching in Web 2.0* (pp. 371–392). Hershey, PA: Information Science Reference; doi:10.4018/978-1-4666-2970-7.ch019

Druzhinina, O., Hvannberg, E. T., & Halldorsdottir, G. (2013). Feedback Fidelities in Three Different Types of Crisis Management Training Environments. [IJSKD]. *International Journal of Sociotechnology and Knowledge Development*, *5*(2), 45–62. doi:10.4018/jskd.2013040104

Eason, K., Waterson, P., & Davda, P. (2013). The Sociotechnical Challenge of Integrating Telehealth and Telecare into Health and Social Care for the Elderly. [IJSKD]. *International Journal of Sociotechnology and Knowledge Development*, *5*(4), 14–26. doi:10.4018/ijskd.2013100102

Edenius, M., & Rämö, H. (2011). An Office on the Go: Professional Workers, Smartphones and the Return of Place. [IJTHI]. *International Journal of Technology and Human Interaction*, *7*(1), 37–55. doi:10.4018/jthi.2011010103

Eke, D. O. (2011). ICT Integration in Nigeria: The Socio-Cultural Constraints. [IJTHI]. *International Journal of Technology and Human Interaction*, *7*(2), 21–27. doi:10.4018/jthi.2011040103

Evett, L., Ridley, A., Keating, L., Merritt, P., Shopland, N., & Brown, D. (2014). Designing Serious Games for People with Disabilities: Game, Set, and Match to the Wii. In J. Bishop (Ed.), *Gamification for Human Factors Integration: Social, Education, and Psychological Issues* (pp. 97–105). Hershey, PA: Information Science Reference; doi:10.4018/978-1-4666-5071-8.ch006

Evmenova, A. S., & Behrmann, M. M. (2014). Communication Technology Integration in the Content Areas for Students with High-Incidence Disabilities: A Case Study of One School System. In Assistive Technologies: Concepts, Methodologies, Tools, and Applications (pp. 26-53). Hershey, PA: Information Science Reference. doi:10.4018/978-1-4666-4422-9.ch003

Evmenova, A. S., & King-Sears, M. E. (2014). Technology and Literacy for Students with Disabilities. In Assistive Technologies: Concepts, Methodologies, Tools, and Applications (pp. 1269-1291). Hershey, PA: Information Science Reference. doi:10.4018/978-1-4666-4422-9.ch067

Ewais, A., & De Troyer, O. (2013). Usability Evaluation of an Adaptive 3D Virtual Learning Environment. [IJVPLE]. *International Journal of Virtual and Personal Learning Environments*, 4(1), 16–31. doi:10.4018/jvple.2013010102

Farrell, H. J. (2014). The Student with Complex Education Needs: Assistive and Augmentative Information and Communication Technology in a Ten-Week Music Program. In K-12 Education: Concepts, Methodologies, Tools, and Applications (pp. 1436-1472). Hershey, PA: Information Science Reference. doi:10.4018/978-1-4666-4502-8.ch084

Fathulla, K. (2012). Rethinking Human and Society's Relationship with Technology. [IJSKD]. *International Journal of Sociotechnology and Knowledge Development*, 4(2), 21–28. doi:10.4018/jskd.2012040103

Fidler, C. S., Kanaan, R. K., & Rogerson, S. (2011). Barriers to e-Government Implementation in Jordan: The Role of Wasta. [IJTHI]. *International Journal of Technology and Human Interaction*, 7(2), 9–20. doi:10.4018/jthi.2011040102

Fischer, G., & Herrmann, T. (2013). Socio-Technical Systems: A Meta-Design Perspective. In J. Abdelnour-Nocera (Ed.), *Knowledge and Technological Development Effects on Organizational and Social Structures* (pp. 1–36). Hershey, PA: Information Science Reference; doi:10.4018/978-1-4666-2151-0.ch001

Foreman, J., & Borkman, T. (2014). Learning Sociology in a Massively Multi-Student Online Learning Environment. In J. Bishop (Ed.), *Gamification for Human Factors Integration: Social, Education, and Psychological Issues* (pp. 216–224). Hershey, PA: Information Science Reference; doi:10.4018/978-1-4666-5071-8.ch013

Fornaciari, F. (2013). The Language of Technoself: Storytelling, Symbolic Interactionism, and Online Identity. In R. Luppicini (Ed.), *Handbook of Research on Technoself: Identity in a Technological Society* (pp. 64–83). Hershey, PA: Information Science Reference; doi:10.4018/978-1-4666-2211-1.ch004

Fox, J., & Ahn, S. J. (2013). Avatars: Portraying, Exploring, and Changing Online and Offline Identities. In R. Luppicini (Ed.), *Handbook of Research on Technoself: Identity in a Technological Society* (pp. 255–271). Hershey, PA: Information Science Reference; doi:10.4018/978-1-4666-2211-1.ch014

Fox, W. P., Binstock, J., & Minutas, M. (2013). Modeling and Methodology for Incorporating Existing Technologies to Produce Higher Probabilities of Detecting Suicide Bombers. [IJORIS]. *International Journal of Operations Research and Information Systems*, 4(3), 1–18. doi:10.4018/joris.2013070101

Franchi, E., & Tomaiuolo, M. (2013). Distributed Social Platforms for Confidentiality and Resilience. In L. Caviglione, M. Coccoli, & A. Merlo (Eds.), *Social Network Engineering for Secure Web Data and Services* (pp. 114–136). Hershey, PA: Information Science Reference; doi:10.4018/978-1-4666-3926-3.ch006

Frigo, C. A., & Pavan, E. E. (2014). Prosthetic and Orthotic Devices. In Assistive Technologies: Concepts, Methodologies, Tools, and Applications (pp. 549-613). Hershey, PA: Information Science Reference. doi:10.4018/978-1-4666-4422-9.ch028

Fuhrer, C., & Cucchi, A. (2012). Relations Between Social Capital and Use of ICT: A Social Network Analysis Approach. [IJTHI]. *International Journal of Technology and Human Interaction*, *8*(2), 15–42. doi:10.4018/jthi.2012040102

Galinski, C., & Beckmann, H. (2014). Concepts for Enhancing Content Quality and eAccessibility: In General and in the Field of eProcurement. In Assistive Technologies: Concepts, Methodologies, Tools, and Applications (pp. 180-197). Hershey, PA: Information Science Reference. doi:10.4018/978-1-4666-4422-9.ch010

Galván, J. M., & Luppicini, R. (2012). The Humanity of the Human Body: Is Homo Cybersapien a New Species? [IJT]. *International Journal of Technoethics*, *3*(2), 1–8. doi:10.4018/jte.2012040101

García-Gómez, A. (2013). Technoself-Presentation on Social Networks: A Gender-Based Approach. In R. Luppicini (Ed.), *Handbook of Research on Technoself: Identity in a Technological Society* (pp. 382–398). Hershey, PA: Information Science Reference; doi:10.4018/978-1-4666-2211-1.ch021

Gill, L., Hathway, E. A., Lange, E., Morgan, E., & Romano, D. (2013). Coupling Real-Time 3D Landscape Models with Microclimate Simulations. [IJEPR]. *International Journal of E-Planning Research*, *2*(1), 1–19. doi:10.4018/ijepr.2013010101

Godé, C., & Lebraty, J. (2013). Improving Decision Making in Extreme Situations: The Case of a Military Decision Support System. [IJTHI]. *International Journal of Technology and Human Interaction*, *9*(1), 1–17. doi:10.4018/jthi.2013010101

Griol, D., Callejas, Z., & López-Cózar, R. (2014). Conversational Metabots for Educational Applications in Virtual Worlds. In Assistive Technologies: Concepts, Methodologies, Tools, and Applications (pp. 1405-1433). Hershey, PA: Information Science Reference. doi:10.4018/978-1-4666-4422-9.ch074

Griol Barres, D., Callejas Carrión, Z., Molina López, J. M., & Sanchis de Miguel, A. (2014). Towards the Use of Dialog Systems to Facilitate Inclusive Education. In Assistive Technologies: Concepts, Methodologies, Tools, and Applications (pp. 1292-1312). Hershey, PA: Information Science Reference. doi:10.4018/978-1-4666-4422-9.ch068

Groba, B., Pousada, T., & Nieto, L. (2014). Assistive Technologies, Tools and Resources for the Access and Use of Information and Communication Technologies by People with Disabilities. In Assistive Technologies: Concepts, Methodologies, Tools, and Applications (pp. 246-260). Hershey, PA: Information Science Reference. doi:10.4018/978-1-4666-4422-9.ch013

Groß, M. (2013). Personal Knowledge Management and Social Media: What Students Need to Learn for Business Life. In M. Pătruţ & B. Pătruţ (Eds.), *Social Media in Higher Education: Teaching in Web 2.0* (pp. 124–143). Hershey, PA: Information Science Reference; doi:10.4018/978-1-4666-2970-7.ch007

Gu, L., Aiken, M., Wang, J., & Wibowo, K. (2011). The Influence of Information Control upon Online Shopping Behavior. [IJTHI]. *International Journal of Technology and Human Interaction, 7*(1), 56–66. doi:10.4018/jthi.2011010104

Hainz, T. (2012). Value Lexicality and Human Enhancement. [IJT]. *International Journal of Technoethics, 3*(4), 54–65. doi:10.4018/jte.2012100105

Harnesk, D., & Lindström, J. (2014). Exploring Socio-Technical Design of Crisis Management Information Systems. In Crisis Management: Concepts, Methodologies, Tools and Applications (pp. 514-530). Hershey, PA: Information Science Reference. doi:10.4018/978-1-4666-4707-7.ch023

Hicks, D. (2014). Ethics in the Age of Technological Change and its Impact on the Professional Identity of Librarians. In *Technology and Professional Identity of Librarians: The Making of the Cybrarian* (pp. 168–187). Hershey, PA: Information Science Reference; doi:10.4018/978-1-4666-4735-0.ch009

Hicks, D. (2014). Technology, Profession, Identity. In *Technology and Professional Identity of Librarians: The Making of the Cybrarian* (pp. 1–20). Hershey, PA: Information Science Reference; doi:10.4018/978-1-4666-4735-0.ch001

Hirata, M., Yanagisawa, T., Matsushita, K., Sugata, H., Kamitani, Y., Suzuki, T., . . . Yoshimine, T. (2014). Brain-Machine Interface Using Brain Surface Electrodes: Real-Time Robotic Control and a Fully Implantable Wireless System. In Assistive Technologies: Concepts, Methodologies, Tools, and Applications (pp. 1535-1548). Hershey, PA: Information Science Reference. doi:10.4018/978-1-4666-4422-9.ch080

Hodge, B. (2014). Critical Electronic Discourse Analysis: Social and Cultural Research in the Electronic Age. In H. Lim & F. Sudweeks (Eds.), *Innovative Methods and Technologies for Electronic Discourse Analysis* (pp. 191–209). Hershey, PA: Information Science Reference; doi:10.4018/978-1-4666-4426-7.ch009

Hoey, J., Poupart, P., Boutilier, C., & Mihailidis, A. (2014). POMDP Models for Assistive Technology. In Assistive Technologies: Concepts, Methodologies, Tools, and Applications (pp. 120-140). Hershey, PA: Information Science Reference. doi:10.4018/978-1-4666-4422-9.ch007

Hogg, S. (2014). An Informal Use of Facebook to Encourage Student Collaboration and Motivation for Off Campus Activities. In G. Mallia (Ed.), *The Social Classroom: Integrating Social Network Use in Education* (pp. 23–39). Hershey, PA: Information Science Reference; doi:10.4018/978-1-4666-4904-0.ch002

Holmqvist, E., & Buchholz, M. (2014). A Model for Gaze Control Assessments and Evaluation. In Assistive Technologies: Concepts, Methodologies, Tools, and Applications (pp. 332-343). Hershey, PA: Information Science Reference. doi:10.4018/978-1-4666-4422-9.ch016

Hsiao, S., Chen, D., Yang, C., Huang, H., Lu, Y., Huang, H., & Lin, Y. et al. (2013). Chemical-Free and Reusable Cellular Analysis: Electrochemical Impedance Spectroscopy with a Transparent ITO Culture Chip. [IJTHI]. *International Journal of Technology and Human Interaction, 8*(3), 1–9. doi:10.4018/jthi.2012070101

Hsu, M., Yang, C., Wang, C., & Lin, Y. (2013). Simulation-Aided Optimal Microfluidic Sorting for Monodispersed Microparticles. [IJTHI]. *International Journal of Technology and Human Interaction, 8*(3), 10–18. doi:10.4018/jthi.2012070102

Huang, W. D., & Tettegah, S. Y. (2014). Cognitive Load and Empathy in Serious Games: A Conceptual Framework. In J. Bishop (Ed.), *Gamification for Human Factors Integration: Social, Education, and Psychological Issues* (pp. 17–30). Hershey, PA: Information Science Reference; doi:10.4018/978-1-4666-5071-8.ch002

Huseyinov, I. N. (2014). Fuzzy Linguistic Modelling in Multi Modal Human Computer Interaction: Adaptation to Cognitive Styles using Multi Level Fuzzy Granulation Method. In Assistive Technologies: Concepts, Methodologies, Tools, and Applications (pp. 1481-1496). Hershey, PA: Information Science Reference. doi:10.4018/978-1-4666-4422-9.ch077

Hwa, S. P., Weei, P. S., & Len, L. H. (2012). The Effects of Blended Learning Approach through an Interactive Multimedia E-Book on Students' Achievement in Learning Chinese as a Second Language at Tertiary Level. [IJCALLT]. *International Journal of Computer-Assisted Language Learning and Teaching*, 2(1), 35–50. doi:10.4018/ijcallt.2012010104

Iglesias, A., Ruiz-Mezcua, B., López, J. F., & Figueroa, D. C. (2014). New Communication Technologies for Inclusive Education in and outside the Classroom. In Assistive Technologies: Concepts, Methodologies, Tools, and Applications (pp. 1675-1689). Hershey, PA: Information Science Reference. doi:10.4018/978-1-4666-4422-9.ch088

Inghilterra, X., & Ravatua-Smith, W. S. (2014). Online Learning Communities: Use of Micro Blogging for Knowledge Construction. In J. Pelet (Ed.), *E-Learning 2.0 Technologies and Web Applications in Higher Education* (pp. 107–128). Hershey, PA: Information Science Reference; doi:10.4018/978-1-4666-4876-0.ch006

Ionescu, A. (2013). Cyber Identity: Our Alter-Ego? In R. Luppicini (Ed.), *Handbook of Research on Technoself: Identity in a Technological Society* (pp. 189–203). Hershey, PA: Information Science Reference; doi:10.4018/978-1-4666-2211-1.ch011

Jan, Y., Lin, M., Shiao, K., Wei, C., Huang, L., & Sung, Q. (2013). Development of an Evaluation Instrument for Green Building Literacy among College Students in Taiwan. [IJTHI]. *International Journal of Technology and Human Interaction*, 8(3), 31–45. doi:10.4018/jthi.2012070104

Jawadi, N. (2013). E-Leadership and Trust Management: Exploring the Moderating Effects of Team Virtuality. [IJTHI]. *International Journal of Technology and Human Interaction*, 9(3), 18–35. doi:10.4018/jthi.2013070102

Jiménez-Castillo, D., & Fernández, R. S. (2014). The Impact of Combining Video Podcasting and Lectures on Students' Assimilation of Additional Knowledge: An Empirical Examination. In J. Pelet (Ed.), *E-Learning 2.0 Technologies and Web Applications in Higher Education* (pp. 65–87). Hershey, PA: Information Science Reference; doi:10.4018/978-1-4666-4876-0.ch004

Jin, L. (2013). A New Trend in Education: Technoself Enhanced Social Learning. In R. Luppicini (Ed.), *Handbook of Research on Technoself: Identity in a Technological Society* (pp. 456–473). Hershey, PA: Information Science Reference; doi:10.4018/978-1-4666-2211-1.ch025

Johansson, L. (2012). The Functional Morality of Robots. In R. Luppicini (Ed.), *Ethical Impact of Technological Advancements and Applications in Society* (pp. 254–262). Hershey, PA: Information Science Reference; doi:10.4018/978-1-4666-1773-5.ch020

Johansson, L. (2013). Robots and the Ethics of Care. [IJT]. *International Journal of Technoethics*, 4(1), 67–82. doi:10.4018/jte.2013010106

Johri, A., Dufour, M., Lo, J., & Shanahan, D. (2013). Adwiki: Socio-Technical Design for Mananging Advising Knowledge in a Higher Education Context. [IJSKD]. *International Journal of Sociotechnology and Knowledge Development*, *5*(1), 37–59. doi:10.4018/jskd.2013010104

Jones, M. G., Schwilk, C. L., & Bateman, D. F. (2014). Reading by Listening: Access to Books in Audio Format for College Students with Print Disabilities. In Assistive Technologies: Concepts, Methodologies, Tools, and Applications (pp. 454-477). Hershey, PA: Information Science Reference. doi:10.4018/978-1-4666-4422-9.ch022

Kaba, B., & Osei-Bryson, K. (2012). An Empirical Investigation of External Factors Influencing Mobile Technology Use in Canada: A Preliminary Study. [IJTHI]. *International Journal of Technology and Human Interaction*, *8*(2), 1–14. doi:10.4018/jthi.2012040101

Kampf, C. E. (2012). Revealing the Socio-Technical Design of Global E-Businesses: A Case of Digital Artists Engaging in Radical Transparency. [IJSKD]. *International Journal of Sociotechnology and Knowledge Development*, *4*(4), 18–31. doi:10.4018/jskd.2012100102

Kandroudi, M., & Bratitsis, T. (2014). Classifying Facebook Usage in the Classroom or Around It. In G. Mallia (Ed.), *The Social Classroom: Integrating Social Network Use in Education* (pp. 62–81). Hershey, PA: Information Science Reference; doi:10.4018/978-1-4666-4904-0.ch004

Kidd, P. T. (2014). Social Networking Technologies as a Strategic Tool for the Development of Sustainable Production and Consumption: Applications to Foster the Agility Needed to Adapt Business Models in Response to the Challenges Posed by Climate Change. In Sustainable Practices: Concepts, Methodologies, Tools and Applications (pp. 974-987). Hershey, PA: Information Science Reference. doi:10.4018/978-1-4666-4852-4.ch054

Kirby, S. D., & Sellers, D. M. (2014). The Live-Ability House: A Collaborative Adventure in Discovery Learning. In Assistive Technologies: Concepts, Methodologies, Tools, and Applications (pp. 1626-1649). Hershey, PA: Information Science Reference. doi:10.4018/978-1-4666-4422-9.ch086

Kitchenham, A., & Bowes, D. (2014). Voice/Speech Recognition Software: A Discussion of the Promise for Success and Practical Suggestions for Implementation. In Assistive Technologies: Concepts, Methodologies, Tools, and Applications (pp. 1005-1011). Hershey, PA: Information Science Reference. doi:10.4018/978-1-4666-4422-9.ch051

Konrath, S. (2013). The Empathy Paradox: Increasing Disconnection in the Age of Increasing Connection. In R. Luppicini (Ed.), *Handbook of Research on Technoself: Identity in a Technological Society* (pp. 204–228). Hershey, PA: Information Science Reference; doi:10.4018/978-1-4666-2211-1.ch012

Koutsabasis, P., & Istikopoulou, T. G. (2013). Perceived Website Aesthetics by Users and Designers: Implications for Evaluation Practice. [IJTHI]. *International Journal of Technology and Human Interaction*, *9*(2), 39–52. doi:10.4018/jthi.2013040103

Kraft, E., & Wang, J. (2012). An Exploratory Study of the Cyberbullying and Cyberstalking Experiences and Factors Related to Victimization of Students at a Public Liberal Arts College. In R. Luppicini (Ed.), *Ethical Impact of Technological Advancements and Applications in Society* (pp. 113–131). Hershey, PA: Information Science Reference; doi:10.4018/978-1-4666-1773-5.ch009

Kulman, R., Stoner, G., Ruffolo, L., Marshall, S., Slater, J., Dyl, A., & Cheng, A. (2014). Teaching Executive Functions, Self-Management, and Ethical Decision-Making through Popular Videogame Play. In Assistive Technologies: Concepts, Methodologies, Tools, and Applications (pp. 771-785). Hershey, PA: Information Science Reference. doi:10.4018/978-1-4666-4422-9.ch039

Kunc, L., Míkovec, Z., & Slavík, P. (2013). Avatar and Dialog Turn-Yielding Phenomena. [IJTHI]. *International Journal of Technology and Human Interaction*, 9(2), 66–88. doi:10.4018/jthi.2013040105

Kuo, N., & Dai, Y. (2012). Applying the Theory of Planned Behavior to Predict Low-Carbon Tourism Behavior: A Modified Model from Taiwan. [IJTHI]. *International Journal of Technology and Human Interaction*, 8(4), 45–62. doi:10.4018/jthi.2012100103

Kurt, S. (2014). Accessibility Issues of Educational Web Sites. In Assistive Technologies: Concepts, Methodologies, Tools, and Applications (pp. 54-62). Hershey, PA: Information Science Reference. doi:10.4018/978-1-4666-4422-9.ch004

Kuzma, J. (2013). Empirical Study of Cyber Harassment among Social Networks. [IJTHI]. *International Journal of Technology and Human Interaction*, 9(2), 53–65. doi:10.4018/jthi.2013040104

Kyriakaki, G., & Matsatsinis, N. (2014). Pedagogical Evaluation of E-Learning Websites with Cognitive Objectives. In D. Yannacopoulos, P. Manolitzas, N. Matsatsinis, & E. Grigoroudis (Eds.), *Evaluating Websites and Web Services: Interdisciplinary Perspectives on User Satisfaction* (pp. 224–240). Hershey, PA: Information Science Reference; doi:10.4018/978-1-4666-5129-6.ch013

Lee, H., & Baek, E. (2012). Facilitating Deep Learning in a Learning Community. [IJTHI]. *International Journal of Technology and Human Interaction*, 8(1), 1–13. doi:10.4018/jthi.2012010101

Lee, W., Wu, T., Cheng, Y., Chuang, Y., & Sheu, S. (2013). Using the Kalman Filter for Auto Bit-rate H.264 Streaming Based on Human Interaction. [IJTHI]. *International Journal of Technology and Human Interaction*, 9(4), 58–74. doi:10.4018/ijthi.2013100104

Li, Y., Guo, N. Y., & Ranieri, M. (2014). Designing an Online Interactive Learning Program to Improve Chinese Migrant Children's Internet Skills: A Case Study at Hangzhou Minzhu Experimental School. In Z. Yang, H. Yang, D. Wu, & S. Liu (Eds.), *Transforming K-12 Classrooms with Digital Technology* (pp. 249–265). Hershey, PA: Information Science Reference; doi:10.4018/978-1-4666-4538-7.ch013

Lin, C., Chu, L., & Hsu, H. (2013). Study on the Performance and Exhaust Emissions of Motorcycle Engine Fuelled with Hydrogen-Gasoline Compound Fuel. [IJTHI]. *International Journal of Technology and Human Interaction*, 8(3), 69–81. doi:10.4018/jthi.2012070107

Lin, L. (2013). Multiple Dimensions of Multitasking Phenomenon. [IJTHI]. *International Journal of Technology and Human Interaction*, 9(1), 37–49. doi:10.4018/jthi.2013010103

Lin, T., Li, X., Wu, Z., & Tang, N. (2013). Automatic Cognitive Load Classification Using High-Frequency Interaction Events: An Exploratory Study. [IJTHI]. *International Journal of Technology and Human Interaction*, 9(3), 73–88. doi:10.4018/jthi.2013070106

Lin, T., Wu, Z., Tang, N., & Wu, S. (2013). Exploring the Effects of Display Characteristics on Presence and Emotional Responses of Game Players. [IJTHI]. *International Journal of Technology and Human Interaction*, 9(1), 50–63. doi:10.4018/jthi.2013010104

Lin, T., Xie, T., Mou, Y., & Tang, N. (2013). Markov Chain Models for Menu Item Prediction. [IJTHI]. *International Journal of Technology and Human Interaction, 9*(4), 75–94. doi:10.4018/ijthi.2013100105

Lin, X., & Luppicini, R. (2011). Socio-Technical Influences of Cyber Espionage: A Case Study of the GhostNet System. [IJT]. *International Journal of Technoethics, 2*(2), 65–77. doi:10.4018/jte.2011040105

Linek, S. B., Marte, B., & Albert, D. (2014). Background Music in Educational Games: Motivational Appeal and Cognitive Impact. In J. Bishop (Ed.), *Gamification for Human Factors Integration: Social, Education, and Psychological Issues* (pp. 259–271). Hershey, PA: Information Science Reference; doi:10.4018/978-1-4666-5071-8.ch016

Lipschutz, R. D., & Hester, R. J. (2014). We Are the Borg! Human Assimilation into Cellular Society. In M. Michael & K. Michael (Eds.), *Uberveillance and the Social Implications of Microchip Implants: Emerging Technologies* (pp. 366–407). Hershey, PA: Information Science Reference; doi:10.4018/978-1-4666-4582-0.ch016

Liu, C., Zhong, Y., Ozercan, S., & Zhu, Q. (2013). Facilitating 3D Virtual World Learning Environments Creation by Non-Technical End Users through Template-Based Virtual World Instantiation. [IJVPLE]. *International Journal of Virtual and Personal Learning Environments, 4*(1), 32–48. doi:10.4018/jvple.2013010103

Liu, F., Lo, H., Su, C., Lou, D., & Lee, W. (2013). High Performance Reversible Data Hiding for Mobile Applications and Human Interaction. [IJTHI]. *International Journal of Technology and Human Interaction, 9*(4), 41–57. doi:10.4018/ijthi.2013100103

Liu, H. (2012). From Cold War Island to Low Carbon Island: A Study of Kinmen Island. [IJTHI]. *International Journal of Technology and Human Interaction, 8*(4), 63–74. doi:10.4018/jthi.2012100104

Lixun, Z., Dapeng, B., & Lei, Y. (2014). Design of and Experimentation with a Walking Assistance Robot. In Assistive Technologies: Concepts, Methodologies, Tools, and Applications (pp. 1600-1605). Hershey, PA: Information Science Reference. doi:10.4018/978-1-4666-4422-9.ch084

Low, R., Jin, P., & Sweller, J. (2014). Instructional Design in Digital Environments and Availability of Mental Resources for the Aged Subpopulation. In Assistive Technologies: Concepts, Methodologies, Tools, and Applications (pp. 1131-1154). Hershey, PA: Information Science Reference. doi:10.4018/978-1-4666-4422-9.ch059

Luczak, H., Schlick, C. M., Jochems, N., Vetter, S., & Kausch, B. (2014). Touch Screens for the Elderly: Some Models and Methods, Prototypical Development and Experimental Evaluation of Human-Computer Interaction Concepts for the Elderly. In Assistive Technologies: Concepts, Methodologies, Tools, and Applications (pp. 377-396). Hershey, PA: Information Science Reference. doi:10.4018/978-1-4666-4422-9.ch019

Luor, T., Lu, H., Johanson, R. E., & Yu, H. (2012). Minding the Gap Between First and Continued Usage of a Corporate E-Learning English-language Program. [IJTHI]. *International Journal of Technology and Human Interaction, 8*(1), 55–74. doi:10.4018/jthi.2012010104

Luppicini, R. (2013). The Emerging Field of Technoself Studies (TSS). In R. Luppicini (Ed.), *Handbook of Research on Technoself: Identity in a Technological Society* (pp. 1–25). Hershey, PA: Information Science Reference; doi:10.4018/978-1-4666-2211-1.ch001

Magnani, L. (2012). Material Cultures and Moral Mediators in Human Hybridization. In R. Luppicini (Ed.), *Ethical Impact of Technological Advancements and Applications in Society* (pp. 1–20). Hershey, PA: Information Science Reference; doi:10.4018/978-1-4666-1773-5.ch001

Maher, D. (2014). Learning in the Primary School Classroom using the Interactive Whiteboard. In K-12 Education: Concepts, Methodologies, Tools, and Applications (pp. 526-538). Hershey, PA: Information Science Reference. doi:10.4018/978-1-4666-4502-8.ch031

Manolache, M., & Patrut, M. (2013). The Use of New Web-Based Technologies in Strategies of Teaching Gender Studies. In M. Pătruţ & B. Pătruţ (Eds.), *Social Media in Higher Education: Teaching in Web 2.0* (pp. 45–74). Hershey, PA: Information Science Reference; doi:10.4018/978-1-4666-2970-7.ch003

Manthiou, A., & Chiang, L., & Liang (Rebecca) Tang. (2013). Identifying and Responding to Customer Needs on Facebook Fan Pages. [IJTHI]. *International Journal of Technology and Human Interaction, 9*(3), 36–52. doi:10.4018/jthi.2013070103

Marengo, A., Pagano, A., & Barbone, A. (2013). An Assessment of Customer's Preferences and Improve Brand Awareness Implementation of Social CRM in an Automotive Company. [IJTD]. *International Journal of Technology Diffusion, 4*(1), 1–15. doi:10.4018/jtd.2013010101

Martin, I., Kear, K., Simpkins, N., & Busvine, J. (2013). Social Negotiations in Web Usability Engineering. In M. Garcia-Ruiz (Ed.), *Cases on Usability Engineering: Design and Development of Digital Products* (pp. 26–56). Hershey, PA: Information Science Reference; doi:10.4018/978-1-4666-4046-7.ch002

Martins, T., Carvalho, V., & Soares, F. (2014). An Overview on the Use of Serious Games in Physical Therapy and Rehabilitation. In Assistive Technologies: Concepts, Methodologies, Tools, and Applications (pp. 758-770). Hershey, PA: Information Science Reference. doi:10.4018/978-1-4666-4422-9.ch038

Mathew, D. (2013). Online Anxiety: Implications for Educational Design in a Web 2.0 World. In M. Pătruţ & B. Pătruţ (Eds.), *Social Media in Higher Education: Teaching in Web 2.0* (pp. 305–317). Hershey, PA: Information Science Reference; doi:10.4018/978-1-4666-2970-7.ch015

Mazzanti, I., Maolo, A., & Antonicelli, R. (2014). E-Health and Telemedicine in the Elderly: State of the Art. In Assistive Technologies: Concepts, Methodologies, Tools, and Applications (pp. 693-704). Hershey, PA: Information Science Reference. doi:10.4018/978-1-4666-4422-9.ch034

Mazzara, M., Biselli, L., Greco, P. P., Dragoni, N., Marraffa, A., Qamar, N., & de Nicola, S. (2013). Social Networks and Collective Intelligence: A Return to the Agora. In L. Caviglione, M. Coccoli, & A. Merlo (Eds.), *Social Network Engineering for Secure Web Data and Services* (pp. 88–113). Hershey, PA: Information Science Reference; doi:10.4018/978-1-4666-3926-3.ch005

McColl, D., & Nejat, G. (2013). A Human Affect Recognition System for Socially Interactive Robots. In R. Luppicini (Ed.), *Handbook of Research on Technoself: Identity in a Technological Society* (pp. 554–573). Hershey, PA: Information Science Reference; doi:10.4018/978-1-4666-2211-1.ch029

McDonald, A., & Helmer, S. (2011). A Comparative Case Study of Indonesian and UK Organisational Culture Differences in IS Project Management. [IJTHI]. *International Journal of Technology and Human Interaction, 7*(2), 28–37. doi:10.4018/jthi.2011040104

McGee, E. M. (2014). Neuroethics and Implanted Brain Machine Interfaces. In M. Michael & K. Michael (Eds.), *Uberveillance and the Social Implications of Microchip Implants: Emerging Technologies* (pp. 351–365). Hershey, PA: Information Science Reference; doi:10.4018/978-1-4666-4582-0.ch015

McGrath, E., Lowes, S., McKay, M., Sayres, J., & Lin, P. (2014). Robots Underwater! Learning Science, Engineering and 21st Century Skills: The Evolution of Curricula, Professional Development and Research in Formal and Informal Contexts. In K-12 Education: Concepts, Methodologies, Tools, and Applications (pp. 1041-1067). Hershey, PA: Information Science Reference. doi:10.4018/978-1-4666-4502-8.ch062

Meissonierm, R., Bourdon, I., Amabile, S., & Boudrandi, S. (2012). Toward an Enacted Approach to Understanding OSS Developer's Motivations. [IJTHI]. *International Journal of Technology and Human Interaction*, 8(1), 38–54. doi:10.4018/jthi.2012010103

Melius, J. (2014). The Role of Social Constructivist Instructional Approaches in Facilitating Cross-Cultural Online Learning in Higher Education. In J. Keengwe, G. Schnellert, & K. Kungu (Eds.), *Cross-Cultural Online Learning in Higher Education and Corporate Training* (pp. 253–270). Hershey, PA: Information Science Reference; doi:10.4018/978-1-4666-5023-7.ch015

Melson, G. F. (2013). Building a Technoself: Children's Ideas about and Behavior toward Robotic Pets. In R. Luppicini (Ed.), *Handbook of Research on Technoself: Identity in a Technological Society* (pp. 592–608). Hershey, PA: Information Science Reference; doi:10.4018/978-1-4666-2211-1.ch031

Mena, R. J. (2014). The Quest for a Massively Multiplayer Online Game that Teaches Physics. In T. Connolly, T. Hainey, E. Boyle, G. Baxter, & P. Moreno-Ger (Eds.), *Psychology, Pedagogy, and Assessment in Serious Games* (pp. 292–316). Hershey, PA: Information Science Reference; doi:10.4018/978-1-4666-4773-2.ch014

Meredith, J., & Potter, J. (2014). Conversation Analysis and Electronic Interactions: Methodological, Analytic and Technical Considerations. In H. Lim & F. Sudweeks (Eds.), *Innovative Methods and Technologies for Electronic Discourse Analysis* (pp. 370–393). Hershey, PA: Information Science Reference; doi:10.4018/978-1-4666-4426-7.ch017

Millán-Calenti, J. C., & Maseda, A. (2014). Telegerontology®: A New Technological Resource for Elderly Support. In Assistive Technologies: Concepts, Methodologies, Tools, and Applications (pp. 705-719). Hershey, PA: Information Science Reference. doi:10.4018/978-1-4666-4422-9.ch035

Miscione, G. (2011). Telemedicine and Development: Situating Information Technologies in the Amazon. [IJSKD]. *International Journal of Sociotechnology and Knowledge Development*, 3(4), 15–26. doi:10.4018/jskd.2011100102

Miwa, N., & Wang, Y. (2011). Online Interaction Between On-Campus and Distance Students: Learners' Perspectives. [IJCALLT]. *International Journal of Computer-Assisted Language Learning and Teaching*, 1(3), 54–69. doi:10.4018/ijcallt.2011070104

Moore, M. J., Nakano, T., Suda, T., & Enomoto, A. (2013). Social Interactions and Automated Detection Tools in Cyberbullying. In L. Caviglione, M. Coccoli, & A. Merlo (Eds.), *Social Network Engineering for Secure Web Data and Services* (pp. 67–87). Hershey, PA: Information Science Reference; doi:10.4018/978-1-4666-3926-3.ch004

Morueta, R. T., Gómez, J. I., & Gómez, Á. H. (2012). B-Learning at Universities in Andalusia (Spain): From Traditional to Student-Centred Learning. [IJTHI]. *International Journal of Technology and Human Interaction, 8*(2), 56–76. doi:10.4018/jthi.2012040104

Mosindi, O., & Sice, P. (2011). An Exploratory Theoretical Framework for Understanding Information Behaviour. [IJTHI]. *International Journal of Technology and Human Interaction, 7*(2), 1–8. doi:10.4018/jthi.2011040101

Mott, M. S., & Williams-Black, T. H. (2014). Media-Enhanced Writing Instruction and Assessment. In J. Keengwe, G. Onchwari, & D. Hucks (Eds.), *Literacy Enrichment and Technology Integration in Pre-Service Teacher Education* (pp. 1–16). Hershey, PA: Information Science Reference; doi:10.4018/978-1-4666-4924-8.ch001

Mulvey, F., & Heubner, M. (2014). Eye Movements and Attention. In Assistive Technologies: Concepts, Methodologies, Tools, and Applications (pp. 1030-1054). Hershey, PA: Information Science Reference. doi:10.4018/978-1-4666-4422-9.ch053

Muro, B. F., & Delgado, E. C. (2014). RACEM Game for PC for Use as Rehabilitation Therapy for Children with Psychomotor Disability and Results of its Application. In Assistive Technologies: Concepts, Methodologies, Tools, and Applications (pp. 740-757). Hershey, PA: Information Science Reference. doi:10.4018/978-1-4666-4422-9.ch037

Muwanguzi, S., & Lin, L. (2014). Coping with Accessibility and Usability Challenges of Online Technologies by Blind Students in Higher Education. In Assistive Technologies: Concepts, Methodologies, Tools, and Applications (pp. 1227-1244). Hershey, PA: Information Science Reference. doi:10.4018/978-1-4666-4422-9.ch064

Najjar, M., Courtemanche, F., Hamam, H., Dion, A., Bauchet, J., & Mayers, A. (2014). DeepKøver: An Adaptive Intelligent Assistance System for Monitoring Impaired People in Smart Homes. In Assistive Technologies: Concepts, Methodologies, Tools, and Applications (pp. 634-661). Hershey, PA: Information Science Reference. doi:10.4018/978-1-4666-4422-9.ch031

Nap, H. H., & Diaz-Orueta, U. (2014). Rehabilitation Gaming. In J. Bishop (Ed.), *Gamification for Human Factors Integration: Social, Education, and Psychological Issues* (pp. 122–147). Hershey, PA: Information Science Reference; doi:10.4018/978-1-4666-5071-8.ch008

Neves, J., & Pinheiro, L. D. (2012). Cyberbullying: A Sociological Approach. In R. Luppicini (Ed.), *Ethical Impact of Technological Advancements and Applications in Society* (pp. 132–142). Hershey, PA: Information Science Reference; doi:10.4018/978-1-4666-1773-5.ch010

Nguyen, P. T. (2012). Peer Feedback on Second Language Writing through Blogs: The Case of a Vietnamese EFL Classroom. [IJCALLT]. *International Journal of Computer-Assisted Language Learning and Teaching, 2*(1), 13–23. doi:10.4018/ijcallt.2012010102

Ninaus, M., Witte, M., Kober, S. E., Friedrich, E. V., Kurzmann, J., Hartsuiker, E., & Wood, G. et al. (2014). Neurofeedback and Serious Games. In T. Connolly, T. Hainey, E. Boyle, G. Baxter, & P. Moreno-Ger (Eds.), *Psychology, Pedagogy, and Assessment in Serious Games* (pp. 82–110). Hershey, PA: Information Science Reference; doi:10.4018/978-1-4666-4773-2.ch005

Olla, V. (2014). An Enquiry into the use of Technology and Student Voice in Citizenship Education in the K-12 Classroom. In K-12 Education: Concepts, Methodologies, Tools, and Applications (pp. 892-913). Hershey, PA: Information Science Reference. doi:10.4018/978-1-4666-4502-8.ch053

Orange, E. (2013). Understanding the Human-Machine Interface in a Time of Change. In R. Luppicini (Ed.), *Handbook of Research on Technoself: Identity in a Technological Society* (pp. 703–719). Hershey, PA: Information Science Reference; doi:10.4018/978-1-4666-2211-1.ch036

Palmer, D., Warren, I., & Miller, P. (2014). ID Scanners and Überveillance in the Night-Time Economy: Crime Prevention or Invasion of Privacy? In M. Michael & K. Michael (Eds.), *Uberveillance and the Social Implications of Microchip Implants: Emerging Technologies* (pp. 208–225). Hershey, PA: Information Science Reference; doi:10.4018/978-1-4666-4582-0.ch009

Papadopoulos, F., Dautenhahn, K., & Ho, W. C. (2013). Behavioral Analysis of Human-Human Remote Social Interaction Mediated by an Interactive Robot in a Cooperative Game Scenario. In R. Luppicini (Ed.), *Handbook of Research on Technoself: Identity in a Technological Society* (pp. 637–665). Hershey, PA: Information Science Reference; doi:10.4018/978-1-4666-2211-1.ch033

Patel, K. K., & Vij, S. K. (2014). Unconstrained Walking Plane to Virtual Environment for Non-Visual Spatial Learning. In Assistive Technologies: Concepts, Methodologies, Tools, and Applications (pp. 1580-1599). Hershey, PA: Information Science Reference. doi:10.4018/978-1-4666-4422-9.ch083

Patrone, T. (2013). In Defense of the 'Human Prejudice'. [IJT]. *International Journal of Technoethics*, 4(1), 26–38. doi:10.4018/jte.2013010103

Peevers, G., Williams, R., Douglas, G., & Jack, M. A. (2013). Usability Study of Fingerprint and Palmvein Biometric Technologies at the ATM. [IJTHI]. *International Journal of Technology and Human Interaction*, 9(1), 78–95. doi:10.4018/jthi.2013010106

Pellas, N. (2014). Theoretical Foundations of a CSCL Script in Persistent Virtual Worlds According to the Contemporary Learning Theories and Models. In E. Nikoi & K. Boateng (Eds.), *Collaborative Communication Processes and Decision Making in Organizations* (pp. 72–107). Hershey, PA: Business Science Reference; doi:10.4018/978-1-4666-4478-6.ch005

Perakslis, C. (2014). Willingness to Adopt RFID Implants: Do Personality Factors Play a Role in the Acceptance of Uberveillance? In M. Michael & K. Michael (Eds.), *Uberveillance and the Social Implications of Microchip Implants: Emerging Technologies* (pp. 144–168). Hershey, PA: Information Science Reference; doi:10.4018/978-1-4666-4582-0.ch006

Pereira, G., Brisson, A., Dias, J., Carvalho, A., Dimas, J., Mascarenhas, S., & Paiva, A. et al. (2014). Non-Player Characters and Artificial Intelligence. In T. Connolly, T. Hainey, E. Boyle, G. Baxter, & P. Moreno-Ger (Eds.), *Psychology, Pedagogy, and Assessment in Serious Games* (pp. 127–152). Hershey, PA: Information Science Reference; doi:10.4018/978-1-4666-4773-2.ch007

Pérez Pérez, A., Callejas Carrión, Z., López-Cózar Delgado, R., & Griol Barres, D. (2014). On the Use of Speech Technologies to Achieve Inclusive Education for People with Intellectual Disabilities. In Assistive Technologies: Concepts, Methodologies, Tools, and Applications (pp. 1106-1117). Hershey, PA: Information Science Reference. doi:10.4018/978-1-4666-4422-9.ch057

Peschl, M. F., & Fundneider, T. (2014). Theory U and Emergent Innovation: Presencing as a Method of Bringing Forth Profoundly New Knowledge and Realities. In O. Gunnlaugson, C. Baron, & M. Cayer (Eds.), *Perspectives on Theory U: Insights from the Field* (pp. 207–233). Hershey, PA: Business Science Reference; doi:10.4018/978-1-4666-4793-0.ch014

Petrovic, N., Jeremic, V., Petrovic, D., & Cirovic, M. (2014). Modeling the Use of Facebook in Environmental Higher Education. In G. Mallia (Ed.), *The Social Classroom: Integrating Social Network Use in Education* (pp. 100–119). Hershey, PA: Information Science Reference; doi:10.4018/978-1-4666-4904-0.ch006

Phua, C., Roy, P. C., Aloulou, H., Biswas, J., Tolstikov, A., Foo, V. S., . . . Xu, D. (2014). State-of-the-Art Assistive Technology for People with Dementia. In Assistive Technologies: Concepts, Methodologies, Tools, and Applications (pp. 1606-1625). Hershey, PA: Information Science Reference. doi:10.4018/978-1-4666-4422-9.ch085

Potts, L. (2011). Balancing McLuhan With Williams: A Sociotechnical View of Technological Determinism. [IJSKD]. *International Journal of Sociotechnology and Knowledge Development*, *3*(2), 53–57. doi:10.4018/jskd.2011040105

Potts, L. (2013). Balancing McLuhan With Williams: A Sociotechnical View of Technological Determinism. In J. Abdelnour-Nocera (Ed.), *Knowledge and Technological Development Effects on Organizational and Social Structures* (pp. 109–114). Hershey, PA: Information Science Reference; doi:10.4018/978-1-4666-2151-0.ch007

Potts, L. (2014). Sociotechnical Uses of Social Web Tools during Disasters. In Crisis Management: Concepts, Methodologies, Tools and Applications (pp. 531-541). Hershey, PA: Information Science Reference. doi:10.4018/978-1-4666-4707-7.ch024

Proença, R., Guerra, A., & Campos, P. (2013). A Gestural Recognition Interface for Intelligent Wheelchair Users. [IJSKD]. *International Journal of Sociotechnology and Knowledge Development*, *5*(2), 63–81. doi:10.4018/jskd.2013040105

Quilici-Gonzalez, J. A., Kobayashi, G., Broens, M. C., & Gonzalez, M. E. (2012). Ubiquitous Computing: Any Ethical Implications? In R. Luppicini (Ed.), *Ethical Impact of Technological Advancements and Applications in Society* (pp. 47–59). Hershey, PA: Information Science Reference; doi:10.4018/978-1-4666-1773-5.ch005

Rambaree, K. (2014). Computer-Aided Deductive Critical Discourse Analysis of a Case Study from Mauritius with ATLAS-ti 6.2. In H. Lim & F. Sudweeks (Eds.), *Innovative Methods and Technologies for Electronic Discourse Analysis* (pp. 346–368). Hershey, PA: Information Science Reference; doi:10.4018/978-1-4666-4426-7.ch016

Ratan, R. (2013). Self-Presence, Explicated: Body, Emotion, and Identity Extension into the Virtual Self. In R. Luppicini (Ed.), *Handbook of Research on Technoself: Identity in a Technological Society* (pp. 322–336). Hershey, PA: Information Science Reference; doi:10.4018/978-1-4666-2211-1.ch018

Rechy-Ramirez, E. J., & Hu, H. (2014). A Flexible Bio-Signal Based HMI for Hands-Free Control of an Electric Powered Wheelchair. [IJALR]. *International Journal of Artificial Life Research*, *4*(1), 59–76. doi:10.4018/ijalr.2014010105

Reiners, T., Wood, L. C., & Dron, J. (2014). From Chaos Towards Sense: A Learner-Centric Narrative Virtual Learning Space. In J. Bishop (Ed.), *Gamification for Human Factors Integration: Social, Education, and Psychological Issues* (pp. 242–258). Hershey, PA: Information Science Reference; doi:10.4018/978-1-4666-5071-8.ch015

Reinhardt, J., & Ryu, J. (2013). Using Social Network-Mediated Bridging Activities to Develop Socio-Pragmatic Awareness in Elementary Korean. [IJCALLT]. *International Journal of Computer-Assisted Language Learning and Teaching*, *3*(3), 18–33. doi:10.4018/ijcallt.2013070102

Revuelta, P., Jiménez, J., Sánchez, J. M., & Ruiz, B. (2014). Automatic Speech Recognition to Enhance Learning for Disabled Students. In Assistive Technologies: Concepts, Methodologies, Tools, and Applications (pp. 478-493). Hershey, PA: Information Science Reference. doi:10.4018/978-1-4666-4422-9.ch023

Ribeiro, J. C., & Silva, T. (2013). Self, Self-Presentation, and the Use of Social Applications in Digital Environments. In R. Luppicini (Ed.), *Handbook of Research on Technoself: Identity in a Technological Society* (pp. 439–455). Hershey, PA: Information Science Reference; doi:10.4018/978-1-4666-2211-1.ch024

Richet, J. (2013). From Young Hackers to Crackers. [IJTHI]. *International Journal of Technology and Human Interaction, 9*(3), 53–62. doi:10.4018/jthi.2013070104

Rigas, D., & Almutairi, B. (2013). An Empirical Investigation into the Role of Avatars in Multimodal E-government Interfaces. [IJSKD]. *International Journal of Sociotechnology and Knowledge Development, 5*(1), 14–22. doi:10.4018/jskd.2013010102

Rodríguez, W. R., Saz, O., & Lleida, E. (2014). Experiences Using a Free Tool for Voice Therapy based on Speech Technologies. In Assistive Technologies: Concepts, Methodologies, Tools, and Applications (pp. 508-523). Hershey, PA: Information Science Reference. doi:10.4018/978-1-4666-4422-9.ch025

Rothblatt, M. (2013). Mindclone Technoselves: Multi-Substrate Legal Identities, Cyber-Psychology, and Biocyberethics. In R. Luppicini (Ed.), *Handbook of Research on Technoself: Identity in a Technological Society* (pp. 105–122). Hershey, PA: Information Science Reference; doi:10.4018/978-1-4666-2211-1.ch006

Rowe, N. C. (2012). The Ethics of Cyberweapons in Warfare. In R. Luppicini (Ed.), *Ethical Impact of Technological Advancements and Applications in Society* (pp. 195–207). Hershey, PA: Information Science Reference; doi:10.4018/978-1-4666-1773-5.ch015

Russo, M. R. (2014). Emergency Management Professional Development: Linking Information Communication Technology and Social Communication Skills to Enhance a Sense of Community and Social Justice in the 21st Century. In Crisis Management: Concepts, Methodologies, Tools and Applications (pp. 651-665). Hershey, PA: Information Science Reference. doi:10.4018/978-1-4666-4707-7.ch031

Sajeva, S. (2011). Towards a Conceptual Knowledge Management System Based on Systems Thinking and Sociotechnical Thinking. [IJSKD]. *International Journal of Sociotechnology and Knowledge Development, 3*(3), 40–55. doi:10.4018/jskd.2011070103

Sajeva, S. (2013). Towards a Conceptual Knowledge Management System Based on Systems Thinking and Sociotechnical Thinking. In J. Abdelnour-Nocera (Ed.), *Knowledge and Technological Development Effects on Organizational and Social Structures* (pp. 115–130). Hershey, PA: Information Science Reference; doi:10.4018/978-1-4666-2151-0.ch008

Saleeb, N., & Dafoulas, G. A. (2014). Assistive Technologies and Environmental Design Concepts for Blended Learning and Teaching for Disabilities within 3D Virtual Worlds and Learning Environments. In Assistive Technologies: Concepts, Methodologies, Tools, and Applications (pp. 1382-1404). Hershey, PA: Information Science Reference. doi:10.4018/978-1-4666-4422-9.ch073

Salvini, P. (2012). Presence, Reciprocity and Robotic Mediations: The Case of Autonomous Social Robots. [IJT]. *International Journal of Technoethics*, *3*(2), 9–16. doi:10.4018/jte.2012040102

Samanta, I. (2013). The Impact of Virtual Community (Web 2.0) in the Economic, Social, and Political Environment of Traditional Society. In S. Saeed, M. Khan, & R. Ahmad (Eds.), *Business Strategies and Approaches for Effective Engineering Management* (pp. 262–274). Hershey, PA: Business Science Reference; doi:10.4018/978-1-4666-3658-3.ch016

Samanta, S. K., Woods, J., & Ghanbari, M. (2011). Automatic Language Translation: An Enhancement to the Mobile Messaging Services. [IJTHI]. *International Journal of Technology and Human Interaction*, *7*(1), 1–18. doi:10.4018/jthi.2011010101

Sarkar, N. I., Kuang, A. X., Nisar, K., & Amphawan, A. (2014). Hospital Environment Scenarios using WLAN over OPNET Simulation Tool. [IJICTHD]. *International Journal of Information Communication Technologies and Human Development*, *6*(1), 69–90. doi:10.4018/ijicthd.2014010104

Sarré, C. (2013). Technology-Mediated Tasks in English for Specific Purposes (ESP): Design, Implementation and Learner Perception. [IJCALLT]. *International Journal of Computer-Assisted Language Learning and Teaching*, *3*(2), 1–16. doi:10.4018/ijcallt.2013040101

Saykili, A., & Kumtepe, E. G. (2014). Facebook's Hidden Potential: Facebook as an Educational Support Tool in Foreign Language Education. In G. Mallia (Ed.), *The Social Classroom: Integrating Social Network Use in Education* (pp. 120–146). Hershey, PA: Information Science Reference; doi:10.4018/978-1-4666-4904-0.ch007

Sayoud, H. (2011). Biometrics: An Overview on New Technologies and Ethic Problems. [IJT]. *International Journal of Technoethics*, *2*(1), 19–34. doi:10.4018/jte.2011010102

Scott, C. R., & Timmerman, C. E. (2014). Communicative Changes Associated with Repeated Use of Electronic Meeting Systems for Decision-Making Tasks. In E. Nikoi & K. Boateng (Eds.), *Collaborative Communication Processes and Decision Making in Organizations* (pp. 1–24). Hershey, PA: Business Science Reference; doi:10.4018/978-1-4666-4478-6.ch001

Scott, K. (2013). The Human-Robot Continuum of Self: Where the Other Ends and Another Begins. In R. Luppicini (Ed.), *Handbook of Research on Technoself: Identity in a Technological Society* (pp. 666–679). Hershey, PA: Information Science Reference; doi:10.4018/978-1-4666-2211-1.ch034

Shasek, J. (2014). ExerLearning®: Movement, Fitness, Technology, and Learning. In J. Bishop (Ed.), *Gamification for Human Factors Integration: Social, Education, and Psychological Issues* (pp. 106–121). Hershey, PA: Information Science Reference; doi:10.4018/978-1-4666-5071-8.ch007

Shen, J., & Eder, L. B. (2011). An Examination of Factors Associated with User Acceptance of Social Shopping Websites. [IJTHI]. *International Journal of Technology and Human Interaction*, *7*(1), 19–36. doi:10.4018/jthi.2011010102

Shrestha, P. (2012). Teacher Professional Development Using Mobile Technologies in a Large-Scale Project: Lessons Learned from Bangladesh. [IJCALLT]. *International Journal of Computer-Assisted Language Learning and Teaching*, *2*(4), 34–49. doi:10.4018/ijcallt.2012100103

Silvana de Rosa, A., Fino, E., & Bocci, E. (2014). Addressing Healthcare On-Line Demand and Supply Relating to Mental Illness: Knowledge Sharing About Psychiatry and Psychoanalysis Through Social Networks in Italy and France. In A. Kapoor & C. Kulshrestha (Eds.), *Dynamics of Competitive Advantage and Consumer Perception in Social Marketing* (pp. 16–55). Hershey, PA: Business Science Reference; doi:10.4018/978-1-4666-4430-4.ch002

Smith, M., & Murray, J. (2014). Augmentative and Alternative Communication Devices: The Voices of Adult Users. In Assistive Technologies: Concepts, Methodologies, Tools, and Applications (pp. 991-1004). Hershey, PA: Information Science Reference. doi:10.4018/978-1-4666-4422-9.ch050

Smith, P. A. (2013). Strengthening and Enriching Audit Practice: The Socio-Technical Relevance of "Decision Leaders". In J. Abdelnour-Nocera (Ed.), *Knowledge and Technological Development Effects on Organizational and Social Structures* (pp. 97–108). Hershey, PA: Information Science Reference; doi:10.4018/978-1-4666-2151-0.ch006

So, J. C., & Lam, S. Y. (2014). Using Social Networks Communication Platform for Promoting Student-Initiated Holistic Development Among Students. [IJISSS]. *International Journal of Information Systems in the Service Sector*, *6*(1), 1–23. doi:10.4018/ijisss.2014010101

Söderström, S. (2014). Assistive ICT and Young Disabled Persons: Opportunities and Obstacles in Identity Negotiations. In Assistive Technologies: Concepts, Methodologies, Tools, and Applications (pp. 1084-1105). Hershey, PA: Information Science Reference. doi:10.4018/978-1-4666-4422-9.ch056

Son, J., & Rossade, K. (2013). Finding Gems in Computer-Assisted Language Learning: Clues from GLoCALL 2011 and 2012 Papers. [IJCALLT]. *International Journal of Computer-Assisted Language Learning and Teaching*, *3*(4), 1–8. doi:10.4018/ijcallt.2013100101

Sone, Y. (2013). Robot Double: Hiroshi Ishiguro's Reflexive Machines. In R. Luppicini (Ed.), *Handbook of Research on Technoself: Identity in a Technological Society* (pp. 680–702). Hershey, PA: Information Science Reference; doi:10.4018/978-1-4666-2211-1.ch035

Spillane, M. (2014). Assistive Technology: A Tool for Inclusion. In Assistive Technologies: Concepts, Methodologies, Tools, and Applications (pp. 1-11). Hershey, PA: Information Science Reference. doi:10.4018/978-1-4666-4422-9.ch001

Stahl, B. C., Heersmink, R., Goujon, P., Flick, C., van den Hoven, J., Wakunuma, K., & Rader, M. et al. (2012). Identifying the Ethics of Emerging Information and Communication Technologies: An Essay on Issues, Concepts and Method. In R. Luppicini (Ed.), *Ethical Impact of Technological Advancements and Applications in Society* (pp. 61–79). Hershey, PA: Information Science Reference; doi:10.4018/978-1-4666-1773-5.ch006

Stern, S. E., & Grounds, B. E. (2011). Cellular Telephones and Social Interactions: Evidence of Interpersonal Surveillance. [IJT]. *International Journal of Technoethics*, *2*(1), 43–49. doi:10.4018/jte.2011010104

Stinson, J., & Gill, N. (2014). Internet-Based Chronic Disease Self-Management for Youth. In Assistive Technologies: Concepts, Methodologies, Tools, and Applications (pp. 224-245). Hershey, PA: Information Science Reference. doi:10.4018/978-1-4666-4422-9.ch012

Stockwell, G. (2011). Online Approaches to Learning Vocabulary: Teacher-Centred or Learner-Centred? [IJCALLT]. *International Journal of Computer-Assisted Language Learning and Teaching*, *1*(1), 33–44. doi:10.4018/ijcallt.2011010103

Stradella, E. (2012). Personal Liability and Human Free Will in the Background of Emerging Neuroethical Issues: Some Remarks Arising From Recent Case Law. [IJT]. *International Journal of Technoethics*, *3*(2), 30–41. doi:10.4018/jte.2012040104

Stubbs, K., Casper, J., & Yanco, H. A. (2014). Designing Evaluations for K-12 Robotics Education Programs. In K-12 Education: Concepts, Methodologies, Tools, and Applications (pp. 1342-1364). Hershey, PA: Information Science Reference. doi:10.4018/978-1-4666-4502-8.ch078

Suki, N. M., Ramayah, T., Ming, M. K., & Suki, N. M. (2011). Factors Enhancing Employed Job Seekers Intentions to Use Social Networking Sites as a Job Search Tool. [IJTHI]. *International Journal of Technology and Human Interaction*, *7*(2), 38–54. doi:10.4018/jthi.2011040105

Sweeney, P., & Moore, C. (2012). Mobile Apps for Learning Vocabulary: Categories, Evaluation and Design Criteria for Teachers and Developers. [IJCALLT]. *International Journal of Computer-Assisted Language Learning and Teaching*, *2*(4), 1–16. doi:10.4018/ijcallt.2012100101

Szeto, A. Y. (2014). Assistive Technology and Rehabilitation Engineering. In Assistive Technologies: Concepts, Methodologies, Tools, and Applications (pp. 277-331). Hershey, PA: Information Science Reference. doi:10.4018/978-1-4666-4422-9.ch015

Tamim, R. (2014). Technology Integration in UAE Schools: Current Status and Way Forward. In K-12 Education: Concepts, Methodologies, Tools, and Applications (pp. 41-57). Hershey, PA: Information Science Reference. doi:10.4018/978-1-4666-4502-8.ch004

Tan, R., Wang, S., Jiang, Y., Ishida, K., & Fujie, M. G. (2014). Motion Control of an Omni-Directional Walker for Walking Support. In Assistive Technologies: Concepts, Methodologies, Tools, and Applications (pp. 614-622). Hershey, PA: Information Science Reference. doi:10.4018/978-1-4666-4422-9.ch029

Tankari, M. (2014). Cultural Orientation Differences and their Implications for Online Learning Satisfaction. In J. Keengwe, G. Schnellert, & K. Kungu (Eds.), *Cross-Cultural Online Learning in Higher Education and Corporate Training* (pp. 20–61). Hershey, PA: Information Science Reference; doi:10.4018/978-1-4666-5023-7.ch002

Tchangani, A. P. (2014). Bipolarity in Decision Analysis: A Way to Cope with Human Judgment. In A. Masegosa, P. Villacorta, C. Cruz-Corona, M. García-Cascales, M. Lamata, & J. Verdegay (Eds.), *Exploring Innovative and Successful Applications of Soft Computing* (pp. 216–244). Hershey, PA: Information Science Reference; doi:10.4018/978-1-4666-4785-5.ch012

Tennyson, R. D. (2014). Computer Interventions for Children with Disabilities: Review of Research and Practice. In Assistive Technologies: Concepts, Methodologies, Tools, and Applications (pp. 841-864). Hershey, PA: Information Science Reference. doi:10.4018/978-1-4666-4422-9.ch042

Terrell, S. S. (2011). Integrating Online Tools to Motivate Young English Language Learners to Practice English Outside the Classroom. [IJCALLT]. *International Journal of Computer-Assisted Language Learning and Teaching, 1*(2), 16–24. doi:10.4018/ijcallt.2011040102

Tiwary, U. S., & Siddiqui, T. J. (2014). Working Together with Computers: Towards a General Framework for Collaborative Human Computer Interaction. In Assistive Technologies: Concepts, Methodologies, Tools, and Applications (pp. 141-162). Hershey, PA: Information Science Reference. doi:10.4018/978-1-4666-4422-9.ch008

Tomas, J., Lloret, J., Bri, D., & Sendra, S. (2014). Sensors and their Application for Disabled and Elderly People. In Assistive Technologies: Concepts, Methodologies, Tools, and Applications (pp. 357-376). Hershey, PA: Information Science Reference. doi:10.4018/978-1-4666-4422-9.ch018

Tomasi, A. (2013). A Run for your [Techno]Self. In R. Luppicini (Ed.), Handbook of Research on Technoself: Identity in a Technological Society (pp. 123-136). Hershey, PA: Information Science Reference. doi:10.4018/978-1-4666-2211-1.ch007

Tootell, H., & Freeman, A. (2014). The Applicability of Gaming Elements to Early Childhood Education. In J. Bishop (Ed.), *Gamification for Human Factors Integration: Social, Education, and Psychological Issues* (pp. 225–241). Hershey, PA: Information Science Reference; doi:10.4018/978-1-4666-5071-8.ch014

Tsai, C. (2011). How Much Can Computers and Internet Help?: A Long-Term Study of Web-Mediated Problem-Based Learning and Self-Regulated Learning. [IJTHI]. *International Journal of Technology and Human Interaction, 7*(1), 67–81. doi:10.4018/jthi.2011010105

Tsai, W. (2013). An Investigation on Undergraduate's Bio-Energy Engineering Education Program at the Taiwan Technical University. [IJTHI]. *International Journal of Technology and Human Interaction, 8*(3), 46–53. doi:10.4018/jthi.2012070105

Tsiakis, T. (2013). Using Social Media as a Concept and Tool for Teaching Marketing Information Systems. In M. Pătruţ & B. Pătruţ (Eds.), *Social Media in Higher Education: Teaching in Web 2.0* (pp. 24–44). Hershey, PA: Information Science Reference; doi:10.4018/978-1-4666-2970-7.ch002

Tu, C., McIsaac, M. S., Sujo-Montes, L. E., & Armfield, S. (2014). Building Mobile Social Presence for U-Learning. In F. Neto (Ed.), *Technology Platform Innovations and Forthcoming Trends in Ubiquitous Learning* (pp. 77–93). Hershey, PA: Information Science Reference; doi:10.4018/978-1-4666-4542-4.ch005

Valeria, N., Lu, M. V., & Theng, L. B. (2014). Collaborative Virtual Learning for Assisting Children with Cerebral Palsy. In Assistive Technologies: Concepts, Methodologies, Tools, and Applications (pp. 786-810). Hershey, PA: Information Science Reference. doi:10.4018/978-1-4666-4422-9.ch040

Van Leuven, N., Newton, D., Leuenberger, D. Z., & Esteves, T. (2014). Reaching Citizen 2.0: How Government Uses Social Media to Send Public Messages during Times of Calm and Times of Crisis. In Crisis Management: Concepts, Methodologies, Tools and Applications (pp. 839-857). Hershey, PA: Information Science Reference. doi:10.4018/978-1-4666-4707-7.ch041

Vargas-Hernández, J. G. (2013). International Student Collaboration and Experiential Exercise Projects as a Professional, Inter-Personal and Inter-Institutional Networking Platform. [IJTEM]. *International Journal of Technology and Educational Marketing*, *3*(1), 28–47. doi:10.4018/ijtem.2013010103

Velicu, A., & Marinescu, V. (2013). Usage of Social Media by Children and Teenagers: Results of EU KIDS Online II. In M. Pătruţ & B. Pătruţ (Eds.), *Social Media in Higher Education: Teaching in Web 2.0* (pp. 144–178). Hershey, PA: Information Science Reference; doi:10.4018/978-1-4666-2970-7.ch008

Vidaurre, C., Kübler, A., Tangermann, M., Müller, K., & Millán, J. D. (2014). Brain-Computer Interfaces and Visual Activity. In Assistive Technologies: Concepts, Methodologies, Tools, and Applications (pp. 1549-1570). Hershey, PA: Information Science Reference. doi:10.4018/978-1-4666-4422-9.ch081

Viswanathan, R. (2012). Augmenting the Use of Mobile Devices in Language Classrooms. [IJCALLT]. *International Journal of Computer-Assisted Language Learning and Teaching*, *2*(2), 45–60. doi:10.4018/ijcallt.2012040104

Wallgren, L. G., & Hanse, J. J. (2012). A Two-Wave Study of the Impact of Job Characteristics and Motivators on Perceived Stress among Information Technology (IT) Consultants. [IJTHI]. *International Journal of Technology and Human Interaction*, *8*(4), 75–91. doi:10.4018/jthi.2012100105

Wang, H. (2014). A Guide to Assistive Technology for Teachers in Special Education. In Assistive Technologies: Concepts, Methodologies, Tools, and Applications (pp. 12-25). Hershey, PA: Information Science Reference. doi:10.4018/978-1-4666-4422-9.ch002

Wang, S., Ku, C., & Chu, C. (2013). Sustainable Campus Project: Potential for Energy Conservation and Carbon Reduction Education in Taiwan. [IJTHI]. *International Journal of Technology and Human Interaction*, *8*(3), 19–30. doi:10.4018/jthi.2012070103

Wang, Y., & Tian, J. (2013). Negotiation of Meaning in Multimodal Tandem Learning via Desktop Videoconferencing. [IJCALLT]. *International Journal of Computer-Assisted Language Learning and Teaching*, *3*(2), 41–55. doi:10.4018/ijcallt.2013040103

Wareham, C. (2011). On the Moral Equality of Artificial Agents. [IJT]. *International Journal of Technoethics*, *2*(1), 35–42. doi:10.4018/jte.2011010103

Warwick, K., & Gasson, M. N. (2014). Practical Experimentation with Human Implants. In M. Michael & K. Michael (Eds.), *Uberveillance and the Social Implications of Microchip Implants: Emerging Technologies* (pp. 64–132). Hershey, PA: Information Science Reference; doi:10.4018/978-1-4666-4582-0.ch004

Welch, K. C., Lahiri, U., Sarkar, N., Warren, Z., Stone, W., & Liu, C. (2014). Affect-Sensitive Computing and Autism. In Assistive Technologies: Concepts, Methodologies, Tools, and Applications (pp. 865-883). Hershey, PA: Information Science Reference. doi:10.4018/978-1-4666-4422-9.ch043

Wessels, B., Dittrich, Y., Ekelin, A., & Eriksén, S. (2014). Creating Synergies between Participatory Design of E-Services and Collaborative Planning. In Assistive Technologies: Concepts, Methodologies, Tools, and Applications (pp. 163-179). Hershey, PA: Information Science Reference. doi:10.4018/978-1-4666-4422-9.ch009

White, E. L. (2014). Technology-Based Literacy Approach for English Language Learners. In K-12 Education: Concepts, Methodologies, Tools, and Applications (pp. 723-740). Hershey, PA: Information Science Reference. doi:10.4018/978-1-4666-4502-8.ch042

Whyte, K. P., List, M., Stone, J. V., Grooms, D., Gasteyer, S., Thompson, P. B., & Bouri, H. et al. (2014). Uberveillance, Standards, and Anticipation: A Case Study on Nanobiosensors in U.S. Cattle. In M. Michael & K. Michael (Eds.), *Uberveillance and the Social Implications of Microchip Implants: Emerging Technologies* (pp. 260–279). Hershey, PA: Information Science Reference; doi:10.4018/978-1-4666-4582-0.ch012

Wilson, S., & Haslam, N. (2013). Reasoning about Human Enhancement: Towards a Folk Psychological Model of Human Nature and Human Identity. In R. Luppicini (Ed.), *Handbook of Research on Technoself: Identity in a Technological Society* (pp. 175–188). Hershey, PA: Information Science Reference; doi:10.4018/978-1-4666-2211-1.ch010

Woodhead, R. (2012). What is Technology? [IJSKD]. *International Journal of Sociotechnology and Knowledge Development, 4*(2), 1–13. doi:10.4018/jskd.2012040101

Woodley, C., & Dorrington, P. (2014). Facebook and the Societal Aspects of Formal Learning: Optional, Peripheral, or Essential. In G. Mallia (Ed.), *The Social Classroom: Integrating Social Network Use in Education* (pp. 269–291). Hershey, PA: Information Science Reference; doi:10.4018/978-1-4666-4904-0.ch014

Yamazaki, T. (2014). Assistive Technologies in Smart Homes. In Assistive Technologies: Concepts, Methodologies, Tools, and Applications (pp. 663-678). Hershey, PA: Information Science Reference. doi:10.4018/978-1-4666-4422-9.ch032

Yan, Z., Chen, Q., & Yu, C. (2013). The Science of Cell Phone Use: Its Past, Present, and Future. [IJCBPL]. *International Journal of Cyber Behavior, Psychology and Learning, 3*(1), 7–18. doi:10.4018/ijcbpl.2013010102

Yang, Y., Wang, X., & Li, L. (2013). Use Mobile Devices to Wirelessly Operate Computers. [IJTHI]. *International Journal of Technology and Human Interaction, 9*(1), 64–77. doi:10.4018/jthi.2013010105

Yartey, F. N., & Ha, L. (2013). Like, Share, Recommend: Smartphones as a Self-Broadcast and Self-Promotion Medium of College Students. [IJTHI]. *International Journal of Technology and Human Interaction, 9*(4), 20–40. doi:10.4018/ijthi.2013100102

Yaseen, S. G., & Al Omoush, K. S. (2013). Investigating the Engage in Electronic Societies via Facebook in the Arab World. [IJTHI]. *International Journal of Technology and Human Interaction, 9*(2), 20–38. doi:10.4018/jthi.2013040102

Yeo, B. (2012). Sustainable Economic Development and the Influence of Information Technologies: Dynamics of Knowledge Society Transformation. [IJSKD]. *International Journal of Sociotechnology and Knowledge Development, 4*(3), 54–55. doi:10.4018/jskd.2012070105

Yu, L., & Ureña, C. (2014). A Review of Current Approaches of Brain Computer Interfaces. In Assistive Technologies: Concepts, Methodologies, Tools, and Applications (pp. 1516-1534). Hershey, PA: Information Science Reference. doi:10.4018/978-1-4666-4422-9.ch079

Zelenkauskaite, A. (2014). Analyzing Blending Social and Mass Media Audiences through the Lens of Computer-Mediated Discourse. In H. Lim & F. Sudweeks (Eds.), *Innovative Methods and Technologies for Electronic Discourse Analysis* (pp. 304–326). Hershey, PA: Information Science Reference; doi:10.4018/978-1-4666-4426-7. ch014

Compilation of References

Aayeshah, W., & Bebawi, S. (2014). The Use of Facebook as a Pedagogical Platform for Developing Investigative Journalism Skills. In G. Mallia (Ed.), *The Social Classroom: Integrating Social Network Use in Education* (pp. 83–99). Hershey, PA: Information Science Reference; doi:10.4018/978-1-4666-4904-0.ch005

Accenture. (2014). *Eighty Percent of Consumers Believe Total Data Privacy No Longer Exists, Accenture Survey Finds*. Retrieved July 26, 2014, from http://www.accenture.com/SiteCollectionDocuments/PDF/Accenture-Survey-Eighty-Percent-Consumers-Believe-Total-Data-Privacy-No-Longer-Exists.pdf

Adelman, I., & Yeldan, E. (2000). Is this the end of economic development? In *Structural Change and Economic Dynamic* (pp. 95-109). Elselvier.

Adi, A., & Scotte, C. G. (2013). Barriers to Emerging Technology and Social Media Integration in Higher Education: Three Case Studies. In M. Pătruţ & B. Pătruţ (Eds.), *Social Media in Higher Education: Teaching in Web 2.0* (pp. 334–354). Hershey, PA: Information Science Reference; doi:10.4018/978-1-4666-2970-7.ch017

Agazzi, E. (2012). How Can the Problems of An Ethical Judgment on Science and Technology Be Correctly Approached? In R. Luppicini (Ed.), *Ethical Impact of Technological Advancements and Applications in Society* (pp. 30–38). Hershey, PA: Information Science Reference; doi:10.4018/978-1-4666-1773-5.ch003

Agina, A. M., Tennyson, R. D., & Kommers, P. (2013). Understanding Children's Private Speech and Self-Regulation Learning in Web 2.0: Updates of Vygotsky through Piaget and Future Recommendations. In P. Ordóñez de Pablos, H. Nigro, R. Tennyson, S. Gonzalez Cisaro, & W. Karwowski (Eds.), *Advancing Information Management through Semantic Web Concepts and Ontologies* (pp. 1–53). Hershey, PA: Information Science Reference; doi:10.4018/978-1-4666-2494-8.ch001

Agrawal, D., Bamieh, B., Budak, C., El Abbadi, A., Flanagin, A., & Patterson, S. (2011). Data-Driven Modeling and Analysis of Online Social Networks. In H. Wang, S. Li, S. Oyama, X. Hu, & T. Qian (Eds.), *Web-Age Information Management: Proceedings of the 2011 International Conference* (LNCS) (Vol. 6897, pp. 3-17). Berlin, Germany: Springer.

Aguilar Castro, V. (2001). *Informe preliminar "Proyecto reconocimiento efectivo de los derechos Ye'kwana y Sanemá sobre los hábitats ocupados en el Caura, Venezuela y elaboración de un programa de manejo sostenible de sus recursos"*. Venezuela: Kuyujani, CIAG-UNEG, FPP, ULA.

Aguilar, J., & Terán, O. (2011). Ciencia y tecnología liberada y liberadora, para una potencia mediana. In E. T. Haiman & F. Fernández (Eds.), Venezuela: Potencia emergente (pp. 357-394). Caracas, Venezuela: Monte Ávila Editores, Centro de Estudios Políticos Económicos y Sociales (CEPES).

Aguilar, J. (2009). Hacia una Tecnología Democrática para Mérida: Bases para un nuevo Paradigma Universitario en la creación de una Facultad en Tecnologías Informáticas. *Revista de la Academia de Mérida, 14*(22), 17–80.

Aguilar, J. (2011). Conocimiento libre y educación emancipadora. *Revista EDUCARE, 15*(1), 84–106.

Aguilar, J. (2011a). Conocimiento libre y educación emancipadora. *Revista EDUCARE., 15*(1), 84–106.

Aguilar, J. (2011b). Para construir un nuevo tipo de Economía Social y Humanista, se requiere reflexionar sobre el Capitalismo Cognitivo. *Revista Sistémica Libre, 1*(1), 3–18.

Aguilar, J. (2012). Autonomía Tecnológica vs. Tecnocracia. In J. Medina & M. Salazar (Eds.), *Tecnología y Poder: Una mirada a las Telecomunicaciones* (pp. 37–60). Caracas, Venezuela: Ediciones A Desalambrar.

Ahrens, A., Bassus, O., & Zaščerinska, J. (2014). Enterprise 2.0 in Engineering Curriculum. In M. Cruz-Cunha, F. Moreira, & J. Varajão (Eds.), *Handbook of Research on Enterprise 2.0: Technological, Social, and Organizational Dimensions* (pp. 599–617). Hershey, PA: Business Science Reference; doi:10.4018/978-1-4666-4373-4.ch031

Akputu, O. K., Seng, K. P., & Lee, Y. L. (2014). Affect Recognition for Web 2.0 Intelligent E-Tutoring Systems: Exploration of Students' Emotional Feedback. In J. Pelet (Ed.), *E-Learning 2.0 Technologies and Web Applications in Higher Education* (pp. 188–215). Hershey, PA: Information Science Reference; doi:10.4018/978-1-4666-4876-0.ch010

Akrich, M. (1992). The De-scription of technical objects. In W. E. Bijker & J. Law (Eds.), *Shaping Technology/ Building Society: Studies in Socio-technical Change*. Cambridge, MA: MIT Press.

Al Hujran, O., Aloudat, A., & Altarawneh, I. (2013). Factors Influencing Citizen Adoption of E-Government in Developing Countries: The Case of Jordan.[IJTHI]. *International Journal of Technology and Human Interaction, 9*(2), 1–19. doi:10.4018/jthi.2013040101

Al Zoubi, O., & Read, R. (2013). Unrest uprising, or revolution? *The Philosophers' Magazine, 2013*(60), 28–29.

Alavi, R., Islam, S., Jahankhani, H., & Al-Nemrat, A. (2013). Analyzing Human Factors for an Effective Information Security Management System.[IJSSE]. *International Journal of Secure Software Engineering, 4*(1), 50–74. doi:10.4018/jsse.2013010104

Alessa, L. N., Laituri, M., & Barton, M. (2006). An "all hands" call to the social science community: Establishing a community framework for complexity modeling using agent based models and cyberinfrastructure. *Journal of Artificial Societies and Social Simulation, 9*(4), 6. Retrieved from http://jasss.soc.surrey.ac.uk/9/4/6.html

Al-Fattal, R. (2013, May 7). *Why the Arab Uprising Will Not Lead to Democracy Any Time Soon - The Métropolitain*. Retrieved February 27, 2015, from http://themetropolitain.ca/articles/view/1285

Al-Hajri, S., & Tatnall, A. (2013). A Socio-Technical Study of the Adoption of Internet Technology in Banking, Re-Interpreted as an Innovation Using Innovation Translation. In A. Tatnall (Ed.), *Social and Professional Applications of Actor-Network Theory for Technology Development* (pp. 207–220). Hershey, PA: Information Science Reference; doi:10.4018/978-1-4666-2166-4.ch016

Altun, N. E., & Yildiz, S. (2013). Effects of Different Types of Tasks on Junior ELT Students' Use of Communication Strategies in Computer-Mediated Communication.[IJCALLT]. *International Journal of Computer-Assisted Language Learning and Teaching, 3*(2), 17–40. doi:10.4018/ijcallt.2013040102

Alves, A. M., & Pessôa, M. (2010). *Brazilian Public Software: beyond Sharing*. Business Complexity and the Global Leader Conference. Retrieved March 1, 2014, from http://businesscomplexity.com/bizcom2010/papers/p584f01r311ed40c.pdf

Amaldi, P., & Smoker, A. (2013). An Organizational Study into the Concept of "Automation Policy" in a Safety Critical Socio-Technical System.[IJSKD]. *International Journal of Sociotechnology and Knowledge Development, 5*(2), 1–17. doi:10.4018/jskd.2013040101

Andacht, F. (2013). The Tangible Lure of the Techno-self in the Age of Reality Television. In R. Luppicini (Ed.), *Handbook of Research on Technoself: Identity in a Technological Society* (pp. 360–381). Hershey, PA: Information Science Reference; doi:10.4018/978-1-4666-2211-1.ch020

Anderson, A., & Petersen, A. (2012). Shaping the Ethics of an Emergent Field: Scientists' and Policymakers' Representations of Nanotechnologies. In R. Luppicini (Ed.), *Ethical Impact of Technological Advancements and Applications in Society* (pp. 219–231). Hershey, PA: Information Science Reference; doi:10.4018/978-1-4666-1773-5.ch017

Anderson, J. L. (2014). Games and the Development of Students' Civic Engagement and Ecological Stewardship. In J. Bishop (Ed.), *Gamification for Human Factors Integration: Social, Education, and Psychological Issues* (pp. 199–215). Hershey, PA: Information Science Reference; doi:10.4018/978-1-4666-5071-8.ch012

Anderson, L. (2011). Demystifying the Arab Spring: Parsing the Differences between Tunisia, Egypt, and Libya. *Foreign Affairs*, *90*, 2.

An, I. S. (2013). Integrating Technology-Enhanced Student Self-Regulated Tasks into University Chinese Language Course.[IJCALLT]. *International Journal of Computer-Assisted Language Learning and Teaching*, *3*(1), 1–15. doi:10.4018/ijcallt.2013010101

Ann, O. C., Lu, M. V., & Theng, L. B. (2014). A Face Based Real Time Communication for Physically and Speech Disabled People. In Assistive Technologies: Concepts, Methodologies, Tools, and Applications (pp. 1434-1460). Hershey, PA: Information Science Reference. doi:10.4018/978-1-4666-4422-9.ch075

Aouragh, M., & Alexander, A. (2011). The Arab Spring| The Egyptian Experience: Sense and Nonsense of the Internet Revolution. *International Journal of Communication*, *5*(0), 15.

Appropiate Framework for Broadband Access to the Internet over Wireline Facilities; Fine Rule 70 Fed. Reg. 60222, 60234 (Oct. 17, 2005) (FCC 05-151) 2005

Appropriate Framework for Broadband Access to the Internet over Wireline Facilities, CC Docket Nos. 02-33, 01-337, 95-20, 98-10, GN Docket No. 00-185, CS Docket No. 02-52, Policy Statement, 20 FCC Rcd 14986 (2005).

Apt, K. R. (1991). Logic programming. In *Handbook of theoretical computer science* (Vol. B, pp. 493–574). Cambridge, MA: MIT Press.

Aricak, O. T., Tanrikulu, T., Siyahhan, S., & Kinay, H. (2013). Cyberbullying: The Bad and the Ugly Side of Information Age. In M. Pǎtruţ & B. Pǎtruţ (Eds.), *Social Media in Higher Education: Teaching in Web 2.0* (pp. 318–333). Hershey, PA: Information Science Reference; doi:10.4018/978-1-4666-2970-7.ch016

Ariely, G. (2011). Boundaries of Socio-Technical Systems and IT for Knowledge Development in Military Environments.[IJSKD]. *International Journal of Sociotechnology and Knowledge Development*, *3*(3), 1–14. doi:10.4018/jskd.2011070101

Ariely, G. (2013). Boundaries of Socio-Technical Systems and IT for Knowledge Development in Military Environments. In J. Abdelnour-Nocera (Ed.), *Knowledge and Technological Development Effects on Organizational and Social Structures* (pp. 224–238). Hershey, PA: Information Science Reference; doi:10.4018/978-1-4666-2151-0.ch014

Arjunan, S., Kumar, D. K., Weghorn, H., & Naik, G. (2014). Facial Muscle Activity Patterns for Recognition of Utterances in Native and Foreign Language: Testing for its Reliability and Flexibility. In Assistive Technologies: Concepts, Methodologies, Tools, and Applications (pp. 1462-1480). Hershey, PA: Information Science Reference. doi:10.4018/978-1-4666-4422-9.ch076

Arling, P. A., Miech, E. J., & Arling, G. W. (2013). Comparing Electronic and Face-to-Face Communication in the Success of a Long-Term Care Quality Improvement Collaborative.[IJRQEH]. *International Journal of Reliable and Quality E-Healthcare*, *2*(1), 1–10. doi:10.4018/ijrqeh.2013010101

Arrow, K. J. (1962). Economic welfare and the allocation of resources for invention. In he rate and direction of inventive activity: economic and social factors (pp. 609–626). Princeton, NJ: Princeton University Press.

Asamblea Legislativa Plurinacional de Bolivia. (2012). *Ley General de Telecomunicaciones, Tecnologías de Información y Comunicación*. Retrieved March 1, 2014, from http://www.softwarelibre.org.bo/wiki/doku.php?id=ley_de_telecomunicaciones_2011

Asamblea Nacional de la RBV. (2013). *Ley de Infogobierno. Gaceta Oficial de la República Bolivariana de Venezuela*. Año CXIII Número 40274. Retrieved March 1, 2014, from http://www.cnti.gob.ve/images/stories/documentos_pdf/leydeinfogob.pdf

Asghari-Oskoei, M., & Hu, H. (2014). Using Myoelectric Signals to Manipulate Assisting Robots and Rehabilitation Devices. In Assistive Technologies: Concepts, Methodologies, Tools, and Applications (pp. 970-990). Hershey, PA: Information Science Reference. doi:10.4018/978-1-4666-4422-9.ch049

Aspradaki, A. A. (2013). Deliberative Democracy and Nanotechnologies in Health.[IJT]. *International Journal of Technoethics*, *4*(2), 1–14. doi:10.4018/jte.2013070101

Asselin, S. B. (2014). Assistive Technology in Higher Education. In Assistive Technologies: Concepts, Methodologies, Tools, and Applications (pp. 1196-1208). Hershey, PA: Information Science Reference. doi:10.4018/978-1-4666-4422-9.ch062

Auer, S., Bizer, C., Kobilarov, G., Lehmann, J., Cyganiak, R., & Ives, Z. (2007). Dbpedia: A nucleus for a web of open data. In The semantic web (pp. 722-735). Springer Berlin Heidelberg.

Auld, G., & Henderson, M. (2014). The Ethical Dilemmas of Social Networking Sites in Classroom Contexts. In G. Mallia (Ed.), *The Social Classroom: Integrating Social Network Use in Education* (pp. 192–207). Hershey, PA: Information Science Reference; doi:10.4018/978-1-4666-4904-0.ch010

Autorité de Régulation des Communications Eléctroniques et des Postes. (2010). *Interview de Stéphane Richard, directeur général de France Télécom*. Retrieved from http://www.arcep.fr/index.php?id=10411

Awwal, M. A. (2012). Influence of Age and Genders on the Relationship between Computer Self-Efficacy and Information Privacy Concerns.[IJTHI]. *International Journal of Technology and Human Interaction*, *8*(1), 14–37. doi:10.4018/jthi.2012010102

Axtell, R., Axelrod, R., Epstein, J. M., & Cohen, M. D. (1996). Aligning simulation models: A case study and results. *Computational & Mathematical Organization Theory*, *1*(2), 123–141. doi:10.1007/BF01299065

Azagra-Caro, J. M., Carayol, N., & Llerena, P. (2006). Patent production at a European research university: Exploratory evidence at the laboratory level. *The Journal of Technology Transfer*, *31*(2), 257–268. doi:10.1007/s10961-005-6110-3

Baldini, N., Grimaldi, R., & Sobrero, M. (2007). To patent or not to patent? A survey of Italian inventors on motivations, incentive and obstacles to university patenting. *Scientometrics*, *70*(2), 333–354. doi:10.1007/s11192-007-0206-5

Ball, S. (1896). The Moral Aspects of Socialism. *Fabian Track No 72*. London: The Fabian Society. Retrieved August 1, 2014, from http://lib-161.lse.ac.uk/archives/fabian_tracts/072.pdf

Ballesté, F., & Torras, C. (2013). Effects of Human-Machine Integration on the Construction of Identity. In R. Luppicini (Ed.), *Handbook of Research on Technoself: Identity in a Technological Society* (pp. 574–591). Hershey, PA: Information Science Reference; doi:10.4018/978-1-4666-2211-1.ch030

Balmas, M., & Sheafer, T. (2010). Candidate Image in Election Campaigns: Attribute Agenda Setting, Affective Priming, and Voting Intentions. *International Journal of Public Opinion Research*, *22*(2), 204–229. doi:10.1093/ijpor/edq009

Baporikar, N. (2014). Effective E-Learning Strategies for a Borderless World. In J. Pelet (Ed.), *E-Learning 2.0 Technologies and Web Applications in Higher Education* (pp. 22–44). Hershey, PA: Information Science Reference; doi:10.4018/978-1-4666-4876-0.ch002

Baptista, A. (2010). *Teoría económica del capitalismo rentístico*. Caracas: Banco Central de Venezuela (BCV) p. 306. Retrieved August 1, 2014, from http://www.bcv.org.ve/Upload/Publicaciones/ABaptistateoria.pdf

Bardone, E. (2011). Unintended Affordances as Violent Mediators: Maladaptive Effects of Technologically Enriched Human Niches.[IJT]. *International Journal of Technoethics*, 2(4), 37–52. doi:10.4018/jte.2011100103

Barge Gil, A., Modrego Rico, A., & Santamaría Sánchez, L. (2006). *El proceso de transferencia tecnológica universidad-empresa*. Barcelona: Fundaciò Empresa i Ciéncia.

Barton, J. H. (1996-1997). Patents and antitrust: A rethinking in light of patent breadth and sequential innovation. *Antitrust Law Journal*, 65, 449–466.

Barwise, J., & Hammer, E. (1995). *Diagrams and Concept of Logical Systems. What is a Logical System?* (D. Gabbay, Ed.). Oxford, UK: Oxford University Press.

Basham, R. (2014). Surveilling the Elderly: Emerging Demographic Needs and Social Implications of RFID Chip Technology Use. In M. Michael & K. Michael (Eds.), *Uberveillance and the Social Implications of Microchip Implants: Emerging Technologies* (pp. 169–185). Hershey, PA: Information Science Reference; doi:10.4018/978-1-4666-4582-0.ch007

Basteiro, D. (2010, May 5). *Bruselas reconoce que estudia la 'tasa Google'*. Publico.es.

Bates, M. (2013). The Ur-Real Sonorous Envelope: Bridge between the Corporeal and the Online Technoself. In R. Luppicini (Ed.), *Handbook of Research on Technoself: Identity in a Technological Society* (pp. 272–292). Hershey, PA: Information Science Reference; doi:10.4018/978-1-4666-2211-1.ch015

Bateson, G. (1972). *Steps to an Ecology of Mind*. New York: Ballantine Books.

Bauer, K. A. (2012). Transhumanism and Its Critics: Five Arguments against a Posthuman Future. In R. Luppicini (Ed.), *Ethical Impact of Technological Advancements and Applications in Society* (pp. 232–242). Hershey, PA: Information Science Reference; doi:10.4018/978-1-4666-1773-5.ch018

Bax, S. (2011). Normalisation Revisited: The Effective Use of Technology in Language Education.[IJCALLT]. *International Journal of Computer-Assisted Language Learning and Teaching*, 1(2), 1–15. doi:10.4018/ijcallt.2011040101

Baya'a, N., & Daher, W. (2014). Facebook as an Educational Environment for Mathematics Learning. In G. Mallia (Ed.), *The Social Classroom: Integrating Social Network Use in Education* (pp. 171–190). Hershey, PA: Information Science Reference; doi:10.4018/978-1-4666-4904-0.ch009

Bayerl, P. S., & Janneck, M. (2013). Professional Online Profiles: The Impact of Personalization and Visual Gender Cues on Online Impression Formation.[IJSKD]. *International Journal of Sociotechnology and Knowledge Development*, 5(3), 1–16. doi:10.4018/ijskd.2013070101

Belknap, M. H. (2001). *The CNN Effect: Strategic Enabler or Operational Risk?* U.S. Army War College Strategy Research Project.

Bell, D., & Shirzad, S. R. (2013). Social Media Business Intelligence: A Pharmaceutical Domain Analysis Study. [IJSKD]. *International Journal of Sociotechnology and Knowledge Development*, 5(3), 51–73. doi:10.4018/ijskd.2013070104

Belson, D. (2010). *The State of the Internet: 3rd Quarter, 2010 Report* (Tech. Rep. No.3 (3)). Cambridge: Akamai.

BEREC (2011). *Guidelines on net neutrality and transparency: Best practices and recommended approaches. Draft for public consultation BOR (11) 44.*

BEREC (2012). *Guidelines for quality of service in the scope of net neutrality: Draft for public consultation BOR (12) 32.*

Bergmann, N. W. (2014). Ubiquitous Computing for Independent Living. In Assistive Technologies: Concepts, Methodologies, Tools, and Applications (pp. 679-692). Hershey, PA: Information Science Reference. doi:10.4018/978-1-4666-4422-9.ch033

Bertolotti, T. (2011). Facebook Has It: The Irresistible Violence of Social Cognition in the Age of Social Networking.[IJT]. *International Journal of Technoethics*, 2(4), 71–83. doi:10.4018/jte.2011100105

Berzsenyi, C. (2014). Writing to Meet Your Match: Rhetoric and Self-Presentation for Four Online Daters. In H. Lim & F. Sudweeks (Eds.), *Innovative Methods and Technologies for Electronic Discourse Analysis* (pp. 210–234). Hershey, PA: Information Science Reference; doi:10.4018/978-1-4666-4426-7.ch010

Bessen, J., Ford, J., & Meurer, M. (2012). The private and social costs of patent trolls. *Regulation, 34*(4), 26–35.

Best, L. A., Buhay, D. N., McGuire, K., Gurholt, S., & Foley, S. (2014). The Use of Web 2.0 Technologies in Formal and Informal Learning Settings. In G. Mallia (Ed.), *The Social Classroom: Integrating Social Network Use in Education* (pp. 1–22). Hershey, PA: Information Science Reference; doi:10.4018/978-1-4666-4904-0.ch001

Bhattacharya, S. (2014). Model-Based Approaches for Scanning Keyboard Design: Present State and Future Directions. In Assistive Technologies: Concepts, Methodologies, Tools, and Applications (pp. 1497-1515). Hershey, PA: Information Science Reference. doi:10.4018/978-1-4666-4422-9.ch078

Bibby, S. (2011). Do Students Wish to 'Go Mobile'?: An Investigation into Student Use of PCs and Cell Phones.[IJCALLT]. *International Journal of Computer-Assisted Language Learning and Teaching, 1*(2), 43–54. doi:10.4018/ijcallt.2011040104

Bishop, J. (2014). The Psychology of Trolling and Lurking: The Role of Defriending and Gamification for Increasing Participation in Online Communities Using Seductive Narratives. In J. Bishop (Ed.), *Gamification for Human Factors Integration: Social, Education, and Psychological Issues* (pp. 162–179). Hershey, PA: Information Science Reference; doi:10.4018/978-1-4666-5071-8.ch010

Bishop, J., & Goode, M. M. (2014). Towards a Subjectively Devised Parametric User Model for Analysing and Influencing Behaviour Online Using Neuroeconomics. In J. Bishop (Ed.), *Gamification for Human Factors Integration: Social, Education, and Psychological Issues* (pp. 80–95). Hershey, PA: Information Science Reference; doi:10.4018/978-1-4666-5071-8.ch005

Biswas, P. (2014). A Brief Survey on User Modelling in Human Computer Interaction. In Assistive Technologies: Concepts, Methodologies, Tools, and Applications (pp. 102-119). Hershey, PA: Information Science Reference. doi:10.4018/978-1-4666-4422-9.ch006

Black, D. (2013). The Digital Soul. In R. Luppicini (Ed.), *Handbook of Research on Technoself: Identity in a Technological Society* (pp. 157–174). Hershey, PA: Information Science Reference; doi:10.4018/978-1-4666-2211-1.ch009

Blake, S., Black, D., Carlson, M., Davies, E., Wang, Z., & Weiss, W. (1998). *An architecture for differentiated services (RFC 2475)*. IETF. Retrieved from http://www.ietf.org/rfc/rfc2475.txt

Blake, S., Winsor, D. L., Burkett, C., & Allen, L. (2014). iPods, Internet and Apps, Oh My: Age Appropriate Technology in Early Childhood Educational Environments. In K-12 Education: Concepts, Methodologies, Tools, and Applications (pp. 1650-1668). Hershey, PA: Information Science Reference. doi:10.4018/978-1-4666-4502-8.ch095

Bleicher, P. (2006). Web 2.0 revolution: Power to the people. *Applied Clinical Trials, 15*(8), 34.

Boghian, I. (2013). Using Facebook in Teaching. In M. Pătruţ & B. Pătruţ (Eds.), *Social Media in Higher Education: Teaching in Web 2.0* (pp. 86–103). Hershey, PA: Information Science Reference; doi:10.4018/978-1-4666-2970-7.ch005

Boldrin, M., & Levine, D. K. (2008). *Against intellectual monopoly*. Cambridge, UK: Cambridge University Press.

Boling, E. C., & Beatty, J. (2014). Overcoming the Tensions and Challenges of Technology Integration: How Can We Best Support our Teachers? In K-12 Education: Concepts, Methodologies, Tools, and Applications (pp. 1504-1524). Hershey, PA: Information Science Reference. doi:10.4018/978-1-4666-4502-8.ch087

Bonanno, P. (2014). Designing Learning in Social Online Learning Environments: A Process-Oriented Approach. In G. Mallia (Ed.), *The Social Classroom: Integrating Social Network Use in Education* (pp. 40–61). Hershey, PA: Information Science Reference; doi:10.4018/978-1-4666-4904-0.ch003

Bongers, B., & Smith, S. (2014). Interactivating Rehabilitation through Active Multimodal Feedback and Guidance. In Assistive Technologies: Concepts, Methodologies, Tools, and Applications (pp. 1650-1674). Hershey, PA: Information Science Reference. doi:10.4018/978-1-4666-4422-9.ch087

Borges Barbosa, D., & Grau-Kuntz, K. (2009). *Exclusions from patentable subject matter and exceptions and limitations to the rights.* WIPO SCP/15/3, Annex III. Retrieved from http://www.wipo.int/edocs/mdocs/scp/en/scp_15/scp_15_3-annex3.pdf

Bottino, R. M., Ott, M., & Tavella, M. (2014). Serious Gaming at School: Reflections on Students' Performance, Engagement and Motivation.[IJGBL]. *International Journal of Game-Based Learning*, 4(1), 21–36. doi:10.4018/IJGBL.2014010102

Braden, R., Clark, D., & Shenker, S. (1994). *Integrated services in the Internet architecture: An overview (RFC 1633).* IETF. Retrieved from http://www.apps.ietf.org/rfc/rfc1633.html

Brad, S. (2014). Design for Quality of ICT-Aided Engineering Course Units.[IJQAETE]. *International Journal of Quality Assurance in Engineering and Technology Education*, 3(1), 52–80. doi:10.4018/ijqaete.2014010103

Braman, J., Thomas, U., Vincenti, G., Dudley, A., & Rodgers, K. (2014). Preparing Your Digital Legacy: Assessing Awareness of Digital Natives. In G. Mallia (Ed.), *The Social Classroom: Integrating Social Network Use in Education* (pp. 208–223). Hershey, PA: Information Science Reference; doi:10.4018/978-1-4666-4904-0.ch011

Bratitsis, T., & Demetriadis, S. (2013). Research Approaches in Computer-Supported Collaborative Learning. [IJeC]. *International Journal of e-Collaboration*, 9(1), 1–8. doi:10.4018/jec.2013010101

Braun, L. (2012). Social Media and Public Opinion. In *Master's Thesis: Interculturalitat i Polítiques Comunicatives en la Societat de la Informació*. University of Valencia.

Brenner *v.* Manson 383 U.S. 519 (1966)

Briceño Guerrero, J. (1977). *La identificación Americana con la Europa Segunda*. Universidad de Los Andes.

Brick, B. (2012). The Role of Social Networking Sites for Language Learning in UK Higher Education: The Views of Learners and Practitioners.[IJCALLT]. *International Journal of Computer-Assisted Language Learning and Teaching*, 2(3), 35–53. doi:10.4018/ijcallt.2012070103

Brown, W. J., Malveau, R. C., McCormick, H. W., & Mowbray, T. J. (1998). *Antipatterns: refactoring software, architectures, and projects in crisis.* New York, NY: John Wiley & Sons.

Bruce, J. W. (1998). Review of tenure terminology. *Tenure Brief*, 1, 1–8.

Buck Cox, S. J. (1985). No tragedy on the commons. *Environmental Ethics*, 7.

Burke, W., Buxbaum, J. N., Chakravarti, A., Horvitz, H. R., Kucherlapati, R., Lawrence, J., … Williamson, A. (2000, March 21). *Letter to the commissioner of patents and trademarks.* Retrieved from http://www.uspto.gov/web/offices/com/sol/comments/utilguide/nih.pdf

Burke, D. (2004). GM food and crops: What went wrong in the UK? *EMBO Reports*, 5(5), 432–436. doi:10.1038/sj.embor.7400160 PMID:15184970

Burke, M. E., & Speed, C. (2014). Knowledge Recovery: Applications of Technology and Memory. In M. Michael & K. Michael (Eds.), *Uberveillance and the Social Implications of Microchip Implants: Emerging Technologies* (pp. 133–142). Hershey, PA: Information Science Reference; doi:10.4018/978-1-4666-4582-0.ch005

Burton, A. M., Liu, H., Battersby, S., Brown, D., Sherkat, N., Standen, P., & Walker, M. (2014). The Use of Motion Tracking Technologies in Serious Games to Enhance Rehabilitation in Stroke Patients. In J. Bishop (Ed.), *Gamification for Human Factors Integration: Social, Education, and Psychological Issues* (pp. 148–161). Hershey, PA: Information Science Reference; doi:10.4018/978-1-4666-5071-8.ch009

Burusic, J., & Karabegovic, M. (2014). The Role of Students' Personality Traits in the Effective Use of Social Networking Sites in the Educational Context. In G. Mallia (Ed.), *The Social Classroom: Integrating Social Network Use in Education* (pp. 224–243). Hershey, PA: Information Science Reference; doi:10.4018/978-1-4666-4904-0.ch012

Busch, C. D., Lorenzo, A. M., Sánchez, I. M., González, B. G., García, T. P., Riveiro, L. N., & Loureiro, J. P. (2014). In-TIC for Mobile Devices: Support System for Communication with Mobile Devices for the Disabled. In Assistive Technologies: Concepts, Methodologies, Tools, and Applications (pp. 345-356). Hershey, PA: Information Science Reference. doi:10.4018/978-1-4666-4422-9.ch017

Business Dictionary. (n.d.). *What are emerging technologies? definition and meaning. BusinessDictionary.com.* Retrieved August 1, 2014, from http://www.business-dictionary.com/definition/emerging-technologies.html

Bute, S. J. (2013). Integrating Social Media and Traditional Media within the Academic Environment. In M. Pătruţ & B. Pătruţ (Eds.), *Social Media in Higher Education: Teaching in Web 2.0* (pp. 75–85). Hershey, PA: Information Science Reference; doi:10.4018/978-1-4666-2970-7.ch004

Butler, J. (2009). *Frames of War.* London: Verso.

Butler-Pascoe, M. E. (2011). The History of CALL: The Intertwining Paths of Technology and Second/Foreign Language Teaching.[IJCALLT]. *International Journal of Computer-Assisted Language Learning and Teaching, 1*(1), 16–32. doi:10.4018/ijcallt.2011010102

Cabrera, L. (2012). Human Implants: A Suggested Framework to Set Priorities. In R. Luppicini (Ed.), *Ethical Impact of Technological Advancements and Applications in Society* (pp. 243–253). Hershey, PA: Information Science Reference; doi:10.4018/978-1-4666-1773-5.ch019

Cacho-Elizondo, S., Shahidi, N., & Tossan, V. (2013). Intention to Adopt a Text Message-based Mobile Coaching Service to Help Stop Smoking: Which Explanatory Variables?[IJTHI]. *International Journal of Technology and Human Interaction, 9*(4), 1–19. doi:10.4018/ijthi.2013100101

Caldelli, R., Becarelli, R., Filippini, F., Picchioni, F., & Giorgetti, R. (2014). Electronic Voting by Means of Digital Terrestrial Television: The Infrastructure, Security Issues and a Real Test-Bed. In Assistive Technologies: Concepts, Methodologies, Tools, and Applications (pp. 905-915). Hershey, PA: Information Science Reference. doi:10.4018/978-1-4666-4422-9.ch045

Camacho, M. (2013). Making the Most of Informal and Situated Learning Opportunities through Mobile Learning. In M. Pătruţ & B. Pătruţ (Eds.), *Social Media in Higher Education: Teaching in Web 2.0* (pp. 355–370). Hershey, PA: Information Science Reference; doi:10.4018/978-1-4666-2970-7.ch018

Camilleri, V., Busuttil, L., & Montebello, M. (2014). MOOCs: Exploiting Networks for the Education of the Masses or Just a Trend? In G. Mallia (Ed.), *The Social Classroom: Integrating Social Network Use in Education* (pp. 348–366). Hershey, PA: Information Science Reference; doi:10.4018/978-1-4666-4904-0.ch018

Campos, P., Noronha, H., & Lopes, A. (2013). Work Analysis Methods in Practice: The Context of Collaborative Review of CAD Models.[IJSKD]. *International Journal of Sociotechnology and Knowledge Development, 5*(2), 34–44. doi:10.4018/jskd.2013040103

Canadian Radio-television and Telecommunications Commission. (2009). *Telecom Regulatory Policy CRTC 2009-657.* Author.

Canals, A. (2005). Knowledge diffusion and complex networks: a model of high-tech geographical industrial clusters. *The Network Science Society.* Retrieved from: http://www.netscisociety.net/biblio?page=1

Candeub, A., & McCartney, D. J. (2010). Network transparency: Seeing the neutral network. *Northwestern University Journal of Technology and Intellectual Property, 8*(2), 227–246.

Canfield, K. (2006). The disclosure of source code in software patents: Should software patents be open source? *The Columbia Science and Technology Law Review, 7*, 1–25.

Cao, G. (2013). A Paradox Between Technological Autonomy and Ethical Heteronomy of Philosophy of Technology: Social Control System. [IJT]. *International Journal of Technoethics, 4*(1), 52–66. doi:10.4018/jte.2013010105

Capel, H. (2003). El drama de los bienes comunes. la necesidad de un programa de investigación. *Biblio 3W, Revista Bibliográfica de Geografía y Ciencias Sociales, 8*(458).

Capotorti, F. (1991). *Etude des droits des personnes appartenant aux minorités ethniques, religieuses et linguistiques.* New York: ONU.

Carmouche, A. (2013, November 29). *New technologies cannot substitute political will.* Retrieved February 27, 2015, from https://www.opendemocracy.net/opensecurity/ayesha-carmouche/new-technologies-cannot-substitute-political-will

Carofiglio, V., & Abbattista, F. (2013). BCI-Based User-Centered Design for Emotionally-Driven User Experience. In M. Garcia-Ruiz (Ed.), *Cases on Usability Engineering: Design and Development of Digital Products* (pp. 299–320). Hershey, PA: Information Science Reference; doi:10.4018/978-1-4666-4046-7.ch013

Carpenter, B. (1996, June). *Architectural principles of the Internet (RFC 1958).* IETF. Retrieved from http://www.ietf.org/rfc/rfc1958.txt

Carpenter, B., & Nichols, K. (2002, March). *Differentiated services (Diffserv) (concluded wg).* IETF. Retrieved from http://datatracker.ietf.org/wg/diffserv/charter/

Carpenter, J. (2013). Just Doesn't Look Right: Exploring the Impact of Humanoid Robot Integration into Explosive Ordnance Disposal Teams. In R. Luppicini (Ed.), *Handbook of Research on Technoself: Identity in a Technological Society* (pp. 609–636). Hershey, PA: Information Science Reference; doi:10.4018/978-1-4666-2211-1.ch032

Carroll, J. L. (2014). Wheelchairs as Assistive Technology: What a Special Educator Should Know. In Assistive Technologies: Concepts, Methodologies, Tools, and Applications (pp. 623-633). Hershey, PA: Information Science Reference. doi:10.4018/978-1-4666-4422-9.ch030

Casey, L. B., & Williamson, R. L. (2014). A Parent's Guide to Support Technologies for Preschool Students with Disabilities. In Assistive Technologies: Concepts, Methodologies, Tools, and Applications (pp. 1340-1356). Hershey, PA: Information Science Reference. doi:10.4018/978-1-4666-4422-9.ch071

Caviglione, L., Coccoli, M., & Merlo, A. (2013). On Social Network Engineering for Secure Web Data and Services. In L. Caviglione, M. Coccoli, & A. Merlo (Eds.), *Social Network Engineering for Secure Web Data and Services* (pp. 1–4). Hershey, PA: Information Science Reference; doi:10.4018/978-1-4666-3926-3.ch001

CC. (2014). *Creative Commons License.* Retrieved from http://creativecommons.org/licenses/

Cevallos, R. (2014). FAO no descarta transgénicos en la lucha contra el hambre. La República.pe. Retrieved from http://www.larepublica.pe/08-05-2014/fao-no-descarta-transgenicos-en-la-lucha-contra-el-hambre

Chadwick, A. (2008). Web 2.0: New Challenges for the Study of E-Democracy in an Era of Informational Exuberance. *I/S: A Journal of Law and Policy for the Information Society, 5*, 9.

Chadwick, D. D., Fullwood, C., & Wesson, C. J. (2014). Intellectual Disability, Identity, and the Internet. In Assistive Technologies: Concepts, Methodologies, Tools, and Applications (pp. 198-223). Hershey, PA: Information Science Reference. doi:10.4018/978-1-4666-4422-9.ch011

Chao, L., Wen, Y., Chen, P., Lin, C., Lin, S., Guo, C., & Wang, W. (2012). The Development and Learning Effectiveness of a Teaching Module for the Algal Fuel Cell: A Renewable and Sustainable Battery. [IJTHI]. *International Journal of Technology and Human Interaction, 8*(4), 1–15. doi:10.4018/jthi.2012100101

Charnkit, P., & Tatnall, A. (2013). Knowledge Conversion Processes in Thai Public Organisations Seen as an Innovation: The Re-Analysis of a TAM Study Using Innovation Translation. In A. Tatnall (Ed.), *Social and Professional Applications of Actor-Network Theory for Technology Development* (pp. 88–102). Hershey, PA: Information Science Reference; doi:10.4018/978-1-4666-2166-4.ch008

Chen, E. T. (2014). Challenge and Complexity of Virtual Team Management. In E. Nikoi & K. Boateng (Eds.), *Collaborative Communication Processes and Decision Making in Organizations* (pp. 109–120). Hershey, PA: Business Science Reference; doi:10.4018/978-1-4666-4478-6.ch006

Chen, R., Xie, T., Lin, T., & Chen, Y. (2013). Adaptive Windows Layout Based on Evolutionary Multi-Objective Optimization.[IJTHI]. *International Journal of Technology and Human Interaction, 9*(3), 63–72. doi:10.4018/jthi.2013070105

Chen, W., Juang, Y., Chang, S., & Wang, P. (2012). Informal Education of Energy Conservation: Theory, Promotion, and Policy Implication.[IJTHI]. *International Journal of Technology and Human Interaction, 8*(4), 16–44. doi:10.4018/jthi.2012100102

Chien, C. V. (2009). Of Trolls, Davids, Goliaths, and Kings: Narratives and evidence in the litigation of high-tech patents. *North Carolina Law Review, 87,* 1571–1615.

Chino, T., Torii, K., Uchihira, N., & Hirabayashi, Y. (2013). Speech Interaction Analysis on Collaborative Work at an Elderly Care Facility.[IJSKD]. *International Journal of Sociotechnology and Knowledge Development, 5*(2), 18–33. doi:10.4018/jskd.2013040102

Chiu, M. (2013). Gaps Between Valuing and Purchasing Green-Technology Products: Product and Gender Differences.[IJTHI]. *International Journal of Technology and Human Interaction, 8*(3), 54–68. doi:10.4018/jthi.2012070106

Chivukula, V., & Shur, M. (2014). Web-Based Experimentation for Students with Learning Disabilities. In Assistive Technologies: Concepts, Methodologies, Tools, and Applications (pp. 1156-1172). Hershey, PA: Information Science Reference. doi:10.4018/978-1-4666-4422-9.ch060

Cho, M., Illangasekare, S., Weaver, M. A., Leonard, D. G. B., & Merz, J. F. (2003). Effects of patents and licenses on the provision of clinical genetic testing services. *The Journal of Molecular Diagnostics, 5*(1), 3–8. doi:10.1016/S1525-1578(10)60444-8 PMID:12552073

Chronister, R., & Hardy, S. (1997). The Limbic System. In D. Haines (Ed.), *Fundamental neuroscience* (pp. 443–454). New York: Churchill Livingstone Inc.

Chun, S., & Luna-Reyes, L. (2012). Social Media in Government. *Government Information Quarterly, 29*(4), 441–445. doi:10.1016/j.giq.2012.07.003

Clarkson, G., & Dekorte, D. (2006). The problem of patent thickets in convergent technologies. *Annals of the New York Academy of Sciences: Covergent Technologies, 1093*(1), 180–200. doi:10.1196/annals.1382.014 PMID:17312259

Clore, G., & Ortony, A. (2000). Cognition in Emotion: l, Sometimes or Never? In R. Lane, L. Nadel, G. Ahern, J. Allen, & A. Kaszniak (Eds.), *Cognitive Neuroscience of Emotion* (pp. 24–61). Oxford University Press.

CNN. (2012). *"Father of the internet": Why we must fight for its freedom.* Retrieved July 26, 2014, from http://edition.cnn.com/2012/11/29/business/opinion-cerf-google-internet-freedom/index.html

CNN. (2013). *Kurdish men in drag promote feminism in the region.* Retrieved July 26, 2014, from http://www.cnn.com/2013/09/11/world/meast/kurd-drag-campaign/index.html

Coakes, E., Bryant, A., Land, F., & Phippen, A. (2011). The Dark Side of Technology: Some Sociotechnical Reflections.[IJSKD]. *International Journal of Sociotechnology and Knowledge Development, 3*(4), 40–51. doi:10.4018/ijskd.2011100104

Cobo, J. (1987). *Estudio del problema de la discriminación contra las poblaciones indígenas.* New York: Organización de las Naciones Unidas.

Cohen, B. (1963). *The press and foreign policy.* New York: Harcourt.

Cole, I. J. (2013). Usability of Online Virtual Learning Environments: Key Issues for Instructors and Learners. In C. Gonzalez (Ed.), *Student Usability in Educational Software and Games: Improving Experiences* (pp. 41–58). Hershey, PA: Information Science Reference; doi:10.4018/978-1-4666-1987-6.ch002

Colombo, B., Antonietti, A., Sala, R., & Caravita, S. C. (2013). Blog Content and Structure, Cognitive Style and Metacognition.[IJTHI]. *International Journal of Technology and Human Interaction, 9*(3), 1–17. doi:10.4018/jthi.2013070101

Combs, C. (2014). These Photos Being Shared From Venezuela Are Fake. *Global Research. Global Research News.* Retrieved from: http://www.globalresearch.ca/these-photos-being-shared-from-venezuela-are-fake/5370091

Comcast v FCC 600 F.3d 642 (D.C. Cir. 2010).

Commission on Intellectual Property Rights. (2002). *Report of the commission on intellectual property rights: Integrating intellectual property rights and development policy.* Retrieved from http://www.iprcommission.org/papers/pdfs/final_report/ciprfullfinal.pdf

Communication from the Commission to the European Parliament, the Council, the Economic and Social Committee and the Committee of the Regions on the open Internet and net neutrality in Europe. COM (2011) 0222 final.

Connotation. (n.d.). *Wikipedia.* Retrieved from: http://en.wikipedia.org/wiki/Connotative

Constantinides, M. (2011). Integrating Technology on Initial Training Courses: A Survey Amongst CELTA Tutors.[IJCALLT]. *International Journal of Computer-Assisted Language Learning and Teaching, 1*(2), 55–71. doi:10.4018/ijcallt.2011040105

Cook, R. G., & Crawford, C. M. (2013). Addressing Online Student Learning Environments and Socialization Through Developmental Research. In M. Khosrow-Pour (Ed.), *Cases on Assessment and Evaluation in Education* (pp. 504–536). Hershey, PA: Information Science Reference; doi:10.4018/978-1-4666-2621-8.ch021

Correa, R. (2008). *Decreto 1014 del Rafael Correa Delgado.* Quito, Ecuador: Presidente Constitucional de la República de Ecuador.

Corritore, C. L., Wiedenbeck, S., Kracher, B., & Marble, R. P. (2012). Online Trust and Health Information Websites. [IJTHI]. *International Journal of Technology and Human Interaction, 8*(4), 92–115. doi:10.4018/jthi.2012100106

Council of the European Union. (2011). Council conclusions on the open Internet and net neutrality in Europe. *3134th Transport, Telecommunications and Energy Council meeting.*

Covarrubias, M., Bordegoni, M., Cugini, U., & Gatti, E. (2014). Supporting Unskilled People in Manual Tasks through Haptic-Based Guidance. In Assistive Technologies: Concepts, Methodologies, Tools, and Applications (pp. 947-969). Hershey, PA: Information Science Reference. doi:10.4018/978-1-4666-4422-9.ch048

Coverdale, T. S., & Wilbon, A. D. (2013). The Impact of In-Group Membership on e-Loyalty of Women Online Shoppers: An Application of the Social Identity Approach to Website Design.[IJEA]. *International Journal of E-Adoption, 5*(1), 17–36. doi:10.4018/jea.2013010102

Crabb, P. B., & Stern, S. E. (2012). Technology Traps: Who Is Responsible? In R. Luppicini (Ed.), *Ethical Impact of Technological Advancements and Applications in Society* (pp. 39–46). Hershey, PA: Information Science Reference; doi:10.4018/978-1-4666-1773-5.ch004

Craig, R. P. (2013). Why Disinformation Works. In America "Truth has no Relevance. Only Agendas are Important". *Global Research.* Retrieved from: http://www.globalresearch.ca/why-disinformation-works-in-america-truth-has-no-relevance-only-agendas-are-important/5336335

Crespo, R. G., Martíne, O. S., Lovelle, J. M., García-Bustelo, B. C., Díaz, V. G., & Ordoñez de Pablos, P. (2014). Improving Cognitive Load on Students with Disabilities through Software Aids. In Assistive Technologies: Concepts, Methodologies, Tools, and Applications (pp. 1255-1268). Hershey, PA: Information Science Reference. doi:10.4018/978-1-4666-4422-9.ch066

Cressey, P., & Kelleher, M. (2003). The conundrum of the learning organization: Instrumental and emancipatory theories of learning. In B. Nyhan, P. Cressey, M. Kelleher, & R. Poell (Eds.), Learning organisations: European perspectives, theories and practices. Luxembourg: CEDEFOP.

Croasdaile, S., Jones, S., Ligon, K., Oggel, L., & Pruett, M. (2014). Supports for and Barriers to Implementing Assistive Technology in Schools. In Assistive Technologies: Concepts, Methodologies, Tools, and Applications (pp. 1118-1130). Hershey, PA: Information Science Reference. doi:10.4018/978-1-4666-4422-9.ch058

Cucchiarini, C., & Strik, H. (2014). Second Language Learners' Spoken Discourse: Practice and Corrective Feedback through Automatic Speech Recognition. In H. Lim & F. Sudweeks (Eds.), *Innovative Methods and Technologies for Electronic Discourse Analysis* (pp. 169–189). Hershey, PA: Information Science Reference; doi:10.4018/978-1-4666-4426-7.ch008

Cummings, D. (2010, November 10). *A new technological democracy? | Dolan Cummings | Independent Battle of Ideas Blogs*. Retrieved July 26, 2014, from http://blogs. independent.co.uk/2010/11/10/a-new-technological-democracy/

Daes, E. I. (2000). *Prevention of discrimination and protection of indigenous peoples and minorities, working paper on discrimination against indigenous peoples submitted by Mrs Erica-Irene Daes, chairperson-rapporteur of the Working Group on Indigenous Populations, in accordance with Sub-commission resolution 1999/20*. Economic and Social Council, United Nations.

Dafoulas, G. A., & Saleeb, N. (2014). 3D Assistive Technologies and Advantageous Themes for Collaboration and Blended Learning of Users with Disabilities. In Assistive Technologies: Concepts, Methodologies, Tools, and Applications (pp. 421-453). Hershey, PA: Information Science Reference. doi:10.4018/978-1-4666-4422-9.ch021

Dai, Z., & Paasch, K. (2013). A Web-Based Interactive Questionnaire for PV Application.[IJSKD]. *International Journal of Sociotechnology and Knowledge Development*, *5*(2), 82–93. doi:10.4018/jskd.2013040106

Daradoumis, T., & Lafuente, M. M. (2014). Studying the Suitability of Discourse Analysis Methods for Emotion Detection and Interpretation in Computer-Mediated Educational Discourse. In H. Lim & F. Sudweeks (Eds.), *Innovative Methods and Technologies for Electronic Discourse Analysis* (pp. 119–143). Hershey, PA: Information Science Reference; doi:10.4018/978-1-4666-4426-7.ch006

Davis, B., & Mason, P. (2014). Positioning Goes to Work: Computer-Aided Identification of Stance Shifts and Semantic Themes in Electronic Discourse Analysis. In H. Lim & F. Sudweeks (Eds.), *Innovative Methods and Technologies for Electronic Discourse Analysis* (pp. 394–413). Hershey, PA: Information Science Reference; doi:10.4018/978-1-4666-4426-7.ch018

De Civrieux, M. (1992). *Watunna*. Caracas, Venezuela: Monte Avila Editores.

de l'Économie, M. de l'industrie et de l'emploi de la République Française. (2010). *Consultation publique sur la neutralité du Net*.telecom.gouv.fr

De la Cruz, R. (2007). The rights of indigenous intellectual property and traditional knowledge of indigenous peoples. In L. Giraudo (Ed.), *Citizenship and indigenous rights in Latin America: Population, states and international order*. Madrid: Academic Press.

Dearing, J., & Rogers, E. (1988). Agenda-setting research: Where has it been, where is it going? *Communication Yearbook*, *11*, 555–594.

Department Of State, The Office of Website Management, B. of P. A. (2011, July 6). *The Open Government Partnership*. Retrieved February 27, 2015, from http:// www.state.gov/j/ogp/

Deskmag, C. E. (2012). *The 2nd Global Coworking Survey*. Retrieved July. 1, 2013, from http://www.deskmag.com/en/first-results-of-global-coworking-survey-171

Díaz, L. (2013). Detección de secuencias asociadas a organismos vivos modificados en semillas de maíz (Zea mays L.) y Soya (Glycine max L. Merryl). Master Degree Work. Facultad de Agronomía. Universidad Central de Venezuela. Maracay. Retrieved from http://saber.ucv.ve/xmlui/bitstream/123456789/4520/1/T026800007886-0-Trabajo_de_grado_Luis_Diaz-000.pdf

Ding, H., & Samadzadeh, M. H. (2004). Extraction of Java program fingerprints for software authorship identification. *Journal of Systems and Software*, *72*(1), 49–57. doi:10.1016/S0164-1212(03)00049-9

Directive 2002/21/EC of the European Parliament and of the Council on a common regulatory framework for electronic communications networks and services, 2002 O.J. (L 108) 33. Amended by Directive 2009/140/EC of the European Parliament and of the Council of 25 November 2009, O.J. (L137) 37.

Directive 2002/22/EC of the European Parliament and of the Council of 7 March 2002 on universal service and users' rights relating to electronic communications networks and services (Universal Service Directive), 2002 O.J. (L108) 51. Amended by Directive 2009/136/EC of the European Parliament and of the Council of 25 November 2009, O.J. (L337) 11.

Dogoriti, E., & Pange, J. (2014). Considerations for Online English Language Learning: The Use of Facebook in Formal and Informal Settings in Higher Education. In G. Mallia (Ed.), *The Social Classroom: Integrating Social Network Use in Education* (pp. 147–170). Hershey, PA: Information Science Reference; doi:10.4018/978-1-4666-4904-0.ch008

Domingo, C. (2008). La Economía de Venezuela. *Entorno-Empresarial.Com*. Retrieved March 1, 2014, from http://www.entorno-empresarial.com/articulo/1769/la-economia-de-venezuela

Donegan, M. (2014). Features of Gaze Control Systems. In Assistive Technologies: Concepts, Methodologies, Tools, and Applications (pp. 1055-1061). Hershey, PA: Information Science Reference. doi:10.4018/978-1-4666-4422-9.ch054

Dorgan, B., Snowe, O., Kerry, J., Boxer, B., Harki, T., Leahy, P., & Clinton, H. et al. (2007). *Internet Freedom Preservation Act. S. 215, 110th Cong. (2007-2008)*

Douglas, G., Morton, H., & Jack, M. (2012). Remote Channel Customer Contact Strategies for Complaint Update Messages.[IJTHI]. *International Journal of Technology and Human Interaction, 8*(2), 43–55. doi:10.4018/jthi.2012040103

Drahos, P. (2007). Makind Deals with Al Capone: Paying Protection Money for Intelectual Property in the Global Knowledge Economy. In P. K. Yu (Ed.), Intellectual Property and Information Wealth: Issues and Practices in the Digital Age, Volumen 4. Academic Press.

Drahos, P. (2010). *The global governance of knowledge: Patent offices and their clients.* New York: Cambridge University Press.

Drake, J. R., & Byrd, T. A. (2013). Searching for Alternatives: Does Your Disposition Matter?[IJTHI]. *International Journal of Technology and Human Interaction, 9*(1), 18–36. doi:10.4018/jthi.2013010102

Dray, A., Perez, P., Jones, N., Le Page, C., D'Aquino, P., White, I., & Auatabu, T. (2006). The AtollGame experience: from knowledge engineering to a computer-assisted role playing game. *Journal of Artificial Societies and Social Simulation, 9*(1), 6. Retrieved from http://jasss.soc.surrey.ac.uk/9/1/6.html

Driouchi, A. (2013). ICTs and Socioeconomic Performance with Focus on ICTs and Health. In ICTs for Health, Education, and Socioeconomic Policies: Regional Cases (pp. 104-125). Hershey, PA: Information Science Reference. doi:10.4018/978-1-4666-3643-9.ch005

Driouchi, A. (2013). Social Deficits, Social Cohesion, and Prospects from ICTs. In ICTs for Health, Education, and Socioeconomic Policies: Regional Cases (pp. 230-251). Hershey, PA: Information Science Reference. doi:10.4018/978-1-4666-3643-9.ch011

Driouchi, A. (2013). Socioeconomic Reforms, Human Development, and the Millennium Development Goals with ICTs for Coordination. In ICTs for Health, Education, and Socioeconomic Policies: Regional Cases (pp. 211-229). Hershey, PA: Information Science Reference. doi:10.4018/978-1-4666-3643-9.ch010

Drula, G. (2013). Media and Communication Research Facing Social Media. In M. Pătruţ & B. Pătruţ (Eds.), *Social Media in Higher Education: Teaching in Web 2.0* (pp. 371–392). Hershey, PA: Information Science Reference; doi:10.4018/978-1-4666-2970-7.ch019

Drummond, R. (1997). Thyroid storm. *Journal of the American Medical Association, 277*(15), 1238–1243. doi:10.1001/jama.1997.03540390068038 PMID:9103350

Druzhinina, O., Hvannberg, E. T., & Halldorsdottir, G. (2013). Feedback Fidelities in Three Different Types of Crisis Management Training Environments.[IJSKD]. *International Journal of Sociotechnology and Knowledge Development, 5*(2), 45–62. doi:10.4018/jskd.2013040104

Eason, K., Waterson, P., & Davda, P. (2013). The Sociotechnical Challenge of Integrating Telehealth and Telecare into Health and Social Care for the Elderly.[IJSKD]. *International Journal of Sociotechnology and Knowledge Development, 5*(4), 14–26. doi:10.4018/ijskd.2013100102

Edenius, M., & Rämö, H. (2011). An Office on the Go: Professional Workers, Smartphones and the Return of Place. [IJTHI]. *International Journal of Technology and Human Interaction, 7*(1), 37–55. doi:10.4018/jthi.2011010103

Edmonds, B. (2000). *The purpose and place of formal systems in the development of science, CPM Report 00-75, MMU, UK.* Retrieved from http://cfpm.org/cpmrep75.html

Edmonds, B., & Hales, D. (2003). Replication, replication and replication - some hard lessons from model alignment. *Journal of Artificial Societies and Social Simulation, 6*(4), 11. Retrieved from http://jasss.soc.surrey.ac.uk/6/4/11.html

Edmonds, B. (2012). Context in social simulation: Why it can't be wished away. *Computational & Mathematical Organization Theory, 18*(1), 5–21. doi:10.1007/s10588-011-9100-z

Edmonds, B., & Hales, D. (2005). Computational simulation as theoretical experiment. *The Journal of Mathematical Sociology, 29*(3), 209–232. doi:10.1080/00222500590921283

Eggertsson, T. (2003). Open access versus common property. In T. L. Anderson & F. S. McChesney (Eds.), Property rights: Cooperation, conflict and law (pp. 73–89). Princeton, NJ: Princeton University Press.

Eisenberg, R. (1987). Propietary rights and the norms of science in biotechnology research. *The Yale Law Journal, 97*(2), 177–231. doi:10.2307/796481 PMID:11660398

Eisenberg, R. (1996). Public research and private development: Patents and technology transfer in government-sponsored research. *Virginia Journal of Law, 8*(8), 1663–1727. doi:10.2307/1073686

Eisenberg, R. (2003). Science and law: Patent swords and shields. *Science, 229*(5609), 1018–1019. doi:10.1126/science.1081790 PMID:12586927

Eke, D. O. (2011). ICT Integration in Nigeria: The Socio-Cultural Constraints.[IJTHI]. *International Journal of Technology and Human Interaction, 7*(2), 21–27. doi:10.4018/jthi.2011040103

Ellickson, R. C. (1993). Property in land. *The Yale Law Journal, 102*(6), 1315–1400. doi:10.2307/796972

Elliot, V. (2001). Who calls the tune? *The Unesco Courier, 54*(11), 21–22.

Ellner, S. (2014). Terrorism in Venezuela and Its "Regime Change" Accomplices. *Global Research.* Retrieved from: http://www.globalresearch.ca/terrorism-in-venezuela-and-its-regime-change-accomplices/5383291

Entman, R. M. (1993). Framing: Toward clarification of a fractured paradigm. *Journal of Communication, 43*(4), 51–58. doi:10.1111/j.1460-2466.1993.tb01304.x

Estévez Araújo, J. A (2008). Que no te den gobernanza por democracia. *Mientras tanto, 108–109*, 33–49.

Europe. (2006). *The impact of Free / Libre / Open Source Software on innovation and Competitiveness of the European Union.* Retrieved March 1, 2007, from http://ec.europa.eu/enterprise/sectors/ict/files/2006-11-20-flossimpact_en.pdf

European Commission (2002). *Towards a reinforced culture of consultation and dialogue - General principles and minimum standards for consultation of interested parties by the Commission.* COM (2002) 704 final.

European Commission (2002b). *An assessment of the implications for basic genetic engineering research of failure to publish, or late publication of, papers on subjects which could be patentable as required under Article 16(b) of Directive 98/44/EC on the legal protection of biotechnological inventions* [SEC(2002) 50]. COM / 2002/0002 final*/.

European Commission (2006). *Public consultation on content online in the single market.*

European Commission (2009). *Telecom reform 2009: Commission declaration on net neutrality.* Official Journal of the European Communities (L337) 69.

European Commission (2010a). *Questionnaire for the public consultation on the open Internet and net neutrality in Europe.*

European Commission (2010b). *Report on the public consultation on the open Internet and net neutrality in Europe.*

European Commission Press Release. (April. 13, 2010). SPEECH/10/153.

European Commission Press Release. (Sept. 10, 2010) SPEECH/10/434.

European Commission Press Release. SPEECH/08/473 (Sept. 09, 2008).

European Commission. (2002a). *Development and implications of patent law in the field of biotechnology and genetic engineering.* COM(2002) 545 Final.

European Commission. (2012). *Public consultation on specifics aspects of transparency, traffic management and switching in an open Internet.*

European Parliament (2011). Resolution of 17 November 2011 on the open Internet and net neutrality in Europe (P7_TA(2011)0511)

European Parliament (2014). Legislative resolution of 3 April 2014 on the proposal for a regulation of the European Parliament and of the Council laying down measures concerning the European single market for electronic communications and to achieve a connected continent, and amending directives 2002/20/EC, 2002/21/EC, 2002/22/EC, and regulations (EC) N° 1211/2009 and (EU) N° 531/2012 (com(2013)0627- c7-0267/2013 - 2013/0309(cod)) (ordinary legislative procedure: first reading).

European Parliament. (2012). Resolution of 11 December 2012 on a digital freedom strategy in EU foreign policy. Retrieved at http://www.europarl.europa.eu/sides/getDoc.do?pubRef=-//EP//TEXT+TA+P7-TA-2012-0470+0+DOC+XML+V0//EN

Evans, G. (2001). Leaving room for dissent. *The Unesco Courier, 54*(11), 17.

Evett, L., Ridley, A., Keating, L., Merritt, P., Shopland, N., & Brown, D. (2014). Designing Serious Games for People with Disabilities: Game, Set, and Match to the Wii. In J. Bishop (Ed.), *Gamification for Human Factors Integration: Social, Education, and Psychological Issues* (pp. 97–105). Hershey, PA: Information Science Reference; doi:10.4018/978-1-4666-5071-8.ch006

Evmenova, A. S., & Behrmann, M. M. (2014). Communication Technology Integration in the Content Areas for Students with High-Incidence Disabilities: A Case Study of One School System. In Assistive Technologies: Concepts, Methodologies, Tools, and Applications (pp. 26-53). Hershey, PA: Information Science Reference. doi:10.4018/978-1-4666-4422-9.ch003

Evmenova, A. S., & King-Sears, M. E. (2014). Technology and Literacy for Students with Disabilities. In Assistive Technologies: Concepts, Methodologies, Tools, and Applications (pp. 1269-1291). Hershey, PA: Information Science Reference. doi:10.4018/978-1-4666-4422-9.ch067

Ewais, A., & De Troyer, O. (2013). Usability Evaluation of an Adaptive 3D Virtual Learning Environment. [IJVPLE]. *International Journal of Virtual and Personal Learning Environments, 4*(1), 16–31. doi:10.4018/jvple.2013010102

Farrell, H. J. (2014). The Student with Complex Education Needs: Assistive and Augmentative Information and Communication Technology in a Ten-Week Music Program. In K-12 Education: Concepts, Methodologies, Tools, and Applications (pp. 1436-1472). Hershey, PA: Information Science Reference. doi:10.4018/978-1-4666-4502-8.ch084

Fathulla, K. (2012). Rethinking Human and Society's Relationship with Technology.[IJSKD]. *International Journal of Sociotechnology and Knowledge Development, 4*(2), 21–28. doi:10.4018/jskd.2012040103

Federal Trade Commission. (2006). *FTC to host workshop on broadband connectivity competition policy.* Retrieved from http://www.ftc.gov/opa/2006/12/broadbandworkshop2.shtm

Feenberg, A. (2002). Democratic rationalization: Technology, power and democracy. In R. Scharff & V. Dusek (Eds.), *Technology and the human condition: A philosophy of technology reader* (pp. 652–665). London: Blackwell.

Feeny, D., Berkes, F., McCay, B. J., & Acheson, J. M. (1990). The tragedy of the commons: Twenty-two years later. *Human Ecology, 18*(1), 1–19. doi:10.1007/BF00889070 PMID:12316894

Feldman, R. (2009). Plain language patents. *Texas Intellectual Property Law Journal, 17*(2), 289–304.

Fidler, C. S., Kanaan, R. K., & Rogerson, S. (2011). Barriers to e-Government Implementation in Jordan: The Role of Wasta.[IJTHI]. *International Journal of Technology and Human Interaction, 7*(2), 9–20. doi:10.4018/jthi.2011040102

Fischer, G., & Herrmann, T. (2013). Socio-Technical Systems: A Meta-Design Perspective. In J. Abdelnour-Nocera (Ed.), *Knowledge and Technological Development Effects on Organizational and Social Structures* (pp. 1–36). Hershey, PA: Information Science Reference; doi:10.4018/978-1-4666-2151-0.ch001

Forbes. (2012). *Social Media Platforms and Liberty: A Two-Edged Sword. Forbes.* Retrieved July 26, 2014, from http://www.forbes.com/sites/timothylee/2012/09/11/social-media-platforms-and-liberty-a-two-edged-sword/

Forbes. (2013a). *Obama Seeks To Free Up Wireless Spectrum (Updated).* Retrieved July 26, 2014, from http://www.forbes.com/sites/larrymagid/2013/06/14/obama-seeks-to-free-up-wireless-spectrum/

Forbes. (2013b). *The Impact Of Mobile On Publishers -- More Consumption, Less Revenue - Forbes.* Retrieved July 26, 2014, from http://www.forbes.com/sites/benjaminboxer/2013/11/14/the-impact-of-mobile-on-publishers-more-consumption-less-revenue/

Foreman, J., & Borkman, T. (2014). Learning Sociology in a Massively Multi-Student Online Learning Environment. In J. Bishop (Ed.), *Gamification for Human Factors Integration: Social, Education, and Psychological Issues* (pp. 216–224). Hershey, PA: Information Science Reference; doi:10.4018/978-1-4666-5071-8.ch013

Fornaciari, F. (2013). The Language of Technoself: Storytelling, Symbolic Interactionism, and Online Identity. In R. Luppicini (Ed.), *Handbook of Research on Technoself: Identity in a Technological Society* (pp. 64–83). Hershey, PA: Information Science Reference; doi:10.4018/978-1-4666-2211-1.ch004

Forrester, J. (1971). Counterintuitive behavior of social systems. *Technology Review, 73*(3), 52–68.

Fowler, M. (2000). *Refactoring: improving the design of existing code.* Upper Saddle River, NJ: Addison-Wesley.

Fox, J., & Ahn, S. J. (2013). Avatars: Portraying, Exploring, and Changing Online and Offline Identities. In R. Luppicini (Ed.), *Handbook of Research on Technoself: Identity in a Technological Society* (pp. 255–271). Hershey, PA: Information Science Reference; doi:10.4018/978-1-4666-2211-1.ch014

Fox, W. P., Binstock, J., & Minutas, M. (2013). Modeling and Methodology for Incorporating Existing Technologies to Produce Higher Probabilities of Detecting Suicide Bombers.[IJORIS]. *International Journal of Operations Research and Information Systems, 4*(3), 1–18. doi:10.4018/joris.2013070101

Framing (social communication theory). (n.d.). *The Free Dictionary.* Retrieved from: http://encyclopedia.thefreedictionary.com/Framing+(communication+theory)

Framing (social sciences). (n.d.), *Wikipedia.* Retrieved from: http://en.wikipedia.org/wiki/Framing_(social_communication_theory)

Franchi, E., & Tomaiuolo, M. (2013). Distributed Social Platforms for Confidentiality and Resilience. In L. Caviglione, M. Coccoli, & A. Merlo (Eds.), *Social Network Engineering for Secure Web Data and Services* (pp. 114–136). Hershey, PA: Information Science Reference; doi:10.4018/978-1-4666-3926-3.ch006

French Constitutional Council. (2009). *Décision Nro. 2009-580 DC du 10 juin (Loi favorisant la diffusion et la protection de la création sur internet).*

Frigo, C. A., & Pavan, E. E. (2014). Prosthetic and Orthotic Devices. In Assistive Technologies: Concepts, Methodologies, Tools, and Applications (pp. 549-613). Hershey, PA: Information Science Reference. doi:10.4018/978-1-4666-4422-9.ch028

Frischmann, B. M. (2012). *Infraestructure: The social value of shared resources.* New York: Oxford University Press. doi:10.1093/acprof:oso/9780199895656.001.0001

Fromer, J. C. (2009). Patent disclosure. *Iowa Law Review, 94,* 539–606.

Frühwirth, T., & Abdennadher, S. (2003). *Essentials of constraint programming.* Springer.

FSF. (2007). *GNU General Public License Version 3, 29.* Free Software Foundation, Inc. Retrieved from http://fsf.org/

FSF. (2014a). *Categories of free and non-free software.* Retrieved from http://www.gnu.org/philosophy/categories.es.html

FSF. (2014b). *Free Software Licenses.* Retrieved from http://www.gnu.org/licenses/licenses.es.html

FSF. (2014c). *The Free Software Definition, GNU.* Retrieved from http://www.gnu.org/philosophy/free-sw.es.html

Fuenmayor, R. (1999). Venezuela: su enfermedad y crisis actual. *Estudios de Derecho P, 335-358.*

Fuenmayor, R. (2000). *Sentido y sinsentido del desarrollo.* Mérida, Venezuela: Consejo de Publicaciones y Consejo de Estudios de Postgrado de la Universidad de Los Andes. Retrieved from http://www.saber.ula.ve/db/ssaber/Edocs/centros_investigacion/csi/publicaciones/monografias/sentido_y_sinsentido.pdf

Fuenmayor, R. (2006). *El estado venezolano y la posibilidad de la ciencia.* Mérida, Venezuela: Fundacite. Gráficas Quintero. Retrieved from http://www.cenditel.gob.ve/node/422

Fuenmayor, R. (2006). *El estado venezolano y la posibilidad de la ciencia.* Universidad de Los Andes, Mérida, Venezuela: Fundacite & Gráficas Quintero. Retrieved from http://www.cenditel.gob.ve/node/422

Fuenmayor, R. (2001). Educación y la reconstitución de un lenguaje madre. *LOGOI, 4,* 39–58.

Fuenmayor, R., Aguilar, J., Anzola, M., Delgado, M., León, L., Mendialdúa, J., & Terán, O. (2007). *El estado venezolano y la posibilidad de la ciencia. En Debate abierto sobre misión ciencia.* Ediciones del Ministerio del Poder Popular para Ciencia y Tecnología.

Fuhrer, C., & Cucchi, A. (2012). Relations Between Social Capital and Use of ICT: A Social Network Analysis Approach.[IJTHI]. *International Journal of Technology and Human Interaction, 8*(2), 15–42. doi:10.4018/jthi.2012040102

Funkhouser, G. (1973). The issues of the sixties: An exploratory study in the dynamics of public opinion. *Public Opinion Quarterly, 37*(1), 62–75. doi:10.1086/268060

Gabriel, C. (2010, April 26,). *Vodafone to petition EU for 'Google tax'.* Rethink Wireless. Geist, M. (200, December 22). *Towards a two-tier Internet.* BBC News. Retrieved from http://news.bbc.co.uk/2/hi/technology/4552138.stm

Galinski, C., & Beckmann, H. (2014). Concepts for Enhancing Content Quality and eAccessibility: In General and in the Field of eProcurement. In Assistive Technologies: Concepts, Methodologies, Tools, and Applications (pp. 180-197). Hershey, PA: Information Science Reference. doi:10.4018/978-1-4666-4422-9.ch010

Galván, J. M., & Luppicini, R. (2012). The Humanity of the Human Body: Is Homo Cybersapien a New Species?[IJT]. *International Journal of Technoethics, 3*(2), 1–8. doi:10.4018/jte.2012040101

Garabedian, T. E. (2002). Nontraditional publications and their effect on patentable inventions. *Nature Biotechnology, 20*(4), 401–402. doi:10.1038/nbt0402-401 PMID:11923849

García-Gómez, A. (2013). Technoself-Presentation on Social Networks: A Gender-Based Approach. In R. Luppicini (Ed.), *Handbook of Research on Technoself: Identity in a Technological Society* (pp. 382–398). Hershey, PA: Information Science Reference; doi:10.4018/978-1-4666-2211-1.ch021

Gaudichaud, F. (2014). Street Violence and the Political Destabilization of Venezuela. US Sponsored "Color Revolution". *Global Research.* Retrieved from: http://www.globalresearch.ca/street-violence-and-the-political-destabilization-of-venezuela-us-sponsored-color-revolution/5376339

Genachowski, J. (2010, May 6). *The third way: A narrowly tailored broadband framework.* Federal Communications Commission. Retrieved from http://www.broadband.gov/the-third-way-narrowly-tailored-broadband-framework-chairman-julius-genachowski.html

Gibbs, W. (1996, November). The price of silence: Does profit-minded secrecy retard scientific progress? *Scientific American, 275*(5), 15–16. doi:10.1038/scientificamerican1196-15

Gill, L., Hathway, E. A., Lange, E., Morgan, E., & Romano, D. (2013). Coupling Real-Time 3D Landscape Models with Microclimate Simulations.[IJEPR]. *International Journal of E-Planning Research, 2*(1), 1–19. doi:10.4018/ijepr.2013010101

GNP. (2013). *Tem(p)i e luoghi del lavoro flessibile.* Retrieved July, 1, 2013, from http://www.giornatanazionaledellaprevidenza.it/terza-giornata-gnp2013

Godé, C., & Lebraty, J. (2013). Improving Decision Making in Extreme Situations: The Case of a Military Decision Support System.[IJTHI]. *International Journal of Technology and Human Interaction, 9*(1), 1–17. doi:10.4018/jthi.2013010101

Godin, B., & Gingras, Y. (2000). The place of universities in the system of knowledge production. *Research Policy, 29*(2), 273–278. doi:10.1016/S0048-7333(99)00065-7

Golden, B. (2005). *Succeeding with Open Source.* Addison-Wesley.

Goldspink, C., Edmonds, B., & Gilbert, N. (2008). *Normative behaviour in Wikipedia.* Paper presented at the 4th International Conference on e-Social Science, Manchester, UK. Retrieved from http://cfpm.org/cpmrep190.html

Golinger, E. (2014). Agents of Destabilization in Venezuela: The Dirty Hand of the National Endowment for Democracy. *Global Research.* Retrieved from: http://www.globalresearch.ca/agents-of-destabilization-the-dirty-hand-of-the-national-endowment-for-democracy-in-venezuela/5379325

Google. (2014). *Google Fiber.* Retrieved July 26, 2014, from https://fiber.google.com/about2/

Gotts, N. M., & Polhill, J. G. (2009). *Narrative scenarios, mediating formalisms, and the agent-based simulation of land use change. In Epistemological Aspects of Computer Simulation in the Social Sciences* (pp. 99–116). Berlin: Springer-Verlag.

Government of the Russian Federation. (2010). *Plan for the transition of federal executive authorities and federal budgetary institutions on the use of free software in 2011 - 2015.* Retrieved March 25, 2014 from http://filearchive.cnews.ru/doc/2010/06/17/2299p.doc

Green, G., Taylor, G., Murphy, S., Arcuri, M., Kosmas, S., & Wilson, C. … Brown, C. (2010, May 24,). *Letter to Julius Genachowski.* Congress of the United States. Retrieved from http://www.policybytes.org/Blog/PolicyBytes.nsf/dx/TitleII_FCC_24May2010.pdf/$file/TitleII_FC__24May2010.pdf

Green, P. (2010). *5 Steps for a Successful Social Knowledge Network Implementation.* Retrieved from: http://www.cmswire.com/cms/enterprise-20/5-steps-for-a-successful-social-knowledge-network-implementation-008423.php

Grimm, V., & Schmolke, A. (2011). *How to read and write TRACE documents.* Helmholtz Centre for Environmental Research – UFZ, Department of Ecological Modelling, Permoserstr. 15, 04318 Leipzig, Germany. Retrieved from http://cream-itn.eu/creamwp/wp-content/uploads/Trace-Guidance-11-03-04.pdf

Grimm, V., Berger, U., Bastiansen, F., Eliassen, S., Ginot, V., Giske, J., & DeAngelis, D. L. et al. (2006). A standard protocol for describing individual-based and agent-based models. *Ecological Modelling, 198*(1–2), 115–126. doi:10.1016/j.ecolmodel.2006.04.023

Grimm, V., Berger, U., DeAngelis, D. L., Polhill, J. G., Giske, J., & Railsback, S. F. (2010). The ODD protocol: A review and first update. *Ecological Modelling, 221*(23), 2760–2768. doi:10.1016/j.ecolmodel.2010.08.019

Griol Barres, D., Callejas Carrión, Z., Molina López, J. M., & Sanchis de Miguel, A. (2014). Towards the Use of Dialog Systems to Facilitate Inclusive Education. In Assistive Technologies: Concepts, Methodologies, Tools, and Applications (pp. 1292-1312). Hershey, PA: Information Science Reference. doi:10.4018/978-1-4666-4422-9.ch068

Griol, D., Callejas, Z., & López-Cózar, R. (2014). Conversational Metabots for Educational Applications in Virtual Worlds. In Assistive Technologies: Concepts, Methodologies, Tools, and Applications (pp. 1405-1433). Hershey, PA: Information Science Reference. doi:10.4018/978-1-4666-4422-9.ch074

Groba, B., Pousada, T., & Nieto, L. (2014). Assistive Technologies, Tools and Resources for the Access and Use of Information and Communication Technologies by People with Disabilities. In Assistive Technologies: Concepts, Methodologies, Tools, and Applications (pp. 246-260). Hershey, PA: Information Science Reference. doi:10.4018/978-1-4666-4422-9.ch013

Groß, M. (2013). Personal Knowledge Management and Social Media: What Students Need to Learn for Business Life. In M. Pătruţ & B. Pătruţ (Eds.), *Social Media in Higher Education: Teaching in Web 2.0* (pp. 124–143). Hershey, PA: Information Science Reference; doi:10.4018/978-1-4666-2970-7.ch007

Grossman, D. (2002, April). *New Terminology and Clarifications for Diffserv (RFC 3260).* IETF. Retrieved from http://www.ietf.org/rfc/rfc2002.txt

Guédon, J. C. (2001). *A l'ombre d'Oldenburg: Bibliothecaires, chercheurs scientifiques, maisons d'edition et le controle des publications scientifiques.* Paper presented at the Association of Research Libraries Meeting, Toronto, Canada. Retrieved from https://halshs.archives-ouvertes.fr/halshs-00395366/document

Guédon, J. C. (2001). *In Oldenburg's Long Shadow. Librarians, Research Scientists, Publishers, and the Control of Scientific Publishing.* Association of Research Libraries. Retrieved March 1, 2014, from http://www.arl.org/storage/documents/publications/in-oldenburgs-long-shadow.pdf

Gu, L., Aiken, M., Wang, J., & Wibowo, K. (2011). The Influence of Information Control upon On-line Shopping Behavior. [IJTHI]. *International Journal of Technology and Human Interaction*, 7(1), 56–66. doi:10.4018/jthi.2011010104

Guss, D. (2014). Descripción of the book: *To weave and sing: Art, symbol, and narrative in the South American rainforest.* Retrieved from http://www.ucpress.edu/book.php?isbn=9780520071858

Guss, D. (1990). *To weave and sing.* Berkeley, CA: University of California Press.

Habermas, J. (1968). *Technik und wissenschaft als "ideologie".* Frankfurt am Main: Suhrkamp.

Habermas, J. (1999). *Ciencia y tecnología como ideología* (2nd ed.). Editorial Tecnos.

Hahn, R. W., & Litan, R. W. (2007). The myth of network neutrality and what we should Do about it. *International Journal of Communication*, 1, 596–606.

Hahn, R. W., & Wallsten, S. (2006). The economics of net neutrality. *The Economists' Voice*, 3(6), 1–7. doi:10.2202/1553-3832.1194

Hainz, T. (2012). Value Lexicality and Human Enhancement. [IJT]. *International Journal of Technoethics*, 3(4), 54–65. doi:10.4018/jte.2012100105

Harari, H. (2013, June). *Technology May Endanger Democracy.* Retrieved February 27, 2015, from http://edge.org/response-detail/23835

Hardin, G. (1968, December). The tragedy of commons. *Science*, 162(3859), 1243–1248. doi:10.1126/science.162.3859.1243 PMID:5699198

Harnesk, D., & Lindström, J. (2014). Exploring Socio-Technical Design of Crisis Management Information Systems. In Crisis Management: Concepts, Methodologies, Tools and Applications (pp. 514-530). Hershey, PA: Information Science Reference. doi:10.4018/978-1-4666-4707-7.ch023

Heggestuen, J. (2013, December 15). *One In Every 5 People In The World Own A Smartphone, One In Every 17 Own A Tablet* [CHART]. Retrieved February 27, 2015, from http://www.businessinsider.com/smartphone-and-tablet-penetration-2013-10

Heidegger, M. (1982). The Question Concerning Technology. In M. Heidegger (Ed.), The Question Concerning Technology, and Other Essays (p. 224). Perennial.

Heidegger, M. (1977). The question concerning technology. In *The question concerning technology and other essays* (pp. 3–35). New York, NY: Harper Torchbooks.

Heller, M. (1998). The tragedy of the anticommons: Property in the transition from Marx to markets. *Harvard Law Review, 111*(3), 621–688. doi:10.2307/1342203

Heller, M. (2008). *The gridlock economy: How too much ownership wrecks markets, stops innovation and costs lives.* New York: Basic Books.

Heller, M., & Eisenberg, R. (1998). Can patents deter innovation? The anticommons in biomedical research. *Science, 280*(5364), 698–701. doi:10.1126/science.280.5364.698 PMID:9563938

Helms, R., Ignacio, R., Brinkkemper, S., & Zonneveld, A. (2010). Limitations of Network Analysis for Studying Efficiency and Effectiveness of Knowledge Sharing. *Electronic Journal of Knowledge Management, 8*(1), 53–67.

Henkel, J., & Reitzgi, M. (2010). *Patent Trolls, the sustainability of 'locking-in-to-extort' strategies, and implications for innovating firms.* Retrieved from http://ssrn.com/abstract=985602

Herman, E., & Chomsky, N. (2010). *Manufacturing Consent: The Political Economy of the Mass Media.* New York: Pantheon Books.

Hess, S. (2013, February 22). *Why Wasn't There a Chinese Spring?* Retrieved February 27, 2015, from http://thediplomat.com/2013/02/why-wasnt-there-a-chinese-spring/

Hess, C., & Ostrom, E. (2001). Artifacts, facilities, and content: Information as a common-pool resource. *Law and Contemporary Problems, 66*, 111–145.

Hess, D. J. (1997). *Science studies: An advanced introduction.* New York: NYU press.

Hettinger, E. C. (1989). Justifying intellectual property. *Philosophy & Public Affairs, 18*(1), 31–52.

Hicks, D. (2014). Ethics in the Age of Technological Change and its Impact on the Professional Identity of Librarians. In *Technology and Professional Identity of Librarians: The Making of the Cybrarian* (pp. 168–187). Hershey, PA: Information Science Reference; doi:10.4018/978-1-4666-4735-0.ch009

Hicks, D. (2014). Technology, Profession, Identity. In *Technology and Professional Identity of Librarians: The Making of the Cybrarian* (pp. 1–20). Hershey, PA: Information Science Reference; doi:10.4018/978-1-4666-4735-0.ch001

Himanen, P. (2001). The hacker ethic and the spirit of the information age. New York, NY: Random House. Retrieved from http://portal.feaa.uaic.ro/isg/Shared%20Documents/The.Hacker.Ethic.pdf

Himanen, P. (2001). The hacker ethic and the spirit of the information age. New York: Random House; Retrieved from http://portal.feaa.uaic.ro/isg/Shared%20Documents/The.Hacker.Ethic.pdf

Hirata, M., Yanagisawa, T., Matsushita, K., Sugata, H., Kamitani, Y., Suzuki, T., . . . Yoshimine, T. (2014). Brain-Machine Interface Using Brain Surface Electrodes: Real-Time Robotic Control and a Fully Implantable Wireless System. In Assistive Technologies: Concepts, Methodologies, Tools, and Applications (pp. 1535-1548). Hershey, PA: Information Science Reference. doi:10.4018/978-1-4666-4422-9.ch080

Hodge, B. (2014). Critical Electronic Discourse Analysis: Social and Cultural Research in the Electronic Age. In H. Lim & F. Sudweeks (Eds.), *Innovative Methods and Technologies for Electronic Discourse Analysis* (pp. 191–209). Hershey, PA: Information Science Reference; doi:10.4018/978-1-4666-4426-7.ch009

Hoey, J., Poupart, P., Boutilier, C., & Mihailidis, A. (2014). POMDP Models for Assistive Technology. In Assistive Technologies: Concepts, Methodologies, Tools, and Applications (pp. 120-140). Hershey, PA: Information Science Reference. doi:10.4018/978-1-4666-4422-9.ch007

Hogg, T., & Huberman, B. (2007). *Solving the organizational free riding problem with social networks.* Technical Report. HP Labs, American Association for Artificial Intelligence. Retrieved from: http://www.hpl.hp.com/research/scl/papers/insurance/AAAIinsurance.pdf

Hogg, S. (2014). An Informal Use of Facebook to Encourage Student Collaboration and Motivation for Off Campus Activities. In G. Mallia (Ed.), *The Social Classroom: Integrating Social Network Use in Education* (pp. 23–39). Hershey, PA: Information Science Reference; doi:10.4018/978-1-4666-4904-0.ch002

Holman, C. M. (2008). Trends in human gene patent litigation. *Science*, *322*(5899), 198–199. doi:10.1126/science.1160687 PMID:18845733

Holmqvist, E., & Buchholz, M. (2014). A Model for Gaze Control Assessments and Evaluation. In Assistive Technologies: Concepts, Methodologies, Tools, and Applications (pp. 332-343). Hershey, PA: Information Science Reference. doi:10.4018/978-1-4666-4422-9.ch016

House, F. (2011). *Freedom on the net 2011: A global assessment of internet and digital media*. New York: Freedom House.

Howkins, J. (2005, September). Enhancing creativity. In Creative Industries: A symposium on culture based development strategies. New Delhi, India: Malvika Singh Editor.

Hsiao, S., Chen, D., Yang, C., Huang, H., Lu, Y., Huang, H., & Lin, Y. et al. (2013). Chemical-Free and Reusable Cellular Analysis: Electrochemical Impedance Spectroscopy with a Transparent ITO Culture Chip.[IJTHI]. *International Journal of Technology and Human Interaction*, *8*(3), 1–9. doi:10.4018/jthi.2012070101

Hsu, M., Yang, C., Wang, C., & Lin, Y. (2013). Simulation-Aided Optimal Microfluidic Sorting for Monodispersed Microparticles.[IJTHI]. *International Journal of Technology and Human Interaction*, *8*(3), 10–18. doi:10.4018/jthi.2012070102

Huang, K. G., & Murray, F. E. (2009). Does patent strategy shape the long-run supply of public knowledge? Evidence from human genetics. *Academy of Management Journal*, *52*(6), 1139–1221. doi:10.5465/AMJ.2009.47084665

Huang, W. D., & Tettegah, S. Y. (2014). Cognitive Load and Empathy in Serious Games: A Conceptual Framework. In J. Bishop (Ed.), *Gamification for Human Factors Integration: Social, Education, and Psychological Issues* (pp. 17–30). Hershey, PA: Information Science Reference; doi:10.4018/978-1-4666-5071-8.ch002

Huesmann, R. (2007). The Impact of Electronic Media Violence: Scientific Theory and Research. *The Journal of Adolescent Health*, *41*(6Supplement), S6–S13. doi:10.1016/j.jadohealth.2007.09.005 PMID:18047947

Huffington Post. (2011, February 11). *Egypt's Facebook Revolution: Wael Ghonim Thanks The Social Network*. Retrieved July 26, 2014, from http://www.huffingtonpost.com/2011/02/11/egypt-facebook-revolution-wael-ghonim_n_822078.html

Huseyinov, I. N. (2014). Fuzzy Linguistic Modelling in Multi Modal Human Computer Interaction: Adaptation to Cognitive Styles using Multi Level Fuzzy Granulation Method. In Assistive Technologies: Concepts, Methodologies, Tools, and Applications (pp. 1481-1496). Hershey, PA: Information Science Reference. doi:10.4018/978-1-4666-4422-9.ch077

Hwa, S. P., Weei, P. S., & Len, L. H. (2012). The Effects of Blended Learning Approach through an Interactive Multimedia E-Book on Students' Achievement in Learning Chinese as a Second Language at Tertiary Level.[IJCALLT]. *International Journal of Computer-Assisted Language Learning and Teaching*, *2*(1), 35–50. doi:10.4018/ijcallt.2012010104

IEEE. (2002). *WG12: Learning Object Metadata*. IEEE Standard for Learning Object Metadata. Retrieved July 1, 2009, from http://ltsc.ieee.org/wg12/

Iglesias, A., Ruiz-Mezcua, B., López, J. F., & Figueroa, D. C. (2014). New Communication Technologies for Inclusive Education in and outside the Classroom. In Assistive Technologies: Concepts, Methodologies, Tools, and Applications (pp. 1675-1689). Hershey, PA: Information Science Reference. doi:10.4018/978-1-4666-4422-9.ch088

Illich, I. (1971). *Deschooling Society*. New York: Harper Colophon Books.

informationactivism.org. (n.d.). *Postage Stamps Document the Revolution*. Retrieved July 26, 2014, from https://informationactivism.org/en/postage-stamps-document-revolution

Inghilterra, X., & Ravatua-Smith, W. S. (2014). Online Learning Communities: Use of Micro Blogging for Knowledge Construction. In J. Pelet (Ed.), *E-Learning 2.0 Technologies and Web Applications in Higher Education* (pp. 107–128). Hershey, PA: Information Science Reference; doi:10.4018/978-1-4666-4876-0.ch006

Input–Output Model . (2014). Retrieved from http://en.wikipedia.org/wiki/Input-output_model

Instituto de Estadística de la UNESCO. (2012). *Uso de TIC en Educación en América Latina y El Caribe. Análisis regional de la integración de las TIC en la educación y de la aptitud digital (e-readiness)*. Retrieved March 25, 2014 from: http://www.uis.unesco.org/Communication/Documents/ict-regional-survey-lac-2012-sp.pdf

International Association of Chiefs of Police. (2013). *Guiding Principles on Cloud Computing in Law Enforcement*. Retrieved 26 February, 2015 from http://www.theiacp.org/Portals/0/documents/pdfs/CloudComputingPrinciples.pdf

Ionescu, A. (2013). Cyber Identity: Our Alter-Ego? In R. Luppicini (Ed.), *Handbook of Research on Technoself: Identity in a Technological Society* (pp. 189–203). Hershey, PA: Information Science Reference; doi:10.4018/978-1-4666-2211-1.ch011

Iyengar, S. (1990). The accessibility bias in politics: Television news and public opinion. *International Journal of Public Opinion Research*, *2*(1), 1–15. doi:10.1093/ijpor/2.1.1

Iyengar, S. (1991). *Is Anyone Responsible? How Television Frames Political Issues*. Chicago: University of Chicago Press.

Iyengar, S., & Kinder, D. (1987). *News that matters: Television and American opinion*. Chicago, IL: University of Chicago Press.

Jackson, M. W. (2010). The patenting of human genes: a cautionary tale. *Cable, 37*(2), 11–14.

Jacobs, P., & Gosselin, P. G. (2000, March 21). Profiteering & shoddy science: Error found in patent of aids gene. *Los Angeles Times*. Retrieved from http://articles.latimes.com/2000/mar/21/news/mn-11091

Jaffe, A. B., & Lerner, J. (2001). Reinventing public R&D: Patent policy and the commercialization of national laboratory technologies. *The Rand Journal of Economics*, *32*(1), 167–198. doi:10.2307/2696403

Jakeman, A. J., Letcher, R. A., & Norton, J. P. (2006). Ten iterative steps in development and evaluation of environmental models. *Environmental Modelling & Software*, *21*(5), 602–614. doi:10.1016/j.envsoft.2006.01.004

James, C. (2013). Situación mundial de los cultivos biotecnológicos/GM: 2012. Executive summary. International Service for the Acquisition of Agri-Biotech Applications. Retrieved from http://www.isaaa.org/resources/publications/briefs/44/executivesummary/pdf/Brief%2044%20-%20Executive%20Summary%20-%20Spanish.pdf

Janssen, M. A., Alessa, L. N., Barton, M., Bergin, S., & Lee, A. (2008). Towards a community framework for agent-based modelling. *Journal of Artificial Societies and Social Simulation, 11*(2), 6. Retrieved from http://jasss.soc.surrey.ac.uk/11/2/6.html

Jan, Y., Lin, M., Shiao, K., Wei, C., Huang, L., & Sung, Q. (2013). Development of an Evaluation Instrument for Green Building Literacy among College Students in Taiwan.[IJTHI]. *International Journal of Technology and Human Interaction*, *8*(3), 31–45. doi:10.4018/jthi.2012070104

Jawadi, N. (2013). E-Leadership and Trust Management: Exploring the Moderating Effects of Team Virtuality. [IJTHI]. *International Journal of Technology and Human Interaction*, *9*(3), 18–35. doi:10.4018/jthi.2013070102

Jiménez-Castillo, D., & Fernández, R. S. (2014). The Impact of Combining Video Podcasting and Lectures on Students' Assimilation of Additional Knowledge: An Empirical Examination. In J. Pelet (Ed.), *E-Learning 2.0 Technologies and Web Applications in Higher Education* (pp. 65–87). Hershey, PA: Information Science Reference; doi:10.4018/978-1-4666-4876-0.ch004

Jin, L. (2013). A New Trend in Education: Technoself Enhanced Social Learning. In R. Luppicini (Ed.), *Handbook of Research on Technoself: Identity in a Technological Society* (pp. 456–473). Hershey, PA: Information Science Reference; doi:10.4018/978-1-4666-2211-1.ch025

Johansson, L. (2012). The Functional Morality of Robots. In R. Luppicini (Ed.), *Ethical Impact of Technological Advancements and Applications in Society* (pp. 254–262). Hershey, PA: Information Science Reference; doi:10.4018/978-1-4666-1773-5.ch020

Johansson, L. (2013). Robots and the Ethics of Care. [IJT]. *International Journal of Technoethics*, *4*(1), 67–82. doi:10.4018/jte.2013010106

Johri, A., Dufour, M., Lo, J., & Shanahan, D. (2013). Adwiki: Socio-Technical Design for Mananging Advising Knowledge in a Higher Education Context.[IJSKD]. *International Journal of Sociotechnology and Knowledge Development, 5*(1), 37–59. doi:10.4018/jskd.2013010104

Jones, M. G., Schwilk, C. L., & Bateman, D. F. (2014). Reading by Listening: Access to Books in Audio Format for College Students with Print Disabilities. In Assistive Technologies: Concepts, Methodologies, Tools, and Applications (pp. 454-477). Hershey, PA: Information Science Reference. doi:10.4018/978-1-4666-4422-9.ch022

Jones, P. (2001). Collaborative Knowledge Management, Social Networks, and Organizational Learning. In *Proceedings of the Ninth International Conference on Human-Computer Interaction* (pp. 310-314). Academic Press.

Kaba, B., & Osei-Bryson, K. (2012). An Empirical Investigation of External Factors Influencing Mobile Technology Use in Canada: A Preliminary Study.[IJTHI]. *International Journal of Technology and Human Interaction, 8*(2), 1–14. doi:10.4018/jthi.2012040101

Kampf, C. E. (2012). Revealing the Socio-Technical Design of Global E-Businesses: A Case of Digital Artists Engaging in Radical Transparency.[IJSKD]. *International Journal of Sociotechnology and Knowledge Development, 4*(4), 18–31. doi:10.4018/jskd.2012100102

Kandroudi, M., & Bratitsis, T. (2014). Classifying Facebook Usage in the Classroom or Around It. In G. Mallia (Ed.), *The Social Classroom: Integrating Social Network Use in Education* (pp. 62–81). Hershey, PA: Information Science Reference; doi:10.4018/978-1-4666-4904-0.ch004

Kathleen, J. (2000). *The interplay of influence.* Belmont, UK: Wadsworth.

Katzman, J. (2002). *4GW: What is 4ᵗʰ generation warfare?.* Retrieved from: http://windsofchange.net/archives/002736.html

Kennedy, J. J. (2012). What Is the Color of a Non-Revolution: Why the Jasmine Revolution and Arab Spring Did Not Spread to China. *Whitehead Journal of Diplomacy and International Relations, 13*, 63.

Kenney, M. (1987). The ethical dilemmas of university - industry collaborations. *Journal of Business Ethics, 6*(2), 127–135. doi:10.1007/BF00382026

Kepler, T. B., Crossman, C., & Cook-Deegan, R. (2010). Metastasizing patent claims on BRCA1. *Genomics, 95*(5), 312–314. doi:10.1016/j.ygeno.2010.03.003 PMID:20226239

Kidd, P. T. (2014). Social Networking Technologies as a Strategic Tool for the Development of Sustainable Production and Consumption: Applications to Foster the Agility Needed to Adapt Business Models in Response to the Challenges Posed by Climate Change. In Sustainable Practices: Concepts, Methodologies, Tools and Applications (pp. 974-987). Hershey, PA: Information Science Reference. doi:10.4018/978-1-4666-4852-4.ch054

Kirby, S. D., & Sellers, D. M. (2014). The LiveAbility House: A Collaborative Adventure in Discovery Learning. In Assistive Technologies: Concepts, Methodologies, Tools, and Applications (pp. 1626-1649). Hershey, PA: Information Science Reference. doi:10.4018/978-1-4666-4422-9.ch086

Kitchenham, A., & Bowes, D. (2014). Voice/Speech Recognition Software: A Discussion of the Promise for Success and Practical Suggestions for Implementation. In Assistive Technologies: Concepts, Methodologies, Tools, and Applications (pp. 1005-1011). Hershey, PA: Information Science Reference. doi:10.4018/978-1-4666-4422-9.ch051

Knuth, D. E. (1992). *Literate Programming.* Center for the Study of Language and Information Publications, Stanford University.

Konrath, S. (2013). The Empathy Paradox: Increasing Disconnection in the Age of Increasing Connection. In R. Luppicini (Ed.), *Handbook of Research on Technoself: Identity in a Technological Society* (pp. 204–228). Hershey, PA: Information Science Reference; doi:10.4018/978-1-4666-2211-1.ch012

Koutsabasis, P., & Istikopoulou, T. G. (2013). Perceived Website Aesthetics by Users and Designers: Implications for Evaluation Practice.[IJTHI]. *International Journal of Technology and Human Interaction, 9*(2), 39–52. doi:10.4018/jthi.2013040103

Kraft, E., & Wang, J. (2012). An Exploratory Study of the Cyberbullying and Cyberstalking Experiences and Factors Related to Victimization of Students at a Public Liberal Arts College. In R. Luppicini (Ed.), *Ethical Impact of Technological Advancements and Applications in Society* (pp. 113–131). Hershey, PA: Information Science Reference; doi:10.4018/978-1-4666-1773-5.ch009

Kriesi, H. (1998). *Le système politique suisse* (2nd ed.). Paris: Económica.

Krimsky, S. (2003). *Science in the private interest: Has the lure of profits corrupted biomedical research.* Lanham: Rowman & Littlefield Publishers.

Krsul, I., & Spafford, E. H. (1997). Authorship analysis: Identifying the author of a program. *Computers & Security, 16*(3), 233–257. doi:10.1016/S0167-4048(97)00005-9

Kulman, R., Stoner, G., Ruffolo, L., Marshall, S., Slater, J., Dyl, A., & Cheng, A. (2014). Teaching Executive Functions, Self-Management, and Ethical Decision-Making through Popular Videogame Play. In Assistive Technologies: Concepts, Methodologies, Tools, and Applications (pp. 771-785). Hershey, PA: Information Science Reference. doi:10.4018/978-1-4666-4422-9.ch039

Kunc, L., Míkovec, Z., & Slavík, P. (2013). Avatar and Dialog Turn-Yielding Phenomena.[IJTHI]. *International Journal of Technology and Human Interaction, 9*(2), 66–88. doi:10.4018/jthi.2013040105

Kuo, N., & Dai, Y. (2012). Applying the Theory of Planned Behavior to Predict Low-Carbon Tourism Behavior: A Modified Model from Taiwan.[IJTHI]. *International Journal of Technology and Human Interaction, 8*(4), 45–62. doi:10.4018/jthi.2012100103

Kurt, S. (2014). Accessibility Issues of Educational Web Sites. In Assistive Technologies: Concepts, Methodologies, Tools, and Applications (pp. 54-62). Hershey, PA: Information Science Reference. doi:10.4018/978-1-4666-4422-9.ch004

Kuypers, J. (2009). Framing Analysis. In K. Jim (Ed.), *Rhetorical Criticism: Perspectives in Action*. Lexington Books.

Kuzma, J. (2013). Empirical Study of Cyber Harassment among Social Networks.[IJTHI]. *International Journal of Technology and Human Interaction, 9*(2), 53–65. doi:10.4018/jthi.2013040104

Kyriakaki, G., & Matsatsinis, N. (2014). Pedagogical Evaluation of E-Learning Websites with Cognitive Objectives. In D. Yannacopoulos, P. Manolitzas, N. Matsatsinis, & E. Grigoroudis (Eds.), *Evaluating Websites and Web Services: Interdisciplinary Perspectives on User Satisfaction* (pp. 224–240). Hershey, PA: Information Science Reference; doi:10.4018/978-1-4666-5129-6.ch013

Latour, B. (2005). *Reassembling the Social: An Introduction to Actor-Network-Theory.* New York: Oxford University Press.

Law, A. M., & Kelton, W. D. (2000). *Simulation Modelling and Analysis.* McGraw Hill Higher Education.

Lee, R., & Coccaro, E. (2007). Neurobiology of Impulsive Aggression: Focus on serotonin and the orbitofrontal cortex. In D. Flannery, A. Vazsonyi & I. Waldman (Eds.), The Cambridge Handbook of Violent Behavior and Aggression (pp. 170-186). Cambridge, UK: Cambridge University Press.

Lee, H., & Baek, E. (2012). Facilitating Deep Learning in a Learning Community.[IJTHI]. *International Journal of Technology and Human Interaction, 8*(1), 1–13. doi:10.4018/jthi.2012010101

Lee, W., Wu, T., Cheng, Y., Chuang, Y., & Sheu, S. (2013). Using the Kalman Filter for Auto Bit-rate H.264 Streaming Based on Human Interaction.[IJTHI]. *International Journal of Technology and Human Interaction, 9*(4), 58–74. doi:10.4018/ijthi.2013100104

Leff, E. (2003). *Epistemología ambiental.* Sao Paulo: Cortez Editora.

Legislatura de la Provincia de Santa Fe. Argentina. (2004). *Ley 12360 del 18 de Noviembre de 2004.* Retrieved March 25, 2014, from http://www.proposicion.org.ar/proyecto/leyes/11134-BRA/texto_aprobado.html

Lemley, M. A. (2011). *The myth of the sole inventor.* Stanford Public Law Working Paper No. 1856610. Retrieved from http://ssrn.com/abstract=1856610

Lemley, M. A. (2008). Are universties patents trolls? *Fordham Intellectual Property. Media & Entertainment Law Journal, 18*, 611–631.

Lemley, M. A., & Lessig, L. (2000). The end of end-to-end: Preserving the architecture of the Internet in the broadband era. *UCLA Law Review. University of California, Los Angeles. School of Law, 48*, 925–972.

León, L. (2004). Software libre y su rol en el desarrollo tecnológico del País. In *Software libre - Uso y desarrollo en la administración pública venezolana. Serie Conocimiento para el desarrollo sustentable.* Caracas, Venezuela: Ministerio de Ciencia y Tecnología.

Ley que privatiza la semilla campesina. (2013, 22 October) [Video file]. Retrieved from http://www.youtube.com/watch?v=uWoZIM0QkdU

Leyton-Brown, K., & Shoham, Y. (2008). *Essentials of Game Theory.* Morgan and Claypool, Publishers.

Lin, C., Chu, L., & Hsu, H. (2013). Study on the Performance and Exhaust Emissions of Motorcycle Engine Fuelled with Hydrogen-Gasoline Compound Fuel.[IJTHI]. *International Journal of Technology and Human Interaction, 8*(3), 69–81. doi:10.4018/jthi.2012070107

Linek, S. B., Marte, B., & Albert, D. (2014). Background Music in Educational Games: Motivational Appeal and Cognitive Impact. In J. Bishop (Ed.), *Gamification for Human Factors Integration: Social, Education, and Psychological Issues* (pp. 259–271). Hershey, PA: Information Science Reference; doi:10.4018/978-1-4666-5071-8.ch016

Lin, L. (2013). Multiple Dimensions of Multitasking Phenomenon.[IJTHI]. *International Journal of Technology and Human Interaction, 9*(1), 37–49. doi:10.4018/jthi.2013010103

Lin, T., Li, X., Wu, Z., & Tang, N. (2013). Automatic Cognitive Load Classification Using High-Frequency Interaction Events: An Exploratory Study.[IJTHI]. *International Journal of Technology and Human Interaction, 9*(3), 73–88. doi:10.4018/jthi.2013070106

Lin, T., Wu, Z., Tang, N., & Wu, S. (2013). Exploring the Effects of Display Characteristics on Presence and Emotional Responses of Game Players.[IJTHI]. *International Journal of Technology and Human Interaction, 9*(1), 50–63. doi:10.4018/jthi.2013010104

Lin, T., Xie, T., Mou, Y., & Tang, N. (2013). Markov Chain Models for Menu Item Prediction.[IJTHI]. *International Journal of Technology and Human Interaction, 9*(4), 75–94. doi:10.4018/ijthi.2013100105

Lin, X., & Luppicini, R. (2011). Socio-Technical Influences of Cyber Espionage: A Case Study of the GhostNet System.[IJT]. *International Journal of Technoethics, 2*(2), 65–77. doi:10.4018/jte.2011040105

Lippmann, W. (1922). *Public Opinion.* New York: Harcourt.

Lipschutz, R. D., & Hester, R. J. (2014). We Are the Borg! Human Assimilation into Cellular Society. In M. Michael & K. Michael (Eds.), *Uberveillance and the Social Implications of Microchip Implants: Emerging Technologies* (pp. 366–407). Hershey, PA: Information Science Reference; doi:10.4018/978-1-4666-4582-0.ch016

Liu, C., Zhong, Y., Ozercan, S., & Zhu, Q. (2013). Facilitating 3D Virtual World Learning Environments Creation by Non-Technical End Users through Template-Based Virtual World Instantiation.[IJVPLE]. *International Journal of Virtual and Personal Learning Environments, 4*(1), 32–48. doi:10.4018/jvple.2013010103

Liu, F., Lo, H., Su, C., Lou, D., & Lee, W. (2013). High Performance Reversible Data Hiding for Mobile Applications and Human Interaction.[IJTHI]. *International Journal of Technology and Human Interaction, 9*(4), 41–57. doi:10.4018/ijthi.2013100103

Liu, H. (2012). From Cold War Island to Low Carbon Island: A Study of Kinmen Island.[IJTHI]. *International Journal of Technology and Human Interaction, 8*(4), 63–74. doi:10.4018/jthi.2012100104

Livet, P., Müller, J.-P., Phan, D., & Sanders, L. (2010). Ontology, a mediator for agent-based modeling in social science. *Journal of Artificial Societies and Social Simulation, 13*(1), 3. Retrieved from http://jasss.soc.surrey.ac.uk/13/1/3.html

Livingston, S. (1997). Clarifying the CNN Effect: An Examination of Media Effects According to Type of Military Intervention. Cambridge, MA: John F. Kennedy School of Government's. Joan Shorenstein Center on the Press, Politics and Public Policy at Harvard University. Retrieved from http://genocidewatch.info/images/1997C larifyingtheCNNEffect-Livingston.pdf

Lixun, Z., Dapeng, B., & Lei, Y. (2014). Design of and Experimentation with a Walking Assistance Robot. In Assistive Technologies: Concepts, Methodologies, Tools, and Applications (pp. 1600-1605). Hershey, PA: Information Science Reference. doi:10.4018/978-1-4666-4422-9.ch084

Li, Y., Guo, N. Y., & Ranieri, M. (2014). Designing an Online Interactive Learning Program to Improve Chinese Migrant Children's Internet Skills: A Case Study at Hangzhou Minzhu Experimental School. In Z. Yang, H. Yang, D. Wu, & S. Liu (Eds.), *Transforming K-12 Classrooms with Digital Technology* (pp. 249–265). Hershey, PA: Information Science Reference; doi:10.4018/978-1-4666-4538-7.ch013

Low, R., Jin, P., & Sweller, J. (2014). Instructional Design in Digital Environments and Availability of Mental Resources for the Aged Subpopulation. In Assistive Technologies: Concepts, Methodologies, Tools, and Applications (pp. 1131-1154). Hershey, PA: Information Science Reference. doi:10.4018/978-1-4666-4422-9.ch059

Luczak, H., Schlick, C. M., Jochems, N., Vetter, S., & Kausch, B. (2014). Touch Screens for the Elderly: Some Models and Methods, Prototypical Development and Experimental Evaluation of Human-Computer Interaction Concepts for the Elderly. In Assistive Technologies: Concepts, Methodologies, Tools, and Applications (pp. 377-396). Hershey, PA: Information Science Reference. doi:10.4018/978-1-4666-4422-9.ch019

Luor, T., Lu, H., Johanson, R. E., & Yu, H. (2012). Minding the Gap Between First and Continued Usage of a Corporate E-Learning English-language Program. [IJTHI]. *International Journal of Technology and Human Interaction*, 8(1), 55–74. doi:10.4018/jthi.2012010104

Luppicini, R. (2013). The Emerging Field of Technoself Studies (TSS). In R. Luppicini (Ed.), *Handbook of Research on Technoself: Identity in a Technological Society* (pp. 1–25). Hershey, PA: Information Science Reference; doi:10.4018/978-1-4666-2211-1.ch001

MacIntyre, A. (1985). *After virtue: a study in moral theory*. London: Duckworth.

Madey v. Duke 307 F.3d 1351, (Fed. Cir. 2002).

Magnani, L. (2012). Material Cultures and Moral Mediators in Human Hybridization. In R. Luppicini (Ed.), *Ethical Impact of Technological Advancements and Applications in Society* (pp. 1–20). Hershey, PA: Information Science Reference; doi:10.4018/978-1-4666-1773-5.ch001

Maher, D. (2014). Learning in the Primary School Classroom using the Interactive Whiteboard. In K-12 Education: Concepts, Methodologies, Tools, and Applications (pp. 526-538). Hershey, PA: Information Science Reference. doi:10.4018/978-1-4666-4502-8.ch031

Maineri, M. (2013). Collaboriamo! Come i social media ci aiutano a lavorare e a vivere bene in tempo di crisi. Milano, Italy: Hoepli.

Manolache, M., & Patrut, M. (2013). The Use of New Web-Based Technologies in Strategies of Teaching Gender Studies. In M. Pătruţ & B. Pătruţ (Eds.), *Social Media in Higher Education: Teaching in Web 2.0* (pp. 45–74). Hershey, PA: Information Science Reference; doi:10.4018/978-1-4666-2970-7.ch003

Manthiou, A., & Chiang, L., & Liang (Rebecca) Tang. (2013). Identifying and Responding to Customer Needs on Facebook Fan Pages.[IJTHI]. *International Journal of Technology and Human Interaction*, 9(3), 36–52. doi:10.4018/jthi.2013070103

Mapa Productivo de Venezuela. (2014). Retrieved from http://http://miv.cenditel.gob.ve/

Marengo, A., Pagano, A., & Barbone, A. (2013). An Assessment of Customer's Preferences and Improve Brand Awareness Implementation of Social CRM in an Automotive Company.[IJTD]. *International Journal of Technology Diffusion*, 4(1), 1–15. doi:10.4018/jtd.2013010101

Martin, I., Kear, K., Simpkins, N., & Busvine, J. (2013). Social Negotiations in Web Usability Engineering. In M. Garcia-Ruiz (Ed.), *Cases on Usability Engineering: Design and Development of Digital Products* (pp. 26–56). Hershey, PA: Information Science Reference; doi:10.4018/978-1-4666-4046-7.ch002

Martins, T., Carvalho, V., & Soares, F. (2014). An Overview on the Use of Serious Games in Physical Therapy and Rehabilitation. In Assistive Technologies: Concepts, Methodologies, Tools, and Applications (pp. 758-770). Hershey, PA: Information Science Reference. doi:10.4018/978-1-4666-4422-9.ch038

Mathew, D. (2013). Online Anxiety: Implications for Educational Design in a Web 2.0 World. In M. Pătruţ & B. Pătruţ (Eds.), *Social Media in Higher Education: Teaching in Web 2.0* (pp. 305–317). Hershey, PA: Information Science Reference; doi:10.4018/978-1-4666-2970-7.ch015

Maurer, S. M. (2006). Inside the anticommons: Academic scientists' struggle to build a commercially self-supporting human mutations database, 1999–2001. *Research Policy*, *35*(6), 839–853. doi:10.1016/j.respol.2006.04.008

Mazzanti, I., Maolo, A., & Antonicelli, R. (2014). E-Health and Telemedicine in the Elderly: State of the Art. In Assistive Technologies: Concepts, Methodologies, Tools, and Applications (pp. 693-704). Hershey, PA: Information Science Reference. doi:10.4018/978-1-4666-4422-9.ch034

Mazzara, M., Biselli, L., Greco, P. P., Dragoni, N., Marraffa, A., Qamar, N., & de Nicola, S. (2013). Social Networks and Collective Intelligence: A Return to the Agora. In L. Caviglione, M. Coccoli, & A. Merlo (Eds.), *Social Network Engineering for Secure Web Data and Services* (pp. 88–113). Hershey, PA: Information Science Reference; doi:10.4018/978-1-4666-3926-3.ch005

McColl, D., & Nejat, G. (2013). A Human Affect Recognition System for Socially Interactive Robots. In R. Luppicini (Ed.), *Handbook of Research on Technoself: Identity in a Technological Society* (pp. 554–573). Hershey, PA: Information Science Reference; doi:10.4018/978-1-4666-2211-1.ch029

McCombs, M., & Reynolds, A. (2002). News influence on our pictures of the world. In J. Bryant, & M. Oliver (Eds.), *Media effects: Advances in theory and research* (pp. 1-18). Retrieved from: http://www.asc.upenn.edu/gerbner/Asset.aspx?assetID=1617

McCombs, M. (2005). A look at agenda-setting: Past, present and future. *Journalism Studies*, *6*(4), 543–557. doi:10.1080/14616700500250438

McCombs, M., & Shaw, D. (1972). The agenda-setting function of mass media. *Public Opinion Quarterly*, *36*(2), 176–187. doi:10.1086/267990

McCombs, M., Shaw, D., & Weaver, D. (Eds.). (1997). *Communication and democracy: exploring the intellectual frontiers in agenda-setting theory*. Mahwah, NJ: Lawrence Erlbaum Associates.

McCullagh, D. (2002). *Tech companies ask for unfiltered Net*. CNET News. Retrieved from http://news.cnet.com/2100-1023-966307.html

McDonald, A., & Helmer, S. (2011). A Comparative Case Study of Indonesian and UK Organisational Culture Differences in IS Project Management. [IJTHI]. *International Journal of Technology and Human Interaction*, *7*(2), 28–37. doi:10.4018/jthi.2011040104

McDonough, J. F. (2006–2007). The myth of the patent troll: An alternative view of the function of patent dealers in an idea economy. *Emory Law Journal*, *56*, 189–228.

McGee, E. M. (2014). Neuroethics and Implanted Brain Machine Interfaces. In M. Michael & K. Michael (Eds.), *Uberveillance and the Social Implications of Microchip Implants: Emerging Technologies* (pp. 351–365). Hershey, PA: Information Science Reference; doi:10.4018/978-1-4666-4582-0.ch015

McGrath, E., Lowes, S., McKay, M., Sayres, J., & Lin, P. (2014). Robots Underwater! Learning Science, Engineering and 21st Century Skills: The Evolution of Curricula, Professional Development and Research in Formal and Informal Contexts. In K-12 Education: Concepts, Methodologies, Tools, and Applications (pp. 1041-1067). Hershey, PA: Information Science Reference. doi:10.4018/978-1-4666-4502-8.ch062

Compilation of References

McManis, C. R., & Noh, S. (2011). *The impact of the Bayh-Dole act on genetic research and development: Evaluating the arguments and empirical evidence.* Washington University in St. Louis Legal Studies Research Paper Series.

Media Influence. (n.d.). *The Free Dictionary.* Retrieved from: http://encyclopedia.thefreedictionary.com/media+influence

Meissonierm, R., Bourdon, I., Amabile, S., & Boudrandi, S. (2012). Toward an Enacted Approach to Understanding OSS Developer's Motivations.[IJTHI]. *International Journal of Technology and Human Interaction, 8*(1), 38–54. doi:10.4018/jthi.2012010103

Melius, J. (2014). The Role of Social Constructivist Instructional Approaches in Facilitating Cross-Cultural Online Learning in Higher Education. In J. Keengwe, G. Schnellert, & K. Kungu (Eds.), *Cross-Cultural Online Learning in Higher Education and Corporate Training* (pp. 253–270). Hershey, PA: Information Science Reference; doi:10.4018/978-1-4666-5023-7.ch015

Melson, G. F. (2013). Building a Technoself: Children's Ideas about and Behavior toward Robotic Pets. In R. Luppicini (Ed.), *Handbook of Research on Technoself: Identity in a Technological Society* (pp. 592–608). Hershey, PA: Information Science Reference; doi:10.4018/978-1-4666-2211-1.ch031

Mena, R. J. (2014). The Quest for a Massively Multiplayer Online Game that Teaches Physics. In T. Connolly, T. Hainey, E. Boyle, G. Baxter, & P. Moreno-Ger (Eds.), *Psychology, Pedagogy, and Assessment in Serious Games* (pp. 292–316). Hershey, PA: Information Science Reference; doi:10.4018/978-1-4666-4773-2.ch014

Meredith, J., & Potter, J. (2014). Conversation Analysis and Electronic Interactions: Methodological, Analytic and Technical Considerations. In H. Lim & F. Sudweeks (Eds.), *Innovative Methods and Technologies for Electronic Discourse Analysis* (pp. 370–393). Hershey, PA: Information Science Reference; doi:10.4018/978-1-4666-4426-7.ch017

Merges, R. P., & Nelson, R. R. (1990). On the complex economics of patent scope. *Columbia Law Review, 90*(4), 839–916. doi:10.2307/1122920

Merton, R. K. (1973). *The sociology of science: Theoretical and empirical investigations.* The University Chicago Press.

Micelli, S. (2011). Futuro artigiano. Venezia, Italy: Marsilio Editore.

Microsoft Corporation. (2010). *Microsoft Announces Patent Agreement With HTC.* Retrieved from http://news.microsoft.com/2010/04/27/microsoft-announces-patent-agreement-with-htc/

Microsoft. (2014). *Microsoft Research Licence Agreement | Microsoft DOS V1.1 and V2.0.* Retrieved March 25, 2014, from http://www.computerhistory.org/_static/atchm/microsoft-ms-dos-early-source-code/agreement/

Microsystems, S. Inc. (n.d.). *Java Research License. Version 1.6.* Retrieved March 1, 2014, from https://www.java.net/jrl.csp

Millán-Calenti, J. C., & Maseda, A. (2014). Telegerontology®: A New Technological Resource for Elderly Support. In Assistive Technologies: Concepts, Methodologies, Tools, and Applications (pp. 705-719). Hershey, PA: Information Science Reference. doi:10.4018/978-1-4666-4422-9.ch035

Ministerio de Economía y Hacienda del Reino de España. (2011). *Proyecto de Ley de Economía Sostenible.*

Ministry of Transport and Communications of Finland (2009). *Decree on the minimum rate of a functional Internet access as a universal service (732/2009).*

Miscione, G. (2011). Telemedicine and Development: Situating Information Technologies in the Amazon. [IJSKD]. *International Journal of Sociotechnology and Knowledge Development, 3*(4), 15–26. doi:10.4018/jskd.2011100102

Miwa, N., & Wang, Y. (2011). Online Interaction Between On-Campus and Distance Students: Learners' Perspectives.[IJCALLT]. *International Journal of Computer-Assisted Language Learning and Teaching, 1*(3), 54–69. doi:10.4018/ijcallt.2011070104

mobilisationlab.org. (2013). *Facebook users convince Hungarian companies to wash GMOs from food supply.* Retrieved July 26, 2014, from http://www.mobilisationlab. org/facebook-users-convince-hungarian-companies-to-wash-gmos-from-food-supply/

Moglen, E., Sullivan, J. D., & Sullivan, I. (2013). An introduction to the most used FOSS license: the GNU GPL license. In *Legal aspects of free and open source software.* European Commission. Retrieved March 1, 2014, from http://www.europarl.europa.eu/document/ activities/cont/201307/20130702ATT68998/20130702 ATT68998EN.pdf

Mohammed, A. (2006, February 7). *Verizon executive calls for end to Google's "free lunch".* The Washington Post. Retrieved from http://www.washingtonpost.com/wpdyn/ content/article/2006/02/06/AR2006020601624.html

Montes, J. (2014, April 23). Social Media Protests in Mexico Shape Telecom Bill. *Wall Street Journal.* Retrieved July 26, 2014, from http://www.wsj.com/articles/SB1000 14240527023047884045795196332200313644

Moore, M. J., Nakano, T., Suda, T., & Enomoto, A. (2013). Social Interactions and Automated Detection Tools in Cyberbullying. In L. Caviglione, M. Coccoli, & A. Merlo (Eds.), *Social Network Engineering for Secure Web Data and Services* (pp. 67–87). Hershey, PA: Information Science Reference; doi:10.4018/978-1-4666-3926-3.ch004

Morgan, M. (2008). Stop looking under the bridge for imaginary creatures: A comment examining who really deserves the title patent troll. *The Federal Circuit Bar Journal, 17*(2), 165–180.

Morueta, R. T., Gómez, J. I., & Gómez, Á. H. (2012). B-Learning at Universities in Andalusia (Spain): From Traditional to Student-Centred Learning.[IJTHI]. *International Journal of Technology and Human Interaction, 8*(2), 56–76. doi:10.4018/jthi.2012040104

Mosindi, O., & Sice, P. (2011). An Exploratory Theoretical Framework for Understanding Information Behaviour. [IJTHI]. *International Journal of Technology and Human Interaction, 7*(2), 1–8. doi:10.4018/jthi.2011040101

Mott, M. S., & Williams-Black, T. H. (2014). Media-Enhanced Writing Instruction and Assessment. In J. Keengwe, G. Onchwari, & D. Hucks (Eds.), *Literacy Enrichment and Technology Integration in Pre-Service Teacher Education* (pp. 1–16). Hershey, PA: Information Science Reference; doi:10.4018/978-1-4666-4924-8. ch001

Mulligan, C., & Lee, T. B. (2012). Scaling the patent system. *NYU Annual Survey of American Law, 68,* 289. Retrieved from http://ssrn.com/abstract=2016968

Mulvey, F., & Heubner, M. (2014). Eye Movements and Attention. In Assistive Technologies: Concepts, Methodologies, Tools, and Applications (pp. 1030-1054). Hershey, PA: Information Science Reference. doi:10.4018/978-1-4666-4422-9.ch053

Munzer, S. R. (2005). The commons and the anticommons in the law and theory of property. In *The Blackwell Guide to the Philosophy of Law and Legal Theory.* Retrieved from http://ssrn.com/abstract=647063

Muro, B. F., & Delgado, E. C. (2014). RACEM Game for PC for Use as Rehabilitation Therapy for Children with Psychomotor Disability and Results of its Application. In Assistive Technologies: Concepts, Methodologies, Tools, and Applications (pp. 740-757). Hershey, PA: Information Science Reference. doi:10.4018/978-1-4666-4422-9.ch037

Muwanguzi, S., & Lin, L. (2014). Coping with Accessibility and Usability Challenges of Online Technologies by Blind Students in Higher Education. In Assistive Technologies: Concepts, Methodologies, Tools, and Applications (pp. 1227-1244). Hershey, PA: Information Science Reference. doi:10.4018/978-1-4666-4422-9.ch064

Nagesh, G. (2010, August 5). *Kerry: Net-neutrality legislation unlikely, FCC must act.* The Hill. Retrieved from http:// thehill.com/blogs/hillicon-valley/technology/112935-kerry-net-neutrality-legislation-unlikely-fcc-must-act

Najjar, M., Courtemanche, F., Hamam, H., Dion, A., Bauchet, J., & Mayers, A. (2014). DeepKøver: An Adaptive Intelligent Assistance System for Monitoring Impaired People in Smart Homes. In Assistive Technologies: Concepts, Methodologies, Tools, and Applications (pp. 634-661). Hershey, PA: Information Science Reference. doi:10.4018/978-1-4666-4422-9.ch031

Nap, H. H., & Diaz-Orueta, U. (2014). Rehabilitation Gaming. In J. Bishop (Ed.), *Gamification for Human Factors Integration: Social, Education, and Psychological Issues* (pp. 122–147). Hershey, PA: Information Science Reference; doi:10.4018/978-1-4666-5071-8.ch008

Nazemroava, M. D. (2014). Rise of the Anti-Government Flash Mobs: First Ukraine, Now Venezuela. *Global Research*. Retrieved from: http://www.globalresearch. ca/rise-of-the-anti-government-flash-mobs-first-ukraine-now-venezuela/5369691

Neira, E. (2008). *Venezuela: 4th & 5th Republics. The Economic Thing*. Universidad de Los Andes. Retrieved March 1, 2014, from http://www.saber.ula.ve/bitstream/123456789/14622/1/econo.pdf

Nelson, R. R. (1959). The simple economics of basic scientific research. *Journal of Political Economy*, *67*(3), 297–306. doi:10.1086/258177

Nelson, T. E., Clawson, R. A., & Oxley, Z. M. (1997). Media framing of a civil liberties conflict and its effect on tolerance. *The American Political Science Review*, *91*(3), 567–583. doi:10.2307/2952075

Nemertes Research. (2007, November 19). *User demand for the Internet could outpace network capacity by 2010*. Retrieved from http://www.nemertes.com/press_releases/ user_demand_internet_could_outpace_network_capacity_2010

Neves, J., & Pinheiro, L. D. (2012). Cyberbullying: A Sociological Approach. In R. Luppicini (Ed.), *Ethical Impact of Technological Advancements and Applications in Society* (pp. 132–142). Hershey, PA: Information Science Reference; doi:10.4018/978-1-4666-1773-5.ch010

Newtactics.org. (2011). *Mobilizing supporters on social media to get the attention of strategic targets | New Tactics in Human Rights*. Retrieved July 26, 2014, from https:// www.newtactics.org/tactic/mobilizing-supporters-social-media-get-attention-strategic-targets

Nguyen, P. T. (2012). Peer Feedback on Second Language Writing through Blogs: The Case of a Vietnamese EFL Classroom.[IJCALLT]. *International Journal of Computer-Assisted Language Learning and Teaching*, *2*(1), 13–23. doi:10.4018/ijcallt.2012010102

Nichols, K., Blake, S., Baker, F., & Black, D. (1998, December). *Definition of the Differentiated Services Field (DS Field) in the IPv4 and IPv6 Headers (RFC 2474)*. IETF. Retrieved from http://www.ietf.org/rfc/rfc2474.txt

Ninaus, M., Witte, M., Kober, S. E., Friedrich, E. V., Kurzmann, J., Hartsuiker, E., & Wood, G. et al. (2014). Neurofeedback and Serious Games. In T. Connolly, T. Hainey, E. Boyle, G. Baxter, & P. Moreno-Ger (Eds.), *Psychology, Pedagogy, and Assessment in Serious Games* (pp. 82–110). Hershey, PA: Information Science Reference; doi:10.4018/978-1-4666-4773-2.ch005

Noelle-Neumann, E. (1977). Turbulances in the climate of opinion: Methodological applications of the spiral of silence theory. *Public Opinion Quarterly*, *4*(2), 143–158. doi:10.1086/268371

Noiville, C. (1997). *Ressources génétiques et droit. Essai sur les régimes juridiques des ressources génétiques marines*. Paris: Editions Pedone.

Nordström, K. A., & Ridderstrale, J. (2007). *Funky business forever: How to enjoy capitalism*. Upper Saddle River, NJ: Pearson Education.

Norling, E., Edmonds, B., & Meyer, R. (2013). Informal approaches to developing simulation models. In B. Edmonds & R. Meyer (Eds.), *Simulating Social Complexity - A Handbook* (pp. 39–55). Springer. doi:10.1007/978-3-540-93813-2_4

Núñez, J. J. (1999). *La ciencia y la tecnología como procesos sociales. Lo que la educación científica no debería olvidar*. La Habana, Cuba: Editorial Félix Varela.

Núñez, J. J. (1999). *La ciencia y la tecnología como procesos sociales: Lo que la educación científica no debería olvidar*. La Habana, Cuba: Editorial Félix Varela.

Núñez, M. (2007). *La agroecología en la soberanía alimentaria venezolana*. Mérida: Ed. IPIAT.

O'Connell, P. (2005, November 7). Online Extra: At SBC, it's all about "scale and scope". *BusinessWeek*. Retrieved from http://www.businessweek.com/print/magazine/content/05_45/b3958092.htm?chan=gl

Obama, B. (2014). Statement on net neutrality. *The White House*. Retrieved from http://www.whitehouse.gov/net-neutrality

OCDE. (2004). *Patents and innovation: Trends and policy challenges*. Retrieved from http://www.oecd.org/science/sci-tech/24508541.pdf

Ochoa, A. (2008). El sentido de las políticas públicas vinculadas al conocimiento para la transformación social. *Reflexiones desde Cenditel, 4*, 5-31.

Ochoa, A. (2006). *Aprendiendo en torno al Desarrollo Endógeno*. Mérida, Venezuela: CDCHT-ULA.

Ochoa, A. (2006). *Aprendiendo en torno al desarrollo endógeno*. Mérida: CDCHT-ULA.

OECD. (2010a). *Fixed and wireless broadband subscriptions per 100 inhabitants*. Retrieved from http://www.oecd.org/dataoecd/21/35/39574709.xls

OECD. (2010b). *Households with broadband access*. Retrieved from http:// www.oecd.org/dataoecd/20/59/39574039.xls

Olivieri, N. F. (2003). Patients' health or company profits? The commercialisation of academic research. *Science and Engineering Ethics, 9*(1), 29–41. doi:10.1007/s11948-003-0017-x PMID:12645227

Olla, V. (2014). An Enquiry into the use of Technology and Student Voice in Citizenship Education in the K-12 Classroom. In K-12 Education: Concepts, Methodologies, Tools, and Applications (pp. 892-913). Hershey, PA: Information Science Reference. doi:10.4018/978-1-4666-4502-8.ch053

Orange, E. (2013). Understanding the Human-Machine Interface in a Time of Change. In R. Luppicini (Ed.), *Handbook of Research on Technoself: Identity in a Technological Society* (pp. 703–719). Hershey, PA: Information Science Reference; doi:10.4018/978-1-4666-2211-1.ch036

Palmer, D., Warren, I., & Miller, P. (2014). ID Scanners and Überveillance in the Night-Time Economy: Crime Prevention or Invasion of Privacy? In M. Michael & K. Michael (Eds.), *Uberveillance and the Social Implications of Microchip Implants: Emerging Technologies* (pp. 208–225). Hershey, PA: Information Science Reference; doi:10.4018/978-1-4666-4582-0.ch009

Pan, G., & Bonk, C. J. (2007). The Emergence of Open-Source Software in China. *International Review of Research in Open and Distance Learning, 8*(1). Retrieved March 1, 2014 from http://www.irrodl.org/index.php/irrodl/article/view/331/0

Papadopoulos, F., Dautenhahn, K., & Ho, W. C. (2013). Behavioral Analysis of Human-Human Remote Social Interaction Mediated by an Interactive Robot in a Cooperative Game Scenario. In R. Luppicini (Ed.), *Handbook of Research on Technoself: Identity in a Technological Society* (pp. 637–665). Hershey, PA: Information Science Reference; doi:10.4018/978-1-4666-2211-1.ch033

Pardo, D. (2014). Los opositores venezolanos que están hartos de las protestas violentas. *BBC Mundo*. Caracas. Retrieved from: http://www.bbc.co.uk/mundo/noticias/2014/04/140409_venezuela_12_guarimba_oposicion_dp.shtml

Pascual, R. (2011, July 16). Con las patentes no habría sido posible la Capilla Sixtina. *El País.com*.

Patel, K. K., & Vij, S. K. (2014). Unconstrained Walking Plane to Virtual Environment for Non-Visual Spatial Learning. In Assistive Technologies: Concepts, Methodologies, Tools, and Applications (pp. 1580-1599). Hershey, PA: Information Science Reference. doi:10.4018/978-1-4666-4422-9.ch083

Patrone, T. (2013). In Defense of the 'Human Prejudice'. [IJT]. *International Journal of Technoethics, 4*(1), 26–38. doi:10.4018/jte.2013010103

Peevers, G., Williams, R., Douglas, G., & Jack, M. A. (2013). Usability Study of Fingerprint and Palmvein Biometric Technologies at the ATM.[IJTHI]. *International Journal of Technology and Human Interaction, 9*(1), 78–95. doi:10.4018/jthi.2013010106

Pellas, N. (2014). Theoretical Foundations of a CSCL Script in Persistent Virtual Worlds According to the Contemporary Learning Theories and Models. In E. Nikoi & K. Boateng (Eds.), *Collaborative Communication Processes and Decision Making in Organizations* (pp. 72–107). Hershey, PA: Business Science Reference; doi:10.4018/978-1-4666-4478-6.ch005

Perakslis, C. (2014). Willingness to Adopt RFID Implants: Do Personality Factors Play a Role in the Acceptance of Uberveillance? In M. Michael & K. Michael (Eds.), *Uberveillance and the Social Implications of Microchip Implants: Emerging Technologies* (pp. 144–168). Hershey, PA: Information Science Reference; doi:10.4018/978-1-4666-4582-0.ch006

Pereira, G., Brisson, A., Dias, J., Carvalho, A., Dimas, J., Mascarenhas, S., & Paiva, A. et al. (2014). Non-Player Characters and Artificial Intelligence. In T. Connolly, T. Hainey, E. Boyle, G. Baxter, & P. Moreno-Ger (Eds.), *Psychology, Pedagogy, and Assessment in Serious Games* (pp. 127–152). Hershey, PA: Information Science Reference; doi:10.4018/978-1-4666-4773-2.ch007

Pérez Pérez, A., Callejas Carrión, Z., López-Cózar Delgado, R., & Griol Barres, D. (2014). On the Use of Speech Technologies to Achieve Inclusive Education for People with Intellectual Disabilities. In Assistive Technologies: Concepts, Methodologies, Tools, and Applications (pp. 1106-1117). Hershey, PA: Information Science Reference. doi:10.4018/978-1-4666-4422-9.ch057

Perozo, N., Aguilar, J., Terán, O., & Molina, H. (2013). A verification method for MASOES. *IEEE Transactions on Systems, Man, and Cybernetics. Part B, Cybernetics*, *43*(1), 64–76. Retrieved from http://ieeexplore.ieee.org/xpl/articleDetails.jsp?arnumber=6211437

Perozo, N., Aguilar, J., Terán, O., & Molina, H. (2013). A verification method for MASOES. *IEEE Transactions on Systems, Man, and Cybernetics. Part B, Cybernetics*, *43*(1), 64–76. Retrieved from http://ieeexplore.ieee.org/xpl/articleDetails.jsp?arnumber=6211437

Peschl, M. F., & Fundneider, T. (2014). Theory U and Emergent Innovation: Presencing as a Method of Bringing Forth Profoundly New Knowledge and Realities. In O. Gunnlaugson, C. Baron, & M. Cayer (Eds.), *Perspectives on Theory U: Insights from the Field* (pp. 207–233). Hershey, PA: Business Science Reference; doi:10.4018/978-1-4666-4793-0.ch014

Petrovic, N., Jeremic, V., Petrovic, D., & Cirovic, M. (2014). Modeling the Use of Facebook in Environmental Higher Education. In G. Mallia (Ed.), *The Social Classroom: Integrating Social Network Use in Education* (pp. 100–119). Hershey, PA: Information Science Reference; doi:10.4018/978-1-4666-4904-0.ch006

Phua, C., Roy, P. C., Aloulou, H., Biswas, J., Tolstikov, A., Foo, V. S., . . . Xu, D. (2014). State-of-the-Art Assistive Technology for People with Dementia. In Assistive Technologies: Concepts, Methodologies, Tools, and Applications (pp. 1606-1625). Hershey, PA: Information Science Reference. doi:10.4018/978-1-4666-4422-9.ch085

Pierce, B. C. (2002). *Types and programming languages*. Cambridge, MA: MIT Press.

Pignotti, E., Polhill, G., & Edwards, P. (2013). Using provenance to analyse agent-based simulations. In *EDBT '13 Proceedings of the Joint EDBT/ICDT 2013 Workshops* (pp. 319-322). New York, NY: ACM. Retrieved from http://www.edbt.org/Proceedings/2013-Genova/papers/workshops/a46-pignotti.pdf

Pignotti, E., Edwards, P., Gotts, N., & Polhill, G. (2010). Enhancing workflow with a semantic description of scientific intent. *Journal of Web Semantics*, *9*(2), 222–244. doi:10.1016/j.websem.2011.05.001

Polhill, J. G., & Edmonds, B. (2007). Open access for social simulation. *Journal of Artificial Societies and Social Simulation, 10*(3), 10. Retrieved from http://jasss.soc.surrey.ac.uk/10/3/10.html

Polhill, J. G., & Gotts, N. M. (2009). Ontologies for transparent integrated human-natural system modelling. *Landscape Ecology*, *24*(9), 1255–1267. doi:10.1007/s10980-009-9381-5

Police Chief Magazine. (2011). *How Location-Based Services Can Improve Policing*. Retrieved August 5, 2014, from http://www.policechiefmagazine.org/magazine/index.cfm?fuseaction=display_arch&article_id=2402&issue_id=62011

Popper, K. (1963). *Conjectures and refutations*. London: Routledge.

Popper, K. (1967). *The open society and its enemies*. London: Hutchinson.

Posey, D. (2004). International Agreements and intellectual property right protection for indigenous peoples. In *COICA, biodiversity, collective rights and sui generis intellectual property regime*. Ecuador: COICA.

Pot, F., & Associates. (2011 September). *Social innovation of work and employment, challenge social innovation*. Paper presented at Workshop: Social Innovation at Work, Wien.

Potts, L. (2014). Sociotechnical Uses of Social Web Tools during Disasters. In Crisis Management: Concepts, Methodologies, Tools and Applications (pp. 531-541). Hershey, PA: Information Science Reference. doi:10.4018/978-1-4666-4707-7.ch024

Potts, L. (2011). Balancing McLuhan With Williams: A Sociotechnical View of Technological Determinism. [IJSKD]. *International Journal of Sociotechnology and Knowledge Development*, *3*(2), 53–57. doi:10.4018/jskd.2011040105

Potts, L. (2013). Balancing McLuhan With Williams: A Sociotechnical View of Technological Determinism. In J. Abdelnour-Nocera (Ed.), *Knowledge and Technological Development Effects on Organizational and Social Structures* (pp. 109–114). Hershey, PA: Information Science Reference; doi:10.4018/978-1-4666-2151-0.ch007

Preserving the Open Internet, GN Docket No. 09-191, WC Docket No. 07-52, *Report and Order*, 25 FCC Rcd 17905 (2010).

Preserving the Open Internet. (2011, September 23). *Final Rule*. 76 (185). *Federal Register*, *59191*, 59235.

Preserving the Open Internet; Broadband Industry Practices, GN Docket No. 09-191, WC Docket No. 07-52, *Notice of Proposed Rulemaking*, 24 FCC Rcd 13064 (2009).

Proença, R., Guerra, A., & Campos, P. (2013). A Gestural Recognition Interface for Intelligent Wheelchair Users. [IJSKD]. *International Journal of Sociotechnology and Knowledge Development*, *5*(2), 63–81. doi:10.4018/jskd.2013040105

Proposal for a Regulation of the European Parliament and of the Council laying down measures concerning the European single market for electronic communications and to achieve a Connected Continent, and amending Directives 2002/20/EC, 2002/21/EC and 2002/22/EC and Regulations (EC) No 1211/2009 and (EU) No 531/2012. COM (2013) 627 final.

Protecting and Promoting the Open Internet, GN Docket No. 14-28, *Notice of Proposed Rulemaking* 29 FCC Rcd. 5561 (2014).

Public Engines. (2012, September 18). *New Mobile App CityConnect™ Lets Local Law Enforcement Connect Directly to Communities*. Retrieved February 27, 2015, from http://www.publicengines.com/company/press/cityconnect-lets-local-law-enforcement-connect-to-communities.php

Public Opinion. (n.d.). *Wikipedia*. Retrieved from: http://en.wikipedia.org/wiki/Public_opinion

Quilici-Gonzalez, J. A., Kobayashi, G., Broens, M. C., & Gonzalez, M. E. (2012). Ubiquitous Computing: Any Ethical Implications? In R. Luppicini (Ed.), *Ethical Impact of Technological Advancements and Applications in Society* (pp. 47–59). Hershey, PA: Information Science Reference; doi:10.4018/978-1-4666-1773-5.ch005

Ragas, M., & Roberts, M. (2009). Agenda Setting and Agenda Melding in an Age of Horizontal and Vertical Media: A New Theoretical Lens for Virtual Brand Communities. *Journalism & Mass Communication Quarterly*, *86*(1), 45–64. doi:10.1177/107769900908600104

Rai, A. K., & Eisenberg, R. (2003). Bayh-Dole: Reform and the progress of biomedicine. *Law and Contemporary Problems*, *66*(1/2), 289–334.

Rambaree, K. (2014). Computer-Aided Deductive Critical Discourse Analysis of a Case Study from Mauritius with ATLAS-ti 6.2. In H. Lim & F. Sudweeks (Eds.), *Innovative Methods and Technologies for Electronic Discourse Analysis* (pp. 346–368). Hershey, PA: Information Science Reference; doi:10.4018/978-1-4666-4426-7.ch016

Ramírez, L. (2012). *El parque automotor en la República Bolivariana de Venezuela, estratos medios de la población y elecciones 2012. período 1990-2011*. Retrieved from http://despertaruniversitario.org/2011/12/24/el-parque-automotor-en-la-republica-bolivariana-de-venezuela-estratos-medios-de-la-poblacion-y-elecciones-2012-periodo-1990-2011-y-parte-ii/

Ratan, R. (2013). Self-Presence, Explicated: Body, Emotion, and Identity Extension into the Virtual Self. In R. Luppicini (Ed.), *Handbook of Research on Technoself: Identity in a Technological Society* (pp. 322–336). Hershey, PA: Information Science Reference; doi:10.4018/978-1-4666-2211-1.ch018

Read, S., & Dew, N. (2012). *Money from Nothing - The Redhat Story*. British Airways Business Life. Retrieved March 1, 2014, from http://www.effectuation.org/article/money-nothing-redhat-story on March 2014.

Rechy-Ramirez, E. J., & Hu, H. (2014). A Flexible Bio-Signal Based HMI for Hands-Free Control of an Electric Powered Wheelchair.[IJALR]. *International Journal of Artificial Life Research*, *4*(1), 59–76. doi:10.4018/ijalr.2014010105

Reiners, T., Wood, L. C., & Dron, J. (2014). From Chaos Towards Sense: A Learner-Centric Narrative Virtual Learning Space. In J. Bishop (Ed.), *Gamification for Human Factors Integration: Social, Education, and Psychological Issues* (pp. 242–258). Hershey, PA: Information Science Reference; doi:10.4018/978-1-4666-5071-8.ch015

Reinhardt, J., & Ryu, J. (2013). Using Social Network-Mediated Bridging Activities to Develop Socio-Pragmatic Awareness in Elementary Korean.[IJCALLT]. *International Journal of Computer-Assisted Language Learning and Teaching*, *3*(3), 18–33. doi:10.4018/ijcallt.2013070102

Revuelta, P., Jiménez, J., Sánchez, J. M., & Ruiz, B. (2014). Automatic Speech Recognition to Enhance Learning for Disabled Students. In Assistive Technologies: Concepts, Methodologies, Tools, and Applications (pp. 478-493). Hershey, PA: Information Science Reference. doi:10.4018/978-1-4666-4422-9.ch023

Ribeiro, J. C., & Silva, T. (2013). Self, Self-Presentation, and the Use of Social Applications in Digital Environments. In R. Luppicini (Ed.), *Handbook of Research on Technoself: Identity in a Technological Society* (pp. 439–455). Hershey, PA: Information Science Reference; doi:10.4018/978-1-4666-2211-1.ch024

Richet, J. (2013). From Young Hackers to Crackers. [IJTHI]. *International Journal of Technology and Human Interaction*, *9*(3), 53–62. doi:10.4018/jthi.2013070104

Richiardi, M., Leombruni, R., Saam, N., & Sonnessa, M. (2006). A common protocol for agent-based social simulation. *Journal of Artificial Societies and Social Simulation*, *9*(1), 15. Retrieved from http://jasss.soc.surrey.ac.uk/9/1/15.html

Rifkin, J. (1998). *The biotech century*. New York: Tarcher/Putnam.

Rigas, D., & Almutairi, B. (2013). An Empirical Investigation into the Role of Avatars in Multimodal E-government Interfaces.[IJSKD]. *International Journal of Sociotechnology and Knowledge Development*, *5*(1), 14–22. doi:10.4018/jskd.2013010102

Risch, M. (2011). Patent troll myths. *Seton Hall Law Review*, *42*, 457–499.

Rivas, M. (2011). *From creative industries to the creative place: Refreshing the local development agenda in small and medium size towns*. URBACT creative clusters project final report. Óbidos, PT.

Rizzoli, A. E., Donatelli, M., Athanasiadis, I. N., Villa, F., & Huber, D. (2008). Semantic links in integrated modelling frameworks. *Mathematics and Computers in Simulation*, *78*(2-3), 412–423. doi:10.1016/j.matcom.2008.01.017

Robinson, S. (2004). *Simulation – The practice of model development and use*. Wiley.

Rodríguez, W. R., Saz, O., & Lleida, E. (2014). Experiences Using a Free Tool for Voice Therapy based on Speech Technologies. In Assistive Technologies: Concepts, Methodologies, Tools, and Applications (pp. 508-523). Hershey, PA: Information Science Reference. doi:10.4018/978-1-4666-4422-9.ch025

Rogers, E., Dearing, J. W., & Bregman, D. (1993). The anatomy of agenda-setting research. *Journal of Communication, 43*(2), 68–84. doi:10.1111/j.1460-2466.1993.tb01263.x

Ross, C. (2013). *The Venezuelan Guarimba (Into Bizarro World)*. Retrieved from: http://www.counterpunch.org/2013/04/17/the-venezuelan-guarimba/

Rothblatt, M. (2013). Mindclone Technoselves: Multi-Substrate Legal Identities, Cyber-Psychology, and Biocyberethics. In R. Luppicini (Ed.), *Handbook of Research on Technoself: Identity in a Technological Society* (pp. 105–122). Hershey, PA: Information Science Reference; doi:10.4018/978-1-4666-2211-1.ch006

Rowe, N. C. (2012). The Ethics of Cyberweapons in Warfare. In R. Luppicini (Ed.), *Ethical Impact of Technological Advancements and Applications in Society* (pp. 195–207). Hershey, PA: Information Science Reference; doi:10.4018/978-1-4666-1773-5.ch015

Roy, O. (2012). The Transformation of the Arab World. *Journal of Democracy, 23*(3), 5–18. doi:10.1353/jod.2012.0056

Ruane, K. A. (2010). *The FCC's authority to regulate net neutrality after Comcast v. FCC* (Tech. Rep.). Congressional Research Service.

Russo, M. R. (2014). Emergency Management Professional Development: Linking Information Communication Technology and Social Communication Skills to Enhance a Sense of Community and Social Justice in the 21st Century. In Crisis Management: Concepts, Methodologies, Tools and Applications (pp. 651-665). Hershey, PA: Information Science Reference. doi:10.4018/978-1-4666-4707-7.ch031

Sajeva, S. (2011). Towards a Conceptual Knowledge Management System Based on Systems Thinking and Sociotechnical Thinking.[IJSKD]. *International Journal of Sociotechnology and Knowledge Development, 3*(3), 40–55. doi:10.4018/jskd.2011070103

Sajeva, S. (2013). Towards a Conceptual Knowledge Management System Based on Systems Thinking and Sociotechnical Thinking. In J. Abdelnour-Nocera (Ed.), *Knowledge and Technological Development Effects on Organizational and Social Structures* (pp. 115–130). Hershey, PA: Information Science Reference; doi:10.4018/978-1-4666-2151-0.ch008

Saleeb, N., & Dafoulas, G. A. (2014). Assistive Technologies and Environmental Design Concepts for Blended Learning and Teaching for Disabilities within 3D Virtual Worlds and Learning Environments. In Assistive Technologies: Concepts, Methodologies, Tools, and Applications (pp. 1382-1404). Hershey, PA: Information Science Reference. doi:10.4018/978-1-4666-4422-9.ch073

Saltzer, J., Reed, D., & Clark, D. (1984). End-to-end arguments in system design. *ACM Transactions on Computer Systems, 2*(4), 277–288. doi:10.1145/357401.357402

Salvini, P. (2012). Presence, Reciprocity and Robotic Mediations: The Case of Autonomous Social Robots. [IJT]. *International Journal of Technoethics, 3*(2), 9–16. doi:10.4018/jte.2012040102

Samanta, I. (2013). The Impact of Virtual Community (Web 2.0) in the Economic, Social, and Political Environment of Traditional Society. In S. Saeed, M. Khan, & R. Ahmad (Eds.), *Business Strategies and Approaches for Effective Engineering Management* (pp. 262–274). Hershey, PA: Business Science Reference; doi:10.4018/978-1-4666-3658-3.ch016

Samanta, S. K., Woods, J., & Ghanbari, M. (2011). Automatic Language Translation: An Enhancement to the Mobile Messaging Services.[IJTHI]. *International Journal of Technology and Human Interaction, 7*(1), 1–18. doi:10.4018/jthi.2011010101

Sandvine. (2008). *Traffic management in a world with network neutrality* (Tech. Rep.).

Sarkar, N. I., Kuang, A. X., Nisar, K., & Amphawan, A. (2014). Hospital Environment Scenarios using WLAN over OPNET Simulation Tool.[IJICTHD]. *International Journal of Information Communication Technologies and Human Development, 6*(1), 69–90. doi:10.4018/ijicthd.2014010104

Sarré, C. (2013). Technology-Mediated Tasks in English for Specific Purposes (ESP): Design, Implementation and Learner Perception.[IJCALLT]. *International Journal of Computer-Assisted Language Learning and Teaching*, *3*(2), 1–16. doi:10.4018/ijcallt.2013040101

Saykili, A., & Kumtepe, E. G. (2014). Facebook's Hidden Potential: Facebook as an Educational Support Tool in Foreign Language Education. In G. Mallia (Ed.), *The Social Classroom: Integrating Social Network Use in Education* (pp. 120–146). Hershey, PA: Information Science Reference; doi:10.4018/978-1-4666-4904-0.ch007

Sayoud, H. (2011). Biometrics: An Overview on New Technologies and Ethic Problems.[IJT]. *International Journal of Technoethics*, *2*(1), 19–34. doi:10.4018/jte.2011010102

Scheufele, D. (2000). Agenda-setting, priming, and framing revisited: Another look at cognitive effects of political communication. *Mass Communication & Society*, *3*(2), 297–316. doi:10.1207/S15327825MCS0323_07

Schiller, H. I. (1976). *Communication and cultural domination*. New York: International Arts and Sciences Press.

Schmolke, A., Thorbek, P., DeAngelis, D. L., & Grimm, V. (2010). Ecological models supporting environmental decision-making: A strategy for the future. *Trends in Ecology & Evolution*, *25*(8), 479–486. doi:10.1016/j.tree.2010.05.001 PMID:20605251

Scott, C. R., & Timmerman, C. E. (2014). Communicative Changes Associated with Repeated Use of Electronic Meeting Systems for Decision-Making Tasks. In E. Nikoi & K. Boateng (Eds.), *Collaborative Communication Processes and Decision Making in Organizations* (pp. 1–24). Hershey, PA: Business Science Reference; doi:10.4018/978-1-4666-4478-6.ch001

Scott, K. (2013). The Human-Robot Continuum of Self: Where the Other Ends and Another Begins. In R. Luppicini (Ed.), *Handbook of Research on Technoself: Identity in a Technological Society* (pp. 666–679). Hershey, PA: Information Science Reference; doi:10.4018/978-1-4666-2211-1.ch034

Sécretariat d'Etat à la Prospective et au Développement de l'économie numérique (2010). *Consultation publique sur la neutralité du net.*

Shapiro, C. (2000). Navigating the patent thicket: Cross licenses, patent pools, and standard-setting. In A. Jaffe, J. Lerner, & S. Stern (Eds.), *Innovation policy and the economy, 1.* Cambridge, MA: MIT Press.

Shasek, J. (2014). ExerLearning®: Movement, Fitness, Technology, and Learning. In J. Bishop (Ed.), *Gamification for Human Factors Integration: Social, Education, and Psychological Issues* (pp. 106–121). Hershey, PA: Information Science Reference; doi:10.4018/978-1-4666-5071-8.ch007

Shen, J., & Eder, L. B. (2011). An Examination of Factors Associated with User Acceptance of Social Shopping Websites.[IJTHI]. *International Journal of Technology and Human Interaction*, *7*(1), 19–36. doi:10.4018/jthi.2011010102

Shiva, V. (2001). *Protect or plunder: Understanding intellectual property rights.* New York: Zed Books.

Shrestha, P. (2012). Teacher Professional Development Using Mobile Technologies in a Large-Scale Project: Lessons Learned from Bangladesh.[IJCALLT]. *International Journal of Computer-Assisted Language Learning and Teaching*, *2*(4), 34–49. doi:10.4018/ijcallt.2012100103

Sichelman, T. (2010). Commercializing patents. *Stanford Law Review*, *62*(2), 341–413.

Silvana de Rosa, A., Fino, E., & Bocci, E. (2014). Addressing Healthcare On-Line Demand and Supply Relating to Mental Illness: Knowledge Sharing About Psychiatry and Psychoanalysis Through Social Networks in Italy and France. In A. Kapoor & C. Kulshrestha (Eds.), *Dynamics of Competitive Advantage and Consumer Perception in Social Marketing* (pp. 16–55). Hershey, PA: Business Science Reference; doi:10.4018/978-1-4666-4430-4.ch002

Simon, H. A. (1982). *Models of Bounded Rationality: Empirically grounded economic reason.* MIT Press.

Smith, M., & Murray, J. (2014). Augmentative and Alternative Communication Devices: The Voices of Adult Users. In Assistive Technologies: Concepts, Methodologies, Tools, and Applications (pp. 991-1004). Hershey, PA: Information Science Reference. doi:10.4018/978-1-4666-4422-9.ch050

Smith, P. A. (2013). Strengthening and Enriching Audit Practice: The Socio-Technical Relevance of "Decision Leaders". In J. Abdelnour-Nocera (Ed.), *Knowledge and Technological Development Effects on Organizational and Social Structures* (pp. 97–108). Hershey, PA: Information Science Reference; doi:10.4018/978-1-4666-2151-0.ch006

Smith, T. (2009). The social media revolution. *International Journal of Market Research*, *51*(4), 559–561. doi:10.2501/S1470785309200773

Snowe, O., Dorgan, B., Inouye, D., & Wyden, R., Leahy, Boxer, B., …, Dayton, M. (2006). *Internet Freedom Preservation Act*. S. 2917, 109th Cong. (2005-2006).

Söderström, S. (2014). Assistive ICT and Young Disabled Persons: Opportunities and Obstacles in Identity Negotiations. In Assistive Technologies: Concepts, Methodologies, Tools, and Applications (pp. 1084-1105). Hershey, PA: Information Science Reference. doi:10.4018/978-1-4666-4422-9.ch056

So, J. C., & Lam, S. Y. (2014). Using Social Networks Communication Platform for Promoting Student-Initiated Holistic Development Among Students.[IJISSS]. *International Journal of Information Systems in the Service Sector*, *6*(1), 1–23. doi:10.4018/ijisss.2014010101

Solum, L. B. (2009). Models of Internet governance. In L. A. Bygrave & J. Bing (Eds.), *Internet governance: Infrastructure and institutions* (pp. 48–91). New York: Oxford University Press. doi:10.1093/acprof:oso/9780199561131.003.0003

Sone, Y. (2013). Robot Double: Hiroshi Ishiguro's Reflexive Machines. In R. Luppicini (Ed.), *Handbook of Research on Technoself: Identity in a Technological Society* (pp. 680–702). Hershey, PA: Information Science Reference; doi:10.4018/978-1-4666-2211-1.ch035

Son, J., & Rossade, K. (2013). Finding Gems in Computer-Assisted Language Learning: Clues from GLoCALL 2011 and 2012 Papers.[IJCALLT]. *International Journal of Computer-Assisted Language Learning and Teaching*, *3*(4), 1–8. doi:10.4018/ijcallt.2013100101

Sowe, S. K., Parayil, G., & Sunami, A. (2012). *Free and Open Source Software Technology for Sustainable Development*. United Nations University Press.

Spengler, T. (2014, April 30). *5 Technology Solutions Worth Government Spending*. Retrieved February 27, 2015, from http://politix.topix.com/story/11820-5-technology-solutions-worth-government-spending

Spillane, M. (2014). Assistive Technology: A Tool for Inclusion. In Assistive Technologies: Concepts, Methodologies, Tools, and Applications (pp. 1-11). Hershey, PA: Information Science Reference. doi:10.4018/978-1-4666-4422-9.ch001

Stahl, B. C., Heersmink, R., Goujon, P., Flick, C., van den Hoven, J., Wakunuma, K., & Rader, M. et al. (2012). Identifying the Ethics of Emerging Information and Communication Technologies: An Essay on Issues, Concepts and Method. In R. Luppicini (Ed.), *Ethical Impact of Technological Advancements and Applications in Society* (pp. 61–79). Hershey, PA: Information Science Reference; doi:10.4018/978-1-4666-1773-5.ch006

Stallman, R. (2013). Misinterpreting Copyright—A Series of Errors. In *Free Software Free Society: Selected Essays of Richard M. Stallman*. Retrieved March 25, 2014, from http://shop.fsf.org/product/free-software-free-society-2/

Stavenhagen, R. (2001). *The ethnic question*. Colegio de México.

Sterman, J. D. (2000). *Business Dynamics: Systems Thinking and Modeling for a Complex World*. New York: McGraw.

Stern, S. E., & Grounds, B. E. (2011). Cellular Telephones and Social Interactions: Evidence of Interpersonal Surveillance.[IJT]. *International Journal of Technoethics*, *2*(1), 43–49. doi:10.4018/jte.2011010104

Stinson, J., & Gill, N. (2014). Internet-Based Chronic Disease Self-Management for Youth. In Assistive Technologies: Concepts, Methodologies, Tools, and Applications (pp. 224-245). Hershey, PA: Information Science Reference. doi:10.4018/978-1-4666-4422-9.ch012

Stockwell, G. (2011). Online Approaches to Learning Vocabulary: Teacher-Centred or Learner-Centred?[IJCALLT]. *International Journal of Computer-Assisted Language Learning and Teaching*, *1*(1), 33–44. doi:10.4018/ijcallt.2011010103

Stradella, E. (2012). Personal Liability and Human Free Will in the Background of Emerging Neuroethical Issues: Some Remarks Arising From Recent Case Law. [IJT]. *International Journal of Technoethics, 3*(2), 30–41. doi:10.4018/jte.2012040104

Stubbs, K., Casper, J., & Yanco, H. A. (2014). Designing Evaluations for K-12 Robotics Education Programs. In K-12 Education: Concepts, Methodologies, Tools, and Applications (pp. 1342-1364). Hershey, PA: Information Science Reference. doi:10.4018/978-1-4666-4502-8.ch078

Suber, P. (2012) *Open Access*. MIT Press. Retrieved March 1, 2014, from https://mitpress.mit.edu/books/open-access

Suki, N. M., Ramayah, T., Ming, M. K., & Suki, N. M. (2011). Factors Enhancing Employed Job Seekers Intentions to Use Social Networking Sites as a Job Search Tool. [IJTHI]. *International Journal of Technology and Human Interaction, 7*(2), 38–54. doi:10.4018/jthi.2011040105

Sweeney, P., & Moore, C. (2012). Mobile Apps for Learning Vocabulary: Categories, Evaluation and Design Criteria for Teachers and Developers.[IJCALLT]. *International Journal of Computer-Assisted Language Learning and Teaching, 2*(4), 1–16. doi:10.4018/ijcallt.2012100101

Szeto, A. Y. (2014). Assistive Technology and Rehabilitation Engineering. In Assistive Technologies: Concepts, Methodologies, Tools, and Applications (pp. 277-331). Hershey, PA: Information Science Reference. doi:10.4018/978-1-4666-4422-9.ch015

Tamayo, F. (1952). Introducción al estudio del fitofolklore venezolano. In *Archivos Venezolanos de Folklore. Year 1, Nº 1. Universidad Central de Venezuela. Facultad de Filosofía y Letras*. Caracas: Faculty of Pharmacy and Language.

Tamim, R. (2014). Technology Integration in UAE Schools: Current Status and Way Forward. In K-12 Education: Concepts, Methodologies, Tools, and Applications (pp. 41-57). Hershey, PA: Information Science Reference. doi:10.4018/978-1-4666-4502-8.ch004

Tan, R., Wang, S., Jiang, Y., Ishida, K., & Fujie, M. G. (2014). Motion Control of an Omni-Directional Walker for Walking Support. In Assistive Technologies: Concepts, Methodologies, Tools, and Applications (pp. 614-622). Hershey, PA: Information Science Reference. doi:10.4018/978-1-4666-4422-9.ch029

Tankari, M. (2014). Cultural Orientation Differences and their Implications for Online Learning Satisfaction. In J. Keengwe, G. Schnellert, & K. Kungu (Eds.), *Cross-Cultural Online Learning in Higher Education and Corporate Training* (pp. 20–61). Hershey, PA: Information Science Reference; doi:10.4018/978-1-4666-5023-7.ch002

Tarrow, S. (1994). *Power in movement: Social movements, collective action and politics*. New York: Cambridge University Press.

Tchangani, A. P. (2014). Bipolarity in Decision Analysis: A Way to Cope with Human Judgment. In A. Masegosa, P. Villacorta, C. Cruz-Corona, M. García-Cascales, M. Lamata, & J. Verdegay (Eds.), *Exploring Innovative and Successful Applications of Soft Computing* (pp. 216–244). Hershey, PA: Information Science Reference; doi:10.4018/978-1-4666-4785-5.ch012

Team, M. (2013, April 29). *Facebook users convince Hungarian companies to wash GMOs from food supply*. Retrieved February 27, 2015, from http://www.mobilisationlab.org/facebook-users-convince-hungarian-companies-to-wash-gmos-from-food-supply/

Tennyson, R. D. (2014). Computer Interventions for Children with Disabilities: Review of Research and Practice. In Assistive Technologies: Concepts, Methodologies, Tools, and Applications (pp. 841-864). Hershey, PA: Information Science Reference. doi:10.4018/978-1-4666-4422-9.ch042

Terán, O., & Ablan, M. (2013). Modelado y simulación de situaciones sociales complejas en Latinoamérica: Contribuyendo al cuidado del bien público. In La emergencia de los enfoques de la complejidad en América Latina: Desafíos, contribuciones y compromisos para abordar los problemas complejos del siglo XXI (pp. 118–135). Buenos Aires: Comunidad de Pensamiento Sistémico; Retrieved from http://www.academia.edu/3366646/Tomo_1._La_emergencia_de_los_enfoques_de_la_complejidad_en_America_Latina._Desafios_contribuciones_y_compromisos_para_abordar_los_problemas_complejos_del_siglo_XXI

Terrell, S. S. (2011). Integrating Online Tools to Motivate Young English Language Learners to Practice English Outside the Classroom.[IJCALLT]. *International Journal of Computer-Assisted Language Learning and Teaching, 1*(2), 16–24. doi:10.4018/ijcallt.2011040102

The C. I. A.'s Plan to Create a "Destabilizing Student Opposition in Venezuela": Interview with Ex-CIA Collaborator. (2014). *Global Research: Global Research News*. Retrieved from: http://www.globalresearch.ca/the-cias-plan-to-create-a-destabilizing-student-opposition-in-venezuela/5376807

Thomas, S. M., Hopkins, M. M., & Brady, M. (2002). Shares in the human genome; the future of patenting DNA. *Nature Biotechnology*, *20*(12), 1185–1188. doi:10.1038/nbt1202-1185 PMID:12454661

Tiwary, U. S., & Siddiqui, T. J. (2014). Working Together with Computers: Towards a General Framework for Collaborative Human Computer Interaction. In Assistive Technologies: Concepts, Methodologies, Tools, and Applications (pp. 141-162). Hershey, PA: Information Science Reference. doi:10.4018/978-1-4666-4422-9.ch008

Tomas, J., Lloret, J., Bri, D., & Sendra, S. (2014). Sensors and their Application for Disabled and Elderly People. In Assistive Technologies: Concepts, Methodologies, Tools, and Applications (pp. 357-376). Hershey, PA: Information Science Reference. doi:10.4018/978-1-4666-4422-9.ch018

Tomasi, A. (2013). A Run for your [Techno]Self. In R. Luppicini (Ed.), Handbook of Research on Technoself: Identity in a Technological Society (pp. 123-136). Hershey, PA: Information Science Reference. doi:10.4018/978-1-4666-2211-1.ch007

Tootell, H., & Freeman, A. (2014). The Applicability of Gaming Elements to Early Childhood Education. In J. Bishop (Ed.), *Gamification for Human Factors Integration: Social, Education, and Psychological Issues* (pp. 225–241). Hershey, PA: Information Science Reference; doi:10.4018/978-1-4666-5071-8.ch014

Torrecuadrada, S. (2001). *Los pueblos indígenas en el orden internacional*. Madrid: Editorial Dykinson.

Touraine, A. (1984). *Le retour de l'acteur*. Paris: Fayard.

Treaty of Lisbon. 2007 O.J. (C306) 01. United States Code.

Treem, J., & Leonardi, P. (2012). Social Media Use in Organizations: Exploring the Affordances of Visibility, Editability, Persistence, and Association. *Communication Yearbook*, *36*, 143–189.

Treibig, C., & Klugl, F. (2009). Elements of a documentation framework for agent-based simulation models. *Cybernetics and Systems*, *40*(5), 441–474. doi:10.1080/01969720902922459

Trosky, L. (1938). Their Morals and Ours. *The New International, 4*(6), 163-173. Retrieved August 1, 2014 from https://www.marxists.org/archive/trotsky/1938/morals/morals.htm

Tsai, C. (2011). How Much Can Computers and Internet Help?: A Long-Term Study of Web-Mediated Problem-Based Learning and Self-Regulated Learning.[IJTHI]. *International Journal of Technology and Human Interaction, 7*(1), 67–81. doi:10.4018/jthi.2011010105

Tsai, W. (2013). An Investigation on Undergraduate's Bio-Energy Engineering Education Program at the Taiwan Technical University.[IJTHI]. *International Journal of Technology and Human Interaction, 8*(3), 46–53. doi:10.4018/jthi.2012070105

Tsiakis, T. (2013). Using Social Media as a Concept and Tool for Teaching Marketing Information Systems. In M. Pătruţ & B. Pătruţ (Eds.), *Social Media in Higher Education: Teaching in Web 2.0* (pp. 24–44). Hershey, PA: Information Science Reference; doi:10.4018/978-1-4666-2970-7.ch002

Tu, C., McIsaac, M. S., Sujo-Montes, L. E., & Armfield, S. (2014). Building Mobile Social Presence for U-Learning. In F. Neto (Ed.), *Technology Platform Innovations and Forthcoming Trends in Ubiquitous Learning* (pp. 77–93). Hershey, PA: Information Science Reference; doi:10.4018/978-1-4666-4542-4.ch005

UNESCO. (1999). *Declaration on science and the use of scientific knowledge*. Paper presented at the World Conference on Science. Definitive version. Retrieved from http://www.unesco.org/science/wcs/eng/declaration_e.htm

Unwin, T. (2014). *Social media and democracy: Critical reflections*. Paper presented at the Commonwealth Parliamentary Conference (Colombo). Retrieved from http://www.cpahq.org/cpahq/cpadocs/Unwin%20CPA%20Social%20media%20and%20democracy.pdf

Uzcátegui, A., & Aguilar, V. (2010). Collective indigenous rights and intellectual property in Venezuela. The case of the Pemon people. *Year, 27*(27), 161–201.

Valeria, N., Lu, M. V., & Theng, L. B. (2014). Collaborative Virtual Learning for Assisting Children with Cerebral Palsy. In Assistive Technologies: Concepts, Methodologies, Tools, and Applications (pp. 786-810). Hershey, PA: Information Science Reference. doi:10.4018/978-1-4666-4422-9.ch040

Van Leuven, N., Newton, D., Leuenberger, D. Z., & Esteves, T. (2014). Reaching Citizen 2.0: How Government Uses Social Media to Send Public Messages during Times of Calm and Times of Crisis. In Crisis Management: Concepts, Methodologies, Tools and Applications (pp. 839-857). Hershey, PA: Information Science Reference. doi:10.4018/978-1-4666-4707-7.ch041

Vanneste, S., Van Hiel, A., Parisi, F., & Depoorter, B. (2006). From 'tragedy' to 'disaster': Welfare effects of commons and anticommons dilemmas. *International Review of Law and Economics*, *26*(1), 104–122. doi:10.1016/j.irle.2006.05.008

Vargas-Hernández, J. G. (2013). International Student Collaboration and Experiential Exercise Projects as a Professional, Inter-Personal and Inter-Institutional Networking Platform.[IJTEM]. *International Journal of Technology and Educational Marketing*, *3*(1), 28–47. doi:10.4018/ijtem.2013010103

Varsavsky, O. (2013). *Estilos tecnológicos. Propuestas para la selección de tecnologías bajo racionalidad socialista*. Buenos Aires, Argentina: Biblioteca Nacional. Colección PLACTED-Ministerio de Ciencia, Tecnología, e Innovación Productiva, Presidencia de la Nación.

Varsavsky, O. (1974). *Estilos Tecnológicos*. Buenos Aires, Argentina: Ediciones Periferia S.R.L.

Varsavsky, O. (2006). *Hacia una política científica nacional*. Caracas, Venezuela: Monte Ávila Editores. (Original work published 1972)

Velicu, A., & Marinescu, V. (2013). Usage of Social Media by Children and Teenagers: Results of EU KIDS Online II. In M. Pătruţ & B. Pătruţ (Eds.), *Social Media in Higher Education: Teaching in Web 2.0* (pp. 144–178). Hershey, PA: Information Science Reference; doi:10.4018/978-1-4666-2970-7.ch008

Verizon v. FCC, 740 F.3d 623, D.C. Cir. 2014.

Vidaurre, C., Kübler, A., Tangermann, M., Müller, K., & Millán, J. D. (2014). Brain-Computer Interfaces and Visual Activity. In Assistive Technologies: Concepts, Methodologies, Tools, and Applications (pp. 1549-1570). Hershey, PA: Information Science Reference. doi:10.4018/978-1-4666-4422-9.ch081

Virtually Blind. (2007, April 24). *Reader Roundtable: "Virtual Rape" Claim Brings Belgian Police to Second Life | Virtually Blind | Virtual Law | Benjamin Duranske*. Retrieved July 26, 2014, from http://virtuallyblind.com/2007/04/24/open-roundtable-allegations-of-virtual-rape-bring-belgian-police-to-second-life/

Viswanathan, R. (2012). Augmenting the Use of Mobile Devices in Language Classrooms.[IJCALLT]. *International Journal of Computer-Assisted Language Learning and Teaching*, *2*(2), 45–60. doi:10.4018/ijcallt.2012040104

Wallerstein, I. (1991). *Histoire et dilemmes des mouvements antisystemiques*. Paris: La Decouverte.

Wallgren, L. G., & Hanse, J. J. (2012). A Two-Wave Study of the Impact of Job Characteristics and Motivators on Perceived Stress among Information Technology (IT) Consultants.[IJTHI]. *International Journal of Technology and Human Interaction*, *8*(4), 75–91. doi:10.4018/jthi.2012100105

Wang, H. (2014). A Guide to Assistive Technology for Teachers in Special Education. In Assistive Technologies: Concepts, Methodologies, Tools, and Applications (pp. 12-25). Hershey, PA: Information Science Reference. doi:10.4018/978-1-4666-4422-9.ch002

Wang, S., Ku, C., & Chu, C. (2013). Sustainable Campus Project: Potential for Energy Conservation and Carbon Reduction Education in Taiwan.[IJTHI]. *International Journal of Technology and Human Interaction*, *8*(3), 19–30. doi:10.4018/jthi.2012070103

Wang, Y., & Tian, J. (2013). Negotiation of Meaning in Multimodal Tandem Learning via Desktop Videoconferencing.[IJCALLT]. *International Journal of Computer-Assisted Language Learning and Teaching*, *3*(2), 41–55. doi:10.4018/ijcallt.2013040103

Wareham, C. (2011). On the Moral Equality of Artificial Agents.[IJT]. *International Journal of Technoethics*, *2*(1), 35–42. doi:10.4018/jte.2011010103

Warwick, K., & Gasson, M. N. (2014). Practical Experimentation with Human Implants. In M. Michael & K. Michael (Eds.), *Uberveillance and the Social Implications of Microchip Implants: Emerging Technologies* (pp. 64–132). Hershey, PA: Information Science Reference; doi:10.4018/978-1-4666-4582-0.ch004

Weingast, B. (2013). e-Study Guide for the Oxford Handbook of Political Economy. Academic Press.

Welch, K. C., Lahiri, U., Sarkar, N., Warren, Z., Stone, W., & Liu, C. (2014). Affect-Sensitive Computing and Autism. In Assistive Technologies: Concepts, Methodologies, Tools, and Applications (pp. 865-883). Hershey, PA: Information Science Reference. doi:10.4018/978-1-4666-4422-9.ch043

Wessels, B., Dittrich, Y., Ekelin, A., & Eriksén, S. (2014). Creating Synergies between Participatory Design of E-Services and Collaborative Planning. In Assistive Technologies: Concepts, Methodologies, Tools, and Applications (pp. 163-179). Hershey, PA: Information Science Reference. doi:10.4018/978-1-4666-4422-9.ch009

White, E. L. (2014). Technology-Based Literacy Approach for English Language Learners. In K-12 Education: Concepts, Methodologies, Tools, and Applications (pp. 723-740). Hershey, PA: Information Science Reference. doi:10.4018/978-1-4666-4502-8.ch042

Whyte, K. P., List, M., Stone, J. V., Grooms, D., Gasteyer, S., Thompson, P. B., & Bouri, H. et al. (2014). Uberveillance, Standards, and Anticipation: A Case Study on Nanobiosensors in U.S. Cattle. In M. Michael & K. Michael (Eds.), *Uberveillance and the Social Implications of Microchip Implants: Emerging Technologies* (pp. 260–279). Hershey, PA: Information Science Reference; doi:10.4018/978-1-4666-4582-0.ch012

Wilenski, U. (1999). *NetLogo*. Center for Connected Learning and Computer-Based Modeling, Northwestern University, Evanston, IL. Retrieved from http://ccl.northwestern.edu/netlogo/

Wilenski, U. (2007). Making models match: Replicating an agent-based model. *Journal of Artificial Societies and Social Simulation, 10*(4), 2. Retrieved from http://jasss.soc.surrey.ac.uk/10/4/2.html

Williams, H. (2010). *Intellectual property rights and innovation: Evidence from the human genome.* National Bureau of Economic Research, Tech. Rep. No. 16213.

Wilson, R. (2012). *GPL V3 - What's New?* OSS Watch. Retrieved from http://oss-watch.ac.uk/resources/gpl3final

Wilson, S., & Haslam, N. (2013). Reasoning about Human Enhancement: Towards a Folk Psychological Model of Human Nature and Human Identity. In R. Luppicini (Ed.), *Handbook of Research on Technoself: Identity in a Technological Society* (pp. 175–188). Hershey, PA: Information Science Reference; doi:10.4018/978-1-4666-2211-1.ch010

WIPO. (2004). *Enlarged Concept of Novelty: Initial Study Concerning Novelty and the Prior Art Effect of Certain Applications under draft Article 8(2) of the Substantive Patent Law Treaty (SPLT).* Retrieved from http://www.wipo.int/export/sites/www/scp/en/novelty/documents/5prov.pdf

WIPO. (2010). *World intellectual property indicators.* Retrieved from http://www.wipo.int/edocs/pubdocs/en/intproperty/941/wipo_pub_941_2010.pdf

WIPO. (2011). *World intellectual property report: The changing face of innovation.* Retrieved from http://www.wipo.int/edocs/pubdocs/en/intproperty/944/wipo_pub_944_2011.pdf

Wittgenstein, L. (1953/2001). *Philosophical Investigations.* Blackwell Publishing.

Wolfram, S. (2002). *A new kind of science.* Wolfram Media.

Woodhead, R. (2012). What is Technology?[IJSKD]. *International Journal of Sociotechnology and Knowledge Development, 4*(2), 1–13. doi:10.4018/jskd.2012040101

Woodley, C., & Dorrington, P. (2014). Facebook and the Societal Aspects of Formal Learning: Optional, Peripheral, or Essential. In G. Mallia (Ed.), *The Social Classroom: Integrating Social Network Use in Education* (pp. 269–291). Hershey, PA: Information Science Reference; doi:10.4018/978-1-4666-4904-0.ch014

World Summit on the Information Society. (2005, November). *Tunis agenda for the information society.* ITU. Retrieved from http://www.itu.int/wsis/docs2/tunis/off/6rev1.pdf

Wu, T. (2010, August 9). Controlling commerce and speech. *The Wall Street Journal*. Retrieved from http://www.nytimes.com/roomfordebate/2010/8/9/who-gets-priority-on-the-web/controlling-commerce-and-speech

Wu, T. (2003). Network neutrality, broadband discrimination. *Journal of Telecommunications and High Tecnology Law*, 2, 141–178.

Xia, Y. (2010). Introduction to software protection under Chinese law. In *The International Free and Open Source Software Law Book*. Open Source Press GmbH. Retrieved March 1, 2014, from http://ifosslawbook.org/china/

Yamazaki, T. (2014). Assistive Technologies in Smart Homes. In Assistive Technologies: Concepts, Methodologies, Tools, and Applications (pp. 663-678). Hershey, PA: Information Science Reference. doi:10.4018/978-1-4666-4422-9.ch032

Yang, Y., Wang, X., & Li, L. (2013). Use Mobile Devices to Wirelessly Operate Computers.[IJTHI]. *International Journal of Technology and Human Interaction*, 9(1), 64–77. doi:10.4018/jthi.2013010105

Yan, Z., Chen, Q., & Yu, C. (2013). The Science of Cell Phone Use: Its Past, Present, and Future.[IJCBPL]. *International Journal of Cyber Behavior, Psychology and Learning*, 3(1), 7–18. doi:10.4018/ijcbpl.2013010102

Yartey, F. N., & Ha, L. (2013). Like, Share, Recommend: Smartphones as a Self-Broadcast and Self-Promotion Medium of College Students.[IJTHI]. *International Journal of Technology and Human Interaction*, 9(4), 20–40. doi:10.4018/ijthi.2013100102

Yaseen, S. G., & Al Omoush, K. S. (2013). Investigating the Engage in Electronic Societies via Facebook in the Arab World.[IJTHI]. *International Journal of Technology and Human Interaction*, 9(2), 20–38. doi:10.4018/jthi.2013040102

Yeo, B. (2012). Sustainable Economic Development and the Influence of Information Technologies: Dynamics of Knowledge Society Transformation.[IJSKD]. *International Journal of Sociotechnology and Knowledge Development*, 4(3), 54–55. doi:10.4018/jskd.2012070105

Yu, L., & Ureña, C. (2014). A Review of Current Approaches of Brain Computer Interfaces. In Assistive Technologies: Concepts, Methodologies, Tools, and Applications (pp. 1516-1534). Hershey, PA: Information Science Reference. doi:10.4018/978-1-4666-4422-9.ch079

Zelenkauskaite, A. (2014). Analyzing Blending Social and Mass Media Audiences through the Lens of Computer-Mediated Discourse. In H. Lim & F. Sudweeks (Eds.), *Innovative Methods and Technologies for Electronic Discourse Analysis* (pp. 304–326). Hershey, PA: Information Science Reference; doi:10.4018/978-1-4666-4426-7.ch014

Ziman, J. (2000). *Real Science: What it is, and what it means*. Cambridge, UK: Cambridge University Press.

About the Contributors

Oswaldo Terán got his Systems Engineering degree and a M. Sc. in Applied Statistics at, and is a full Professor of, the University of Los Andes in Venezuela. His Ph.D was in Computational Modeling at the Centre for Policy Modeling of the Manchester Metropolitan University, UK. He was a Post-doctoral researcher at the University of Toulouse-1, from April 2013 to March 2014, in the Project Emotes, related with modeling morality and emotions in organizational settings. He has been directive of FUNDACITE-Merida and CENDITEL, where he has promoted (via diverse projects) free, pertinent and liberating knowledge, methodologies and technologies. His main research subjects are Social Simulation, Strategic Planning and Organizational Studies.

Jose Aguilar received the B. S. degree in 1987 (Universidad de Los Andes-Venezuela), the M. Sc. degree in 1991 (Universite Paul Sabatier-France), and the Ph.D degree in 1995 (Universite Rene Descartes-France). He was a Postdoctoral Research Fellow in the Department of Computer Sciences at the University of Houston (1999-2000). He is full Professor at the Universidad de Los Andes, Venezuela; member of the Mérida Science Academy and of the IEEE CIS Technical Committee on Neural Networks. Also, currently he is Prometeo Researcher at the Technical University of Loja (UTPL) and Yachay-EP, Ecuador. He has published more than 400 papers and 9 books, in the field of parallel and distributed systems, computational intelligence, science and technology management, etc. Dr. Aguilar has been a visiting research/professor in different universities/laboratories, coordinator or inviting research in more than 20 research/industrial projects, and supervised more than 40 M.S. and Doctoral theses.

* * *

Vladimir Aguilar Castro is a Lawyer and Political Scientist. He is a Doctor in International Policy Studies Development references and DEA in History and International Politics at the University of Geneva, Switzerland. He got a Master in International Relations from the Central University of Venezuela. Dr. Aguilar Castro is professor at the Faculty of Law and Political Science at the University of Los Andes. In addition, he is currently developing processes accompanying with indigenous peoples and communities of the indigenous land rights, as Coordinator of the Center for Political and Social Studies of Latin America (CEPSAL) and researcher-head of the Working Group on Indigenous Affairs (GTAI), of the Universidad de Los Andes.

Eitan Altman received the B.Sc. degree in electrical engineering (1984), the B.A. degree in physics (1984) and the Ph.D. degree in electrical engineering (1990), all from the Technion-Israel Institute, Haifa. In (1990) he further received his B.Mus. degree in music composition in Tel-Aviv University. Since 1990, Dr. Altman has been a researcher at INRIA (National Institute for Research in Computer Science and Control) in Sophia-Antipolis, France. He has been in the editorial boards of several scientific journals: Wireless Networks (WINET), Computer Networks (COMNET), Computer Communications (Comcom), J. Discrete Event Dynamic Systems (JDEDS), SIAM J. of Control and Optimisation (SICON), Stochastic Models, and Journal of Economy Dynamic and Control (JEDC). He received the best paper award in the Networking 2006, in Globecom 2007, in IFIP Wireless Days 2009 and in CNSM 2011 (Paris) conferences. His areas of interest include network engineering games, social networks and their control. He received in 2012 the Grand Prix de France Telecom from the French Academy of Sciences. On 2014 he received the ISAACS award from the International Society of Dynamic Games.

Jacinto Dávila got his PhD in Logic and Artificial Intelligence, Imperial College, UK, MSc en Foundations of Advanced Information Technology, Imperial College, UK and System Engineer, Universidad de Los Andes, Venezuela. Tenure Professor at Universidad de Los Andes, cooperated in funding a graduate programme in modelling and simulation and a distance education system in computing. (co) Developer of Resumidor, Gloria, Galatea, Bioinformantes and InMemorian, he has served as supervisor for 14 undergraduate, 16 MSc and 6 doctoral thesis. He also leads the community service project ULAnux/ULAnix and the open studies community "comunidad de aprendizaje sobre servicios públicos" at the polytechnic, territorial university of Mérida "Kléber Ramírez".

Bruce Edmonds is the director of the Centre for Policy Modelling (CPM), and Professor of Social Simulation, both at the Manchester Metropolitan University. His first degree was in Mathematics at Oxford, and his Doctorate in the Department of Philosophy at the University of Manchester, on the meaning and definition of complexity. Since 1994 he has been working at the CPM, developing it with its founder, Scott Moss, into one of the world-leading teams in the field of social simulation. He publishes widely across computer science, social science, and philosophy. Recently he co-edited the first handbook on "Simulating Social Complexity". More about him can be found at http://cfpm.org/~bruce

Giulio Focardi worked as business consultant, trainer and social designer in Europe and South America. His research interests focus on Social Business, Collaborative Economy and Social Innovation.

Carlos Grimaldo Lorente is a Lawyer, professor at the Faculty of Law and Political Science at the University of Los Andes (ULA), Mérida Venezuela, Department of Private Law. He got a Master in Intellectual Property Rights at the University of Los Andes (ULA), and a Master in International Law and International Relations, International University Menéndez Pelayo, Spain (2013).

Amir Manzoor holds a bachelor's degree in engineering from NED University, Karachi, an MBA from Lahore University of Management Sciences (LUMS), and an MBA from Bangor University, United Kingdom. He has many years of diverse professional and teaching experience working at many renowned national and internal organizations and higher education institutions. His research interests include electronic commerce and technology applications in business.

Gary Polhill did a degree in Computing and Artificial Intelligence at Sussex, and a PhD on guaranteeing generalisation in neural networks at St. Andrews. He spent 18 months in industry as a professional programmer, before joining the Macaulay Land Use Research Institute in 1997 to work on agent-based modelling of land use systems. The Macaulay Land Use Research Institute merged with the Scottish Crop Research Institute in 2011 to form The James Hutton Institute, where Gary now works on agent-based modelling of various human-environmental systems, including agri-environmental incentive schemes, everyday pro-environmental behaviour, sustainable lifestyles, and socio-environmental transitions.

Leandro Rabindranath Leon is a Programmer and Professor of Distributed Systems and Algorithms at the University of Los Andes in Venezuela. He has a degree in Systems Engineering from the University of Los Andes. He did his graduate and postgraduate studies at the University Pierre et Marie Curie, Paris, France, where he got a Doctoral degree in Computer Science oriented to Programming; Semantic, Proofs and Programming Languages. In his country, he has been a strong activist and advocate of free knowledge. Currently he works on the mathematical models and algorithms for the observation, analysis and simulation of large production chains.

Julio Rojas-Mora has a systems engineering degree from the University of Los Andes (Venezuela). His academic career includes an Advanced Studies Diploma (D.E.A.) in Statistics and Operations Research from the Universidade de Santiago de Compostela (Spain) in 2006, and a Ph.D. from the Business Economics and Organization Department of the Universitat de Barcelona (Spain) in 2011. After finishing a postdoctoral fellowship at the UMR Espace CNRS of the Université d'Avignon et des Pays de Vaucluse (France), he joined the Institute of Statistics of the Universidad Austral de Chile. His research partially focuses on the study of the problems that the information society, as well as the free, open and neutral Internet, are facing in a minefield of economic rights and archaic business models.

Lorenza Salati used to work for several mainstream media companies, before shifting to independent movie making and documentaries. Her main areas of interest are visual anthropology and innovative use of filmmaking as a tool for community development and construction of personal and group identity.

Torrecuadrada Soledad Garcia-Lozano is a Professor of Public International Law and International Relations at the Autonomous University of Madrid (2000) – Professor accredited by resolution of the Ministry of Education on July 4, 2012. She graduated in law from the Autonomous University of Madrid (1989), got a Master MA in International Relations from the University Research Institute Ortega y Gasset in Madrid (1992), received her Doctorate in Law from the Autonomous University of Madrid (1996), and acquired a Diploma from the Centre for Studies and Research in International Law and International Relations of the Academy of International Law The Hague (1996).

Sulan Wong is a lawyer who graduated "Cum Laude" from the University of Los Andes (Venezuela). She got her Advanced Studies Diploma (DEA) and Doctorate in Public Freedoms and Fundamental Rights at the University of A Coruña (Spain). She has been a visiting researcher at the Department of Law Philosophy of the Universitat de Barcelona (Spain), as well as at the MAESTRO Team of INRIA (France). She is an associated researcher of the GRC Filosofia del Dret, Moral i Política of the Universitat de Barcelona (Spain), and has recently joined the Faculty of Law of the Universidad Católica de Temuco (Chile) in 2014, where she is a researcher of the Grupo de Investigaciones Jurídicas (GIJ).

Index

Information Resources Management Association

Become an IRMA Member

Members of the **Information Resources Management Association (IRMA)** understand the importance of community within their field of study. The Information Resources Management Association is an ideal venue through which professionals, students, and academicians can convene and share the latest industry innovations and scholarly research that is changing the field of information science and technology. Become a member today and enjoy the benefits of membership as well as the opportunity to collaborate and network with fellow experts in the field.

IRMA Membership Benefits:

- **One FREE Journal Subscription**

- **30% Off Additional Journal Subscriptions**

- **20% Off Book Purchases**

- Updates on the latest events and research on Information Resources Management through the IRMA-L listserv.

- Updates on new open access and downloadable content added to Research IRM.

- A copy of the Information Technology Management Newsletter twice a year.

- A certificate of membership.

IRMA Membership $195

Scan code to visit irma-international.org and begin by selecting your free journal subscription.

Membership is good for one full year.

Printed in the United States
By Bookmasters